Tolley's Employment Handbook

Elizabeth A Slade MA *(Oxon)*
of the Inner Temple, Barrister

Sixth Edition

by

Elizabeth A Slade
and
Nigel D Giffin BA *(Oxon)*
of the Inner Temple, Barrister

Tolley Publishing Company Limited
A UNITED NEWSPAPERS PUBLICATION

Published by
Tolley Publishing Company Limited
2 Addiscombe Road
Croydon Surrey CR9 5AF England
01-686 9141

Typeset in Great Britain by
C Leggett & Son Ltd
Mitcham Surrey

Printed by:
UNWIN BROTHERS LIMITED
The Gresham Press, Old Woking, Surrey
A Member of the Martins Printing Group

ISBN 0 85459 419-1

Preface

The months since the publication of the Fifth Edition of this book have witnessed a number of important statutory and case-law developments. In the summer of 1989 there was an upsurge of industrial action, and when employers resorted to the courts several significant decisions followed. It seems that the Government intends to bring forward further legislation in the field of collective employment law in the near future. The *Employment Act 1989* deals principally with the individual employment relationship. Its major consequence is the removal of certain restrictions upon the employment of women and young persons. Since the last Preface was written, the remainder of the *Employment Act 1988* has come into force. There is increasing awareness of the fundamental importance of the statutory scheme governing the transfer of undertakings, strongly emphasised by the decision of the House of Lords in *Litster v Forth Dry Dock & Engineering Co Ltd [1989] ICR 341*. Meanwhile, detailed proposals for employment-related legislation are awaited from the Commission of the EC, and it remains to be seen whether the U.K. Government can successfully resist such proposals, as it will seek to do.

We have taken the opportunity to make some changes to the structure of the book. Partly this has consisted of eliminating the duplication of material which appeared in more than one chapter, both by further cross-referencing and by combining the chapters on dismissal, notice and termination of employment. The law on restraint of trade and confidential information is now so important in practice that it has been given a chapter to itself, and chapters have been added dealing with directors as employees and with employees in the public sector. The treatment of unfair dismissal has been further subdivided for the sake of clarity.

We seek to state the law of England and Wales at 1 September 1989, with later developments incorporated where possible. The two usual warnings still apply: readers need to be aware of recent changes in the law, and in cases of real doubt or complexity they should consult a professional adviser.

Eric Harvey has recently retired from full-time work with Tolley, and we are most grateful to him for his involvement with past editions. This is the second edition which has been edited by Stephen Barc, and his skill and care have been just as much evidenced and appreciated this time as on the previous occasion. As usual, Tolley's experts have contributed the chapters dealing with benefits in kind and PAYE. Our colleagues at the Bar, Martin Rodger and Alistair McGregor, very kindly checked the sections in which they are expert, service lettings and employee inventions respectively.

Finally, we should thank and dedicate this edition to Anthony Stern and Samantha Ward, who had to put up with us whilst we wrote it.

Elizabeth Slade
Nigel Giffin

Inner Temple
London EC4

17 November 1989

Contents

Contents

Table of Statutes

Table of Statutes

Table of Statutes

Table of Statutes

Unfair Contract Terms Act 1977 40.5
ss 2, 11 40.5

Table of EC Legislative Material

Table of Statutory Instruments

Conduct of Employment Agencies and Employment Businesses Regulations 1976 (SI 1976 No 715)	48.2
Control of Industrial Major Accident Hazards Regulations 1984 (SI 1984 No 1902 as amended by SI 1988 No 1462)	25.5
Control of Lead at Work Regulations 1980 (SI 1980 No 1248)	30.1
Control of Substances Hazardous to Health Regulations 1988 (SI 1988 No 1657)	25.2, 25.11, 30.1
Criminal Penalties etc. (Increase) Order 1984 (SI 1984 No 447)	1.10
Data Protection (Fees) Regulations 1988 (SI 1988 No 1969)	13.12
Data Protection (Subject Access) (Fees) Regulations 1987 (SI 1987 No 1507)	13.12
Disabled Persons (Designated Employments) Order 1946 (SR&O 1946 No 1257)	12.5
Disabled Persons (Registration) Regulations 1945 (SR&O 1945 No 938)	12.3
Disabled Persons (Special Percentage) (No 1) Order 1946 (SR&O 1946 No 236)	12.6
Disabled Persons (Standard Percentage) Order 1946 (SR&O 1946 No 1258)	12.6
Employers' Health and Safety Policy Statements (Exception) Regulations 1975 (SI 1975 No 1584)	25.3
Employers' Liability (Compulsory Insurance) General Regulations 1971 (SIs 1971 No 1117; 1974 No 208; 1975 Nos 194, 1443), Regs 5, 6	24.2
Employment Act 1988 (Commencement No 1) Order 1988 (SI 1988 No 1118)	6.1
Employment Appeal Tribunal Rules 1980 (SI 1980 No 2035)	27.28
Employment Appeal Tribunal (Amendment) Rules 1985 (SI 1985 No 29) and 1988 (SI 1988 No 2072)	27.28
Employment Protection (Handling of Redundancies) Variation Order 1979 (SI 1979 No 958)	39.4
Employment Protection (Offshore Employment) Order 1976 (SI 1976 No 766)	54.15
Employment Protection (Recoupment of Unemployment Benefit) Regulations 1977 (SI 1977 No 674) and 1980 (SI 1980 No 1608)	56.6
Employment Protection (Variation of Limits) Order 1988 (SI 1988 No 276)	38.15, 56.7

Table of Statutory Instruments

Table of Statutory Instruments

Table of Cases

Table of Cases

Table of Cases

Table of Cases

Table of Cases

Table of Cases

Table of Cases

Table of Cases

Abbreviations and References

ABBREVIATIONS – GENERAL

ACAS	= Advisory, Conciliation and Arbitration Service
CA	= Court of Appeal
CAC	= Central Arbitration Committee
COIT	= Central Office of the Industrial Tribunals
DE	= Department of Employment
DSS	= Department of Social Security
EAT	= Employment Appeal Tribunal
EEC	= European Economic Community
EC	= European Community
Pt	= Part
Sch	= Schedule
SI	= Statutory Instrument
SR & O	= Statutory Rules and Orders

ABBREVIATIONS – STATUTES

EA	= Employment Act (with date)
EPA	= Employment Protection Act 1975
EPCA	= Employment Protection (Consolidation) Act 1978
EqPA	= Equal Pay Act 1970
FA	= Finance Act (with date)
HSWA	= Health and Safety at Work etc. Act 1974
ICTA	= Income and Corporation Taxes Act 1988
OLA	= Occupiers' Liability Act 1957
OSRPA	= Offices, Shops and Railway Premises Act 1963
RRA	= Race Relations Act 1976
SBA	= Supplementary Benefits Act 1976
SDA	= Sex Discrimination Act 1975
SDA 1986	= Sex Discrimination Act 1986
SSA	= Social Security Act 1975
SSA 1986	= Social Security Act 1986
SSHBA	= Social Security and Housing Benefits Act 1982
SSPA	= Social Security Pensions Act 1975
TUA	= Trade Union Act 1984
TULRA	= Trade Union and Labour Relations Act 1974
TULR(A)A	= Trade Union and Labour Relations (Amendment) Act 1976
WA	= Wages Act 1986

LAW REPORTS – SERIES REFERRED TO

AC	= Law Reports, Appeal Cases
AER	= All England Law Reports
ATC	= Annotated Tax Cases
BCLC	= Butterworths Company Law Cases
Ch	= Law Reports, Chancery Division
Cr App R	= Criminal Appeal Reports
ICR	= Law Reports, Industrial Cases Reports
IRLR	= Industrial Relations Law Reports

Abbreviations and References

ITR	=	Industrial Tribunal Reports
LJKB	=	Law Journal Reports, New Series, King's Bench (ended 1949)
Lloyd's Rep	=	Lloyd's List Law Reports
L S Gaz	=	Law Society's Gazette
QB/KB	=	Law Reports, Queen's (King's) Bench Division
TLR	=	Times Law Reports (last year of publication 1952)
WLR	=	Weekly Law Reports

1 Introduction

1.1 SCOPE AND AIMS OF THIS BOOK

Employment law is fully recognised today as a subject of the greatest importance. Legislation passed in recent years has transformed the law and created entirely new statutory rights and obligations. Inevitably, a wealth of reported tribunal and court decisions on the meaning and effect of these new provisions has also built up.

This handbook seeks to explain the legislation in its context, along with the common law on employment matters. It is intended as a reference guide for the employer, company secretary, manager or personnel officer involved daily in decisions concerning the rights of employees. It is also intended to serve as a comprehensive handbook on employment law for solicitors, employees, trade union officials and all kinds of advisers and professional people.

The remainder of this chapter serves as an introduction to the subject by examining a number of fundamental aspects of current employment law. It concludes with a checklist of the areas of law relevant to the various stages of employment.

1.2 Employment law and trade union law

The emphasis of this book is on the law affecting the individual employment relationship, i.e. directly applying to employers and their employees. It therefore provides detailed coverage of the law governing the contract of employment, termination of employment, redundancy, unfair dismissal, etc. The importance of trade unions is nonetheless fully recognised, and the status, functions and liabilities of trade unions and the rules governing closed shop agreements are considered in appropriate chapters. However, it has not been possible, in the space available, to cover trade union law in the depth accorded to individual employment law.

1.3 WHAT CONSTITUTES EMPLOYMENT?

One of the most fundamental questions asked is whether a particular worker is an employee or not. An employee is a person who agrees to work for another person pursuant to a *contract of employment* (or 'contract of service' to use the more traditional term). It is important to be able to distinguish a contract of employment from other types of agreement under which services are rendered, and there are a number of characteristics which enable a contract of employment to be identified. One problem which can often arise is deciding whether a particular person doing work for another is working as an employee, i.e. under a contract of employment, or as an independent contractor (or 'self-employed' person) under a contract *for services*. These matters are discussed further in EMPLOYEE OR SELF-EMPLOYED? (15).

1.4 The contract of employment

The most important matters to be borne in mind are the following.

(*a*) In general, the parties are free to agree whatever contractual terms they wish – this means, among other things, that they may agree that the person doing the work is either an employee or an independent contractor.

(*b*) However, *all the terms* of the contract, and the way in which it is performed, will be looked at in deciding whether it is a contract of employment or not, so it will not be sufficient, for example, merely to agree that the contract is a contract for services and not a contract of employment.

(*c*) Whether or not the contract is a contract of employment certain further terms may be implied, if not expressly agreed.

(*d*) If the contract *is* a contract of employment, all the statutory employment rights are capable of applying, if the pre-conditions are satisfied, and (subject to limited exceptions) any term of the contract excluding these rights is *ineffective*.

(*e*) If the contract *is not* a contract of employment, the main statutory employment rights cannot apply, because they apply only for the benefit of people working under a contract of employment.

For further details, see CONTRACT OF EMPLOYMENT (10) and EMPLOYEE OR SELF-EMPLOYED? (15).

1.5 SOURCES OF EMPLOYMENT LAW

The legal rules governing employment law are derived from two principal sources

(*a*) the terms of the contract of employment, as modified, restricted or extended by the law of contract;

(*b*) Acts of Parliament and regulations, which operate outside the contract (e.g. the law on unfair dismissal) and, of increasing importance, European legislation.

These two categories are considered briefly below, but they are not exhaustive. For example, the law of 'torts' (wrongful acts which cause damage or loss) is important in relation to civil liability for industrial accidents, civil liability for strikes, etc.

There are two additional sources which are of importance in the operation of employment law

(i) COLLECTIVE AGREEMENTS (8);

(ii) CODES OF PRACTICE (7).

1.6 Terms of the contract of employment

Generally, the employer and employee are free to agree whatever terms they wish. Therefore, the most basic legal rules governing the employment relationship are those agreed by the parties themselves, for example the type of work to be done, place of work, rate of pay, etc. In practice, the more detailed terms and conditions of the contract are sometimes not discussed and agreed individually with each employee. Many employers have written standard terms and conditions of employment for all employees, sometimes drawn up and agreed in consultation with officials of recognised trade unions.

In cases where a disagreement arises, the main problem is often evidential. If an employer does not provide written particulars of the terms and conditions of employment, or if a particular matter was agreed orally but never put in writing, years later memories will have faded and there may be no reliable evidence of precisely what was agreed. This is why employers are under a statutory obligation to provide a written resumé of the main contractual terms to each employee within a short time after he begins his job. They must notify changes in the same way. (See 10.7 CONTRACT OF EMPLOYMENT.)

1.7 Employment legislation

The main statutory employment rights are now to be found in

Employment Protection (Consolidation) Act 1978, as amended.

The principal amending Acts are the *Employment Act 1980* , the *Employment Act 1982* and the *Employment Act 1988*.

In addition, there is a considerable amount of anti-discrimination legislation affecting employment. The three main Acts are

Equal Pay Act 1970, as amended
Sex Discrimination Act 1975, as amended
Race Relations Act 1976.

The main Acts governing trade unions and trade disputes are

Trade Union and Labour Relations Act 1974,
as amended.
Employment Act 1980
Employment Act 1982
Trade Union Act 1984
Employment Act 1988
Employment Act 1989

This book provides an account of the effect of all of these main legislative provisions, with references to the specific provisions and to decided cases. However, a reader who is called upon to consider the law in detail would probably be well advised to obtain copies of the Acts themselves in addition. The Acts are obtainable from the HMSO or through bookshops. For people requiring a complete reprint of all the relevant legislation, compendia of employment legislation are published commercially by a number of law publishers. As mentioned in the Preface, in a particular case of doubt or difficulty the reader should consult a professional adviser.

Leaflets. The Department of Employment produces a large number of free explanatory leaflets dealing with particular aspects of employment legislation (e.g. unfair dismissal, redundancy payments). This book gives the name and reference number of each leaflet at the beginning of the relevant chapter. They may also be useful, for example, to provide to employees to explain their rights. Leaflets become out of date when the law changes and they are then reprinted or discontinued. There is a very real danger in using a leaflet that is out of date: it is important to ensure that any leaflet being used is the latest reprint available.

European Legislation. Where English domestic legislation has failed fully to implement EC Treaty obligations, individuals may rely in the English courts upon the EC Treaty, and, where the employer is the State, upon certain EC directives.

In the employment context, this has been done to establish claims for equal pay and equal treatment. The main European legislation dealing with equal pay and equal treatment is

Article 119 EC Treaty
Directive 76/207

EC legislation is also important where a business is transferred from one employer to another. See *Directive 77/187*, implemented in the United Kingdom by the *Transfer of Undertakings (Protection of Employment) Regulations 1981 (SI 1981 No 1794)*, and TRANSFER OF UNDERTAKINGS (53).

1.8 GEOGRAPHICAL SCOPE OF THIS BOOK

This book seeks to explain the law applying in England and Wales. Much of the relevant legislation applies, without significant differences, to *Scotland*. However, Scotland has a quite different legal system from that of England and Wales, and different legal traditions. It also has a separate system of courts and tribunals. This book should not be regarded as authoritative on the law applying in Scotland because specific matters of Scottish law have not been taken into consideration. For example, the explanation of attachment of earnings for payment of debts (Chapter 32) relates to England and Wales only: different procedures apply in Scotland.

The legal system and legal traditions of *Northern Ireland* are much more similar to those of England and Wales, but the legislation discussed in this book generally does not apply to Northern Ireland. Northern Ireland has a separate legislative code, although on employment law its provisions are co-ordinated with those of Great Britain. The province also has a separate system of courts and tribunals. Therefore, while the law will often be similar, this book is not authoritative on Northern Ireland employment law and any reader in Northern Ireland is advised to consult the specific Northern Ireland legal sources on any particular issue.

This book does not contain an account of the laws relating to employment applying in the Channel Islands or the Isle of Man.

1.9 STAGES OF EMPLOYMENT — CHECKLIST

The chapters of this book are arranged in alphabetical order to assist the reader in tracing all the areas of law that may relate to a particular problem. The following checklist sets out the chronological stages of employment, from selection for appointment to termination, and beyond, together with a list of chapters relevant to each stage. (The order of these topics should not be taken as a prophecy of doom!)

All stages	
General	Contract of Employment (10) Employee or Self-Employed? (15)
Discrimination	Equal Pay (19) Racial Discrimination (37) Sex Discrimination – I and II (44, 45)
Statutory rights	Continuous Employment (9) 'A Week's Pay' (58)

Chronological stages

Selection for appointment	Children and Young Persons (5) Disabled Employees (12) Employee's Past Criminal Convictions (17) Foreign Employees (22)
Terms of engagement	Contract of Employment (10) Employee or Self-Employed? (15) Engagement of Employees (18) Probationary Employees (35)
Duration of employment	Continuous Employment (9) Temporary and Seasonal Employees (48) Transfer of Undertakings (53)
Pay, etc.	Benefits in Kind (3) Equal Pay (19) Pay – I and II (31, 32) Pay As You Earn (33) Sickness and Sick Pay (46) Wages Councils (57)
Terms and conditions (other than pay)	Collective Agreements (8) Contract of Employment (10) Directors (11) Equal Pay (19) Holidays (26) Public Sector Employees (36) Restraint of Trade and Confidential Information (41) Service Lettings (43) Transfer of Undertakings (53) Wages Councils (57)
Safety and welfare	Children and Young Persons (5) Education and Training (14) Health and Safety at Work – I and II (24, 25) Maternity Rights (29) Medical Suspension Payments (30) Sickness and Sick Pay (46) Time off Work (50)
General management	Advisory, Conciliation and Arbitration Service (2) Codes of Practice (7) Employee Participation (16)
Trade unions	Closed Shop (6) Disclosure of Information (13) Health and Safety at Work – II (25) Trade Unions – I and II (51, 52)
Trade disputes	Advisory, Conciliation and Arbitration Service (2) Central Arbitration Committee (4) Codes of Practice (7) Picketing (34) Strikes and Industrial Action (47)

Lay-offs	Guarantee Payments for Workless Days (23) Redundancy – I (38)
Discipline and breach of contract	Termination of Employment (49) Unfair Dismissal – II (55)
Termination of employment (generally)	Closed Shop (6) Maternity Rights (29) References (40) Restraint of Trade and Confidential Information (41) Termination of Employment (49) Transfer of Undertakings (53) Unfair Dismissal – I, II and III (54, 55, 56) Wrongful Dismissal (59)
Redundancy	Redundancy – I and II (38, 39) Unfair Dismissal – II (55)
Retirement	Retirement (42)
Claims against employer – Dismissals	Industrial Tribunals (27) Redundancy – I and II (38, 39) Unfair Dismissal – I, II and III (54, 55, 56) Wrongful Dismissal (59)
Insolvency of employer	Insolvency of Employer (28)

1.10 STANDARD SCALE OF FINES

At various points in the book, reference is made to the standard scale of maximum fines which may be imposed upon conviction of an adult of a summary offence.

These are at present as follows:

Level on the scale	*Amount of fine (£)*
1	50
2	100
3	400
4	1,000
5	2,000

(*Criminal Justice Act 1982, s 37*; *Criminal Penalties etc. (Increase) Order 1984 (SI 1984 No 447)*).

2 Advisory, Conciliation and Arbitration Service (ACAS)

2.1 The Advisory, Conciliation and Arbitration Service was established pursuant to powers conferred by the *Employment Protection Act 1975 (EPA)*. Its duties are to bring about an improvement in industrial relations and in particular to encourage the extension, development and reform of the machinery for collective bargaining. [*EPA s 1(2)*].

2.2 CONSTITUTION

The Secretary of State for Employment appoints the members of ACAS in accordance with the requirements laid down in *EPA 1 Sch*. Those requirements ensure that both employers' organisations and workers' organisations are consulted before appointments are made and that a balance is maintained between employers' and workers' interests.

2.3 CONCILIATION

The most important function of ACAS is to conciliate in trade disputes. ACAS may appoint either an independent person or an officer of the Service to offer assistance to the parties to the dispute. No payment is required for such assistance. During the course of conciliation the parties will be encouraged to use any existing procedures to resolve the conflict. [*EPA s 2*].

2.4 Conciliation on industrial tribunal complaints

ACAS appoints conciliation officers to conciliate on matters which are or could be the subject of proceedings before an industrial tribunal.

Conciliation officers may (and must if required to do so by a party to the complaint) take action to conciliate on most claims which can be brought before an industrial tribunal, including claims of sex or race discrimination. [*EPCA ss 133, 134; Sex Discrimination Act 1975 (SDA), s 64; Race Relations Act 1976 (RRA), s 55*]. Either the person making the complaint or the person against whom the complaint or application is made may request the assistance of a conciliation officer.

Before a complaint is presented to an industrial tribunal, the conciliation officer will only take action if requested to do so by a party to the potential complaint. [*EPCA ss 133(3), 134(3); SDA s 64(2); RRA s 55*]. He must conciliate if requested to do so by both parties to the potential complaint, or if he considers that he could conciliate with a reasonable prospect of success. He may conciliate (at the request of either party) as soon as action has been taken in respect of which a person could present a complaint to an industrial tribunal. [*EPCA s 134(3); EA 1980, 1 Sch 18*]. Once a complaint has been presented to an industrial tribunal, a conciliation officer must conciliate whether or not he is requested to do so if he considers that he could conciliate with a reasonable prospect of success, or when he is requested to do so by both parties. [*EPCA ss 133(2), 134(1); SDA s 64(1); RRA s 55(1)*].

Where the complaint is one of unfair dismissal, and the complainant has ceased to be employed by the employer against whom the complaint is made, the conciliation officer is required to seek the complainant's reinstatement or re-engagement. Where the complainant does not wish for either of these remedies, or where reinstatement or re-engagement is not practicable, the conciliation officer will attempt to obtain for him a sum by way of compensation. [*EPCA s 134(2)*].

Thus, if a complaint is presented to an industrial tribunal, the respondent employer will often be contacted by a conciliation officer. The conciliation officer will usually outline the complainant's grievance and may convey the respondent's comments back to the complainant. If the respondent does not want his comments conveyed to the complainant he should make this clear to the conciliation officer. No comment of a conciliation officer may be referred to at any tribunal hearing. In addition, nothing communicated to a conciliation officer, in connection with the performance of his functions, is admissible in evidence in any proceedings before an industrial tribunal, except with the consent of the person who communicated it to the officer. [*EPCA ss 133(6), 134(5); SDA s 64(4); RRA s 55(4)*].

The important role of conciliation officers is emphasised by the fact that an agreement to settle an industrial tribunal complaint will only be binding on the parties if the agreement relates to a complaint or potential complaint where a conciliation officer has taken action in accordance with his statutory powers. Unless an agreement to settle a claim or a potential claim is made in a case where a conciliation officer has taken action under his statutory powers, the agreement is unenforceable, leaving the complainant free to pursue his claim before an industrial tribunal. [*EPCA s 140(2)(d)(e)(g); SDA s 77(4)(a); RRA s 72(4)(a)*]. In *Duport Furniture Products Ltd v Moore* [*1982*] *ICR 84*, a conciliation officer was considered to have taken such action in circumstances where the parties had already reached a settlement. In that case the officer ascertained that they had truly reached agreement, which he then recorded in writing on a form designed for the purpose (form COIT 3). Where a conciliation officer assisted the parties in reaching an oral agreement, that agreement was held to be binding, notwithstanding that it had not been recorded in writing. (*Gilbert v Kembridge Fibres Ltd* [*1984*] *ICR 188*; see also *Hennessy v Craigmyle & Co Ltd* [*1986*] *ICR 461*). A conciliation officer is not under a duty to advise an employee on the relevant legislation, but an agreement reached with his assistance may be set aside if he acts partially or adopts unfair methods. (*Slack v Greenham (Plant Hire) Ltd* [*1983*] *ICR 617*).

Thus, in order to ensure that an agreement to settle a complaint or potential complaint is enforceable, parties should seek the assistance of a conciliation officer to promote a settlement and have him record the agreement on the appropriate form.

2.5 ARBITRATION

If conciliation fails in a trade dispute, ACAS may, with the consent of all parties to the dispute, refer the matters in dispute for the arbitration of

(*a*) an independent arbitrator, not being an employee of ACAS; or

(*b*) the CENTRAL ARBITRATION COMMITTEE (4).

[*EPA s 3*].

An award by an arbitrator may be published if ACAS so decides and all the parties concerned consent. [*EPA s 3(4)*].

Arbitration Act 1950, Part 1 does not apply to such an arbitration and the arbitrator's determinations are not legally binding upon the parties. [*EPA s 3(5)*].

2.6 ADVICE

ACAS is empowered, on request or on its own initiative, to offer advice to employers, workers and their organisations on any matter concerned with industrial relations or employment policies, including the following

(*a*) the organisation of workers or employees for the purpose of collective bargaining;

(*b*) the recognition of trade unions by employers;

(*c*) machinery for the negotiation of terms and conditions of employment and for joint consultation;

(*d*) procedures for avoiding and settling disputes and workers' grievances;

(*e*) questions relating to communication between employers and workers;

(*f*) facilities for officials of trade unions;

(*g*) procedures relating to the termination of employment;

(*h*) disciplinary matters;

(*j*) manpower, planning, labour turnover and absenteeism;

(*k*) recruitment, retention, promotion and vocational training of workers;

(*l*) payment systems, including job evaluation and equal pay.

[*EPA s 4(1)*].

ACAS has the right, without the consent of interested parties, to publish its findings on any of these topics. This advice will be of a general nature, not relating to specific employers or employees. [*EPA s 4(2)*].

2.7 INQUIRY

ACAS may, if it thinks fit, inquire into any question relating to industrial relations generally or to industrial relations in any particular industry or in any particular undertaking or part of any undertaking. [*EPA s 5(1)*].

The findings of such an inquiry, together with any advice given in connection with those findings, may be published by ACAS if it appears to it that publication is desirable for the improvement of industrial relations. Before deciding whether to publish, ACAS must send a draft of the findings to all the parties appearing to ACAS to be concerned, and take account of their views. [*EPA s 5(2)*].

2.8 Relationship between advice and inquiry

Although, as can be seen, there is considerable overlap between the provisions of *EPA ss 4 and 5*, it is thought that the advice given under *Sec 4* (see 2.6 above) will be of a general nature with little or no reference to particular employers or employees, and which can therefore be published without obtaining their consent, whereas the findings of an inquiry under *Sec 5* will refer to particulars, and for that reason certain restrictions on publication are imposed.

2.9 CODES OF PRACTICE

ACAS has a general power to issue new Codes of Practice to give practical guidance for promoting the improvement of industrial relations. [*EPA s 6*]. It has issued three Codes of Practice so far

No 1: Disciplinary Practice and Procedures in Employment.

No 2: Disclosure of Information.

No 3: Time Off for Trade Union Duties.

In November 1985, ACAS issued a consultative document on a draft code concerned with disciplinary and other employment procedures. However, the document has eventually been issued as an advisory handbook rather than a formal Code. This is discussed more fully in the chapter on CODES OF PRACTICE (7).

These Codes (but not the advisory handbook) are set out in full in the Appendix. For the legal effect of these Codes of Practice, see 7.3 CODES OF PRACTICE.

2.10 CONTACTING ACAS

ACAS headquarters are at 27 Wilton Street, London SW1X 7AZ. Tel. 01-210 3000. However, for enquiries, leaflets etc. a person should contact his or her regional office, as listed below.

Regional offices

Northern Region
Westgate House, Westgate Road, Newcastle-upon-Tyne NE1 1TJ
Tel: 091-261 2191

Cumbria	Tyne and Wear	Cleveland
Northumberland	Durham	

Yorkshire and Humberside Region
Commerce House, St Albans Place, Leeds LS2 8HH
Tel: (0532) 431371

North Yorkshire	South Yorkshire	Humberside
West Yorkshire		

London Region
Clifton House, 83-117 Euston Road, London NW1 2RB
Tel: 01-388 5100

South East Region
Westminster House, 125 Fleet Road, Fleet, Hants GU13 8PD
Tel: (0252) 811868

Cambridgeshire	Hertfordshire	Hampshire (except Ringwood)
Norfolk	Essex	
Suffolk	Berkshire	Isle of Wight
Oxfordshire	Surrey	East Sussex
Buckinghamshire	Kent	West Sussex
Bedfordshire		

South West Region
Regent House, 27a Regent Street, Clifton, Bristol BS8 4HR
Tel: (0272) 744066

Gloucestershire	Cornwall	Dorset
Avon	Devon	Ringwood
Wiltshire	Somerset	

Midlands Region
Alpha Tower, Suffolk Street, Queensway, Birmingham B1 1TZ
Tel: 021-631 3434

Northamptonshire (except Corby)	Staffordshire (except Burton-on-Trent)	Hereford & Worcester
Shropshire	West Midlands	Warwickshire

Nottingham Office: 66-72 Houndsgate, Nottingham NG1 6BA
Tel: (0602) 415450

Derbyshire (except High Peak District)	Leicestershire	Lincolnshire
Nottinghamshire	Corby	Burton-on-Trent

North West Region
Boulton House, 17-21 Chorlton Street, Manchester M1 3HY
Tel: 061-228 3222

Lancashire	High Peak District of Derbyshire	Greater Manchester
Cheshire		

Merseyside Office: Cressington House, 249 St Mary's Road, Garston, Liverpool L19 0NF
Tel: 051-427 8881

Scotland
Franborough House, 123-157 Bothwell Street, Glasgow G2 7JR
Tel: 041-204 2677

Wales
Phase 1, Ty Glas Road, Llanishen, Cardiff CF4 5PH
Tel: (0222) 762636

3 Benefits in Kind

3.1 OUTLINE

For income tax purposes, the emoluments of an office or employment are chargeable to tax under Schedule E. 'Emoluments' include 'all salaries, fees, wages, perquisites and profits whatsoever'. [*Income and Corporation Taxes Act 1988, s 131(1)*]. All perquisites, or benefits in kind, in money or money's worth are taxable under this general provision unless specifically exempt (or otherwise taxed); but the provision does not cover benefits not in money or money's worth. Certain other types of benefit, however, are specifically made taxable, and certain further ones are made taxable if received by directors or higher paid employees (see 3.2 and 3.5 below). In general terms, the amount assessable in respect of a benefit is its cash value or its cost to the employer less any amount made good by the employee (see 3.6 below).

Detailed information on the tax treatment of benefits in kind is to be found in *Tolley's Income Tax 1989/1990* (or later edition). Concise factual information, in tabular form, is contained in *Tolley's Tax Data 1989/1990* (or later edition). A brief account of general principles in relation to those benefits most commonly derived from employment is given in 3.3-3.6 below. Special rules applying to employee share schemes are outlined briefly in 3.7-3.9 below.

Note that a knowing failure to declare benefits to tax may preclude a party from relying upon the contract in the court or tribunal (see 10.14 CONTRACT OF EMPLOYMENT).

3.2 'Directors and higher-paid employees'

For the purposes of the special charging provisions mentioned in 3.1 above, a 'director or a higher-paid employee' is either of the following

(*a*) A director of a company unless

  (i) he has no material interest (i.e. his interest does not exceed 5% with or without associates) in the company; and

  (ii) either he is a full-time working director or the company is non-profit making or a charity.

(*b*) An employee (including a director) whose earnings are £8,500 per year or more, inclusive of all benefits in kind and before deduction of any necessary expenses of the employment. The £8,500 figure has not been altered since 1979.

[*ICTA 1988, s 167*].

3.3 GENERAL RULES

Taxable benefits

(*a*) Cash vouchers – taxed on their redemption value.

(*b*) Non-cash vouchers – taxed on the cost to the employer of providing them.

(*c*) Credit tokens – taxed on the cost to the employer of the money, goods or services obtained.

(*d*) Expense allowances – taxable subject to relief for actual expenses; see 3.6 below.

(*e*) 'Living accommodation' – taxed on the annual value (as defined) or the actual rent paid by the employer if greater, subject to exemptions (e.g. where the employee is a representative occupier). For accommodation costing in excess of £75,000, a higher value is attributed to the excess.

(*f*) Shares – an employee who is given shares, or allowed to acquire shares on terms more favourable than those available to the public, is taxed on the value of the benefit he receives. Special rules impose additional charges to tax in relation to certain share option and share incentive schemes.

(*g*) Nursery facilities – taxed on the cost to the employer.

3.4 Tax-free benefits

(*a*) Meals provided in a canteen – not assessable, but taxable on directors and higher-paid employees if not provided for the staff generally.

(*b*) Luncheon vouchers – not taxable up to 15 pence per day.

(*c*) Approved superannuation or pension schemes – contributions by an employer are not taxable.

(*d*) Medical insurance premiums – but taxable on directors and higher-paid employees, see 3.5(*a*) below.

(*e*) Use of employers' assets (e.g. loans at low interest rates or interest-free, or the use of a company car) – not taxable under the general rules, provided they are not in money or money's worth (but they will be assessable for directors and higher-paid employees, see 3.5(*b*) to (*d*) below).

3.5 ADDITIONAL RULES FOR 'DIRECTORS AND HIGHER-PAID EMPLOYEES'

For directors and higher-paid employees (as defined, see 3.2 above), the following benefits are also taxable.

(*a*) Medical insurance premiums, unless for treatment outside the UK while the employee is working abroad.

(*b*) Company cars (pooled cars, subject to conditions) as follows

(i) Preponderant business use (at least 18,000 business miles per year) – taxed at half the scale rate described in (ii) below.

(ii) Substantial business use (over 2,500 and under 18,000 business miles per year) – taxed at the scale rate dependent on the value, engine capacity and age of car.

(iii) Insubstantial business use (not more than 2,500 business miles per year) or a 'second' car – taxed at one and a half times the scale rate described in (ii) above.

(iv) Car fuel – taxed at a scale rate (based on the value and engine capacity of the car) if provided for private motoring (in a company car). There are no special rules for 'second' cars and insubstantial use; but the rate is halved for a car within (i) above. Contrary to the general rule that taxable benefits can be reduced by any reimbursement by the employee (see 3.6 below), this benefit can only be cancelled by the employee being required to make good (and making good) the cost of all the fuel provided for private use.

The charges under (i) to (iv) above include all benefits in connection with the car except the provision of a driver. They are time-apportioned if the car is not made available for any period, or for at least 30 consecutive days is incapable of being used.

(*c*) Loans – the taxable benefit is the difference between the interest paid (if any) and notional interest at a rate prescribed by the Treasury. There are certain reliefs for loans made at fixed rates not below market value when made, and loans for some specified purposes (mainly loans up to £30,000 for house purchase and improvements). A difference of £200 or less is disregarded.

(*d*) Use of assets other than money, cars and living accommodation – taxed annually at 20% of the market value when first provided for the employee. If ownership is later transferred to him, he is taxed on the market value then, or (if greater) on the excess of the market value when he first used the asset over the total of the yearly charges made.

3.6 REDUCTION OF ASSESSABLE BENEFITS

In all the above cases except car fuel (see 3.5(*b*)(iv) above), the assessable benefit may be reduced by payments made by the employee to the employer and/or by a claim for relief for expenses incurred wholly, exclusively and necessarily in the performance of the duties. The latter is an especially difficult test to satisfy.

3.7 EMPLOYEE SHARE SCHEMES

Profit sharing schemes

ICTA 1988, ss 186, 187 and 9 Sch enable a particular kind of share acquisition scheme to be set up by a company for its employees and directors, the benefits of which will be free of income tax provided that the scheme is approved by the Board of Inland Revenue and the appropriate rules are observed. The basis of the scheme is the establishment of a trust to which the company transfers funds annually (subject to limits) which enable the trustees to acquire shares in the company or its holding company. The shares are earmarked for ('appropriated to') the individual participants, but they continue to be held by the trustees for a minimum 'period of retention' (two years or until earlier death, retirement etc.). Income tax is chargeable at a reduced level if the trustees dispose of the shares (on the employee's instructions) after the period of retention but within five years of appropriation; income tax is not chargeable on disposals five years or more after appropriation. While the trustees retain the shares, they must follow the participant's instructions as to take-overs, etc. and they must pay over to him any dividends (which are taxable in the usual way).

3.8 Savings-related share option schemes

FA 1980, s 47 (now *ICTA 1988, s 185*) introduced a savings-related share option scheme whereby a company may establish a scheme for its employees to obtain options to acquire the company's shares without charge to income tax either on the value of the options or on any subsequent increase in the value of the shares before the options are exercised. For capital gains tax purposes, the market value is not substituted for the consideration given. The scheme must be linked to an approved savings scheme (subject to monthly monetary limits) to provide the funds for the acquisition of the shares when the option is exercised.

3.9 Approved share option schemes

ICTA 1988, s 185 and 9 Sch provides for the establishment of an approved share option scheme under which selected full-time directors and employees can be granted options to purchase shares, without income tax liability arising either on the grant of the option or on the purchase of the shares. In the case of a close company, an individual who has a material interest (10%) in the company is excluded. The purchase price of the shares must be not less than their market value at the time of the grant; and at that time their total value must not exceed £100,000 or, if greater, four times the employee's remuneration. The option must be exercised between 3 and 10 years after being granted. The allowable cost for capital gains tax is the aggregate of the cost of the option (if any) and the cost of the shares.

For a thorough discussion of the schemes outlined in 3.7-3.9 above, see *Tolley's Share Options and Incentives for Directors and Employees*.

4 Central Arbitration Committee (CAC)

4.1 The Central Arbitration Committee (CAC) was established pursuant to *Sec 10(1)* of *Employment Protection Act 1975 (EPA)*.

4.2 CONSTITUTION

The Secretary of State for Employment is responsible for appointing members of the CAC whom he selects from persons nominated by ACAS as being experienced in industrial relations and who include both employers' and workers' representatives. In addition the Secretary of State appoints a chairman and may appoint one or more deputy chairmen after consultation with ACAS. [*EPA 1 Sch Part II*].

4.3 FUNCTIONS

(*a*) Arbitration in trade disputes (see 4.4 below).

(*b*) Resolution of complaints that an employer has failed to disclose information which he was required to disclose by *EPA s 17* (see 13.3 DISCLOSURE OF INFORMATION) [*EPA s 19(1)*] (see 4.5 below).

(*c*) Determination of questions previously referred to the Industrial Arbitration Board. [*EPA s 10(2)*]. (The Board was the successor of the Industrial Court created by the *Industrial Courts Act 1919*, to which trade disputes of various kinds could be referred.)

4.4 ARBITRATION

The CAC may arbitrate on trade disputes at the request of one or more parties to the dispute and provided that all parties consent to the arbitration. The request for arbitration is made to ACAS in the first instance, who may refer the matter to the CAC. [*EPA s 3(1)(b)*]. The award or decision of the CAC on an arbitration is not legally binding upon the parties. [*EPA s 3(5)*].

4.5 COMPLAINT OF FAILURE TO DISCLOSE INFORMATION

The CAC may hear and determine complaints made by an independent trade union recognised for collective bargaining purposes that the employer by whom it is recognised has not disclosed information to which the union is statutorily entitled (see 13.3 DISCLOSURE OF INFORMATION). [*EPA s 19*]. The CAC is only empowered to make an order if the union is recognised by the employer for the particular purpose to which the information relates. (*R v CAC, ex parte BTP Tioxide* [*1982*] *ICR 843*). If the CAC finds the complaint well founded it will specify the information which must be disclosed, the date upon which the employer refused or failed to disclose it and the period within which it must be disclosed. [*EPA s 19(6)*].

If the employer fails to comply with the order of the CAC the union may present a further complaint which may be coupled with, or followed by, a claim regarding the terms and conditions of employees for which and on whose behalf the union is recognised by the employer. [*EPA ss 20, 21*].

If the CAC finds the further complaint well-founded, it may make an award that, in respect of any description of employees specified in the claim, the employer shall from a certain date observe either the terms and conditions specified in the claim or other terms and conditions which the CAC considers appropriate. [*EPA s 21(3)*]. These terms and conditions have effect as part of the contract of employment of any such employee. [*EPA s 21(6)*].

4.6 APPEAL

There is no appeal against an award of the CAC but its decision may be challenged by judicial review proceedings in the High Court and set aside if it can be shown that the CAC

(*a*) misdirected itself in law or exceeded its jurisdiction; or

(*b*) failed to take into account relevant considerations or took into account irrelevant ones; or

(*c*) acted unreasonably, or acted in breach of natural justice.

5 Children and Young Persons

The employment of children and young persons is restricted by legislation, the most important of which is summarised below. A number of such restrictions have been removed by *Employment Act 1989, s 10*. The Youth Training Scheme is considered briefly at the end of the chapter.

5.1 DEFINITIONS

Child. For the purposes of the statutory provisions relating to the employment of children, a child is a person not over compulsory school age (at present 16 years). [*Education Act 1944, s 58; Employment of Children Act 1973, s 3*].

Young person. A person who has ceased to be a child and who is under the age of 18 years. [*Education Act 1944, s 114(1)*].

5.2 RESTRICTIONS ON EMPLOYMENT OF CHILDREN

In general, no child may be employed whether paid or not

(*a*) if he is under the age of 13 years; or

(*b*) before the close of school hours on any day on which he is required to attend school; or

(*c*) before seven o'clock in the morning or after seven o'clock in the evening on any day; or

(*d*) for more than two hours on any day on which he is required to attend school; or

(*e*) for more than two hours on any Sunday; or

(*f*) to lift, carry or move anything so heavy as to be likely to cause injury to him.

[*Children and Young Persons Act 1933, s 18 as amended; Employment of Children Act 1973, 1 Sch Pt 2, 1(1)].*

The Education (Work Experience) Act 1973, s 1 provides that, with certain exceptions, the enactments relating to the prohibition or regulation of the employment of a child in his last year of compulsory schooling shall not apply where the employment is in pursuance of arrangements made or approved by the local education authority. However, the enactments regulating the employment of young persons apply to a child on a work experience programme. [*Sec 1(3)*].

The Secretary of State has power to repeal statutory provisions relating to the employment of persons or classes of persons who have not attained the age of 18 (or a specified lower age not less than 16); he may also amend such provisions so that they refer to school-leaving age rather than a specific age [*EA 1989, s 10(3)(b)(c)*]. But the exercise of those powers may not affect provisions relating to the employment of persons under school-leaving age [*EA 1989, s 10(4)*].

5.3 Local authority powers

Each local education authority is given power to supervise the employment of children in its area.

(*a*) *Requiring particulars.* It may require particulars of how the child is employed, or about to be employed, and at what times and for what periods from

(i) the child's parent or guardian or a person who has actual custody of the child; or

(ii) the person appearing to have the child in his employment or to be about to employ him.

[*Employment of Children Act 1973, s 2(2)*].

(*b*) *Prohibiting or restricting employment.* If it appears to the authority that a child is currently employed, or is about to become employed, in a way (or at times or for periods) which is not unlawful but is unsuitable for the child (by reference to his age or state of health), or otherwise prejudicial to his education, it may by a notice served on either the parent or the employer

(i) prohibit the child's employment in any manner specified in the notice; or

(ii) require his employment to be subject to such conditions (specified in the notice and to be complied with by the person served with it) as the authority thinks fit to impose in the interests of the child.

[*Employment of Children Act 1973, s 2(3)*].

Local authorities are empowered under the *Children and Young Persons Acts 1933-1969* to pass bye-laws restricting the employment of children. The employer who breaches such a bye-law will be guilty of a criminal offence as will any person (other than the person employed) by whose act or default a contravention took place. [*Children and Young Persons Act 1933, s 21*].

In *Portsea Island Mutual Co-operative Society Ltd v Leyland* [*1978*] *IRLR 556*, the Divisional Court quashed the convictions recorded against the company under *Sec 21*. A milk roundsman, exceeding his authority and contrary to the company's instructions, had engaged a boy ten years of age to deliver milk on a Sunday before 9 a.m., contrary to the local authority's bye-laws. Talbot J held ([*1978*] *IRLR* at p 558) that an employer can be liable for such a contravention only if either he employed the child or if an agent of his who is engaged to take persons into his employment (e.g. a personnel manager) did so.

5.4 Special provisions

(*a*) No child may be employed in any industrial undertaking, nor in any British sea-going ship or boat, unless the undertaking or the ship is one in or on which only members of the same family are employed. [*Employment of Women, Young Persons and Children Act 1920, ss 1(1)(2), 3(2), Sch*].

(*b*) Special provisions regulate the employment of children in entertainment. [*Children and Young Persons Act 1933, ss 23-26* as amended by *EA 1989, 3 Sch Part III; Children and Young Persons Act 1963, ss 37-42*].

5.5 EMPLOYMENT OF YOUNG PERSONS

The employment of young persons in factories and shops is governed by the *Shops Act 1950*, the *Factories Act 1961* and the *Offices, Shops and Railway Premises Act 1963 (OSRPA)*, as amended by *EA 1989*. However, *OSRPA* does not apply to premises where only close relatives of the employer are employed. [*OSRPA s 2(1)*]. The *Young Persons (Employment) Act 1938 (YPEA)* governed a wide variety of employments, but is repealed (from two months after Royal Assent) by *EA 1989*, which also repeals many of the restrictions contained in the *Factories Act 1961*.

5.6 **TRAINING PROGRAMMES**

Youth Training Scheme

The principal provision made for young people is the Youth Training Scheme (YTS). YTS provides training and work experience for school leavers. 16 year-olds are given two years of training and 17 year-olds, one year.

The two-year programme involves at least 20 weeks off-the-job training (in a college or training centre) in addition to on-the-job training and planned work experience. 16 year-old entrants receive a tax-free allowance of £29.50 a week in their first year, but this will increase to £35.00 in their second year. Those joining on a one-year entitlement will receive £29.50 for the first three months and £35.00 for the other nine months.

A range of grants is available to employers and organisations who become YTS providers. It is most unlikely that young people participating in YTS will as such be regarded as employees (although the employer may now opt to give his YTS trainees express employed status). In *Daley v Allied Suppliers Ltd* [*1983*] *ICR 90*, the EAT held that a participant in the YOP scheme, the predecessor of the YTS, was not an employee because 'the underlying purpose of any contract between (the young person and the company with whom she was placed) was not to establish a relationship of an employer and employee but to enable her to acquire certain skills and experience'. Similar observations may be made of the YTS.

However, for the purposes of health and safety legislation, YTS trainees, who are not employed under a contract of employment, are to be treated as being the employee of the person whose undertaking is providing training. [*Health and Safety (Youth Training Scheme) Regulations 1983 (SI 1983 No 1919)*]. Trainees are entitled to 1½ days paid holiday per month and to 3 weeks paid sick leave.

Information about YTS may be obtained from a local Careers office or Jobcentre.

6 Closed Shop

(See the Department of Employment Code of Practice: Closed Shop Agreements and Arrangements; see also DE booklet No. 7 'Union membership rights and the closed shop including the union labour only provisions of the *Employment Act 1982*' (PL 754). N.B. these reflect the position prior to the *Employment Act 1988*.)

Cross-references. For the general nature and liabilities of a trade union see TRADE UNIONS – I (51) and for the rights of members, TRADE UNIONS – II (52); see 55.3 UNFAIR DISMISSAL – II for the general rules on 'union-related' dismissals.

6.1 The *Industrial Relations Act 1971* gave the right to employees to belong to the trade union of their choice or not to belong to a trade union at all. That Act was repealed by the *Trade Union and Labour Relations Act 1974 (TULRA)*, which enabled an employer lawfully to enforce a closed shop by a 'union membership agreement' made with a trade union or trade unions. The *Employment Acts 1980* and *1982* subsequently imposed certain restrictions and conditions on the closed shop. The *Employment Act 1988* has now effectively outlawed dismissals to enforce a closed shop. Dismissals taking effect on or after 26 July 1988 to enforce a union membership agreement are automatically unfair. [*EA 1988, s 11; Employment Act 1988 (Commencement No 1) Order 1988 (SI 1988 No 1118)*]. Employers will now have to confine compliance with union membership agreements to recruitment (as opposed to dismissals), or be prepared to pay heavy compensation.

6.2 DISMISSAL AND THE CLOSED SHOP

The dismissal of an employee will automatically be regarded as unfair if the principal reason for the dismissal was that he was not a member of any trade union, or of a particular trade union, or of one of a number of particular trade unions, or had refused or proposed to refuse to become or remain a member. [*EPCA s 58(1); amended by EA 1982 s 3; EA 1988 s 11(b)*]. (See 55.3 UNFAIR DISMISSAL – II).

'Proposing to refuse to remain a member' covers the situation where the proposed refusal is contingent upon a particular event. (*Crosville Motor Services Ltd v Ashfield* [*1986*] *IRLR 475*).

For the relevance of the employer's belief in the employee's membership or non-membership, see *Leyland Vehicles v Jones* [*1981*] *ICR 428*.

Compensation for the dismissal is assessed as described in 6.4 below.

Note that there is no minimum qualifying period of employment before an employee is entitled to make such a complaint of unfair dismissal.

6.3 FAILURE TO MAKE PAYMENTS

Instead of being a member of a trade union, an employee may be subject to a requirement to make a payment, for example to a charity. If such an employee who is not or ceases to be a union member refuses, in breach of a requirement, to make such a payment and is dismissed for that reason, he will be treated as dismissed for failure to become or remain a member of a trade union. The same is true if he is dismissed for objecting to a provision which entitles his employer to deduct such a payment from his wages. [*EPCA s 58(13)*]. A dismissal for failure to make such a payment or for objecting to such a provision will be regarded as automatically unfair, and will be compensated as described in 6.4 below.

6.4 COMPENSATION FOR DISMISSALS RELATED TO UNION MEMBERSHIP

For the detailed rules on compensation see 56.6-56.19 UNFAIR DISMISSAL – III. Note in particular, however, that *in addition* to the general rules governing unfair dismissal awards, the following apply to 'automatically' unfair dismissals where a closed shop agreement exists.

(*a*) There is a minimum basic award of £2,520 (£2,400 for dismissals before 1 April 1989), though the compensatory award is calculated in the normal way.

(*b*) A special award is made where the employee requests reinstatement or re-engagement and this request is not met.

(i) If the Tribunal does not order reinstatement or re-engagement the special award is 104 weeks' pay or £12,550 (£11,950 for dismissals before 1 April 1989) whichever is the greater up to a maximum of £25,040 (£23,850 for dismissals before 1 April 1989).

(ii) If the Tribunal does order reinstatement or re-engagement but the order is not complied with, the amount of the special award is increased to 156 weeks' pay or £18,795 (£17,900 for dismissals before 1 April 1989) whichever is the greater.

(*c*) There is provision that conduct of the employee in refusing to join a union or to make payments in lieu of joining, or in objecting to such payments, should be disregarded in assessing contributory fault for possible reduction of any part of the award.

(*d*) The employee may request that a third party (e.g. a union) be joined in the unfair dismissal proceedings if pressure by it has induced the dismissal and the award may be made wholly or partly against that third party.

[*EPCA ss 72(c), 72A, 73(4A)(4B), 75A(1)-(4), 76A; EA 1982, ss 4-7*; *Unfair Dismissal (Increase of Limits of Basic and Special Awards) Order 1989 (SI 1989 No 528)*]. (See 56.8, 56.16-56.19, 56.21 UNFAIR DISMISSAL – III.)

6.5 ACTION SHORT OF DISMISSAL

Every employee has the right not to have action short of dismissal taken against him by his employer for the purpose of compelling him to be or become a member of a trade union or a particular trade union, or for the purpose of enforcing a requirement that in the event of his failing to become or ceasing to be a member he must make one or more payments. [*EPCA s 23(1)(c), (1A)*]. Infringement of this right entitles the employee to complain to an industrial tribunal and seek a declaration and compensation. [*EPCA s 24*].

6.6 THE CODE OF PRACTICE

A Code of Practice giving practical guidance on the formulation and operation of closed shop agreements has been issued by the Secretary of State exercising powers under *EA 1980, s 3*. (See further 7.4-7.5 CODES OF PRACTICE.)

The general approach of the Code is that any agreement on union membership 'should protect basic individual rights; should enjoy the overwhelming support of those affected; and should be flexibly and tolerantly applied.' (*Section A, para 3*). However, the *Employment Act 1988* has meant that the Code is no longer of great practical significance.

6.7 INDUSTRIAL ACTION AND THE CLOSED SHOP

The statutory immunity for industrial action is inapplicable where the purpose of the action is to impose union membership requirements or to enforce a closed shop. For a more detailed account of the relevant provisions, see 47.6 STRIKES AND INDUSTRIAL ACTION.

6.8 THE PRE-ENTRY CLOSED SHOP

At present there are no restrictions upon an employer's recruitment policy other than the laws relating to sex and race discrimination. Therefore an employer is entitled to have a policy that he will recruit only members of a particular trade union, although he cannot now fairly dismiss an employee who subsequently resigns his or her union membership. This situation is known as a pre-entry closed shop. If it is prevalent in a particular industry, it allows the union concerned some measure of control over the supply of labour to that industry.

The Government has now published a Green Paper, 'Removing Barriers to Employment' (Cm 655), which is expected to lead to legislation being introduced in the autumn of 1989. It proposes to give individuals a statutory right not to be refused engagement on the ground of non-membership of a trade union, or of refusing to agree to join a union after starting employment. There would be a right of complaint to an industrial tribunal, which would award compensation on the same basis as in discrimination cases (see RACIAL DISCRIMINATION (37) and SEX DISCRIMINATION – II (45)).

7 Codes of Practice

(See Appendix for full text of eight principal Codes of Practice.)

Cross-references. See 13.4 DISCLOSURE OF INFORMATION for details of ACAS Code No 2; 25.14 HEALTH AND SAFETY AT WORK – II for the HSC Code on Safety Representatives and Safety Committees; 50.2, 50.3 and 50.8 TIME OFF WORK for ACAS Code No 3 and the HSC Code on Time Off for Training of Safety Representatives.

7.1 The first Code of Practice was introduced under powers conferred by the *Industrial Relations Act 1971*. Since then a number of other Codes have been issued. Codes of Practice are written in clear terms for the layman in order to give practical guidance. Employers are advised to read the existing and any new Codes of Practice issued and to follow their provisions whenever applicable. Although following a Code of Practice does not guarantee success in any potential claim in an industrial tribunal, the employer who can show that he has followed its provisions will be on firm ground.

In broad terms these Codes of Practice are all 'non-statutory' and cannot be enforced by law. Nor does breach of a Code *of itself* give rise to any liability. This chapter considers the powers which exist enabling specified bodies or people to issue Codes and the particular legal effect of the different Codes.

7.2 THE INDUSTRIAL RELATIONS CODE OF PRACTICE AND CODES ISSUED BY ACAS

Power to issue the Codes

The *Industrial Relations Code of Practice*, which came into effect on 28 February 1972, was issued under the *Industrial Relations Act 1971* and continued in force on the repeal of that Act by *TULRA 1 Sch Pt I*, and then by *EPA 17 Sch 4*. Its purpose is to give practical guidance for promoting good industrial relations in accordance with certain general principles such as freely conducted collective bargaining and orderly procedures for settling disputes. It emphasises the need for planned employment policies. The greater part of the Code remains in force although certain paragraphs have since been superseded by the three ACAS Codes of Practice, as noted where appropriate in the text of the *Industrial Relations Code* in the Appendix.

The *Employment Protection Act 1975, s 6* gave ACAS the power to issue Codes of Practice, subject to approval by both Houses of Parliament. Three such Codes have been issued

ACAS Code of Practice No 1 on Disciplinary Practice and Procedures in Employment

ACAS Code of Practice No 2 on Disclosure of Information to Trade Unions for Collective Bargaining Purposes

ACAS Code of Practice No 3 on Time Off for Trade Union Duties and Activities.

ACAS Code No 1 has particular relevance for unfair dismissal claims.

ACAS issued a consultative document, entitled 'Disciplinary and Other Procedures in Employment', in November 1985. It was intended to supersede

Code No 1, but in January 1987 the necessary Ministerial approval was refused. Instead, ACAS has issued an advisory handbook, 'Discipline at Work', which draws heavily on the abortive draft Code. The handbook does not have the legal status of a Code (see 7.3 below), but employers should be familiar with it, and there seems to be no reason why a tribunal should not be referred to it. The handbook is quite lengthy and is not included in the Appendix of this book. However, copies can be obtained from: ACAS, 27 Wilton Street, London, SW1X 7AZ, or from any of the regional offices of ACAS, the addresses of which can be found at 2.10.

7.3 **Legal effect**

TULRA 1 Sch 3 specified that a failure on the part of any person to observe a provision of the *Industrial Relations Code of Practice* shall not of itself render him liable to any proceedings. *EPA 17 Sch 4* preserved the *Industrial Relations Code of Practice* and confirmed that the Code is admissible in evidence and any provision which appears to the tribunal to be relevant is to be taken into account by it.

Similarly, *EPA s 6(11)* states that breach of the ACAS Codes does not render a person liable to proceedings, but that the Codes shall be admissible and are to be taken into account if relevant in any proceedings before an industrial tribunal or the Central Arbitration Committee (CAC).

Non-compliance with a Code will not necessarily render a dismissal unfair, but 'a failure to follow a procedure prescribed in the Code may lead to the conclusion that a dismissal was unfair, which, if that procedure had been followed, would have been held to have been fair' (*W. Devis & Sons Ltd v Atkins [1977] AC 931* at *p 955*).

However, a tribunal does not err in law if it fails to take account of the Codes in a case where their provisions are not relied upon by the parties (*Shakespeare and another v British Coal Corporation, The Times, 5 April 1988*).

7.4 CODES ISSUED BY THE DEPARTMENT OF EMPLOYMENT

Power to issue the Codes

The *Employment Act 1980, s 3* empowers the Secretary of State for Employment to issue Codes of Practice, after consultation with ACAS, to be approved by both Houses of Parliament. Two such Codes have been issued, the *Code on Picketing*, in force from 17 December 1980, and the *Code on Closed Shop Agreements and Arrangements*, which came into force on 18 May 1983, replacing the earlier *Code on Closed Shops* to take into account the provisions of the *Employment Act 1982*, but itself largely superseded by the *Employment Act 1988*. A draft *Code on Trade Union Industrial Action Balloting* has been issued for consultation (see STRIKES AND INDUSTRIAL ACTION (47)).

The Department of Employment Codes may supersede any part of or all of a Code issued by ACAS or the *Industrial Relations Code of Practice*. [*EA 1980, s 3(7)*].

7.5 **Legal effect**

The Codes issued by the Secretary of State are specified to be admissible in evidence and to be taken into account, if relevant, in any proceedings not only before an industrial tribunal or the CAC but also *in any court*. [*EA 1980, s 3(8)*].

7.6 Codes of Practice

7.6 **CODES ISSUED BY THE COMMISSION FOR RACIAL EQUALITY**

Power to issue the Codes

The *Race Relations Act 1976, s 47* empowers the Commission for Racial Equality to issue codes of practice containing practical guidance for either or both of the following purposes

(*a*) the elimination of discrimination in the field of employment;

(*b*) the promotion of equality of opportunity in that field between persons of different racial groups.

The Commission for Racial Equality has issued a Code of Practice which came into force on 1 April 1984. (See RACIAL DISCRIMINATION (37) and Appendix.)

7.7 **Legal effect**

The *Race Relations Act 1976, s 47(10)* provides that a failure to observe any provision in a code of practice shall not of itself render a person liable to proceedings. However, such codes are admissible in evidence and where relevant are to be taken into account in any proceedings before an industrial tribunal.

7.8 **CODES ISSUED BY THE EQUAL OPPORTUNITIES COMMISSION**

Power to issue the Codes

The *Sex Discrimination Act 1975, s 56A* empowers the Equal Opportunities Commission to issue codes of practice containing practical guidance for either or both of the following purposes

(*a*) the elimination of discrimination in the field of employment;

(*b*) the promotion of equality of opportunity in that field between men and women.

The Equal Opportunities Commission has issued a Code of Practice which came into force on 30 April 1985. (See SEX DISCRIMINATION II (45).)

7.9 **Legal effect**

The *Sex Discrimination Act 1975, s 56A* provides that a failure to observe any provision in a code of practice shall not of itself render a person liable to proceedings. However, such codes are admissible in evidence and where relevant are to be taken into account in any proceedings before an industrial tribunal.

7.10 **CODES APPROVED OR ISSUED BY THE HEALTH AND SAFETY COMMISSION**

Power to issue the Codes

Regulations made under the *Health and Safety at Work etc. Act 1974 (HSWA)* are sometimes supplemented by Codes of Practice approved and/or issued by the Health and Safety Commission (for details of which see 25.14 HEALTH AND SAFETY AT WORK – II). [*HSWA s 16*]. A full consideration of these Codes is beyond the scope of this book. Two such Codes are directly relevant to employment law, the HSC *Code of Practice on Safety Representatives and Safety Committees* and the HSC *Code of Practice on Time Off for Training Safety Representatives*. They both supplement the *Safety Representatives and Safety Committees Regulations 1977 (SI 1977 No 500)*, made under *HSWA*.

7.11 **Legal effect**

Non-compliance with a relevant HSC Code does not of itself render a person liable to any civil or criminal proceedings. However, where in any criminal proceedings a person is alleged to have committed an offence by contravening a provision for which a code of practice was in force, if breach of the code is established, the offence is proved unless the court is satisfied that the requirement or prohibition was complied with otherwise than by observance of the code. [*HSWA s 17*].

7.12 CODE ISSUED BY THE TRAINING COMMISSION

Power to issue the Code

The Training Commission, formerly the Manpower Services Commission, was empowered to issue Codes at the request of the Government. It issued a *Code of Good Practice on the Employment of Disabled People*. The Commission is dissolved by *EA 1989*.

Content

The Code is concerned with all disabled workers and not only those registered as disabled under the *Disabled Persons (Employment) Act 1944*. The Code sets out specific and realistic objectives for which employers, employees and their representatives can aim and then describes the assistance already available to help achieve these objectives.

Legal effect

Observance of the Code is voluntary.

8 Collective Agreements

8.1 In large industries, the wage rates and terms and conditions of employment of workers in those industries are frequently determined by collective agreements. These are negotiated by the trade unions and employers or employers' associations in the industry concerned. The collective agreements may form the basis for the individual worker's contract of employment if it is agreed between the parties that they should do so.

8.2 Legal effect

Any collective agreement made before 1 December 1971, or after 16 September 1974, will be conclusively presumed not to have been intended by the parties to the agreement to be a legally enforceable contract unless the agreement

(*a*) is in writing; and

(*b*) contains a provision which (however expressed) states that the parties intend that the agreement shall be a legally enforceable contract,

in which event it is conclusively presumed to be legally enforceable. [*TULRA s 18 (1)(2)*]. Condition (*b*) is not satisfied by a mere statement in the agreement that the parties are to be bound by it. (*NCB v NUM* [*1986*] *ICR 736*). To be legally enforceable, a collective agreement must contain a statement, however expressed, that the parties intend that the agreement is to be legally enforceable (see [*1986*] *ICR* at pp *759-60*).

8.3 Effect on individual contracts of employment

Although most collective agreements will not be legally enforceable by the union against the employer or vice versa for the reasons given in 8.2 above, they may have legally binding consequences as between the employer and the individual employee. Their terms may be incorporated into individual contracts of employment either because the contract expressly provides for such incorporation, or because incorporation is an implied term of the contract deriving from custom and practice in the industry. In either case, the collective agreement will be incorporated notwithstanding that the particular employee may not approve of what the union has negotiated, or may even have ceased to belong to the relevant union (see e.g. *Tocher v General Motors (Scotland) Ltd* [*1981*] *IRLR 55*). In *Marley v Forward Trust Group Ltd* [*1986*] *ICR 891* the Court of Appeal held that an employee could enforce the terms of a collective agreement on redundancy which was incorporated into his contract, even though the agreement itself was expressed to be 'binding in honour only'.

However, some terms of collective agreements, such as the terms of conciliation schemes, may not be apt to become enforceable by or against individual employees, and will not be treated as incorporated. (*NCB v NUM* [*1986*] *ICR 736*).

8.4 Changes to collective agreements

Once the terms of a collective agreement are incorporated into individual contracts, the relevant contractual terms are in principle unaffected by the termination of the collective agreement. (*Robertson v British Gas Corporation* [*1983*] *ICR 351; Gibbons v Associated British Ports* [*1985*] *IRLR 376*). However, the true construction of the contract of employment may be that it incorporates the collective agreement between employer and union which is for the time being in force. In such a case, agreed variations in the collective agreement will be effective to alter the terms of the individual contracts of employment.

Where the document which is incorporated is not a collective agreement but a set of rules promulgated by the employer, and the employer is entitled unilaterally to amend those rules, the employee cannot enforce any contractual rights where the employer changes the rules so as to withdraw benefits under them. (*Cadoux v Central Regional Council [1986] IRLR 131*).

8.5 'No strike' clauses

Any provision of a collective agreement which prohibits or restricts the right of workers to engage in a strike or other industrial action, or has the effect of prohibiting or restricting that right, will by law be excluded from forming any part of the contract of employment of an individual worker with an individual employer. This restriction will apply unless the collective agreement

(*a*) is in writing; and

(*b*) contains a provision stating that those terms shall or may be incorporated in such a contract; and

(*c*) is reasonably accessible at his place of work to the worker to whom it applies and is available for him to consult during working hours; and

(*d*) is one where each trade union which is a party to the agreement is an independent trade union (see 51.15 TRADE UNIONS – I); and

(*e*) the individual contract with the worker expressly or impliedly incorporates those terms of the collective agreement relating to strikes.

[*TULRA s 18(4)*].

Despite the fact that a collective agreement and an individual's contract of employment may comply with all the requirements of *Sec 18(4)*, no court will order specific performance of a contract of employment or grant an injunction restraining a breach, or threatened breach, of such a contract which would have the effect of compelling an employee to do any work or attend at any place for the doing of any work. [*TULRA s 16*].

8.6 Miscellaneous

Subject to certain preconditions, collective agreements are automatically transferred from vendor to purchaser on the transfer of an undertaking. [*Transfer of Undertakings (Protection of Employment) Regulations 1981 (SI 1981 No 1794, Reg 6(a))*]. (See TRANSFER OF UNDERTAKINGS (53).)

Terms in collective agreements which are discriminatory between men and women are void. [*Sex Discrimination Act 1986 s 6*]. (See SEX DISCRIMINATION – I (44).)

9 Continuous Employment

(See DE booklet No. 11 'Rules governing continuous employment and a week's pay' (PL 711).)

9.1 Many of the statutory employment protection rights such as the right to claim a redundancy payment and compensation for unfair dismissal are conferred only on those employees who have accrued sufficient continuous employment. Further, the calculation of a redundancy payment and of the basic award in unfair dismissal proceedings is based on the employee's length of continuous service. With some minor exceptions, the length of an employee's period of continuous employment is calculated according to the provisions of *EPCA s 151 and 13 Sch* as amended by *EA 1982, s 20 and 2 Sch*.

The more important provisions relating to continuity of employment are set out in this chapter.

9.2 EMPLOYMENT ACT 1982 AMENDMENTS

Since the relevant provisions of the *Employment Act 1982* came into force on 2 January 1983, questions arising as to whether an employee's employment is of a kind which counts towards a period of continuous employment, or whether periods are to be treated as forming a single period of continuous employment, are still to be determined week by week, but the length of an employee's period of employment is to be computed in *calendar months* and *years of twelve months.* [*EPCA s 151(1)(2); EA 1982, 2 Sch 7(1)*].

9.3 Beginning and end of a period of continuous employment

Subject to the provisions of *EPCA s 151*, as amended (see 9.5 and 9.10 below), an employee's period of continuous employment for the purpose of calculating his entitlement to any right under *EPCA* begins with the day on which he actually starts work and ends with the day by reference to which the length of his period of continuous employment falls to be ascertained for the purposes of the employment right in question. [*EPCA s 151(3); EA 1982, 2 Sch 7(1)*]. In *General of the Salvation Army v Dewsbury* [*1984*] *ICR 498*, the EAT held that 'starts work' in *Section 151(3)* was not intended to refer to the undertaking of the full-time duties of employment but was intended to refer to the beginning of the employee's employment under her contract of employment, which in that case was earlier than the former date.

9.4 EVENTS AFFECTING A PERIOD OF EMPLOYMENT

The rest of this chapter sets out the events which may affect the period of employment. The following matters are considered

- weeks which count (see 9.6 below);
- change of employer (see 9.8 below);
- weeks, or part weeks, which do not count but which do not break continuity (see 9.9 below);
- events which break continuity (see 9.11 below).

9.5 PRELIMINARY POINTS

References in the rest of the chapter are to *EPCA 13 Sch as amended by EA 1982, 2 Sch, para 7(2)* unless otherwise specified.

Presumption of continuity. A person's employment is presumed to have been continuous unless the contrary is shown. [*Para 1(3)*]. Except as otherwise specifically provided, any week which does not count in computing a period of employment breaks the continuity of the period of employment. [*Para 1(1)*].

Employment under 18. For the purpose of calculating the length of qualifying employment for the amount of the payment for redundancy purposes only, an employee's period of continuous employment will be treated as beginning on his eighteenth birthday if that date is later than the actual commencement date of his employment. [*EPCA s 151(4); EA 1982, 2 Sch 7(1)*].

9.6 WEEKS WHICH COUNT

The following weeks count towards a period of continuous employment. (Note that the Secretary of State may by Order substitute a number of hours less than 16 or 8 in the following provisions. [*Para 8*].)

(*a*) Any week in which the employee is employed for 16 hours or more. [*Para 3*].

(*b*) Any week during the whole or part of which the employee's relations with his employer are governed by a contract of employment which normally involves employment for 16 hours or more weekly. [*Para 4*]. In *Lewis v Surrey County Council [1987] ICR 982* the House of Lords held that in calculating the number of hours of employment per week normally involved in a contract of employment for the purposes of *paragraph 4*, regard could be had only to the particular contract of employment in relation to which the complaint of unfair dismissal or redundancy had been made and not to other concurrent contracts with the same employer. Thus, a teacher employed under three separate concurrent contracts was not able to aggregate the number of hours worked under each for the purposes of *paragraph 4*. Continuity of employment may be maintained if there exists a 'global' or 'umbrella' contract which imposes mutually binding obligations during periods when the employee is not performing work for the employer. (See observations in *Nethermere (St Neots) Ltd v Gardiner [1984] ICR 612* and *Hellyer Brothers Ltd v McLeod [1987] ICR 526*, although no such contracts were held to exist in those cases.)

(*c*) Any week governed by a contract which normally involves employment for 8 hours or more (but less than 16 hours), if the employee had previously worked under a contract involving employment for 16 hours or more weekly.

Not more than 26 weeks of employment under a contract involving employment for 8 hours or more weekly (but less than 16 hours), count between 2 periods of employment under a contract requiring work for 16 hours a week or more. [*Para 5*]. (The Employment Appeal Tribunal in *Opie v John Gubbins (Insurance Brokers) Ltd [1978] IRLR 540* held that a similar provision in the *Contracts of Employment Act 1972* was *not* satisfied in a case where an employee worked more than 16 hours in one week and less than 16 hours in another but so as to give an average of more than 16 hours over a period.)

(*d*) An employee who has been continuously employed for 5 years or more under a contract normally involving employment for, or who has actually worked for, 8 hours or more weekly (but less than 16 hours), is considered to have satisfied the requirements of (*a*) or (*b*) above. [*Para 6*]. In considering whether a contract 'normally' involves employment for 16 hours or more weekly, an industrial tribunal will not only consider the terms of the contract at the date of dismissal, but also the terms of the contract as originally drawn and the variations made to its terms during the period the contract was in being. (*Secretary of State for Employment v Deary and others* [*1984*] *ICR 413*). In *Letheby & Christopher Ltd v Bond* [*1988*] *ICR 480*, the EAT held that an employee who was employed under a separate individual contract each week that she worked could not rely on *paragraph 6* to preserve her continuity of employment in weeks when she worked for less than 16 hours.

(*e*) Periods in which there is no contract of employment may count as a period of employment in certain circumstances. If in any week the employee is, for the whole or part of the week,

(i) incapable of work in consequence of illness or injury; or

(ii) absent from work on account of a temporary cessation of work; or

(iii) absent from work in circumstances such that, by arrangement or custom, he is regarded as continuing in the employment of his employer for all or any purposes; or

(iv) absent from work wholly or partly because of pregnancy or confinement,

that week will count as a period of employment. [*Para 9*].

Not more than 26 weeks count under (*e*)(i) above or, subject to the exercise of the right to return to work after pregnancy or confinement, under (*e*)(iv) above, between any periods of employment which themselves count for continuity purposes. The problems arising from *paragraph 9* are considered in 9.7 below.

(*f*) Absence preceding exercise of the right to return to work after pregnancy or confinement counts. If an employee returns to work in accordance with *EPCA s 47* (see 29.17 MATERNITY RIGHTS) after a period of absence from work wholly or partly occasioned by pregnancy or confinement, every week during that period counts in computing a period of employment. [*Para 10*].

(*g*) Intervals in employment where employment is deemed to continue by the provisions of *EPCA ss 55(5), 90(3) and 84(1)* also count. *Secs 55(5) and 90(3)* operate to treat an employee's employment as continuing until the expiry of the statutory minimum period of notice in circumstances where notice should have been given but was not, and the employee was thereby deprived of the minimum qualifying period of employment for claims for unfair dismissal and redundancy payments. *Sec 84(1)* operates to preserve continuity where an employee dismissed for redundancy has his contract renewed or is re-engaged after an interval of not more than four weeks. If a dismissed employee is reinstated or re-engaged in consequence of the presentation of a complaint of unfair dismissal, or as a result of action taken by a conciliation officer under *EPCA s 134(3)*, the employee's continuity of employment is preserved and the weeks in any intervening period count. Further, if the employee has been paid a redundancy payment and it is a term of his reinstatement or re-engagement that he repay that sum, the continuity of his employment for redundancy payments purposes is not broken. [*Labour Relations (Continuity of Employment) Regulations 1976 (SI 1976 No 660); EPCA 13 Sch 20*].

9.7 Periods of 'no employment'

The true meaning of *paragraph 9* (see (*e*) above) has given rise to difficulty in interpretation. Do its provisions apply only where there is no contract of employment in existence, or do they also apply where there is a contract of employment in existence, but the employee is not required to perform any work under that contract? *Paragraph 9* is headed 'Periods in which there is no contract of employment'. Lord Upjohn in *Fitzgerald v Hall, Russell & Co Ltd [1970] AC 984*, at p 1000 ignored the cross-heading; however, the House of Lords in that case held that the provisions could apply to preserve continuity in circumstances in which one contract had come to an end and there was an interval before a new contract was entered into. More recently in *Ford v Warwickshire County Council [1983] ICR 273*, Lord Diplock in the House of Lords held that since *paragraph 9* only applied to an interval of time between the coming to an end of one contract of employment and the beginning of a fresh contract of employment, the expression 'absent from work' where it appeared in *paragraph 9(1)(b)(c) and (d)* must mean not only that the employee was not doing any actual work for his employer but that there was no contract of employment subsisting between him and his employer that would entitle the latter to require him to do any work.

In *Ford* the House of Lords held that the continuity of employment of a teacher whose contract came to an end at the end of every summer term but who was re-engaged in the autumn term was preserved during the summer vacation by *paragraph 9*. Lord Diplock at p 285 said that 'temporary' meant lasting only for a relatively short time, and that it was necessary to ask whether the interval between the two contracts was short in relation to their combined duration. This has become known as the 'mathematical' approach. In *Flack and others v Kodak Ltd [1986] ICR 775* the Court of Appeal had to consider whether six workers in the photo-finishing department of Kodak Ltd had sufficient continuous employment to pursue their employment protection rights. They had been employed intermittently over a number of years. Their period of employment depended on the extent of the department's work. The court decided that the correct approach in deciding whether a gap in an employee's employment, during which he is absent from work on account of a cessation of work, is a temporary cessation for the purposes of *paragraph 9(1)(b)*, is to take into account all the relevant circumstances and in particular to consider the length of the period of absence in the context of the period of employment as a whole. The court held that the periods of absence did not break the continuity of employment. However, in *Sillars v Charringtons Fuels Ltd [1989] IRLR 152* the Court of Appeal held that it was still open to an industrial tribunal, after considering the matter in the round, to conclude that the 'mathematical' approach should be applied in an appropriate case (for example, where there was a systematic pattern of events). That there was an intention to re-employ the applicant later did not necessarily mean that the cessation of work was temporary in the sense of being for a relatively short time.

The 'cessation of work' must involve a reduction in the employer's overall quantum of work, and not merely a decision to allocate work to some other employee. (*Byrne v Birmingham City District Council [1987] ICR 519*). *Byrne* was followed in *Letheby & Christopher Ltd v Bond [1988] ICR 480*. It was also held in

Letheby that an employee employed under single separate contracts (rather than an 'umbrella' contract – see 9.6(*b*) above) who went on holiday at a time convenient to her employers was not absent from work in circumstances such that by arrangement or custom she was regarded as continuing in employment.

In *Ingram v Foxon [1984] ICR 685*, the period between an employee's dismissal and his reinstatement on terms that his continuity of employment would be regarded as unbroken was held to be a period in which the employee was absent from work in circumstances that by arrangement he was regarded as continuing in his employment within the meaning of *paragraph 9(1)(c)* of *Schedule 13* and therefore his continuity of employment was preserved.

9.8 CHANGE OF EMPLOYER

Normally, to be continuous, employment must be with one employer. However, note the following points.

(*a*) If an employee of an employer is taken into the employment of another employer who, at the time when the employee enters his employment is an 'associated' employer of the former employer, that change will not break the continuity of the employee's employment. [*Para 18*].

For the purposes of *EPCA* any two employers are to be treated as associated if one is a company of which the other (directly or indirectly) has control, or if both are companies of which a third person (directly or indirectly) has control. [*EPCA s 153(4)*]. 'Control' in *Section 153(4)* means voting control by a majority of shares. (*Hair Colour Consultants Ltd v Mena [1984] ICR 671*; see also *South West Launderettes Ltd v Laidler [1986] ICR 455*). One view is that the common majority shareholding may be an aggregate of the shareholdings of more than one person and that if this is the case evidence to establish whether the shareholders always vote in the same way will be relevant. (*Harford v Swiftrim Ltd [1987] ICR 439*). However, the EAT in *Strudwick v IBL [1988] ICR 796* declined to follow *Harford*, suggesting that the third party must be a single person, and holding that in any event control would have to be exercised by the same persons in the case of each company, and not by varying combinations of persons. The Court of Appeal in *Payne v Secretary of State for Employment [1989] IRLR 352* held that whilst voting control is the usual and normal test for determining whether two employers are associated within the meaning of *Sec 153(4)*, that test is not conclusive. Shares may be held by nominees and the person who has the legal right to control the exercise of votes has 'control'.

For a discussion of the concepts of a company and of control as applied to statutory corporations and government departments, see *Hasley v Fair Employment Agency [1989] IRLR 106*.

(*b*) If a trade or business of an undertaking is transferred from one person to another, the period of employment of an employee in the trade or business or undertaking at the time of the transfer counts as a period of employment with the transferee and is regarded as unbroken. [*Para 17(2)*]. In *Dabell v Vale Industrial Services (Nottingham) Ltd [1988] IRLR 439*, the Court of Appeal upheld a tribunal's decision that there was such a transfer when there was a substantive handing over of the business but no finally concluded agreement as to the transfer of ownership. (See also *Transfer of Undertakings (Protection of Employment) Regulations 1981 (SI 1981 No 1794)* and TRANSFER OF UNDERTAKINGS (53).)

(*c*) A change in partners, personal representatives or trustees does not break the continuity of an employee's employment. [*Para 17(5)*].

9.9 WEEKS WHICH DO NOT COUNT BUT WHICH DO NOT BREAK CONTINUITY

The following weeks do not count in the computation but do not break continuity. (This applies also where the events occur in only part of the week.)

(*a*) Any week during which the employee takes part in a strike. [*Para 15(1)*].

(*b*) Any week during which the employee is absent from work because of a lock out. [*Para 15(4)*].

(*c*) For the purpose of calculating the qualifying period for pursuing a claim to a redundancy payment and for the purpose of calculating the amount of the payment, any week during which the employee was employed outside Great Britain. [*Para 14(1)*].

9.10 'Postponement' of start of employment

If an employee's period of continuous employment includes one or more periods which do not count in computing the length of the period but do not break continuity, the beginning of the period is treated as *postponed* by the number of days falling within that intervening period, or, as the case may be, by the aggregate number of days falling within those periods. [*EPCA s 151(5); EA 1982, 2 Sch 7(1)*].

9.11 EVENTS WHICH BREAK CONTINUITY

Except as is otherwise provided in *EPCA 13 Sch*, any week which does not count in the computation breaks the continuity of a period of employment.

The receipt of a redundancy payment breaks continuity for redundancy qualification and payment purposes. [*Para 12*].

9.12 TABLE OF QUALIFYING PERIODS FOR STATUTORY EMPLOYMENT PROTECTION RIGHTS

Employment right	*Qualifying period*
	N.B. Not all statutory employment protection rights require a qualifying period of continuous employment.
Guarantee payments Payments during medical suspension	One month ending with the day before the period for which guarantee payment etc. is claimed. [*Section 13 of EPCA as amended by EA 1982, 2 Sch 1*] An employee employed under either a contract for three months or less, or a contract for the performance of a specific task which is not expected to last more than three months, will not qualify unless he has been continuously employed for three months ending with the day before the period for which the guarantee payment etc. is claimed. [*Section 20 of EPCA as amended by EA 1982, 2 Sch 2*]

9.12 Continuous Employment

Employment right	*Qualifying period*
Minimum period of notice	One month [*Sections 49 and 50 of EPCA as amended by EA 1982, 2 Sch 3*] Any contract of a person who has been employed for three months which is a contract for a fixed term of one month or less is deemed to have effect as if it were for an indefinite period and thus subject to the notice provisions. Sections 49(1) and (2) do not apply to a contract made for the performance of a specific task which is not expected to last for more than three months unless the employee has been employed for more than three months. [*Section 49(4) of EPCA as amended by EA 1982, 2 Sch 3*]
Written reasons for dismissal	Six months ending with the effective date of termination. [*Section 53 of EPCA as amended by EA 1982, 2 Sch 4*]. To be increased to two years by *EA 1989, s 15(1)*.
Unfair dismissal	Two years [*Section 64 of EPCA as amended by EA 1982, 2 Sch 5 and SI 1985 No 782*] If an employee is dismissed by reason of a medical suspension requirement or recommendation (cf. *Section 20*) the qualifying period is one month [*Section 63(2)*]. If an employee is dismissed for membership or non-membership of a trade union or for trade union activities, there is no qualifying period [*Section 64(3)*].
Redundancy payment	Two years [*Section 81(1)(4)*]
Consultation of trade union representatives and notification of Secretary of State on redundancy	Three months [*Section 119(7) of EPA as amended by EA 1982, 2 Sch 6*]

10 Contract of Employment

(See also DE booklet No. 1 'Written statement of main terms and conditions of employment' (PL 700).)

Cross-references. See CHILDREN AND YOUNG PERSONS (5) for statutory restrictions on their employment; RESTRAINT OF TRADE, CONFIDENTIALITY AND EMPLOYEE INVENTIONS (41); COLLECTIVE AGREEMENTS (8) and WAGES COUNCILS (57) for their respective effects on individual contracts; 19.4 EQUAL PAY for the statutory equality clause; 31.5 PAY – I for illegal deductions from wages; 44.31 SEX DISCRIMINATION – I for contract terms made void; 47.8 STRIKES for the effect of industrial action on contracts; and 56.2-56.5 UNFAIR DISMISSAL – III for reinstatement and re-engagement orders. See TERMINATION (49) and WRONGFUL DISMISSAL (59) for termination of contract rules. For restrictions on contracting out of statutory provisions, see 19.15 EQUAL PAY, 37.33 RACIAL DISCRIMINATION, 38.13 REDUNDANCY – I, 44.32 SEX DISCRIMINATION – I and 54.18 UNFAIR DISMISSAL – I.

10.1 The contract between an employer and an employee is usually referred to as a contract of employment. Three different categories of question may arise regarding a contract of employment.

(*a*) The question whether a particular agreement under which a person works is a 'contract of employment' or not, which is considered in EMPLOYEE OR SELF-EMPLOYED? (15).

(*b*) Questions relating to the terms or form of a particular contract of employment, which are considered in this chapter. This chapter also considers the requirement to provide certain written particulars of the contract terms if there is no written contract (see 10.4-10.8 below).

(*c*) Questions relating to the remedies available for breach of the contract of employment (see 10.20 below).

10.2 FREEDOM TO EMPLOY

An employer may engage or refuse to engage any person, subject only to the statutory provisions relating to CHILDREN AND YOUNG PERSONS (5), discrimination on grounds of race or sex (see RACIAL DISCRIMINATION (37), SEX DISCRIMINATION – I (44)) and the provisions relating to the employment of foreign nationals (see FOREIGN EMPLOYEES (22)).

10.3 THE FORM OF THE CONTRACT

A contract of employment may be either written or oral or a mixture of the two. This means that its form may range from a document drawn up by solicitors and signed by both parties, to a chat over a cup of tea in the canteen. It is usual for senior executives to be employed pursuant to written agreements drafted by solicitors to meet the specific circumstances. These agreements are usually for a fixed term. Note that a provision for the employment of a director for more than 5 years is void, unless the term has the prior approval of the company in general meeting. A term enabling termination on reasonable notice will be substituted. (*Companies Act 1985, s 319*). Such agreements frequently contain provisions dealing with the tenure by the employee of a directorship of the employing company. They may also contain restrictive covenants (see RESTRAINT OF TRADE,

CONFIDENTIALITY AND EMPLOYEE INVENTIONS (41)). Less senior employees may be asked to sign a standard form of contract of employment. In other cases, the contract will be contained in an exchange of letters, or terms may be agreed orally at an interview. Provided that the parties are in agreement over the essential terms of the contract such as hours and wages there will be a valid contract of employment enforceable by either party. However, an employer is under a duty to give his employees particulars *in writing* of certain important terms of their contracts (see 10.4 below).

10.4 WRITTEN PARTICULARS OF CONTRACT

Although the law does not require the contract itself to be in writing, every employer is required by *EPCA s 1* to give each employee a written statement of particulars of certain terms of his contract not later than thirteen weeks after the beginning of the employee's employment.

10.5 Particulars which must be given

The written statement must

(*a*) identify the parties to the contract; and

(*b*) specify the date when the employment began; and

(*c*) specify the date on which the employee's period of *continuous* employment began (taking into account any employment with a previous employer which counts towards that period).

(For the day on which employment 'begins' see 9.3 CONTINUOUS EMPLOYMENT.)

[*EPCA s 1(2); EA 1982, 2 Sch 8(1)*].

It must also give particulars of the following information which is currently applicable on, or not more than one week before, the date the statement is given

(*d*) the scale or rate of remuneration, or the method of calculating remuneration;

(*e*) the intervals at which remuneration is paid (that is whether weekly, or monthly or by some other period);

(*f*) any terms and conditions relating to hours of work (including any terms and conditions relating to normal working hours);

(*g*) any terms and conditions relating to

- (i) entitlement to holidays, including public holidays and holiday pay (the particulars being sufficient to enable the employee's entitlement, including any entitlement to accrued holiday pay on the termination of employment, to be precisely calculated);
- (ii) incapacity for work due to sickness or injury, including any provisions for sick pay;
- (iii) pensions and pension schemes except any state pension schemes;

(*h*) the length of notice which the employee is obliged to give and entitled to receive to determine his contract of employment, or in the case of a fixed term contract, the date of expiry;

(*j*) the title of the job which the employee is employed to do.

[*EPCA ss 1(3), 2(2)*].

Contracting-out certificate. The written particulars must include a note stating whether a contracting-out certificate is in force for the particular employment concerned. [*EPCA s 1(4)(d)*].

Disciplinary and complaints procedures. *EPCA* further requires that every statement given to an employee shall contain a note

(A) specifying any disciplinary rules applicable to the employee, or referring to a document which is reasonably accessible to the employee and which specifies such rules;

(B) specifying, by description or otherwise

  (i) a person to whom the employee can apply if he is dissatisfied with any disciplinary decision relating to him; and

  (ii) a person to whom the employee can apply for the purpose of seeking redress of any grievance relating to his employment and the manner in which any such application should be made;

and where there are further steps to be taken in any such application, explaining those steps or referring to a document which is reasonably accessible to the employee and which explains them. [*EPCA s 1(4)*].

This requirement does not apply to rules, disciplinary decisions, grievances or procedures relating to HEALTH AND SAFETY AT WORK – II (25). [*EPCA s 1(5)*]. Nor will it apply, except for the requirement to identify a person from whom redress of a grievance may be sought, if, on the date when the employment began, the employer together with any associated employer employed fewer than twenty persons. [*EPCA s 2A*, inserted by *EA 1989, s 13(3)*].

EPCA does not require there to be provisions in the contract on all these matters. It simply requires notice of such provisions that do exist to be given to the employee. *Where there are no provisions relating to any of the matters listed above that fact must be stated*; e.g. where no contractual sick pay is provided. [*EPCA s 2(1)*].

In *Robertson v British Gas Corporation* [*1983*] *ICR 351*, the Court of Appeal approved as being correct the statement of law by the EAT in *System Floors (UK) Ltd v Daniels* [*1982*] *ICR 54* that the statutory written statement of particulars is neither the contract itself nor conclusive evidence of it. For obvious reasons, however, an employer may have difficulty in going behind the written statement.

10.6 Alternatives to written statement of particulars

EPCA provides that instead of such a written statement of particulars

(*a*) a written contract of employment may be given to an employee or made reasonably accessible to him which contains express terms relating to all the particulars required to be given; or

(*b*) a notice may be given to an employee referring him to a document which the employee has reasonable opportunities of reading in the course of his employment or which is made readily accessible to him in some other way and which contains the details required by statute.

[*EPCA s 2(3)*].

10.7 **Changes in contract terms**

Any changes in the contractual terms or in other matters of which written particulars must be given, must be communicated to the employee in writing not more than one month after the change. If the employer does not leave a copy of the amendments with the employee, he must make the amended statement reasonably accessible to him. [*EPCA s 4(1)*]. No change in an employee's contractual terms may be made without his consent (see 10.20).

10.8 **Exceptions**

The requirement to give written particulars applies to all employees except

(*a*) seamen of various kinds [*EPCA s 144*];

(*b*) employees engaged in work wholly or mainly outside Great Britain, unless they ordinarily work in Great Britain and the work outside Great Britain is for the same employer [*EPCA s 141(1)*];

(*c*) a person who already has a written contract of employment giving all the necessary particulars [*EPCA s 5; EA 1989 s 9(5)*];

(*d*) a person re-employed by the same employer after a gap of six months or less who was originally given a statement of particulars. (Changes must still be notified.) [*EPCA s 2(4); EA 1982, 2 Sch 8(2); EA 1989, s 13(2)*].

Part-time workers. There is no duty to give written particulars in respect of a period of employment during which the employee's normal hours of employment are less than 16 per week, except as follows. An employee is entitled to written particulars if he normally works less than 16 hours per week but more than eight and he has been continuously employed for five years or more. There are other minor exceptions. [*EPCA s 3, 13 Sch*].

10.9 **Employees' remedies for failure to give particulars**

An employee who has not been provided with the particulars specified in the Act may make a complaint relating to the failure to an industrial tribunal. [*EPCA s 11(1)(2)*]. An application may be made if no written particulars have been given or if the statement given is incomplete or inaccurate. If it is necessary for the tribunal to *imply a term* it must consider all the facts and circumstances of the relationship between the employer and the employee concerned, including the way in which they had worked the particular contract of employment since it was made. (*Mears v Safecar Security Ltd* [*1982*] *ICR 626*). The tribunal will, if it finds such a complaint well founded, state the particulars which should have been given and the employer will be deemed to have given a statement including those particulars. [*EPCA s 11(5)(6)*]. If the employer has been in breach of any of those terms, the employee may bring an action against him in the county court or the High Court. The right to present a complaint for failure to provide written particulars may be exercised by an employee who has been employed for more than thirteen weeks.

10.10 **TERMS OF THE CONTRACT**

Freedom to agree

The parties are free to agree any terms they wish, subject to certain limitations set out below. If an industrial tribunal is called upon to interpret the terms of a contract, it must apply the same principles as an ordinary court. This means, for example, that the parties' subsequent conduct is not admissible in construing their original written agreement (*Hooper v British Railways Board* [*1988*] *IRLR 517*).

10.11 Express or implied terms

The terms of the contract may be express or implied. Express terms are those that the parties specifically deal with and agree upon. The parties may agree upon certain points by reference to a document such as a collective agreement which thereby becomes incorporated into the agreement between the parties (see 8.2 COLLECTIVE AGREEMENTS).

10.12 Common implied terms

Frequently, many terms of the contract will not be specifically set out or stated. There may be many rights and obligations on either side which are left unexpressed and unspecified. The general rule is that a term will be implied into a contract if it is *necessary* to give it business efficacy or if it was too *obvious* for the parties to need to make it explicit. If it is essential to imply *some* term, the court or tribunal will imply a term which is reasonable (*Courtaulds Northern Spinning Ltd v Sibson and another* [*1988*] *ICR 451*). Terms also may be implied if they are customary in the trade or calling.

Terms commonly implied are the *employee's* duties of

(*a*) fidelity;

(*b*) obedience;

(*c*) working with due diligence and care;

and the *employer's* duty

(*d*) not to destroy the relationship of trust and confidence between the employer and the employee;

(*e*) and the duty of *both parties* to give a reasonable period of notice of termination, when no specific notice has been agreed.

The above list is not exhaustive: other duties can arise in various circumstances. Some of them are dealt with below.

Employee's duties. An employee has a duty to serve his employer faithfully and not to act against the interests of the employer's business. Thus, it would be in breach of an implied term of the contract of employment for the employee to set up a rival business to that of his employer during the period of his employment unless he had been expressly permitted to do so. The employee is also obliged by the implied terms of his contract of employment to obey the reasonable instructions of his employer and to carry out his work conscientiously and honestly. In *Sybron Corporation v Rochem Ltd* [*1984*] *Ch 112*, it was held that the terms and nature of a particular employment might be such that there was a contractual duty to disclose the misconduct of other employees.

In *Cresswell v Board of Inland Revenue* [*1984*] *ICR 508* it was held that an employee was expected to adapt to new methods and techniques in performing his duties, provided the employer arranged for him to receive the necessary training in the new skills and the nature of the work did not alter so radically that it was outside the contractual obligation of the employee.

There must be some contractual term, express or implied, dealing with the place where the employee may be required to work. If there is no express term, that term will be implied which the parties would have agreed if they had directed their minds to the problem. All the circumstances of the case will be considered, including the nature of the business, the nature of the employee's duties and his status, what the employee was told when employed and whether he has in fact been moved from time to time, and whether there is any provision for the payment of expenses for working away from home. The term implied may be that the employee can be required to work anywhere within reasonable daily travelling distance of his home. (*O'Brien v Associated Fire Alarms Ltd [1969] 1 AER 93; Jones v Associated Tunnelling Co Ltd [1981] IRLR 477; Courtaulds Northern Spinning Ltd v Sibson [1988] ICR 451*). See also *Little v Charterhouse Magna Assurance Co Ltd [1980] IRLR 19; Rank Xerox Ltd v Churchill [1988] IRLR 280; McAndrew v Prestwick Circuits Ltd [1988] IRLR 514*.

Employer's duties. Cases on constructive dismissal (see 54.7 UNFAIR DISMISSAL – I), relating to conduct on the part of an employer entitling an employee to resign and claim that he was dismissed, show that the courts are ready to imply a term that an employer will not act so as to destroy the relationship of confidence and trust which should exist between employer and employee. (See e.g. *Lewis v Motorworld Garages Ltd [1985] IRLR 465*.) The contract of employment will also be held to include an implied term that the employer will take reasonable steps to ensure the employee's safety. (See comments in *Dutton & Clark Ltd v Daly [1985] IRLR 363*.)

In *Wigan Borough Council v Davies [1979] ICR 411* a term was implied that the employer in the circumstances of that case should render reasonable support to an employee.

Another implied term which is frequently relied upon by employees is the requirement, where no specific agreement on notice has been reached, that one party should give the other a reasonable period of notice to terminate the employment. What is reasonable will depend upon all the circumstances of the employment (see 49.8 TERMINATION OF EMPLOYMENT).

In the normal case there is no duty upon an employer to provide work. In other words, so long as the employee is fully remunerated, the employer can ask him to stay at home without being in breach of contract. However, there may be exceptions to this rule where earnings vary according to the work done, where an individual such as an actor is dependent upon publicity, or where the employee has skills which may atrophy through lack of use. See *Langston v AUEW (Nos 1 and 2) [1974] ICR 180* and *510; Breach v Epsylon Industries Ltd [1976] ICR 316; Spencer v Marchington [1988] IRLR 392*; and cf. *Warren v Mendy [1989] IRLR 210*.

10.13 Terms automatically varied by statute

Terms which, although they are agreed between the parties, are in breach of certain statutory provisions take effect as if varied to comply with those provisions. For example

(*a*) terms relating to pay which are less advantageous to the employee than those contained in an applicable wages order (see 57.4 WAGES COUNCILS);

(*b*) terms which are less advantageous than those which apply to a member of the opposite sex doing the same or like work, or work of equal value (see 19.5 EQUAL PAY), or which infringe the law on sex discrimination (see 44.31 SEX DISCRIMINATION – I);

(*c*) terms providing for the employment of directors for a fixed period of more than 5 years, which are varied by *Companies Act 1985, s 319* to enable termination on the giving of reasonable notice.

10.14 **Terms which are unlawful or contrary to public policy**

A contract the terms of which are unlawful (e.g., to do an unlawful act) or which are contrary to public policy (e.g., a contract for an immoral purpose) is unenforceable in a court of law. For example, contracts which are a fraud on the Inland Revenue cannot be relied upon to pursue claims for wrongful or unfair dismissal. (*Napier v National Business Agency Ltd [1951] 2 AER 264; Tomlinson v Dick Evans 'U Drive' Ltd* [1978] *ICR 639*). If the employee was not aware of the fact that the contract was being performed unlawfully by the employer (by, for example, not deducting tax from remuneration) the employee may rely on the contract for the purposes of claiming employment protection rights. (*Newland v Simons and Willer (Hairdressers) Ltd* [1981] *ICR 521*). However, ignorance of the law as opposed to the facts is no excuse (*Miller v Karlinski (1945) 62 TLR 85*). If in the course of performing an otherwise lawful contract, the employee commits an unlawful or immoral act he may nonetheless bring a claim for unfair dismissal. (*Coral Leisure Group Ltd v Barnett* [1981] *ICR 503*).

10.15 **UNENFORCEABLE TERMS**

Certain terms, while not being unlawful in the sense of rendering an employer liable to criminal prosecution or a civil action, may be unenforceable by him, as set out in 10.16-10.19 below.

10.16 **Restrictions upon contracting out of certain statutory provisions**

With some exceptions, for instance where a conciliation officer (see 2.3 ADVISORY, CONCILIATION AND ARBITRATION SERVICE) has exercised his statutory powers in the settlement of certain claims, an employer or employee may not contract out of

Sex Discrimination Act 1975
Equal Pay Act 1970
Race Relations Act 1976
Employment Protection Act 1975
Employment Protection (Consolidation) Act 1978
Employment Act 1980
Wages Act 1986 Part I.

Any attempt to do so will be ineffective.

10.17 **Discriminatory terms**

A term in a contract which is contrary to *Sex Discrimination Act 1975* is void and unenforceable against the person discriminated against [*SDA 1975, s 77*]. (There is an equivalent provision in *Race Relations Act 1976, s 72*). Similarly any discriminatory term in a collective agreement is void and unenforceable against the party discriminated against. (See *SDA 1986, s 6*).

10.18 **Terms in restraint of trade**

Sometimes, a contract will contain a term restricting the employee's freedom after he leaves his employment to enter into any similar employment which may be in any way in competition with that of his present employer. Such terms will be regarded as 'in restraint of trade' and therefore unenforceable if their main purpose is simply to restrain competition. However, if the main purpose is to protect something in which the employer has a legitimate interest, such as trade secrets or confidential information, or to protect the employer's goodwill or '*customer connection*' (as it is called in this context), then such a term may be enforceable. These questions are discussed in more detail in RESTRAINT OF TRADE, CONFIDENTIALITY AND EMPLOYEE INVENTIONS (41).

10.19 **Restrictions on industrial action**

Provisions in collective agreements which purport to restrict the right to take industrial action cannot form part of the individual contract of employment unless certain conditions are satisfied (see 8.5 COLLECTIVE AGREEMENTS).

10.20 CHANGE IN TERMS OF CONTRACT

No change in the terms of an employee's contract may be made without his consent. Such consent may be *express*, by the employee agreeing to the change orally, or preferably in writing. Alternatively it may be *implied*, by the employee continuing to work for the employer without protest for a significant period of time whilst being aware of the change.

If the change in contractual terms is of great importance to the employer, the only course of action open to him in circumstances in which the employee does not consent, is to give notice to terminate the original contract and offer new terms. Great care must be taken to adhere to a fair procedure when doing this so as to avoid a successful claim for unfair dismissal. (See UNFAIR DISMISSAL – I (54)).

10.21 REMEDIES FOR BREACH OF CONTRACT OF EMPLOYMENT

Employee's remedies

If an employer is in breach of contract his employee may bring proceedings in the High Court or the county court for sums due under the contract. The employee may refuse to accept the employer's breach as bringing his contract to an end, and can bring such an action while remaining in employment. If the employer's breach of contract is serious and the employee leaves, he can bring proceedings for his prospective loss (see WRONGFUL DISMISSAL (59)) as well as for any sums outstanding at the date of dismissal. The courts are also able to grant declaratory relief.

In certain circumstances, the courts will grant an employee an injunction to restrain the employer from taking action in breach of contract. This is most commonly done to restrain the implementation of a dismissal where a disciplinary or disputes procedure has not been exhausted. (See e.g. *Irani v Southampton and South-West Hampshire Health Authority* [*1985*] *ICR 590* and observations in *R v BBC ex parte Lavelle* [*1983*] *ICR 99*.) An injunction has also been granted to restrain the enforcement of an instruction the employer was not contractually entitled to give (see *Hughes v London Borough of Southwark* [*1988*] *IRLR 55*). However, an injunction will only be granted in the exceptional case where the employer still has full confidence in the employee's continuing ability and other necessary attributes (*Powell v Brent London Borough Council* [*1988*] *ICR 176*). The employer must have rational grounds for saying that he has lost confidence in the employee, and the mere existence of a dispute will not constitute such grounds. Similarly, if new working practices are introduced in breach of contract, an injunction will not be granted where for practical purposes the old system cannot be restored (*MacPherson v London Borough of Lambeth* [*1988*] *IRLR 470*). See also *Dietman v Brent London Borough Council* [*1988*] *ICR 842*, *Ali v London Borough of Southwark* [*1988*] *ICR 567*.

The court will usually be asked to grant an *interlocutory* injunction, i.e. one which seeks to restrain the alleged breach of contract pending the trial (which may not happen for several months or even longer). At the interlocutory stage the judge does not hear oral evidence and will not have time to determine complex questions which may arise. The correct approach is therefore to decide, first, whether there is a serious question to be tried (in other words, is it obvious that one side is going to win?), and, secondly, whether any injustice caused by granting or refusing to grant the injunction could be properly compensated by an award of damages later. If there is a serious question and damages would not be an adequate remedy, the court should base its decision upon the 'balance of convenience'. This will often lead it to preserve the status quo. (See *American Cyanamid Co v Ethicon Ltd* [*1975*] *AC 396*.)

Employer's remedies

If an employee does not perform any of his contractual duties he is not entitled to his contractual wage. Thus an employee is not entitled to be paid for days when he is on strike.

If the employee refuses to perform the full range of his contractual duties, particularly if this refusal is in pursuance of industrial action, the purpose of which is to disrupt the employer's business, the employee will not be entitled to his full contractual wage. (See *Miles v Wakefield Metropolitan District Council* [*1987*] *ICR 368*.) In *Wiluszynski v London Borough of Tower Hamlets* [*1989*] *IRLR 259*, the Court of Appeal held that the Council was entitled to withhold the whole of the employee's wages when the employee refused to perform a substantial part of his duties and it was clear that the employer was not accepting the work which was performed as substantial performance of the contract.

Alternatively, the employer may be able to deduct from the employee's wages a sum representing the financial loss suffered by him as a result of the employee's breach of contract. (See *Sim v Rotherham Metropolitan Borough Council* [*1986*] *ICR 897*).

(See also 31.8 PAY - I below.)

If the employee is in fundamental breach of his contractual obligations, the employer can accept the breach and bring the contract to an end.

An employer may bring proceedings against an employee for damages for breach of contract (see e.g. *Janata Bank v Ahmed* [*1981*] *ICR 791*). Situations which may give rise to such proceedings are a breach of the employee's duty of fidelity, breach of his duty of care and failure to give the notice of termination he is contractually obliged to give. In practice, such claims are rare. What is more common is an application for an injunction to restrain disclosure of confidential information or to enforce a restrictive covenant (see 10.18 above).

In no circumstances may the employee be compelled to work by injunction or specific performance being ordered. That was the common law, and the principle is enacted in *TULRA s 16*. That applies also if such compulsion will be the practical result of granting an injunction against a third party, e.g. the only alternative employer (*Warren v Mendy* [*1989*] *IRLR 210*): the court will not make an order which would reduce the employee to starvation or idleness. However, the Court of Appeal held in *Evening Standard Co. Ltd v Henderson* [*1987*] *ICR*

588 that it may be possible to restrain an employee who does not give proper notice (see 49.18 TERMINATION OF EMPLOYMENT) from working elsewhere during his notice period so long as the employer will provide him with all his contractual benefits without his actually having to work. The *Henderson* principle was approved in *Provident Financial Group PLC and Whitegates Estate Agency Ltd v Hayward [1989] ICR 160*, where an express contractual prohibition was relied upon. However, the Court of Appeal indicated that no injunction would be granted if the plaintiff's business had nothing to do with that of the new employer. It also recognised that an employee might need to work and exercise his skills (the employer in *Hayward* had put the employee on 'garden leave' during his notice period, whereas in *Henderson* work was available if the employee wanted it), and refused to grant an injunction after considering the nature of the job and the length of the notice period (see also *Warren*, and see 10.12 above).

The same general principles relating to the grant of interlocutory injunctions apply as are discussed under 'Employee's remedies', above.

11 Directors

11.1 Directors of companies are subject to many duties both at common law and under statute which are beyond the scope of this book, as is the law governing their appointment, removal, replacement and disqualification. This chapter seeks to draw attention to some of the main questions which may arise in considering the position of a director *qua* employee. (For a more detailed discussion of these questions, see *Tolley's Company Law*.)

11.2 DIRECTORS AS EMPLOYEES

The directors of a company are not automatically its employees; as such, they are merely office-holders. However, they may also have contracts of employment. This is usual in the case of managing directors, and common in the case of other executive directors. In general, a director who devotes all or most of his time to the company and receives a salary will be an employee.

11.3 DIRECTORS' SERVICE CONTRACTS

A director's contract of employment will have to be approved by the board, unless for example the managing director has been given power to fix the terms of employment of other executive directors. Any provisions in the contract which conflict with the company's articles of association will be ineffective, because the board has no power to override the articles.

The company must keep, either at its registered office or at the place where its register of members is kept or at its principal place of business, copies of the contracts of employment of its own directors and of the directors of its subsidiaries (and variations thereto), or written memoranda of the terms if the contracts themselves are not in writing. [*Companies Act 1985, s 318*]. This provision also applies to contracts of employment of 'shadow directors', i.e. those persons in accordance with whose directions or instructions the directors are accustomed to act. [*Secs 318(6), 741(2)*]. The copies must be open for inspection by members. [*Sec 318(7)*]. The requirements are modified if the contract requires the director to work wholly or mainly outside the United Kingdom [*Sec 318(5)*], and excluded if the contract will expire or can be terminated by the company without compensation within the next twelve months. [*Sec 318(11)*].

By *Companies Act 1985, s 319*, a company is prohibited from entering into contracts with its directors which it cannot terminate by notice (or which it can terminate only in specified circumstances) for a period exceeding five years, unless the term is first approved by a resolution of the company in general meeting. A term not so approved is void, and is replaced by a deemed term entitling the company to terminate the employment upon reasonable notice. [*Sec 319(6)*]. The provision applies to shadow directors, and to directors of holding companies employed within the group. If a new contract is concluded more than six months before the expiry of the old one, the further period under the new contract is to be added to the unexpired period of the old contract for these purposes. [*Sec 319(2)*].

11.4 REMUNERATION

Directors' fees are governed by the articles of association and any resolutions passed pursuant thereto. Salaries of employee directors will be in accordance with the terms of their contracts. See also BENEFITS IN KIND (3). The company's annual accounts must give details of the directors' aggregate emoluments, pensions and the aggregate amounts of any compensation paid to directors for loss of office. [*Companies Act 1985, s 232, 6 Sch Part I*, as amended by *Companies Act 1989*].

Remuneration paid to directors must not be free of income tax, or calculated by reference to or vary in accordance with their income tax liabilities. [*Companies Act 1985, s 311*].

11.5 DUTIES TO THE COMPANY

A director is under a *fiduciary duty* to the company. This is distinct from and goes beyond the ordinary employee's duty of fidelity (see 10.2 CONTRACT OF EMPLOYMENT). By way of brief summary, it means that he must at all times act *bona fide* in the best interests of the company, and he must not put himself in a position where his interests and those of the company conflict, at any rate without disclosing the potential conflict. A director who makes a profit from his position may have to account for that profit to the company, i.e. disgorge the entire profit, and not merely pay damages for any loss suffered by the company. See e.g. *Regal (Hastings) Ltd v Gulliver [1942] 1 AER 378*; *Industrial Development Consultants Ltd v Cooley [1972] 1 WLR 443*.

11.6 REMOVAL AND DISMISSAL

If a director is validly removed from the board in accordance with the articles of association, that removal takes effect notwithstanding that his contract of employment may not have been properly terminated. Indeed, unless it is an express or an implied term of the contract that he is to be a director, he will simply continue to be employed as an ordinary employee. Conversely, dismissal from the company's employment does not automatically entail removal from the board; the proper procedures must be followed. Note that *Companies Act 1985, s 303* permits a director to be removed by ordinary resolution of the company in general meeting notwithstanding any contrary provision in the articles or in any agreement between the company and the director.

If the true construction of the contract of employment is that it terminates upon removal from the board, then an employee who is so removed without due notice under the contract may sue for WRONGFUL DISMISSAL (59). But where at the time of appointment the articles contain a provision whereby he will cease to hold office upon the happening of a certain event, that provision will normally be incorporated into the contract of employment so that there is no claim for damages when it is terminated accordingly. See *Nelson v James Nelson & Sons Ltd [1914] 2 KB 770*; *Shindler v Northern Raincoat Co [1960] 1 WLR 1038*.

Payments to directors for compensation for loss of office or on retirement which are not *bona fide* payments by way of damages for breach of contract, or by way of pension in respect of past services, require the prior approval of members of the company. [*Companies Act 1985, ss 312, 313, 316(3)*]. Therefore payments on settlement of a director's claim for wrongful dismissal which contain an element of bounty require prior shareholder approval.

12 Disabled Employees

(See MSC leaflet DPL1 'The Disabled Person's Register'.)

12.1 The *Disabled Persons (Employment) Act 1944 (DPEA)* provides for the registration of disabled persons and obliges certain employers to have a quota of disabled persons in their employment.

12.2 DEFINITION OF DISABLED PERSON

A 'disabled person' is a person who, on account of injury, disease or congenital deformity, is substantially handicapped in obtaining or keeping employment (or undertaking work on his own account) of a kind which would be suitable for his age, experience and qualifications were it not for that injury, disease or deformity. [*DPEA s 1(1)*].

12.3 CERTIFICATE OF REGISTRATION

There is a register of disabled persons, who are issued with a certificate of registration. [*DPEA s 6(1)*]. Entry on the register shows that the registered person is capable of entering into and keeping some form of employment or work. [*DPEA s 7(1)*]. Apart from failing to come within the provisions for registration, a person may be disqualified if he is

(*a*) an inmate of a prison; or

(*b*) a whole-time patient at a hospital, sanatorium or similar institution in circumstances which make it impossible for him to undertake employment or work on his own account or to attend for industrial training; or

(*c*) of habitual bad character.

[*Disabled Persons (Registration) Regulations 1945 (SR&O 1945 No 938), para 6*].

12.4 DISTRICT ADVISORY COMMITTEE

District advisory committees are established throughout Great Britain to advise the Secretary of State on matters relating to the employment of disabled persons. [*DPEA s 17(1)(b)*]. The district advisory committee can be contacted through any local Jobcentre or Department of Employment office

12.5 EMPLOYER'S OBLIGATIONS

Designated employments

Certain work has been designated by the Secretary of State as being especially suitable for disabled persons under *DPEA s 12(1)*. Employment as an attendant of an electrically operated passenger lift or of a car park have been so designated. [*Disabled Persons (Designated Employments) Order 1946 (SR&O 1946 No 1257), paras 1 and 2*]. Only registered disabled persons may be engaged in these employments. [*DPEA s 12(2)*]. If an employer wishes to engage a person who is not disabled in a designated employment, he must make an application for a permit to the Secretary of State. [*DPEA s 9(4)*].

12.6 Other employments – the 'Quota'

Every employer who has in his employment 20 or more employees, is obliged to give employment to a quota of registered disabled persons and to allocate vacancies for that purpose. [*DPEA s 9(1)*]. The extent of the obligation is determined by applying to the number of employees either the 'standard percentage' or the 'special percentage'. The standard percentage is 3 per cent. [*Disabled Persons (Standard Percentage) Order 1946 (SR&O 1946 No 1258), para 2*]. The special percentage is only applicable to employment on a British ship (see Schedule) and is 0.1 per cent. [*Disabled Persons (Special Percentage) (No 1) Order 1946 (SR&O 1946 No 236), para 2*]. Both these percentages may be reduced for a period not exceeding twelve months in respect of an individual employer by the Secretary of State on advice from the district advisory committee. [*DPEA s 10(5)*].

An employer, to whom the provisions of *DPEA s 9* apply, must not discontinue the employment of a registered disabled person unless he has reasonable cause for doing so, if, immediately after the discontinuance, the number of registered disabled people employed by him falls below the quota. [*DPEA s 9(5)*]. A dismissal which is fair on normal principles (see UNFAIR DISMISSAL – II (55)) is likely to be for reasonable cause within *DPEA*. See also *Seymour v British Airways Board* [*1983*] *IRLR 55*.

If an employer is unable to fulfil the quota of registered persons in his employment he should apply to the Secretary of State for Employment for a permit allowing the employment of non-registered persons.

An employer who is obliged to employ a quota of disabled persons must keep records to show the measure of compliance with that obligation. [*DPEA s 14(1)*].

Contravention of the provisions of the Act is an offence punishable, if tried in a magistrates' court, with a fine not exceeding level 3 on the standard scale or imprisonment for a term not exceeding three months or both in the case of an individual, and a fine not exceeding level 5 on the standard scale for a company. [*DPEA ss 9(6), 12(4), 19(3);* and see 1.10 INTRODUCTION].

In 1984, a Code of Practice was issued by the MSC (since dissolved), at the request of the Government, on the employment of disabled people. It is concerned with the employment of all disabled persons, see 7.12 CODES OF PRACTICE. The Council of the EC has issued a recommendation to member States (*Recommendation 86/376/EEC of 24 July 1986*) on the employment of disabled people in the EC.

12.7 Company reports

Companies which employ, on average, more than 250 employees in the financial year are obliged to include in their annual report a policy statement on the employment of disabled persons. [*Companies Act 1985, 7 Sch 9*].

12.8 REMUNERATION OF REGISTERED DISABLED PERSONS

In certain industries WAGES COUNCILS (57) specify a statutory minimum wage. The *Wages Councils Act 1979* made provision for Wages Councils to grant permits (on application from an employer) whereby a disabled person could be paid less than the minimum specified in the wages order. Following the repeal of the *Wages Councils Act 1979* by the *Wages Act 1986* no new permits will be granted but permits already in force continue until the expiry of the wages order in question.

12.9 DISMISSAL OF REGISTERED DISABLED PERSONS

While an employer cannot necessarily expect the same standard or speed of working from a registered disabled person as from a normally healthy employee, if the disabled person performs far worse than can reasonably be expected or causes excessive disruption he may be fairly dismissed provided that a proper procedure is adopted. (*Pascoe v Hallen & Medway [1975] IRLR 116*).

A registered disabled person is entitled to special consideration by his employer. However, the extent to which, if at all, such a person should be given preference over an unregistered disabled or an able-bodied employee in a redundancy situation must depend upon all the circumstances. (*Seymour v British Airways Board [1983] IRLR 55*). There are statutory restrictions on the dismissal of a registered disabled person (see 12.6 above).

13 Disclosure of Information

(See also ACAS Code of Practice No. 2, set out in the Appendix.)

13.1 An employer is under a duty to disclose certain information to his employees and their representatives, by virtue of the *Employment Protection Act 1975* (see 13.2-13.6 below), *the Transfer of Undertakings* (*Protection of Employment*) *Regulations 1981* (*SI 1981 No 1794*) and the *Health and Safety at Work etc. Act 1974* (see 13.7-13.8 below). If the employer is a company it has to disclose or make available certain information by virtue of the *Companies Act 1985*. The trustees of occupational pension schemes are put under certain duties of disclosure by virtue of the *Occupational Pension Schemes (Disclosure of Information) Regulations 1986 (SI 1986 No 1046)*. Duties to afford access to certain records (as well as other obligations) arise from the *Data Protection Act 1984* and the *Access to Medical Reports Act 1988*. It is possible that in the future more extensive duties will be imposed by EC law: the draft Social Charter (see 20.9 EUROPEAN COMMUNITY LAW) contemplates such changes.

13.2 INFORMATION FOR COLLECTIVE BARGAINING

The *Employment Protection Act 1975 (EPA)* imposes an obligation on an employer to disclose information necessary for collective bargaining. He can no longer be in the advantageous position of withholding information about such matters as profits and wages when negotiating. The right to enforce such an obligation is given to trade unions recognised for the particular group of employees in whose interests the information is sought. The sanctions for non-disclosure are wide; if the information required for negotiation is not disclosed, the Central Arbitration Committee (CAC) may order that the terms and conditions under negotiation become part of the individual employee's contract of employment. The CAC may order these terms to take effect as claimed or in a modified form. If the employer refuses to implement these terms the employees affected may bring an action for breach of contract in the county court or High Court.

13.3 Duty to disclose

If at any stage of collective bargaining, a representative of a trade union which is recognised by the employer requests, either orally or, if required by the employer in writing, information which is both

(*a*) information without which the trade union representative would be, to a material extent, impeded in carrying on with the employer such collective bargaining; and

(*b*) information which it would be in accordance with good industrial relations practice that the employer should disclose for the purposes of collective bargaining;

the employer must disclose such information unless it falls within one of the exceptions below. [*EPA s 17*].

Exceptions. The employer need not disclose the information where

(i) it would be against the interests of national security; or

(ii) it is information which he could not disclose without contravening a prohibition imposed by or under an enactment; or

(iii) it is information which has been communicated to the employer in confidence, or which the employer has otherwise obtained in consequence of the confidence reposed in him by another person; or

(iv) it is information relating specifically to an individual and he has not consented to its being disclosed; or

(v) it is information the disclosure of which would cause substantial injury to the employer's undertaking for reasons other than its effect on collective bargaining; or

(vi) it is information obtained by the employer for the purpose of bringing, prosecuting or defending any legal proceedings.

[*EPA s 18(1)*].

An employer will not be required

(A) to produce, or allow inspection of, any document (other than a document prepared for the purpose of conveying or confirming the information) or to make a copy of, or extracts from, any document; or

(B) to compile or assemble any information where the compilation or assembly would involve an amount of work or expenditure out of reasonable proportion to the value of the information in the conduct of collective bargaining.

[*EPA s 18(2)*].

A union only has the right to information concerning matters which are relevant to collective bargaining for which it is recognised. Thus, although a union may have the right to represent a certain class of employee, unless it has a right to represent them *for the purpose of collective bargaining* it does not enjoy the statutory right to information. (*R v Central Arbitration Committee ex parte BTP Tioxide Ltd* [*1982*] *ICR 843*).

Furthermore, information which would not assist collective bargaining need not be disclosed. Thus, the High Court refused to order the disclosure of figures obtained by the Ministry of Defence showing detailed tenders submitted by contract labour cleaners. (*Civil Service Union v Central Arbitration Committee* [*1980*] *IRLR 274*).

13.4 Code of Practice

ACAS issued its Code of Practice No. 2, on 'Disclosure of Information', in 1977. The Code does not provide a complete list of items which should be disclosed as these will vary according to the circumstances, but merely provides some examples of information which should be considered for disclosure. Some of the categories of negotiations for which information may have to be disclosed are set out below. (The full text of the Code is given in the Appendix.)

(*a*) Negotiations over pay and benefits.

(*b*) Negotiations on conditions of service.

(*c*) Negotiations over manpower.

(*d*) Negotiations over performance.

(*e*) Financial negotiations.

The extent of the duty, and the exceptions, will be matters for interpretation in individual cases. A common sense view of what information is necessary in all the circumstances will be taken.

13.5 **Consequences of failure to comply with a request for information**

Initial failure to give information. If an employer fails to comply with a request for information from an independent trade union, the union may present a complaint to the CAC. If conciliation seems a possibility, the CAC will refer the matter to ACAS. If ACAS fails in its attempt at conciliation, or if the complaint is not considered initially suitable for conciliation, the CAC will proceed to hear and determine the complaint. The trade union and employer concerned are entitled to be heard, as well as any person whom the CAC considers to have a proper interest in the complaint. [*EPA s 19(1)(2)(4)(5)*].

If the CAC finds the complaint wholly or partly well-founded, it will make a declaration specifying the following

(*a*) the nature of the information which it considers should originally have been provided;

(*b*) the date (or, if more than one, the earliest date) on which the employer refused or failed to disclose that information or to confirm it in writing;

(*c*) a period (not being less than one week from the date of the declaration) within which the employer must disclose the information or confirm it in writing.

[*EPA s 19(6)*].

Continued failure to give information. If the employer persists in failing to disclose the information within the specified time limit, the trade union may present a further complaint to the CAC who will hear and determine the further complaint. The trade union and employer concerned are again entitled to be heard as is any person whom the CAC considers has a proper interest in the complaint. If it finds the complaint well-founded, the CAC will issue a declaration specifying the nature of the information which it considers should originally have been provided. [*EPA s 20(1)-(4)*].

On or after presenting a further complaint, the trade union may also present a claim relating to the terms and conditions of employment of employees of a description specified in the original claim for information (and in relation to whom the trade union is recognised) [*EPA s 21(1)*]. If the CAC finds or has found the further complaint well-founded, it may make an award that there be incorporated into those employees' contracts of employment

(i) the terms and conditions specified in the claim; or

(ii) other terms and conditions which it considers appropriate.

[*EPA s 21(3)*]. The award may be back-dated to the date on which the CAC declared that the employer refused or failed to disclose (or confirm in writing) the information. [*EPA s 21(4)*].

However, if at any time after a trade union has presented a claim under *EPA s 21(1)* to the CAC and before the CAC has made its award, the employer gives the union the required information, the claim is treated as withdrawn. [*EPA s 21(2)*].

Such terms remain in force until they are superseded or varied

(*a*) by a subsequent award under this procedure;

(*b*) by a collective agreement between the employer and the union;

(*c*) by express or implied agreement between the employees and the employer improving any terms and conditions awarded under this procedure.

[*EPA s 21(6)*].

13.6 POINTS TO NOTE

— An employer is only obliged to disclose information to representatives of a trade union which is recognised by him in respect of the class of workers for whose benefit the information is required.

— If such a request is made to an employer, he should, so far as is reasonably practicable, comply with the request if he considers that he is legally obliged to do so.

— If he fails to comply with the request, the trade union may present a complaint to the CAC upon the hearing of which the CAC may order the information to be supplied and state the time limit for so doing.

— If the employer persists in refusing to supply the information required, the trade union may present a further complaint to the CAC and include with it a claim, for example, for improved wages or conditions for the employees it represents. The CAC may order those terms to be incorporated in individual contracts of employment or substitute such other terms as it considers reasonable.

— If the employer fails to observe the terms adjudicated upon by the CAC, the employees may sue the employer for breach of contract.

It will be seen from this procedure that it is essential for an employer to disclose and present in a comprehensible form all relevant information at the earliest possible opportunity. Failure to do so could involve him in having, for example, to pay higher wages for the relevant group of employees without the advantage of further negotiations.

13.7 TRANSFER OF UNDERTAKINGS REGULATIONS

The Transfer of Undertakings (Protection of Employment) Regulations 1981 (SI 1981 No 1794) impose obligations on employers to disclose information to recognised trade unions when there is a transfer to which the *Regulations* apply. Both the vendor and the purchaser must inform representatives of recognised trade unions of certain specified matters which arise on the transfer. [*Regs 10 and 11*]. Further, obligations to disclose information which arise from trade union recognition are transferred from the vendor to the purchaser in certain circumstances. [*Reg 9*]. (See TRANSFER OF UNDERTAKINGS (53).)

13.8 INFORMATION NECESSARY FOR HEALTH AND SAFETY PURPOSES

Employers are obliged by the *Health and Safety at Work etc. Act 1974 (HSWA)* to provide their employees with information necessary to ensure, so far as is possible, their health and safety at work. [*HSWA s 2(2)(c)*]. An employer must prepare and, when appropriate, revise a written statement of his general policy with respect to the health and safety at work of his employees and the organisation and arrangements for the time being in force for carrying out that policy, and bring the statement and any revision of it to the notice of all his employees. [*HSWA s 2(3)*]. Failure to provide such written information is an offence which carries a maximum fine of £2,000 on conviction in a magistrates' court, and an unlimited fine on conviction in the Crown Court. [*HSWA s 33(1)(3); Magistrates' Courts Act 1980, s 32(2)*, and see 1.10 INTRODUCTION].

13.9 **Safety representatives**

Safety representatives, appointed by a recognised trade union, were given statutory powers to obtain certain information by the *Safety Representatives and Safety Committees Regulations 1977 (SI 1977 No 500), Reg 7*. They are entitled, after giving the employer reasonable notice, to inspect and take copies of any document which the employer is legally obliged to keep, except a document consisting of or relating to any health record of an identifiable individual. [*Reg 7(1)*]. In addition, an employer is obliged to make available to safety representatives any information within his knowledge relating to health, safety or welfare, which is necessary to enable them to fulfil their functions, *except*

(*a*) any information the disclosure of which would be against the interests of national security; or

(*b*) any information which he could not disclose without contravening a prohibition imposed by or under an enactment; or

(*c*) any information relating specifically to an individual, unless he has consented to its being disclosed; or

(*d*) any information the disclosure of which would, for reasons other than its effect on health, safety or welfare at work, cause substantial injury to the employer's undertaking or, where the information was supplied to him by some other person, to the undertaking of that other person; or

(*e*) any information obtained by the employer for the purpose of bringing, prosecuting or defending any legal proceedings.

[*Reg 7(2)(3)*].

13.10 **COMPANIES ACT 1985**

The *Companies Act 1985* contains several provisions requiring the disclosure of information which may concern employees. The most important of these are the requirements that the directors' report contain the following:

(*a*) where the average number of persons employed in the financial year exceeded 250, information concerning the employment of disabled persons;

(*b*) in the case of companies such as may be prescribed by regulations made by the Secretary of State, information about the health, safety and welfare at work of the company's employees (no such regulations have yet been made);

(*c*) where the average number of persons employed in the financial year exceeded 250, information about employee involvement.

For the information to be supplied, see *Companies Act 1985, 7 Sch paras 9, 10 and 11*.

13.11 OCCUPATIONAL PENSION SCHEMES

Under the *Occupational Pension Schemes (Disclosure of Information) Regulations 1986 (SI 1986 No 1046)* the trustees of such schemes must make available to members and prospective members, and (in most instances) to their spouses, and to beneficiaries and independent recognised trade unions, various categories of information. These include the constitution of the scheme [*reg 4*], basic information about the scheme [*reg 5* and *1 Sch*], information about entitlements [*reg 6* and *2 Sch*] and audited accounts [*reg 9*]. Each of these Regulations details the categories of persons and (where applicable) trade unions to whom the information is to be furnished.

13.12 DATA PROTECTION ACT 1984

If information about an employee is stored on a computer, the employer must comply with the *Data Protection Act 1984*, passed in response to the Council of Europe's Convention for the Protection of Individuals with regard to Automatic Processing of Personal Data. This will entail:

(*a*) registration with the Data Protection Registrar [*Sec 5(1)*] – the registration fee is currently £56 [*Data Protection (Fees) Regulations 1988 (SI 1988 No 1969)*];

(*b*) restrictions upon use or disclosure of the data other than for the purposes and to the persons entered upon the register [*Sec 5(2)*];

(*c*) adherence to the 'data protection principles', which provide that the employee should be informed that he is the subject of personal data and allowed access to such data, and that the data should be corrected or erased where appropriate [*1 Sch Part I, 7*];

(*d*) informing employees whether personal data are kept on them, and supplying a copy of the relevant information [*Sec 21*] – a maximum fee of £10 may be charged [*Data Protection (Subject Access) (Fees) Regulations 1987 (SI 1987 No 1507*];

(*e*) paying compensation where damage is caused by reason of the inaccuracy, loss or unauthorised disclosure of data [*Sec 22, 23*].

Payrolls and accounts are exempt from certain of the provisions of the Act. [*Sec 32*].

The Registrar has powers of supervision and enforcement under the Act. He has issued eight guideline booklets to assist parties to understand their rights and obligations. These can be obtained free of charge from the Data Protection Registrar, Springfield House, Water Lane, Wilmslow, Cheshire SK9 5AX (enquiry service: 0625-535777).

13.13 ACCESS TO MEDICAL REPORTS ACT 1988

The *Access to Medical Reports Act 1988* gives individuals a right of access to medical reports relating to them which are supplied by medical practitioners for employment purposes. [*Sec 1*]. An employer may not apply to a medical practitioner for such a report without the employee's consent. [*Sec 3(1)*]. The ACAS handbook 'Discipline at Work' includes a model letter of enquiry to an employee's doctor. The employee is entitled to see the report *before* it is supplied [*Sec 4*] and to withhold consent to the report being supplied [*Sec 5(1)*]. There is also provision for the correction of errors. [*Sec 5(2)*].

13.13 Disclosure of Information

The statutory definition of 'medical report' refers to a medical practitioner who is or has been responsible for the clinical care of the individual. Therefore a report obtained from a company doctor after an examination carried out for a particular purpose is unlikely to be subject to the Act.

Medical reports obtained by an employer should obviously be kept confidential.

14 Education and Training

14.1 An employer has no obligation at common law to provide facilities for the education and training of his employees unless they are engaged under a contract of apprenticeship or their contract of employment provides otherwise. Similarly he does not have to allow employees time off for day-release or sandwich courses. However, an employer should not ask his employee to carry out a task requiring special skill unless he has ensured that the employee possesses those skills or unless the employer has undertaken to train the employee. (If he does so and an accident occurs he may be liable, see 24.6-24.8 HEALTH AND SAFETY AT WORK - I.) For the income tax treatment of training costs, see *ICTA 1988 ss 588, 589.*

Various bodies and schemes have been created by government to encourage the education and training of employees and those seeking employment. Changes have occurred frequently in recent years. Many recent changes and current proposals can be ascertained from the December 1988 White Paper 'Employment for the 1990s' (Cm 540). The most notable recent development is the dissolution of the Training Commission, previously known as the Manpower Services Commission, which was formally accomplished by *EA 1989 s 22*. Its functions have been performed directly by the Department of Employment, but the Government now proposes to create a National Training Task Force, on which employers will have majority representation.

Up to date information may be obtained from Job Centres, Careers Offices and the Department of Employment.

14.2 APPRENTICESHIPS

Apprenticeships offer what must be the oldest form of training in skilled trades for young people.

The apprenticeship is normally for a fixed term of years, the apprentice, his parent or guardian, (if he is a minor), and the employer entering into a written agreement. The agreement will usually be in a form common to all apprenticeships for the trade concerned. In general the apprentice will have time off to attend college and take examinations.

If they satisfy the necessary qualifying conditions, apprentices enjoy the statutory employment protection rights [*EPCA s 153(1); Sex Discrimination Act 1975, s 82(1); Race Relations Act 1976, s 78(1)*].

The Employment Appeal Tribunal, on the basis of the evidence before it that the Law Society recommended the operation of a dual system whereby a clerk was articled to an individual partner in a firm of solicitors under a deed of articles but was employed by the firm under a contract of employment, held that an articled clerk was engaged under such a system. (*Oliver v J P Malnick & Co* [*1983*] *ICR 708*).

14.3 INDUSTRIAL TRAINING BOARDS

The Industrial Training Boards are established by the Secretary of State for Employment under the *Industrial Training Act 1982 (ITA)*, as amended (most recently by *EA 1989*), which repealed and replaced the *Industrial Training Act 1964*, as amended, except as that Act applies to the Agricultural Training Board.

14.4 Education and Training

The law relating to the Agricultural Training Board is now consolidated in the *Agricultural Training Board Act 1982*, as amended. Industrial Training Boards are administered by the Secretary of State. The Boards exist to encourage adequate training of persons employed or intending to be employed in certain industries, and may therefore

(*a*) provide or secure the provision of such courses and other facilities (which may include residential accommodation) for the training of those persons whom the Board consider adequate, having regard to any alternative courses or facilities available;

(*b*) approve alternative courses and facilities;

(*c*) publish recommendations regarding the length and nature of courses and standards to be attained in training;

(*d*) make tests for ascertaining the standards recommended and award certificates of the attainment of those standards;

(*e*) assist persons in finding facilities for being trained for employment in the industry;

(*f*) carry out, or assist others to carry out, research into any matter relating to training for employment in the industry;

(*g*) provide advice about training connected with the industry.

[*ITA s 5(1)*].

An Industrial Training Board may enter into contracts of service or apprenticeship with persons who intend to be employed in the industry and to attend courses or avail themselves of other facilities provided or approved by the Board. [*ITA s 5(2)*].

Industrial Training Boards may provide advice on training. They may also

(i) pay maintenance and travelling allowances to persons attending courses provided or approved by the Board;

(ii) make grants or loans to persons providing courses or other facilities approved by the Board, to persons who investigate the provision of such courses or facilities, and to persons who maintain arrangements to provide such courses or facilities which are not for the time being in use;

(iii) pay fees to persons providing further education in respect of persons who receive it in association with their training in courses provided or approved by the Board;

(iv) make payments to persons in connection with arrangements under which they or employees of theirs make use of courses or other facilities provided or approved by the Board.

[*ITA s 5(4)*].

It has been proposed that most or all of the seven remaining statutory Boards should become fully independent organisations supported by employers in the relevant sector, and amendments have been made to *ITA* by *EA 1989* to facilitate this.

14.4 Levies and exemption certificates

In order to encourage adequate training in a particular industry, the Industrial Training Board may, in accordance with an order made by the Minister, impose a levy on employers in the industry. The Industrial Training Board may, and shall at or before the time when it submits proposals for a levy, submit to the Secretary of State proposals for the issue of certificates giving exemption from part or all of the levy to those employers who have made adequate arrangements for the training of employees. [*ITA s 13(1)*]. Such a certificate, which will remain in force for a period of not longer than three years, may require the employer to comply with certain conditions relating to training. An employer may request the Board in writing to reconsider a question on which he is dissatisfied in relation to the issue or non-issue of an exemption certificate.

A further appeal lies to the Referees established under the *Industrial Training (Levy Exemption References) Regulations 1974 (SI 1974 No 1335)*. The Referees consist of a President and representatives of employers and employees. [*ITA s 14(6)(8)*].

14.5 Grants

An Industrial Training Board may make grants or loans to persons providing courses or facilities approved by the Board. Thus, although an employer may be liable to pay a levy, he may be able to recoup a grant if he satisfies the Board that he is providing adequate training for his employees. Forms are available from the relevant Industrial Training Board for the employer to provide the information enabling him to claim such a grant. [*ITA s 5(4)(b)*].

14.6 Information

An Industrial Training Board, with the approval of the Minister, may require employers to furnish returns and other information, to keep certain records and to produce them for examination by the Board. [*ITA s 6(1)*]. Penalties may be imposed for the infringement of any of these provisions. Penalties also exist for knowingly or recklessly furnishing false records or information.

14.7 EMPLOYMENT TRAINING

The principal training programme for adults is now Employment Training. It is a programme designed to meet the needs of the long-term adult unemployed by providing up to 12 months' training and work experience. Eligibility is normally dependent upon being aged between 18 and 60 and having been unemployed for at least six months, but certain people with special needs (e.g. the disabled, those whose first language is not English, those who have been absent from the labour market for domestic reasons and ex-servicemen) may also participate. Priority is given first to those aged between 18 and 24 and unemployed for between 6 and 12 months, and then to those aged under 50 and unemployed for more than two years.

A training allowance is paid through the Department of Social Security. The amount paid is £10 per week more than the trainee's benefit allowance, or £10 if he or she is not receiving benefit. Help may also be given with travel costs and child-care. Further details are given in the Training Agency pamphlet 'Eligibility and Allowances on Employment Training' (M42, revised May 1989).

Following the abolition of the Training Commission, there is to be created a network of about 100 local Training and Enterprise Councils, on which employers will fill the majority of places, but there will also be representation of trade unions, local authorities and voluntary organisations.

Other relevant programmes include 'Enterprise Training', involving various schemes to assist those who are self-employed or running small businesses, and 'Business Growth through Training', which will attempt to assist small and medium-sized companies in meeting their training needs.

The Skilled Training Agency, a part of the Training Agency, operates 60 Skillcentres across the country.

For the Youth Training Scheme, see 5.6 CHILDREN AND YOUNG PERSONS.

14.8 **SERVICES FOR SCHOOL-LEAVERS**

Local Education Authorities are charged, under the *Employment and Training Act 1973*, with the duty of assisting persons who are attending full-time or part-time educational institutions in Great Britain, other than universities, to advise them on careers and training. [*ETA s 8*].

15 Employee or Self-Employed?

Cross-reference. See also CONTRACT OF EMPLOYMENT (10).

15.1 The difference between an employee and a self-employed person is of great importance. The legal rights enjoyed by each differ in many ways. For example, an employee will enjoy the statutory employment protection rights discussed elsewhere in this book if he meets the necessary qualifying requirements: a self-employed person will not. An employee's earnings are liable to tax under Schedule E to the *Income and Corporation Taxes Act 1988*, and tax is deducted under the PAYE system, whereas a self-employed person is liable to tax under Schedule D.

The question of whether a person is an employee or self-employed is determined by reference to the contract under which he works – is it a contract of employment or a contract 'for services'?

15.2 CONTRACT OF SERVICE AND CONTRACT OF EMPLOYMENT

The terms 'contract of service' and 'contract of employment' are identical in meaning. The former is the more archaic term which was used when the parties to the contract were known as 'master' and 'servant'. The term 'contract of employment' for the purposes of *EPCA* includes a contract of apprenticeship. [*EPCA s 153(1)*].

15.3 DISTINGUISHING A CONTRACT OF EMPLOYMENT FROM A CONTRACT FOR SERVICES

Contracts of employment may be distinguished from those of agency and partnership and these distinctions usually present little difficulty. They may also be distinguished from a contract of apprenticeship the main purpose of which is for the apprentice to be bound to the master for a period of time to learn the skills of a certain trade or calling. Much more complex is the distinction between a *contract of service* and a *contract for services* – the distinction between an employee and an independent contractor or consultant. The courts will not pay much regard to the labels used by the parties in their agreement, as these are often created to avoid the consequences of the legislation referred to above, but will look to the reality of the relationship. There is one fundamental prerequisite of a contract of employment. There must be mutual obligations on the employer to provide work for the employee and on the employee to perform work for the employer. (*Nethermere (St Neots) Ltd v Gardiner and another [1984] ICR 612*; see also *Hellyer Brothers Ltd v McLeod [1987] ICR 526*). If those mutual obligations are present, the court or tribunal will engage upon what has been called a balancing exercise, weighing the following factors in coming to a conclusion whether the individual concerned is an employee or not. It will consider whether

(*a*) he works under the orders of another who controls not only what he must do, but also how and when he must do it;

(*b*) he is employed as part of the business of the employer and his work is done as an integral part of that business;

(*c*) he provides his own equipment;

(*d*) he hires his own helpers;

(*e*) he takes a degree of financial risk;

(*f*) he has responsibility for investment and management;

(*g*) and how far he has the opportunity of profiting from sound management in performing his task.

(*Market Investigations Ltd v Minister of Social Security [1969] 2 QB 173 per* Cooke J at p *185*).

The greater the degree of personal responsibility an individual undertakes in any of these matters, the more likely he is to be considered an independent contractor rather than an employee. In *Addison v London Philharmonic Orchestra Ltd [1981] ICR 261*, other tests were considered including the incidence of tax and national insurance, the traditional structure of the profession (or business) and the intention of the parties. However, the way that a worker is treated for tax and national insurance purposes is by no means conclusive (see e.g. *Tyne and Clyde Warehouses Ltd v Hamerton [1978] ICR 661*).

Some other factors sometimes indicate the existence of a contract of employment such as

(A) remuneration by way of payment of wages or salary (although piece workers may of course be employees);

(B) payment during absence for illness;

(C) paid holidays;

(D) membership of a company pension scheme;

(E) control by a disciplinary code laid down by the employer;

(F) a prohibition on working for other companies or individuals.

Where the nature of the relationship between the parties is in doubt or is ambiguous, it is open to the parties, by agreement, to stipulate what the legal situation between them is to be. (*Massey v Crown Life Insurance Co Ltd [1978] ICR 590*). However, all the circumstances of the relationship must be considered, and the courts will look behind the parties' intentions, and labels, to ascertain the true nature of the agreement. (*Young & Woods Ltd v West [1980] IRLR 201*).

Note also that a full-time working director of his family firm (who drew fees rather than being paid a salary) was held to be self-employed (*Parsons v Albert J Parsons & Sons Ltd [1979] ICR 271*), as were musicians with a London orchestra (*Winfield v London Philharmonic Orchestra Ltd [1979] ICR 726* and *Addison*, above), and a sub-postmaster (*Hitchcock v Post Office [1980] ICR 100*). A police cadet was held not to be an employee or an apprentice. (*Wiltshire Police Authority v Wynn [1980] ICR 649*). A Presbyterian minister was held not to be an employee. (*Davies v Presbyterian Church of Wales [1986] ICR 280*).

There may be contracts which are neither contracts of employment nor contracts for services, but fall into an intermediate category (*Construction Industry Training Board v Labour Force Ltd [1970] 3 AER 220, Ironmonger v Morefield Ltd [1988] IRLR 461*). It is thought that a person who works under such a contract will for most purposes be in the same position as one who is self-employed.

In *O'Kelly v Trusthouse Forte plc [1983] ICR 728*, the majority of the Court of Appeal held that an appellate court could only interfere with a decision of an industrial tribunal on the question of whether an individual was an employee if it could be shown that the industrial tribunal had erred in law or reached a perverse conclusion.

15.4 SOME LEGAL CONSEQUENCES OF THE DISTINCTION

(The lists set out below are not exhaustive.)

For the employee

Rights

An employee enjoys (subject to satisfaction of the qualifying conditions) the following rights

Unfair dismissal protection
Redundancy payment entitlement
Written particulars of terms of employment
Statutory minimum period of notice
Guarantee payment
Medical suspension payment
Protection from racial and sex discrimination
Equal pay
Maternity rights
Time off for trade union activities, duties, etc.
Not to be unreasonably excluded or expelled from a trade union with which the employer has a closed shop
To be employed for the agreed period or be given the agreed length of notice
To be provided with a safe place of work and to have reasonable care taken of his safety
To be paid statutory sick pay

Obligations

To obey the employer's lawful orders
To work faithfully and with due diligence
To give the contractually agreed or statutory minimum period of notice to terminate the employment
To pay income tax by way of deductions under the PAYE scheme
To pay employee's national insurance contributions

For the employer

Rights

To benefit from the employee's obligations set out above

Obligations

To observe the employee's rights set out above
To deduct tax under the PAYE scheme
To keep the necessary statutory sick pay records
To make the appropriate national insurance contributions

15.4 Employee or Self-Employed?

Self-employed — the self-employed person

Rights

To benefit from all his contractual entitlements
Not to be discriminated against on grounds of race or sex
Where applicable to be provided with a safe place and safe system of work

Obligations

To fulfil his contractual obligations
To work with due skill and diligence
To pay income tax under Schedule D
To pay self-employed person's national insurance contributions

Self-employed — the person who engages a self-employed person

Rights

To benefit from the self-employed person's contractual obligations

Obligations

To observe the self-employed person's rights set out above.

16 Employee Participation

16.1 Although there has been much discussion on the subject of the participation of employees in the affairs of the businesses for which they work, there is as yet little statutory provision for such participation. Some legislation in the 1970s (the *Health and Safety at Work etc. Act 1974* and the *Employment Protection Act 1975*) compelled employers to consult with their employees on such matters as health and safety, disclosure of information and on redundancies (see appropriate chapters for details).

Employee participation (also referred to in broad terms as 'industrial democracy') was considered in the Report of the Committee of Inquiry on Industrial Democracy, chaired by Lord Bullock ('the Bullock Report'), published in January 1977 (*Cmnd 6706*). This was followed by a White Paper in May 1978, but no legislation was introduced before the change of government in 1979. The Conservative government has preferred to pursue participation by encouraging employee share ownership and profit-related pay. However, two specific legislative provisions have been introduced (see below).

16.2 DIRECTORS TO HAVE REGARD FOR INTERESTS OF EMPLOYEES

By the *Companies Act 1985*, the directors of a company are to have regard to the interests of the employees as well as of the shareholders. [*CA 1985, s 309(1)*]. However, by *Sec 309(2)* that duty is owed not to the employees but to the company alone, and the employees cannot thus complain if the directors give greater priority to the interests of the shareholders.

16.3 DIRECTORS' REPORT

The directors' report of any company employing an average number of 250 employees in the United Kingdom in the financial year must now contain a statement describing the action that has been taken during the financial year to introduce, maintain or develop arrangements aimed at

(*a*) providing employees systematically with information on matters of concern to them as employees;

(*b*) consulting employees or their representatives on a regular basis so that the views of employees can be taken into account in making decisions which are likely to affect their interests;

(*c*) encouraging the involvement of employees in the company's performance through an employees' share scheme or by some other means;

(*d*) achieving a common awareness on the part of all employees of the financial and economic factors affecting the performance of the company.

[*CA 1985, s 234(4), 7 Sch 11*, as amended by *CA 1989*].

16.4 EUROPEAN COMMUNITY PROPOSALS

The most likely source of future legislation in this area, at least before the next General Election, is the EC. Proposals for employee participation and consultation are contained both in the draft Company Statute and in the draft Social Charter (see 20.9 EUROPEAN COMMUNITY LAW). The United Kingdom government is expected to resist such proposals, but attempts may be made to adopt them under a majority voting procedure.

17 Employee's Past Criminal Convictions

17.1 SPENT CONVICTIONS

The *Rehabilitation of Offenders Act 1974* provides that after a period of time, people who have been convicted of criminal offences and who have served their sentences are, with some exceptions (see 17.4 below), not obliged to disclose those convictions. The length of time which must elapse before a person's conviction becomes 'spent' in this way depends upon the nature of the sentence imposed and runs from the date of sentence. Certain sentences, such as imprisonment or custody for life, sentences of imprisonment, youth custody or corrective training for a term exceeding 30 months, and detention during Her Majesty's pleasure, can never become spent. [*Sec 5(1); Criminal Justice Act 1982, ss 77, 78, 14 Sch 36, 16 Sch*]. An offender whose conviction has become spent is known as a 'rehabilitated person'.

17.2 Non-disclosure of spent convictions

A rehabilitated person is not obliged to disclose

(*a*) a spent conviction;

(*b*) the offence for which he was sentenced; or

(*c*) any circumstances surrounding the conviction,

in any judicial proceedings, in answer to any question relating to his past behaviour or by virtue of any law or agreement requiring him to disclose such information. Neither is a person required to answer questions about or to disclose information relating to someone else's spent criminal convictions. [*Sec 4(1)–(3)*].

In relation to employment, these provisions are important since they can apply, for example, in respect of questions asked at job interviews or information required to be given on an application form (see 17.5 below).

These rules do not apply, among other things, to questions asked in the course of criminal proceedings. [*Sec 7(2)(a)*]. However, *Practice Note* [*1975*] *2 AER 1072* relating to the Crown Court provides that courts and counsel should give effect to the general intention of Parliament by not making any reference to spent convictions when such reference can reasonably be avoided. Further, no-one should refer in open court to a spent conviction without the authority of the judge, which authority should not be given unless the interests of justice so require. A person who reveals another's spent criminal convictions may raise the defence of justification (i.e. truth) in any subsequent action for libel or slander, provided that the revelation was not made with malice. [*Sec 8(3)(5)*].

17.3 Spent convictions and dismissal

A spent conviction or a failure to disclose such a conviction are not proper grounds for dismissing or excluding a person from any office, profession, occupation or employment or for prejudicing him in any way in any occupation or employment. [*Sec 4(3)(b)*]. Thus, an employer may not dismiss an employee merely because he discovers that the employee has a conviction which has become spent. In *Hendry v Scottish Liberal Club* [*1977*] *IRLR 5*, a Scottish industrial tribunal held that a spent conviction for possession of cannabis had to some extent influenced the club's decision to dismiss the employee. Therefore, the reason for the dismissal could not fall within the range of permitted reasons (now contained in *EPCA s 57(1)(b), (2)*) and the dismissal was unfair. A security officer is not an occupation excluded from the benefit of the 1974 Act (see 17.4 below), and consequently, an employer who dismissed two security officers for failing to disclose a spent conviction was held to have dismissed them unfairly. (*Property Guards Ltd v Taylor and Kershaw [1982] IRLR 175*).

Furthermore, the fact that a person has a spent conviction is not a proper ground for an employer to refuse to engage that person, unless the person falls within a category to which the *Exceptions Order* applies (see below). [*Sec 4(3)(b)*]. However, it is not clear what remedy there would be for such a refusal.

17.4 EXCEPTIONS

The *Rehabilitation of Offenders Act 1974 (Exceptions) Order 1975 (SI 1975 No 1023)* provides that people following certain occupations and professions are obliged (despite the provisions of *Sec 4(2)*) to disclose any spent convictions and may be dismissed or excluded from employment because of such a conviction (despite the provisions of *Sec 4(3)*). Those professions and occupations include: doctors, nurses, midwives, dentists, barristers, solicitors, accountants, teachers and police officers. The *Rehabilitation of Offenders Act 1974 (Exceptions) (Amendment) Order 1986 (SI 1986 No 1249)*, which took effect on 18 July 1986, amends the *(Exceptions) Order 1975 (SI 1975 No 1023)* by substituting for a number of specific excepted occupational groups a general exception covering any office or employment which is concerned in the provision of accommodation, care, leisure and recreational facilities, schooling, social services, supervision or training to persons under 18 years, where the holder of the office or employment would have access to such minors in the normal course of his duties, or if the duties are carried out wholly or partly on the premises where such provision takes place.

By virtue of the 1975 Order, as amended, an applicant for, or candidate for admission to, any profession or occupation specified in the Order, or which falls within the general exception referred to above, is no longer statutorily excused from the obligation to disclose spent convictions where a question is asked in order to assess his suitability for any profession, occupation, office or employment in the circumstances described, if the question relates to the applicant for such a post, or (where applicable) if it relates to a person who lives in the same household as the applicant, and the provision of the services mentioned would normally take place in that household.

17.5 EFFECT OF PROVISIONS FOR REHABILITATION

If, for example, at an interview for the post of chargehand in a factory, an applicant is asked whether he has any criminal convictions, a negative answer may mean

(i) that he has no previous convictions;

(ii) that he has convictions but they are spent;

(iii) that he has convictions which are not spent and he is not telling the truth.

If the employer subsequently discovers, after engaging the applicant, that he has previous convictions (*a*) if these are not spent, he may consider the man for dismissal if such a dismissal would be fair in all the circumstances (see 55.4 UNFAIR DISMISSAL – II); or

(*b*) if these are spent, he may not take any action, unless there are other reasons which justify him in doing so.

If the applicant reveals at an interview that he has previous convictions

(i) if the convictions are spent, they do not form a good reason for refusing the applicant the job;

(ii) if they are not spent, they may form good grounds for refusing the applicant the job.

Any agreement or arrangement that an applicant must reveal past convictions is ineffective so far as spent convictions are concerned. [*Sec 4(3)(a)*].

Applicants for any position in a profession or occupation excluded from the protection of the Act (see 17.4 above) must answer questions relating to previous convictions and may be refused or dismissed from such employment for a conviction or for failing to disclose such a conviction.

17.6 REHABILITATION PERIODS

The period of rehabilitation is related to the length of the sentence which was passed on the offender. The main rehabilitation periods are set out below.

Sentence	Rehabilitation period	
Imprisonment, custody, detention for life, or detention at Her Majesty's pleasure.	Not applicable	
Imprisonment, youth custody or corrective training for a term exceeding 30 months.	Not applicable	
Imprisonment, youth custody or corrective training for between 6 and 30 months.	10 years	Rehabilitation periods subject to reduction by half for persons under 17.
Imprisonment or youth custody for 6 months or less	7 years	
Fine	5 years	
Detention under the *Children and Young Persons Act 1933, s 53* for between 6 and 30 months.	5 years	
Detention under above Act for 6 months or less.	3 years	
Conditional discharge, probation, care or supervision order.	1 year or the duration of the order, if longer.	

17.6 Employee's Past Criminal Convictions

Sentence	Rehabilitation period
Disqualification from driving.	Period of disqualification.
Absolute discharge.	6 months.

[*Sec 5*]

18 Engagement of Employees

18.1 Advertising

When advertising for prospective employees, an employer must be careful not to infringe the provisions of the *Sex Discrimination Act 1975* (see 44.7 SEX DISCRIMINATION – I) and the *Race Relations Act 1976* (see 37.10 RACIAL DISCRIMINATION).

18.2 Interviewing and selection

An employer may use any interviewing and selection procedures he wishes provided that they are not discriminatory within the meaning of the *Sex Discrimination Act 1975* and the *Race Relations Act 1976*. He is free to select whomsoever he chooses, subject to the following

(*a*) the restrictions on the employment of CHILDREN AND YOUNG PERSONS (5);

(*b*) the restrictions on the employment of women in certain industries, notably the lead and pottery industries;

(*c*) the restrictions on the employment of FOREIGN EMPLOYEES (22);

(*d*) the requirement that employers employing 20 or more workers must employ a quota of registered disabled people (3% of their workforce). [*Disabled Persons (Employment) Act 1944, s 9; Disabled Persons (Standard Percentage) Order 1946, Art 2*; and see DISABLED EMPLOYEES (12)];

(*e*) the restriction on excluding a person from any office, profession, occupation or employment by reason of a spent conviction (see EMPLOYEE'S PAST CRIMINAL CONVICTIONS (17)).

The Government also now intends to outlaw the pre-entry CLOSED SHOP (6).

18.3 Engagement

An employer should inform a new employee of the terms and conditions under which he is to work and his commencement date and time. This should be done by letter. He is obliged by law to give the employee written particulars of those terms and conditions within 13 weeks of the commencement of his employment (see 10.4 CONTRACT OF EMPLOYMENT).

The *actual day* on which employment commences has importance under the rules for computing continuity of employment (see 9.3 CONTINUOUS EMPLOYMENT) irrespective of whether the employee actually performs any duties on that day (see *General of the Salvation Army v Dewsbury* [*1984*] *ICR 498*).

18.4 Employment agencies

For the law regulating employment agencies, and the status of those recruited through such agencies, see 48.2 TEMPORARY AND SEASONAL EMPLOYEES.

19 Equal Pay

(See also DE booklets 'Equal Pay – A Guide to the Equal Pay Act 1970' (PL 743) and 'Equal pay for women: what you should know about it' (PL 739, revised).)

Cross-reference. See 44.6 SEX DISCRIMINATION – I for the rules forbidding discrimination on grounds of sex in matters other than pay.

19.1 Since the coming into force on 29 December 1975 of the *Equal Pay Act 1970 (EqPA)*, women have been able to claim equal pay with men. The accession of Great Britain to the Treaty of Rome on 1 January 1973 also affected women's rights to equal pay since *Article 119* provides that 'Each member State shall during the first stage ensure and subsequently maintain the application of the principle that men and women should receive equal pay for equal work.' *Article 119* and *Directive No. 75/117* ('the Equal Pay Directive') provide a European underpinning of rights to equal pay. These provisions have been relied upon increasingly as an aid to construction of domestic law, and, where the rights conferred by domestic law fall short of the rights conferred by *Article 119*, to provide a right of action where none exists in domestic law.

The EC provisions and their effect on United Kingdom law are considered at the end of the chapter (see 19.16-19.17 below, and EUROPEAN COMMUNITY LAW (20)).

19.2 EQUAL PAY ACT 1970 – RIGHT TO EQUAL PAY

EqPA provides the legal framework to eliminate discrimination between the sexes in the terms of their contracts of employment. The *EqPA* and the examples set out below are framed with reference to women but they are to be read as applying equally to men. The Act has been subsequently amended by the *Sex Discrimination Act 1975*, the *Equal Pay (Amendment) Regulations 1983 (SI 1983 No 1794)* (*EqP Regulations*) and the *Sex Discrimination Act 1986*.

The *EqP Regulations* were introduced in an attempt to bring the United Kingdom into conformity with EC requirements. They introduced for the first time the right to claim equal pay for work of equal value in circumstances in which the jobs of the claimant and the comparator have not been rated as equivalent under a job evaluation scheme.

19.3 Employees who may benefit

The right to equal pay applies

(*a*) to women employed in an establishment in Great Britain whether they are British or not and regardless of the law governing their contract of employment [*EqPA s 1(1)(11)*];

(*b*) to men as well as women [*EqPA s 1(13)*].

It does not apply to members of the armed services. [*EqPA s 1(9)*].

'Employed' in equal pay legislation is defined as 'employed under a contract of service or of apprenticeship or a contract personally to execute any work or labour' [*EqPA s 1(6)(a)*]. The definition therefore includes contracts to perform personal services (cf 15.3 EMPLOYEE OR SELF-EMPLOYED?).

19.4 Equality clause

The *EqPA* implies a clause known as an 'equality clause' into every woman's contract of employment, provided that the contract does not already include such a clause. [*EqPA s 1(1)*]. The clause modifies the woman's contract in any situation where the woman is engaged on *like work* to a man, on *work rated as equivalent* to work done by a man, or on work of *equal value* to that done by a man.

An equality clause operates so that

(i) if any term of a woman's contract is, or becomes, less favourable to the woman than a term of a similar kind in a contract under which a man is employed, that term in the woman's contract is modified to become as favourable as the corresponding term in the man's contract; or

(ii) if at any time a woman's contract does not include a beneficial term which is in a man's contract, the woman's contract will be modified so as to include that term.

[*EqPA s 1(2)(a),(b) (c)*].

Thus, for example, if a man and a woman are engaged on like work and the man is paid £120 per week for that work, but the woman only £100, the equality clause will operate so as to entitle the woman to £120 per week. Also, if the man's contract contains a clause which entitles him to be paid during absence from work due to sickness, but the woman's contract contains no such clause, the woman's contract will be considered by law to include such a clause. The equality clause applies to all terms and conditions of employment and not only to pay (e.g. *Sun Alliance and London Insurance Ltd v Dudman [1978] ICR 551*, relating to a contractual term granting a mortgage interest allowance).

In *Hayward v Cammell Laird Shipbuilders Ltd [1988] 2 WLR 1134* the House of Lords rejected the argument that the 'total remuneration package' must be taken into account when making the comparison between a woman's pay and a man's. What must be compared is each distinct provision of the contract dealing with pay and benefits in kind. The applicant was thus entitled to the same rate of basic pay and overtime pay as her male comparator even if she was more favourably treated in other respects, in this case paid meal breaks, additional holidays and better sickness benefits. However, it was suggested that the 'material factor' defence under *EqPA s 1(3)* (see 19.10 below) might be available to an employer who could show that the unfavourable character of the term in the woman's contract was due to the more favourable character of the other terms.

The clause is applied in cases in which a member of one sex is employed under a contract which contains a term or terms less beneficial than those enjoyed by a comparator of the opposite sex. The employee does not have to establish that the reason for the difference is the difference in sex; it is for the employer to show that the reason for the difference is a genuine material factor other than sex (see 19.10 below). *EqPA* applies only to cases of direct discrimination i.e. to contractual terms which are different for men and for women. It does not apply to cases of indirect discrimination i.e. to contractual terms which are unisex but which make contractual benefits subject to conditions which exclude a far greater number of women than men. However, European law may provide a remedy in such situations (see 19.17 below).

19.5 Like work

A woman is regarded as employed on like work with men if, but only if, her work and theirs is of the same or of a broadly similar nature and the differences (if any) between the things she does and the things they do are not of practical importance in relation to the performance of her contract of employment. In comparing her work with theirs, the nature and extent of the differences will be considered, as will the frequency or otherwise with which such differences occur in practice. [*EqPA s 1(4)*].

Thus, although the job descriptions of male and female employees or their written job specifications may be different, if in practice the differences in their duties are of no practical importance, the women will be considered to be employed on like work with the men. The question of what is or is not a difference of practical importance will always be one of fact and degree depending upon the particular circumstances of the case. If, for example, male guillotine operators in a paper mill are required once in two weeks to lift reams of paper whereas women are not, the lifting is purely incidental to their main employment and is not of practical importance. Accordingly, it is not a difference which would prevent the women's right to equal pay.

The Employment Appeal Tribunal (EAT) has stated in *Capper Pass Ltd v Lawton [1977] ICR 83*, that 'In deciding whether the work done by a woman and the work done by a man is "like work" within the meaning of section 1(4) of the *Equal Pay Act* the industrial tribunal has to make a broad judgment. The intention is that the industrial tribunal should not be required to undertake too minute an examination, or be constrained to find that work is not like work merely because of insubstantial differences. In order to be like work within the Act's definition the work need not be of the same nature; it need only be broadly similar.' In that case a cook in the directors' dining room was held to be engaged on like work with the assistant chefs of the company's factory canteen. The fact that women do their work at a different time of the day from men may not prevent them from claiming that they are engaged upon like work. (*Dugdale v Kraft Foods Ltd [1977] ICR 48; National Coal Board v Sherwin [1978] ICR 700*; contrast with *Thomas v National Coal Board [1981] ICR 757* in which the EAT held that a male canteen worker on permanent night shift was not employed on like work with female day shift canteen workers.)

However, the duties actually performed are not the only considerations to be taken into account in deciding whether a woman is engaged on like work. In *Eaton Ltd v Nuttall [1977] ICR 272*, the EAT held that 'In considering whether there is like work, though the most important point is what the man does and what the woman does, the circumstances in which they do it should not be disregarded. One of the circumstances properly to be taken into account is the degree of responsibility involved in carrying out the job.'

If a woman's work is more onerous or more responsible than a man's, she may not be considered to be engaged on like work, even though less well paid (*Waddington v Leicester Council for Voluntary Service [1977] ICR 266*). However she may now be able to obtain equal pay on the basis described in *Murphy v Bord Telecom Eireann [1988] ICR 445*. (See also 19.7 below.)

19.6 Work rated as equivalent

A woman may claim equivalence with a man even though she is not engaged on like work, if a job evaluation scheme has been carried out in respect of his work and hers, and her job has been rated as equivalent to the man's. [*EqPA s 1(5)*].

The principal methods of job evaluation are set out in ACAS Guide No 1. They are known as job ranking, paired comparison, job classification, points assessment and factor comparison. A job evaluation must be carried out on an objective basis. The principles were set out in *Eaton Ltd v Nuttall* (see above). The job of each worker covered by the study must be valued in terms of the demand made on the worker under the various headings (e.g. effort, skill, responsibility) in the study (*Bromley and others v H & J Quick Ltd [1988] ICR 623*). Thus it will not suffice simply to compare 'whole jobs'. The assessment should be qualitative, not quantitative – matters such as a difference in the number of hours worked go to the defence of material factor (see 19.10 below), not to evaluation of the job (*Leverton v Clwyd County Council [1989] ICR 33*). Whilst the study as a whole must be objective, it is permissible for it to contain certain subjective elements, so long as they are not themselves inadvertently discriminatory. It is for the employer to explain how any job evaluation study worked and what was taken into account at each stage (see also *Rummler v Dato-Druck GMBH [1987] ICR 774*). The validity of a job evaluation scheme which is not impartial or which is not conducted on a scientific basis may be challenged if reliance is placed on such a scheme to claim equal pay. If no job evaluation scheme has been carried out, there is no legal requirement for an employer to conduct one. However, once a job evaluation study has been undertaken and has resulted in a conclusion that the job of a woman is of equal value to that of a man, the woman may claim equal pay, despite the fact that the employers may not have implemented the scheme. (*O'Brien v Sim-Chem Ltd [1980] ICR 573*). But, for work to be rated as equivalent under the *EqPA* there must be a *completed* job evaluation study, and there is no complete job evaluation study unless and until the parties who have agreed to the carrying out of the study have accepted its validity. (*Arnold v Beecham Group Ltd [1982] ICR 744*).

19.7 Work of equal value

Where a woman is employed on work which is not like work or work which has been rated as equivalent to that of a male comparator, she may now claim equal pay with a man if her work is of equal value to his, in terms of the demands made on her, for example under such headings as effort, skill and decision (*EqPA s 1(2)(c)*). Relying upon EC law, she may also claim equal pay where she is doing work of *greater* value (*Murphy and others v Bord Telecom Eireann (Case 157/86) [1988] ICR 445*). Following the approach of the House of Lords in *Pickstone* and in *Litster v Forth Dry Dock and Engineering Co Ltd [1989] ICR 341*, it may be that *EqPA* will be construed so as to allow such a claim in English law. Employees of one sex may use *Sec 1(2)(c)* to claim equal pay with those of the other sex doing a quite different job. Using this provision a female cook employed as a canteen assistant succeeded in a claim for equal pay with male skilled tradesmen (see *Hayward v Cammell Laird Shipbuilders Ltd [1988] 2 WLR 1134*). The fact that one man is being paid the same as a woman for doing like work to hers is no longer a bar to the woman claiming equal pay with another man doing a different job of equal value to hers (see *Pickstone v Freemans plc [1988] 3 WLR 265*). The House of Lords in *Pickstone* held that the construction of *EqPA* which enabled them to achieve this result was consistent with EC law. (For the procedure to be adopted on claims based on work of equal value see *Industrial Tribunals (Rules of Procedure) Regulations 1985 (SI 1985 No 16) 2 Sch* and 19.14 below).

19.8 Persons with whom an employee may claim equivalence

A woman may claim equivalence with a male employee of her employer at her workplace. If that employer has several establishments in Great Britain she may claim parity with a man working at a different establishment from her own, provided that common conditions of employment are observed at all the employer's establishments in Great Britain either generally or for employees of the relevant classes. The concept of common terms and conditions of employment observed differently at different establishments necessarily contemplates terms and conditions applicable to a wide range of employees whose individual terms will vary greatly. Terms and conditions governed by the same collective agreement are an example of common terms and conditions. (*Leverton v Clwyd County Council [1989] ICR 33*).

If two or more employers are associated (i.e. if one is a company of which the other directly or indirectly has control or if both are companies of which a third person directly or indirectly has control; see 9.8 CONTINUITY OF EMPLOYMENT) a woman working in a factory owned by Company A can claim equivalence with a man working in another factory owned by an associated company, Company B, provided that the same terms and conditions of employment apply either generally or for employees of the class of which the woman is a member. [*EqPA s 1(6)(c)*].

An employee may not claim equal pay with a predecessor under the *EqPA* but may do so under *Article 119* of the EC Treaty. (*Macarthys Ltd v Smith [1979] ICR 785; [1980] ICR 672*). It may be that the *EqPA* is to be treated as amended by *Article 119* in which case such claims could be admitted under the *EqPA*. (*Albion Shipping Agency v Arnold [1982] ICR 22 at p 29*). The argument that *EqPA* should, if possible, be construed so as to achieve consistency with EC law has support in the approach of the House of Lords in *Pickstone*.

There is no requirement that the selected comparator be representative of a group, or that his position should not be an anomalous one (*Thomas and others v National Coal Board [1987] ICR 757*).

19.9 Exclusions from equal pay rights

An equality clause does not operate in relation to terms

(*a*) affected by compliance with the laws regulating the employment of women (although certain restrictions on working hours for women in particular employments have been repealed by *SDA 1986*); or

(*b*) affording special treatment to women in connection with pregnancy or childbirth; or

(*c*) relating to death or retirement, except terms which, in relation to retirement, afford access to opportunities for promotion, transfer or training or provide for dismissal or demotion.

[*EqPA s 6(1)(1A); SDA 1986, s 2(4)*].

A discriminatory retirement age (e.g. 60 for women, 65 for men), which is now unlawful by virtue of *SDA 1986, s 2(1)*, cannot be used to justify pay differentials of any kind.

Where contributions into a pension scheme required of men but not of women were compensated for by additions to male employees' salary, *EqPA s 6* excluded the women's claim under English law. However, the women succeeded in a claim under *Article 119* before the European Court of Justice ('ECJ') (see *Worringham and Humphreys v Lloyds Bank Ltd [1982] ICR 299* and 19.17 below).

19.10 Defence of 'material factor'

Although a woman may establish that she is engaged on like work, work rated as equivalent to that of a man or work of equal value, she will not be able to claim equivalence with that man if the employer can show that the variation between the woman's contract and the man's contract is genuinely due to a material factor which is not the difference of sex. [*EqPA s 1(3)*]. In the case of equality claimed on the basis of *like work* or *work rated as equivalent*, that factor *must* be a material difference between the woman's case and the man's. [*EqPA s 1(3)(a)*]. In the case of equality claimed on the basis of *work of equal value*, that factor *may* be a material difference between the woman's case and the man's. [*EqPA s 1(3)(b)*]. Thus, in establishing a defence to a claim based on like work or work rated as equivalent, any difference in terms must be justified by a difference between the woman's case and the man's case. In a claim based on work of equal value the defence includes but is not limited to such differences. Once an employee has shown that she is engaged on like work, work rated as equivalent to that of a man, or work of equal value to that of a man it is for the employer to prove that he has a defence under *Sec 1(3)*.

The House of Lords in *Rainey v Greater Glasgow Health Board [1987] ICR 129* has resolved earlier doubts upon the matters which may be taken into account in considering a defence of 'material difference' under *Sec 1(3)*. At p 140, Lord Keith stated:

> 'The difference must be "material", which I would construe as meaning "significant and relevant", and it must be between "her case and his". Consideration of a person's case must necessarily involve consideration of all circumstances of that case. These may well go beyond what is not very happily described as "the personal equation", i.e. the personal qualities by way of skill, experience or training which the individual brings to the job. Some circumstances may on examination prove to be not significant or not relevant, but others may do so, though not relating to the personal qualities of the employee. In particular, where there is no question of intentional sex discrimination whether direct or indirect (and there is none here) a difference which is connected with economic factors affecting the efficient carrying on of the employer's business or other activity may well be relevant.'

He held that the defence available in *Sec 1(3)* is equivalent in scope to that held by the European Court in *Bilka-Kaufhaus Gmbh v Weber von Hartz (Case 170/84) [1987] ICR 110* to be available under *Article 119* of the *Treaty of Rome*. A relevant difference for the purposes of *Sec 1(3)* may relate to circumstances other than the personal qualifications or merits of the male and female workers who are the subject of comparison. The House of Lords disapproved the restrictive approach adopted to *Sec 1(3)(a)* by the Court of Appeal in *Fletcher v Clay Cross (Quarry Services) Ltd [1979] ICR 1* which held that the wording of the section required an analysis of 'the personal equation of the woman as compared with the man, to what appertained to her in her job and to him in his', and considered that extrinsic factors such as market forces could not justify a pay differential.

The material difference or factor relied upon must be one which exists throughout the period during which there is a difference in pay. For example, where a woman was appointed at a lower rate of pay than existing male employees because of financial constraints, there was no defence to her equal pay claim after those constraints had ceased to exist. (*Benveniste v University of Southampton [1989] IRLR 122*). The material difference must not itself be the result of sex discrimination. (*Re Equal Opportunities Commission for Northern Ireland's Application [1989] IRLR 57*).

The House of Lords held in *Leverton v Clwyd County Council [1989] ICR 33* that, if there was no significant difference between the hourly rates of pay of the applicant and her male comparator, it would be a legitimate if not a necessary inference that the difference between their total salaries was due to and justified by the difference in the number of hours worked.

For other cases on *Sec 1(3)* see *Snoxall and Davies v Vauxhall Motors Ltd and Charles Early & Marriott (Witney) Ltd v Smith and Ball [1977] 3 WLR 189; National Vulcan Engineering Insurance Group Ltd v Wade [1978] ICR 800; Methven v Cow Industrial Polymers Ltd [1980] ICR 463; Jenkins v Kingsgate (Clothing Productions) Ltd [1981] ICR 715* and *Albion Shipping Agency v Arnold [1982] ICR 22*.

19.11 EQUAL PAY ACT 1970 – REMEDIES FOR UNEQUAL PAY

Any claim brought by virtue of the *EqPA*, whether for arrears of remuneration or damages, may be brought before an industrial tribunal. [*EqPA s 2(1)*].

The parties who may refer a case to the tribunal are as follows.

(*a*) An employee claiming the benefit of the Act.

(*b*) An employer who may apply to the tribunal for an order declaring his and the employee's rights in relation to an equality clause.

(*c*) The Secretary of State may take action on behalf of an aggrieved employee where it is not reasonable to expect the parties to take steps to have the question determined.

(*d*) A court in which any proceedings are pending may direct that a claim or counter-claim in respect of the operation of an equality clause may be struck out where it appears that they would more conveniently be disposed of separately by an industrial tribunal.

(*e*) Alternatively, a court may on application of any party or on its own motion refer a question to an industrial tribunal and stay the proceedings meanwhile.

[*EqPA s 2(1A)(2)(3)*].

No claim in respect of an equality clause may be referred to an industrial tribunal otherwise than by virtue of (*d*) above unless the woman has been employed in the employment within the six months preceding the date of the reference. [*EqPA s 2(4)*].

If the claim is successful, the amount awarded will be the difference in pay between that of the claimant and the 'equal' or 'equivalent' employee. Arrears of pay for *up to two years* before the proceedings were instituted may be recovered (but it has been doubted whether such limits can necessarily be relied upon where a claim is based directly upon European law. See 45.6 SEX DISCRIMINATION – II). The proceedings will be so instituted on the date the industrial tribunal receives the application. [*EqPA s 2(5)*].

19.12 Collective agreements

Prior to the coming into force of *SDA 1986* a collective agreement containing differing provisions for men and women could by *EqPA s 3* be referred (at the request of any party to the agreement or the Secretary of State) to the Central Arbitration Committee which had jurisdiction to modify contracts governed by the collective agreement. *EqPA s 3* is now repealed by *SDA 1986* which provides that collective agreements (whether they would otherwise be legally enforceable or not) are deemed automatically unenforceable and void insofar as they provide for the inclusion in a contract of employment of a provision which contravenes *EqPA s 1*. Discriminatory collective agreements can be referred to a county court by a person interested in the agreement. The court may remove or modify any unenforceable term [*SDA 1975, s 77*; *SDA 1986, s 6*]. Declarations made by the CAC prior to the repeal of *EqPA s 3* continue in force [*SDA 1986, s 9*].

19.13 **Agricultural Wages Orders**

If such an order contains any discriminatory terms, it may be referred by the Secretary of State to the CAC for amendment. He may be requested to do so by employer or worker representatives on the Agricultural Wages Board or may do so on his own motion. If the CAC decide the amendments should be made, the Agricultural Wages Board must make an order giving effect to those amendments not later than five months from the date of the decision. [*EqPA s 5*].

19.14 PROCEDURE IN EQUAL PAY CLAIMS

The *Industrial Tribunals (Rules of Procedure) Regulations 1985 (SI 1985 No 16)* ('*the IT Regulations*') govern the procedure relating to all applications before industrial tribunals instituted on or after 1 March 1985 (see INDUSTRIAL TRIBUNALS (27)).

Schedule 2 to the *Regulations* sets out additional rules of procedure which apply only in proceedings involving an equal value claim. An important and unique feature of the procedure in these claims is the obtaining by the tribunal of an expert's report. Proceedings in equal value claims are started in the same way as all proceedings before industrial tribunals, by the filing of an Originating Application. [*IT Regulations 1 Sch, Reg 1*]. The Respondent enters a Notice of Appearance. [*IT Regulations 1 Sch, Reg 3*]. The tribunal has power to order the discovery and inspection of documents and the attendance of witnesses. [*IT Regulations 1 Sch, Reg 4; 2 Sch, Reg 4*]. The tribunal may determine an equal value claim without calling for an expert's report if it is satisfied that there are no reasonable grounds for determining that the work is of equal value. [*EqPA s 2A(1)(a)*]. If that submission is made, it *must* be adjudicated upon before an expert is appointed (*Sheffield Metropolitan District Council v Siberry* [*1989*] *ICR 208*).

One reason for holding that there are no such reasonable grounds is if the work of the applicant and the work of the male comparator have been given different values on a job evaluation study, and there are no reasonable grounds for determining that the evaluation contained in the study was made on a system which discriminates on grounds of sex. [*EqPA s 2A(2)*]. *On the application of a party*, if in the circumstances it thinks it appropriate to do so, the tribunal may consider a defence of *genuine material factor* (see 19.10 above) before asking for an expert's report (see e.g. *Reed Packaging v Boozer* [*1988*] *ICR 391*). [*IT Regulations 2 Sch, Reg 8(2E)*].

In all other contested cases the tribunal must adjourn the proceedings and refer the question of whether the applicant's work is of equal value to the comparator, to a member of the panel of independent experts appointed by ACAS to prepare a report. [*EqPA s 2A(1)(b)(4); IT Regulations 2 Sch, Reg 7A(4)*].

The expert must take account of all information and relevant representations made to him. [*IT Regulations 2 Sch, Reg 7A(3)(a)*]. Before drawing up his report, he must produce, and send to the parties, a written summary of the information and representations, inviting their comments. [*Reg 7A(3)(b)*]. His report to the tribunal must set out the summary and contain a brief account of any representations received from the parties, any conclusion he may have reached and the reasons for that conclusion. [*Reg 7A(3)(c)*]. He must take no account of the difference of sex and at all times act fairly. [*Reg 7A(3)(d)*].

When the tribunal has received the report, it will immediately send a copy to each of the parties and fix a date for the resumed hearing. Unless the tribunal decides that the expert has not complied with the rules or has reached a perverse conclusion, or that for some other material reason the report is unsatisfactory, it will be admitted in evidence. [*Reg 7A(7)(8)*]. The tribunal must take into account any representations of the parties and may permit evidence to be called in deciding upon whether, on the grounds set out above, the report should be excluded. [*Reg 7A(9)*].

The industrial tribunal may, and must, if requested by a party to the proceedings, require the attendance of the expert at the resumed hearing. At any time after the tribunal has received the report any party may, on giving reasonable notice, call one witness to give expert evidence on the equal value question. [*Reg 8(2B)*]. There is no power in the tribunal to compel an applicant to be interviewed by the employer's expert (*Lloyds Bank PLC v Fox* [*1989*] *ICR 80*), although interrogatories may be served for written answer. With certain exceptions, no party may give evidence upon, or question any witness upon, any matter of fact upon which a conclusion in the report of the independent expert is based. [*Reg 8(2C)*]. This restriction upon new evidence and cross-examination does not mean that the tribunal is bound to *accept* his findings of fact or his conclusion, and the parties can make submissions on the independent expert's report. (*Tennants Textile Colours Ltd v Todd* [*1989*] *IRLR 3*). Even if the defence of *genuine material factor* may have failed at an earlier stage, a respondent may raise it again at the resumed hearing. [*Reg 8(2E)*]. In all other respects the proceedings are conducted in the same way as any other application.

The burden of proving a claim under *EqPA* is on the applicant. The burden does not in law become heavier if the independent expert's report is against the applicant. Nor is the burden of proof transferred to the employer if the report is in favour of the applicant (see *Tennants Textile Colours Ltd*).

An employer may commission a job evaluation study in order to obtain material with which to resist an equal pay claim. However the fact that an employer was initiating and would implement an independent job evaluation was not considered sufficient grounds for granting a stay of proceedings on an equal pay claim. (*Avon County Council v Foxall* [*1989*] *ICR 407*).

The tribunal will give full written reasons for its decision [*Reg 9(3)(4)*].

19.15 EQUAL PAY ACT 1970 – NO CONTRACTING OUT

A term in a contract which purports to exclude or limit any provision of the *EqPA* is unenforceable by any person in whose favour the term would operate. [*Sex Discrimination Act 1975, s 77(3)*]. However, a contract settling a complaint to an industrial tribunal will be upheld if it was made with the assistance of a conciliation officer. [*Sex Discrimination Act 1975, s 77(4)*]. Thus, an agreement by a woman that she will not bring a claim for equal pay will be void, and the payment of any sum to compromise such a claim will not prevent her continuing with her complaint unless the conciliation officer has assisted in the agreement (see 2.3 ADVISORY, CONCILIATION AND ARBITRATION SERVICE).

19.16 EC PROVISIONS

The foundation of the right to equal pay in EC law is contained in *Article 119* of the Treaty of Rome (the EC Treaty) which provides:

'Each Member State shall during the first stage ensure and subsequently maintain the application of the principle that men and women should receive equal pay for equal work.

For the purposes of this Article, "pay" means the ordinary basic or minimum wage or salary and any other consideration, whether in cash or in kind, which the worker receives, directly or indirectly, in respect of his employment from his employer.

Equal pay without discrimination based on sex means

(*a*) that pay for the same work at piece rates shall be calculated on the basis of the same unit of measurement;

(*b*) that pay for work at time rates shall be the same for the same job.'

There are several Directives of the Council of the European Community dealing with the general implementation of the principle of equal pay and equal treatment of men and women in specific areas.

In the area of pay, the Council of the EC has adopted *Directive No 75/117* (the '*Equal Pay Directive*') on the approximation of the laws of Member States relating to the application of the principle of equal pay for men and women. It has also adopted *Directive No 86/378* on the progressive implementation of the principle of equal treatment for men and women in occupational social security schemes, including pension schemes.

Directive No 76/207 (the '*Equal Treatment Directive*') provides by *Article 5.1*

'Application of the principle of equal treatment with regard to working conditions, including the conditions governing dismissal, means that men and women shall be guaranteed the same conditions without discrimination on grounds of sex.'

See 20 EUROPEAN COMMUNITY LAW, 44 and 45 SEX DISCRIMINATION.

19.17 Application in the United Kingdom

European Communities Act 1972 (*ECA*) (as amended by *European Communities (Amendment) Act 1986*) which makes provision relating to the accession of the United Kingdom to EC, by *section 2* provides that rights and obligations conferred by the EC Treaty should be given legal effect in the United Kingdom. *Section 2(4)* provides that any enactment passed or to be passed is to be construed and have effect subject to that stated principle.

United Kingdom legislation has sought to implement the Article and the Directives by the enactment of the *Equal Pay Act 1970,* the *Equal Pay (Amendment) Regulations 1983*, the *Sex Discrimination Act 1975* and the *Sex Discrimination Act 1986*. EC law is used as an aid to the construction of ambiguous UK legislation. Further, it can be used to interpret unambiguous legislation enacted to comply with EC requirements (see *Pickstone v Freemans plc* [*1988*] *ICR 697*). Where domestic legislation falls short of a directly enforceable EC provision (i.e. *Article 119* in the area of equal pay), and cannot be construed or amended to comply with it, then that provision will be directly enforceable in member states of the EC. (*Defrenne v Sabena* [*1976*] *ICR 547;*

Worringham and Humphreys v Lloyds Bank Ltd [*1982*] *ICR 299; Garland v British Rail Engineering Ltd* [*1982*] *ICR 420*). (See also *Hasley v Fair Employment Agency* [*1989*] *IRLR 106*.) More recently in *Hammersmith & Queen Charlotte's Special Health Authority v Cato* [*1988*] *ICR 132* an applicant succeeded in relying directly on *Article 119* to claim the same contractual redundancy payment as a man (but see *Secretary of State for Employment v Levy* [*1989*] *IRLR 469* for a decision that a statutory redundancy payment is not 'pay' within *Article 119*; the case is under appeal). However in *Leverton v Clwyd County Council* [*1988*] *IRLR 239* the Court of Appeal held that there can be no directly enforceable rights under *Article 119* where the terms of the *Article* are too imprecise to be applied without further definition by national or Community measures. In Mrs Leverton's case, neither *Article 119* nor the *Equal Pay Directive* dealt with the problem of how the principle of equal pay is to operate if the applicant and her male comparator work at different establishments. The House of Lords at [*1989*] *ICR 33* did not need to deal with this point. EC law may also be relied upon to claim equal pay to remedy indirect discrimination. (*Bilka-Kaufhaus GmbH v Weber von Hartz* [*1987*] *ICR 110*). See also the very important recent decision of the ECJ in *Rinner-Kühn v FWW Spezial-Gebäudereinigung GmbH & Co KG* [*1989*] *IRLR 493*.

Where English law is inconsistent with Community law which is directly applicable in this country, Community law takes precedence. In a number of cases on equal pay the English courts have referred questions to the European Court of Justice for determination and given judgment in accordance with its decision. (*Macarthys Ltd v Smith* [*1980*] *ICR 672; Jenkins v Kingsgate (Clothing Productions) Ltd* [*1981*] *ICR 715; Worringham and Humphreys v Lloyds Bank Ltd* [*1982*] *ICR 299*).

20 European Community Law

20.1 THE EUROPEAN COMMUNITY AND ITS LAW

European Community (EC) law has applied to the United Kingdom since its accession to the European Community on 1 January 1973. [*European Communities Act 1972; European Communities (Amendment) Act 1986*]. There are three basic sources of EC law

(i) the provisions of the EC Treaty itself (the Treaty of Rome of 1957, as amended by the Single European Act in 1986), which sets out the fundamental principles of the EC;

(ii) EC legislation;

(iii) decisions of the European Court of Justice (ECJ).

EC legislation takes the form of regulations and directives. Regulations are the closest equivalent to an Act of Parliament (in that they are 'directly applicable', i.e. they do not need to be implemented by national legislation) whereas directives are instructions to member States to bring their national legislation into conformity with EC requirements.

20.2 THE EFFECT OF EC LAW

EC law is having an ever increasing effect on domestic litigation. In certain circumstances it is taken into account in the construction of domestic legislation and in others it can give rise to independent rights which can be pursued before UK courts.

EC law is used as an aid to the construction of English legislation where the legislation is ambiguous or unclear. Where legislation has been enacted to give effect to EC law the domestic legislation will be construed so as to give effect to it (*Garland v British Rail Engineering Ltd* [*1982*] *ICR 420*, *Pickstone v Freemans plc* [*1988*] *ICR 697*) even if this means reading words into the statute which are not there (*Litster v Forth Dry Dock and Engineering Co Ltd* [*1989*] *ICR 341*).

However where it was not the intention of Parliament to give effect to EC law in domestic legislation and the wording of the legislation is clear, on the current state of House of Lords authority, the English legislation will not be modified to give effect to EC law (*Duke v GEC Reliance Systems Ltd* [*1988*] *ICR 339*).

Where domestic law rights fall short of EC rights which are enforceable by individuals in the Courts of member States, individuals can bring claims based on EC law in UK courts. The question of whether claims based solely on EC law are subject to domestic procedural and jurisdictional limits such as limits on compensation is yet to be decided by the higher courts. When *Marshall* was remitted to the industrial tribunal for compensation to be assessed ([*1988*] *IRLR 325*) the English limit on compensation was exceeded. The EAT overturned the award of interest [*1989*] *IRLR 459* but there was no appeal against the decision of the tribunal to exceed the English limit on compensation.

Certain Articles of the EC Treaty (e.g. *Article 119*, see 20.6 below) have direct effect in member States and can be enforced by individuals in UK courts. Similarly, some directives can be relied on by individuals, but only if their employer is the State (see *Marshall v Southampton and South West Hampshire*

Area Health Authority (Teaching) [*1986*] *ICR 335; Foster v British Gas PLC* [*1988*] *ICR 584*). Also, the individual concerned must be a citizen of a member State. (*R v Immigration Appeal Tribunal Ex parte Bernstein, The Times, 11 June 1988*). However, the questions of 'direct effect' and 'direct applicability' are too complex to be dealt with fully here.

The European Community has its own court, the European Court of Justice ('ECJ'), which sits in Luxembourg and is not to be confused with the European Court of Human Rights in Strasbourg (see EUROPEAN CONVENTION ON HUMAN RIGHTS (21)). Questions relating to European Community law may be referred to the European Court by UK courts. There is a growing body of decisions by the European Court on matters affecting UK law and EC law is becoming increasingly important in considering domestic employment matters. This importance will certainly not lessen as the EC moves towards its objective of a completed internal market by 1992.

20.3 EC REQUIREMENTS AFFECTING EMPLOYMENT LAW

All relevant Community law requirements concerning employment law are derived from the EC Treaty and legislation made under it. The most notable requirements include

(*a*) free movement of labour;

(*b*) equal access to social security benefits;

(*c*) equal pay and equal treatment;

(*d*) holidays;

(*e*) redundancy procedure;

(*f*) rights on the transfer of a business.

These are examined in the following paragraphs.

Other EC requirements affect specific employments such as that of transport drivers. Information about relevant EC legislation may be obtained from the Department of Employment or from the office of the Commission of the EC at 8 Storey's Gate, London SW1.

20.4 FREE MOVEMENT OF LABOUR

Articles 48-50 of the EC Treaty require member States to permit the free movement of workers between member States. No discrimination based on nationality may be exercised against EC nationals in relation to employment, remuneration or other conditions of work and employment. Directives and regulations relating to these Articles have been passed. Great Britain has complied with these requirements so that EC nationals have a right to enter the country to take or seek work without the necessity of obtaining a work permit. They have the right to remain here and to bring their families with them (see also FOREIGN EMPLOYEES (22)).

20.5 EQUAL ACCESS TO SOCIAL SECURITY BENEFITS

EC Article 5 provides for the passing by the Council of the EC of measures to ensure the aggregation of social security benefits which may have been paid in different member States, and for the payment of benefit in one member State where contributions have been made in another member State. Such regulations have been passed. (*Regulation 1408/71*, as amended). The regulations also ensure that the rules about liability to pay national insurance in the UK while working elsewhere in the EC are in line with the rules applied by the other member States. (See generally DSS leaflet SA 29 'Your social security and pension rights in the European Community'.)

20.6 EQUAL PAY AND EQUAL TREATMENT

EC Article 119 obliges each member State to ensure and maintain the principle that men and women should receive equal pay for equal work. (See also *Article 1 of Council Directive 75/117/EEC of 10 February 1975*.) Further, *Council Directive 76/207/EEC of 9 February 1976* requires member States to take the measures necessary to implement the principle of equal treatment for men and women in relation to the following stages of employment: engagement, training, promotion, working conditions and dismissal.

The UK sought to comply with those requirements. However, in three cases, the ECJ has held that the UK had failed to comply fully with its EC obligations.

In *Commission of the European Communities v United Kingdom of Great Britain and Northern Ireland* [*1982*] *ICR 578*, the ECJ held that the UK had failed to comply fully with the equal pay Directive because under *EqPA* a right to claim equal pay for work of equal value was only given where a job evaluation study had been carried out with the consent of the employer (see 19.6 EQUAL PAY). The Government has complied with the ruling of the ECJ by amending the *EqPA* to enable claims based upon work of equal value to be made without the necessity of establishing that an agreed job evaluation study has been carried out. [*Equal Pay (Amendment) Regulations 1983 (SI 1983 No 1794)* now contained in the *Industrial Tribunals (Rules of Procedure) Regulations 1985 (SI 1985 No 16)*].

In *Commission of the European Communities v United Kingdom of Great Britain and Northern Ireland* [*1984*] *ICR 192*, the ECJ held that the United Kingdom had failed to comply fully with its EC obligations since there was no provision in the United Kingdom legislation declaring discriminatory terms in collective agreements void, or amending them. Further, it held that the exclusion from rights under the *Sex Discrimination Act 1975* of persons in private households, and those whose employers employed no more than five workers, infringed the Directive. The *Sex Discrimination Act 1986* amends the *Sex Discrimination Act 1975* so as to give effect to the judgment of the ECJ and thus brings the English legislation into conformity with the Directive. However, further changes to the EC legislation cannot be ruled out.

In *Marshall v Southampton and South West Hampshire Area Health Authority (Teaching)* [*1986*] *ICR 335*, an individual successfully relied upon *Directive 76/207*. She could only do so because her employer was conceded to be the State. Employees of employers who are not the State cannot rely upon Directives. In *Marshall*, the ECJ held that a policy of dismissing female employees at 60 and male employees at 65 infringed the Directive. Miss Marshall could not succeed in pursuing her claim under the English statute because claims based on provisions in relation to retirement were then excluded from protection by *Sec 6(4)* of the *Sex Discrimination Act 1975*. The *Sex Discrimination Act 1986 (Sec 2)* amended *Sec 6(4)* of the *1975 Act* so as to give effect to the ECJ decision in *Marshall*.

Further, in *Johnston v Chief Constable of the Royal Ulster Constabulary (Case 222/84)* [*1987*] *ICR 83*, the ECJ declared that a provision in a Northern Ireland Order similar to that contained in *SDA s 52(2)*, which specifies that a certificate signed by or on behalf of a Minister certifying that an act was done for the purpose of safeguarding national security is to be conclusive evidence that it was done for that purpose, deprived complainants of an effective remedy in domestic courts and was contrary to *Article 6 EC Directive 76/207* (see 44.18 SEX DISCRIMINATION - I).

For decisions on the application of *Article 119* see *Defrenne v Sabena [1976] ICR 547, Jenkins v Kingsgate (Clothing Productions) Ltd [1981] ICR 715, Worringham and Humphreys v Lloyds Bank Ltd [1982] ICR 229, Bilka-Kaufhaus Gmbh v Weber Von Hartz [1987] ICR 110, Leverton v Clwyd County Council [1989] ICR 33, Hasley v Fair Employment Agency [1989] IRLR 106* and 19.17 EQUAL PAY.

In a highly significant recent case, the ECJ has held that *Article 119* is contravened by a statutory restriction (so that the restriction can be avoided) if it affects a considerably greater number of women than men and is not shown to be justified by objective factors unrelated to discrimination on the ground of sex. (*Rinner-Kühn v FWW Spezial-Gebäudereinigung GmbH & Co KG [1989] IRLR 493*).

20.7 HOLIDAYS

EC Article 120 provides that member States should endeavour to maintain the existing equivalence between paid holiday schemes. *Council Recommendation 75/457/EEC* of 22 July 1975 recommends that member States ensure, whether by means of legislation or by encouraging collective agreements or by other means, a 40-hour working week and 4 weeks' annual paid holiday. A recommendation is not binding upon member States.

20.8 REDUNDANCY PROCEDURE

Directive 75/129/EEC contains requirements for the approximation of the laws of member States relating to collective redundancies. This has been complied with by the enactment of *EPA ss 99-107* (see 39.3-39.6 REDUNDANCY - II).

20.9 RIGHTS ON TRANSFER OF BUSINESS

The *Transfer of Undertakings (Protection of Employment) Regulations 1981 (SI 1981 No 1794)* implement the requirements of *Directive 77/187/EEC* (see 38.5 REDUNDANCY - I and TRANSFER OF UNDERTAKINGS (53)).

20.10 SOCIAL CHARTER

The Commission of the EC has produced a draft 'Community Charter of Fundamental Social Rights' (COM(89)248). If adopted by the Council of Ministers, this broad statement of principles will provide the framework for detailed legislation, some of which may be of great importance to English employment law.

Matters referred to in the draft Charter include: fair remuneration for all employment; a maximum duration to the working week; the right to strike; the opportunity to continue vocational training throughout working life; rights of information, consultation and participation for workers; vocational training during working hours for young people; and the fullest possible integration of the disabled into working life.

21 European Convention on Human Rights

21.1 EFFECT OF THE CONVENTION

The European Convention on Human Rights and Fundamental Freedoms is an international treaty which was drawn up in 1950 and came into force in 1953. The Convention sets out in broad terms a number of fundamental rights and freedoms. It also established the *European Commission of Human Rights* and the *European Court of Human Rights*, both based in Strasbourg. It should be emphasised that the Convention and its institutions are entirely separate from the law and institutions of the European Community. The subscribing states are the members of the Council of Europe. Also, unlike European Community Law, the provisions of the Convention are not part of domestic law; they only bind the Government. The main text of the Convention, which has been amended by several protocols, can be found in Command Paper *Cmd 8969* (1953), published by HMSO.

If a State which is a party to the Convention interferes with or abrogates any of the rights or freedoms enshrined in the Convention, a complaint may be made by any other party State. More importantly, the Convention allows for a right of direct complaint by an *individual* affected by an alleged breach of the Convention (such an individual right of complaint is very rare in international law). The Government of the United Kingdom ratified the Convention in 1950. However, it was not until 1966 that the UK Government recognised the jurisdiction of the European Court of Human Rights and accepted the right of an individual in the UK to petition the Court.

21.2 Procedure for petition by an individual

In outline the procedure is as follows. The aggrieved individual must pursue every remedy available under UK law. When he has exhausted these 'domestic' remedies, without having his complaint satisfactorily resolved, he may present his petition to the European Commission of Human Rights. The Commission investigates the complaint. If it decides that there is, or may be, a breach of the Convention and that the complaint is admissible, it will endeavour to obtain a settlement between the parties. If no settlement is reached, the Commission will refer the case, together with its report, to the European Court of Human Rights. The Court will then proceed to decide on the complaint.

21.3 CLOSED SHOPS AND THE FREEDOM OF ASSOCIATION

The most important case concerning UK employment law to reach the European Court of Human Rights was the British Rail closed shop case, *Young, James and Webster v United Kingdom* [*1981*] *IRLR 408,* [*1983*] *IRLR 35.*

Article 11 of the Convention provides:

> '1. Everyone has the right to . . . freedom of association with others, including the right to form and to join trade unions for the protection of his interests.
>
> '2. No restrictions shall be placed on the exercise of these rights . . . [certain exceptions permitted].'

In the *Young, James and Webster* case, the Court held that the requirement on the applicants to join one of the unions specified in the closed shop agreement between British Rail and the railway unions, in circumstances where there had been no such requirement at the time when they were engaged, amounted to a restriction on the freedom guaranteed by *Article 11* because the alternative to their joining was that they would lose their jobs. (*[1981] IRLR 408* at *p 409*). The Court made substantial monetary awards to the applicants.

The decision leaves the general question of the consistency of closed shop agreements with *Article 11* unclear. Now that the right of individuals not to join a specified trade union has been entrenched by the *Employment Act 1982* and the *Employment Act 1988* (see CLOSED SHOP (6)), it seems unlikely that this aspect of the Convention will be tested further under the present Government. A complaint by workers at GCHQ that they were not permitted to belong to trade unions was not referred to the Court by the Commission, which accepted the Government's argument based upon national security.

21.4 THE CONVENTION AS AN AID TO INTERPRETATION

Despite numerous attempts in Parliament, the Convention has not been incorporated into English law and cannot be relied upon directly in domestic courts and tribunals. However, it may, like other treaties, be cited on the basis that Parliament is presumed to have intended to legislate consistently with the UK's international obligations unless the contrary intention appears (see for example *R v Secretary of State for the Home Department Ex parte Bhajan Singh [1976] QB 198*; and see also *Attorney-General v Guardian Newspapers Ltd (No 2) [1988] 3 WLR 776* at p *805*).

21.5 OTHER INTERNATIONAL OBLIGATIONS

The Council of Europe has also promulgated, and the United Kingdom has ratified, the *European Social Charter*, which contains provisions relating to, for example, annual holidays and the right to strike. This should not be confused with the Social Charter currently proposed by the EC (see 20.9 above). There is a recent Additional Protocol which has not been signed by the UK.

The International Labour Organisation is a specialist body of the United Nations. It has issued a number of conventions, some of which have been ratified by the United Kingdom. They deal with matters such as health and safety, freedom of association and racial discrimination.

22 Foreign Employees

(See also DE leaflets 'Guide for Employers (Training and Work Experience Scheme) – Employment of overseas nationals in the United Kingdom' (OW21), 'Guide for Employers – Employment of overseas workers in the United Kingdom' (OW5), 'Employment in the UK' (OW17).)

22.1 A distinction is drawn in the procedure adopted for the admission of foreign workers to employment in the UK between nationals of member States of the European Community (EC) and others. The different procedures are set out in the *Department of Employment Leaflet OW5 (1989)* relating to the non-EC members, and 'A guide for workers from abroad – Employment in the UK' (OW17) relating also to EC nationals. The comments below are drawn from those leaflets with the kind permission of the Controller of Her Majesty's Stationery Office.

The Department of Employment has recently issued a consultation paper which aims to reduce the burden of making applications for work permits and to speed up the processing of such applications. The main proposal is to create a two-tier system: in the case of workers who are senior executives transferring within firms, or who clearly bring substantial investment and job creation to the UK, or who have high level qualifications and experience which are in short supply, there would be the minimum of checks and it would not be necessary to search for resident labour. The second tier would cover all other applications and would still be dependent on a search of the EC labour force.

22.2 NATIONALS OF THE EUROPEAN COMMUNITY

Nationals of EC countries, except for nationals of Spain and Portugal, are free to come to England, Scotland, Wales and Northern Ireland to seek or take up employment without the necessity of first obtaining a work permit. The family of an EC worker may also come to this country without any restriction on their right of entry. EC nationals are entitled to the same treatment as UK nationals with regard to pay, working conditions, access to housing and property, training, social security and trade union rights. They are free, if unemployed, to seek unemployment benefit.

Although EC nationals do not require work permits to take up employment in this country, nationals of member States (other than nationals of the Republic of Ireland) who are in work and wish to stay in the UK for longer than six months need a residence permit. The application forms for a residence permit are available from the Home Office, at offices of the Department of Employment and at police stations. The completed form should be sent to the Home Office with two recent passport size photographs, a valid passport or identity card and the notice of leave to enter given to the EC national on arrival in the UK.

The period of validity of residence permits for EC nationals is normally limited to the duration of the employment if this is expected to be more than three months but to be less than twelve months. If the employment is expected to be for more than a year, the residence permit will normally be valid for five years. A person issued with a residence permit valid for five years who has remained in employment in the United Kingdom for four years, and continues to do so, may at that stage apply to the Home Office to have his or her residence permit endorsed showing permission to remain in the United Kingdom indefinitely.

Note that in some respects nationals of Spain and Portugal (the most recent members of the EC) do not yet benefit in full from the provisions relating to free movement of labour.

22.3 NON-EC NATIONALS

Non-EC nationals who are subject to immigration control must obtain work permits in order to be able to take up employment in the UK, unless the Immigration Rules provide otherwise. Certain limited categories of persons do not require work permits.

A person who wishes to take up employment for which he believes a permit may not be needed should first make enquiries of a UK representative overseas and obtain entry clearance if appropriate.

22.4 APPLICATIONS FOR WORK PERMITS

If an employer wishes to employ a foreign national he must first apply for a work permit on his behalf. The conditions which must be satisfied before a work permit can be issued are that

(*a*) the employment falls within the categories set out in 22.5 below;

(*b*) a genuine vacancy exists;

(*c*) there is no suitable resident labour available to fill the post offered;

(*d*) the employer has made adequate efforts to find a worker from suitable resident labour or from other member states of the European Community;

(*e*) the application is for a named worker for a specific post;

(*f*) the pay and other conditions of employment offered are at least as good as those offered in the area for similar work.

The overseas worker should normally be between 23 and 54 years of age. The lower age limit does not apply to sportsmen or sportswomen and neither limit applies to entertainers.

The worker will also normally be expected to have an adequate command of the English language and to have acquired his qualifications, skills and experience outside the United Kingdom.

22.5 WORKERS ELIGIBLE FOR PERMIT

Permits are issued only to certain categories of workers. The categories are

(*a*) those holding recognised professional qualifications;

(*b*) administrative and executive staff;

(*c*) highly qualified technicians having specialised experience;

(*d*) other key workers with a high or scarce qualification in an industry or occupation requiring expert knowledge or skills;

(*e*) highly skilled and experienced workers for senior posts in hotel and catering work who have successfully completed full-time training courses of at least two years' duration at approved schools abroad or, exceptionally, have acquired other specialised or uncommon skills or experience relevant to the industry;

(*f*) established entertainers, including self-employed entertainers coming to fulfil engagements;

(*g*) sportsmen and sportswomen who meet the appropriate skills criteria (professional sportsmen and sportswomen taking part in competitions of international standing do not normally require permits);

(*h*) people coming for a limited period of training or work experience approved by the Department of Employment (see leaflet OW21);

(*j*) other persons only if, in the opinion of the Secretary of State for Employment, their employment is in the national interest.

22.6 Procedure

(i) *Proving no suitable resident labour.* In order to satisfy condition 22.4(*c*) above, an employer must

(A) consider carefully whether the vacancy can be filled by the promotion or transfer of an existing worker, perhaps after suitable training;

(B) advertise the vacancy in the local, national and/or EC press and in any appropriate trade and professional journals;

(C) send copies of any such advertisements with the application for the permit and give full details of the results of such advertising;

(D) be willing to pay the travel expenses of any worker resident in this country coming from a distance for a pre-arranged interview or to take up employment.

A full explanation must be given if the prospective employer considers that it would be unproductive to search the resident and/or EC labour market.

(ii) *Time for application.* The employer must submit an application on form OW1 for a work permit at least eight weeks before the permit is required. The forms are available at employment offices, Jobcentres and should be returned, when completed, to the appropriate address given on the form.

(iii) *Issue of permit.* When an application is approved the work permit is issued together with a copy of 'Employment in the United Kingdom' OW17, a booklet of guidance for workers from non-EC countries. In the case of Commonwealth citizens, the documents are sent direct to them through official channels and the employer is notified when this is done. In the case of other overseas workers, the documents are generally sent to the employer, who is responsible for forwarding them to the workers concerned.

(iv) *Arrival of worker.* When workers arrive in the UK they must present the permit together with a valid passport (not an identity card) to the immigration authorities. Nationals of certain foreign countries also require visas. Without these documents they may be refused entry. Leave to enter will usually be given for the period specified on the work permit, which can be for up to twelve months.

(v) *Change of job.* If a permit holder wishes to change his job he will usually only be permitted to take up employment of a type similar to that for which the permit was originally issued. Application must be made on his behalf to the Department of Employment for permission for the change of job, the application being made by the new employer on form OW1. Consent to a change of employment is subject to the same conditions as the issue of a work permit and changes of employment authorised by the Department of Employment will be recorded in a certificate of employment for Commonwealth citizens and in the police certificate of registration for other overseas workers. Application must also be made, and permission obtained, for a change of place of employment with the same employer.

(vi) *Registering with police*. Overseas workers who are not Commonwealth citizens are generally required to register with the police if they are given leave to enter for employment lasting more than three months.

(vii) *Extensions of stay* may be granted by the Home Office to permit holders who remain in approved employment. After four years in approved employment they may apply to the Home Office for the removal of the time limit on their stay. If the time limit is removed there will be no conditions attached to their stay and they are free to take any employment without reference to the Department of Employment.

22.7 FURTHER INFORMATION

More detailed information about the work permit scheme can be obtained from any local office of the Training Commission or from

Department of Employment
Overseas Labour Section
Caxton House
Tothill Street
London SW1A 9HF tel: 01-273 5336

Information and advice about all other aspects of the law on immigration can be obtained from

The Home Office
Immigration and Nationality Department
Lunar House
Wellesley Road
Croydon CR9 2BY tel: 01-686 0688

23 Guarantee Payments for Workless Days

(See also DE booklet No. 9 'Guarantee payments' (PL 724).)

23.1 The *Employment Protection Act 1975* created certain rights to payment when no work is done owing to circumstances beyond the control of the employee. These provisions were re-enacted in the *Employment Protection (Consolidation) Act 1978* and amended by the *Employment Acts 1980* and *1982*. These are of benefit, chiefly, to hourly paid employees and to workers on piece rates.

23.2 RIGHT TO GUARANTEE PAYMENT

Workless day

Where any employee, throughout a day during any part of which he would normally be required to work in accordance with his contract of employment, is not provided with work by his employer by reason of

(*a*) a diminution in the requirements of the employer's business for work of the kind which the employee is employed to do; or

(*b*) any other occurrence affecting the normal working of the employer's business in relation to work of the kind which the employee is employed to do;

he is, subject to certain exceptions, entitled to a guarantee payment. [*EPCA s 12(1)*].

A threatened power cut is such an occurrence. (*Miller v Harry Thornton (Lollies) Ltd [1978] IRLR 430*).

If a worker can turn down work given to her she is normally not 'required to work' within the meaning of the section and is not entitled to a guarantee payment when not provided with any work. (*Mailway (Southern) Ltd v Willsher [1978] ICR 511*).

If an employer provides some although not the usual amount of work during a day, that is not considered a 'workless day' for which an employee is entitled to a guarantee payment. Examples of situations which may cause a day to be 'workless' are a lack of orders, under (*a*), or any other occurrence such as a power strike affecting the normal working of the employer's business in relation to work of the kind which the employee is employed to do, under (*b*).

Where employment begins before midnight and extends into the next day, the period of employment for the purpose of deciding which is the workless day is defined as follows

(i) if the employment before midnight is, or would normally be, of longer duration than that after midnight, that period of employment is treated as falling wholly on the first day; and

(ii) in any other case, that period of employment is treated as falling wholly on the second day.

[*EPCA s 12(2)*].

23.3 Qualifying period

In order to qualify for the entitlement, an employee must have been continuously employed for one month ending with the day before the workless day. [*EPCA s*

13(1); EA 1982, 2 Sch 1]. In calculating the period of continuous employment, a week is counted (generally speaking) where

(*a*) the employee actually worked for 16 hours or more during the week; or

(*b*) the employment is under a contract which normally involves employment for 16 hours or more weekly; or

(*c*) the employee has been continuously employed for five years or more and the employment is under a contract which normally involves employment for eight hours or more weekly.

The legislation sets out the rules in more detail. [*EPCA s 151 and 13 Sch; EA 1982, 2 Sch 7*]. (See CONTINUOUS EMPLOYMENT (9).)

'Normal working hours' are not to be equated with average working hours. (*Mailway (Southern) Ltd v Willsher [1978] ICR 511*).

An employee who is employed

(i) under a contract for a fixed term of three months or less; or

(ii) under a contract made in contemplation of the performance of a specific task which is not expected to last for more than three months,

is not entitled to a guarantee payment unless he has been continuously employed for a period of more than three months ending with the day before that in respect of which the guarantee payment is claimed. [*EPCA s 13(2); EA 1982, 2 Sch 1*].

23.4 Exclusions

Trade disputes. An employee is not entitled to a guarantee payment in respect of a workless day if the failure to provide him with work occurs in consequence of a trade dispute involving any employee of his employer or of an associated employer. [*EPCA s 13(3); EA 1982, 2 Sch 1*]. 'Trade dispute' and 'associated employer' have the same meaning as in the *Trade Union and Labour Relations Act 1974, s 29* (see 47.3 STRIKES AND INDUSTRIAL ACTION). Thus, a dispute with his employer involving members of another union at his workplace or of employees of his employer at a factory in another part of the country, which causes a halt in production, disentitles an employee from receiving a guarantee payment.

Offer of suitable alternative work. An employee is not entitled to a guarantee payment in respect of a workless day if

(*a*) his employer has offered to provide alternative work for that day which is suitable in all the circumstances (whether or not it is work which the employee is employed to perform under his contract) and the employee has unreasonably refused that offer; or

(*b*) he does not comply with reasonable requirements imposed by his employer with a view to ensuring that his services are available.

[*EPCA s 13(4); EA 1982, 2 Sch 1*].

Both objective and subjective tests are involved in deciding what is 'suitable' and 'reasonable' within the meaning of (*a*) above. No general rules can be laid down, but what tribunals will have in mind are pay, hours, geographical location and skill required. So far as (*b*) is concerned, clearly, if an employer asked an employee to telephone to find out whether work was available, that would be considered a reasonable requirement.

23.5 AMOUNT OF PAYMENT

The amount of the guarantee payment payable in respect of any day is the sum produced by multiplying the *number of normal working hours* in that day by the *guaranteed hourly rate*. [*EPCA s 14(1)*].

The 'guaranteed hourly rate' is the amount of one week's pay (see 'A WEEK'S PAY' (58)) divided by the number of normal working hours in that week. In calculating 'normal working hours' where the number of working hours in a week fluctuate, one takes the average number of working hours over the 12 weeks ending with the last complete week before the day in respect of which the guarantee payment is payable. If the employee has not been employed for 12 weeks, a calculation is made having regard to

(*a*) the average number of normal working hours in a week which the employee could expect in accordance with the terms of his contract;

(*b*) the average number of such hours of other employees engaged in relevant comparable employment with the same employer.

[*EPCA s 14(2)*].

If any employee's contract has been varied or a new contract has been entered into for short-time working, the calculation is made by reference to the last day that the original contract was in force. [*EPCA s 14(3)*].

The amount of a guarantee payment payable to an employee in respect of any day will not exceed £11.85 (£11.30 before 1 April 1989) and such payments cannot exceed five days in any period of three months. The present maximum annual liability is therefore £237. [*EPCA s 15; EA 1980, s 14(1); Employment Protection (Variation of Limits) Order 1989 (SI 1989 No 526)*]. Any contractual remuneration paid to an employee in respect of a workless day goes towards discharging any statutory liability of the employer to pay a guarantee payment in respect of that day and, conversely, any guarantee payment paid in respect of a day goes towards discharging any liability of the employer to pay contractual remuneration in respect of that day. [*EPCA s 16(2)*]. Thus, if any employee is paid on a weekly or monthly basis, irrespective of the work actually done, these payments will go towards discharging any statutory liability. Contractual payments made in respect of any workless days are to be taken into account when calculating the maximum number of days within the three-month period for which the employee is entitled to a payment. (*Cartwright v G Clancey Ltd* [*1983*] *ICR 552*).

The Secretary of State may by order exempt certain industries from these provisions where there is in force a collective agreement or wages order which complies with certain conditions. [*EPCA s 18*]. For example, by the *Guarantee Payments (Exemption) (No 22) (Amendment) Order 1985 (SI 1985 No 1270)* which amended a previous order (*SI 1983 No 571*), the Secretary of State excluded from the right to a guarantee payment employees to whom the Substantive Agreement of the Joint Negotiating Council for the UK Confectionery Division of Rowntree Mackintosh plc applies.

23.6 REMEDY FOR FAILURE TO MAKE PAYMENT

An employee may present a complaint to an industrial tribunal that his employer has failed to pay the whole or any part of a guarantee payment to which he is entitled. The tribunal, if it finds the complaint well-founded, will order the employer to pay the complainant the amount of guarantee payment which it finds due to him. [*EPCA s 17(1)(3)*]. Such a complaint must be presented to a tribunal before the end of the period of *three months* beginning with the workless day (or within such further period as the tribunal considers reasonable, when it is satisfied that it was not reasonably practicable for the complaint to be presented within the period of three months). [*EPCA s 17(2)*].

24 **Health and Safety at Work – I:** Employers' Duties and Liability

(See also HSC leaflets HSC2 'The Act outlined', HSC3 'Advice to employers', HSC5 'Advice to employees', HSC6 on employers' policy statements and HSC7 on regulations, codes and guidance literature; see also HSC booklets HSC9 'Time off for the training of Safety Representatives' and HSC8 on Safety Committees where the employees are not members of a recognised union. These are all free of charge. Other detailed guidance notes are also available from HMSO for a small charge.)

Cross-reference. See HEALTH AND SAFETY AT WORK – II (25) for the statutory obligations under the *Health and Safety at Work etc. Act 1974*.

24.1 An employer is under a common law duty to have regard to the safety of his employees. He is also liable at common law for accidents caused by acts of his employees where the employees were acting in the course of their employment. In addition to these common law duties, statutory obligations are imposed upon employers in certain circumstances by such enactments as

Occupiers' Liability Act 1957 (see 24.13 below)
Factories Act 1961 (see 24.17 below)
Offices, Shops and Railway Premises Act 1963 (see 24.21 below)
Health and Safety at Work etc. Act 1974 (see HEALTH AND SAFETY AT WORK – II (25))

Failure by an employer to attend to the safety duties owed by him to an employee may entitle the employee to resign and complain of unfair dismissal (see 24.26 below). An employee has a duty to abide by his employer's safety rules, and he may in principle be fairly dismissed for a breach of those rules (see 24.26 below and 25.7 HEALTH AND SAFETY AT WORK – II).

24.2 Compulsory insurance against liability

The *Employers' Liability (Compulsory Insurance) Act 1969*, as amended, obliges every employer carrying on a business in Great Britain to maintain insurance, under one or more approved policies with an authorised insurer, against liability for bodily injury or disease sustained by employees and arising out of and in the course of their employment in Great Britain. An employer is not obliged to insure members of his family. [*Sec 2(2)(a)*]. Insurance companies issue annual certificates which must be displayed at every place where the employer carries on business so that they may be easily seen and read by every person employed there. [*Employers' Liability (Compulsory Insurance) General Regulations 1971, as amended (SIs 1971 No 1117; 1974 No 208; 1975 Nos 194, 1443), Regs 5, 6*].

There is generally no duty upon the employer to protect his employees from economic loss as opposed to physical injury. Hence it was not a breach of duty to fail to arrange or advise insurance for an employee sent to work in a country without compulsory motor insurance (*Reid v Rush & Tompkins Group PLC [1989] IRLR 265*).

24.3 THE COMMON LAW DUTY

An employer is obliged to take such steps as are reasonably necessary to ensure the safety of his employees. The duty is not an absolute one and the mere occurrence of an accident does not of itself necessarily impose liability on the employer. All the circumstances of the accident will be investigated in deciding whether the employer acted reasonably or not. If an accident occurs as a result of the employer's failure to comply with his duty to his employees, he is liable for any resulting injury or damage.

Where a job has inherent risks to health and safety which are not commonly known but of which the employer is or ought to be aware, and if the employer cannot guard against those risks by taking precautionary measures, then he has a duty to inform prospective employees of the risks if knowledge of them would be likely to affect a sensible and level-headed person's decision on whether or not to accept the job. (*White v Holbrook Precision Castings* [*1985*] *IRLR 215*).

The employer's compliance with his common law duty of care is usually tested under the following headings:

(*a*) providing a safe place of work;

(*b*) providing a safe means of access to the place of work;

(*c*) providing a safe system of work;

(*d*) providing adequate equipment and materials;

(*e*) employing competent fellow employees;

(*f*) protecting employees from unnecessary risk of injury.

However, these are simply specific aspects of the employer's overall general duty not to be negligent, and so should be viewed as examples of ways in which employers can take steps to ensure that their employees are reasonably safe at work.

24.4 Safe place of work

An employer is obliged to see that the place where his employees work is reasonably safe in all the circumstances. A place of work must be safely constructed and adequately maintained in a reasonable state of repair. An employer would be as guilty of failing to provide a safe place of work if, for example, a platform high above the ground on which men were required to stand was not adequately fenced as if one of the planks provided for the platform were rotten and liable to give way.

So far as construction of the work place is concerned, it is not sufficient to show that the employer engaged a competent contractor to provide a safe place. (*Paine v Colne Valley Electrical Supply Co Ltd and British Insulated Cables Ltd* [*1938*] *4 AER 803,* per Goddard LJ at p 807). This reflects the general principle that the employer's duty of care to his employees is non-delegable (see 24.10 below). If, however, an employer maintains an adequate system of inspection of the work place and despite inspection, as in the example, a part of the work place becomes inadequate or defective, the employer will probably not have been in breach of his common law duty. (He may nevertheless be in breach of a statutory provision which imposes a stricter duty, see 24.13 et seq. below.)

Temporary conditions affecting the work place. A place of work which is intrinsically safe may become unsafe by the occurrence of certain events. Liquid may be spilt on a workshop floor making it slippery, a fence may be temporarily removed or an object placed in an unfamiliar position. All these events could cause accidents. The employer's liability will depend upon whether a reasonable employer would in the particular circumstances have taken measures to avoid the accident or different measures from those in fact taken What is reasonable will vary according to the facts of the case. If a man slips on an oil slick at his work place and thereby injures himself, his employer's potential liability may well vary according to how long the oil had been present (or according to the frequency with which such spillages occur, as in *Bell v Department of Health and Social Security, The Times, 13 June 1989*). If the oil had been spilt just a few minutes before the accident there may well be no liability, whereas if it had been there for half a day, the position would be different. In *Thomas v Bristol Aeroplane Co [1954] 2 AER 1*, an employer was held not to be in breach of the common law duty of care in failing to take steps to remove from the entrance to the factory frozen snow which had fallen about a quarter of an hour before the factory opened. However, there may be a breach of the relevant duties under e.g. the *Factories Act 1961* (see 24.17 below) even if there is no breach of the common law duty of care (see e.g. *Powley v Bristol Siddeley Engines Ltd [1965] 3 AER 612*).

Employee working on other premises. An employer owes a general duty to his employee to provide him with a safe place of work whether he is employed on the employer's own premises or elsewhere. However, the extent of that duty when the employee is on other premises may well be less than when he is on his employer's premises. The test again is: did the employer in question act as a reasonable employer would have acted in the circumstances? Thus, if an employer sends a window-cleaner to premises he knows to be unsafe, he may well be held liable for any accident caused as a result of the state of the premises. If he does not know whether the premises are safe or not, then, depending on the convenience of inspection and the degree of risk involved, he may be held negligent in failing to inspect and, if necessary, make those premises safe.

24.5 Safe means of access

It is the duty of every employer to provide his employees with a safe means of access to their place of work. Thus, if access to a factory is by means of a footpath, that footpath should be kept in a reasonable state of repair.

Sometimes it is hard to distinguish the means of access to the place of work from the place of work itself. A painter may use a ladder to reach a position from where to carry on his decorating. The ladder may in certain circumstances be considered the means of access and in others the place of work. In any event the common law duty of care in relation to both is the same.

24.6 Safe system of work

A system of work is the method used for carrying out the work, the sequence of events followed. It includes such things as manning of operations, provision of equipment, and supervision. It may be that the system used by an employer is intrinsically unsafe or it may be that there is in existence a suitable system of work but that the system itself is applied unsatisfactorily. For example, an employer who provides insufficient men to carry out a task may be held liable for any accident caused thereby.

The *Factories Act 1961*, and the regulations made thereunder (see also 24.17 below), contain several provisions which relate to the system of work. These statutory provisions complement rather than supersede the common law provisions relating to safety.

One defect in an otherwise unimpeachable system may render the whole system unsafe. If, for example, the procedures for carrying out blasting in a quarry were adequate but the warning given to workers in the quarry to leave was too short, the whole system would thereby be rendered unsafe. Similarly, it would be considered an unsafe system to require men who had insufficient training or supervision to carry out a task which would otherwise be considered safe.

Employers who require their workers to carry out manoeuvres which involve several actions should first check to see whether there are any relevant statutory requirements relating to the procedure. Before devising a system of working they should consult the employees who are to work the system or their representatives. Where the workforce is unionised, the employer has a duty to consult with union-appointed safety representatives. If the procedure is at all complicated, employers should consult the Health and Safety Executive (see 25.11 HEALTH AND SAFETY AT WORK–II).

Duty based on reasonable steps. The duty to provide a safe system of work is not an absolute one. The duty is to take reasonable steps to provide a system which will be reasonably safe, having regard to the dangers necessarily inherent in the operation. In deciding what is reasonable, long established practice in the trade (although not necessarily conclusive) is generally regarded as strong evidence in support of reasonableness. (*General Cleaning Contractors Ltd v Christmas [1953] AC 180* per Lord Tucker at *195*). Thus, in deciding the extent of the duty the courts will take into account (i) the size of the danger (ii) the likelihood of an accident occurring (iii) the possible consequences of the occurrence of an accident and (iv) the steps needed to eliminate all risk and the cost of doing so.

Ensuring implementation of safety measures. It is not sufficient to provide a safe system of work. An employer should take such steps as are reasonably practicable to see that the system is implemented. If it is within his knowledge that a piece of safety equipment is persistently not used, he should take reasonable steps to encourage his workers to use it. (*Bux v Slough Metals [1974] 1 AER 262*). However, this duty is not so onerous as the duty to provide the safety equipment etc. in the first place. As Lord Radcliffe said in *Qualcast (Wolverhampton) Ltd v Haynes [1959] AC 743 at 753*: 'the courts should be circumspect in filling out that duty with the much vaguer obligation of encouraging, exhorting or instructing workmen or a particular workman to make regular use of what is provided'. In *Crouch v British Rail Engineering Ltd [1988] IRLR 404* it was held to be insufficient on the facts merely to make safety goggles available for collection from a point about five minutes away. The failure to have them available where they were needed encouraged the taking of risks.

Some workers are notoriously reluctant to use certain safety equipment or safety clothing and it has been held to be a good defence to a claim based on a failure to provide protective clothing to show that the workman would probably not have used it in any event (e.g. *McWilliams v Sir William Arroll & Co Ltd [1962] 1 AER 623; Wigley v British Vinegars [1964] AC 307*).

24.7 Safe equipment and materials

An employer is under a common law duty to provide equipment, materials and clothing to enable his workmen to carry out their duties in safety. As with the system of work, the duty is not an absolute one. It may be, for example, that goggles costing £300 per pair are marginally safer than those costing £50 per pair. In deciding whether an employer was in breach of his duty in failing to provide his employees with the more expensive goggles the court would have regard to the difference in effectiveness between the cheaper and the more expensive goggles, the degree of risk involved, and the additional cost.

When an employer bought materials from a reputable supplier, and injury was caused by an undetected defect in those materials, his failure to examine the materials would not render him liable for the accident at common law. However, since 25 October 1969, when the *Employers' Liability (Defective Equipment) Act 1969* came into force, if an employee is injured by reason of a defect in the equipment, the injury is by statute deemed to be attributable to the fault of the employer. This does not affect the employer's right to allege that the accident was wholly or partly due to negligence on the part of the employee; nor does it affect any remedy the employer may have against his supplier. Thus, if an employee is injured by a piece of metal flying from a defective high pressure hose, supplied to him by his employer, he could succeed in a claim against the employer for his injury. The employer could only seek to reduce the damages awarded against him by showing that the accident was caused or contributed to by the fault of the employee and/or by claiming against the supplier of the hose.

Under *Section 1(3)* of the *1969 Act* 'equipment' includes any plant, machinery, vehicle, aircraft and clothing. A ship is 'equipment' for the purposes of *Section 1(3)*. (*Coltman and another v Bibby Tankers Ltd (The Derbyshire) [1988] ICR 67*).

24.8 Fellow workers

An employer is under a duty to provide competent fellow workers. Thus, if an employee of his is injured because of the known inadequacy of a fellow worker, the employer is liable to that employee in damages for the injury caused by the fellow worker. Even if the employee's action is untypical, the employer may nevertheless be held liable by reason of his vicarious liability (see 24.10 below).

An employer may not contract out of his liability to his employees for the negligence of fellow workers. The *Law Reform (Personal Injuries) Act 1948, s 1(3)* renders void any agreement to that effect.

24.9 Protection from risk of injury

An employer is under a duty to take reasonable care to see that his employees are not subjected to any unnecessary risks of injury. In *Charlton v Forrest Printing Ink Co Ltd [1980] IRLR 330*, the Court of Appeal held that an employer has a duty to take steps to eliminate a risk which he knows or ought to know is a real risk and not a mere possibility which would never influence the mind of a reasonable man. On the facts of that case, injuries caused to an employee by criminals in a wages snatch, the employers were held not to be negligent in not using a security firm since the sums involved were small.

Where a risk is not obvious, the employee will succeed only if he can show that the state of knowledge in the relevant industry at the relevant time was such that the employer knew or ought to have known of that risk. But an employer must keep reasonably abreast of developing knowledge, and if he has greater than average knowledge of the risks, he may have to take greater than average precautions (*Stokes v Guest Keen & Nettlefold (Bolts and Nuts) Ltd [1968] 1 WLR 1776*).

In cases of industrial disease, it may often be difficult to determine whether the employee's illness was *caused* by the employer's breach of duty. For recent decisions of the House of Lords on similar problems, see *Hotson v East Berkshire Area Health Authority [1987] AC 750* and *Wilsher v Essex Area Health Authority [1988] 2 WLR 557*.

24.10 VICARIOUS LIABILITY FOR ACTS OF EMPLOYEES

An employer is liable for the acts of his employee if they are committed in the course of the employee's employment. This is known as 'vicarious liability'. Thus, if a van delivery driver drives negligently while in the normal course of his duties and causes an accident, his employer is held liable for the damage or injury resulting. Similarly, if an employee closes a hatch on a ship without warning, thereby trapping a fellow employee's fingers, the employer will be made liable for his employee's negligence. (*Hopkins v Shaw Savill & Albion Co Ltd [1968] 1 Lloyd's Rep 103*).

Although the general rule is that the employer is not liable for torts committed by a person who is not an employee, there are exceptions. The nature of the employer's duty is personal with respect to each employee, and if he delegates that duty to another, whether or not that person is his employee, the employer will be liable for any injury caused through the negligence of the person to whom he delegated the duty. (*McDermid v Nash Dredging & Reclamation Co Ltd [1987] ICR 917*).

24.11 'In the course of the employment'

The employer may seek to avoid being made vicariously liable by alleging that the acts complained of were not authorised by him. However, vicarious liability may be imposed not only where the employer does not expressly authorise the acts in question, but even where he has prohibited such acts. He will be liable if the acts occur in the course of employment as that concept has been interpreted by the courts.

In *Rose v Plenty [1976] 1 WLR 141*, the defendant's employees were expressly instructed not to employ young people to assist in their duties as milk roundsmen. An employee of the defendant contravened the instruction and allowed a boy to help. The boy was injured partly through the negligence of the employee, and the defendant employer was vicariously liable because the employee's conduct in allowing the boy to help with milk delivery was within the scope of his employment, despite being prohibited. Lord Denning said: '. . . the prohibition affects only the conduct within the sphere of the employment and did not take the conduct outside the sphere altogether'. But in the remarkable case of *General Engineering Services Ltd v Kingston and St. Andrew Corporation [1989] ICR 88* the Privy Council held that for firemen to drive slowly to a fire pursuant to a go-slow was not a mere mode of performance, but was the very antithesis of the act they were authorised to do. Thus the fire authority was held not to be vicariously liable.

An employer is not liable for the torts of an employee who has gone so far outside the scope of his duties as to have embarked on what has been described as a 'frolic of his own'. Similarly the employer cannot be liable for acts such as assaults by his employees unless they were perpetrated in the course of the employment and in pursuance of express or implied authority vested in him. It used to be thought that an employer could not be made liable for theft by his employee, but in *Morris v C W Martin & Sons Ltd [1966] 1 QB 716*, a dry-cleaning company was held liable to the owner of a fur coat stolen by one of its employees in the course of handling by the company. There must, though, be some nexus other than mere opportunity between the criminal act and the circumstances of the employment (*Heasmans v Clarity Cleaning Co. [1987] ICR 949*). In that case, the employee of a contractor engaged to clean offices made use of a telephone in those offices for international calls. The Court of Appeal held that his employers were not vicariously liable for his acts.

In *Aldred v Nacanco [1987] IRLR 292* the Court of Appeal approved the following test (taken from *Salmond on Torts*, 18th edition, p 437):

> 'If a servant does negligently that which he was authorised to do carefully, or if he does fraudulently that which he was authorised to do honestly, or if he does mistakenly that which he was authorised to do correctly, his master will answer for that negligence, fraud or mistake. On the other hand, if the unauthorised and wrongful act of the servant is not so connected with the authorised act as to be a mode of doing it, but is an independent act, the master is not responsible; for in such a case the servant is not acting in the course of his employment but has gone outside of it.'

An employer may be held vicariously liable for the act of his employee, even if the employee is not at work, in circumstances in which the employee is being paid for his time, in which he is carrying out the instructions of his employer or in which the employer is entitled to direct how the employee is to act. In such circumstances the House of Lords held an employer vicariously liable for the negligence of his employee while driving a workmate home to Staffordshire after completing a job in Pembroke (*Smith v Stages and another [1989] ICR 272*). The speeches of Lord Goff and Lord Lowry contain extensive analyses of vicarious liability for the acts of travelling employees.

24.12 Independent contractors

With the exception of the statutory occupier's liability (see 24.13 below), in general an employer is not liable for acts of an independent contractor engaged by him, provided that he exercised due diligence in selecting the contractor for the task.

24.13 OCCUPIERS' LIABILITY ACT 1957

Apart from the common law duties of an employer to provide his employees with a safe place of work, as an occupier of premises he owes his employees, and other visitors, the common duty of care imposed by the *Occupiers' Liability Act 1957 (OLA)*. The extent of the duty which is owed to trespassers is defined by the *Occupiers' Liability Act 1984*. An outline is given below of the duties imposed on an employer, as the occupier of premises, to employees and other visitors by the *OLA*.

24.14 Meaning of 'occupier'

An occupier of premises may be the owner, the lessor, or the licensee (a person who merely has permission to occupy). An occupier need not have exclusive control over premises in order to have a duty to persons who visit those premises; more than one person may owe a duty in respect of the same premises. For example, both an employer and an independent contractor may be held to be occupiers of premises where the employer has engaged the independent contractor to carry out work on the premises.

24.15 Duty of occupier

The extent of the duty of care is defined in *OLA s 2(2)* as

> 'a duty to take such care as in all the circumstances of the case is reasonable to see that the visitor is reasonably safe in using the premises for the purposes for which he is invited or permitted by the occupier to be there.'

In defining the extent of the duty, the courts will take into account the *degree of control over the premises actually enjoyed* by the occupier and, if applicable, the division of duties between the two occupiers of the same premises. Thus, if a harbour authority leases a certain wharf to a shipping company and an employee of that company suffers an accident due to the state of repair of the wharf, the apportionment of blame will depend on the actual degree of control exercised by the harbour authority and the shipping company.

Children and persons pursuing a calling. OLA s 2(3) provides a little help in defining the extent of the duty of care to be exercised in relation to children and to persons on the premises in pursuance of a particular calling.

> 'The circumstances relevant for the present purpose include the degree of care, and of want of care, which would ordinarily be looked for in such a visitor, so that (for example) in proper cases
>
> (*a*) an occupier must be prepared for children to be less careful than adults; and
>
> (*b*) an occupier may expect that a person, in the exercise of his calling, will appreciate and guard against any special risks ordinarily incident to it, so far as the occupier leaves him free to do so.'

Thus, a scaffolder must guard against the ordinary hazards of his job, but the occupier would be liable if, for example, a piece of scaffolding on premises which should have been tested by him proved defective and caused an accident.

24.16 Faulty work by independent contractor

If an accident occurs as a result of faulty work by an independent contractor employed at the premises which the employer occupies, *OLA s 2(4)(b)* provides that

> 'the occupier is not to be treated without more ["without more" in the sense of "on those facts alone"] as answerable for the danger if in all the circumstances he had acted reasonably in entrusting the work to an independent contractor and had taken such steps (if any) as he reasonably ought in order to satisfy himself that the contractor was competent and that the work had been properly done.'

Thus, if injury is caused to a visitor to the premises by the fault of an independent contractor, the occupier will not be held liable for the injury or damage so caused if he can show that

(*a*) he acted reasonably in entrusting the work to the independent contractor (it may be held to be reasonable to employ an independent contractor where the work to be done is of a skilled or specialist nature and is beyond the capabilities of the employer); and

(*b*) he exercised a reasonable degree of care in selecting the independent contractor to see that he was competent to do the task entrusted to him; and

(*c*) he checked so far as was possible to see that the work was properly carried out.

For example, an employer may need to have his factory rewired. He may have no electricians in his employ, and therefore need to engage an outside firm. If he has reasonable grounds for regarding that firm as competent, he will not ordinarily be expected to supervise the firm's activities in order to ensure that a safe system of work is being used. But if he knows or has reason to suspect that the firm is using an unsafe system of work, it may well be reasonable for him to take steps to see that it is made safe. If he does not, he might be liable to one of his own or the firm's employees injured e.g. by receiving an electric shock (*Ferguson v Welsh and others* [*1988*] *IRLR 112*, on different facts). He may also be liable to the employee for breach of other statutory provisions, e.g. *Factories Act 1961*, see 24.17 below.

24.17 FACTORIES ACT 1961

The *Factories Act 1961* is an important piece of consolidating legislation which lays down specific provisions regulating such things as safety measures, lighting and cleanliness in factories. Parts of the Act have, however, been replaced or modified by powers conferred by the *Health and Safety at Work etc. Act 1974* (see HEALTH AND SAFETY AT WORK – II (25)). For more detail about the provisions of the Act itself and the many regulations thereunder see *'Redgrave's Health and Safety in Factories' (2nd ed)*.

The provisions of the *Factories Act 1961* apply to all 'factories'. [*Factories Act 1961, s 172*]. The expression 'factory' is defined in *Factories Act 1961, s 175 (1)(2)*.

In addition to leading to civil liability for breach of statutory duty (see below), breaches of certain sections of the Act are criminal offences. [*Factories Act 1961, s 155*].

The provisions of the Act apply to protect all persons working in a factory, whether they are employed by the occupier of the factory or not.

24.18 Duties under the Act

The principal duties imposed by the Act include the following:

(i) to keep the factory clean [*Sec 1*];

(ii) the prevention of overcrowding [*Sec 2*];

(iii) to maintain a reasonable temperature [*Sec 3*], adequate ventilation [*Sec 4*] and sufficient lighting [*Sec 5*];

(iv) to fence machinery [*Sec 12 et seq*];

(v) to maintain floors, passages and stairs, to keep them free from obstructions and from substances likely to cause persons to slip, and to provide handrails etc. where the Act requires [*Sec 28*]; and

(vi) to provide and maintain safe access to, and to make and keep safe, every place where any person has to work [*Sec 29*].

24.19 Employer's liability for breach of the Act

If an employee can establish (i) that the Act applies to him, (ii) that his employer was in breach of a provision of the Act and (iii) that he has thereby suffered injury or damage, he may bring an action for damages for breach of statutory duty. However, breach of a provision of the Act does not automatically entitle a plaintiff to damages. In order successfully to pursue a claim for breach of statutory duty, the employee must establish that the breach caused the accident. In *McWilliams v Sir William Arrol & Co Ltd* [*1962*] *1 AER 623*, a widow brought an action against the occupiers of a shipbuilding yard alleging a breach of *Factories Act 1937, s 26(2)* (now *Factories Act 1961, s 29*) for failure to provide her deceased husband with a safety belt. It was established by the employers on a balance of probabilities that had the deceased been provided with a safety belt he would not have used it, and therefore it was not their failure to provide the belt that caused the accident. It may also be necessary to consider whether some foolish or unpredictable intervention by the plaintiff or a third party operates to break the chain of causation (see *McGovern v British Steel Corporation* [*1986*] *ICR 608*).

Some provisions of the Act merely oblige the employer to take reasonable steps to achieve a particular result, but others impose an absolute duty.

As with all other statutory provisions considered here, the provisions of the *Factories Act 1961* do not exclude the common law duty of care, but rather are complementary to it, so that a certain action may be both negligent and a breach of statutory duty. (*Franklin v Gramophone Co Ltd* [*1948*] *1 KB 542*). In that case Evershed LJ said at p 561 '. . . as a matter of general principle, it does not seem to me that the imposition . . . of statutory obligations absolves the factory owner or occupier from his common law duty.'

24.20 Enforcement

The provisions of the *Factories Act 1961* are enforced by the Health and Safety Executive. (See further 25.15 HEALTH AND SAFETY AT WORK – II.)

24.21 THE OFFICES, SHOPS AND RAILWAY PREMISES ACT 1963

As with the *Factories Act 1961* the general intention of the *Offices, Shops and Railway Premises Act 1963 (OSRPA)* is to ensure the health, safety and welfare of all those who work in the defined premises.

The general effect of *OSRPA* is similar to that of the *Factories Act 1961* in that it imposes similar statutory duties. If an employee is injured as a result of a failure to observe the provisions of the Act then he may bring a claim based upon a breach of the Act in addition to any common law claim he may have against the occupier and/or other persons responsible for the contravention. The premises to which *OSRPA* applies are defined in *Sec 1*.

24.22 Workers protected

Some of the provisions of *OSRPA* define specifically the class of persons to whom they apply, in others the words 'persons employed' are used. For example, *OSRPA s 17(1)* specifically applies to every person working in the premises whether he be employed by the occupier or an independent contractor, whereas the phrase 'persons employed' used in other sections may be subject to a different interpretation. The provisions of the Act do not however protect persons not working at the premises, such as customers in a shop.

Exceptions. The provisions of the Act do not apply to

(*a*) premises where only the husband, wife, parent, grandparent, son, daughter, grandchild, brother or sister of the employer are working [*OSRPA s 2(1)*];

(*b*) a dwelling house even where a resident such as a housekeeper is employed to work by an employer who does not reside there [*OSRPA s 2(2)*];

(*c*) premises where work is not normally carried on for more than 21 hours a week [*OSRPA s 3*].

24.23 Enforcement

It is the duty of every local authority to enforce within their area the provisions of the *Offices, Shops and Railway Premises Act 1963*. [*Health and Safety (Enforcing Authority) Regulations 1977 (SI 1977 No 746), Regs 2, 3*]. (See further 25.16 HEALTH AND SAFETY AT WORK – II.)

24.24 OTHER LEGISLATION

Other legislation governs the safety of other occupations; for example, the *Agriculture (Safety, Health and Welfare Provisions) Act 1956* applies to employment in agriculture and the *Mineral Workings (Offshore Installations) Act 1971* to employment on offshore installations.

Moreover, certain categories of worker, such as women and young persons, may be the subject of special provision under the *Factories Act 1961*. The restrictions relate to hours and times of work, and do not apply to women holding responsible management positions who are not ordinarily engaged in manual work. [*Factories Act 1961, s 95*]. Many such restrictions are abolished by the *Employment Act 1989*.

The main objective of the legislation was to protect vulnerable workers. However, the effect may sometimes be to exclude women from work which they would otherwise be able to do. Therefore, certain restrictions on the employment of women have been removed by the *Sex Discrimination Act 1986* and orders made thereunder [*Factories Act (Hours of Employment Orders and Regulations) Revocation and Amendment Order 1986 (SI 1986 No 2312)*].

24.25 HEALTH AND SAFETY AT WORK ETC. ACT 1974

The Act introduced a new system of legal rights and duties applying generally to all forms of employment. (See HEALTH AND SAFETY AT WORK – II (25).)

24.26 BREACH OF SAFETY REGULATIONS AND UNFAIR DISMISSAL

A failure by an employer to have regard for the safety of his employees can be considered a fundamental breach of contract entitling the employee to resign and claim that he has been constructively dismissed. In *British Aircraft Corporation Ltd v Austin [1978] IRLR 332*, the Employment Appeal Tribunal held that the employer's failure to give consideration to the employee's request that she should be provided with protective goggles incorporating the prescription lenses of her spectacles amounted to conduct entitling the employee to resign, and, when she did resign, to claim that she had been constructively dismissed under *EPCA s 55(2)(c)*. The EAT in *Dutton & Clark Ltd v Daly [1985] IRLR 363* considered that the test for ascertaining whether an employer is in fundamental breach of contract is to ask whether his actions are outside the band of reasonable responses of the reasonable employer. However, it is doubted whether this is a correct approach, although the reasonableness of the employer's conduct may well be relevant to whether it constitutes a breach of an implied contractual term.

An employer may fairly dismiss an employee for breach of safety regulations if he brought to the attention of the employee and made clear to him the fact that such a breach would lead to dismissal. (*Martin v Yorkshire Imperial Metals [1978] IRLR 440*).

24.27 CONTRIBUTORY NEGLIGENCE

In any successful action against the employer for breach of duty at common law or under some enactment, the amount of damages may be reduced in proportion to the degree to which the employee failed to take reasonable steps for his own safety. [*Law Reform (Contributory Negligence) Act 1945, s 1(1)*]. However, in cases where it is clear that the employee was, in practical terms, entirely at fault the court will not make fine distinctions about respective degrees of blame, and will decide that the employee was 100% at fault. This is so even where the statute which was breached by the employer was intended, *inter alia*, to provide protection for the employee against his own folly. (*Jayes v IMI (Kynoch) Ltd [1985] ICR 155*).

24.28 SIKHS ON CONSTRUCTION SITES

Note that no statutory provision or rule of law is to be taken as imposing, upon a Sikh on a construction site, any requirement to wear a safety helmet at any time when he is wearing a turban. [*EA 1989, s 11*]. However, a Sikh who does not comply with a requirement that would otherwise have been imposed, and is injured, may recover damages in tort only to the extent that he would have suffered injury even if wearing a helmet. [*EA 1989, s 11(5)*]. A person who does require a Sikh to wear a safety helmet on a construction site will probably be guilty of indirect RACIAL DISCRIMINATION (37), and if he has no reasonable grounds to believe that the Sikh would not wear a turban at all times when on site, he will not be permitted to justify that requirement. [*EA 1989, s 12(1)*]. Nor will special treatment afforded to a Sikh in consequence of *Sec 11* constitute racial discrimination against anyone else. [*EA 1989, s 12(2)*].

24.29 ACQUIRED IMMUNE DEFICIENCY SYNDROME (AIDS)

The spread of AIDS may be a cause of concern to employers. The Department of Employment has published a booklet 'AIDS and Employment' (PL 811). It is thought that, because the risk of contracting the disease in most normal employment situations is very slight, the employer will not normally be in breach of his duty of care to other employees (see 24.8, 24.9 above) if he permits an AIDS sufferer to continue working. Indeed, it may well be unfair to dismiss a sufferer (see UNFAIR DISMISSAL – I (54)), even in response to pressure from fellow employees, although such pressure will be irrelevant to the reasonableness of the dismissal (see also 55.16 UNFAIR DISMISSAL – II). An employer who revealed the fact that an individual was an AIDS sufferer might in certain circumstances be liable to the sufferer for a breach of confidence.

25 **Health and Safety at Work – II:** Health and Safety at Work etc. Act 1974

Cross-reference. See HEALTH AND SAFETY AT WORK – I (24) for safety duties at common law and for other systems of statutory duties.

25.1 The *Health and Safety at Work etc. Act 1974 (HSWA)* lays down general principles to be followed by employers governing the health and safety at work of employees. It also establishes the Health and Safety Commission ('the Commission') and the Health and Safety Executive ('the Executive'), gives powers to inspectors to issue improvement notices and prohibition notices, and imposes certain civil and criminal liabilities upon employers.

25.2 HEALTH, SAFETY AND WELFARE

The provisions of *HSWA Part I* (as expressed in *Sec 1(1)*) are designed to have the effect of

(*a*) securing the health, safety and welfare of persons at work;

(*b*) protecting persons other than persons at work against risks to health or safety arising out of, or in connection with, the activities of persons at work;

(*c*) controlling the keeping and use of explosive or highly flammable or otherwise dangerous substances, and generally preventing the unlawful acquisition, possession and use of such substances; and

(*d*) controlling the emission into the atmosphere of noxious or offensive substances from premises of a class prescribed by the *Health and Safety (Emissions into the Atmosphere) Regulations 1983 (SI 1983 No 943*, as amended by *SI 1989 No 319*).

Regulations and codes of practice are issued under *HSWA* to give effect to the general principles set out and also to enforce the provisions of a large body of health and safety legislation (including the *Factories Act 1961*) which is set out in *1 Schedule* to the Act. Two examples of regulations made under *HSWA* are the *Health and Safety (First-Aid) Regulations 1981 (SI 1981 No 917)* and the *Reporting of Injuries, Diseases and Dangerous Occurrences Regulations 1985 (SI 1985 No 2023*). There are also many regulations dealing with specific problems such as asbestos at work. However, as from 1 October 1989 a large number of outdated statutory instruments have been replaced upon the coming into force of the *Control of Substances Hazardous to Health Regulations 1988 (SI 1988 No 1657)* (*COSHH*). *COSHH* has been described as 'the most far-reaching health and safety legislation since 1974'. (See 25.11 below.)

As will be seen below, inspectors appointed under the Act have powers to enforce the legislation set out in *1 Schedule* as well as the provisions of the Act itself and health and safety regulations.

The protection of *HSWA* is extended to those training under Employment Training, the Youth Training Scheme and various other arrangements by *Health and Safety (Training for Employment) Regulations 1988 (SI 1988 No 1222)*.

25.3 Employer's obligations

HSWA contains provisions broadly equivalent to the common law duty of care of an employer to his employees (see 24.3 HEALTH AND SAFETY AT WORK – I). [*HSWA s 2(1)(2)*]. A failure by an employer to comply with the requirements relating to the safety of his employees may in certain circumstances constitute a fundamental breach of contract entitling the employee to resign and claim that he was constructively dismissed. (*British Aircraft Corporation Ltd v Austin* [*1978*] *IRLR 332*).

Health and safety policy statement. Employers are obliged to prepare (and if necessary revise) a written statement of their general policy with respect to the health and safety at work of their employees and the organisation and arrangements for carrying out that policy. In addition, employers must bring such information to the notice of all of their employees. [*HSWA s 2(3)*]. The length and complexity of the notice required will depend on the nature of the employer's undertaking. Such information should in all cases be placed on an easily accessible notice board.

Employers who carry on undertakings in which for the time being they employ less than five employees are exempted from the requirement of *Sec 2(3)* by the *Employers' Health and Safety Policy Statements (Exception) Regulations 1975 (SI 1975 No 1584)*.

Safety representatives and safety committees. Employers must recognise, afford facilities and allow time off for the training of safety representatives appointed in accordance with the *Safety Representatives and Safety Committees Regulations 1977 (SI 1977 No 500)* made under *HSWA s 2(4)*. Safety representatives are appointed by a trade union recognised by an employer from among the employees of a unionised workforce, with certain exceptions, e.g. members of the British Actors' Equity Association or of the Musicians' Union who need not be employees. [*Regs 3(1), 8(2)*]. The representative should, if possible, either have been employed by his employer throughout the preceding two years or have had at least two years' experience in similar employment. [*Reg 3(4)*].

Safety representatives represent the employees in consultations with the employer over arrangements for their health and safety at work. In addition, they have other functions, including the investigation of potential hazards and complaints about health, safety or welfare. They can make representations about such matters and attend meetings of safety committees. [*Reg 4(1)*]. (See also 13.8 DISCLOSURE OF INFORMATION.) Employers must allow safety representatives time off with pay to perform these functions. [*Reg 4(2)*]. An employer must also permit safety representatives time off with pay to undergo training to fulfil these duties. (See 50.8-50.9 TIME OFF WORK and see Appendix for *Code of Practice on Time off for the Training of Safety Representatives*.)

25.4 Employers and the self-employed

Employers and self-employed people are obliged to conduct their undertakings, so far as is reasonably practicable, in a way which will ensure that persons who may be affected, not being their employees, are not exposed to risks to health or safety. [*HSWA s 3(1)(2)*]. The conduct of the undertaking extends to the manner in which equipment is made available for use by employees outside business hours (*R v Mara* [*1987*] *ICR 165*).

Regulations may be introduced compelling such people to give information relating to health and safety to people (not being their employees) who may be affected by the way in which they conduct their undertakings. [*HSWA s 3(3)*]. No such regulations have yet been made.

25.5 Duties of occupiers

(*a*) Obligations are imposed on occupiers of 'non-domestic' premises in respect of persons who are not their employees but who are working on their premises or using plant or substances provided for use on the premises. [*HSWA s 4*]. Thus, in *Westminster City Council v Select Management [1985] ICR 353*, the defendants were obliged to ensure that lifts and other 'non-domestic' parts of their premises were safe and without risk to health. These provisions would apply to protect workers who were sent by their employer, for example, to re-decorate a client's factory.

(*b*) Those in control of prescribed premises (i.e. prescribed by regulation by the Secretary of State) must use the best practical means for preventing the emission into the atmosphere from the premises of noxious or offensive substances and for rendering harmless and inoffensive such substances as may be so emitted. [*HSWA s 5*]. Premises and substances which fall within these provisions are those prescribed in the *Health and Safety (Emission into the Atmosphere) Regulations 1983 (SI 1983 No 943*, as amended by *SI 1989 No 319)*.

Occupiers whose industrial activities involve the use of dangerous substances are required to take steps to prevent and limit the effects of accidents arising from those activities. [*Control of Industrial Major Accident Hazards Regulations 1984 (SI 1984 No 1902)*, as amended by *SI 1988 No 1462*].

25.6 Duties of manufacturers

Manufacturers, designers, importers and suppliers of articles or substances for use at work are placed under a duty to ensure so far as is reasonably practicable that the design of their product is safe, to carry out necessary tests for so ensuring and to provide adequate information about the use of the product and the conditions necessary for its safe use. [*HSWA s 6*, as amended by *Consumer Protection Act 1987 s 36* and *3 Sch*]. The manufacturers, designers, importers or suppliers of articles for use at work are exempt from such duties if they obtain a written undertaking from their customers that the customer will take specified steps sufficient to ensure, so far as is reasonably practicable, that the article will be safe and without risk to health when properly used. [*HSWA s 6(8)*]. This exemption is qualified where the goods are imported [*HSWA s 6(8A)*].

25.7 Duties of employees

Every employee while at work has the duty

(*a*) to take reasonable care for the health and safety of himself and of other persons who may be affected by his acts or omissions at work; and

(*b*) to co-operate with his employer, or any other person, in ensuring that requirements or duties imposed by the relevant statutory provisions (including those specified in *1 Schedule*) are complied with.

[*HSWA s 7*].

Thus, if an employer is required to provide his workers with goggles, foremen should ensure that, if that task is delegated to them, adequate goggles are available. Also, the workers themselves are under an obligation to wear them.

25.8 Interference with safety measures

No person may intentionally or recklessly interfere with or misuse anything provided in the interests of health, safety or welfare in pursuance of any of the relevant statutory provisions. [*HSWA s 8*]. Thus, an employee who removes a safety guard provided by his employer, in breach of the regulations, is in breach of *Sec 8* and is guilty of an offence for which in a magistrates' court he may be fined up to level 5 on the standard scale and in the Crown Court there may be an unlimited fine. [*HSWA s 33(1)(b), (3)(b)*; see 1.10 INTRODUCTION].

Such conduct may also justify dismissal, provided the employee was properly instructed about the safety measures and had been made aware that interference could lead to dismissal. (*Martin v Yorkshire Imperial Metals Ltd* [*1978*] *IRLR 440*).

25.9 No charge for safety measures

An employer may not charge any employee of his for anything done or supplied in compliance with any of the relevant statutory provisions. [*HSWA s 9*]. If, for example, an employer is required to provide an employee of his with a mask, he may not require that employee to contribute towards the cost of that mask.

25.10 REPORTING AND RECORDING OF ACCIDENTS

Notification of industrial injuries. An employee who suffers an 'industrial injury' which results in him being incapable of work for four consecutive days or more must report the accident to his employer. Notice of the accident may be given orally or in writing, and may be given by someone else on the employee's behalf. It is sufficient notice if the accident is recorded in the accident book (see below). The employer is required to take reasonable steps to investigate the accident and must, on request, provide all information uncovered to the Department of Social Security, who will in turn inform the Health and Safety Executive. Failure by an employee to notify an accident may jeopardise his entitlement to industrial injury benefits.

Accident book. Every employer who normally employs ten or more persons on or about the same premises in connection with a trade or business must keep an accident book in which specified particulars of accidents may be recorded, as must (however few employees they have) all employers who are owners or occupiers of a mine or quarry or of a 'factory' within the meaning of the *Factories Act 1961*.

Notification of accidents and dangerous occurrences. The current regulations governing the notification and recording of accidents are *The Reporting of Injuries, Diseases and Dangerous Occurrences Regulations 1985 (SI 1985 No 2023)*.

An employer must notify the Executive or local authority, whichever is in the circumstances the enforcing authority (see 25.16 below), of

(*a*) any accident arising out of or in connection with work which results in the death of or major injury to any person (for another category of 'notifiable accident', see below);

(*b*) any 'notifiable dangerous occurrence' specified in *1 Schedule*;

(*c*) the death of an employee within one year of being injured as the result of a notifiable accident or notifiable dangerous occurrence (this applies whether or not the accident was reported at the time it occurred);

(*d*) any person at work who suffers from one of the diseases specified in *2 Schedule*, and who works in a specified category of occupation;

(*e*) any 'gas incident' as specified in *Reg 6*.

[*Regs 3-6*].

In cases under (*a*) and (*b*) the enforcing authority must be notified by the fastest practicable means in the first instance, and a report on the prescribed form must be sent to that authority within seven days. [*Reg 3*].

Road accidents are not covered by the Regulations, except where they result from exposure to a substance which is being transported, the loading or unloading of vehicles or specified roadworks. [*Reg 10*].

Examples of notifiable injuries are amputation of the hand, foot, digit or toe, loss of vision of an eye along with chemical, hot metal burn or penetrating injury to an eye, and fractures of the skull, pelvis, spine and bones of the arm, wrist, leg or ankle. Any injury other than of a type specified in the Regulations will be reportable if it results in the injured person being immediately admitted to hospital for more than 24 hours. [*Reg 3(2)*].

Where an accident at work incapacitates a person for more than three consecutive days, excluding the day of the accident but including days on which the person would not have worked, a written report, on the appropriate form, must be sent to the enforcing authority within seven days of the accident. [*Reg 3(3)*].

Records must be kept of all notifiable accidents, dangerous occurrences and reportable diseases, containing the necessary particulars set out in the Regulations. They must be kept at the place of work to which they relate or at the usual place of business of the responsible person as defined in the Regulations for a period of three years from the date the details were entered in the records. [*Reg 7*].

Accidents to self-employed persons are covered if they were working under the control of someone else, in which case the obligations attach to the person in control of the premises where the accident occurred.

Special rules are applied specifically to mines, quarries, railways and pipe-lines.

25.11 SUBSTANCES HAZARDOUS TO HEALTH

References in this section are to the provisions of *COSHH* (see 25.2 above) unless stated.

The definition of a substance hazardous to health is contained in *Reg 2(1)*, and includes:

(*a*) substances listed as dangerous for supply and whose specified nature of risk is very toxic, toxic, harmful, corrosive or irritant;

(*b*) substances for which there is a maximum exposure limit specified in *1 Sch* (e.g. arsenic and formaldehyde) or for which the HSC has approved an occupational exposure standard;

(*c*) micro-organisms which create a hazard to the health of any person;

(*d*) dust of any kind, when present at a substantial concentration in air;

(*e*) other substances which create a comparable hazard to the health of any person.

Employers owe duties under *COSHH* to their employees and, so far as reasonably practicable and with certain exceptions, to other persons who may be affected by the work which they carry on [*Reg 3*]. The Executive has powers to grant exemption certificates. [*Reg 14*].

An employer may not carry on any work liable to expose any employees to any substance hazardous to health unless he has made a suitable and sufficient assessment of the risks to their health and of the steps necessary to meet the requirements of *COSHH*. The assessment must be reviewed forthwith if there is reason to suspect that it is no longer valid or if there has been a significant change in the work to which it relates. [*Reg 6*].

The employer must ensure that the exposure of his employees to hazardous substances is either prevented or, where this is not reasonably practicable, adequately controlled. [*Reg 7(1)*]. So far as reasonably practicable, that is to be secured by measures *other* than the provision of personal protective equipment, although that is also to be provided where necessary. [*Reg 7(2)(3)*].

Employers are under a duty to take all reasonable steps to ensure that control measures, protective equipment etc. are properly used or applied, and employees are under a duty to make full and proper use of such facilities and to report any defects to their employer. [*Reg 8(1)(2)*]. The employer must maintain control measures and equipment in an efficient state, in efficient working order and in good repair, and keep records of tests carried out on them. [*Reg 9*].

In appropriate cases the employer must ensure that the exposure of employees to hazardous substances is monitored [*Reg 10*] and/or that the relevant employees are under suitable health surveillance. In certain specified cases that must include medical surveillance, as a result of which the employer may be barred from engaging an employee on the work concerned. [*Reg 11*].

Employees whose work may expose them to hazardous substances are to be provided with suitable and sufficient information, instruction and training to enable them to know the risks of exposure and the precautions which should be taken. [*Reg 12*].

The Health and Safety Commission has approved a number of relevant Codes of Practice: 'Control of Substances Hazardous to Health'; 'Control of Carcinogenic Substances'; 'Control of Substances Hazardous to Health in Fumigation Operations'; and 'Control of Vinyl Chloride at Work'. The Executive has published 'COSHH assessments: a step by step guide to assessment and the skills needed for it'.

25.12 THE HEALTH AND SAFETY COMMISSION AND EXECUTIVE

HSWA s 10 establishes the Health and Safety Commission and the Health and Safety Executive. The Commission is made up of both employer and employee representatives and the Executive is made up of three of the Commission's appointees approved by the Secretary of State for Employment, one of whom is first chosen as the director of the Executive and who is consulted as to the appointment of the other two members. The Commission's chief function is to advise, authorise research and make suggestions for the implementation of the provisions of the *HSWA*. It may make suggestions for the passing of regulations. The Executive also has the duty of providing information and advice to any government minister who requests it.

The address for inquiries, leaflets, etc. is Health and Safety Executive (Inquiry Room), Baynards House, 1 Chepstow Place, London W2 4TF, tel: 01-229 3456.

25.13 Inquiries

The Commission may either direct the Executive or authorise any other person to investigate and make a special report on any accident, occurrence, situation or other matter that the Commission thinks is necessary or expedient to investigate, or (with the consent of the Secretary of State) direct an inquiry to be held into any such matter. [*HSWA s 14(1)(2)*]. The *Health and Safety Inquiries (Procedure) Regulations 1975, as amended (SIs 1975 No 335; 1976 No 1246)* lay down the procedure for the conduct of such inquiries. Since civil or criminal liability for an accident may depend on the outcome of such an inquiry, proper representation is essential.

25.14 Information

HSWA s 27 enables the Commission to obtain information necessary for the discharge of its functions, or for provision to an enforcing authority (e.g. the Executive or an inspector) of information necessary to discharge its duties.

25.15 Codes of Practice

The Commission is empowered by *HSWA s 16* to approve and issue Codes of Practice for the enforcement of *Secs 2-7* or of health and safety regulations introduced under the Act, or any other existing statutory provisions. The Commission has to date issued several Codes of Practice including one on Safety Representatives and Safety Committees and one on Time Off for the Training of Safety Representatives (both of which are reprinted in the Appendix), as well as those referred to in 25.11 above.

25.16 ENFORCING AUTHORITIES AND INSPECTORS

The Executive and local authorities are responsible for the enforcement of the Act and are known as 'enforcing authorities'. [*HSWA s 18; Health and Safety (Enforcing Authority) Regulations 1977 (SI 1977 No 746) as amended by the Health and Safety (Enforcing Authority) (Amendment) Regulations 1985 (SI 1985 No 1107)* – to be replaced by *SI 1989 No 1903* from 1 April 1990]. With certain exceptions, where the main activities carried on in premises are those set out in *1 Schedule*, the enforcing authority will be the local authority.

The enforcement powers under *HSWA* cover all the 'relevant statutory provisions', which comprise the provisions of *HSWA Part I*, all the enactments specified in *HSWA 1 Schedule* (e.g. the *Factories Act 1961* and *OSRPA*) and regulations made under them, and any health and safety and agricultural health and safety regulations. [*HSWA s 53(1)*].

25.17 Powers of inspectors

Every enforcing authority has the power to appoint inspectors. An inspector has many powers to enforce the statutory provisions for which his enforcing authority has responsibility. He may enter premises, if necessary accompanied by a police constable, take measurements and photographs and make other records, and take samples of articles or substances found in any premises which he has power to enter and of the atmosphere in or near such premises. If he fears that an article or substance found on premises which he has power to enter has caused or is likely to cause danger to health or safety, he may have it dismantled or subjected to any process or test. He may not destroy it unless that action is necessary for the performance of his duties. The inspector may take possession of a dangerous or potentially dangerous article or substance to examine it, to ensure that it is not tampered with or to ensure that it is available for use as evidence in any proceedings under the *HSWA*. When he takes possession of any article, the inspector must fix in a conspicuous position, a notice giving particulars of the article or substance and stating that he has taken possession of it. [*HSWA s 20(2)(a)-(i), (4)*].

An inspector may require persons to answer questions in the course of his investigations and to sign a declaration of the truth of their answers. He may require the production of books and documents and take copies of them. If he requires any facilities or assistance in the course of his investigations, he may require the person able to do so to provide him with such facilities. [*HSWA s 20(2)(j)-(l)*]. No answer given by a person to an inspector is admissible in evidence against that person or the husband or wife of that person. [*HSWA s 20(7)*]. The section does not compel a person to disclose a document which could be withheld on grounds of legal professional privilege in High Court proceedings (such as an opinion of counsel). [*HSWA s 20(8)*].

Where an inspector has reasonable cause to believe that an article or substance on premises he is empowered to enter is a cause of imminent danger of serious personal injury, he may seize it and cause it to be rendered harmless. [*HSWA s 25(1)*].

25.18 IMPROVEMENT AND PROHIBITION NOTICES

Improvement notices

If an inspector is of the opinion that a person

(*a*) is contravening one or more of the relevant statutory provisions (see 25.15 above); or

(*b*) has contravened one or more of those provisions in circumstances that make it likely that the contravention will continue or be repeated,

he may serve on that person a notice (referred to as 'an improvement notice'). [*HSWA s 21*].

An improvement notice must (i) state that he is of that opinion; (ii) specify the provisions which in his opinion are being or have been contravened; (iii) give particulars of the reasons for his opinion; and (iv) require that person to remedy the contravention within a specified period.

The specified period in (iv) above is not to be shorter than that allowed for an appeal to an industrial tribunal (which is 21 days from the date of the service on the appellant of the notice appealed against; see *Industrial Tribunals (Improvement and Prohibition Notices Appeals) Regulations 1974 (SI 1974 No 1925)*).

25.19 Prohibition notices

If an inspector regards any activities as involving or potentially involving *a risk of serious personal injury*, he may serve on the person in control of those activities a notice known as 'a prohibition notice'. [*HSWA s 22*].

A prohibition notice must

(*a*) state the opinion of the inspector;

(*b*) specify the matters which in his opinion give or, as the case may be, will give rise to the risks;

(*c*) where in his opinion any of those matters involves or will involve a contravention of any of the relevant statutory provisions, state that he is of that opinion, specify the relevant provision or provisions, and give particulars of the reasons why he is of that opinion; and

(*d*) direct that the activities to which the notice relates shall not be carried on by or under the control of the person on whom the notice is served unless the matters specified in the notice and any associated contraventions so specified have been remedied.

A direction given in pursuance of (*d*) above takes effect immediately if the inspector is of the opinion, and states it, that the risk of serious personal injury is or will be imminent. In any other case, it takes effect at the end of the period specified in the notice. [*HSWA s 22(4)*].

Improvement and prohibition notices may make reference to any approved Code of Practice (see 25.15 above). [*HSWA s 23(2)(a)*].

25.20 Withdrawal of notices

Where an improvement notice or a prohibition notice which is not to take immediate effect has been served, the notice may be withdrawn by an inspector at any time before it takes effect and the period before it takes effect may be extended or further extended by an inspector at any time when an appeal against the notice is not pending. [*HSWA s 23(5)*].

25.21 APPEALS AGAINST THE NOTICES

A person on whom an improvement or prohibition notice is served may within 21 days appeal to an industrial tribunal. [*Industrial Tribunals (Improvement and Prohibition Notices Appeals) Regulations 1974 (SI 1974 No 1925), Reg 2(1)*]. A tribunal may extend the period for lodging an appeal (on an application made in writing to the Secretary of the Tribunals either before or after the expiration of the time limit) if it is satisfied that it is not or was not reasonably practicable for an appeal to be brought within that time. [*Reg 2(2)*].

One or more assessors may be appointed for the purposes of any such appeals brought before an industrial tribunal. [*HSWA s 24(4)*].

The tribunal may either cancel or affirm the notice and, if it affirms it, may do so either in its original form or with such modifications as the tribunal may in the circumstances think fit. [*HSWA s 24(2)*].

25.22 Suspension of notices pending appeal hearing

Where an appeal is brought within the time limit allowed –

(*a*) *improvement notice*: the bringing of the appeal has the effect of suspending the operation of the notice until the appeal is finally disposed of or, if the appeal is withdrawn, until the withdrawal of the appeal;

(*b*) *prohibition notice*: the bringing of the appeal will not affect the notice unless, on application by the appellant, the tribunal so directs, in which case the prohibition notice will be suspended from the time that the tribunal gives its direction.

25.23 Cost of remedy required

In deciding whether an improvement notice which required the cleaning and repainting of walls should be cancelled or not, an industrial tribunal sitting at Shrewsbury held that the company's financial position was irrelevant and evidence relating to its financial position would not be admitted. (*T C Harrison (Newcastle-under-Lyme) Ltd v K Ramsey (HM Inspector)* [*1976*] *IRLR 135*). It may therefore be no ground for appeal against such notices that the company cannot afford to remedy the defects.

25.24 CRIMINAL PROCEEDINGS

HSWA s 33 lists various offences including

(*a*) failure to discharge a duty under *Secs 2-7* (see 25.3-25.7 above) [*HSWA s 33(1)(a)*];

(*b*) contravention of any health and safety regulations or any requirement or prohibition imposed under such a regulation [*HSWA s 33(1)(c)*];

(*c*) contravention of any requirement or prohibition imposed by an improvement notice or a prohibition notice (including any such notice as modified on appeal) [*HSWA s 33(1)(g)*];

(*d*) intentionally to obstruct an inspector in the exercise or performance of his powers or duties [*HSWA s 33(1)(h)*].

Criminal offences are triable either summarily (i.e. in the magistrates' court) or on indictment (i.e. in the Crown Court) or 'either way' (i.e. where the defendant may normally elect the mode of trial). The maximum fine for *HSWA* offences tried in the magistrates' court is at level 5 on the standard scale. On indictment the penalty may be a fine unlimited in amount and/or, for certain offences, imprisonment for up to two years. [*HSWA s 33(2)-(4);* see 1.10 INTRODUCTION].

Any explosive article or substance may be forfeited by order of the court and may be destroyed. [*HSWA s 42(4)*].

Breaches of Codes of Practice approved by the Health and Safety Commission (see 25.15 above) are not in themselves criminal offences. However, if in a prosecution for a contravention of the Act or the Regulations, it is shown that there was a failure to observe any relevant Code, then that contravention will be considered proven unless the court is satisfied that the requirement or prohibition was complied with in an alternative, acceptable manner. [*HSWA s 17(2)*].

25.25 Continuing offences

Where a person is convicted of contravening any requirement or prohibition imposed by an improvement or prohibition notice [*HSWA s 33(1)(g)*] or of failure to comply with an order to remedy a default (see 25.26 below) [*HSWA s 33(1)(o)*], and he continues the contravention in respect of which he was convicted, he is guilty of a further offence and liable in respect thereof to a fine not exceeding £100 for each day on which the contravention continues. [*HSWA s 33(5); Criminal Law Act 1977, 1 Sch*].

25.26 Order to remedy default

If a person is convicted of an offence and it appears to the court that the matter is one which it is in his power to remedy, the court may, in addition to or instead of imposing any punishment, order him (within such time as may be fixed by the order) to take such steps as may be specified in the order to remedy the situation. The time fixed by such an order may be extended or further extended by order of the court on an application made before the end of the time originally fixed or as extended. [*HSWA s 42(1)(2)*].

25.27 Time for bringing proceedings

Summary proceedings may be brought at any time within six months from the date on which there comes to the knowledge of an enforcing authority evidence to justify a prosecution [*HSWA s 34(3)*]. A failure to do something required by the Act is treated as continuing until the requirement is complied with, so that the six-month period runs from the last day on which the requirement was not complied with. [*HSWA s 34(2)*]. The time limit is extended in cases where there is a special report under *Sec 14(2)(a)*, a report of an inquiry under *Sec 14(2)(b)*, a coroner's inquest, a public inquiry (in Scotland) into a death, to three months from the making of the report or three months from the conclusion of the inquest or inquiry. [*HSWA s 34(1)*].

25.28 Defence

Many of the statutory provisions contain the modification 'so far as is reasonably practicable', or 'practicable' or to use 'the best practicable means to do something'. In those cases the onus is on the accused to prove that it was not practicable or not reasonably practicable to do more than was in fact done to satisfy the duty or requirement, or that there was no better practicable means than was in fact used to satisfy the duty or requirement. [*HSWA s 40*]. However, where proceedings are brought under *HSWA s 33(1)(g)* for contravention of an improvement notice, the offence is established if there has been a non-compliance with a requirement of the notice irrespective of whether compliance was reasonably practicable. (*Deary (HM Inspector of Factories) v Mansion Hide Upholstery Ltd* [*1983*] *IRLR 195*).

25.29 CIVIL LIABILITY

Breaches of *HSWA ss 2-8* cannot form the basis of a civil action [*HSWA s 47(1)(a)*] but breach 'of a duty imposed by health and safety regulations . . . shall, so far as it causes damage, be actionable except in so far as the regulations provide otherwise'. [*HSWA s 47(2)*]. In other words a civil action can be brought where a breach of the health and safety regulations causes damage, unless the regulations prevent such an action from being brought.

Any provision in any agreement to contract out of liability for such breaches is void unless the health and safety regulations provide otherwise. [*HSWA s 47(5)*].

25.30 NOISE AT WORK

It has not been possible in this edition to deal in detail with the important *Noise at Work Regulations 1989 (SI 1989 No 1790)*, which implement *EC Directive 86/188*, and come into force on 1 January 1990.

26 Holidays

26.1 The right of an employee to a period of paid holiday is regulated, subject to certain exceptions, by his contract. Wages orders, made by wages councils, had power under *Wages Councils Act 1979, s 14(1)(b)* to determine holiday entitlement. However, since the repeal of the 1979 Act and its replacement by the *Wages Act 1986*, wages councils no longer have the power to make orders determining entitlement to holidays. Existing orders ceased to have effect at the end of the period of six months beginning with the date of the passing of the Act (25 July 1986), or at the end of the period of twelve months beginning with the date of the coming into force of the order, whichever was the later. [*Wages Act 1986, s 24*]. However, accrued rights to holiday and holiday pay were preserved by the *Wages Councils (Preservation of Accrued Rights under Wages Orders) Order 1986 (SI 1986 No 2282)*.

26.2 STATUTORY RULES

The only notable remaining statutory provision affecting the right to a holiday is the *Agricultural Wages Act 1948, s 3*, as substituted by *EPA 1975, s 97(1), 9 Sch Pt I*, which enables the Agricultural Wages Board to direct that holidays be allowed and that certain rates of pay be given for holidays. An agreement inconsistent with the order is void. [*Sec 11*]. Failure to allow holidays or give holiday pay specified in the order gives rise to a right to a claim by the employee as well as liability for a criminal offence [*Sec 4*] and a fine of level 3 on the standard scale (see 1.10 INTRODUCTION), continuing at £5 per day after conviction where the offence consists of a failure to pay wages.

Factories Act 1961, s 94 which specified minimum entitlement to holidays for young persons working in factories, is repealed by *EA 1989 s 10(1)(a)*.

26.3 CONTRACT

The contract of employment usually makes express provision for paid holidays to be given. Where contractual terms are determined by reference to a collective agreement, that agreement will usually specify holiday entitlement. Holiday entitlement is quite often related to length of service. It is thought that today the right to annual holiday accrues *pro rata* so that if an employee leaves half way through a holiday year, having taken no holiday, he will be entitled to half his annual entitlement. However, it was held in *Hurt v Sheffield Corporation (1916) 85 LJ KB 1684*, that the right to a holiday accrued only at the end of the year in the absence of any express provision to the contrary. It is thought unlikely that this decision would now be followed.

Usually, express provision is made that in addition to annual holiday, bank holidays will be given. It is thought likely that in most industries, in the absence of express provision, it will be held to be an implied term that bank holidays may be taken.

In *Tucker v British Leyland Motor Corporation Ltd [1978] IRLR 493* at *p 496*, a county court judge decided that '. . . if no express contractual provision or regular usage to the contrary is established an hourly paid employee is entitled to a day's holiday on recognised public holidays without fear of dismissal as an absentee; and that if he is entitled to a guaranteed minimum weekly wage he is entitled to be paid for that day without having to work additional hours in that week'. So, unless the contrary is agreed with an employee, expressly or impliedly because of custom and practice, he must be allowed to take time off on any statutory holidays and be paid for the time taken.

If an employee is required, and consents, to forgo all or part of his holiday, he will usually be entitled to be paid his holiday pay in addition to his normal remuneration for that period or to be given a day off in lieu. If, however, of his own volition and not at his employer's request, he forgoes his holiday, he will not be entitled to holiday pay in addition to his normal remuneration. The time at which annual holidays are to be taken is a matter for agreement between employer and employee. Unless the employer has the right to dictate when the employee takes his holiday, it is thought that he is contractually obliged to pay the employee his accrued holiday pay when he leaves his employment.

26.4 Implied terms

If no provision is agreed relating to holidays, it is thought that a term providing for a reasonable holiday period will be implied into the contract of employment. The question should not however arise, as particulars of holiday entitlement are amongst those the employer is obliged by the *Employment Protection (Consolidation) Act 1978, s 1(3)(d)(i)* to supply in writing to the employee (see 10.5(*g*) CONTRACT OF EMPLOYMENT).

26.5 EUROPEAN COMMUNITY PROVISIONS

The Treaty of Rome provides for the maintenance by member States of the equivalence between paid holiday schemes. [*EC Treaty Article 118, and Council Recommendation 75/457/EEC of 22 July 1975 (OJ L199/32 of 30 July 1975)*, for four weeks' paid holiday]. (See 20.6 EUROPEAN COMMUNITY LAW.)

27 Industrial Tribunals: Practice and Procedure

(See also DE leaflets 'Industrial tribunals procedure – for those concerned in industrial tribunal proceedings' ITL 1 (1986), 'Facing an unfair dismissal claim?' (PL 734), and ITL 19 for appeals concerning improvement or prohibition notices under the *Health and Safety at Work etc. Act 1974*.)

27.1 Industrial tribunals hear applications under

Employment Protection (Consolidation) Act 1978
Employment Act 1980
Employment Act 1988
Equal Pay Act 1970
Health and Safety at Work etc. Act 1974
Sex Discrimination Act 1975, s 63
Race Relations Act 1976, s 54
Wages Act 1986, s 5

They also deal with certain matters beyond the scope of this book, such as appeals against the imposition of industrial training levies.

The procedure of all industrial tribunals for applications instituted on or after 1 March 1985 is governed by the *Industrial Tribunals (Rules of Procedure) Regulations 1985 (SI 1985 No 16)* (the '*IT Regs*') except where different regulations are specified (as, for example, for appeals against prohibition and improvement notices, see 25.21 HEALTH AND SAFETY AT WORK – II). The Rules are set out in Schedule 1 to the Regulations. Additional complementary rules of procedure for claims under *Equal Pay Act 1970* which are based upon an allegation of work of equal value are set out in Schedule 2 to the Regulations. These are not set out below but are summarised in 19.14 EQUAL PAY.

A person who wishes to bring a claim in an industrial tribunal, 'the Applicant', commences proceedings by lodging an 'Originating Notice of Application'. The defendant to the claim, who is known as 'the Respondent', then serves his answer in the form of a 'Respondent's Notice of Appearance'. Before the hearing, the tribunal Chairman may give orders for the giving of particulars by one party to the other, for the attendance of witnesses and for the production (discovery) of documents. At the hearing both sides produce their evidence and a decision is made. The industrial tribunal is the court of first instance for most of the remedies granted by recent employment legislation.

27.2 ORIGINATING NOTICE OF APPLICATION

All applications are started by an *Originating Notice of Application* which must be in writing and must set out

(*a*) the name and address of the applicant;

(*b*) the names and addresses of the person or persons against whom relief is sought or of the parties to the proceedings before the tribunal;

(*c*) the grounds, with particulars, on which relief is sought.

[*IT Regs, Rule 1(1)*].

An Originating Notice of Application known as Form IT1 should be used to institute proceedings in an industrial tribunal. However a letter will be accepted provided it contains all the information required by *Rule 1(1)*. (*Smith v Automobile Proprietary Ltd [1973] ICR 306*). The grounds of the application may be set out shortly, or at length, depending on the circumstances. A failure to complete the section in the IT1 for particularising grounds of complaint was held by the EAT, in *Dodd v British Telecommunications plc [1988] ICR 116*, not to render an originating application a nullity when the nature of the complaint was made clear elsewhere in the form. Nevertheless care should be taken to complete the form fully and accurately. If the applicant gives evidence which differs from his originating application, he may be challenged to explain the inconsistency. In redundancy cases it is sensible to add a claim for unfair dismissal. (*British Newspaper Printing Corporation (North) Ltd v Kelly [1989] IRLR 222*; and see 55.11 UNFAIR DISMISSAL – II). Form IT1 may be obtained from any industrial tribunal office or from the local Department of Employment office and when completed should be submitted to the specified Secretary of the Tribunals.

27.3 Time limits for applications

All the applications brought before an industrial tribunal must be brought within a certain time limit. In some cases the tribunal has jurisdiction to hear late applications. Such applications for unfair dismissal may be heard within such further period as the tribunal considers reasonable if it considers that it was not 'reasonably practicable for the applicant to have presented it in time'. [*EPCA s 67(2)*]. Out of time claims alleging sex or race discrimination may be heard if in all the circumstances of the case, the industrial tribunal considers it is just and equitable to do so. [*SDA s 76(5); RRA s 68(6)*]. When considering time limits, the following points should be borne in mind.

(*a*) In each case the time limit for the particular application should be ascertained as the limit will vary according to the remedy sought, e.g. six months for a redundancy application, three months for an application based on unfair dismissal. If an application seeking a particular remedy is lodged in time, and the applicant later seeks an additional or alternative remedy, the question is not whether the time limit for seeking that remedy has expired, but 'what are the relevant hardships expected to be suffered by the parties if the amendment is or is not to be allowed?'. (*British Newspaper Printing Corporation (North) Ltd v Kelly [1989] IRLR 222*).

(*b*) Time starts to run from and including the day on which the employee actually ceases to work if he is summarily dismissed or if he is paid in lieu of notice in respect of a period of time running beyond that date. (*Dedman v British Building and Engineering Appliances Ltd [1974] ICR 53*). However, if the employer gives notice to terminate a contract of employment but does not require the employee to work during the notice period, the effective date of termination is not the date on which the employee ceases work, but the date on which the notice expires. If the employee has invoked an internal appeal procedure, time starts to run from the date of the original dismissal, *not* the date of the dismissal of the appeal, unless the contract provides otherwise. (*J Sainsbury Ltd v Savage [1981] ICR 1*). (See also 54.13 UNFAIR DISMISSAL – I.)

(*c*) The question of whether an application was presented in time is a question of jurisdiction and must be considered by the tribunal even though the party resisting the application, the respondent, may not wish to take advantage of the point. It is considered as a preliminary issue upon which the respondent may cross-examine the applicant, give evidence and make submissions.

(*d*) Where a complaint has to be presented within a period 'beginning with' a particular date, such as a complaint of unfair dismissal, that date is included in the calculation. (*Hammond v Haigh Castle & Co Ltd [1973] ICR 148*). If an employee is dismissed on 1 April, the last date for the presentation of his complaint of unfair dismissal is 30 June.

(*e*) A claim is presented to an industrial tribunal when it is received by the tribunal and not when it is posted. (*Hammond v Haigh Castle & Co Ltd [1973] ICR 148*). If the originating application arrives at the tribunal office before midnight on the last day of the three-month limitation period it is presented on time. (*Post Office v Moore [1981] ICR 623*). Since an application is presented if it is placed through a letterbox or dealt with in some way held out by a regional office as a means whereby it would receive communications, when the limitation period ends on a non-working day the time limit is not automatically extended to the next working day. (*Hetton Victory Club Ltd v Swainston [1983] ICR 341*). However, where there was no letter-box or other authorised means by which a complaint could have been presented on a day when the tribunal office was closed, the time for presenting the complaint was extended to the next working day. (*Ford v Stakis Hotels & Inns Ltd [1987] ICR 943*. See also *Lang v Devon General Ltd [1987] ICR 4*.)

(*f*) If an applicant does not discover his right to present a claim for unfair dismissal until after the time limit for presenting such a complaint has passed, the tribunal may consider that it was not reasonably practicable for him to bring the complaint within the time limit for so doing. If it is shown that the applicant ought reasonably to have known of his right to claim for unfair dismissal, then it will probably be held that it *was* reasonably practicable for him to present a complaint within the time limit, whether he in fact knew of his right or not. (*Porter v Bandridge Ltd [1978] ICR 943, per* the majority of the Court of Appeal). It will now be rare for an employee to be able to persuade a tribunal that he ought not reasonably to have known of the unfair dismissal legislation. It is not reasonably practicable for an employee to bring a complaint of unfair dismissal until he has knowledge of the facts giving him grounds to apply to the tribunal (*Machine Tool Industry Research Association v Simpson [1988] ICR 558*). The Employment Appeal Tribunal in *Foster v South Glamorgan Health Authority [1988] ICR 526* remitted a case to an industrial tribunal on the basis that a change in the law could render it just and equitable to hear an out of time complaint of sex discrimination. This case represents a significant development. Leave to appeal was granted.

(*g*) If the applicant instructs solicitors or advisers to act on his behalf and through their default the application is not presented in time, the tribunal will consider that it was reasonably practicable for the application to be presented in time and will not entertain the application. As Lord Denning MR said in *Dedman v British Building and Engineering Appliances Ltd* (see (*b*) above) at p 61

> 'I would suggest that in every case the tribunal should inquire into the circumstances and ask themselves whether the man or his advisers were at fault in allowing [the time limit] to pass by without presenting the complaint. If he was not at fault, nor his advisers – so that he had just cause or excuse for not presenting his complaint within [the time limit] – then it was "not practicable" for him to present it within that time.'

(See also *Wall's Meat Co Ltd v Khan [1979] ICR 52*, *Riley v Tesco Stores Ltd [1980] ICR 323* and *Croydon Health Authority v Jaufurally [1986] ICR 4*.) In *Harvey's Household Linens v Benson [1974] ICR 306* it was held that Department of Employment officials were not 'advisers' for this purpose, so their error ought not to be attributed to an applicant who followed their advice.

An applicant who loses the opportunity to have his case heard by the tribunal because of his advisers' negligence is able to sue them in the ordinary court. An assessment of the prospects of success in the tribunal is made when calculating damages.

27.4 RESPONDENT'S 'NOTICE OF APPEARANCE'

If a respondent wishes to defend any application, he must complete and return a written Notice of Appearance within 14 days of receiving a copy of the Originating Application. Forms for entering a Notice of Appearance are available at all tribunal offices.

In the notice the respondent must

(*a*) set out his full name and address;

(*b*) state whether or not he intends to resist the application;

(*c*) if he does intend to resist, state on what grounds, giving sufficient particulars.

[*IT Regs, Rule 3(1)*].

The respondent should set out with some care the grounds upon which he wishes to resist the application, because if he omits a ground and wishes to raise it at any subsequent tribunal hearing, the applicant may successfully apply for an adjournment, possibly at the respondent's expense, to consider the additional matter. (See also *Hotson v Wisbech Conservative Club [1984] IRLR 422*.) Also, as with the applicant's Originating Notice of Application, any statement made by a respondent in his Notice of Appearance may be challenged at the hearing. The grounds of resistance should be thought through carefully and a resumé of the facts set out upon which the respondent will rely.

If the Notice of Appearance is not entered in time, the respondent is not entitled to take any further part in the proceedings. He may, however, apply to the tribunal, either before or after the expiry of the time limit, for an extension of time for filing the Notice. He may also apply for further particulars of the Originating Application, make application for a review, be called as a witness and receive a copy of the decision. [*IT Regs, Rule 3(2)*].

27.5 PRE-HEARING ASSESSMENTS

If a party to the proceedings, or the tribunal itself, considers that an originating application is unlikely to succeed or that any contention of a party appears to have no reasonable prospect of success, a pre-hearing assessment may be held. A party wishing to apply for a pre-hearing assessment must do so in writing to the Secretary of the Tribunals. Notice of the holding of a pre-hearing assessment is sent to all parties, who may submit written representations and put forward oral argument. No oral *evidence* is heard at pre-hearing assessments but quite frequently documents are produced. If a tribunal on a pre-hearing assessment forms the view that the originating application, or a contention of a party, has no reasonable prospect of success, it may indicate its opinion that if the party pursues the application, or persists in the contention, an order for costs may be made against him at the hearing if the application or contention fails. The tribunal's opinion will then be recorded in writing and copies will be sent to the parties. Copies of the opinion will be placed before the tribunal at the full hearing of the case. If a tribunal does indicate an opinion that an application or contention has no reasonable prospect of success, no member of that tribunal may be a member of the tribunal which hears the substantive case. [*IT Regs, Rule 6*].

In *Mackie v John Holt Vintners Ltd [1982] ICR 146*, the EAT considered that in principle there was a right of appeal against the opinion expressed by an industrial tribunal on a pre-hearing assessment. However, it held that there are great practical difficulties in such an appeal being heard since the tribunal does not have to give reasons for its opinion nor is there any evidence or finding by the tribunal as to the oral argument on the basis of which it reached its opinion.

EA 1989 s 20 allows regulations to be made which provide for a 'pre-hearing review', and in particular for the person or tribunal carrying out such a review to require a party to pay a deposit of up to £150 as a condition of continuing to participate in the proceedings. It is thought that such reviews will probably be by tribunal Chairmen sitting alone, and will include the giving of various directions for the conduct of the proceedings.

27.6 ORDERS FOR PARTICULARS, WITNESSES AND DISCOVERY OF DOCUMENTS

Particulars

When one party receives an Originating Notice of Application or a respondent's Notice of Appearance, he may wish to know more details about the allegations made in the Notice or require clarification of some vagueness or ambiguity. A request should be made to the other party in writing. If the request is not satisfied, application may be made to the tribunal for an order that the particulars be supplied. The tribunal will only make an order if the particulars requested are shown to be relevant to the issues in the case. An industrial tribunal may also make such an order on its own motion, without being requested to do so by a party to the proceedings. [*IT Regs, Rule 4(1)*].

If a party refuses to give the particulars, having been ordered to do so, the tribunal may, before or at the hearing, dismiss the application or strike out the whole or part of the Notice of Appearance, and may direct that the respondent be debarred from defending altogether. Before such a step is taken, the party who has not complied with the order must be given an opportunity to make representations. [*IT Regs, Rule 4(4); Beacard Property Management and Construction Co Ltd v Day [1984] ICR 837*].

27.7 Discovery of documents

If a party considers that the other party has in his possession a document which is relevant to the case, he should first write requesting to see the document or to be sent a copy of it. If the keeper of the document fails or refuses to produce it, an application should be made to the tribunal which has power to order discovery (production) of the document, provided that it is not 'privileged' (e.g. because it is a communication with a legal adviser). The tribunal has a considerable discretion as to whether such an order is granted or not. Where the order would compel the discovery of reports given and received in confidence, relevance alone does not provide an automatic test for ordering discovery, the ultimate test being whether discovery is necessary for disposing fairly of the proceedings. (*Science Research Council v Nasse; Vyas v Leyland Cars Ltd [1979] ICR 921; West Midlands Passenger Transport Executive v Singh [1988] ICR 614*). A person who, without reasonable excuse, fails to comply with such an order for discovery is liable on conviction in a magistrates' court to a fine. [*IT Regs, Rule 4(3)*].

In the absence of a formal order for discovery, there is no general duty on a party to proceedings before an industrial tribunal to disclose any document in his possession. However, the EAT held in *Birds Eye Walls Ltd v Harrison [1985] ICR 279* that a party should not withhold a document if its suppression would render a disclosed document misleading. Further, industrial tribunals should use their powers to ensure that a party is not unfairly disadvantaged by the non-disclosure. It is also thought that if the withholding of a document would cause oral evidence to be misleading, there is an obligation on a party to disclose that document.

If a relevant document is in the possession of someone who is not a party to the proceedings, and he refuses to produce the document, application may be made to the tribunal for an order that he attend as a witness and bring the document with him. [*IT Regs, Rule 4(1)(b)*].

A recent Department of Employment consultation paper proposed that the tribunal should be able to order discovery or the attendance of witnesses of its own motion, that is without the application of either party.

27.8 Attendance of witnesses

If a party considers that the testimony of a certain person may be relevant to the case but that person is unwilling to attend the hearing, he may apply to the tribunal for an order that the person attend the hearing as a witness. It should be borne in mind, however, that if a witness has to be compelled by a tribunal to give evidence he may not be helpful to the case.

If a witness order is granted and the person fails, without reasonable excuse, to comply with the order he is liable on conviction in a magistrates' court to a fine. [*IT Regs, Rule 4(3)*]. If the applicant has obtained an order for the attendance of a witness who is still employed by the respondent, the respondent must on no account dissuade or attempt to dissuade him from attending.

See 27.7 above for the tribunal's proposed new power to make orders of its own motion.

27.9 BEFORE THE HEARING

It is essential that a party to an application before a tribunal prepares his case well in advance of the hearing so that all the necessary evidence, statements from witnesses or documents may be obtained. If the fact that there has been a dismissal is not in dispute the employer (respondent) will normally have to open the case and thus should be prepared to present his evidence first (see 27.19 below) in an unfair dismissal application. Whoever is to represent the respondent, whether it is a member of that company or firm, a legal representative, or some other person, should, if the case is complex, prepare a brief opening statement. In that statement the size and general field of operation of the company or firm should be set out. Then the role of the applicant in the company or firm should be explained giving a brief history of his commencement date, any promotions and the date (if relevant) of his dismissal, stating whether the dismissal was summary or on notice. If the claim is one for unfair dismissal, the relevant facts establishing the reason for the dismissal and its fairness should be set out as specifically as possible, giving the dates of any warning if appropriate. At the end of the opening speech, the respondent should be prepared to summarise his case referring to any relevant statutes or cases. In a straightforward case the tribunal may not wish to hear an opening statement. If the fact of dismissal is disputed (e.g. in a constructive dismissal case, see 54.7 UNFAIR DISMISSAL – I) it will normally be for the employee (applicant) to open the case, and he should be ready to give an opening statement setting out the basis in fact and law for his claim. It is also usual for the employee to open cases of alleged sex or race discrimination.

27.10 Documentary evidence

Parties should always make six copies of any document they propose to adduce in evidence, three for the members of the tribunal, one for the other party, one for the witness and one for themselves. They should also have the original document available to be produced. The respondent should have available the letter of engagement, the written particulars of the terms of employment (see 10.4 CONTRACT OF EMPLOYMENT), any written warnings, the letter of dismissal, and any appeal documents where relevant. If several documents are to be produced it is convenient to have them held together in a chronological, paginated bundle. Lists of documents to be produced should be exchanged with the opposing party well before the hearing, and if requested, the bundle of documents to be relied upon should be supplied. An applicant in unfair dismissal proceedings should take to the tribunal evidence of wages earned or benefits received, and of attempts made to find work since the dismissal.

According to the strict rules of evidence, the author of a document is (with certain exceptions) the only person who can adduce it in evidence. However, a document which is not produced by the author may be introduced in evidence if the other side agree. It is in any event more convenient to agree a bundle of documents to be produced with the other side so that they do not all have to be strictly proved. The industrial tribunals are not bound by the strict rules of evidence but may adhere to them on an important point.

27.11 Oral evidence

The parties should ensure that persons present at all relevant events or discussions should be available to give evidence. They should be asked to write down their recollection of those events and conversations so that they may be asked questions within their knowledge. Witnesses are not allowed to refer to notes when giving their evidence unless those notes were made contemporaneously (i.e. at the time the events or the conversations took place and while they were fresh in the witness's memory). If such records are taken, they should be introduced by first asking the witness whether the events were fresh in his memory when he made the notes and whether they were made at the earliest possible opportunity. The tribunal then will usually allow the witness to refresh his memory from the notes.

Witnesses are entitled to recover travelling and other expenses and lost wages on a set scale from the Department of Employment. The tribunal clerk will provide the necessary forms.

27.12 Affidavit evidence

If a witness is unable for good reason to give oral evidence, a tribunal may admit an affidavit from him. Exceptionally, a tribunal may admit an unsworn statement from a witness. The weight attached to such written evidence is usually less than that given to oral evidence which can be tested in cross-examination.

27.13 **Legal representation**

Parties should consider as soon as possible whether they wish to be legally represented and should then give all their preparatory work to their representatives. The fact that it does not appear from a Notice of Application that a party is legally represented does not necessarily mean that he will appear unrepresented at the hearing. Legal aid is not available for tribunal cases. Hence appearances by, for example, CAB workers and trade union officials are common. There are no restrictions on who may represent a party before a tribunal.

27.14 **Communication with the Central Office of Tribunals**

All correspondence relating to a case in an industrial tribunal should be directed to the Secretary of Tribunals at the relevant Central Office of Tribunals. The tribunal office should, as a matter of course, send a copy of any letter or communicate its contents to the other side. All requests for adjournments should be sent in good time, together with reasons for the request, to the Secretary of Tribunals. If it seems that the case will take more than one day, a request should be made to the Secretary of Tribunals for the necessary time to be set aside. If this is not done, the case may proceed with several weeks elapsing between two hearing dates. The Secretary of Tribunals will notify the parties of any order, such as for particulars, discovery of documents or attendance of witnesses, made by the Chairman. He will also notify the parties of the hearing date for the case.

27.15 SETTLEMENT OF CLAIM

In some cases, once an Originating Notice of Application has been lodged, a conciliation officer will contact the parties to see whether a compromise can be reached. If any compromise is reached (whether before or after an application has been lodged) the conciliation officer should be asked to assist in promoting or concluding a settlement. This action may be restricted to endorsing the settlement on a form produced by him (currently numbered COT 3). (See *Duport Furniture Products Ltd v Moore and Advisory, Conciliation and Arbitration Service* [*1982*] *ICR 84*.) If this is not done, the agreement will be unenforceable and the applicant free to pursue his claim before the tribunal. [*EPCA s 140(1), (2)(d)(e)*]. If a compromise is agreed whilst the parties are actually at the tribunal, the tribunal can make an order disposing of the proceedings on those terms.

27.16 THE TRIBUNAL HEARING

The tribunal hearings are usually conducted in modern rooms with the three members of the tribunal sitting at a table on a slightly raised dais and the applicant and respondent sitting at the tables facing the tribunal. There is a table at which the witness sits to give evidence. The tribunal is composed of a legally qualified Chairman, one member with management experience and one member with trade union experience. If any tribunal member has any connection with either of the parties, that fact should be made known to all concerned at the outset, and the case relisted before a fresh tribunal if necessary (see e.g. *University College of Swansea v Cornelius* [*1988*] *ICR 735*. See also 27.29 below.) In sex discrimination cases both sexes will normally be represented on the tribunal, and in race discrimination cases at least one member should have special knowledge of race relations; however, these are not mandatory requirements. A clerk is also present to whom a list of cases on which a party will base his argument, if any, should be given before the proceedings start. The Chairman of the tribunal is addressed as Sir or Madam. Proceedings are formal, but considerably less so than in an ordinary court.

The Chairman examines the Originating Application and the Notice of Appearance. He checks to see that both parties agree over such essentials as the name of the respondent company and the dates of commencement and termination of employment of the applicant. He may make necessary amendments to the Originating Application or the respondent's Notice. Whether amendments should be allowed depends upon what justice requires in all the circumstances of the case (see *Cocking v Sandhurst (Stationers) Ltd [1974] ICR 650*).

27.17 Jurisdiction

Preliminary issues which may affect the jurisdiction of the tribunal are dealt with as a separate matter and usually on a different day from the hearing of the main issues in the case. If, for example, a respondent to an unfair dismissal claim alleges that the tribunal has no jurisdiction to hear the claim because the applicant ordinarily worked abroad, that issue will be dealt with before the tribunal go on to consider whether the dismissal was fair or unfair. Even if a respondent does not wish to rely upon the fact that the tribunal may have no jurisdiction, the tribunal itself will investigate the matter.

27.18 The party who begins the case

In general, the party upon whom the burden of proof lies, opens the case. If the respondent in an unfair dismissal or redundancy case denies that the applicant has been dismissed, it is for the applicant to begin, as he must establish that he was dismissed. If the fact of dismissal is admitted, the respondent will begin, as the burden of establishing the reason for the dismissal (or that it was not due to redundancy) lies on him. Similarly, in equal pay cases, the applicant must begin if the respondent denies that she was engaged on like work, or work of equal value, as that of a man earning more than her. If, however, the respondent concedes that she is engaged on like work, or work of equal value, but seeks to show that the difference in pay is due to a 'genuine material difference' other than that of sex (see 19.10 EQUAL PAY), the burden of proving that fact lies on him and he must begin. The applicant will usually begin in cases of sex and race discrimination.

27.19 ARGUMENTS AND EVIDENCE

The tribunal may conduct the hearing in such a way as it considers most suitable to the clarification of the issues before it and generally to the just handling of the proceedings. Subject to this wide discretion, a person entitled to appear is entitled to give evidence, call witnesses, to question any witness and to address the tribunal. [*IT Regs, Rule 8*]. Where a party disrupts the proceedings the tribunal may adjourn the hearing indefinitely. (*O'Keefe v Southampton City Council [1988] ICR 419*). The EAT has recently stressed that, wide though the tribunal's discretion is, total informality can be counter-productive, and the generally recognised rules of procedure and evidence should normally be adhered to. (*Aberdeen Steak Houses Group plc v Ibrahim [1988] ICR 550*). That case sets out certain useful guidelines as to what will normally be proper procedure. A

Department of Employment consultation paper proposes that *Rule 8* be amended so as to encourage tribunals to be more investigative. The usual procedure is as follows

(*a*) the party called upon to open

(i) may sometimes give an outline of the case; and

(ii) calls his evidence;

(*b*) the other party

(i) calls his evidence; and

(ii) makes a closing speech;

(*c*) the party who opened the case then makes a closing speech.

If an opening speech is required or permitted by the tribunal a party should mention briefly

(A) if he is a respondent to the application

(i) the size and scope of operation of the company or employer concerned;

(ii) the position and responsibilities of the applicant with the company;

(iii) the facts upon which the respondent bases his case;

(iv) the statutes and decided cases which are applicable.

(B) if he is an applicant

(i) his role in the company, and the history of his employment;

(ii) the facts upon which he bases his case;

(iii) the statutes and decided cases which are applicable.

Witnesses are examined on oath. They give their evidence seated at a table and should address the Chairman of the tribunal as Sir or Madam. Their evidence-in-chief should be elicited by a series of short questions dealing with all the relevant points in the case including all the matters in the notices of application and appearance. When the representative of one party cross-examines the witness of the other party he should put a series of questions to the witness and not a series of comments or statements. It must be remembered that there is a dual purpose to cross-examination. One is to test the truth and the reliability of the witness; the other is to put the questioner's version of the facts to the witness so far as it concerns him, so that he has an opportunity of commenting on it. A failure to do this may prejudice the cross-examiner's case.

The Chairman and tribunal members may ask additional questions of each witness. Where an applicant is unrepresented, the Chairman may ask several questions to elicit relevant matters in order to assist.

Documents should be introduced in the evidence in chronological order and explained by the witness who can best deal with them (see also 27.10 above).

In a closing speech, the representative of each party should sum up the relevant facts and the law, answering any points raised by the opposing party or the Chairman or members of the tribunal.

In determining the terms of a contract of employment, industrial tribunals are not free to apply principles of law in any sense different from those applicable in ordinary courts. (*Hooper v British Railways Board [1988] IRLR 517*).

In *Iggesund Converters Ltd v Lewis [1984] ICR 544*, the EAT suggested ways in which industrial tribunals could deal with evidence and argument on the reduction of an award for contributory fault.

For the sake of certainty, it is best to obtain from the industrial tribunal at the commencement of the hearing, directions as to whether it will consider liability and remedy separately, and when it will consider evidence and argument on contributory fault. It is unusual for a tribunal to hear evidence relating solely to compensation before it has reached a decision on liability.

27.20 THE DECISION

The tribunal may reach a unanimous or majority decision. It may announce it on the day of the hearing, but in difficult cases may reserve its decision.

Written reasons are sent to all parties after the hearing even if oral reasons are given at the time. The tribunal will give its reasons either in full or in summary form. The tribunal must give full reasons in cases of alleged sex or race discrimination, equal pay claims and claims brought pursuant to the *Employment Act 1980* alleging the wrongful exclusion or expulsion from a trade union where there is a closed shop. [*IT Regs, Rule 9(5)(a)*]. The tribunal will also give full reasons where it appears to it that they should be given or if a party to the proceedings requests them. A party must request full written reasons if he wishes to appeal. [*EAT Rule 3(1)(c)*; see 27.28 below]. Such request may be at the hearing or in writing within 21 days of the date on which the summary reasons were sent to the parties. [*IT Regs, Rule 9(5)(b)(c)(d)*].

The appellate courts will be slow to overturn a tribunal's decision on the grounds that the reasons given are inadequate, and no detailed analysis of the facts is required. However, the following recent statement by Bingham LJ in *Meek v City of Birmingham District Council [1987] IRLR 250* should be observed:

> 'It has on a number of occasions been made plain that the decision of an Industrial Tribunal is not required to be an elaborate formalistic product of refined legal draftsmanship, but it must contain an outline of the story which has given rise to the complaint and a summary of the Tribunal's basic factual conclusions and a statement of the reasons which have led them to reach the conclusion which they do on those basic facts. The parties are entitled to be told why they have won or lost. There should be sufficient account of the facts and of the reasoning to enable the EAT . . . to see whether any question of law arises; and it is highly desirable that the decision of an Industrial Tribunal should give guidance both to employers and trade unions as to practices which should or should not be adopted.'

In *Lamont v Fry's Metals Ltd [1985] ICR 566* the Court of Appeal assumed, without deciding the point, that an industrial tribunal can recall its decision before it is entered in the register. However, it should give both parties an opportunity of addressing further argument to the tribunal (see also *Arthur Guinness Son and Co (GB) Ltd v Green [1989] ICR 241*).

27.21 INTEREST

The Secretary of State may now make an order specifying that sums awarded by, or on appeal from, industrial tribunals which exceed a specified amount shall, in certain circumstances, carry interest at a prescribed rate. [*EPCA 9 Sch 6A; EA 1982, 3 Sch 7*]. Despite judicial criticism on more than one occasion, no such order has been made and interest may not be awarded. However, the recent Department of Employment consultation paper proposed that simple interest at the normal judgment rate (currently 15%) should start to run 28 days *after* the promulgation of the decision containing the award, and it was announced during parliamentary debates on *EA 1989* that this proposal was to be acted upon later in the year.

27.22 COSTS

Costs are awarded to a successful party only in exceptional circumstances.

(*a*) If a party, in the opinion of the tribunal, has acted frivolously, vexatiously or otherwise unreasonably in bringing or conducting proceedings, costs may be awarded against him. A respondent may have costs awarded against him if he defends a case which is not reasonably defensible. (*Davidson v John Calder (Publishers) Ltd* [*1985*] *ICR 143*). The order may be that he pay the whole or part of that party's costs or expenses as taxed (by a county court taxing officer) if not otherwise agreed. He may also be ordered to pay to the Secretary of State the whole or a part of witness allowances paid by the Secretary of State to a witness for his attendance at the tribunal. [*IT Regs, Rule 11(1)*].

An application for costs should be made within a reasonable time of the proceedings. If the decision is not reserved, the successful party should apply forthwith. Where the decision is reserved, a party who anticipates victory should inform the tribunal that he is applying for costs now and is inviting the tribunal to deal with costs in its decision. (*Johnson v Baxter* [*1984*] *ICR 675*).

If there had been a pre-hearing assessment in the case, in deciding whether to make an award of costs, an industrial tribunal may take into account any opinion on costs expressed by the tribunal which determined the pre-hearing assessment. [*IT Regs, Rule 6(2)(3)*].

(*b*) Costs may be awarded against or in favour of a party if a hearing has to be postponed or adjourned. [*IT Regs, Rule 11(2)*].

(*c*) In the following complaints of unfair dismissal costs may also be awarded

(i) where the applicant has expressed a wish to be reinstated or re-engaged which has been communicated to the respondent at least seven days before the hearing of the complaint; or

(ii) where the proceedings arise out of the respondent's failure to permit the applicant to return to work after an absence due to pregnancy or confinement.

If, in these cases, any postponement or adjournment of the hearing has been caused by the respondent's failure, without a special reason, to adduce reasonable evidence as to the availability of the job from which the applicant was dismissed, or, as the case may be, which she held before her absence, or of comparable or suitable employment, the tribunal will make an order against the respondent as respects any costs or expenses incurred or any allowances paid as a result of the postponement or adjournment. [*IT Regs, Rule 11(3)*].

It should be noted that legal aid is not available for proceedings in industrial tribunals, although it may be available to individuals on appeal.

See 27.11 above, for witnesses' expenses.

27.23 MISCELLANEOUS POWERS OF TRIBUNALS

A tribunal has wide statutory powers to regulate its own procedure (but no inherent, non-statutory powers: *Kelly v Ingersoll Rand Co Ltd [1982] ICR 476*). It may

(*a*) extend the time appointed by the rules for doing any act notwithstanding that the time appointed may have expired;

(*b*) postpone the day or time fixed for, or adjourn, any hearing;

(*c*) if the applicant gives notice of the withdrawal of his Originating Notice of Application, dismiss the proceedings;

(*d*) except in certain proceedings, if both or all the parties (and the Secretary of State, where appropriate, if he is not a party) agree in writing upon the terms of a decision to be made by the tribunal, decide accordingly;

(*e*) at any stage of the proceedings order to be struck out or amended any Originating Notice of Application or Notice of Appearance or anything in such Application or Notice of Appearance, on the ground that it is scandalous, frivolous or vexatious;

(*f*) on the application of the respondent, or of its own motion, order to be struck out any Originating Application for want of prosecution.

[*IT Regs, Rule 12(1)(2)*]. Before exercising its powers under (*e*) or (*f*) above, the tribunal must give the party against whom the order may be made the opportunity to make representations.

Applications to stay tribunal proceedings are often made, and frequently granted, where there are concurrent proceedings in the High Court and the industrial tribunal arising out of the same employment. In such cases, the EAT should only interfere with the tribunal's decision to postpone or continue with the proceedings before it if that decision resulted from an error of law or if it was perverse. (*Carter v Credit Change Ltd [1979] ICR 908; Automatic Switching Ltd v Brunet [1986] ICR 542*). For a discussion of the factors to be taken into consideration, see *First Castle Electronics Ltd v West [1989] ICR 72*. One reason for staying tribunal proceedings in such cases is that the doctrine of *res judicata* (i.e. that findings of fact cannot be relitigated) may apply so as to bind the High Court later. This will only be true if precisely the same issue arises in both sets of proceedings (see *Munir v Jang Publications Ltd [1989] ICR 1*).

27.24 JOINDER AND REPRESENTATIVE RESPONDENTS

A tribunal may at any time, either upon the application of any person or of its own motion, direct that any person against whom any relief is sought be joined as a party to the proceedings. [*IT Regs, Rule 14(1)*].

When either the employer or the complainant claims that dismissal was due to union pressure (see 55.16 UNFAIR DISMISSAL – II) a tribunal must grant an application to join a person as a party to proceedings if it is made before the hearing of the complaint, and may do so if the application is made after the commencement of the hearing but before an award is made. [*EPCA s 76A; EA 1982, s 7*].

Either on the application of a party, or of its own motion, a tribunal may order that any respondent named in the originating application, who appears not to be directly interested in the subject of the application, be dismissed from the proceedings. [*IT Regs, Rule 14(2)*].

Where there are many people having the same interest in an originating application, one or more of them may be cited as the person or persons against whom relief is sought, or may be authorised by the tribunal, before or at the hearing, to defend on behalf of all the persons so interested. [*IT Regs, Rule 14(3)*].

27.25 CONSOLIDATION OF PROCEEDINGS

A tribunal may consolidate two or more applications in which the same question of law or fact arises or if the remedy claimed in them arises out of the same set of facts, such as if several workers claim redundancy payments on the closure of a business, or if for some other reason it is desirable to consolidate the applications. [*IT Regs, Rule 15*].

27.26 TRANSFER OF PROCEEDINGS

Where an application is pending before an industrial tribunal in England or Wales which could be determined by a tribunal in Scotland, and it is more convenient to do so, the application can be transferred to Scotland, and vice versa. [*IT Regs, Rule 16*].

27.27 REVIEW OF DECISION

A tribunal can review or vary its decision on any of the following grounds:

(*a*) the decision was wrongly made as a result of an error on the part of the tribunal staff;

(*b*) a party did not receive notice of the date of the hearing and thus did not attend;

(*c*) the decision was made in the absence of a party or person entitled to be heard;

(*d*) new evidence has become available since the making of the decision which could not have been reasonably known of or foreseen;

(*e*) the interests of justice require such a review.

[*IT Regs, Rule 10(1)*].

An application for a review may be made at the hearing. If the application is not made at the hearing, such an application must be made to the Secretary of Tribunals within 14 days from the date of the entry of a decision in the Register. The application must be in writing stating in full the grounds for the review. [*IT Regs, Rule 10(2)*]. An application for a review may be refused by the President of Industrial Tribunals, or by the Chairman of the tribunal which decided the case or by a Regional Chairman if in his opinion it has no reasonable prospect of success. [*IT Regs, Rule 10(3)*].

If an application for a review is not refused under *Rule 10(3)*, it will either be heard by the tribunal which decided the case or, where it is not practicable for it to be heard by that tribunal or where the decision was made by a Chairman acting alone, by a tribunal appointed either by the President of Industrial Tribunals or a Regional Chairman. If the application is granted, the tribunal will either vary the decision or revoke it and order a re-hearing. [*IT Regs, Rule 10(4)*].

The review procedure enables errors which occur in the course of the proceedings to be corrected regardless of whether the error is major or minor, but it ought not to be invoked when an error of law is alleged after the parties have had a fair opportunity to present their case without procedural mishap. (*Trimble v Supertravel Ltd [1982] ICR 440*).

27.28 APPEALS

Institution of appeals

An appeal from the decision of an industrial tribunal is heard by the Employment Appeal Tribunal (EAT). An appeal can only be brought on a point of law. Parties, therefore, would be well advised to seek legal advice promptly before instituting an appeal. Legal aid is available to individuals for appeals from industrial tribunals, subject to the normal conditions.

The procedure for appeals to the EAT is governed by the *Employment Appeal Tribunal Rules 1980 (SI 1980 No 2035)* as amended by the *Employment Appeal Tribunal (Amendment) Rules 1985 (SI 1985 No 29)* and the *Employment Appeal Tribunal (Amendment) Rules 1988 (SI 1988 No 2072)*, called '*EAT Rules*' here, and the EAT Practice Direction of 17 February 1981 (*[1981] ICR 287*), referred to below as the '*Practice Direction*'. The EAT has issued further Practice Directions the most important of which is *Practice Direction (EAT Preliminary Hearing) [1985] ICR 684*.

Appeals to the EAT must be instituted by serving a Notice of Appeal in the prescribed form (Form 1) to the EAT within 42 days of the date on which the document recording the decision or order appealed from was sent to the appellant. The Notice of Appeal must be accompanied by (i) a copy of the decision or order of an industrial tribunal which is the subject of the appeal, and (ii) a copy of the full written reasons for that decision or order. [*EAT Rule 3(1)*]. Time limits will be strictly enforced. (*Duke v Prospect Training Services Ltd [1988] ICR 521*). Every appeal lodged out of time must be accompanied by an application for an extension of time setting out the reasons for the delay. The Registrar of the EAT will usually hear and determine the application. [*Practice Direction para 4*]. Any party aggrieved by the Registrar's decision may appeal to a judge of the EAT within five days. [*EAT Rule 17*]. The use of a document other than the prescribed form will be permitted only in exceptional cases (*Martin v British Railways Board [1989] ICR 24*, in which the EAT reiterated the warning given in *Marshall v Harland and Wolff Ltd (Practice Note) [1972] ICR 97* that the fact that an application for legal aid is pending does not of itself justify an extension of time for appealing).

The respondent to an appeal who wishes to resist the appeal must set out his grounds of resistance, and cross-appeal where applicable, in Form 3 and deliver it to the EAT within the time specified by the Registrar. [*EAT Rule 6(2)*].

27.29 Preliminary matters

The Registrar may notify an appellant that the grounds of appeal do not give the EAT jurisdiction to entertain the appeal. [*EAT Rule 3(2)*]. When such a notice is served, an appellant may serve a fresh Notice of Appeal within the time limit remaining for serving a Notice of Appeal, or within 28 days from the date on which the Registrar's notification was sent to him, whichever is the longer. [*EAT Rule 3(3)*]. Where an appellant expresses dissatisfaction in writing with the reasons given by the Registrar for his opinion that the grounds of appeal stated in the Notice of Appeal do not give the Appeal Tribunal jurisdiction to entertain the appeal, the Registrar will place the papers before the President or a judge for his direction. [*EAT Rule 3(5)*].

Upon the hearing of an appeal an appellant will not ordinarily be allowed to contend that 'the decision was contrary to the evidence' or that 'there was no evidence to support the decision', or to advance similar contentions, unless full and sufficient particulars identifying the particular matters relied upon have been supplied to the Appeal Tribunal. [*Practice Direction para 5(b)*].

The *Practice Direction, para 6* provides for a special procedure to deal with appeals which appear to disclose no arguable point of law. This procedure has been suspended since 1 October 1985 and replaced by a procedure for a preliminary hearing. (See *Practice Direction (EAT: Preliminary Hearing) [1985] ICR 684*.) Appeals which appear to the Registrar to depend solely or principally upon a plea that the industrial tribunal took an erroneous view of the evidence or reached an unreasonable conclusion upon the facts will be listed for a preliminary hearing. Since 1 March 1987 the practice has been that only the appellant appears at such a hearing. If the appellant fails to establish a fairly arguable case, the appeal will be dismissed.

The EAT will not normally consider complaints of bias or of the conduct of an industrial tribunal unless full and sufficient particulars are set out in the grounds of appeal. In any such case the Registrar may inquire of the party making the complaint whether it is the intention to proceed with the complaint, in which case the Registrar will give directions. Such directions may include the filing of affidavits dealing with the matters upon the basis of which the complaint is made or for giving further particulars. The Chairman of the tribunal will be given the opportunity of commenting upon the complaints made against him. No such complaint of bias will be heard by the EAT unless the correct procedure has been followed. [*Practice Direction para 12*]. Where there is an allegation of bias based on the conduct of one of the members of a tribunal at a hearing, the test is an objective one: would the reasonable observer present at the hearing, not being a party or associated with a party to the proceedings but knowing the issues, reasonably gain the impression of bias. (*Peter Simper & Co Ltd v Cooke [1986] IRLR 19*).

27.30 The hearing

The EAT consists of a High Court judge and two lay members. The EAT will have before it the grounds of appeal, the respondent's answer, the decision of the industrial tribunal and any documents which were before the industrial tribunal and which are relevant to the appeal. The Chairman's notes of evidence are no longer automatically supplied to the parties. An application for the notes of evidence to be supplied will only be granted where the applicant shows that they are relevant for the purposes of the appeal. (*Webb v Anglian Water Authority [1981] ICR 811*). Applications should be made promptly and accompanied by reasons. (*Burnett v Value Travel Agency Ltd [1989] ICR 79*). However, a party seeking to show that no reasonable tribunal could have reached such a conclusion on the evidence will almost certainly require the notes of evidence. The hearing before the EAT consists of legal argument. A party may not be permitted to raise points of law which were abandoned or never raised before the industrial tribunal especially where such points would require further investigation of the facts. (*Secretary of State for Employment v Newcastle-upon-Tyne City Council* [*1980*] *ICR 407*).

The EAT can only overturn the decision of an industrial tribunal if the tribunal can be shown to have erred in law. The error of law may be an express misdirection or it may be inferred from the fact that the conclusion of the tribunal was one which no reasonable industrial tribunal, properly directing itself, could have reached. Even if the EAT would have come to a different conclusion, it must not interfere with the decision of the industrial tribunal unless an error of law is identified. (*Retarded Children's Aid Society Ltd v Day* [*1978*] *ICR 437*). When an industrial tribunal has not erred in law, neither the EAT nor the Court of Appeal should disturb its decision on the fairness of a dismissal under *EPCA s 57(3)* unless one could say in effect: 'My goodness, that was certainly wrong'. (*Neale v Hereford and Worcester County Council* [*1986*] *ICR 471*). However, where an error of law is identified, the EAT must allow the appeal unless the conclusion of the industrial tribunal was plainly and unarguably right, notwithstanding the misdirection. (*Dobie v Burns International Security Services (UK) Ltd* [*1984*] *ICR 812*).

A failure by an industrial tribunal to give reasons for its decision may amount to an error of law rendering the decision liable to be overturned on appeal. In *Yusuf v Aberplace Ltd* [*1984*] *ICR 850*, the EAT took the unusual course of dealing with the inadequacy of a tribunal decision by holding that it was entitled to require an industrial tribunal to amplify any findings and reasons which were incomplete or obscure.

Where both the parties to an application to an industrial tribunal agree that the decision of the tribunal was in error and reach a proposed settlement, the parties may not themselves reverse that decision but must refer the matter to the EAT. The parties should draw up a formal order and request the EAT to accept it, ratify it and make it part of the order of the Appeal Tribunal. (*Comet Radiovision Services Ltd v Delahunty* [*1979*] *ICR 182*; see also *British Publishing Co Ltd v Fraser* [*1987*] *ICR 517*).

27.31 Powers of the Employment Appeal Tribunal

For the purpose of disposing of an appeal the EAT may exercise any powers of the body or officer from whom the appeal was brought. [*EPCA 12 Sch 21(1)*]. On rare occasions this power has been used to admit new oral evidence. However, it must be shown that the new evidence could not with reasonable diligence have been obtained for use at the original hearing, and that it is likely to have an important influence on the result of the case. (*Wileman v Minilec Engineering Ltd* [*1988*] *ICR 318*). This provision also enables the EAT in appropriate circumstances to direct that a party shall not proceed with part of his claim. (*Dean (Saif) v Islamic Foundation* [*1983*] *ICR 36*).

Apart from allowing or dismissing an appeal the EAT may remit the case to the same or a different tribunal for further evidence on certain matters or for the case to proceed along the lines laid down by the EAT. In general, it will allow an appeal from a decision which has been demonstrated to be perverse, and remit a case where there has been a misdirection on the law or the evidence. It may award costs where it appears that any proceedings were 'unnecessary, improper or vexatious' or that there has been unreasonable delay or other unreasonable conduct in bringing or conducting the proceedings. [*EAT Rule 27*]. Where a case is remitted, the tribunal may consider a point not previously raised if it would be just to do so. (*Hooper v British Railways Board* [*1988*] *IRLR 517*).

27.32 Review and further appeal

The EAT may review any order made by it on the grounds that

(*a*) the order was wrongly made as the result of an error on the part of the EAT or its staff; or

(*b*) a party did not receive proper notice of the proceedings leading to the order; or

(*c*) the interests of justice require such review.

[*EAT Rule 26*].

The circumstances in which the review procedure can be invoked are rare (see *Stannard & Co (1969) Ltd v Wilson* [*1983*] *ICR 86*).

Unless the EAT so orders, a transcription of the judgment of the EAT will only be provided free of charge to a party to the appeal if application is made at the hearing or within 14 days of the hearing. [*EAT Practice Direction, 1 September 1981* [*1981*] *ICR 690*].

A further appeal may be taken to the Court of Appeal on a point of law but only with leave from the EAT or the Court of Appeal. [*EPCA s 136(4)*].

In appeals from the EAT, the Court of Appeal is a second-tier appellate court and is concerned with whether the decision of the industrial tribunal was right, not with whether the EAT was right. (*Hennessy v Craigmyle & Co Ltd* [*1986*] *ICR 461; Campion v Hamworthy Engineering Ltd* [*1987*] *ICR 966*).

The time limit for lodging an appeal to the Court of Appeal is four weeks from the date on which the order or judgment of the EAT was drawn up. [*Rules of the Supreme Court Order 59, Rule 4(1)*].

A further appeal lies to the House of Lords if the Court of Appeal or the House of Lords gives leave. A number of special rules govern House of Lords appeals.

Where the outcome of an application or an appeal turns on a question of EC law, the answer to which is unclear, the tribunal or court may, or if it is a court of final appeal must, refer the question to the European Court of Justice under *Article 177* of the Treaty of Rome. The parties to the application or appeal can request a reference in these circumstances.

28 Insolvency of Employer

(See also DE booklet No. 3 'Employee's rights on insolvency of employer' (PL 718).)

28.1 In the event of insolvency, certain claims by an employee against his employer for some time have had precedence over other claims. The right to claim priority for specified sums due to employees on insolvency is now set out in the *Insolvency Act 1986*, whether the employer is a company or an individual. (As to personal insolvency in Scotland, see the *Bankruptcy (Scotland) Act 1985*.) Employees may also make claims on the Redundancy Fund for other payments if their employer becomes insolvent. Detailed provisions relating to both corporate and individual insolvency in England and Wales are contained in the *Insolvency Rules 1986 (SI 1986 No 1925)*, as amended by the *Insolvency (Amendment) Rules 1987 (SI 1987 No 1925)*. (Detailed provisions relating to corporate insolvency in Scotland are contained in the *Insolvency (Scotland) Rules 1986 (SI 1986 No 1915)* as amended.) A detailed analysis of the law of insolvency is beyond the scope of this book (see *Tolley's Company Law* for a detailed treatment of corporate insolvency). A brief outline of the provisions affecting employees is set out below. Before December 1986 similar provisions applied, which were to be found in the *Companies Act 1985, s 614, 19 Sch* and *Bankruptcy Act 1914, s 33*.

28.2 CLAIMS GIVEN PRECEDENCE BY INSOLVENCY ACT 1986

In the winding-up of a company or in the distribution of a bankrupt's estate, the following debts are amongst those given priority over others.

(*a*) Remuneration (including commission) of employees and ex-employees owed in respect of the whole or any part of the period of four months immediately preceding the date on which an administration order was made, a provisional liquidator appointed, a winding-up order made, or a resolution for the winding-up of a company passed, or, in the case of an individual, the date on which an interim receiver was first appointed after the presentation of the bankruptcy petition or the making of a bankruptcy order.

Claims for remuneration have priority up to a total of £800 per employee, or such other amount as may be prescribed by the Secretary of State.

(*b*) Accrued holiday remuneration owed in respect of any period of employment before the date referred to in (*a*) above, to a person whose employment by the debtor has been terminated, whether before, on or after that date. For ascertaining entitlement to a holiday, account is taken of any statutory or contractual period of notice to which the employee was entitled but not given.

Any remuneration payable by the debtor to a person in respect of a period of holiday or of absence from work through sickness or other good cause is deemed to be wages or salary in respect of services rendered to the debtor in that period.

[*Insolvency Act 1986, ss 175, 328, 386, 387, 6 Sch 9-11, 13-15; Insolvency Proceedings (Monetary Limits) Order 1986 (SI 1986 No 1996)*].

The following are deemed to be remuneration within 28.2(*a*) above if they are due in respect of the period referred to in (*a*)

(i) a GUARANTEE PAYMENT (23);

(ii) a MEDICAL SUSPENSION PAYMENT (30);

(iii) any payment for TIME OFF WORK (50) under *EPCA s 27(3)* (trade union duties), *s 31(3)* (looking for work etc.) or *s 31A* (ante-natal care);

(iv) statutory sick pay (see SICKNESS AND SICK PAY (46));

(v) remuneration under a protective award made by an industrial tribunal (see REDUNDANCY - II (39)).

These payments have priority up to the maximum of £800 per employee, or such other amount as may be fixed by the Secretary of State (see (*a*) above).

Each individual claim under (*a*), (*b*) and (i)-(v) above ranks equally and is to be paid in equal proportions to other such claims if the assets are insufficient to pay the claims in full.

[*Insolvency Act 1986, ss 175, 328*].

In order to determine whether a worker is an employee under (*a*) above, the test of whether he has a contract for services or a contract of employment is applied (see *Eaton v Robert Eaton Ltd* [*1988*] *ICR 302* and 15.3 EMPLOYEE OR SELF-EMPLOYED?).

28.3 OTHER CLAIMS

An employee may have other contractual or statutory claims against his employer which do not enjoy the preference accorded to wages etc. by the provisions mentioned in 28.2 above.

The *Insolvency Rules 1986 (SI 1986 No 1925)*, as amended, contain detailed provisions for proving debts in a company's winding-up or an individual's bankruptcy in England and Wales.

28.4 PAYMENTS OUT OF THE REDUNDANCY FUND

Redundancy payments

An employee who claims that his employer is liable to pay him a redundancy payment, and that his employer is insolvent and the whole or part of the payment remains unpaid, may apply to the Secretary of State for Employment for payment. [*EPCA s 106(1)*]. If such a payment is made to the employee out of the Redundancy Fund, all subsequent rights to recover the redundancy payment from the employer then rest with the Secretary of State. [*EPCA s 106(3)*].

28.5 Statutory maternity pay

Where an employee is unable to obtain her entitlement to statutory maternity pay from her employer, she may claim such payment from the Secretary of State (see 29.15 MATERNITY RIGHTS).

28.6 Other rights of recovery

In addition to an application for a redundancy payment an employee may also make application to the Secretary of State for Employment for various other payments from the Redundancy Fund.

28.6 Insolvency of Employer

If, on an application made to him in writing by an employee, the Secretary of State is satisfied

(*a*) that the employer of that employee has become insolvent;

(*b*) that the employment of the employee has been terminated; and

(*c*) that on the relevant date the employee was entitled to be paid the whole or part of any debt covered by (i) to (v) below;

then the Secretary of State must pay him his entitlement out of the Redundancy Fund. [*EPCA s 122(1)*]. 'Relevant date' in relation to arrears of pay and holiday pay means the date on which the employer becomes insolvent. In relation to a protective award and to a basic award of compensation for unfair dismissal, it is the latest of –

(1) the date on which the employer became insolvent;

(2) the date of the termination of the employee's employment; and

(3) the date on which the award was made.

In relation to any other debt, the relevant date is the later of the dates mentioned in (1) and (2) above. [*EPCA s 122(2); Insolvency Act 1985, s 218*]. An employee may therefore only claim unpaid wages and holiday pay which accrued before the insolvency of his employer.

This right applies to the following debts:

(i) any arrears of pay in respect of one or more (but not more than eight) weeks;

(ii) any amount which the employer is liable to pay the employee for the statutory minimum period of notice, or for any failure of the employer to give the period of notice required;

(iii) any holiday pay due for a period or periods of holiday not exceeding six weeks in all, and to which the employee became entitled during the twelve months ending with the relevant date;

(iv) any basic award of compensation for unfair dismissal (see 56.7 UNFAIR DISMISSAL – III);

(v) any reasonable sum by way of reimbursement of the whole or any part of any fee or premiums paid by an apprentice or articled clerk.

[*EPCA s 122(3); EA 1982, 3 Sch 4*].

For the purpose of a claim, the following are deemed to be arrears of pay: a guarantee payment, a medical suspension payment, any payment for time off for trade union duties, to seek alternative employment when under notice of redundancy or for ante-natal care, and remuneration under a protective award. [*EPCA s 122(4) as substituted by Insolvency Act 1985, s 218(4)*].

The total amount payable to an employee in respect of any debt referred to above, where that debt is calculated according to a period of time, may not exceed £172 (£164 if the relevant date (see above) was before 1 April 1989) for any one week or such amount as the Secretary of State may order (or proportionately less for a period less than one week). [*EPCA s 122(5); Employment Protection (Variation of Limits) Order 1989 (SI 1989 No 526)*]. The employee must be placed in no worse position than if notice had been given or pay in lieu of notice made. Therefore, in making a payment under *Sec 122*, the Secretary of State was entitled to deduct unemployment benefit and earnings related supplement only to the extent that there had been a net gain to the employee after taking into account the premature termination of his employment. (*Westwood v Secretary of State for Employment* [*1985*] *ICR 209*).

Where a liquidator or receiver has been appointed in a liquidation or bankruptcy, the employee must first apply to him for payment. The liquidator or receiver then must make a statement to the Secretary of State for Employment of the amounts appearing to him to be owing to the applicant. The Secretary of State then makes the payment. He may do so without having received the statement if it appears to him that he can determine the amount of the unpaid debt without it. [*EPCA s 122(10)(11) as substituted by EA 1989, s 18(2)*]. Where the amount of a week's pay exceeds the statutory maximum payable under *Sec 122*, the statutory benefit limit is applied to the gross week's pay. Tax and national insurance contributions are to be deducted from that amount (see *Morris v Secretary of State for Employment* [*1985*] *ICR 522*). Thus, in that case Mr Morris was entitled, *inter alia*, to six days' arrears of wages in the sum of £183.29. The Secretary of State was held entitled to reduce the sum claimed to the maximum allowed for a week's pay (then £140, now £172) and to deduct from *that* figure of £140, sums for income tax and national insurance payments.

When calculating the amount of an order against the Secretary of State under *EPCA s 122*, the amount of salary an employee should have received during the period of notice is to be reduced by the amount of the employee's earnings during the period and is to be based on pay net of tax. (*Secretary of State for Employment v Jobling* [*1980*] *ICR 380*). Sums earned in mitigation should also be deducted (*Secretary of State for Employment v Cooper* [*1987*] *ICR 766*).

The rights and remedies of the employee in respect of the debt will be transferred to the Secretary of State [*EPCA s 125* as amended]. But he has no right to be paid in priority to other creditors (*Re Urethane Engineering Products Ltd, The Times, 7 April 1989*).

28.7 Unpaid contributions to occupational pension schemes

The Secretary of State may make payments out of the Redundancy Fund into an occupational pension scheme if he is satisfied that an employer has become insolvent and that at the time he became insolvent there remained unpaid relevant contributions falling to be paid by him to the scheme. Application for payment is to be made by the person competent to act in respect of the pension scheme. [*EPCA s 123(1)*]. 'Relevant contributions' are defined as contributions to be paid by the employer on his own behalf or on behalf of an employee from whose pay a deduction has been made for that purpose. [*EPCA s 123(2)*].

The amount payable in respect of contributions of an employer on his own behalf is the least of the following:

(*a*) the balance of relevant contributions remaining unpaid on the date when the employer became insolvent and payable by the employer on his own account to the scheme in respect of the twelve months immediately preceding that date;

(*b*) the amount certified by an actuary to be necessary for the purpose of meeting the liability of the scheme on dissolution to pay the benefits provided by the scheme to or in respect of the employees of the employer;

(*c*) an amount equal to 10% of the total amount of remuneration paid or payable to those employees in respect of the twelve months immediately preceding the date on which the employer became insolvent.

[*EPCA s 123(3)*].

The sum payable in respect of unpaid contributions on behalf of an employee may not exceed the amount deducted from the pay of the employee in respect of the employee's contributions to the occupational pension scheme during the twelve months immediately preceding the date on which the employer became insolvent. [*EPCA s 123(5)*].

The liquidator, receiver or trustee in bankruptcy must make a statement to the Secretary of State of the amounts so owing before any payment out of the Redundancy Fund may be made. However, the Secretary of State may make a payment from the Redundancy Fund if he is satisfied that he does not require such a statement in order to determine the relevant amounts. [*EPCA s 123(9) as substituted by EA 1989, s 18(3)*].

The rights and remedies of the persons competent to act in respect of the scheme will be transferred to the Secretary of State [*EPCA s 125(3)* as amended].

28.8 **Remedy**

A person who has applied for payment under 28.6 or 28.7 above may, within the period of three months beginning with the date on which the decision of the Secretary of State on that application was communicated to him (or if that is not reasonably practicable, within such further period as is considered reasonable), present a complaint to an industrial tribunal that

(*a*) the Secretary of State has failed to make any such payment; or

(*b*) any such payment by him is less than the amount which should have been paid.

[*EPCA s 124*].

If the industrial tribunal finds the complaint well-founded it makes a declaration to that effect and states the amount due from the Secretary of State.

Disputes relating to payments applied for under 28.4 above are to be referred to the industrial tribunal under *EPCA s 108*. The EAT has suggested that it may be proper on such occasions to join the company in liquidation for the purposes of discovery (*Bradley v Secretary of State for Employment* [*1989*] *ICR 69*).

28.9 INSOLVENCY AND REDUNDANCY

Insolvency frequently necessitates the dismissal of the employees formerly engaged by the insolvent business. Insolvency of itself does not absolve employers from the duty to have consultation with the unions and employees before the dismissal notices are sent out. In *Clarks of Hove Ltd v Bakers' Union* [*1978*] *ICR 1076*, the Court of Appeal held that insolvency is not by itself a special circumstance rendering it not reasonably practicable for an employer to comply with the redundancy consultation provisions in *EPA s 99* (see 39.4 REDUNDANCY–II).

The *Transfer of Undertakings (Protection of Employment) Regulations 1981 (SI 1981 No 1794), Reg 4* makes special provision with regard to the transfer of a company's undertaking by a receiver or liquidator to a wholly-owned subsidiary. *EC Council Directive No 80/987/EEC of 20 October 1980* specified minimum rights for employees of insolvent employers. Pursuant to that directive, employees ordinarily working inside the territory of the EC member States have enjoyed the benefit of the *EPCA* provisions relating to insolvency since 1 June 1983. [*Insolvency of Employer (Excluded Classes) Regulations 1983 (SI 1983 No 624)*].

29 Maternity Rights

(See also DE booklet No. 4 'Employment rights for the expectant mother' (PL 710).)

Cross-references. See UNFAIR DISMISSAL – I and II (54, 55) for the general rules on unfair dismissal; EQUAL PAY (19) and SEX DISCRIMINATION – I (44) for the rules prohibiting discrimination against women.

29.1 The *Employment Protection Act 1975* created new statutory rights for women employees. These provisions were re-enacted in the *Employment Protection (Consolidation) Act 1978* (*EPCA*). An additional right, the right to paid time off for ante-natal care, was conferred by *Employment Act 1980*, which also amended the existing provisions. With the exception of the law relating to statutory maternity pay (which is contained in *Social Security Act 1986, Part V*), all the relevant legislation is to be found in the *EPCA*, as amended, and references below are therefore to that Act, save where otherwise appears.

Women employees who can satisfy the relevant qualifying conditions enjoy the following statutory rights:

(*a*) paid time off to receive ante-natal care;

(*b*) protection from dismissal by reason of pregnancy;

(*c*) maternity pay;

(*d*) return to work after confinement.

[*EPCA ss 31A, 33, 45-48, 56, 60, 2 Sch; Social Security Act 1986, ss 46-50, 4 Sch*].

The European Community is considering proposals for a parental leave directive which would allow either parent three months' unpaid leave during the first five months of a child's life. See also *SSA 1989, 5 Sch 2, 5, 6.*

29.2 TIME OFF FOR ANTE-NATAL CARE

An employee who is pregnant and who has, on the advice of a registered medical practitioner, registered midwife or registered health visitor, made an appointment to attend at any place for the purpose of receiving ante-natal care, has the right not to be unreasonably refused time off during her working hours to enable her to keep the appointment [*EPCA s 31A(1)*], and to be paid for the period of absence at the appropriate hourly rate. [*EPCA s 31A(4)*].

29.3 Qualifying requirements

Except for the first appointment for ante-natal care, the employee must, if requested by the employer, produce for his inspection

(*a*) a certificate from a registered medical practitioner, registered midwife or registered health visitor stating that the employee is pregnant; and

(*b*) an appointment card or some other document showing that the appointment has been made.

[*EPCA s 31A(2)(a)(b)*].

There is no minimum qualifying period of employment for the enjoyment of this right. If an employer could reasonably refuse to allow an employee time off to attend an ante-natal appointment – for example if she was a part-time employee and could arrange to attend during her time off – yet he allows her time off, it is thought that he is not obliged to pay her during the period of her absence provided that he obtains her agreement and makes it clear that the time is not being given in satisfaction of a statutory obligation. The reason for this qualification is that if an employee is entitled to take time off in accordance with the provisions of *EPCA s 31A(1)*, she is automatically entitled to be paid for the time taken. [*EPCA s 31A(4)*]. (See *Gregory v Tudsbury Ltd* [*1982*] *IRLR 267*.)

29.4 Amount

The employee is entitled to payment from the employer for the period of absence at the appropriate hourly rate. That is the amount of one week's pay divided by

(*a*) the number of normal working hours in a week for that employee when employed under the contract of employment in force on the day when the time off is taken; or

(*b*) where the number of such normal working hours differs from week to week or over a longer period, the average number of such hours, calculated by reference to the hours worked during the period of twelve weeks ending with the last complete week before the day on which the time off is taken; or

(*c*) where the number of hours worked in a week differs, but the employee has not been employed long enough for the twelve-week calculation to be made, a number which fairly represents the number of normal working hours in a week taking into account the employee's contract and the average number of hours worked by other employees of the same employer in comparable employment.

[*EPCA s 31A(5)*].

29.5 Remedies

An employee may present a complaint to an industrial tribunal to the effect that her employer has unreasonably refused her time off as required by *EPCA s 31A(1)* or has failed to pay her the whole or part of any amount to which she is entitled under *EPCA s 31A(4)*. [*EPCA s 31A(6)*]. Such a complaint must be presented within the period of three months beginning with the date of the appointment concerned, or within such further period as the tribunal considers reasonable in a case where it is satisfied that it was not reasonably practicable for the complaint to be presented within the period of three months. [*EPCA s 31A(7)*]. By analogy with the time limit in unfair dismissal cases, it is thought that it will not be considered to be reasonably practicable for an employee to present a claim until she is aware or ought reasonably to be aware of her rights. (See 27.3(*f*) INDUSTRIAL TRIBUNALS.) Where an industrial tribunal finds a complaint well-founded it will make a declaration to that effect and make an order for payment of the amount of money due under the statutory provisions. [*EPCA s 31A(8)*]. The employee's statutory right to remuneration does not affect her contractual right, but any contractual remuneration will go to discharge her statutory entitlement and vice versa. [*EPCA s 31A(9), (10)*].

29.6 PROTECTION FROM DISMISSAL BY REASON OF PREGNANCY

An employee with the necessary length of employment is automatically held to be unfairly dismissed if the reason or the principal reason for the dismissal is either (*a*) that she is pregnant; or

(*b*) any other reason connected with her pregnancy; unless

  (i) at the effective date of termination of her contract of employment she is or will have become, because of her pregnancy, incapable of adequately doing the work which she is employed to do; or

  (ii) that, because of her pregnancy, she cannot or will not be able to continue after that date to do that work without contravention (either by her or her employer) of a duty or restriction imposed by or under any enactment.

[*EPCA s 60(1)*].

The House of Lords has held that a pregnant employee selected for redundancy because she would require maternity leave was unfairly dismissed, applying *EPCA s 60(1)* (*Brown v Stockton-on-Tees Borough Council [1988] ICR 410*).

29.7 Suitable vacancy available

Even if an employee is incapable of carrying out her duties because of her pregnancy, whether on ground (i) or ground (ii) in 29.6 above, her dismissal will be considered unfair if there is a suitable available vacancy for her but her employer does not make her an offer of new employment to fill that vacancy before or on the effective date of termination of her existing employment. [*EPCA s 60(2)*]. Where such an offer is made and accepted, the new employment must

(*a*) take effect immediately on the ending of employment under the previous contract;

(*b*) be such that the work to be done under the contract is of a kind which is both suitable in relation to the employee and appropriate for her to do in the circumstances, and

(*c*) be such that the provisions of the new contract as to the capacity and place in which she is to be employed and as to the other terms and conditions of her employment are not substantially less favourable to her than the corresponding provisions of the previous contract.

[*EPCA s 60(3)*].

Such words as 'suitable', 'appropriate' and 'substantially less favourable' are open to various interpretations. In order to establish that an employee has been fairly dismissed when she has become incapable of performing her job by reason of her pregnancy and she alleges that there was a suitable vacancy which was not offered to her, the onus will be on the employer to show that he has offered her a suitable vacancy or that there was no suitable vacancy for her. [*EPCA s 60(4)*]. In order to safeguard themselves, employers should make written offers of available employment if the pregnant employee may be capable of performing such work.

29.8 Qualifying period

The qualifying period for this right is, as for other claims for unfair dismissal, two years. The period is calculated by reference to the effective date of termination of the employment. (See 54.13 UNFAIR DISMISSAL–I.)

29.9 Exceptions

(*a*) If an employee, who is dismissed by reason of her incapacity to do her work or because her continued employment would lead to breach of the law, gives notice to terminate her contract within the notice period given by her employer, she will not be entitled to claim for unfair dismissal. (This is an exception to *EPCA s 55(3)* which provides that an employee who terminates his contract during a period of notice given by his employer will still be considered dismissed by the employer.) [*EPCA s 60(5)*].

(*b*) An employee is not entitled to claim for unfair dismissal from employment under a contract for a fixed term of one year or more where the dismissal consists only of the expiry of that term without its being renewed, and before the term so expires, the employee has agreed in writing to exclude any right to claim for unfair dismissal. [*EPCA s 142(1)*].

(*c*) An employee is not entitled to claim compensation for unfair dismissal from employment which is excluded from unfair dismissal protection by *EPCA ss 141(2)(5), 144(2), 145(2)* (see 54.15 UNFAIR DISMISSAL–I).

29.10 STATUTORY MATERNITY PAY

On 6 April 1987 the provisions in the *EPCA* conferring a right to maternity pay were repealed and replaced by the *Social Security Act 1986, Part V*. The *SSA 1986* introduced a system of statutory maternity pay (SMP), payable for 18 weeks to a woman absent from work because of pregnancy, and to be recouped by her employer from the State, as in the case of statutory sick pay.

Various regulations have been made under *SSA 1986*, of which the most important are the *Statutory Maternity Pay (General) Regulations 1986 (SI 1986 No 1960)*.

(See DSS leaflets NI 257 'Employer's Guide to Statutory Maternity Pay' and NI 17A 'Maternity Benefits' and *Tolley's Guide to Statutory Maternity Pay*.)

29.11 Qualifying requirements

An employee must normally satisfy four conditions before she can qualify for SMP:

(*a*) she must have been continuously employed by her employer for at least 26 weeks ending with the week immediately preceding the 14th week before the expected week of confinement;

(*b*) she must have ceased to work for the employer wholly or partly because of pregnancy or confinement;

(*c*) her normal weekly earnings, for the period of 8 weeks ending with the week immediately preceding the 14th week before the expected week of confinement, must be not less than the lower limit for the payment of national insurance contributions;

(*d*) she must have become pregnant and reached, or been confined before reaching, the start of the 11th week before the expected week of confinement.

[*SSA 1986, s 46(1) (2)*].

'Confinement' is defined as labour resulting in the issue of a living child, or labour after 28 weeks of pregnancy resulting in the issue of a child whether alive or dead. [*SSA 1986, s 50(1)*].

There are certain exceptions to the above requirement of continuous employment. Thus the employer remains liable if the period of continuous employment was not less than 8 weeks and he brought the contract of employment to an end solely or mainly for the purpose of avoiding his liability for SMP. [*SI 1986 No 1960, Reg 3*]. Again, the right to SMP survives if the woman is dismissed before the 15th week before the expected week of confinement on the ground that she is physically or legally incapable of doing the work (i.e. a fair dismissal within *EPCA s 60(1)*), or if she is confined more than 14 weeks before the expected date of confinement, and would, but for her dismissal or confinement, otherwise have qualified. [*SI 1986 No 1960, Reg 4*].

For the purpose of calculating continuity of employment, it is the existence of the contract of employment which is crucial, and not whether the employee is in fact working. In *Secretary of State for Employment v Doulton Sanitaryware Ltd* [*1981*] *ICR 477* (a case decided under the previous law relating to maternity pay) it was held on the facts that the parties intended the contract to continue even though the employee had stopped working (she had been put on a list of 'prolonged absentees').

It is clearly intended that the right to SMP should not be conditional upon an intention to return to work after the confinement.

Members of Her Majesty's forces are excluded from the right to SMP. [*SSA 1986, s 79(5)*]. The right extends to persons working within the EC and to certain mariners, but not to persons outside the EC. [*Statutory Maternity Pay (Persons Abroad and Mariners) Regulations 1987 (SI 1987 No 418)*].

SSA 1986, s 46(6) provides that any agreement is void in so far as it purports to exclude or limit the right to SMP.

29.12 Period of entitlement

SMP is payable in respect of each week during the 'maternity pay period'. The maternity pay period will not exceed 18 weeks. In general, when it starts depends upon when the employee gives notice and stops work. However, the first week of the period will not be earlier than the 11th week, nor later than the 6th week, before the expected week of confinement. Therefore an employee who works beyond the 6th week before the expected week of confinement reduces the amount of SMP which she can expect to receive from the employer. [*SSA 1986, s 47; SI 1986 No 1960, Reg 2*].

29.13 Procedure for making a claim

The employee must give her employer 21 days' prior notice of her absence from work because of her pregnancy, or if that is not reasonably practicable, such notice as is reasonably practicable. That notice must be in writing if the employer so requests. However, notice is dispensed with in cases where the employee leaves the job, after the beginning of the 15th week before the expected week of confinement, for a reason unconnected with the pregnancy, and also where she is dismissed because her pregnancy makes it legally or physically impossible for her to continue. [*SSA 1986, s 46(4)(5); SI 1986 No 1960, Reg 23*].

The employee must also provide a maternity certificate signed by a doctor or midwife as evidence of her pregnancy and of the expected date of confinement, and there is a prescribed form for such certificates. [*SSA 1986, 4 Sch 6; Statutory Maternity Pay (Medical Evidence) Regulations 1987 (SI 1987 No 235)*].

29.14 Amount of payments

SSA 1986, s 48 provides for two rates of payment. The higher rate is payable only for 6 weeks of the maternity pay period, and then only to an employee whose continuous employment in the period ending with the 15th week before the expected week of confinement is at least two years, if she is normally employed for 16 or more hours weekly, or at least five years, if she is normally employed for 8 or more hours weekly (and see *SI 1986 No 1960, Reg 16*). It is calculated as being 9/10ths of the employee's normal weekly earnings for the period of 8 weeks immediately preceding the 14th week before the expected week of confinement. (See also *SI 1988 No 532*.) The lower rate, which prevails for the rest of the maternity pay period and where the employee does not qualify for higher rate, is a flat rate. It was set at £34.25 per week by the *Social Security Benefits Up-rating (No 2) Order 1987* (*SI 1987 No 1978*). With effect from 2 April 1989, this was increased to £36.25 per week by the *Social Security Benefits Up-rating Order 1989 (SI 1989 No 43)*.

SMP should be paid in the like manner and at the same time as the employee would normally be paid, or if there is no agreement as to a pay day, or no normal pay day, on the last day of a calendar month. [*SI 1986 No 1960, Regs 27, 29*]. It does not exclude any contractual benefits to which the employee may be entitled, but the employer is entitled to set off SMP against contractual remuneration in respect of the same period and vice versa. [*SSA 1986, 4 Sch 12*]. In other words, the employer has to meet the more onerous of the contractual and statutory burdens, but not both of them. Similarly, tax, national insurance contributions and any other regular deductions fall to be deducted from SMP.

29.15 Remedy for non-payment

If the employer fails to make payments of SMP to which the employee believes herself to be entitled, the employee may first of all require the employer within a reasonable time to supply her with a written statement of the position which he is adopting. [*SSA 1986, 4 Sch 7*]. If the dispute is not resolved, either the employee or the DSS may refer the matter to an adjudication officer. From that officer an appeal lies to the Social Security Appeal Tribunal and thence to a Social Security Commissioner. [*SSA 1986, s 52; Social Security (Adjudication) Regulations 1986 (SI 1986 No 2218)*]. An employer's continued refusal to pay after an adverse determination is an offence.

If the employee is unable to obtain her entitlement from the employer (which may be because he has become insolvent), she is entitled to look to the Secretary of State for payment. [*SI 1986 No 1960, Regs 7, 30*].

29.16 Recoupment by employer

The system whereby the employer recoups payments of SMP made by him is similar to that which applies to STATUTORY SICK PAY (46). In short, the relevant moneys are deducted by the employer from national insurance contributions which would otherwise fall to be remitted by him. He may deduct an additional 7½% of the SMP paid, representing the expense incurred by him in paying national insurance contributions on the SMP paid out.

The system of recoupment is governed by the *Statutory Maternity Pay (Compensation of Employers) Regulations 1987 (SI 1987 No 91)*, as amended by the *Statutory Maternity Pay (Compensation of Employers) Amendment Regulations 1988 (SI 1988 No 430)* and the *Statutory Maternity Pay*

(Compensation of Employers) and *Statutory Sick Pay (Additional Compensation of Employers) Amendment Regulations 1989 (SI 1989 No 286)*.

29.17 THE RIGHT TO RETURN TO WORK

An employee who has been absent from work wholly or partly because of pregnancy or confinement is entitled to return to work with her original employer or, where appropriate, his successor, in the job in which she was employed and under the contract under which she worked immediately before the beginning of her absence. She can return at any time before the end of the period of 29 weeks beginning with the week in which the date of confinement falls and must be offered her original employment on terms not less favourable than they would have been had she not been absent. [*EPCA ss 45(1), 153(1)*]. Therefore she must benefit from any pay rise granted to the same category of employee in her absence, or if the only employee in her category, must benefit from any customary rise although she is absent on the relevant date. She must not lose seniority or pension rights as a result of the absence. [*EPCA s 45(2); SSA 1989, 5 Sch 15*].

If it is not practicable, by reason of redundancy, for the employer to permit the employee to return to her original job, she is entitled, where there is a suitable available vacancy, to be offered a new contract of employment with her employer or an associated employer which is

(i) suitable to her and appropriate for her to do in the circumstances;

(ii) in its terms and conditions not substantially less favourable to her than if she had returned to her original employment.

[*EPCA s 45(3)(4)*].

29.18 Qualifying requirements

In order to claim the right to return to work an employee must

(*a*) continue to be employed by her employer (whether or not she is at work) until immediately before the beginning of the 11th week before the expected week of confinement;

(*b*) at the beginning of that 11th week have been continuously employed for a period of not less than two years; and

(*c*) inform her employer in writing at least 21 days before her absence begins or, if that is not reasonably practicable, as soon as reasonably practicable

  (i) that she will be (or is) absent from work wholly or partly because of pregnancy or confinement;

  (ii) that she intends to return to work with her employer; and

  (iii) of the expected week of confinement or, if the confinement has occurred, the date of confinement

[*EPCA s 33(3)*];

(*d*) give her employer written confirmation of her intention to return to work within 14 days of being requested in writing to do so by her employer or his successor or, if that is not reasonably practicable, she must reply as soon as reasonably practicable. [*EPCA s 33(3A)*]. The employer's written request must be accompanied by a statement, also in writing, warning the employee of the consequences of failure to comply [*EPCA s 33(3B)*];

(*e*) give written notice to her employer, at least 21 days before the day on which she proposes to return. That day is referred to as the 'notified day of return'. [*EPCA s 47(1)*].

The statutory requirements must be strictly complied with. (*Lavery v Plessey Telecommunications Ltd* [*1983*] *ICR 534; Dowuona v John Lewis plc* [*1987*] *ICR 788*). An employee who has both a statutory and a contractual right to return to work, may not exercise the two rights separately but may take advantage of whichever right is in any particular respect the more favourable. [*EPCA s 48(1)*]. An employee may not, however, claim a right to return to an amalgamation of her former job (to which she would be statutorily entitled to return) and a job to which she is contractually entitled to return. (*Bovey v Board of Governors of the Hospital for Sick Children* [*1978*] *ICR 934*).

29.19 Postponement of date of return

(*a*) An employer may postpone an employee's return to work until a date not more than four weeks after the notified date of return if he informs her of the reasons for doing so before the notified date of return. [*EPCA s 47(2)*].

(*b*) An employee may postpone the date of return or, where no day of return has been notified, extend the time during which she may exercise her right to return, for a period of up to 4 weeks from the notified date of return or from the period of 29 weeks beginning with the week in which the date of confinement falls, if she gives the employer a medical certificate of her incapacity. [*EPCA s 47(3)*]. In *Kelly v Liverpool Maritime Terminals Ltd* [*1988*] *IRLR 311* the Court of Appeal held that there was no dismissal where the employee failed to return to work after the 4 week period has expired, but sent the employer further medical certificates before she was eventually informed that she would not be permitted to return.

(*c*) Apart from the circumstances set out in (*b*) above an employee may return to work after the expiration of the 29th week from the beginning of the week in which the date of confinement falls if

(i) a date of return has been notified to the employer, but work has been interrupted by, for example, a strike, which renders it unreasonable for her to return, in which case she may return when work resumes, or as soon as reasonably practicable thereafter [*EPCA s 47(5)*]; or

(ii) the employee has not notified a date of return and there is an interruption of work, such as a strike, which renders it unreasonable to expect her to return to work, in which case the employee may return to work at any time before the end of the period of 28 days from the end of the interruption. [*EPCA s 47(6)*].

29.20 Remedies

If an employer fails to permit an employee on her notified date of return to exercise her right to return, she will be treated for the purposes of the provisions relating to unfair dismissal and redundancy as having been dismissed on that day for the reason for which she was not permitted to return. [*EPCA s 56*]. That reason may be acceptable or not according to the circumstances. If she is dismissed because another employee has been engaged in her position that will not be an acceptable reason for her dismissal. (*McFadden v Greater Glasgow Passenger Transport Executive* [*1977*] *IRLR 327*). If it is not practicable by reason of redundancy to permit a woman to return to work, and she is not offered suitable alternative employment by her employer or by an associated employer where a vacancy exists, she will be treated as unfairly dismissed. [*EPCA s 45(3), 2 Sch 2(2)*]. Apart from this and other provisions which automatically deem certain dismissals to be unfair (such as the provisions relating to dismissals for trade union activities or selection for redundancy in contravention of an agreed procedure), the question whether the dismissal was fair or unfair will depend on whether the employer can satisfy the tribunal that in the circumstances he would have been acting reasonably in treating the reason as a sufficient reason for dismissing the employee if she had not been absent from work. [*EPCA 2 Sch 2(1)*].

EPCA s 56 does not apply in relation to an employee if

(*a*) (i) immediately before her absence began the number of employees employed by her employer added to the number employed by any associated employer of his, did not exceed five; and

(ii) it is not reasonably practicable for the employer (who may be the same employer or a successor of his) to permit her to return to work in her previous job on no less favourable terms and conditions of employment than would have applied had she not been absent, or for him or an associated employer to offer her employment under a contract providing her with suitable work which it is appropriate for her to do in the circumstances and which is on terms not substantially less favourable than her previous employment

[*EPCA s 56A(1)(3)*];

or if

(*b*) (i) it is not reasonably practicable for a reason other than redundancy for the employer (who may be the same employer or a successor of his) to permit her to return to her previous job on no less favourable terms and conditions than would have applied if she had not been absent; and

(ii) he or an associated employer offers her employment under a contract of employment providing her with suitable work which it is appropriate for her to do in the circumstances and which is on terms not substantially less favourable than her previous employment; and

(iii) she accepts or unreasonably refuses that offer.

[*EPCA s 56A(2)(3)*].

It is for the employer to establish that he has satisfied these statutory defences. [*EPCA s 56A(4)*].

Once an industrial tribunal has come to the conclusion that a vacancy exists, it will not consider whether it was economic or reasonable to offer the vacancy to the employee (*Community Task Force v Rimmer [1986] ICR 491*).

For the purposes of claims for redundancy payments, the 'relevant date' in these circumstances will be the notified date of return (see 38.4 REDUNDANCY–I). [*EPCA 2 Sch 4(1)(a)*].

If an employee who is entitled to return to work, and whose contract of employment is still subsisting, is dismissed during her absence after the beginning of the eleventh week before the expected week of confinement, she is entitled to claim compensation for unfair dismissal. Such a dismissal does not affect the employee's right to return to work, but (*a*) compensation in any unfair dismissal proceedings arising out of that dismissal will be assessed without regard to the employee's right to return; and

(*b*) the right to return may be exercised only on her repaying any redundancy payment or compensation for unfair dismissal paid in respect of that dismissal, if the employer requests such repayment.

[*EPCA 2 Sch 6*].

The time limits for the presentation of complaints of unfair dismissal and redundancy are three and six months respectively beginning with the date deemed to be the effective date of termination or the relevant date.

It is reasonably practicable for an employee who knows of her rights but is undecided or changes her mind as to whether to exercise them, to present her claim within the time limit. (*Nu-Swift International Ltd v Mallinson [1979] ICR 157*). In that case the EAT decided that the guidance of the Court of Appeal, on the meaning of the words 'reasonably practicable' for the purposes of the time limit on unfair dismissal claims, indicates the kind of approach which the court should take and the factors which ought to be taken into account in relation to maternity rights.

See 29.18 above for the position where an employee has a right to return to work both under statute and by reason of the terms of her contract of employment.

29.21 Dismissal of replacement

Where an employer engages an employee to take the place of one who is absent due to pregnancy, the subsequent dismissal of that employee upon the return to work of the original employee will be considered to be a dismissal for a substantial reason (see 55.14 UNFAIR DISMISSAL - II) only if the employer informs the employee in writing, on engaging her, that her employment will be terminated on the return to work of another employee who is, or will be, absent wholly or partly because of pregnancy or confinement. [*EPCA s 61*]. However, this fact does not, in itself, make the dismissal fair. The industrial tribunal will consider whether the dismissal was fair in all the circumstances (see further 55.4 UNFAIR DISMISSAL - II).

30 Medical Suspension Payments

(See DE leaflet No. 5 'Suspension on medical grounds under health and safety regulations' (PL 705).)

30.1 Statutes and regulations safeguard workpeople from exposure to health hazards. They may provide, for example, that a factory be closed when the atmosphere in it becomes contaminated. Before 1 June 1976 when *Employment Protection Act 1975, s 29* came into effect, if a factory closed down in compliance with regulations relating to the health of the factory workers, the workers were not entitled to be paid for the time lost unless their contracts provided otherwise. However, now where an employee is suspended from work by his employer on medical grounds in compliance with any law or regulation concerning the health and safety of workers, he may be entitled to be paid remuneration by his employer while he is so suspended for a period not exceeding 26 weeks. The provision which leads to him being suspended must be one of those for the time being specified in *EPCA 1 Sch* [*EPCA s 19(1)*]. At present only the *Control of Lead at Work Regulations 1980 (SI 1980 No 1248), reg 16*, the *Ionising Radiations Regulations 1985 (SI 1985 No 1333)* and the *Control of Substances Hazardous to Health Regulations 1988 (SI 1988 No 1657), reg 11*, are so specified.

30.2 QUALIFYING CONDITIONS

An employee will be regarded as suspended from work only if, and so long as, he continues to be employed by his employer but is not provided with work or does not perform the work he normally performed before the suspension. [*EPCA s 19(2)*].

In order to be entitled to claim a medical suspension payment, the employee must have been continuously employed for a period of one month ending with the day before that on which the suspension begins. [*EPCA ss 20(1), 143(2); EA 1982, 2 Sch 2*].

An employee who is employed

(*a*) under a contract for a fixed term of three months or less; or

(*b*) under a contract made in contemplation of the performance of a specific task which is not expected to last for more than three months,

is not entitled to a medical suspension payment unless he has been continuously employed for a period of more than three months ending with the day before that on which the suspension begins. [*EPCA s 20(2); EA 1982, 2 Sch 2*].

30.3 EXCLUSIONS FROM RIGHT TO PAYMENT

(*a*) An employee will not be entitled to a medical suspension payment in respect of any period during which he is incapable of work by reason of disease or bodily or mental disablement. [*EPCA s 20(3); EA 1982, 2 Sch 2*].

(*b*) An employee is not entitled to a medical suspension payment in respect of any period during which (i) his employer offered to provide him with suitable alternative work, whether or not it was work the employee was engaged to perform, and (ii) the employee unreasonably refused to perform that work. [*EPCA s 20(4)(a); EA 1982, 2 Sch 2*]. If, for example, a man is engaged as a machine operator in the toolroom of a factory and the toolroom has to be closed for medical reasons for a few weeks, it may be considered unreasonable for the operative to refuse to work on a similar type of machine in a different part of the factory, provided he is offered the same rate of pay as that which he had previously received.

(*c*) An employee is not entitled to a medical suspension payment in respect of any period during which he did not comply with reasonable requirements imposed by his employer with a view to ensuring that his services were available. [*EPCA s 20(4)(b); EA 1982, 2 Sch 2*]. Therefore, if an employer sent a man home because his workplace was medically unsafe but asked him to telephone each day to find out whether his services were required, and the employee failed to do so, he may be deprived of his right to a medical suspension payment.

30.4 AMOUNT OF PAYMENT

The employee is entitled to a week's pay in respect of every week of suspension (with proportionate reduction for part of a week). [*EPCA s 21(1)*]. A week's pay is calculated in accordance with *EPCA 14 Sch* (see 'A WEEK'S PAY' (58)). If an employee is entitled to payment during suspension on medical grounds by a term of his contract, he will only be able to claim from the employer the additional amount by which his statutory entitlement exceeds the contractual entitlement. Any payment under a contract goes to discharge the statutory liability and vice versa. [*EPCA s 21(2)(3)*]. Thus, if an employee's week's pay is £130 and on suspension from work on medical grounds he is contractually entitled to £90, he can claim £40 as a statutory medical suspension payment.

30.5 REMEDY FOR FAILURE TO MAKE PAYMENT

If an employer fails to make a medical suspension payment, an employee may present a complaint to an industrial tribunal in respect of that payment. [*EPCA s 22(1)*].

The complaint must be presented to the tribunal within three months beginning with the day in respect of which the claim is made (or within such further period as the tribunal considers reasonable, in a case where it is satisfied that it was not reasonably practicable for the complaint to be presented within the period of three months). [*EPCA s 22(2)*].

Where an industrial tribunal finds a complaint well founded it will order the employer to pay the complainant the amount of remuneration which it finds is due to him. [*EPCA s 22(3)*].

31 Pay – I: Payments and Pay Statements

(See also DE booklets No. 8 'Itemised pay statement' (PL 704) and 'The law on payment of wages and deductions' (PL 810).)

Cross-references. See PAY – II (32) for statutory deductions from pay; EQUAL PAY (19) for the rules against sex discrimination in pay.

31.1 The rate of pay and the intervals at which payment is made are governed by the individual employee's contract of employment, which also provides for any bonuses, commission, overtime, holiday pay or sick pay which may be payable. Such matters must be included in the written particulars of the contract of employment given by the employer to the employee, see 10.4 CONTRACT OF EMPLOYMENT.

Since 1 January 1987 the relevant statute has been the *Wages Act 1986*, which regulates the deductions which may be made from employees' pay, and makes special provision for employees in retail employment. The *Wages Act 1986* supersedes the old *Truck Acts*. However, where the relevant contract of employment was made before 1 January 1987, it may still be necessary to have regard to the *Truck Act 1831* in relation to the method of payment (see 31.4 below).

The employee has a statutory right to an itemised pay statement (see 31.10 below).

31.2 PAYMENT OF WAGES: THE TRUCK ACTS

Until 1 January 1987 all wages payable to a manual labourer for work done by him, with certain exceptions, had to be paid to him in current coin of the realm or, if he so requested, by payment into a bank account, cheque, postal order or money order. [*Truck Act 1831, s 3; Payment of Wages Act 1960, s 1*]. Any agreement to the contrary was illegal, null and void. If an employer acted in breach of the *Truck Acts*, for example, by payment in kind by the delivery of goods, or by payment by cheque against the employee's wishes,

(*a*) the employee could sue for the wages due, no allowance being made for the value of the goods supplied; and

(*b*) the employer was guilty of an offence.

[*Truck Act 1831, s 9*].

A foreman did not fall within the protection of the *Truck Acts*. (*Brooker v Charrington Fuel Oils Ltd* [*1981*] *IRLR 147*).

31.3 Exceptions

(i) The provision of medicine or medical attendance, fuel materials, tools and accommodation could form part of the consideration for the employee's services. [*Truck Act 1831, s 23*].

(ii) Payments to domestic servants did not need to comply with the requirements as to payment in coin. [*Truck Act 1831, s 20*].

(iii) Contracts for the provision for agricultural workers of food, non-intoxicating drink, a cottage or other similar allowances or privileges were not illegal if money wages were paid in addition to these benefits. [*Truck Amendment Act 1887, s 4*].

31.4 PAYMENT OF WAGES : WAGES ACT 1986

All references in paragraphs 31.4-31.7 are to the *Wages Act 1986 (WA)* unless otherwise stated. *Section 11* removes restrictions on the way in which payment of wages to manual and other workers may be made. The method of payment is now to be determined by the contract. It will be either the subject of express agreement or determined by an implied term. If no express agreement is reached it is likely that the method of payment impliedly agreed will be that which is customary in the industry.

The new provisions replaced the old restrictions on the payment of wages contained in the *Truck Acts* and the *Payment of Wages Act 1960*. *Sec 11* came into force on 1 January 1987. [*The Wages Act 1986 (Commencement) Order 1986 (SI 1986 No 1998)*]. However, it is thought that, because *Sec 1* of the *Truck Act 1831* operated by implying into the contract of employment a term that wages were payable in coin and not otherwise, the contractual terms thus created survive the repeal of the Act. In other words, where the worker was employed before 1 January 1987, it remains necessary to refer to 31.2 and 31.3 above, but the requirement is now contractual rather than statutory and may be varied by consent.

31.5 DEDUCTIONS FROM WAGES: WAGES ACT 1986

No deduction from a worker's wages may be made unless either

(*a*) it is required or permitted by a statutory or contractual provision; or

(*b*) the worker has given his prior written consent to the deduction.

If the deduction is made pursuant to a contractual provision, the terms of the contract must have been shown to the worker or, if not in writing, its effect notified in writing to the worker before the deduction is made.

The above provisions do not apply to deductions

(*a*) made pursuant to any statutory disciplinary proceedings;

(*b*) which are statutory payments due to a public authority;

(*c*) payable to third parties, for example trade union dues, made either pursuant to a contractual term to whose inclusion the worker has agreed in writing, or otherwise with his prior written agreement or consent (but note that the employer is under a duty to ensure that no further union dues are paid after the employee certifies that his membership of the union has terminated – *EA 1988, s 7*);

(*d*) made from a worker's wages for taking part in a strike or other industrial action.

[*Sec 1*].

'Deductions' are very broadly defined by *Sec 8(3)* to include any failure to pay the amount properly due, other than when the deficiency is attributable to an error of computation.

31.6 DEDUCTIONS FROM WAGES OF, AND RECEIPT OF PAYMENTS FROM, WORKERS IN RETAIL EMPLOYMENT

Special provisions of the *WA* apply to deductions from the wages of workers in retail employment and to payments by such workers, on account of cash shortages or stock deficiences. Retail employment is defined as employment involving the carrying out by workers of retail transactions – the sale or supply of goods, or the supply of services (including financial services) – directly with members of the public. [*Sec 2(2)*].

The employer of a worker in retail employment may not deduct for cash shortages or stock deficiencies more than one-tenth of gross wages payable to the worker on a particular pay day. [*Sec 2(1)*]. The employer must make such a deduction not more than twelve months after the date when he discovered or ought reasonably to have discovered the shortage or deficiency. [*Sec 2(3)*].

If such a worker's pay is calculated by reference to cash shortages or stock deficiencies, the difference between the payment made when there are shortages and when there are not is treated as a deduction and the difference may not be more than one-tenth on any pay day. [*Sec 2(4)*].

In addition, the employer of a worker in retail employment may not receive from the worker any payment on account of a cash shortage or stock deficiency, unless certain requirements are met. The employer must

(*a*) notify the worker in writing of his total liability to him in respect of that shortage or deficiency;

(*b*) make a demand for payment which is

- (i) in writing; and
- (ii) on a pay day.

[*Sec 3(1)(2)*].

The demand must be made not earlier than the first pay day on or after the date of the written notification, and not later than twelve months after the date when the employer discovered or ought reasonably to have discovered the shortage or deficiency. [*Sec 3(3)*].

The amount demanded on a particular pay day must not exceed one-tenth of the gross wages remaining after any deductions on account of cash shortages or stock deficiencies. [*Sec 3(4)*].

The restriction of deductions to one-tenth of gross wages (and the requirements referred to in (*a*) and (*b*) above) do not apply to deductions made from the final payment of wages. Nor does *Sec 3* apply to payments made after the final payment of wages. [*Sec 4*]. However, after the twelve-month time limit referred to above has expired, the employer may neither receive payments (even after the final payment of wages), nor bring legal proceedings for recovery without first having made a demand in accordance with *Sec 3* within that time limit. [*Sec 4(3)(4)*].

Even if legal proceedings are taken against a worker still in retail employment, a court which finds him liable to pay sums in respect of a shortage or deficiency must make provision so that the rate of payment does not exceed that at which the employer could recover under *Sec 3*. [*Sec 4(5)*].

31.7 REMEDIES

The worker's remedy for breach by his employer of the statutory provisions outlined above is to present a complaint to an industrial tribunal. A complaint may be made that

(*a*) an unauthorised deduction has been made contrary to *Sec 1(1)*;

(*b*) an unauthorised payment has been received by the employer contrary to *Sec 1(2)* or *3(1)*;

(*c*) deductions exceeding the limit set by *Sec 2(1)* have been made;

(*d*) the employer has received more than the limit set by *Sec 3(4)*.

[*WA s 5(1)*].

The time limit for presenting a complaint to an industrial tribunal under *WA* is three months beginning with the date of the deduction or the receipt of which complaint is made. The tribunal has jurisdiction to extend the time limit where it is satisfied that it was not reasonably practicable for the complaint to be presented within the relevant period of three months.

Where a series of deductions or payments are made, in certain circumstances, the time limit runs from the date of the last payment. [*Sec 5(3)*].

Where an industrial tribunal finds that a complaint under *Sec 5* is well-founded, it will make a declaration to that effect and, where an unlawful deduction or payment has been made, will order the employer to pay (or, as the case may be, repay) to the worker the amount of the deduction or payment. [*Sec 5(4)*].

If the provisions of *WA* have been satisfied in respect of an amount less than the deduction, the employer will be ordered to pay the worker the difference between the amount actually deducted and that which could lawfully have been deducted. [*Sec 5(5)*].

In making the order the tribunal will take into account payments or repayments already made to the worker. [*Sec 5(6)*].

Where a tribunal has ordered an employer to pay or repay a worker any amount (the relevant amount), the amount which the employer is entitled to recover in respect of the matter which gave rise to the deduction or payment (including cash shortages or stock deficiencies) is reduced by the relevant amount. [*Sec 5(7)(8)*].

Where an order is made under *WA s 5* and *EPCA s 11* (see 32.14 below) the aggregate of the amount ordered to be paid by the employer to the worker will not exceed the amount of the deduction. [*Sec 6(2)*].

Parties cannot, by agreement, exclude or limit the operation of *Sec 5* except where agreement has been reached to refrain from presenting or continuing with a complaint where a conciliation officer has taken action in accordance with *Sec 133(2)* or *(3)* of *EPCA*. [*Sec 6(3)*].

These provisions do not apply to employment where under his contract the person employed ordinarily works outside Great Britain. [*Sec 30(1)*].

31.8 OTHER DEDUCTIONS FROM WAGES

In *Sim v Rotherham Metropolitan Borough Council* [1986] *ICR 897* it was held that the principle of equitable set-off applied to contracts of employment. In other words, where an employee's breach of contract has caused the employer loss, the employer is in principle entitled to retain for himself sums representing the amount of that loss when he pays the employee's wages. This saves the employer from paying the full wage and suing for damages for breach of contract. However, the court retains a discretion to disallow the set-off.

The leading authority on the employer's right to make deductions from wages where the employee refuses to carry out all his contractual duties is now the decision of the House of Lords in *Miles v Wakefield Metropolitan District Council [1987] ICR 368*. A superintendent registrar with a normal working week of 37 hours, including 3 hours on Saturday mornings, took industrial action and refused to conduct weddings on Saturdays. He worked normally during the rest of the week. It was held that the council was entitled to deduct 3/37ths from his normal salary, even though the registrar would have been willing to perform duties other than the conduct of weddings on Saturdays (in fact the council instructed him to work normally or not at all).

Lord Brightman and Lord Templeman took the view that a worker not performing the full range of his contractual duties was not entitled to his full wages, but to a *quantum meruit* payment based upon the value of the work actually done. An employer placed in such a position must make it clear to the employee that he is not waiving that employee's breach of contract in failing to perform the full range of his contractual duties. He should state that whilst the breach continues, he will make a specified adjustment to the employee's wages. However, an employer cannot be *compelled* to accept and pay for something significantly less than the efficient performance of all the employee's contractual duties. (*MacPherson v London Borough of Lambeth [1988] IRLR 470*). In *Wiluszynski v London Borough of Tower Hamlets [1989] IRLR 259* the Court of Appeal, dealing with a council employee who had refused to perform a material part of his duties, held that the council was entitled to withhold the whole of his pay. This decision was arrived at only because the council had clearly informed the employee that if he attempted to undertake limited work, he would not be paid for it.

31.9 OVERPAYMENT

If an employer makes an overpayment of wages under a mistake of fact, and the employee is led to believe that he can treat the overpaid money as his own, and in reliance on that representation has spent some of it, the employer cannot recover the sum overpaid. (*Avon County Council v Howlett [1983] 1 WLR 605*).

31.10 ITEMISED PAY STATEMENTS

An employer must give any employee of his, at or before the time at which any payment of wages or salary is made to him, a pay statement in writing containing the following particulars

(*a*) the gross amount of the wages or salary;

(*b*) the amounts of any variable and any fixed deductions from that gross amount and the purposes for which they are made, unless a statement of fixed deductions has been given to the employee (see 31.11 below);

(*c*) the net amount of wages or salary payable;

(*d*) where different parts of the net amount are paid in different ways, the amount and method of payment of each part payment.

[*EPCA s 8*].

Tips paid by customers to a waiter in a restaurant were held not to be wages within the meaning of *EPCA s 8*, and his employers were therefore not required to give particulars of such tips or of payments from them to the manager of the restaurant. (*Cofone v Spaghetti House Ltd* [*1980*] *ICR 155*).

31.11 **Statement of fixed deductions**

Provided that the employer has given in writing a standing statement of fixed deductions, there is no need to itemise fixed deductions on an employee's pay statement, but simply to state the total amount of the deductions. This standing statement should give the following information

(*a*) the amount of each deduction;

(*b*) the intervals at which the deduction is to be made; and

(*c*) the purpose for which it is made.

[*EPCA s 9(1)*].

A statement of fixed deductions may be amended, whether by addition of a new deduction or by a change in the particulars or cancellation of an existing deduction, by notice in writing containing particulars of the amendment given by the employer to the employee. [*EPCA s 9(2)*].

It must be remembered that a standing statement of fixed deductions only remains effective for twelve months from the date on which it is given to the employee. Before the expiry of the twelve-month period, the employer must re-issue the statement, together with any amendments, in consolidated form. [*EPCA s 9(3)*].

31.12 **Exclusions**

The requirement for an employer to provide an employee with a pay statement does not apply

(*a*) to persons engaged in police service [*EPCA s 146(2)*];

(*b*) where the employee is engaged under a contract of employment which involves work for less than 16 hours weekly, unless he works 8 hours or more but less than 16 hours and has been continuously employed for 5 years or more [*EPCA s 146(4)(7)*];

(*c*) to employment as a merchant seaman, or as a master or member of the crew of a fishing vessel where the employee is remunerated only by a share in the profits or gross earnings of the vessel [*EPCA s 144(2)(4)*];

(*d*) where the employee ordinarily works outside Great Britain [*EPCA s 141(2)*].

31.13 **APPLICATION TO AN INDUSTRIAL TRIBUNAL**

If an employer does not give any employee of his a pay statement, the employee may refer the matter to an industrial tribunal to determine what particulars ought to have been included in a statement so as to comply with the requirements in 32.10 above. [*EPCA s 11(1)*]. An employee may also apply to a tribunal, as may an employer, to determine provisions which should have been included in a pay statement or a standing statement of fixed deductions, but which have been omitted. [*EPCA s 11(2)(b)*].

Any application concerning a pay statement must be brought while the employee is still employed by the relevant employer, or within three months of the date on which the employment ceased. [*EPCA s 11(9)*].

31.14 **Tribunal order**

Where, on a reference under these provisions, an industrial tribunal finds that an employer has failed to give an employee a pay statement or that a pay statement or standing statement of fixed deductions does not, in relation to a deduction, contain the particulars required to be included in that statement, the tribunal will make a declaration to that effect.

Where the tribunal further finds that any unnotified deductions have been made from the pay of the employee during the period of 13 weeks immediately preceding the date of the application (whether or not such deductions were made in breach of the contract of employment), the tribunal may order the employer to pay the employee a sum not exceeding the aggregate of the unnotified deductions so made. [*EPCA s 11(8)*].

For example, an employee may be required by his contract of employment to pay subscriptions to a sports club of £1.00 per week. If the employer does not notify the employee of this deduction, either in a note with his pay packet or in a statement of fixed deductions, then, on an application to an industrial tribunal, the tribunal may order the employer to repay the employee a sum of up to £13, which is equivalent to the employee's subscriptions for the previous 13 weeks.

In *Milsom v Leicestershire County Council [1978] IRLR 433*, an industrial tribunal held that an employer was in breach of the requirement to give an itemised pay statement. A sum had been deducted from the employee's wages, the only explanation being that it was a 'miscellaneous deduction/payment'. The tribunal ordered the employer to pay £25 to the employee for the failure to give a proper statement, despite the fact that the employee was well aware of the reason for the deduction and that the employer was entitled under the contract between the parties to make such a deduction.

However, in *Scott v Creager [1979] ICR 403*, the EAT held that where an employer had made unnotified deductions, an industrial tribunal had not erred in awarding a sum to the employee equal to the amount by which the pay she actually received fell short of the net pay she should have received.

31.15 PAY ON TERMINATION OF EMPLOYMENT

Upon termination of employment, an employer should pay to the former employee any of the following sums which may be due, depending upon the circumstances: wages in lieu of notice; accrued holiday pay; reimbursement of expenses; other contractual payments; redundancy pay.

32 Pay – II: Attachment of Earnings

32.1 An *attachment of earnings order* is a means of enforcing a court order that a person must pay a sum of money. The order is made by the court and operates as an instruction to that person's employer to deduct sums from his earnings and pay them directly to the court office. The employer must also notify the court of certain matters. The *Attachment of Earnings Act 1971 (AEA)* sets out the obligations of employers and the methods of calculating the deductions.

An attachment of earnings order may be made by a court if it appears to it that a person has failed, or is likely to fail, to pay in a satisfactory way sums due from him. Orders may be made for the payment of

(*a*) **maintenance**

(i) if under a High Court maintenance order, an attachment of earnings order may be made in the High Court or the county court;

(ii) if under a county court maintenance order, an order may be made in the county court;

(iii) if under a magistrates' court maintenance order, an order may be made in a magistrates' court;

(*b*) **judgment debts exceeding £5** – county court;

(*c*) **payments under an administration order** (dealing with a number of debts owed by the same person) – county court;

(*d*) **payment of any sum ordered to be paid on conviction** or treated as so ordered to be paid, e.g. a fine or compensation order – magistrates' court;

(*e*) **payment under a legal aid contribution order** – magistrates' court.

[*AEA s 1(1)-(3)*].

The person who is obliged to make the deduction is the employer. No obligation rests on someone who as servant or agent makes payments to the employee. [*AEA s 6(2)*].

32.2 EARNINGS FROM WHICH THE DEDUCTIONS ARE MADE

Earnings, for the purposes of attachment of earnings, include wages or salary together with bonuses, commission, overtime pay and other emoluments payable under a contract of employment in addition to wages or salary. Pensions, annuities and compensation for loss of office are also included as is statutory sick pay. [*AEA s 24(1) as amended by Social Security Act 1985, s 21, 4 Sch 1; Social Security Act 1986, 10 Sch 102*].

The following payments are not taken into account

(*a*) income payable by any public department of a territory outside the United Kingdom;

(*b*) pay or allowances payable to the debtor as a member of Her Majesty's forces;

(*c*) pensions, allowances or benefits payable under any social security enactment;

(*d*) pensions or allowances payable in respect of disablement or disability;

(*e*) except in relation to a maintenance order, wages payable to a person as a seaman, other than wages payable to him as a seaman of a fishing boat.

[*AEA s 24(2); Merchant Shipping Act 1979, s 39*].

In order to determine whether payments made by him are earnings, an employer may apply to the court which made the order. [*AEA s 16(1)(2)*]. While such an application, or an appeal from the finding on such an application, is pending, an employer will not incur any liability for non-compliance with the order to which the application relates. [*AEA s 16(3)*].

32.3 DEDUCTIONS FROM PAY

Where an employer receives an attachment of earnings order which relates to one of his employees, he must make such deductions from his employee's pay as are specified in the order. [*AEA s 6*].

The court may use the following terms.

'*Attachable earnings*': that part of the employee's earnings to which an attachment of earnings order applies (usually income after statutory deduction).

'*Normal deductions*': the sum to be deducted from the employee's income on each pay day.

'*Protected earnings*': the earnings below which no deduction may be made.

32.4 Calculating the deduction

If an attachment of earnings order is made, then the employer must, on pay day

(*a*) if the attachable earnings are greater than the protected earnings,

  (i) make the normal deduction; and

  (ii) deduct any *arrears* still outstanding;

(*b*) if the attachable earnings are equal to or less than the protected earnings, take no action (but the arrears are increased by the amount due).

[*AEA 3 Sch Pt I*].

Example. Bill Jones earns, on average, £90 per week after tax, national insurance, etc. but because he is on piece work his weekly earnings may vary. The court has ordered him to pay £300 at a *normal deduction rate* of £15 per week, and has decided that his *protected earnings rate* is to be £60 (in other words he will always be allowed to take home £60, provided that he earns that much).

The following table shows his pay, and the deductions over a five-week period.

Week no.	Attachable earnings	Deductions under the order	Take home	Comments
	£	£	£	
1	90	15	75	Normal deduction
2	95	15	80	Normal deduction
3	70	10	60	Only £10 deducted, Jones takes home his protected earnings

Week no.	Attachable earnings	Deductions under the order	Take home	Comments
	£	£	£	
4	95	20	75	Normal deduction plus £5 of arrears
5	100	15	85	Normal deduction

32.5 Priority of orders

Where there are two or more orders in existence, which are not to secure either the payment of judgment debts or payments under an administration order, then the employer must deal first with the first in time and apply the residue of the debtor's earnings over and above his protected earnings to subsequent orders, dealing with them in date order. Where there are several types of orders in existence, those to satisfy judgment debts or administration orders must be dealt with after the rest. [*AEA 3 Sch Pt II paras 7, 8*].

32.6 Time limits

It should be noted that the following notices should be complied with, within seven days

(*a*) an attachment of earnings order [*AEA s 7(1)*];

(*b*) a variation [*AEA s 9(2)*];

(*c*) a notice of cessation or discharge [*AEA s 12(3)*].

32.7 EMPLOYER'S OBLIGATIONS TO NOTIFY COURT

An employer must notify the relevant court as follows.

(*a*) Where a person is served with an attachment of earnings order directed to him and the debtor is not in his employment, *or subsequently ceases to be in his employment*, he must within ten days give notice of that fact to the court. [*AEA s 7(2)*].

(*b*) If the court orders him to do so, the employer must give the court, within a specified period, a statement signed by him or on his behalf of the debtor's earnings and anticipated earnings. [*AEA s 14(1)(b)*].

(*c*) If he *becomes* the debtor's employer and knows that the order is in force and by what court it was made, he must within seven days of his becoming the debtor's employer or acquiring that knowledge (whichever is the later) notify that court in writing that he is the debtor's employer and include in his notification a statement of the debtor's earnings and anticipated earnings. [*AEA s 15(c)*].

32.8 PENALTIES FOR NON-COMPLIANCE

If an employer, required to comply with any of the above provisions relating to deductions or notice, fails to do so, he may be liable on conviction in a magistrates' court to a fine of not more than level 2 on the standard scale (see 1.10 INTRODUCTION) or he may be fined up to £100 by a judge of the High Court or the county court. [*AEA s 23, as amended*]. Furthermore, if he gives a notice or makes any statement on these matters which he knows to be false in a material particular then, in addition to being fined, he may be imprisoned for not more than 14 days.

It will be a defence for an employer to prove

(*a*) that he took all reasonable steps to comply with the attachment of earnings order; or

(*b*) that he did not know and could not reasonably be expected to know that the debtor was not in his employment, or had ceased to be so, and that he gave the required notice as soon as reasonably practicable after that fact came to his knowledge.

[*AEA s 23(5)*].

32.9 OTHER MATTERS

Clerical costs. When an employer makes a deduction in compliance with an order from an employee's earnings, he is entitled to deduct 50p (or such sum as is currently applicable) for clerical and administration costs. [*AEA s 7(4)(a); SI 1980 No 558*]. The employer must give the employee a statement in writing of the deduction. [*AEA s 7(4)(b)*].

Pay statements. The employee must be given a pay statement showing, among other things, deductions from his pay. An employer need not, on each occasion upon which a payment of wages is made, give separate particulars of a fixed deduction. It is sufficient if he supplies a statement of the aggregate amount of fixed deductions having supplied a standing statement in writing of fixed deduction stating

(*a*) the amount of the deduction; and

(*b*) the intervals at which the deduction is to be made; and

(*c*) the purpose for which it is made.

[*EPCA ss 8, 9*]. (See further 31.10 PAY – I.)

If an employer requires advice or information concerning an attachment of earnings order or subsequent procedures he should contact the court where the order was made.

33 Pay As You Earn (PAYE)

[*ICTA 1988, s 203; Income Tax (Employments) Regulations (SIs 1973 No 334; 1974 No 2102; 1975 No 728; 1976 Nos 381, 950; 1977 No 700; 1978 Nos 326, 1196; 1979 No 747; 1980 No 505; 1981 Nos 44, 1648; 1982 Nos 1, 66; 1984 No 1858; 1985 No 350; 1986 No 2212; 1988 No 637)*].

33.1 GENERAL OUTLINE

Definition and earnings limits

PAYE is the statutory system of deducting income tax from the emoluments (widely defined) of an employee at the time they are paid by the employer so as to secure, as far as possible, that the income tax liability in respect of the emoluments is satisfied by the deductions made. In addition, the PAYE system collects National Insurance contributions of both employee and employer. The PAYE system applies to all payments of emoluments assessable to income tax under Schedule E in excess of certain defined limits. These limits (the 'PAYE thresholds') are as laid down from time to time by the Inland Revenue. For a person with one employment only, the PAYE threshold is broadly aligned with the weekly/monthly equivalent of the single person's allowance for income tax.

33.2 Source of information

Detailed instructions on the operation of PAYE are contained in the Inland Revenue booklet 'Employer's Guide to PAYE' (P 7) and supplements issued from time to time. This guide is provided to all operators of PAYE as a matter of course, but additional copies may be obtained from any tax office. The guide complements the general PAYE instructions which accompany documents (see 33.3 below) sent to employers prior to 6 April each year.

33.3 Method of deduction

Employers are provided with (amongst other documents) a deductions working sheet (P 11(New)) for each employee known to be earning amounts above the PAYE threshold. Special arrangements can be made instead for employers with computerised payrolls etc., by providing a list of employees and their codes. The code shown on the deductions working sheet (or list) determines the appropriate amount of tax to be deducted from that employee's wages. The calculation of tax due is made on the deductions working sheet from tax tables provided by the Inland Revenue; alternatively, such computations can be done by and stored in computer installations where computerised payrolls are in operation.

Approved superannuation contributions are deducted from the gross pay before calculation of tax due.

33.4 SPECIAL SITUATIONS

Employees joining after 6 April

(*a*) *Employees holding form P 45 from previous employer.* The form P 45 will show details of cumulative pay and tax paid to the date of leaving the last employment, and the employee's code. These figures are entered on a deductions working sheet for the employee and the normal procedure is followed from the first pay day in the new employment with these figures incorporated into the cumulative totals on that day. Where a refund of tax falls to be made, specific authority must be sought from the Tax Office if this repayment exceeds £50.

(*b*) *New employees, with no form P 45, earning in excess of the PAYE threshold (including existing employees earning over this threshold for the first time).* The employer must operate the code specified for Emergency use on the non-cumulative (Week or Month 1) basis until he is notified by the tax office of the correct code. The employer must notify the tax office as soon as possible after taking on such new employees. Employees taking up employment for the first time following full-time education are dealt with on a cumulative, rather than non-cumulative, Emergency coding basis. On the other hand, employees having other employment should have basic rate tax deducted from earnings. In either case, deductions must continue to be made on the appropriate basis until the correct code is notified.

33.5 Employee leaving or dismissed

The employer must send to the tax office form P 45, giving details of the employee's total pay to date and tax deducted therefrom. The employee is given two copies of this form which he should pass over to his new employer, or if unemployed, to the Unemployment Benefit Office dealing with his benefit claim.

Pay in lieu of notice. Where an employee is dismissed with pay in lieu of notice, the payment in lieu is probably not taxable unless the contract of employment contains an express term conferring a right to such a payment. In the normal case, therefore, tax is not deductible under PAYE. (For further details, see 49.11 TERMINATION OF EMPLOYMENT.)

33.6 Employee retiring on pension from employer

The employer must notify the tax office within 14 days and continue operating the code but on the non-cumulative basis until revised instructions are received from the tax office. However, if the pension is to be paid by the trustees of a pension scheme etc., the employee should be treated as leaving (see 33.5 above).

33.7 Employee dies

The employer must send to the tax office all three copies of form P 45, completed as in 33.5 above, and in addition tell the tax office the name and address of the deceased employee's personal representative, if known.

33.8 Students employed during vacations

The general rules apply, except that under certain arrangements the tax office may notify the employer that tax need not be deducted. These arrangements require a signed statement from the student and a declaration on form P 38(S) by the employer, following which the tax office will notify that a deductions working sheet need only be prepared for national insurance purposes.

33.9 Employees working abroad

Special provisions apply which are detailed in the 'Employer's Guide to PAYE'. Because of the complexities involved, reference to the Tax Office is essential, and it may often be advisable to obtain professional advice in particular cases.

33.10 **Refunds of tax when employee is away from work**

Because of the cumulative nature of the PAYE system, periods during which no emoluments are received may give rise to a right to repayments of tax. In the case of such an absence, e.g. unpaid leave, a repayment may be made by the employer to the employee. This procedure is unlikely to apply to short absences caused by sickness since, from 6 April 1983, the statutory sick pay (see 46.6 SICKNESS AND SICK PAY) required to be paid by an employer is taxable in the usual way. Tax is also chargeable on any payment made by the employer (or by a third party under arrangements made by the employer) through a sick pay scheme.

An employer must not refund tax to an employee who is absent from work in consequence of a trade dispute in which the employee is involved, until the dispute has ended.

Where an employee becomes unemployed (see 33.5 above) and claims unemployment benefit or income support, any tax refund due to him will be made by the Unemployment Benefit Office or DHSS office. However, because these benefits are taxable, payment of any refund will be withheld until the person obtains a new job or, if earlier, until the end of the tax year.

33.11 PAYMENT OF TAX BY EMPLOYER

The employer must pay to the Collector of Taxes, within 14 days of the end of every tax month, all tax and national insurance contributions deducted (net of any refund of tax properly made) and the employer's national insurance contributions, less any gross statutory sick pay (see 46.6 SICKNESS AND SICK PAY). A single remittance is sufficient although a breakdown of the payment, as between income tax and national insurance contributions, is required. Failure to remit amounts due may result in proceedings for recovery against the employer.

33.12 END OF YEAR PROCEDURE

(*a*) *Employee's certificates.* The employer must give each employee in office on 5 April a certificate (P 60 or P 60 (substitute)), showing the following details: the tax year to which the certificate applies, total taxable emoluments, net tax deducted, the code in use on 5 April, the employer's PAYE reference, the employee's name and national insurance number, and the employer's name and address.

In the case of an employee engaged after 6 April, the certificate should include details of pay and tax of the previous employment, insofar as they were taken into account in computing the tax due under this employment.

(*b*) *Returns.* Within 14 days of the end of the tax year, the employer must give to the Collector the End of Year Return (P 14 or substitute) which for each employee (including any employee who has left during the year) gives details of the total emoluments, total net tax deducted, and National Insurance contributions together with amounts of any statutory sick pay (see 33.10 and 33.11 above) included in total emoluments. This form must be accompanied by a covering certificate on form P 35, containing a declaration and statement by the employer.

In addition, details must be given of all emoluments paid otherwise than in money, payments made on behalf of an employee and not repaid, and emoluments paid during the tax year but relating to a different tax year. Within 30 days of the end of the tax year, the employer must give to the

Collector details of expenses payments to, sums put at the disposal of and paid away by, and expenses incurred in providing benefits for, employees who are directors or whose remuneration is at the rate of £8,500 a year or more. Directors who have no material interest in the company (i.e. an interest not exceeding 5% control) are treated solely as employees if either they are full-time working directors or the company is non-profit-making (see 3.2 BENEFITS IN KIND).

Value added tax paid, if any, must be included in the above details of payments etc., even though such tax may have been refunded to the employer.

33.13 RECORDS

All records which the PAYE regulations require the employer to maintain, but not to send to the Revenue, must be retained for not less than three years after the end of the year to which they relate.

34 Picketing

(See the Department of Employment Code of Practice: Picketing, reproduced in full in the Appendix.)

Cross-reference. See STRIKES AND INDUSTRIAL ACTION (47) for general rules relating to industrial action.

34.1 THE RIGHT TO PICKET

If it were not for certain statutory immunities, a person who pickets or who organises picketing would normally be liable to an action in tort. Any successful picket can be expected to involve the *prima facie* commission of the torts of inducing a breach of contract or of interference with contract by unlawful means (see *Union Traffic Ltd v Transport and General Workers Union* [*1989*] *ICR 98*). Picketing may also involve the torts of nuisance and intimidation (especially if it is mass picketing), or of trespass (see *Mersey Dock & Harbour Co v Verrinder* [*1982*] *IRLR 152, Thomas v National Union of Mineworkers (South Wales Area)* [*1985*] *ICR 886, News Group Newspapers Ltd v SOGAT (1982)* [*1987*] *ICR 181*). As well as individuals, trade unions may be liable in tort for unlawful picketing, provided that certain conditions are satisfied. [*EA 1982, s 15*; see 51.8 TRADE UNIONS–I]. The statutory immunity for picketing is contained in the *Trade Union and Labour Relations Act 1974 (TULRA), s 15* as substituted by the *Employment Act 1980, s 16* and amended by the *Employment Act 1982, s 12*. 'Picketing' is not defined. To enjoy statutory immunity from an action in tort, a person must be picketing

(*a*) in contemplation or furtherance of a trade dispute; *and*

(*b*) at a specified place, namely

- (i) at or near his own place of work; or
- (ii) if he is unemployed and either his last employment was terminated in connection with a trade dispute or if the termination was one of the circumstances giving rise to a trade dispute, at or near his former place of work; or
- (iii) if he does not work at any one place or if the place is in a location such that attendance there for picketing is impracticable, at any premises of his employer from which he works or from which his work is administered; or
- (iv) if he is an *official of a trade union*, at or near the place of work or former place of work of a member of that union whom he is accompanying and whom he represents; *and*

(*c*) for the purpose only of peacefully obtaining or communicating information or peacefully persuading any person to work or abstain from working.

Any person who pickets outside these limits will lose the immunity from actions in tort. Accordingly, he will be liable to a claim for an injunction and/or damages if, in the course of such picketing, he commits a tort. A picket who does not have immunity under *TULRA s 15* also does not enjoy the more general immunity conferred on acts done in contemplation or furtherance of a trade dispute which interfere with the performance of contracts conferred by *TULRA s 13* (see *TULRA s 15* and 47.2 STRIKES AND INDUSTRIAL ACTION).

The definition of a trade dispute in *TULRA s 29* has been limited by *EA 1982, s 18* so that now it only covers disputes between workers and *their employer* relating wholly or mainly to one or more of the matters set out in *Sec 29* (see 47.3 STRIKES AND INDUSTRIAL ACTION).

The purpose of condition (*b*) above is to remove the immunity from 'flying pickets'. The Court of Appeal has considered its effects in two recent cases. In *Union Traffic Ltd v Transport and General Workers Union [1989] ICR 98* it was held that lorry drivers were not entitled to picket depots at which they frequently called for deliveries, repairs and the like, because they were not the bases from which the drivers worked. In *Rayware Ltd v Transport and General Workers Union [1989] IRLR 134* a gate leading to a private trading estate but some way from the employer's premises on that estate was 'near' the place of work as a matter of common sense since it was the nearest the pickets could get to their place of work without committing a trespass.

In addition, even if picketing falls within conditions (*a*)-(*c*) above, the pickets will only enjoy immunity under *TULRA s 13* if

(A) their actions do not constitute secondary industrial action within the meaning of *EA 1980, s 17(2)*; or

(B) their actions do constitute secondary action, but either

   (i) the pickets are employed, or if unemployed were last employed, by a party to the trade dispute; or

   (ii) they are trade union officials whose attendance is lawful by reason of (*b*)(iv) above.

[*EA 1980, s 17(5)*].

Inducing a breach of contract etc. EA 1982, s 14 removes statutory immunity from actions in tort from individuals who induce (or attempt to induce) another to incorporate a term in a contract to which the other is a party requiring union membership or recognition, or to exclude a person from a list of suppliers or to terminate a contract of supply on the grounds of union membership. (These provisions are dealt with fully in 47.6 STRIKES AND INDUSTRIAL ACTION.) Thus, for example, picketing which constituted an attempt, whether successful or not, to induce the employer to terminate a contract of supply of goods on the grounds of union membership would lose the pickets the immunity of *TULRA s 13*, even though it was within the provisions of *TULRA s 15*.

The Secretary of State for Employment has, under the power conferred on him by *EA 1980, s 3*, issued a Code of Practice on picketing (see CODES OF PRACTICE (7)). Breach of the Code does not give rise to any liability but the Code will be taken into account in any proceedings concerning picketing. One of the most notable provisions of the Code is that, in general, the number of pickets should not exceed six at any entrance to a workplace. (See Code of Practice: Picketing, para 31, in the Appendix.)

It remains to be seen whether *articles 10 and 11* of the EUROPEAN CONVENTION ON HUMAN RIGHTS (21), which deal with freedom of expression and assembly, have any impact upon the law relating to picketing.

34.2 Broome's case

In *Broome v Director of Public Prosecutions [1974] ICR 84*, the defendant, a picket during an industrial dispute, stood holding a placard in front of a vehicle on a highway, urging the driver not to go to a nearby site and preventing him from so doing for some nine minutes. The Divisional Court reversed the decision of the Stockport magistrates acquitting the defendant and convicted him of obstructing the highway. The House of Lords affirmed the conviction. The law which their Lordships had to consider was *Industrial Relations Act 1971, s 134* (which was framed, for these purposes, in similar terms to the present *TULRA s 15*). Lord Reid said of the defendant's conduct (at p 89)

> '. . . his attendance there is only made lawful by subsection (2) if he attended only for the purpose of obtaining or communicating information or "peacefully persuading" the lorry driver. Attendance for that purpose must I think include the right to try to persuade anyone who chooses to stop and listen, at least in so far as this is done in a reasonable way with due consideration for the rights of others. A right to attend for the purpose of peaceful persuasion would be meaningless unless this were implied.
>
> But I see no ground for implying any right to require the person whom it is sought to persuade to submit to any kind of constraint or restriction of his personal freedom.'

Lord Salmon made similar observations.

Thus, police officers acted within their powers when they prevented pickets from approaching a lorry carrying 'strike breakers' during an industrial dispute because they feared an obstruction or a breach of the peace. (*Kavanagh v Hiscock [1974] ICR 282*).

34.3 CRIMINAL LIABILITY

Action taken by pickets may give rise to criminal liability. For example, if pickets are guilty of assaults or commit nuisances they may be prosecuted under the *Conspiracy and Protection of Property Act 1875*, which provides (in *Sec 7(4)*) that a person who: 'Watches or besets the house or other place where such other person resides, or works, or carries on business, or happens to be, or the approach to such house or place' shall, on summary conviction, be liable to a fine not exceeding level 2 on the standard scale, or up to three months' imprisonment. [*Conspiracy and Protection of Property Act 1875, s 7(4); Criminal Justice Act 1982, ss 37, 46;* see 1.10 INTRODUCTION]. Other criminal charges for assault, criminal damage and offences under the *Public Order Act 1986* (especially *ss 1-5*) may arise if the pickets behave unlawfully. In such cases *TULRA s 15* cannot provide them with a defence. *Public Order Act 1986 Part II* gives the police certain powers to impose conditions upon public processions and assemblies, in addition to their common law powers to take such action as may be necessary to prevent a breach of the peace.

34.4 Obstructing the highway

Any action which does not fall within the provisions of *TULRA s 15* constitutes an offence if the obstruction takes place on the public highway, since the *Highways Act 1980, s 137(1)* provides

> 'If a person, without lawful authority or excuse, in any way wilfully obstructs the free passage along a highway he is guilty of an offence . . .'

For the definition of obstruction, see *Cooper v Metropolitan Police Commissioner (1985) 82 Cr App R 238*. However, picketing may take place outside factory gates which are on private property. In such a case, the pickets cannot be guilty of obstructing the highway but may be liable for a private trespass.

34.5 REDRESS AVAILABLE

If an employer believes that unlawful picketing is taking place outside his premises he may

(*a*) call upon the ADVISORY, CONCILIATION AND ARBITRATION SERVICE (2) to conciliate; and/or

(*b*) if the action is outside the provisions of *TULRA s 15*

(i) apply to the High Court for an injunction to prevent the continuance of the unlawful action; and/or

(ii) issue proceedings to claim damages; and/or

(*c*) if the pickets are obstructing the highway, or endangering persons or property, call the police.

Note that *TULRA s 17(1)* requires that any application for an injunction must be brought to the attention of the other party if it seems likely that he may claim that he is acting in contemplation or furtherance of a trade dispute. Unless the court is satisfied that all reasonable steps have been taken, an injunction will not be granted. In deciding whether or not to grant the injunction, a court will have regard to the likelihood of the defendant succeeding in establishing a defence, for example, lawful picketing under *TULRA s 15*. [*TULRA s 17(2)*].

35 Probationary Employees

35.1 LEGAL STATUS

Many employers when engaging new employees state that they will initially be employed for a 'probationary' period. It is a commonly held but mistaken belief that giving a new employee the status of probationer enables the employer to dispense with that employee's services, if he is found to be unsatisfactory, without the normal hazards of dismissal, such as a claim for unfair dismissal. The labelling of an employee as a 'probationer' has virtually no effect on the employer/employee relationship. If a probationer is dismissed so that his notice expires within two years of the commencement of his employment he will not be able to claim compensation for unfair dismissal. [*EPCA s 64(1)(a)*]. (See 55.3 UNFAIR DISMISSAL – II.) If, however, he is dismissed after that period has elapsed, he may bring a claim for unfair dismissal as may any other employee in a similar situation. The fact that he only had probationer status will not automatically make the dismissal fair. It is merely a circumstance which the tribunal will take into account in deciding whether the dismissal was fair or unfair. If the probationer's contract is not renewed after the expiry of a fixed term, provided he has the necessary qualifying period of employment, he can claim for unfair dismissal unless he has contracted out of his right to claim. An agreement to contract out of the right to claim for unfair dismissal is enforceable only in certain circumstances (see 54.18 UNFAIR DISMISSAL – I).

In the case of dismissal relating to trade union activities there is no qualifying period. Further, employees who are dismissed on the grounds of their sex or race can bring claims under *SDA 1975* or *RRA 1976* without establishing any qualifying period of employment.

35.2 EAT guidelines

In *Post Office v Mughal* [*1977*] *ICR 763* at p *768* the Employment Appeal Tribunal laid down guidelines for industrial tribunals considering the fairness of the dismissal of an employee during a probationary or trial period. They considered that the following question should be asked: 'Have the employers shown that they took reasonable steps to maintain appraisal of the probationer throughout the period of probation, giving guidance by advice or warning when such is likely to be useful or fair; and that an appropriate officer made an honest effort to determine whether the probationer came up to the required standard, having informed himself of the appraisals made by supervising officers and any other facts recorded about the probationer?'.

However, in *Anandarajah v Lord Chancellor's Department* [*1984*] *IRLR 131*, the EAT cautioned against reliance on previous authority – in that case *Mughal* – in assessing the fairness of a dismissal. The preferred approach was to apply the statutory test set out in *Employment Protection (Consolidation) Act 1978, s 57(3)* to the circumstances of each case.

However, it is thought that the matters referred to in *Mughal* remain useful considerations to take into account in assessing the fairness of the dismissal of a probationer.

35.2 Probationary Employees

With the increase in the qualifying period to two years, unfair dismissal claims by probationary employees will become rare, except, perhaps, where an employee is given a probationary period in a new job with an employer by whom he has been employed for some time.

36 Public Sector Employees

36.1 Many people are employed in the public sector, either in the Civil Service, or by local authorities, or by other agencies or in areas such as the National Health Service. Alternatively, they may work in industries which are publicly owned, although the number of such industries has steadily diminished under the present Government. Much of the law described in other chapters of this book applies equally to such people. However, there may sometimes be special factors to bear in mind when dealing with or advising upon public sector employment.

36.2 **Special statutory provisions**

In some cases the employment legislation provides specifically for particular categories of public sector employee. The following paragraphs give some indication of the subject-matter of the provisions. It will be important to look carefully at the statutory section concerned when dealing with a particular case.

EPCA s 138 is, broadly speaking, designed to bring the position of Crown employees into line with that of ordinary employees under the employment protection legislation (see *Sec 138(1)* for their status). (For their status at common law see 36.3 below.) This does not, however, extend to the right to written particulars of the terms of employment (see 10.4 CONTRACT OF EMPLOYMENT), nor to the right to a minimum notice period (see 49.9 TERMINATION OF EMPLOYMENT), nor of course to rights which arise on INSOLVENCY OF EMPLOYER (28). Crown employment is defined by *EPCA s 138(2)* as employment under or for the purposes of a government department or any officer or body exercising statutory functions on behalf of the Crown. *Sec 138* does not apply to service as a member of the armed forces [*Sec 138(3)*] or to any employment in respect of which there is in force a certificate issued by a Minister excepting that service from the provisions of *Sec 138* for the purpose of safeguarding national security. [*Sec 138(4)*]. For certain purposes including unfair dismissal provisions, employment by National Health Service bodies including regional and district health authorities is not regarded as Crown employment. [*Sec 138(5), 5 Sch*].

For continuity of Crown employment, see *EPCA 13 Sch 19*; and see generally CONTINUOUS EMPLOYMENT (9). For the right of Crown employees to statutory maternity pay (see generally 29.10 MATERNITY RIGHTS) and to statutory sick pay (see generally 46.3 SICKNESS AND SICK PAY), see *Social Security Act 1986, s 79(4)* and *Social Security and Housing Benefits Act 1982, s 27* respectively.

NHS employees are deemed to be ordinary employees for most purposes under *EPCA* [*EPCA s 138(5), 5 Sch*], but are expressly excluded from the right to a redundancy payment [*EPCA s 99*] and implicitly excluded from the rights to minimum notice and to written particulars of employment. In fact, statutory instruments governing their terms and conditions of employment supply these apparent deficiencies.

For the continuity of employment of local education authority staff on transfers within one LEA's jurisdiction, see *EPCA 13 Sch 18A*. See also *EPCA s 81(2A)* for the application of the test of whether there is a redundancy situation to LEAs.

For the position of policemen, see *EPCA s 146(2)(3)*; *SDA s 17*; *RRA s 16*; and see *Sheikh v Chief Constable of Greater Manchester Police* [*1989*] *ICR 373*. Prison officers also fall within the scope of statutory provisions relating to persons with 'the powers or privileges of a constable'. (*Home Office v Robinson and The Prison*

Officers' Association [*1982*] *ICR 31*). It is a breach of discipline for the police to strike, and a criminal offence under the *Police Act 1964, s 53* to induce a breach of discipline, which would include the organisation of a strike. Nor may policemen join a trade union other than the Police Federations. [*Police Act 1964, s 47*]. The armed forces are similarly disentitled to organise collectively and to take industrial action.

There are also many statutory instruments which in certain classes of public sector employment prescribe matters which in the private sector would be left wholly or partly to the contractual arrangements between the parties. Statutory instruments of this kind can be found dealing with questions such as superannuation, redundancy, discipline and remuneration. See e.g. *Local Government Superannuation Regulations 1974 (SI 1974 No 520)*; *Police (Discipline) Regulations 1985 (SI 1985 No 518)*.

36.3 Status of Crown servants

Crown servants have a special status in the eyes of the law. The term includes civil servants, and apparently also (for example) those who work in the National Health Service. (*Wood v United Leeds Hospitals* [*1974*] *ICR 535*).

At common law, the Crown servant is employed at the pleasure of the Crown. That is, he can be dismissed at will — without notice and without the need to show cause or to follow any particular procedure (see *Dunn v The Queen* [*1896*] *1 QB 116*; *Council of Civil Service Unions v Minister for the Civil Service* [*1985*] *AC 374*). However, the effect of *EPCA s 138* is to extend to Crown servants the right of an ordinary employee not to be subjected to UNFAIR DISMISSAL (54).

There has for many years been a controversy as to whether Crown servants in fact have a CONTRACT OF EMPLOYMENT (10) at all. By *EA 1988, s 30*, they are deemed to have one for certain purposes (principally, those of liability for torts involving the inducement or threatened inducement of a breach of contract (see 47.2 STRIKES AND INDUSTRIAL ACTION), and of certain provisions of *EA 1988*). The question has recently been considered by the Divisional Court in *R v Civil Service Appeal Board Ex parte Bruce* [*1988*] *ICR 649*. It was suggested that there was nothing unconstitutional in a Crown servant having a contract of employment: the question was whether that was the intention of the Crown when the employment began. The evidence suggested no such intention in relation to civil servants prior to 1985, but a likelihood that future civil service appointments *would* be on the basis of contract. Such a contract was consistent with the right to dismiss at will — indeed, (per Roch J) the Crown could not by contract deprive itself of the prerogative power to dismiss. When the case went to the Court of Appeal ([*1989*] *ICR 171*), it was said that these remarks of the Divisional Court were only *obiter dicta*, and the court declined to express an opinion of its own.

36.4 Availability of judicial review

Those who work in the public sector may sometimes seek to assert their rights, not simply in an industrial tribunal or in an action for tort or breach of contract in the ordinary courts, but by way of an application for judicial review. This is a means of challenging the unlawful actions and decisions of public authorities and bodies exercising statutory power. The possible grounds for such challenge include failure to observe natural justice or a statutorily prescribed procedure, the taking into account of irrelevant considerations (or the failure to consider all matters which ought to be considered), acting for an improper purpose, and extreme irrationality. Applications are heard in the Crown Office list of the High Court, and the procedure is governed by *Rules of the Supreme Court, Order 53*. Its features include a need to obtain leave to proceed from the court, and a strict time limit.

However, the courts have held that the judicial review procedure *must* be used when a *public* right is being asserted, but *must not* be used when the subject-matter is a *private* right. (*O'Reilly v Mackman [1983] 2 AC 237; Davy v Spelthorne Borough Council [1984] AC 262*). This distinction between public and private rights, which is often difficult to draw, applies to employment-related cases. If the claim is really founded upon a contract, in the sense that that is the sole basis of the relationship between the parties, judicial review will not be appropriate (*R v East Berkshire Health Authority Ex parte Walsh [1984] ICR 743*; see also *R v British Broadcasting Corporation Ex parte Lavelle [1983] 1 WLR 23*). But in other cases the relationship may have some 'statutory underpinning' which means that the dispute is a public law matter (see e.g. *R v Home Secretary Ex parte Benwell [1984] ICR 723*, where a prison officer was dismissed without the benefit of the fair application of a *statutory* disciplinary code). See also *R v Liverpool City Corporation Ex parte Ferguson and Ferguson [1985] IRLR 501*.

It should also be remembered that the court hearing an application for judicial review has an overriding discretion as to whether any relief should be granted. One possible reason for refusing relief is that some alternative remedy was available and should have been pursued. Thus in *Bruce* (see 36.3 above) the Divisional Court accepted that there was a sufficient public law element for an unsuccessful appeal against dismissal to the Civil Service Appeal Board to be judicially reviewable, but held that only in exceptional cases would it be right not to confine the applicant to his remedy in an industrial tribunal. The Court of Appeal upheld the refusal of relief on the facts without expressing a view on the general proposition.

In public law there is a doctrine of 'legitimate expectation', which means that, where a public authority has given the impression, by its words or by its consistent past practice, that it will follow a particular course of action, it may not be permitted to go back on that, at least without consulting those who are affected. For a recent successful attempt to invoke this doctrine in the employment field, see the Northern Ireland case *Re NUPE and COHSE's Application [1989] IRLR 202*, where it was held that the health service unions whose members were affected by proposed hospital closures had a legitimate expectation of consultation before such decisions were taken. See also *Council of Civil Service Unions v Minister for the Civil Service [1985] AC 374*.

36.5 European Community law

All employment relationships are now affected by EUROPEAN COMMUNITY LAW (20). However, public sector employees may find themselves in a special position because of the way in which the doctrine of 'direct effect' is applied. Some categories of EC legislation (the Treaties themselves, and regulations) become applicable once promulgated without any need for further action by member States. In the case of *directives*, however, the intention is that member States should, within a given time, take such steps as they consider appropriate to implement the directive in their territory. The European Court of Justice has frequently held that, if a State fails to comply with its obligation (either because it does nothing or because what it does is held not to achieve all that the directive requires), then, although that directive cannot be relied upon in proceedings against private persons, provided that the directive is clear and unconditional, it may be relied upon against the State. The State may not take advantage of its own wrong in failing to introduce measures to implement the directive. In order for a person to be able to rely on a directive against the State, the terms of the directive must be apt to confer rights on individuals and it must require no further implementing measures or time before it is intended to have effect.

It was this doctrine which enabled the applicant in *Marshall v Southampton & South West Hampshire Area Health Authority (Teaching) [1986] ICR 335* to succeed in her claim of unlawful sex discrimination based on discriminatory retiring ages at a time before the *Sex Discrimination Act 1986* was passed. The health authority which employed her was agreed to be an organ of the State, so that she could rely directly upon *Directive 76/207/EEC* (see 20.5 EUROPEAN COMMUNITY LAW; 44.20 SEX DISCRIMINATION - I). The question of whether a nationalised industry (since privatised) is the State for these purposes fell to be considered in *Foster v British Gas [1988] ICR 584*. The Court of Appeal held that it was not. On appeal, the House of Lords referred the question to the European Court of Justice, and the hearing of the reference is awaited.

37 Racial Discrimination

(See also DE leaflet 'The Race Relations Employment Advisory Service. A specialist service for employers' (PL 748).)

37.1 Discrimination on racial grounds is made unlawful by the *Race Relations Act 1976 (RRA)* which repealed and replaced the *Race Relations Acts 1965* and *1968*. Its provisions are similar to those relating to SEX DISCRIMINATION (44) in the *Sex Discrimination Act 1975 (SDA)*, and readers should refer to decisions under that Act as well as to the *RRA*.

The Commission for Racial Equality (CRE) was established by the 1976 Act to replace the Race Relations Board. The purpose and powers of the Commission are considered in 37.24-37.32 below.

37.2 MEANING OF DISCRIMINATION

Discrimination may take place in any one of three ways: direct discrimination, indirect discrimination and discrimination by way of victimisation. In deciding whether a person has been discriminated against, his position will be compared with that of someone of similar ability and qualifications in similar circumstances: like must be compared with like. [*RRA s 3(4)*; and see *Dhatt v McDonalds Hamburgers Ltd* [*1988*] *ICR 591*].

37.3 Direct discrimination

A person discriminates directly if, on racial grounds, he treats one person less favourably than he treats or would treat other persons. [*RRA s 1(1)(a)*].

37.4 Indirect discrimination

A person discriminates indirectly if, on racial grounds, he applies to one person a requirement or condition which he applies or would apply equally to persons not of the same racial group as that person but

(*a*) which is such that the proportion of persons in that racial group who can comply with it is considerably smaller than the proportion of persons not of that racial group who can comply with it; and

(*b*) which he cannot show to be justifiable irrespective of the colour, race, nationality or ethnic or national origins of the person to whom it is applied; and

(*c*) which is to the detriment of that other person because he cannot comply with it.

[*RRA s 1(1)(b)*].

Thus, if an employer capriciously and for no good reason required applicants for a clerical job to be wine connoisseurs, that requirement may be considered discriminatory against Moslems who are forbidden by their religion to drink alcohol. Such a requirement may not be discriminatory in considering applicants for the job of a wine waiter whose duties include the tasting of wine.

An upper age limit of 32 for applicants for the post of administrative trainee was considered to be unlawful indirect discrimination where evidence established that the proportion of 'coloureds' in the complainant's office who could comply with the limit was zero. (*Perera v Civil Service (No 2) [1982] ICR 350*). However, Mr Perera's complaint of direct and indirect discrimination in failing to appoint him as a legal assistant was rejected. (*[1983] ICR 428*). It was held in *Perera* that, in order to establish unlawful indirect discrimination, the requirement or condition relied upon must be mandatory, so that failure to comply with it constituted (in that context) an absolute bar to employment. This was applied in *Meer v Tower Hamlets London Borough Council [1988] IRLR 399*, with the result that one criterion amongst several used in shortlisting for a job could not be relied upon to found a successful claim. The importance of properly identifying the racial group for the purpose of ascertaining whether indirect discrimination has taken place was emphasised by the EAT in *Tower Hamlets London Borough Council v Qayyum [1987] ICR 729*. This decision casts doubt on whether it is legitimate to treat black or coloured people in general as the relevant group.

Whether a person 'can' comply with a condition or requirement is to be judged by what he can in practice do when the condition is invoked. (*Commission for Racial Equality v Dutton [1989] IRLR 8*).

In order to establish the defence of justification set out in (*b*) above, a respondent has to show not that the condition which he seeks to apply is a necessary condition but that it is justifiable without regard to the ethnic origins of the person to whom it is applied. This involves striking an objective balance between its discriminatory effect and the reasonable needs of the respondent. (*Mandla (Sewa Singh) v Dowell Lee [1983] ICR 385*, at *p 394; Ojutiku v Manpower Services Commission [1982] ICR 661; Panesar v Nestlé Co Ltd (Note) [1980] ICR 144; Hampson v Department of Education and Science [1989] ICR 179*). The question of whether indirect discrimination is justifiable is one of fact for the industrial tribunal (*Singh v British Rail Engineering [1986] ICR 22*), but in *Hampson* the case was remitted on appeal because the tribunal had failed to identify the standards by which it was testing justification (leave was given to appeal from the Court of Appeal to the House of Lords).

For requirements or conditions that Sikhs who wear turbans should wear safety helmets on construction sites, see 24.28 HEALTH AND SAFETY AT WORK – I.

37.5 Discrimination by victimisation

'A person ("the discriminator") discriminates against another person ("the person victimised") in any circumstances relevant for the purposes of [the] Act if he treats the person victimised less favourably than in those circumstances he treats or would treat other persons, and does so by reason that the person victimised has –

(*a*) brought proceedings against the discriminator or any other person under [the] Act; or

(*b*) given evidence or information in connection with proceedings brought by any person against the discriminator or any other person under [the] Act; or

(*c*) otherwise done anything under or by reference to [the] Act in relation to the discriminator or any other person; or

(*d*) alleged that the discriminator or any other person has committed an act which . . . would amount to a contravention of [the] Act,

or by reason that the discriminator knows that the person victimised intends to do any of those things, or suspects that the person victimised has done, or intends to do, any of them.' [*RRA s 2(1)*].

(See in particular the decision of the Court of Appeal in *Aziz v Trinity Street Taxis Ltd* [*1988*] *ICR 534*.)

A person is not protected under (*d*) above where it is established that the allegation made by him was false and not made in good faith. [*RRA s 2(2)*].

37.6 Racial grounds

Discrimination is only unlawful pursuant to *RRA* if it is on racial grounds.

'Racial grounds' are defined in *RRA s 3(1)* as any of the following grounds: colour, race, nationality or ethnic or national origins. A distinction is drawn between racial origin and citizenship. (*Ealing London Borough Council v Race Relations Board* [*1972*] *AC 342; Tejani v Superintendent Registrar for Peterborough* [*1986*] *IRLR 502*).

Discrimination is on racial grounds if the substantial or effective, though not necessarily the sole or intended, reason for the discriminatory treatment was the person's race, colour or ethnic origin. (See *R v Commission for Racial Equality Ex parte Westminster City Council* [*1984*] *ICR 770*; affirmed in part [*1985*] *ICR 827*.)

An employee may be discriminated against on racial grounds whether the racial characteristics in question are those of the person concerned or of some other person. The only question in each case is whether the unfavourable treatment afforded to the claimant was caused by racial considerations (see *Showboat Entertainment Centre Ltd v Owens* [*1984*] *ICR 65* at *p* 71H in which a white manager of an entertainment centre was dismissed for refusing to obey an instruction to exclude all black customers; and also *Zarczynska v Levy* [*1979*] *ICR 184*).

In *Simon v Brimham Associates* [*1987*] *ICR 596* the Court of Appeal reached the somewhat surprising conclusion that an industrial tribunal was entitled to find that a Jew who had withdrawn a job application, when he learned that to be Jewish might preclude his selection, was not discriminated against, in circumstances in which the interviewer had merely asked him the same question about his religion as he would have asked any candidate, not knowing whether or not he was Jewish.

37.7 FURTHER DEFINITIONS

'Racial group' means a group of persons defined by reference to colour, race, nationality or ethnic or national origins and references to a person's racial group refer to any racial group into which he falls. [*RRA s 3(1)*]. Jews are members of a racial group (see, for example, *Seide v Gillette Industries Ltd* [*1980*] *IRLR 427*). So are gypsies in the sense of those who belong to the Romany race, though mere habitual wanderers are not. (*Commission for Racial Equality v Dutton* [*1989*] *IRLR 8*). The House of Lords in *Mandla (Sewa Singh) v Dowell Lee* [*1983*] *ICR 385* held that 'ethnic . . . origins' in the definition of 'racial group' meant a group which was a segment of the population distinguished from others by a sufficient combination of shared customs, beliefs, traditions and characteristics derived from a common or presumed common past, even if not drawn from what in biological terms was a common racial stock. On that basis, it held that Sikhs were a racial group entitled to the protection of the *RRA*. The language factor alone cannot be decisive. Thus Welshmen are not divided into two racial groups according to whether or not they are Welsh-speaking. (*Gwynedd County Council v Jones and another* [*1986*] *ICR 833*).

Segregating a person from other persons on racial grounds is treating him less favourably than they are treated. [*RRA s 1(2)*]. Thus, it is not open to an employer to argue that the provision of segregated facilities for his coloured employees is not discriminatory even though the facilities provided for coloured workers are equal to if not better than those provided for his white employees.

37.8 DISCRIMINATION IN EMPLOYMENT

An employer is prohibited from discriminating on grounds of race at every stage of employment *at an establishment in Great Britain*. 'Establishment' is not defined by the Act. 'Employment' is defined in *RRA s 78(1)* as employment under a contract of service or of apprenticeship or a contract personally to execute any work or labour. A sub-postmaster who was responsible for seeing that the work of the Post Office was carried out but was not obliged to carry out the work himself was held not to be an employee within the meaning of the Act. (*Tanna v The Post Office* [*1981*] *ICR 374*). A person working under the Youth Opportunities Programme was held not to be employed within the meaning of *RRA s 78*. (*Daley v Allied Suppliers Ltd* [*1983*] *ICR 90*) (but see 37.15(*d*) below). A special constable is not employed under a contract to execute work or labour but is deemed to be in employment by virtue of *Sec 16(1)* and thus enjoys the protection of *RRA*. (*Sheikh v Chief Constable of Greater Manchester Police* [*1989*] *ICR 373*). No qualifying period of employment is necessary in order to bring a claim based on discrimination in employment.

37.9 'At an establishment in Great Britain'

Employment is to be regarded as being at an establishment in Great Britain unless the employee does his work wholly or mainly outside Great Britain. [*RRA s 8(1)*]. Where work is not done at an establishment as in the case of plumbers who are sent out on assignments, it is treated as done at the establishment from which the workers are sent out.

If employees neither work at nor from a particular establishment, such as market researchers who work from their homes, the work will be considered to be done at the establishment with which it has the closest connection. [*RRA s 8(4)*].

Employment on board a British registered ship, aircraft or hovercraft which is operated by a person who has his principal place of business in, or is ordinarily resident in, Great Britain (other than an aircraft or hovercraft which is so operated in pursuance of a contract with a person who has his principal place of business outside, or is ordinarily resident outside, the United Kingdom) is to be considered employment at an establishment in Great Britain, unless the employee does his work wholly outside Great Britain. [*RRA s 8(2)(3)*].

Employment on the continental shelf may, by statutory instrument, be deemed employment at an establishment in Great Britain. [*RRA s 8(5)*]. The *Race Relations (Offshore Employment) Order 1987 (SI 1987 No 929)* has been made pursuant to this power.

37.10 Advertisements

An employer may not cause to be published an advertisement which indicates, or might reasonably be understood as indicating, an intention to discriminate unlawfully. [*RRA s 29*].

If the discrimination would be lawful, for example on the grounds that being of a particular race is a genuine occupational qualification for the job (see 37.14 (*d*) below), the advertisement may lawfully be placed. Therefore, a restaurateur may lawfully advertise for Chinese waiters for his Chinese restaurant.

The restrictions on discriminatory advertisements do not apply to an advertisement for employment outside Great Britain which discriminates otherwise than by reference to colour, race, or ethnic or national origin. [*RRA s 29(3)*].

Thus, an employer may not advertise for English applicants only for employment overseas, although he may lawfully advertise for applicants with a public school education (which might well be indirectly discriminatory) and may lawfully select only English applicants for such employment.

37.11 Engagement

An employer may not discriminate on racial grounds in relation to

(*a*) the arrangements he makes for the purpose of determining who should be offered employment; or

(*b*) the terms on which he offers employment; or

(*c*) refusing or deliberately omitting to offer employment.

[*RRA s 4(1)*]. (See, for example, *Owen and Briggs v James [1982] ICR 618.*)

37.12 Training and other facilities

An employer may not discriminate on racial grounds in the terms of employment he affords an employee, or in the way he affords him access to opportunities for promotion, transfer or training, or to any other benefits, facilities or services, or by refusing or deliberately omitting to afford him access to them. [*RRA s 4(2)(a), (b)*]. (*Ojutiku v Manpower Services Commission [1982] ICR 661*).

37.13 Dismissal or subjection to any other detriment

It is unlawful for an employer to discriminate, on racial grounds, against an employee of his by dismissing him, or subjecting him to any other detriment. [*RRA s 4(2)(c)*]. Dismissal on racial grounds is also almost certainly unfair. See UNFAIR DISMISSAL – I (54). In order to bring a claim under this section an applicant needs no qualifying period of employment, unlike in the case of claims for unfair dismissal. In *De Souza v the Automobile Association [1986] ICR 514*, the Court of Appeal held that the Employment Appeal Tribunal had correctly concluded that Mrs De Souza had not been subjected to a 'detriment' within the meaning of *RRA s 4(2)(c)* as a result of overhearing a manager say to another manager, about her, to get his typing done by 'the wog'. The Court held that before an employee can be said to have been subjected to a 'detriment' it must be found that by reason of the acts complained of, a reasonable worker would or might take the view that he had thereby been disadvantaged in the circumstances in which he had thereafter to work. (See also *B L Cars Ltd v Brown [1983] ICR 143.*) The EAT in *Barclays Bank PLC v Kapur [1989] ICR 142* (appeal allowed, *[1989] IRLR 387*) suggested, in a passage which was not a necessary part of its decision, that the words 'any other detriment' related to acts in connection with dismissal or disciplinary proceedings and were not wholly general in their scope. The correctness of this construction is, with respect, doubted.

For dismissal of an employee for refusing to comply with unlawful instructions to discriminate, see 37.18 below.

37.14 EXCEPTIONS

As a matter of principle, these exceptions ought to be narrowly or strictly construed. (*Lambeth London Borough Council v Commission for Racial Equality [1989] IRLR 379*).

(*a*) Employment outside Great Britain

With the exception of advertisements indicating direct discrimination, the provisions relating to discrimination do not apply where the employee does his work wholly or mainly outside Great Britain or on a British registered ship, aircraft or hovercraft, wholly outside Great Britain. [*RRA ss 4, 8(1)(2)*]. In deciding whether an employee does his work wholly outside Great Britain, a court will consider whether it was within the contemplation of the parties that his duties would be performed wholly outside Great Britain. (*Deria v General Council of British Shipping [1986] ICR 172*).

(*b*) Private household

Except for discrimination by way of victimisation, the provisions relating to discrimination do not apply to employment for the purposes of a private household. [*RRA s 4(3)*]. *Sec 4 (3)* deals with employment which is for the purposes of a private household *to a substantial degree*. Thus, an applicant for a job as a chauffeur whose primary task was to drive a car for a company chairman could bring a complaint of racial discrimination. (*Heron Corporation Ltd v Commis [1980] ICR 713*).

(*c*) Facilities provided to public

The provisions relating to discrimination in the giving of benefits, facilities or services [*RRA s 4(2)*] do not apply if the employer is concerned with the provision (for payment or not) of benefits, facilities or services of that description to the public, or to a section of the public comprising the employee in question, unless

(i) that provision differs in a material respect from the provision of the benefits, facilities or services by the employer to his employees; or

(ii) the provision of the benefits, facilities or services to the employee in question is regulated by his contract of employment; or

(iii) the benefits, facilities or services relate to training.

[*RRA s 4(4)*].

Thus, a bank which provides loans to members of the public and to most employees on the same terms may not be taken to an industrial tribunal by an employee who is denied a loan on racial grounds if the employee is not entitled to the loan under his contract of employment. However, it will be liable to an action by that employee in the county court under the provisions of *RRA s 20* (discrimination in provision of goods, facilities or services).

(*d*) Genuine occupational qualification

An employer may lawfully discriminate in the arrangements he makes for selecting employees for a job where being a member of a particular racial group is a genuine occupational qualification for the job. (This also applies to training and promotion or transfer.) [*RRA s 5*].

Being of a particular racial group is a genuine occupational qualification for a job only where

(i) the job involves participation in a dramatic performance or other entertainment in a capacity for which a person of that racial group is required for reasons of authenticity; or

(ii) the job involves participation as an artist's or photographic model in the production of a work of art, visual image or sequence of visual images for which a person of that racial group is required for reason of authenticity; or

(iii) the job involves working in a place where food or drink is (for payment or not) provided to and consumed by the members of the public or a section of the public in a particular setting for which, in that job, a person of that racial group is required for reasons of authenticity (thus an employer may lawfully discriminate in selecting waiters for an Indian or Chinese restaurant); or

(iv) the holder of the job provides persons of that racial group with personal services promoting their welfare, and those services can most effectively be provided by a person of that racial group. The scope of this exception was discussed in *Tottenham Green Under-Fives' Centre v Marshall* [*1989*] *ICR 214* and in *Lambeth London Borough Council v Commission for Racial Equality* [*1989*] *IRLR 379*.

[*RRA s 5(2)*].

The exception applies where some of the duties fall within (i) to (iv) above as well as where all of them do.

However, where an employer already has employees of a particular racial group who are capable of carrying out the duties of a vacant post and whom it would be reasonable to employ on those duties and whose numbers are sufficient to meet his likely requirements in respect of those duties without undue inconvenience, then he may not discriminate by giving the job to a person of that particular racial group, despite the fact that the vacancy may fall within (i) to (iv) above. [*RRA s 5(4)*].

(*e*) Acts done under statutory authority

The Act does not prohibit acts of discrimination carried out pursuant to any enactment, Order in Council or statutory instrument, or in order to comply with a ministerial condition or requirement imposed pursuant to statute. [*RRA s 41(1)*].

The scope of this provision was considered by the Court of Appeal in *Hampson v Department of Education and Science* [*1989*] *ICR 179*. It held that the application of the defence was not restricted to acts done in the necessary performance of an express obligation contained in an instrument, but extended to discretionary acts carried out by the Secretary of State in circumstances where he had a positive public duty to exercise his discretion.

(*f*) **Skills to be exercised outside Great Britain**

The Act does not prohibit discriminatory training of a person not ordinarily resident in Great Britain where he is being trained in skills intended to be exercised wholly outside Great Britain. [*RRA s 6*].

(*g*) **Seamen recruited abroad**

Seamen recruited abroad for employment on any ship may lawfully be discriminated against, except if their work is concerned with exploration of the sea bed or subsoil (or the exploitation of their natural resources) on the continental shelf, save for those parts of the continental shelf in which the law of Northern Ireland applies. [*RRA s 9(1)(3)*].

(*h*) **Positive discrimination**

Positive discrimination in favour of a particular racial group, in affording access to training and encouragement to apply for particular work, is permitted to employers if at any time within the twelve months immediately preceding the doing of the act

(i) there were no persons of that group among those doing that work at that establishment; or

(ii) the proportion of persons of that group among those doing that work at that establishment is small in comparison with the proportion of persons of that group among

(A) all those employed by the employer there; or

(B) the population of the area from which that employer normally recruits persons for work in his employment at that establishment. [*RRA s 38(1)(2)*].

Certain persons concerned with the provision of vocational training may also discriminate in favour of racial groups in similar circumstances. [*RRA s 37*].

Positive discrimination is also permitted to encourage membership of and postholding in trade unions and employers' organisations where there are no or proportionally few postholders or members of the relevant racial group. [*RRA s 38(3)(4)*].

37.15 NON-EMPLOYERS COVERED BY THE EMPLOYMENT RULES

(*a*) **Partnerships**

It is unlawful for a firm consisting of six or more partners, in relation to a position as partner in the firm, to discriminate against a person

(i) in the arrangements they make for the purpose of determining who should be offered that position; or

(ii) in the terms on which they offer him that position; or

(iii) by refusing or deliberately omitting to offer him that position; or

(iv) in a case where the person already holds that position

(A) in the way they afford him access to any benefits, facilities or services, or by refusing or deliberately omitting to afford him access to them; or

(B) by expelling him from that position, or subjecting him to any other detriment.

[*RRA s 10*].

A partnership may nevertheless lawfully discriminate in the arrangements it makes for determining who should be offered the job or by refusing or deliberately omitting to offer a person a position, where, if the partnership were employment, being of a particular racial group would be a genuine occupational qualification for the job. [*RRA s 10(3)*].

(*b*) **Trade unions etc.**

Trade unions, organisations of workers and employers' organisations may not discriminate against a person who is not a member of the organisation

(i) in the terms on which they are prepared to admit him to membership; or

(ii) by refusing, or deliberately omitting to accept, his application for membership.

[*RRA s 11*].

Such organisations may not discriminate against a member

(A) in the way they afford him access to any benefits, facilities or services, or by refusing or deliberately omitting to afford him access to them; or

(B) by depriving him of membership, or varying the terms on which he is a member; or

(C) by subjecting him to any other detriment.

[*RRA s 11(3)*].

(*c*) **Bodies conferring professional or trade qualifications**

It is unlawful for an authority or body, which can confer an authorisation or qualification which is needed for or facilitates engagement in a particular profession or trade, to discriminate against a person

(i) in the terms on which it is prepared to confer on him that authorisation or qualification; or

(ii) by refusing or deliberately omitting to grant his application for it; or

(iii) by withdrawing it from him or varying the terms on which he holds it.

[*RRA s 12*].

(*d*) **Persons concerned with provision of vocational training**

It is unlawful, in the case of an individual seeking or undergoing training which would help fit him for employment, for any person who provides, or makes arrangements for the provision of, facilities for such training to discriminate against him

(i) in the terms on which that person affords him access to any training course or other facilities concerned with such training, or

(ii) by refusing or deliberately omitting to afford him such access, or

(iii) by terminating his training, or

(iv) by subjecting him to any detriment during the course of his training.

[*RRA s 13; EA 1989, s 7(2)*].

These provisions apply to persons concerned with the provision of vocational training. They do not apply to the provision of training by employers to their employees to whom *RRA s 4(1) and (2)* apply to prohibit *inter alia* discrimination in access to training.

(*e*) **Employment agencies**

It is unlawful for an employment agency to discriminate against a person

(i) in the terms on which the agency offers to provide any of its services; or

(ii) by refusing or deliberately omitting to provide any of its services; or

(iii) in the way it provides any of its services.

[*RRA s 14*].

Nevertheless, an employment agency can discriminate lawfully if the prospective employer could lawfully refuse employment, for example, on the ground that being of a particular racial group is a genuine occupational qualification for the job.

37.16 CONTRACT WORKERS

It is unlawful for the hirer of contract labour to discriminate against a contract worker

(*a*) in the terms on which he allows him to work; or

(*b*) by not allowing him to work or continue working; or

(*c*) in the way he affords him access to any benefits, facilities or services or by refusing or deliberately omitting to afford him access to them; or

(*d*) by subjecting him to any other detriment.

[*RRA s 7(1)*].

The hirer of contract labour can lawfully discriminate in the same circumstances as can an employer. [*RRA s 7(3)(5)*].

37.17 OTHER UNLAWFUL ACTS

Discriminatory practice

The application of discriminatory practices, namely the application of any requirement or condition which results in any act of discrimination made unlawful by the provisions of the Act relating to employment, is in itself unlawful. [*RRA s 28*].

37.18 **Instructions to discriminate**

It is unlawful for one person who has authority over another, or in accordance with whose wishes that other person is accustomed to act, to instruct him to do any act which is unlawful under the Act or to procure or attempt to procure the doing by him of any such act. [*RRA s 30*].

An instruction to discriminate unlawfully, which is followed by dismissal for disobedience of the instruction, may give rise to two possible consequences. They are proceedings by the CRE in the county court for breach of *Sec 30*, and proceedings by the individual in an industrial tribunal under *Sec 4(2)(c)*. (See *Zarczynska v Levy* [*1979*] *ICR 184*.)

37.19 **Pressure to discriminate**

It is unlawful to induce, or attempt to induce, a person to do anything which is unlawful by virtue of the Act. [*RRA s 31(1)*]. An attempted inducement is not prevented from being unlawful because it is not made directly to the person in question, if it is made in such a way that he is likely to hear of it. [*RRA s 31(2)*]. Thus if A, a managing director, tells B, one of his employees, that another employee, C, will be promoted if C discriminates against X in selecting applicants for a job, A is guilty of an unlawful act. In *Commission for Racial Equality v Imperial Society of Teachers of Dancing* [*1983*] *ICR 473*, the Employment Appeal Tribunal held that a prospective employer was in breach of *Sec 31* for telling the head of careers at a school that he would prefer that the school did not put forward any coloured applicants.

37.20 **Liability for unlawful act of employee**

Any unlawful act (other than a criminal offence) under *RRA* committed by an employee in the course of his employment is treated as also having been done by his employer whether or not it was done with the employer's knowledge or approval. [*RRA s 32(1)*]. (See, for example, *Kingston v British Railways Board* [*1982*] *ICR 392*, and contrast *Irving and Irving v Post Office* [*1987*] *IRLR 289*.) The employer will have a defence if he can prove that he took such steps as were reasonably practicable to prevent his employee from doing that act, or from doing that kind of act during the course of his employment. [*RRA s 32(3)*].

In deciding whether an employer has taken such steps, an industrial tribunal and the CRE may have regard to such matters as whether the employer has issued a written policy to employees on race discrimination, whether it has given its managers training in such matters and whether it has taken steps to discipline employees if they have been guilty of race discrimination.

37.21 **Liability for unlawful act of agent**

Any unlawful act committed by an agent with the express or implied authority (whether precedent or subsequent) of his principal is treated (except as regards offences under *RRA*) as also having been done by his principal. [*RRA s 32(2)*].

37.22 **Aiding unlawful acts**

A person who knowingly aids another to do an act made unlawful by the Act is treated as if he himself did that unlawful act. [*RRA s 33(1)*]. It is a defence for a person to show that

(*a*) he acted in reliance on a statement made to him by that other person that the act would not be unlawful; and (*b*) it was reasonable for him to rely on that statement.

[*RRA s 33(3)*].

37.23 **False or misleading statements**

A person who knowingly or recklessly makes a statement mentioned in 37.22 (*a*) above, which in a material respect is false or misleading, commits an offence and is liable on conviction in a magistrates' court to a fine not exceeding level 5 on the standard scale. [*RRA s 33(4)*; see also *RRA ss 14(6), 29(5)* and 1.10 INTRODUCTION].

37.24 COMMISSION FOR RACIAL EQUALITY

The Act established a Commission for Racial Equality (the CRE) whose members are appointed by the Secretary of State to

(*a*) work towards the elimination of discrimination;

(*b*) promote equality of opportunity, and good relations, between persons of different racial groups and

(*c*) to keep under review the working of the Act.

[*RRA s 43(1)*].

37.25 **Codes of practice**

The CRE may issue codes of practice containing practical guidance for

(*a*) the elimination of discrimination in the field of employment; and/or

(*b*) the promotion of equality of opportunity in that field for persons of different racial groups.

[*RRA s 47(1)*].

The CRE issued a code of practice entitled *Code of Practice on Race Relations* which came into force on 1 April 1984. This is reproduced in the Appendix. A breach of the Code does not of itself render a person liable to proceedings, but any relevant provision of the Code may be taken into account by an industrial tribunal. [*RRA s 47(10)*].

37.26 ENFORCEMENT

Except as specifically provided by the Act, no civil or criminal proceedings may be taken against any person. [*RRA s 53(1)*]. This provision does not restrict the making of an order of *certiorari, mandamus* or *prohibition*. [*RRA s 53(2)*]. The CRE alone may issue non-discrimination notices (see 37.29 below) and take certain other action to enforce the provisions of *RRA ss 29-31*.

37.27 **Enforcement by an individual: application to an industrial tribunal**

A person may present a complaint to an industrial tribunal that he has been discriminated against in relation to any of the provisions relating to employment. [*RRA s 54(1)*]. The time limit for the presentation of such a complaint is three months from the time that the act complained of was done. [*RRA s 68(1)*]. The tribunal may nevertheless consider a complaint which is out of time if, in all the circumstances of the case, it considers that it is just and equitable to do so [*RRA s 68(6)*], but in *Barclays Bank PLC v Kapur* [*1989*] *ICR 142* (appeal allowed, [*1989*] *IRLR 387*) the EAT advocated a strict approach

For the purposes of deciding when an act was done, in calculating the time limit

(*a*) where the inclusion of any term in any contract renders the making of the contract an unlawful act, that act shall be treated as extending throughout the duration of the contract; and

(*b*) any act extending over a period shall be treated as done at the end of that period; and

(*c*) a deliberate omission shall be treated as done when the person in question decided upon it.

If the cause for complaint is an omission rather than an act, the omission will be considered to have been decided upon when a person does something inconsistent with the omitted act or when the period within which he would reasonably have done the act has expired. [*RRA s 68(7)*].

In *Barclays Bank PLC v Kapur* [*1989*] *ICR 142*, the EAT held that *Sec 68(7)(b)* was intended to cover situations where an employer committed a continuing act or where there was a continuing offer to employees. In *Kapur* the EAT held that a refusal to allow the applicants access to pension benefits accrued during their African service was not therefore an act extending over a period and *Sec 68(7)(b)* did not apply. However, the decision of the EAT was reversed by the Court of Appeal ([*1989*] *IRLR 387*), which held that such a refusal was a continuing act, because it adversely affected the applicants for as long as it was maintained; *Sec 68(7)(b)* was therefore applicable.

In pursuing a claim before an industrial tribunal, an applicant may ask for the disclosure of documents by his employer or prospective employer. However, in *Vyas v Leyland Cars* [*1979*] *ICR 921*, the House of Lords held that tribunals should not order the disclosure of reports or references given and received in confidence except when it is necessary for disposing fairly of the proceedings that the confidence should be overridden. In *West Midlands Passenger Transport Executive v Singh* [*1988*] *ICR 614* the Court of Appeal upheld an industrial tribunal's order for discovery of a schedule of statistics showing the ethnic origins of candidates for promotion and those actually promoted during the period preceding the alleged discrimination. The decision also gives guidance as to when discovery should be refused because, although relevant, it would be oppressive. The Court of Appeal further held that it might be possible firstly to infer from statistics that there had been discrimination against members of a racial group in general, and then to infer (in the absence of a satisfactory explanation in the particular case) that the applicant as a member of that group was discriminated against.

The courts have recognised that direct evidence of discrimination will be rare, and that the industrial tribunal must be allowed to draw inferences from the particular circumstances. (*Owen and Briggs v James* [*1982*] *ICR 618; Khanna v Ministry of Defence* [*1981*] *ICR 653*). Evidence of events subsequent to the alleged act of discrimination is admissible if there is a real probability that it will affect the outcome of the complaint. (*Chattopadhyay v Headmaster of Holloway School* [*1982*] *ICR 132*; *North West Thames Regional Health Authority v Noone* [*1989*] *ICR 813*). But these cases should not be taken to mean that the burden of proof shifts to the employer in such circumstances. Ultimately, it is always the claimant who must prove discrimination on the balance of probabilities. (*Barking and Dagenham London Borough Council v Camara* [*1988*] *ICR 865*).

The conciliation officer (see 2.3 ADVISORY, CONCILIATION AND ARBITRATION SERVICE) may consult both parties to the complaint with a view to bringing about a settlement. [*RRA s 55*].

Remedies available from industrial tribunals. If an industrial tribunal finds that a complaint is well-founded, it will make such of the following orders as it considers just and equitable.

(*a*) *Declaratory order* – an order declaring the rights of the complainant and the respondent in relation to the act complained of.

(*b*) *Compensation* – an order requiring the respondent to pay to the complainant compensation of an amount including damages for injured feelings. For decisions relating to the assessment of compensation see *Alexander v The Home Office [1988] ICR 685* and *North West Thames Regional Health Authority v Noone [1988] ICR 813*.

(*c*) *Recommending remedial action* – a recommendation that the respondent take, within a specified period, action appearing to the tribunal to be practicable for the purpose of obviating or reducing the adverse effect on the complainant of any act of discrimination complained of.

[*RRA s 56(1)*].

However, where statutory rules governed an appointment, a tribunal cannot recommend an applicant's appointment. It can merely recommend that the appointing body be made aware of the need to comply with *RRA* and of other relevant matters. (*North West Thames Regional Health Authority v Noone [1988] ICR 813*).

The maximum amount of compensation is that imposed by *EPCA s 75(1)*. [*RRA s 56(2); EPCA 16 Sch 25*]. The limit for acts which occurred after 1 April 1989 is £8,925. [*Unfair Dismissal (Increase of Compensation Limit) Order 1989 (SI 1989 No 527)*]. Previously it was £8,500. Where compensation is awarded both under the *Sex Discrimination Act 1975* and the *Race Relations Act 1976* in respect of one act of discrimination, the aggregate amount of compensation cannot exceed the limit above. [*RRA s 56(3)*].

If, without reasonable justification, the respondent to a complaint fails to comply with a recommendation by an industrial tribunal that he take certain action then, if it thinks it just and equitable to do so, the tribunal may increase the amount of compensation to an amount up to the maximum, or, if no order for compensation had previously been made, make such an order. [*RRA s 56(4)*].

37.28 **Enforcement by the CRE: investigations**

The CRE may conduct investigations into alleged discriminatory practices and for that purpose may compel persons to attend to give evidence and may order the production of documents. [*RRA s 48*]. These may be general investigations or investigation into the activities of persons named in the terms of reference ('named persons investigations'). Before embarking on a named person investigation, the CRE must have already formed a suspicion that the persons named might have committed some unlawful act of discrimination and had at least some grounds for so suspecting. If they do not, the investigation and any non-discrimination notice based upon it may be challenged. (*Commission for Racial Equality v Prestige Group plc [1984] ICR 473; R v Commission for Racial Equality, Ex parte Hillingdon London Borough Council [1982] AC 779*). A person named in the terms of reference of the investigation may be represented by counsel or solicitor or another suitable person. [*RRA s 49(4)*]. The CRE prepare a report from their findings and make recommendations. [*RRA s 51*].

37.29 Issue of non-discrimination notices

If the CRE during the course of a formal investigation (see 37.28 above) becomes satisfied that a person is committing, or has committed an unlawful discriminatory act, an unlawful discriminatory practice, or has been guilty of placing or publishing an unlawful discriminatory advertisement, given instructions or applied pressure to discriminate unlawfully, or as an employer or principal is liable for the discriminatory act of his servant or agent, it may serve a non-discrimination notice on him requiring him

(*a*) not to commit any such acts; and

(*b*) where, in order to comply with the notice he has to change any practices or arrangements, to inform the CRE that he has made those changes and what those changes are, and to take such steps as may be reasonably required by the notice for the purpose of affording that information to other persons concerned.

[*RRA s 58(2)*].

The CRE may also require information to verify compliance with the notice, which must be supplied within a specified time not later than five years from the date the notice became final. [*RRA s 58(4)*].

Before serving a non-discrimination notice the CRE must first

(*a*) give the person concerned notice that they are minded to issue a non-discrimination notice in his case, specifying the grounds on which they contemplate doing so; and

(*b*) offer him an opportunity of making oral or written representations within a period of not less than 28 days specified in the notice; and

(*c*) take account of any representation made by him.

[*RRA s 58(5)*].

The persons concerned are not entitled to cross-examine witnesses. (*R v Commission for Racial Equality, Ex parte Cottrell & Rothon* [*1980*] *1 WLR 1580*).

Appeal. After a non-discrimination notice has been served on him, the employer has six weeks to appeal to an industrial tribunal. [*RRA s 59(1)*]. The Court of Appeal in *Commission for Racial Equality v Amari Plastics Ltd* [*1982*] *ICR 304* approved a procedure formulated by the EAT to be adopted on such appeals. The CRE ought to state the facts on which they relied, and the employer, in answer, ought to say which of those findings of fact are challenged. On appeal, the tribunal may quash or vary the notice. [*RRA s 59(2)(3)*].

The procedure regulating such appeals is set out in the *Industrial Tribunals (Non-discrimination Notices Appeals) Regulations 1977 (SI 1977 No 1094)*. In appropriate cases a non-discrimination notice may be challenged by way of application for judicial review using the procedure of Order 53 of the Rules of the Supreme Court (*Hillingdon London Borough Council v Commission for Racial Equality* [*1982*] *ICR 799; R v Commission for Racial Equality, Ex parte Westminster City Council* [*1984*] *ICR 770;* [*1985*] *ICR 827*).

A register is kept of non-discrimination notices which have become final. [*RRA s 61*]. A non-discrimination notice or a finding by a court or tribunal becomes final when an appeal against the notice or finding is dismissed, withdrawn or abandoned or when the time for appealing expires without an appeal having been brought. [*RRA s 78(4)*].

37.30 Persistent discrimination

If during the period of five years beginning on the date on which a non-discrimination notice or a finding by an industrial tribunal became final, it appears to the CRE that unless restrained any person is likely to commit an unlawful act, it may apply to a county court for an injunction restraining that person from doing so. [*RRA s 62(1)*].

37.31 Enforcement of Sections 29-31

Unlawful acts relating to discriminatory advertisements are dealt with in *Sec 29*, instructions to discriminate in *Sec 30*, and pressure to discriminate in *Sec 31* (see 37.10, 37.18 and 37.19 above). The CRE may make an application to an industrial tribunal for a decision that a contravention of any of *Secs 29-31* has occurred. [*RRA s 63(2)*]. Such an application must be made before the end of the period of six months, beginning when the act to which it relates was done. [*RRA s 68(4)*]. After an industrial tribunal has made such a finding, the CRE may also apply to a county court for an injunction if it appears that further unlawful acts will be done. [*RRA s 63(4)*]. An application under *Sec 63(4)* must be made before the end of the period of five years, beginning when the act to which it relates was done. [*RRA s 68(4)*]. A court may nevertheless consider any such complaint, claim or application which is out of time if, in all the circumstances of the case, the court considers that it is just and equitable to do so. [*RRA s 68(6)*]. *Secs 29-31* may be enforced only by the CRE.

37.32 HELP FOR PERSONS SUFFERING DISCRIMINATION

The Secretary of State has prescribed forms which complainants can use to obtain information from employers relating to alleged discrimination. [*RRA s 65*]. The forms and procedure governing the service of the forms (known as questionnaires) are set out in the *Race Relations (Questions and Replies) Order 1977 (SI 1977 No 842)*. In proceedings before an industrial tribunal, a questionnaire will only be admissible as evidence under *RRA s 65(2)(a)*

(*a*) where it was served before the presentation of a complaint, if it was served within the period of three months beginning when the act complained of was done;

(*b*) where it was served when a complaint had been presented, either if it was so served within the period of 21 days beginning with the day on which the complaint was presented, or if it was so served later with leave of the tribunal, within the period specified by the tribunal.

[*Article 5*].

A questionnaire may be obtained from offices of the Department of Employment or the CRE.

The CRE may give advice or assistance to complainants in difficult or important cases. [*RRA s 66*]. Their address is The Commission for Racial Equality, Elliot House, 10/12 Allington Street, London SW1E 5EH, tel. 01-828 7022.

37.33 NO CONTRACTING OUT

A term in a contract which purports to exclude or limit any provision of the Act is unenforceable by any person in whose favour the term would operate. [*RRA s 72(3)*].

Contracts settling a complaint. Contracts settling a complaint relating to discrimination in employment are enforceable only where the contract is made with the assistance of a conciliation officer. [*RRA s 72(4)(a)*]. Thus, it is most important to have the assistance of a conciliation officer when settling such a complaint, otherwise, despite a sum to settle the complaint having been paid, a complainant may still pursue his application to an industrial tribunal.

38 Redundancy – I: The Right to a Redundancy Payment

(See also DE booklets No. 16 'Redundancy Payments' (PL 808) and No. 10 'Employment rights on the transfer of an undertaking' (PL 699); leaflets RPL1 'Offsetting Pensions against Redundancy Payments'; RPL2 'Ready Reckoner' (see below); also booklet No. 6 'Facing redundancy? – Time off for job hunting or to arrange training' (PL 703).)

Cross-references. TRANSFER OF UNDERTAKINGS (53). See 55.11 UNFAIR DISMISSAL – II for dismissal on grounds of redundancy, and 'A WEEK'S PAY' (58) for details of the calculation of the employee's weekly pay.

38.1 The *Redundancy Payments Act 1965 (RPA)* introduced the right of employees who lost their jobs in certain circumstances to a payment from their employers irrespective of whether they had another job to go to. The *RPA* was amended by the *Employment Protection Act 1975 (EPA)* and the provisions, as amended, were re-enacted in the *Employment Protection (Consolidation) Act 1978 (EPCA)*.

38.2 PRE-CONDITIONS FOR PAYMENT

The conditions which must be fulfilled for a person to be entitled to a redundancy payment are

(*a*) that he was an employee;

(*b*) that he had been continuously employed for the requisite period;

(*c*) that he was dismissed (as defined); and

(*d*) that the dismissal was by reason of redundancy.

Certain employees are excluded from the right to a redundancy payment (see 38.10 below).

38.3 APPLICANT MUST HAVE BEEN AN EMPLOYEE

Only 'employees' are entitled to claim a redundancy payment. Thus, those engaged under a contract for services are not entitled to make such a claim. 'Employee' is defined as

> 'an individual who has entered into or works under (or, where the employment has ceased, worked under) a contract of employment'. [*EPCA s 153(1)*].

See EMPLOYEE OR SELF-EMPLOYED? (15).

If the respondent to an application for a redundancy payment (i.e. the employer) disputes the fact that the applicant was an employee, it is for the applicant to prove that he was.

38.4 CONTINUOUS EMPLOYMENT FOR THE REQUISITE PERIOD

In order to be entitled to a redundancy payment, an applicant must have been *continuously employed for a period of two years ending with the relevant date* (see below for 'relevant date'). An employee who commences employment before his

18th birthday is treated as if his employment commenced on that date. [*EPCA s 81(4); EA 1982, 2 Sch 7*].

The general rule is that a week during the whole or part of which an employee worked under a contract of employment normally involving work for 16 hours or more counts in the computation. An employee who has been employed for 5 years or more under a contract normally involving employment for 8 hours or more but less than 16 hours, is considered as working under a contract involving work for 16 hours or more. [*EPCA 13 Sch 6(1)*]. Certain events such as a transfer of the trade or business do not break continuity. The rules for computing continuous employment are dealt with in detail in CONTINUOUS EMPLOYMENT (9).

The following events do not break continuity.

(*a*) *Change in job with the same employer.* If an employee changes his job, whether because his original position became redundant or for any other reason, but he remains with the same employer albeit in different employment, the continuity of his employment is not broken.

(*b*) *Transfer of an undertaking.* A transfer of an undertaking or part of an undertaking does not terminate the contract of employment of any person who was employed by the transferor in the undertaking transferred immediately before the transfer. [*Transfer of Undertakings (Protection of Employment) Regulations 1981 (SI 1981 No 1794), Reg 5(1)*]. (See 38.5 and TRANSFER OF UNDERTAKINGS (53)). See also *EPCA 13 Sch 17(2)* for provisions on the transfer of a trade or business.

(*c*) *Engagement by an associated employer.* (See 9.7(*a*) CONTINUOUS EMPLOYMENT.)

(*d*) *Absence.* Periods of absence from work for reasons of sickness, injury, absence due to pregnancy or confinement of less than 26 weeks, or periods of absence due to temporary cessation of work or absence during which, by custom or arrangement, the employee is regarded as continuing in employment count as periods of employment for the purposes of entitlement to redundancy payments. [*EPCA 13 Sch 9(1)(2)*]. (See further 9.6(*e*),(*f*) CONTINUOUS EMPLOYMENT.)

(*e*) *Participation in a strike.* (See 9.8 CONTINUOUS EMPLOYMENT.)

(*f*) *Dismissal followed by reinstatement or re-engagement.* If an employer reinstates or re-engages an employee after he has been dismissed, the continuity of the employee's employment is maintained if such action was taken as a result of an application by the employee to an industrial tribunal or as a result of an agreement brought about by a conciliation officer. [*Labour Relations (Continuity of Employment) Regulations 1976 (SI 1976 No 660); EPCA 13 Sch 20*]. Reinstatement is re-employment in the same job from which the employee was dismissed. Re-engagement is employment in a different job. (See also 9.6(*g*) CONTINUOUS EMPLOYMENT.)

The relevant date. The relevant date in relation to the dismissal of an employee

(i) where his contract of employment is terminated by notice, whether given by his employer or by the employee, means the date on which that notice expires;

(ii) where his contract of employment is terminated without notice, means the date on which the termination takes effect;

(iii) where he is employed under a contract for a fixed term and that term expires, means the date on which that term expires.

[*EPCA s 90*].

Thus, if an employer dismisses an employee with notice and requires him to work out his notice period, the *relevant date* is the date on which the notice expires. If the employer dismisses the employee with notice, but waives the requirement that the employee work during the notice period, the relevant date remains the date upon which the notice expires. If, however, there is an immediate dismissal with pay in lieu of notice, the relevant date is the date of the dismissal, not the expiry of the period in respect of which the salary in lieu is paid. (*Robert Cort and Son v Charman* [*1981*] *ICR 816*, in which the Employment Appeal Tribunal considered a similar provision relating to the qualifying period for unfair dismissal, cf. 54.13 UNFAIR DISMISSAL – I; see also *Dedman v British Building & Engineering Appliances Ltd* [*1974*] *ICR 53*.) The 'effective date' of termination in *EPCA s 55(4)* was held to be the actual date of termination of the employment, whether or not the employee was wrongfully dismissed. (*Stapp v The Shaftesbury Society* [*1982*] *IRLR 326*). If an employee is dismissed with no notice or less than the statutory minimum period of notice, for the purposes, *inter alia*, of calculating the qualifying period of employment, the relevant date will be the date upon which the statutory minimum period of notice would have expired had it been given. [*EPCA s 90(3)*]. (See 49.9 TERMINATION OF EMPLOYMENT.) However, this provision does not affect the employer's right to dismiss without notice for an employee's gross misconduct. [*EPCA s 49(5)*]. In the event of such a dismissal, the statutory minimum period of notice will not be added on for the purpose of computing the length of continuous employment.

38.5 Changes in the ownership of the business

The *Transfer of Undertakings (Protection of Employment) Regulations 1981 (SI 1981 No 1794)* are complex and a detailed discussion is beyond the scope of this book, but for a full summary of their main provisions see TRANSFER OF UNDERTAKINGS (53). By virtue of the Regulations, on a 'relevant transfer' of an undertaking the existing employees' contracts of employment are not terminated. On completion of such a transfer all the transferor's rights, powers, duties and liabilities under or in connection with any such contract are transferred to the transferee. [*Transfer of Undertakings Regs, Reg 5(2)(a)*]. Therefore, such an employee will be deemed not to have been dismissed by the transferor and the continuity of his employment will be preserved. It is considered that the test as to whether a relevant undertaking has been transferred will be similar to the test as to whether there has been a change in the ownership of a business for the purposes of *EPCA s 94(1)* and *13 Sch 17(2)*. A business is considered to have been transferred for these purposes if it is handed over as a going concern. (*Kenmir v Frizzell (1968) 3 ITR 159; Lloyd v Brassey (1969) 4 ITR 100*). A transfer of assets alone without the transfer of goodwill and customer connection is not considered to be a transfer of a business for redundancy payments purposes. (*Melon v Hector Powe Ltd* [*1981*] *ICR 43*). The Court of Appeal has held that if there has been a substantive handover of a business, there may have been a transfer of an undertaking within the meaning of *EPCA 13 Sch 17(2)* even though the proposed merger or sale in pursuance of which the handover took place is not in fact completed. (*Dabell v Vale Industrial Services (Nottingham) Ltd* [*1988*] *IRLR 439*). Any provision in an agreement which purports to exclude or limit the operation of *Regulation 5* is void. [*Transfer of Undertakings Regs, Reg 12*]. Where the Regulations apply it is considered that *EPCA ss 84* and *94* cease to apply and

EPCA 13 Sch 17(2) (which preserves continuity of employment in such circumstances) is unnecessary – see 'The Transfer of Undertakings (Protection of Employment) Regulations' by Hepple, Industrial Law Journal, March 1982.

Where, however, the transfer is not of an undertaking as defined in the *Regulations* but is of a business within the meaning of *EPCA*, the *EPCA* will continue to apply. If the new owner of the business offers an employee of the transferor employment, the provisions relating to offer of alternative employment apply (see 38.12 below). If, however, no suitable alternative employment is offered to him, and he is dismissed by reason of redundancy, he may claim a redundancy payment from the transferor. If he accepts employment with the transferee his continuity of employment is preserved. [*EPCA 13 Sch 17(2)*].

38.6 THE EMPLOYEE MUST HAVE BEEN 'DISMISSED'

There is no presumption of dismissal and, if the employer disputes the fact, it is for the employee to prove it. For redundancy payments purposes, dismissal has a statutory meaning instead of merely meaning termination of the contract by the employer. Sub-paragraph (*a*) below reflects the common law position (see 49.7 TERMINATION OF EMPLOYMENT), and occurs most frequently in practice, while (*b*) would not be a dismissal at common law. In addition, certain forms of termination of the contract at common law are disregarded for redundancy payments purposes (see below).

An employee will be taken to be dismissed by his employer if, but only if

(*a*) the contract under which he is employed by the employer is terminated by the employer, whether it is terminated by notice or without notice; or

(*b*) where under that contract he is employed for a fixed term, that term expires without being renewed under the same contract; or

(*c*) the employee terminates that contract with or without notice in circumstances such that he is entitled so to terminate it without notice by reason of the employer's conduct (not being termination by reason of a lock-out).

[*EPCA s 83*].

The statutory definition of dismissal for redundancy payments purposes is the same as for the purposes of unfair dismissal (see UNFAIR DISMISSAL – I (54)).

In order to terminate a contract, an employer must clearly communicate to the employee concerned that on a certain date (which may in certain circumstances be immediately), his employment will come to an end. To constitute an advance notice of dismissal which is to operate on a future date 'the notice must specify that date, or at least certain facts from which that date is ascertainable'. (*Morton Sundour Fabrics Ltd v Shaw (1966) 2 ITR 84*). A contract with no prior fixed date of determination other than completion of the job at some time in the future was considered not to be capable of being a fixed term contract in *Ryan v Shipboard Maintenance Ltd* [*1980*] *ICR 88*. Similarly in *Brown and others v Knowsley Borough Council* [*1986*] *IRLR 102*, the Employment Appeal Tribunal held that there was no dismissal when a temporary lecturer's contract came to an end when funding was withdrawn. Her contract provided that the appointment would last only as long as sufficient funds were provided either by the Manpower Services Commission or by other firms or sponsors. A consensual termination is not a dismissal (see e.g. *Birch v University of Liverpool* [*1985*] *ICR 470*).

Constructive dismissal. Sub-paragraph (*c*) above applies where the employer is in repudiatory breach of contract, such as in *Marriott v Oxford and District Co-operative Society Ltd (No 2) (1969) 4 ITR 377*, where the employer sought unilaterally to reduce the employee's wages. He may also be guilty of repudiatory conduct in reducing the employee's status without his consent. (*Skillen v Eastwoods Froy Ltd (1967) 2 ITR 112*). In order to determine whether the employer is in breach of contract, the obligations of the employee under the contract must first be defined. The contract of employment may enable an employee to be transferred from one place to another (see e.g. *Courtaulds Northern Spinning Ltd v Sibson and another* [*1988*] *ICR 451*). If it does, the fact that he has been working at a particular location for many years does not stop the employer from transferring him. If, however, the employee is employed specifically at one place, insistence by the employer that he transfer to another work place may be repudiatory conduct entitling the employee to terminate the contract. (From the employer's point of view, contracts of employment should therefore be cast in the widest possible terms whilst being an accurate definition of the employee's obligations.)

Where an employee is entitled to return to work after a period of pregnancy (see 29.17 MATERNITY RIGHTS) and has exercised her right to return, but is not permitted to return to work, she is treated as if she had been continuously employed until her notified date of return, and she will be treated as if she was dismissed on that day for the reason for which she was not permitted to return. [*EPCA s 86*].

Situations where no dismissal occurs. An employee is deemed not to have been dismissed in certain circumstances where a dismissal by reason of redundancy has in fact taken place. Three examples are given below.

(i) *Renewal or re-engagement.* If an employee's contract is renewed or he is re-engaged under a new contract of employment and

(A) the offer, whether in writing or not, is made before the ending of the existing contract; and

(B) it is to take effect either immediately on the ending of the original employment or within a period of not more than four weeks thereafter (if the contract ends on Friday, Saturday or Sunday, the new employment must take effect four weeks from the following Monday),

no dismissal will be deemed to have taken place in respect of the termination of the original contract. [*EPCA s 84(1)*].

If the terms and conditions of the new employment differ wholly or in part from the original contract, the employee has a trial period of four weeks from the ending of the original employment, or such longer period as may be agreed in writing, within which to decide whether to accept or reject the offer (see also 38.12 below). Four weeks means four calendar weeks, whether or not the business is working for the whole of that period. (*Benton v Sanderson Kayser Ltd* [*1989*] *ICR 136*). If he rejects the offer or if the employer terminates or gives notice to terminate the contract for a reason connected with the change in contractual terms, within that period, the employee will be taken to have been dismissed on the date of termination of the original contract for the reason that contract was terminated. [*EPCA s 84(3)-(6)*]. However, if the employer terminates the employment during the trial period, when considering a claim for unfair dismissal, an industrial tribunal will consider the fairness of the dismissal at the end of the trial period, rather than at the end of the original contract. (*Hempell v W H Smith & Sons Ltd* [*1986*] *ICR 365*).

Although the *EPCA* no longer requires the employer, in making the offer, to give the employee details of the changes in terms and conditions in writing, where applicable, employers may still find it useful to do so. The employer, however, remains obliged to give written particulars of the main terms of an employee's employment within one month of the change. [*EPCA s 4(1)*]. (See 10.7 CONTRACT OF EMPLOYMENT.)

(ii) *Offers of employment by associated companies.* It should be noted that where the employer is a company, any reference to re-engagement by the employer is construed as reference to re-engagement by *that company or by an associated company*, and any reference to an offer made by the employer is construed as including a reference to an offer made by an associated company. [*EPCA s 84(7)*]. For the meaning of 'associated company', see 9.8 CONTINUITY OF EMPLOYMENT.

(iii) *Offers of employment by new owners of the business.* No dismissal is deemed to have taken place where an employer terminates the employment of his employee on the sale of the business to another and the purchaser renews the employee's contract or re-engages him, provided that the renewal or re-engagement complies with *EPCA s 84*. [*EPCA s 94(3)*].

Thus, if company B acquires the business of company A and the employment of a mechanic at a garage at a particular place is terminated and B re-engages the employee at the same place, no dismissal will be regarded as having occurred. [*EPCA ss 84(1), 94*]. Similarly if, with the employee's agreement and following an offer made before the termination of the old employment, B employs the man at his garage at another place, no dismissal will be regarded as having occurred although his terms and conditions of employment may have changed. However, these provisions do not apply to a case governed by the *Transfer of Undertakings (Protection of Employment) Regulations 1981 (SI 1981 No 1794)*. See 38.5 above and TRANSFER OF UNDERTAKINGS (53).

Employee who leaves prematurely. An employee who leaves his employment before his employer's notice of dismissal expires may lose his right to a redundancy payment. If the employee gives written notice to terminate his employment on a date earlier than that given by his employer, he will not lose his right to a redundancy payment if the employer does not object to his premature departure. If, however, the employer does object and serves on the employee a written request to withdraw his notice, warning him that if he does not do so the employer will contest any liability to make a redundancy payment, he may lose the right to such a payment. If the employer withholds the redundancy payment, the employee may apply to an industrial tribunal which will decide whether the employee is entitled to the full payment, or no payment, or part of the payment. The tribunal will consider whether the employee's action in leaving prematurely was reasonable or unreasonable in the circumstances. [*EPCA s 85*]. If, however, the parties agree by mutual consent to substitute some other date of termination for the date specified by the employer, no question of *Sec 85* arises. (*CPS Recruitment Ltd v Bowen and Secretary of State for Employment* [*1982*] *IRLR 54*).

38.7 REDUNDANCY MUST BE THE REASON FOR DISMISSAL

In order to be entitled to a redundancy payment the employee must be dismissed by reason of redundancy. An employee who has been dismissed by his employer is, unless the contrary is proved, presumed to have been dismissed by reason of redundancy for the purposes of any claim for a redundancy payment. [*EPCA s 91(2)*]. It is therefore for the employer to prove that the reason for the dismissal was other than redundancy or that for some reason the employee is not entitled to the payment. If, therefore, the fact of dismissal is admitted in an application for a redundancy payment and no evidence is presented, the employee will be awarded the appropriate payment provided that he had been continuously employed under a contract of employment for the requisite period.

'Redundancy' is defined as follows

> 'For the purposes of this Act an employee who is dismissed shall be taken to be dismissed by reason of redundancy if the dismissal is attributable wholly or mainly to –
>
> (*a*) the fact that his employer has ceased, or intends to cease, to carry on the business for the purposes of which the employee was employed by him, or has ceased, or intends to cease, to carry on that business in the place where the employee was so employed, or
>
> (*b*) the fact that the requirements of that business for employees to carry out work of a particular kind . . . in the place where he was so employed, have ceased or diminished or are expected to cease or diminish.'

[*EPCA s 81(2)*].

Sub-paragraph (*a*) covers the situation in which the business at the place or places where the employee could be required under his contract to work, is closed down (see *Rank Xerox Ltd v Churchill and others [1988] IRLR 280*). Under sub-paragraph (*b*) it must be considered whether the business requires so many employees to carry out certain work. In deciding whether there has been a cessation or diminution in the requirements of the business for employees to carry out work of a particular kind, the courts will look at whether there was such a cessation or diminution in the requirements for the specific type of work which the employee was obliged to perform under his contract. (*Cowen v Haden Ltd [1983] ICR 1*). If the employer is reducing his staff and decides that he only requires two mechanics instead of three, the third will be dismissed by reason of redundancy. It is irrelevant if a few weeks or months later business recovers and he decides to employ a third mechanic. The test is whether at the time of the dismissal his requirements for employees to do work of that particular kind had or were expected to cease or diminish. There is a redundancy situation where the amount of work remains the same but an event such as reorganisation of the workforce discloses that overmanning exists. (*McCrea v Cullen & Davison Ltd [1988] IRLR 30*).

Night-shift work may be 'work of a particular kind'. (*Macfisheries Ltd v Findlay and others [1985] ICR 160*).

An employee may be dismissed by reason of redundancy despite the fact that the employer still requires the same number of employees to do his particular job. If Smith is to be dismissed because his employer no longer requires men to do his job, but instead of dismissing him, the employer puts him into Brown's job and dismisses Brown, then Brown is dismissed by reason of redundancy. A similar result occurs where Smith and Brown are employed by associated companies. (See, for example, *W Gimber & Sons Ltd v Spurrett (1967) 2 ITR 308*.)

38.8 REDUNDANCY PAYMENTS FOR LAY-OFF AND SHORT TIME

Special provisions relating to redundancy claims by piece-workers who are laid off or put on short time are contained in *EPCA ss 87-89*. An employee is considered to be *laid off* during a particular week if under his contract he gets no pay of any kind from his employer for that week because there is no work for him to do although he is available for work. [*EPCA s 87(1)*]. An employee is considered to be on short time for a week if during that week he gets less than half a week's pay. [*EPCA s 87(2)*].

A redundancy payment may only be claimed by a worker laid off or on short time if he gives notice in writing to his employer of his intention to claim and the claim is submitted within four weeks of

(*a*) the end of a continuous period of lay-off or short time of four or more weeks' duration; or

(*b*) the end of a period of six weeks' lay-off or short time out of thirteen weeks (where not more than three weeks were consecutive).

[*EPCA s 88(1)*].

He must then terminate his contract of employment by giving the contractual period of notice or one week's notice, whichever is the greater. [*EPCA s 88(2)(a)*]. Even if an employee fails to comply with these statutory requirements, he may claim that he has been constructively dismissed for redundancy if he is laid off for more than a reasonable period. (*A Dakri & Co Ltd v Tiffen and others [1981] ICR 256*).

The notice to terminate must be given within the following time limits

(*a*) if the employer does not give a counter-notice within seven days after the service of the notice of intention to claim, that period is three weeks after the end of those seven days;

(*b*) if the employer gives a counter-notice (see 38.9 below) within those seven days, but withdraws it by a subsequent notice in writing, that period is three weeks after the service of the notice of withdrawal;

(*c*) if the employer gives a counter-notice within those seven days and does not so withdraw it, and a question as to the right of the employee to a redundancy payment in pursuance of the notice of intention to claim is referred to a tribunal, that period is three weeks after the tribunal has notified to the employee its decision on that reference.

[*EPCA s 89(5)*].

38.9 Counter-notice

If the employer wishes to contest his liability to make a redundancy payment, he must give written notice of that fact to the employee within seven days of the employee's notice. An employer should serve such a notice if he reasonably expects to be able to provide the employee with a period of employment of not less than thirteen weeks during which he would not be laid off or kept on short time. The period of employment must be expected to begin not later than four weeks from the date of service of the employee's notice. [*EPCA, s 88(3), (4)*].

If the employee wishes to pursue his claim after the service of a counter-notice, an industrial tribunal must be asked to determine whether the grounds for the counter-notice are well founded. If they are, the employee will not be entitled to a redundancy payment. [*EPCA, s 89(4)*].

38.10 EXCLUSIONS FROM RIGHT TO PAYMENT

The following are excluded from the right to a redundancy payment.

(*a*) Employees who have attained the normal retiring age (see 54.14 UNFAIR DISMISSAL – I), provided that there is such an age in the business, that it is less than 65 and that it is the same for men and women. [*EPCA s 82(1)(a)* as substituted by *EA 1989 s 16(1)*].

(*b*) Where (*a*) does not apply, employees who have attained the age of 65. [*EPCA s 82(1)(b)* as substituted by *EA 1989 s 16(1)*].

(*c*) Masters or crew of a fishing vessel who are not remunerated otherwise than by a share of the profits or gross earnings of the vessel. [*EPCA s 144(2)* (see *Goodeve v Gilsons (a firm)* [*1985*] *ICR 401*)].

(*d*) Civil servants and other public employees. [*EPCA s 99*].

(*e*) Employees who are outside Great Britain on the relevant date unless under their contracts of employment they ordinarily work in Great Britain. [*EPCA s 141(3)*].

(*f*) Employees who ordinarily work outside Great Britain unless on the relevant date they are in Great Britain in accordance with instructions given by the employer. [*EPCA s 141(4)*].

(*g*) Employees who have been offered employment on the same terms and conditions as their original employment or offered *suitable alternative employment* and in either case have *unreasonably refused the offer* (see 38.12 below). [*EPCA s 82(3), (5)*].

(*h*) Employees who have been offered suitable alternative employment, and have unreasonably terminated their contracts during the statutory trial period (see 38.12 below). [*EPCA s 82(3), (6)*].

(*j*) Employees who are dismissed for misconduct. If notice is given for this reason it must be accompanied by a statement in writing that the employer would, because of the employee's conduct, be entitled to terminate the contract without notice. [*EPCA s 82(2)*]. This provision does not apply where the dismissal is for taking part in a strike. [*EPCA s 92*].

(*k*) Employees who are dismissed if an *exemption order* is in force. [*EPCA s 96*]. An exemption order is an order made by the Secretary of State for Employment exempting an employer or a group of employers from liability to make redundancy payments under the Act where they have similar or more advantageous agreements with their employees for making payments on redundancy.

(*l*) Employees who receive a lump sum or a pension payable on leaving their employment or within 90 weeks thereafter where the provisions of *Redundancy Payments Pensions Regulations 1965 (SI 1965 No 1932)* are satisfied (see 38.14 below).

(*m*) Employees who are employed under a fixed term contract of more than two years entered into before 6 December 1965 not being a contract of apprenticeship. [*EPCA 15 Sch 12*]. This provision can now be considered obsolete.

(*n*) Employees who are employed under a fixed term contract of two years or more entered into after 5 December 1965 (including a contract of apprenticeship for such a term), where the dismissal consists of the expiry of that term without its being renewed, if before the term so expires the employee has agreed in writing to exclude any right to a redundancy payment in that event. [*EPCA s 142(2)*].

38.11 TIME LIMIT FOR CLAIMS

Employees are not entitled to a redundancy payment unless, before the end of the period of six months beginning with the relevant date

(*a*) the payment has been agreed and paid; or

(*b*) the employee has made a claim for the payment by notice in writing given to the employer; or

(*c*) a question as to the right of the employee to the payment, or as to the amount of the payment, has been referred to an industrial tribunal; or

(*d*) a complaint of unfair dismissal has been presented by the employee to a tribunal.

[*EPCA s 101(1)*].

If, however, within the *next* six months, the employee takes the action in (*b*), (*c*) or (*d*), a tribunal may award a redundancy payment if it considers it just and equitable to do so having regard to the reason for the delay. [*EPCA s 101(2)*].

An application for a redundancy payment is 'referred' to an industrial tribunal when it is received by the tribunal office and not when it is sent by the employee. (*Secretary of State for Employment v Banks & others* [*1983*] *ICR 48*).

38.12 UNREASONABLE REFUSAL OF SUITABLE ALTERNATIVE EMPLOYMENT

An employee who is dismissed by reason of redundancy loses his right to a redundancy payment if he unreasonably refuses an offer of suitable alternative employment. The offer of alternative employment

(*a*) must be made by his original employer or an associated employer [*EPCA s 82(3)(7)*; and see 9.8 CONTINUITY OF EMPLOYMENT];

(*b*) must be made before the ending of his employment under his previous contract [*EPCA s 82(3)*];

(*c*) may be oral or in writing;

(*d*) must take effect either immediately on the ending of the employment under the previous contract or after an interval of not more than four weeks thereafter [*EPCA s 82(3)*]; (The alternative employment will be treated as taking effect immediately on the ending of the employment under the previous contract if that employment ends on a Friday, Saturday or Sunday, and the alternative employment is to commence on or before the next Monday. The interval of four weeks is calculated accordingly [*EPCA s 82(4)*].)

(*e*) must be either

(i) on the same terms and conditions as the previous contract; or

(ii) of suitable employment in relation to the employee.

[*EPCA s 82(5)*].

If the terms and conditions of the renewed or new contract of employment differ (wholly or in part) from the corresponding provisions of his previous contract, the employee has a statutory trial period of four weeks beginning with the ending of his previous employment, in which to decide whether the alternative employment is suitable for him. This four-week period may be extended by agreement. Such an agreement must

(A) be made before the employee starts work under the renewed or new contract;

(B) be in writing;

(C) specify the date of the end of the trial period;

(D) specify the terms and conditions of employment which will apply in the employee's case after the end of that period.

[*EPCA s 84(5)*].

An employee whose contract was repudiated by his employers was held to be entitled, in accordance with the common law, to a reasonable period in which to decide whether to enter into a new contract or to treat himself as dismissed (see TERMINATION OF EMPLOYMENT (49)). It was only after that period had expired and a new contract, or the old contract with variations, was in force that the statutory trial period began to run. (*Turvey and others v C W Cheney & Son Ltd [1979] ICR 341*).

If the employee accepts the alternative employment, which was offered before the termination of his original employment and which takes effect not more than four weeks thereafter, he is deemed not to have been dismissed on the termination of the original employment. [*EPCA s 84(1)*].

If the employee terminates a contract during the statutory trial period, he will be treated as having been dismissed on the date upon which his original contract came to an end. [*EPCA s 84(6)*]. For this purpose, there need not be four weeks' actual trial. Thus eleven days when the factory was closed over Christmas had to be taken into account (see *Benton v Sanderson Kayser Ltd [1989] ICR 136*). If his termination is unreasonable he will not be entitled to a redundancy payment. [*EPCA s 82(6)*].

There has been much discussion, both by academics and in the courts, as to the meaning of the two tests of suitable alternative employment and unreasonable refusal. In considering what is suitable alternative employment, the tribunals may have regard to the pay, conditions and status of the alternative employment offered and in considering whether it was unreasonably refused or not regard may be had to the personal and domestic circumstances of the employee concerned. However, the Court of Appeal in *Spencer and Griffin v Gloucestershire County Council [1985] IRLR 393* has said that in evaluating the separate questions of suitability of employment and reasonableness of refusal, the industrial tribunal is entitled to look at factors which may prove, on analysis, to be common to both. In that case, the Court of Appeal, in upholding a decision of an industrial tribunal, considered that a refusal by an employee to do work of a lower standard than the employee considered reasonable, may be a reason for holding that the work offered is not suitable or has been reasonably refused.

38.13 RESTRICTION ON CONTRACTING OUT

Except in the special circumstances of 38.10(*n*) above, any provision in any agreement (whether a contract of employment or not) is void insofar as it purports to exclude or limit any provisions relating to redundancy. [*EPCA s 140(1)*].

38.14 AMOUNT OF THE PAYMENT

The amount of the redundancy payment is based upon the employee's age, length of continuous employment and gross average wage. See the Table below.

The calculation of continuity is made in accordance with *EPCA 13 Schedule* as amended by *EA 1982, 2 Sch 7*. For the computation rules see 38.4 above and CONTINUOUS EMPLOYMENT (9).

Contractual agreements relating to continuity of employment cannot affect an employer's statutory liability to make a redundancy payment. (*Secretary of State for Employment v Globe Elastic Thread Co Ltd* [*1979*] *ICR 706*). Therefore, if an employer agrees to preserve an employee's continuity of employment where there is no continuity in accordance with the statutory provisions, he will be contractually liable to make a redundancy payment calculated in accordance with his agreement.

The amount of the redundancy payment is calculated by reference to the period, ending with the relevant date, during which the employee has been continuously employed. (For the meaning of *relevant date* see 38.4 above.) There is then allowed

(*a*) one and a half week's pay for each such year of employment which consists wholly of weeks in which the employee was not below the age of 41;

(*b*) one week's pay for each such year of employment (not falling within (*a*) above) which consists wholly of weeks in which the employee was not below the age of 22; and

(*c*) half a week's pay for each such year of employment not falling within either of the preceding sub-paragraphs.

[*EPCA 4 Sch 1, 2*].

In the case of employees over the age of 64, the amount payable is reduced by one twelfth for each month by which her or his age exceeds 64. [*EPCA 4 Sch 4* as amended by *EA 1989, s 16(2)*].

By the *Redundancy Payments Pensions Regulations 1965 (SI 1965 No 1932)* the employer may in some circumstances be able to pay a pension instead of a redundancy payment. For a recent case on this, see *Royal Ordnance PLC v Pilkington* [*1989*] *IRLR 489*. It was held in *Pilkington* that pension rights accruing over the whole period of continuous employment, including those in respect of a period with another employer, could be set off against the redundancy payment, but the claim to set off failed on other grounds. The employer must notify the employee of his claim to exclude or reduce the right to a redundancy payment. (*British Telecommunications plc v Burwell* [*1986*] *ICR 35*).

38.15 WEEK'S PAY

A week's pay is calculated in accordance with *EPCA 14 Schedule*. The calculation is based on average wages without deduction of tax, not taking into account

Ready Reckoner for Redundancy Payments

To use the Table — read off employee's age and number of complete years service. Any week which began before the employee attained the age of 18 does not count. The Table will then show how many weeks' pay the employee is entitled to.

For an employee aged between 64 and 65, the cash amount due is to be reduced by one-twelfth for every complete month by which the age exceeds 64.

	SERVICE (years)																		
	2	**3**	**4**	**5**	**6**	**7**	**8**	**9**	**10**	**11**	**12**	**13**	**14**	**15**	**16**	**17**	**18**	**19**	**20**
AGE (years) **20**	1	1	1	1	—														
21	1	1½	1½	1½	1½	—													
22	1	1½	2	2	2	2	—												
23	1½	2	2½	3	3	3	3	—											
24	2	2½	3	3½	4	4	4	4	—										
25	2	3	3½	4	4½	5	5	5	5	—									
26	2	3	4	4½	5	5½	6	6	6	6	—								
27	2	3	4	5	5½	6	6½	7	7	7	7	—							
28	2	3	4	5	6	6½	7	7½	8	8	8	8	—						
29	2	3	4	5	6	7	7½	8	8½	9	9	9	9	—					
30	2	3	4	5	6	7	8	8½	9	9½	10	10	10	10	—				
31	2	3	4	5	6	7	8	9	9½	10	10½	11	11	11	11	—			
32	2	3	4	5	6	7	8	9	10	10½	11	11½	12	12	12	12	—		
33	2	3	4	5	6	7	8	9	10	11	11½	12	12½	13	13	13	13	—	
34	2	3	4	5	6	7	8	9	10	11	12	12½	13	13½	14	14	14	14	—
35	2	3	4	5	6	7	8	9	10	11	12	13	13½	14	14½	15	15	15	15
36	2	3	4	5	6	7	8	9	10	11	12	13	14	14½	15	15½	16	16	16
37	2	3	4	5	6	7	8	9	10	11	12	13	14	15	15½	16	16½	17	17
38	2	3	4	5	6	7	8	9	10	11	12	13	14	15	16	16½	17	17½	18
39	2	3	4	5	6	7	8	9	10	11	12	13	14	15	16	17	17½	18	18½
40	2	3	4	5	6	7	8	9	10	11	12	13	14	15	16	17	18	18½	19
41	2	3	4	5	6	7	8	9	10	11	12	13	14	15	16	17	18	19	19½
42	2½	3½	4½	5½	6½	7½	8½	9½	10½	11½	12½	13½	14½	15½	16½	17½	18½	19½	20½
43	3	4	5	6	7	8	9	10	11	12	13	14	15	16	17	18	19	20	21

44	3	4½	5½	6½	7½	8½	9½	10½	11½	12½	13½	14½	15½	16½	17½	18½	19½	20½	21½
45	3	4½	6	7	8	9	10	11	12	13	14	15	16	17	18	19	20	21	22
46	3	4½	6	7½	8½	9½	10½	11½	12½	13½	14½	15½	16½	17½	18½	19½	20½	21½	22½
47	3	4½	6	7½	9	10	11	12	13	14	15	16	17	18	19	20	21	22	23
48	3	4½	6	7½	9	10½	11½	12½	13½	14½	15½	16½	17½	18½	19½	20½	21½	22½	23½
49	3	4½	6	7½	9	10½	12	13	14	15	16	17	18	19	20	21	22	23	24
50	3	4½	6	7½	9	10½	12	13½	14½	15½	16½	17½	18½	19½	20½	21½	22½	23½	24½
51	3	4½	6	7½	9	10½	12	13½	15	16	17	18	19	20	21	22	23	24	25
52	3	4½	6	7½	9	10½	12	13½	15	16½	17½	18½	19½	20½	21½	22½	23½	24½	25½
53	3	4½	6	7½	9	10½	12	13½	15	16½	18	19	20	21	22	23	24	25	26
54	3	4½	6	7½	9	10½	12	13½	15	16½	18	19½	20½	21½	22½	23½	24½	25½	26½
55	3	4½	6	7½	9	10½	12	13½	15	16½	18	19½	21	22	23	24	25	26	27
56	3	4½	6	7½	9	10½	12	13½	15	16½	18	19½	21	22½	23½	24½	25½	26½	27½
57	3	4½	6	7½	9	10½	12	13½	15	16½	18	19½	21	22½	24	25	26	27	28
58	3	4½	6	7½	9	10½	12	13½	15	16½	18	19½	21	22½	24	25½	26½	27½	28½
59	3	4½	6	7½	9	10½	12	13½	15	16½	18	19½	21	22½	24	25½	27	28	29
60	3	4½	6	7½	9	10½	12	13½	15	16½	18	19½	21	22½	24	25½	27	28½	29½
61	3	4½	6	7½	9	10½	12	13½	15	16½	18	19½	21	22½	24	25½	27	28½	30
62	3	4½	6	7½	9	10½	12	13½	15	16½	18	19½	21	22½	24	25½	27	28½	30
63	3	4½	6	7½	9	10½	12	13½	15	16½	18	19½	21	22½	24	25½	27	28½	30
64	3	4½	6	7½	9	10½	12	13½	15	16½	18	19½	21	22½	24	25½	27	28½	30

'NOTES

1 Service Calendar RPL 4 should always be used when total service or (in the case of an employee whose service covers his 22nd or 41st birthday) service from 22 to 40 years inclusive, or at age 41 years and above, falls short of a whole number of calendar years by

(1) less than 14 days *or*

(2) 31 days or less if total service (or the relevant part of service) exceeds five calendar years.

2 Exceptionally, an employee whose 20th birthday falls within a few days of the Saturday of the week in which his employment was terminated, may have the necessary 104 weeks qualifying service after the week which began before he attained the age of 18.')

overtime, unless the employer is contractually bound to provide and the employee to work such overtime. (See A WEEK'S PAY (58) for full details.)

The maximum number of years to be taken into account in calculating a redundancy payment is 20. [*EPCA 4 Sch 3*]. The maximum amount of a week's pay allowed in computing a redundancy payment since 1 April 1989, has been £172. [*EPCA 14 Sch 8(1)(c); Employment Protection (Variation of Limits) Order 1989 (SI 1989 No 526)*]. The current maximum redundancy payment is therefore £5,160.

Between 1 April 1988 and 31 March 1989 inclusive, the maximum week's pay was £164. (*SI 1988 No 276*).

38.16 THE EMPLOYER'S REBATE

See 39.1 REDUNDANCY – II.

39 Redundancy – II: Practice and Procedure

(See DE booklet No. 2 'Redundancy consultation and notification' (PL 833).)

Cross-reference. See REDUNDANCY – I (38) for the right to a redundancy payment.

39.1 If an employer dismisses an employee by reason of redundancy, he has a number of statutory obligations in addition to that of making the employee a redundancy payment. He may be liable in a claim of unfair dismissal unless he acts fairly. He must allow the employee reasonable time off work to look for alternative employment. If the proposed dismissal is of an employee of a class for which a trade union is recognised for collective bargaining purposes, the employer must consult with the union.

This chapter considers the following

— The relevant provisions in the *Industrial Relations Code of Practice* (see 39.2 below).

— The requirements for consultation before making an employee redundant (see 39.3-39.8 below).

— The basic 'fair dismissal' considerations relating to proposed redundancies (see 39.9-39.13 below).

The chapter ends with a checklist of redundancy dismissal procedure.

An employer was formerly entitled to claim rebates on redundancy payments from the Department of Employment. That right was restricted to those with fewer than ten employees by *Wages Act 1986* and is abolished altogether by *EA 1989 s 17.*

39.2 THE CODE OF PRACTICE AND REDUNDANCIES

In considering the fairness of a dismissal for the purposes of a claim for unfair dismissal, an industrial tribunal will have regard to any relevant provisions of the *Industrial Relations Code of Practice* (the full text of which is given in the Appendix). The provisions relating to redundancies in the *Code of Practice* are set out below.

'44 Responsibility for deciding the size of the work force rests with management, but before taking the final decision to make any substantial reduction, management should consult employees or their representatives, unless exceptional circumstances make this impossible.

'45 A policy for dealing with reductions in the work force, if they become necessary, should be worked out in advance so far as practicable and should form part of the undertaking's employment policies. As far as is consistent with operational efficiency and the success of the undertaking, management should, in consultation with employee representatives, seek to avoid redundancies by such means as

(i) restrictions on recruitment;

(ii) retirement of employees who are beyond the normal retiring age;

(iii) reductions in overtime;

(iv) short-time working to cover temporary fluctuations in manpower needs;

(v) re-training or transfer to other work.

'46 If redundancy becomes necessary, management in consultation, as appropriate, with employees or their representatives, should

(i) give as much warning as practicable to the employees concerned and to the Department of Employment;

(ii) consider introducing schemes for voluntary redundancy, retirement, transfer to other establishments within the undertaking, and a phased rundown of employment;

(iii) establish which employees are to be made redundant and the order of discharge;

(iv) offer help to employees in finding other work in co-operation, where appropriate, with the Department of Employment, and allow them reasonable time off for the purpose;

(v) decide how and when to make the facts public, ensuring that no announcement is made before the employees and their representatives and trade unions have been informed.'

These paragraphs provide a sensible guide to good industrial relations practice which, if followed, may help an employer to resist any claim for unfair dismissal by an employee dismissed by reason of redundancy. Some of these principles have been approved in case law; see *Vokes v Bear [1974] ICR 1* and *Williams v Compair Maxam Ltd* [*1982*] *ICR 156* (considered in 39.9 below), and some have been confirmed in statutes such as the provisions relating to time off work to seek alternative employment (see 50.6 TIME OFF WORK).

39.3 CONSULTATION AND NOTIFICATION REQUIREMENTS

The *Employment Protection Act 1975* imposes far-reaching obligations on employers to notify both recognised trade unions and the Secretary of State for Employment of forthcoming redundancies. In addition the *Transfer of Undertakings (Protection of Employment) Regulations 1981 (SI 1981 No 1794)* impose new obligations on employers to consult trade union representatives about the transfer of relevant undertakings. (These Regulations are considered further in 39.7 below.) Consultation is a factor taken into account in proceedings for unfair dismissal. As set out above, the Industrial Relations Code of Practice para 46 recommends the warning of and consultation with individuals over impending redundancies. For the need to consult employees not represented by a trade union, see *Freud v Bentalls Ltd* [*1983*] *ICR 77* and *Polkey v AE Dayton Services Ltd* [*1988*] *ICR 142*. An industrial tribunal may hold a redundancy dismissal to be unfair because of failure to consult with individual employees even where agreement has been reached with their union on a redundancy selection procedure. (*Walls Meat Co Ltd v Selby,* [*1989*] *ICR 601*).

39.4 Notification to trade unions

An employer who proposes to dismiss, as being redundant, any employee of a class in respect of which a trade union is recognised by him must consult with the representatives of that union at the earliest opportunity. [*EPA s 99(1)*]. 'Recognition' is defined by *EPA s 126* as meaning the recognition of the union by an employer, or two or more associated employers, to any extent, for the purpose of collective bargaining. In *National Union of Gold, Silver & Allied Trades v Albury Brothers Ltd* [*1979*] *ICR 84*, the Court of Appeal held that recognition should not be held to be established unless there was clear and unequivocal evidence of an express agreement, or conduct from which recognition should be inferred which involved not a mere willingness to discuss but a positive decision to negotiate on one or more of the issues specified in *TULRA s 29(1)*.

In order to comply with the requirements of *EPA s 99*, the employer must begin consultations before giving individual notices of dismissal. (*National Union of Teachers v Avon County Council* [*1978*] *IRLR 626*). Consultation must not be a sham exercise; there must be time for the union representatives, who are consulted, to consider properly the proposals that are being put to them. (*Transport & General Workers' Union v Ledbury Preserves (1928) Ltd* [*1985*] *IRLR 412*). Further, the consultation envisaged by *Sec 99* cannot begin until the information required by the section has been given. (*E Green & Son (Castings) Ltd v Association of Scientific, Technical and Managerial Staffs* [*1984*] *ICR 352*).

In addition

(*a*) if an employer is proposing to dismiss *more than one hundred* employees at any one establishment within a period of ninety days or less, the consultation must begin at least *ninety* days before the first of those dismissals take effect;

(*b*) if more than *ten* employees are to be made redundant within a period of thirty days, consultation must begin at least thirty days before the first of those dismissals take effect. [*EPA s 99(3); Employment Protection (Handling of Redundancies) Variation Order 1979 (SI 1979 No 958)*].

For the purposes of the consultation, the employer must disclose in writing to the trade union representatives

(i) the reasons for his proposals;

(ii) the number and descriptions of employees whom it is proposed to dismiss as redundant;

(iii) the total number of employees of any such description employed by the employer at the establishment in question;

(iv) the proposed method of selecting the employees who may be dismissed; and

(v) the proposed method of carrying out the dismissals with due regard to any agreed procedure, including the period over which the dismissals are to take effect.

[*EPA s 99(5)*].

The employer must consider any representations made by the trade union, reply to those representations and, if he rejects any of them, state his reasons. [*EPA s 99(7)*].

Failure to consult with the recognised trade union, or to do so within the stipulated time, may lead to the employer being held liable to pay each redundant employee a protective award (see 39.5 below). Such a failure will also almost certainly render the dismissals unfair. (*Kelly v Upholstery and Cabinet Works*

(Amesbury) Ltd [*1977*] *IRLR 91; North East Midlands Co-operative Society Ltd v Allen* [*1977*] *IRLR 212; Polkey v AE Dayton Services Ltd* [*1988*] *ICR 142*).

39.5 **Protective award**

If an employer fails to comply with any of the requirements for consultation or fails to do so within the appropriate time, the trade union concerned may apply to an industrial tribunal for a *protective award* and a *declaration* that the employer has not complied with the statutory requirements. [*EPA s 101(1)*].

It is a defence to such an application for an employer to show that there were special circumstances which rendered it not reasonably practicable for him to comply with the requirements, and that he took such steps as he was able to take in the circumstances. [*EPA s 101(2)*]. An unforeseen financial crisis may make it necessary to close down a plant at short notice so that consultations can only take place during a shorter period than that prescribed by law. If an employer is compelled to make his employees redundant in circumstances where full consultation is not possible, he must take such steps as he can to comply with the requirements. In *Clarks of Hove Ltd v Bakers' Union* [*1978*] *ICR 1076*, the Court of Appeal held that insolvency is not on its own a special circumstance and that it depends entirely on the course of the insolvency whether the circumstances can be described as special or not. (See also *Angus Jowett & Co (in liquidation) v NUTGW* [*1985*] *ICR 646*.)

Where a tribunal finds a trade union's complaint well-founded it makes a declaration to that effect and may also make a protective award. [*EPA s 101(3)*]. In deciding whether to make a monetary protective award, an industrial tribunal will have to consider the loss of days of consultation which have occurred and the seriousness of the employer's breach. (*Spillers – French (Holdings) Ltd v Union of Shop Distributive and Allied Workers* [*1980*] *ICR 31*).

A protective award is an order that an employer make payments for the protected period in respect of specified employees who have been dismissed, or whom it is proposed to dismiss, as redundant without complying with the statutory requirements for consultation. The amount of the award will be what is considered to be reasonable by the tribunal in the circumstances and will be

(*a*) up to 90 days' pay where 90 days' minimum notice should have been given; or

(*b*) up to 30 days' pay where 30 days' minimum notice should have been given; or

(*c*) in any other case up to 28 days' pay.

The period for payment of the award (known as the protected period) begins on the date on which the first of the dismissals to which the complaint relates was proposed to take effect, or the date of the award, whichever is the earlier. [*EPA s 101(5)*]. See *Transport and General Workers' Union v Ledbury Preserves (1928) Ltd* [*1986*] *ICR 855; E Green & Son (Castings) Ltd v Association of Scientific, Technical and Managerial Staffs* [*1984*] *ICR 352*.

If an employee, specified in the award, receives payments under his contract of employment during the protected period those payments will go to discharge his employer's liability under the protective award and vice versa. [*EPA s 102(3)*]. The employer is entitled to deduct the gross amount paid (*Vosper Thorneycroft (UK) Ltd v Transport and General Workers' Union* [*1988*] *ICR 270*). Payments received during the protected period from another employer will not be taken into account. (*Spillers-French,* above).

Disallowance of payment under award. If an employee remains employed during a protected period and

(i) he is fairly dismissed by his employer for a reason other than redundancy; or

(ii) he unreasonably terminates the contract of employment; or

(iii) he unreasonably refuses an offer of suitable alternative employment made to take effect before or during the protected period,

he will not be entitled to payment under the protective award in respect of any period during which he would have been employed but for the dismissal, termination or refusal of employment. [*EPA s 102(5)-(7)*]. If the offer of alternative employment embodies terms which differ from those under which he previously worked, the employee has a trial period of four weeks beginning with the commencement date of the new contract (or by agreement in writing, a longer period). [*EPA s 102(8)(9)(10)*; see also 38.6 REDUNDANCY – I]. If during the trial period, the employment is terminated by the employer for a reason connected with the change to the new or renewed employment, or by the employee, the employee remains entitled to his protective award unless he acted unreasonably in terminating or giving notice to terminate the contract. [*EPA s 102(11)*].

Remedy for non-payment of award. If an employer fails to pay a protective award, the employee concerned may present a complaint to an industrial tribunal which will order the employer to make the payment. [*EPA s 103(1)*]. The time limit for the presentation of a complaint by a trade union for a protective award, or by an individual for failure to pay a protective award, is three months from the dismissal or proposed dismissals or the failure to make the payment, or such further period as the tribunal considers reasonable in a case where it is satisfied that it was not reasonably practicable for the complaint to be presented within the period of three months. [*EPA ss 101(6), 103(2)*].

39.6 NOTIFICATION TO THE DEPARTMENT OF EMPLOYMENT

An employer must send written notification of certain redundancies to the Department of Employment. If he proposes to make one hundred or more employees redundant at one establishment within a period of ninety days or less, he must give at least ninety days notice before the first of those dismissals takes effect. If he proposes to make ten or more employees redundant at one establishment within a period of thirty days or less, he must give at least thirty days notice. [*EPA s 100(1)*]. The notice must be in a prescribed form and sent to the specified office. Forms are available from the local Department of Employment office. If consultation with a trade union is required, the trade union concerned must be identified and the date when consultations began must be stated. [*EPA s 100(3)*]. Where the notice relates to employees of any description, in respect of whom an independent trade union is recognised by the employer, he must give a copy of the notice to representatives of that union. [*EPA s 100(1)*]. If there are special circumstances which make it impossible for the employer to comply with any of the requirements of notifying the Department of Employment or the trade union concerned, he must take such steps to comply as are reasonably practicable in the circumstances. [*EPA s 100(6)*]. Ignorance of the statutory obligation to notify the Department of Employment cannot constitute such special circumstances. (*Secretary of State for Employment v Helitron Ltd [1980] ICR 523*).

Failure to notify the Department of Employment may lead to a conviction and fine of up to level 5 on the standard scale in a magistrates' court. [*EPA s 105(1);* and see 1.10 INTRODUCTION].

39.7 THE TRANSFER OF UNDERTAKINGS (PROTECTION OF EMPLOYMENT) REGULATIONS 1981

An employer who recognises a trade union for the purpose of collective bargaining must inform and consult representatives of that trade union about any transfer of an undertaking in which employees represented by that union are employed. [*Transfer of Undertakings (Protection of Employment) Regulations 1981 (SI 1981 No 1794), Reg 10*; see generally TRANSFER OF UNDERTAKINGS (53)]. Long enough before a relevant transfer (see 38.4 (*b*) REDUNDANCY – I) to enable consultations to take place, such an employer must inform the union representatives of

(*a*) the fact that the relevant transfer is to take place, when, approximately, it is to take place and the reasons for it; and

(*b*) the legal, economic and social implications of the transfer for the affected employees; and

(*c*) the measures which he envisages he will take in connection with the transfer in relation to those employees, or if he envisages that no measures will be so taken, that fact; and

(*d*) if the employer is the transferor, the measures which the transferee envisages he will take, in connection with the transfer, in relation to such of those employees as, by reason of *Reg 5*, become employees of the transferee after the transfer or, if he envisages that no measures will be so taken, that fact.

The transferee must give the transferor such information at such a time as will enable the transferor to perform the duty imposed on him by virtue of (*d*) above. *Reg 10(4)* provides that the information is to be delivered to the union representatives, or sent by post to the union's head office or to an address notified by the representatives.

In addition to the obligation to inform, if an employer envisages that he will be taking measures in relation to any employees whose trade union is independent and recognised for collective bargaining by him, he must enter into consultations with the representatives of that union and

(i) consider any representations made by the trade union representatives; and

(ii) reply to those representations and, if he rejects any of those representations, state his reasons.

If there are special circumstances which render it not reasonably practicable for an employer to perform a duty imposed on him by *Reg 10*, he must take all such steps towards performing that duty as are reasonably practicable in the circumstances.

Note that many of the relevant obligations were restrictively construed in *Institute of Professional Civil Servants v Secretary of State for Defence [1987] IRLR 373*. However, the facts in this case were somewhat unusual.

39.8 Complaint by trade union or employee to an industrial tribunal

If an employer fails to inform or consult a representative of a trade union in accordance with the provisions of *Reg 10* as above, that trade union may present a complaint to an industrial tribunal. [*Reg 11*]. In such proceedings the burden of establishing

(*a*) that there were special circumstances which rendered it not reasonably practicable for him to perform the duty, and

(*b*) that he took all such steps towards its performance as were reasonably practicable in those circumstances,

rests on the employer.

A transferor will not be able to allege that he was unable to perform his duty because the transferee had failed to give him the requisite information unless he gives the transferee notice of his intention to make such an allegation. The giving of the notice makes the transferee a party to the proceedings.

Where a tribunal finds the complaint of a trade union well founded it will make a declaration to that effect and may do either of the following –

(i) order the employer to pay appropriate compensation to such affected employees as may be specified in the award; or

(ii) if the transferor, having served due notice on the transferee, shows that the default was due to a failure of the transferee, order the transferee to pay appropriate compensation.

'Appropriate compensation' is defined in *Reg 11(11)* as such sum, not exceeding two weeks' pay for the employee in question, as the tribunal considers just and equitable having regard to the seriousness of the failure of the employer to comply with his duty. Any compensation so awarded goes to reduce any protective award made in respect of the same employees and vice versa. (See 39.5 above.)

If an employer fails to pay an employee compensation in accordance with an award, the employee may present a complaint to an industrial tribunal on that ground. [*Reg 11(5)*].

A complaint under *Reg 11* must be presented to an industrial tribunal before the end of the period of three months beginning with

(A) the date on which the relevant transfer is completed, in the case of a complaint by a trade union; or

(B) the date of the tribunal's order, in the case of an individual employee's complaint.

An appeal to the Employment Appeal Tribunal from the decision of an industrial tribunal on the Regulations lies on a point of law. [*Reg 11(10)*].

Any provision in an agreement which purports to limit the operation of *Regs 10 and 11* is void. [*Reg 12*]. *Regs 10 and 11* do not apply to employment where under his contract of employment the employee ordinarily works outside the United Kingdom. [*Reg 13(1)*].

39.9 FAIRNESS OF THE DISMISSAL

Where redundancy is the reason for a dismissal the employer will be liable in a claim for unfair dismissal in addition to the redundancy payment if he fails to act fairly (see UNFAIR DISMISSAL – III (56).) The fairness of a dismissal on notice will be decided having regard to events starting with the giving of notice and ending with the expiry of the notice. If a suitable vacancy arises during the notice period it should be offered to the otherwise redundant employee. (*Stacey v Babcock Power Ltd [1986] ICR 221*). An employer should bear in mind his statutory obligations, the Industrial Relations Code of Practice and the principles of good industrial relations practice.

The EAT in *Williams v Compair Maxam Ltd [1982] ICR 156*, laid down in very general terms current good industrial practice. It identified the following principles of good practice.

(*a*) The employer will try to give as much warning as possible of impending redundancies.

(*b*) The employer will consult with the union, in particular with a view to agreeing criteria for selection.

(*c*) The employer will establish objective criteria for selection for redundancy.

(*d*) The employer will try to ensure that the selection is made fairly in accordance with the criteria.

(*e*) The employer will try to find the employee alternative employment.

However, in *Rolls-Royce Motors Ltd v Dewhurst [1985] ICR 869*, the EAT gave a reminder that *Williams* was not laying down, like an Act of Parliament, the rules for selection for redundancy, the breach of which would necessarily give rise to a claim for unfair dismissal. What the Tribunal was seeking to do was to give very general guidance as to which matters should be considered in a redundancy situation (see also *Grundy (Teddington) Ltd v Plummer and another [1983] ICR 367*). However, the House of Lords in *Polkey v AE Dayton Services Ltd [1988] ICR 142* has re-emphasised the importance of following a fair procedure (see 55.11 UNFAIR DISMISSAL – II). An industrial tribunal may find a dismissal unfair for lack of consultation with individuals affected, even if there have been consultations with trade union representatives (*Walls Meat Co Ltd v Selby, [1989] ICR 601*). Where there is no union representation, consultation with the individuals affected should still take place. (*Freud v Bentalls Ltd [1983] ICR 77*).

39.10 Selection for redundancy

When a number of dismissals for redundancy seem likely, the employer should decide upon objective criteria for selecting employees for redundancy. Dismissal of an employee selected for redundancy in contravention of a customary arrangement or agreed procedure is unfair [*EPCA s 59*], so employers should first of all look to see if there is such a customary arrangement or agreed procedure. A customary arrangement has been described as 'something which is so well known, so certain and so clear as to amount in effect to an implied "agreed procedure", as contrasted with the express "agreed procedure" which is the alternative contemplated by the paragraph'. (*Bessenden Properties Ltd v Corness [1973] IRLR 365*, affirmed *[1974] IRLR 338*). However, in *Henry v Ellerman Lines plc [1985] ICR 57*, the Court of Appeal held that 'agreed procedure' in *Sec 59* is not limited to an express agreed procedure. However, the procedure must be capable of being defined with reasonable certainty (*Suflex Ltd v Thomas [1987] IRLR 435*; see also *Rogers v Vosper Thorneycroft (UK) Ltd [1988] ICR 305*). The most usual customary arrangement or agreed procedure is that of 'last in, first out' (known as

LIFO). Even in the absence of such an agreement or customary arrangement it may be wise when considering selection for redundancy to dismiss first the employees who joined the company most recently. (See also 55.11(a) UNFAIR DISMISSAL – II.)

For the purpose of consultations with a recognised trade union (see 39.4 above) the employer's proposed selection procedure is one of the items of information which he is required to disclose to trade union representatives. [*EPA s 99(5)(d)*]. If possible, the criteria for selection should be agreed with the trade union.

39.11 Warning of redundancy

Employers should give advance warning of redundancies and in particular should give warning as far in advance as possible to those selected for redundancy. (*IR Code of Practice, para 46*, see 39.2 above). (It should be noted that a *warning* that redundancies are likely, or even that a specific person is likely to be dismissed for redundancy, does not constitute notice of dismissal, which must among other things refer to a specific date of termination.) Employers should also allow employees under notice of dismissal reasonable time off work to look for another job, if no suitable alternative work can be offered by the employer (see 39.12 below). They *must* allow such time off where the employee has been continuously employed for two years. [*EPCA s 31*]. (See 50.6 TIME OFF WORK.)

39.12 Investigating possible alternative jobs

An employer should ascertain whether his firm or company, or other companies in the same group, will have any vacancies in posts which might be suitable for the employees whom he proposes to dismiss as being redundant. A failure to do so may well render the dismissal unfair (see, e.g., *Vokes v Bear* [*1974*] *ICR 1*). An employer may be held to have acted unfairly if he fails to offer a vacancy to an employee even if the vacancy is in a job of lower status and salary than in his previous post. (See e.g. *Avonmouth Construction Co Ltd v Shipway* [*1979*] *IRLR 14*).

39.13 CHECKLIST OF REDUNDANCY DISMISSAL PROCEDURE

In practical terms, the first step in the redundancy dismissal procedure is the business decision on the necessity of making one or more employees redundant. Thereafter the following actions should be considered and undertaken as necessary.

(*a*) *Preliminary procedure*. (Not necessarily in chronological order.)

(i) Consult with representatives of any recognised trade unions within the appropriate time limits on the measures to be taken which are set out below. Provide them with all necessary information. Consult unrepresented employees.

(ii) Decide on the number of employees to be made redundant.

(iii) Invite volunteers for redundancy.

(iv) Consider whether alternative jobs are available within the organisation or group. If it should be necessary to retrain employees for those jobs, consider practicability of doing this.

(v) Select employees to be made redundant in accordance with any customary arrangement or agreed procedure. If no such arrangement or procedure exists, establish, if possible with the agreement of the relevant unions, objective criteria for selection, and apply them.

(vi) Consult with individuals affected before a final decision is taken.

(vii) Inform those employees as soon as possible of their impending redundancies.

(viii) Allow them time off to look for other employment.

(ix) Notify the Department of Employment of impending redundancies within the appropriate time limits.

(*b*) *Dismissal notices* (taking due note of the time limits – see below).

NB. Consultations must take place before notices of dismissal are sent out.

Time limits. The date on which the dismissal is to take effect should be fixed having regard to the obligations of the employer as regards notice (see TERMINATION OF EMPLOYMENT (49)) and with an eye on the following time limits.

For step (*a*)(i)

(A) 'at the earliest opportunity' in all cases

and in any event

(B)	90 days before first dismissal	100 + employees in one establishment to be dismissed within 90 days
(C)	30 days before first dismissal	10-99 employees in one establishment to be dismissed within 30 days

For step (*a*)(ix), as (B) and (C) for step *(a)*(i) above.

40 References

40.1 An employer may be requested to provide a general reference or specific details about an employee or ex-employee of his by that employee, by a prospective employer or by any other person interested in obtaining such information. (For example, the employee may need a reference in order to obtain a mortgage or obtain a lease of residential premises.) The request may be for a reference to be given over the telephone, but more usually it will be for a written document.

40.2 THE EMPLOYER'S OBLIGATION

An employer is *not obliged* to provide such a reference but, as the consequences of a failure to do so may be grave for an employee, the circumstances in which an employer or ex-employer will refuse to supply a reference are probably rare. However, as one of the terms of settlement of a claim or a potential claim before an industrial tribunal, an employer may agree to provide a reference, and he will then be bound to do so, assuming the agreement to be enforceable (see 40.7 below).

40.3 CONTENTS

If the enquiry for a reference poses certain questions then clearly those issues should be dealt with. If, however, the request is a general one, for example from a prospective employer, an employer should consider dealing with the following matters.

(*a*) Length of service.

(*b*) Positions held.

(*c*) Competence in the job.

(*d*) Honesty.

(*e*) Time-keeping.

(*f*) Reason for leaving.

(*g*) Any other particular remarks about the employee, such as long periods of absence due to sickness.

(*h*) Any relevant remarks of a more personal nature about the employee.

For references relating to a certain level of employee, some employers complete a form dealing with these matters. However, for a more senior employee such a form may give an inadequate picture and a full letter should be written.

40.4 EMPLOYER'S LIABILITIES

To the employee

References given by one employer to a prospective employer may not be made the grounds for a libel action by the employee even if the information given proves to be inaccurate, provided that the employer believes the information to be correct and gives it without malice. This is because the employer (or ex-employer) and the prospective employer have a common interest in the statement made about the employee, and the statement is protected by what is known as 'qualified privilege'. As Lord Ellenborough CJ said in 1818: 'In the case of master and servant, the convenience of mankind required that what is said in fair communication between man and man, upon the subject of character, should be privileged, if made bona fide and without malice. If, however, the party giving the character knows what he says to be untrue, that may deprive him of the protection which the law throws around such communications.' (*Hodgson v Scarlett (1818) 1 B & Ald 239*; see also *Sutherland v British Telecommunications plc, The Times, 30 January 1989*). The defence of qualified privilege will, however, be lost if the statement is not merely passed between people having a mutuality of interest in the subject matter but falls into the hands of a third person. Thus, all references should be carefully marked 'private and confidential'.

It has been held that a reference negligently given which adversely affects the employee, so that, for example, he is not offered a job he would have obtained had the correct information been given, may form a good ground for the employee claiming damages against the writer of the reference quite apart from any claim he may have in defamation. (*Lawton v B.O.C. Transhield Ltd [1987] ICR 7*). But it was also stated in *Lawton* that an employer is always free to decline to give a reference.

40.5 To the recipient

If an employer or ex-employer undertakes to supply a reference, he must exercise a reasonable degree of care and skill to ensure that the reference conveys an accurate impression of the employee. It is reasonably foreseeable that the recipient of a reference will act on its contents and if he relies on a reference which is inaccurate because it was carelessly drawn up and thereby suffers loss, the giver of the reference may be held liable to pay the recipient damages on account of his negligence. (Cf. *Hedley Byrne & Co Ltd v Heller & Partners Ltd [1964] AC 465*.)

There is no sure way of avoiding the possibility of liability for negligent mis-statements in references since the *Unfair Contract Terms Act 1977 (UCTA)*. Disclaimers such as 'The above information is given in confidence and in good faith. No responsibility, however, can be accepted for any errors, omissions or inaccuracies in the information or for any loss or damage that may result from reliance being placed upon it' may have been effective to exclude liability before the Act came into force, but now such a disclaimer will only be effective insofar as it 'satisfies the requirement of reasonableness'. [*UCTA s 2(2)*]. The 'explanatory provisions' of the Act state that such a notice of disclaimer will satisfy this requirement of reasonableness where it is 'fair and reasonable to allow reliance upon it, having regard to all the circumstances obtaining when the liability arose or (but for the notice) would have arisen'. [*UCTA s 11(3)*]. If the reference purports to give facts which are ordinarily within the knowledge of an employer, it is thought that liability cannot now be excluded for negligent mis-statement of those facts. If, however, it contains an opinion as to the employee's suitability for a certain post which he has not filled in the past, it may be considered reasonable to insert a disclaimer for such a statement of opinion.

40.6 Data Protection Act 1984

If information about an employee is stored on a computer, the provisions of the *Data Protection Act 1984* must be complied with. See 13.12 DISCLOSURE OF INFORMATION.

40.7 REFERENCES AND EMPLOYMENT PROTECTION RIGHTS

Although employees do not have a statutory right to a reference, references may affect proceedings in industrial tribunals. A good reference may be powerful evidence against an employer who tries to justify the dismissal of an employee on grounds of misconduct or incompetence. Similarly a reference which is inconsistent with written reasons for a dismissal supplied to an employee may be persuasive in enabling the employee to show that those written reasons were inadequate or untrue, thus entitling him to an award under *EPCA s 53* (see 49.15 TERMINATION OF EMPLOYMENT).

A reference may sometimes be used to compromise a claim for unfair dismissal. If a reference is given in such circumstances, care should be taken to ensure that the reference is accurate and complete and the compromise reached with the assistance of a conciliation officer (see 2.4 ADVISORY, CONCILIATION AND ARBITRATION SERVICE).

41 Restraint of Trade, Confidentiality and Employee Inventions

41.1 The law relating to restraint of trade, confidentiality and employee inventions is complex and a detailed exposition is beyond the scope of this book. What is set out below is an outline of the principles involved.

Employers often wish to control competing activities by present or, more usually, past employees. Present employees are impliedly under certain duties in this respect. To impose more extensive duties upon present employees or to exert any control over the activities of past employees, express agreement is required. However, the law is that, as a matter of public policy, such contractual provisions in *restraint of trade* will only be upheld to the extent that they are reasonably required for the protection of the employer's legitimate interests.

Neither past nor present employees may misuse confidential information belonging to their employers, whether or not their contracts expressly prohibit them from doing so.

This chapter also summarises intellectual property rights which arise or subsist in relation to inventions by and work done by employees.

41.2 COMPETING ACTIVITIES OF CURRENT EMPLOYEES

Implied terms

The employee owes his employer an implied duty of fidelity (see 10.12 CONTRACT OF EMPLOYMENT). One aspect of this duty is that it will be a breach of contract for him to compete with his employer whilst the employment relationship subsists, whether on his own account or by working for or assisting a rival concern. (*Thomas Marshall (Exports) Ltd v Guinle [1978] ICR 905; Provident Financial Group plc and Whitegates Estate Agency Ltd v Hayward* [*1989*] *ICR 160*). It will also be a breach to attempt to persuade customers to transfer their business when the employee leaves. (*Wessex Dairies Ltd v Smith* [*1935*] *2 KB 80*). It may not matter that the activities to which objection is taken are carried out in the employee's spare time, if they are such as to harm the employer's business. (*Hivac Ltd v Park Royal Scientific Instruments Ltd* [*1946*] *Ch 169*; cf *Nova Plastics Ltd v Froggatt* [*1982*] *IRLR 146*).

Such a breach will probably both justify summary dismissal at common law (see 49.14 TERMINATION OF EMPLOYMENT) and constitute grounds for fair dismissal (see UNFAIR DISMISSAL – II (55)).

41.3 Preparing to compete

There is authority to the effect that an employee who merely takes steps in his own time towards being able to compete with the employer after the employment ends is *not* in breach of contract. (*Laughton and Hawley v Bapp Industrial Supplies Ltd* [*1986*] *ICR 634*, an unfair dismissal case. See also *G D Searle & Co Ltd v Celltech Ltd* [*1982*] *FSR 92*).

However, the line between legitimate and illegitimate activities is obviously a fine one. A rigorous view of the employee's obligations was taken in *Sanders v Parry* [*1967*] *1 WLR 753*. Further, it is thought that employees who are also directors, and therefore under stricter duties, may not even prepare to compete unless they resign from the board first (see DIRECTORS (11)). It is clear that an employee may not in any event misuse confidential information (see 41.10 below).

41.4 **Express terms**

Employers frequently wish their senior employees to enter into express covenants restraining them from engaging in competing activities during their employment. Such employees may also enter into positive obligations to devote their whole time and attention to the employer's business and negative obligations not to undertake any other business profession or occupation during their employment. Whether or not restraint of trade principles (see 41.5 below) apply to such clauses, the courts will exercise their discretion in deciding whether to enforce them by way of injunction. The court will take into account such matters as the harm likely to be suffered by the employer, and whether the granting of the injunction will force idleness upon the employee in circumstances in which he has a concern to exercise his skills. (*Warner Bros Inc v Nelson* [*1937*] *1 KB 209; Schroeder (A) Music Publishing Co Ltd v Macaulay* [*1974*] *1 WLR 1308; Provident Financial Group plc and Whitegates Estate Agency Ltd v Hayward* [*1989*] *ICR 160*).

41.5 **DOCTRINE OF RESTRAINT OF TRADE**

Covenants in contracts which restrict an employee's activities, especially after his employment has ended, are considered *prima facie* void as being contrary to public policy. Two conditions must be fulfilled if the restraint is to be held valid. First, the restraint must be reasonable in the interests of the contracting parties, and, secondly, it must be reasonable in the interests of the public. (*Nordenfelt v Maxim Nordenfelt Co* [*1894*] *AC 535; Herbert Morris Ltd v Saxelby* [*1916*] *AC 688*). More emphasis is usually placed upon the first condition than the second. Employers' interests which are capable of protection by covenant fall into two categories; customer connection and trade secrets (see below). Once the existence of the protectable interest is established, the covenant must, in order to be upheld, be shown to be no wider than is reasonably necessary for the protection of that interest.

41.6 **Types of restrictive covenant**

Amongst the types of covenant used to protect these interests are the following.

(*a*) *Non-solicitation covenants* — restraints which prohibit the former employee from soliciting the custom of clients of the employer. The pool of prohibited clients should usually be limited to those with whom the former employee dealt personally within a defined and reasonable period immediately preceding the termination of his employment. The prohibition should be for a reasonable period of time (see e.g. *Marley Tile Co Ltd v Johnson* [*1982*] *IRLR 75*).

(*b*) *Non-dealing covenants* — restraints which prohibit the former employee from dealing with clients of the employer, irrespective of whether the ex-employee initiated the approach as in (*a*) above. The restriction is greater than that imposed by (*a*) but may in certain circumstances be justified where a non-solicitation covenant would be impossible to police.

(*c*) *Area covenants* — restraints which prohibit the former employee from working in the business in which he worked for the employer, in a defined geographical area for a certain period of time. This type of covenant is much more restrictive than that in (*a*) or (*b*) and is usually only upheld where the employer establishes that he has a large client pool to protect and that those clients are present in a high concentration in the prescribed area. These covenants are seen most often in occupations such as estate agency, employment agency and hairdressing where there is a significant client base in a particular geographical area. Even if the justification for this type of restraint is established in particular circumstances, its reasonableness will depend to a certain extent upon the density of population and competition in the area covered by the restraint: a one-mile radius restriction in Gloucestershire may be reasonable whilst such a restriction in the City of London may not be. (See e.g. *Spencer v Marchington [1988] IRLR 392.*)

(*d*) *Working for a trade rival* — although the courts will not enforce a covenant which prohibits the former employee from competing with the employer, an employer can in certain circumstances protect his trade secrets or confidential information by taking a covenant from the employee that he will not work for a rival in the trade, and the courts will uphold such a covenant if it is limited to a reasonable period. (*Littlewoods Organisation Ltd v Harris [1977] 1 WLR 1472*).

(*e*) *Non-solicitation of other employees* — sometimes employers seek to place restraints on the recruitment by an ex-employee of his former colleagues. It is not clear whether and in what circumstances such covenants will be enforced. (See Philip Sales, Law Quarterly Review, October 1988 at p 600.)

(*f*) *Indirect restraints* — the rule that restraints going beyond the reasonable protection of legitimate interests are void applies to indirect as well as to direct restraints. For example, it was applied in *Sadler v Imperial Life Assurance Co of Canada Ltd [1988] IRLR 388* so as to strike down a provision that outstanding commission would not be paid after the termination of employment if the employee joined a competitor.

41.7 Reasonableness of restrictive covenants

The following factors are amongst those which will be considered in judging reasonableness.

(i) *The nature of the employee's work.* Is his job such that customers will tend to identify him with the business? Does it bring him into contact with confidential information which can only be effectively protected by means of a covenant restricting his subsequent employment?

(ii) *How widely is the class of 'prohibited' customers defined?* The covenant may be unreasonable if it is expressed so as to catch only those who were customers of the employer a long time ago, or those with whom the employee would not normally have dealt.

(iii) *For how long does the restraint last after the employment terminates?* A restraint of a year or less is likely to be easier to justify than one of more than, say, two or three years' duration.

41.8 Interpretation of restrictive covenants by the courts

In construing restrictive covenants the courts apply the following tests:

(*a*) covenants may be held void for uncertainty – for example, in certain circumstances the meaning of 'customer' may be unclear (*Spafax (1965) Ltd v Dommett (1972) 116 SJ 711*);

(*b*) the reasonableness of the covenant is judged at the time when the contract is concluded (*Commercial Plastics Ltd v Vincent [1965] 1 QB 623*);

(*c*) covenants should be strictly construed (*Commercial Plastics Ltd v Vincent [1965] 1 QB 623*), but in *G W Plowman & Son Ltd v Ash [1964] 1 WLR 568*, *Home Counties Dairies Ltd v Skilton [1970] 1 WLR 526* and *Littlewoods Organisation Ltd v Harris [1977] 1 WLR 1472* the court construed clauses to exclude improbable and unlikely events;

(*d*) covenants will not be rewritten by the court so as to render them enforceable, nor can an employee be effectively restrained by a covenant in the form 'so far as the law allows'. (*Davies v Davies (1887) 36 Ch D 359*). For example, if a restraint lasting two years would be the most that was reasonable in a particular case, but the relevant covenant is expressed to last four years, then no order at all can be obtained;

(*e*) an unenforceable covenant or part of a covenant may be 'blue pencilled' or severed, provided that what is left makes independent sense without the need for modifying the wording and that the sense of the contract is not changed. For recent discussions of the principles governing severance, see *Sadler v Imperial Life Assurance Co of Canada Ltd [1988] IRLR 388* and *Rex Stewart Jeffries Parker Ginsberg Ltd v Parker [1988] IRLR 483*.

The drafting of restrictive covenants is a matter upon which the lay reader should seek specialist advice. There are many cases on the enforceability of such covenants. Some recent examples, apart from those mentioned above, are *John Michael Design plc v Cooke [1987] ICR 445* and *Lawrence David Ltd v Ashton [1989] ICR 123*.

41.9 **Wrongful dismissal**

If the employer dismisses the employee in breach of contract (which will generally be because the requisite notice has not been given), or if the employee resigns in response to the employer's repudiatory breach of contract, the employer will not thereafter be entitled to enforce any restrictive covenants contained in the contract. (*General Billposting Co Ltd v Atkinson [1909] AC 118*).

In this context it should be noted that to dismiss an employee and pay him in lieu of notice may well amount to a breach of contract unless either there is contractual provision allowing the employer to adopt this course or the employee consents to it (see *Lawrence David Ltd v Ashton [1989] ICR 123*). Thus, although the pay in lieu would ensure that the employee had no outstanding claim in damages, it can possibly be argued that the breach allows him to escape from the restrictive covenants.

41.10 **CONFIDENTIALITY**

Breach of confidence is an independent wrong at common law, not confined to the employment relationship or indeed to cases where there is a contract between the parties. Both current and former employees are under an implied obligation not to use or disclose information if it amounts to a trade secret or is so highly confidential that it requires the same protection as a trade secret. The duty of fidelity upon current employees goes further, so as to prevent them from disclosing or using information which falls into a secondary category, being confidential but not to such an extent as to amount to a trade secret (see *Faccenda Chicken*, below). Such 'secondary category' information may be used by ex-employees to the extent that they inevitably carry it away in their heads. (*Roger Bullivant Ltd v Ellis [1987] ICR 464*). This does not mean that any information so carried away is not a trade secret. (*Johnson & Bloy (Holdings) Ltd and another v Wolstenholme Rink plc and Fallon [1987] IRLR 499*).

The obligation not to disclose confidential information is in principle one of unlimited duration. However a time is likely to come when the information loses its confidential character, either because it becomes out of date, or because it enters the public domain (see e.g. *Attorney General v Guardian Newspapers (No 2) [1988] 3 WLR 776*). The test of whether information has ceased to be confidential through disclosure is whether it has become known to a substantial number of people. (*Stephens v Avery [1988] FSR 510*).

Third parties to whom confidential information is disclosed, whether lawfully or otherwise, also become bound by the obligation if they are aware that the information is intended to be kept secret (see the two cases cited above).

Note that an employee will not be restrained from disclosing confidential information about his employer's affairs to a regulatory body or the Inland Revenue in order that an investigation may take place (*Re a Company's Application [1989] 3 WLR 265*), although the employer would no doubt have a remedy if it later proved that the employee was motivated by malice.

41.11 **Confidential information**

The question of what constitutes confidential information was considered by the Court of Appeal in *Faccenda Chicken Ltd v Fowler [1986] ICR 297*. There, a sales manager formed his own company and recruited several of the ex-employer's 'van salesmen'. Use was made of their knowledge of their old sales routes, the identities and needs of their customers, and of the ex-employer's pricing policies. It was held that this knowledge was not in the nature of a trade secret. All the circumstances of the particular case had to be considered, but the following factors were likely to be important.

(i) Did the employee work in a job where he regularly handled such information? If so, he may more readily be expected to recognise and respect its sensitivity.

(ii) Did the employer impress upon the employee the confidentiality of the information?

(iii) How restricted was the circulation of the information within the firm?

(iv) Could the allegedly confidential information be readily isolated from other information which the employee was free to use?

It has been said that restrictive covenants cannot be employed so as to prohibit the use or disclosure after employment ends of information which is not truly a trade secret and falls within the secondary category referred to above (*Faccenda Chicken*). However, this was doubted by Scott J in *Balston Ltd v Headline Filters Ltd [1987] FSR 330*, and a suitably drafted covenant in the employee's contract may in any event help to make clear that particular categories of information are indeed treated as confidential.

41.12 **REMEDIES**

There are two basic remedies which may be sought where a restrictive covenant is violated or there is a misuse of confidential information.

(*a*) *Damages*. The claim may be brought against the employee, for breach of contract or breach of confidence. Also, it may be possible in an appropriate case to sue his new employer for inducing a breach of contract (if he knew of its terms) or for breach of confidence (if he used the information in question knowing its confidential character). The problems with this course of action are that it may often be very difficult to prove what loss has occurred, and that the employee may be unable to meet an award of damages.

(*b*) *An injunction*. The most effective remedy which an employer can obtain is an injunction restraining the ex-employee or employee from breaking the express or implied terms of his contract or misusing information in breach of confidence. Application may be made for an interlocutory injunction before trial of the action. In cases of extreme urgency application may be made *ex parte* without notice to the defendant, although (unless to do so would be demonstrably damaging to the plaintiff's interests) it is preferable that notice of the application be given. Applications for injunctions should be made as soon as evidence of a breach has come to light. If the application is made *ex parte*, the plaintiff must make full and frank disclosure to the court of all material facts, including those unfavourable to his case. If the injunction is granted, the defendant will have an opportunity to apply to the court to seek to have it discharged after argument on both sides.

Whether or not an interlocutory injunction is granted will depend upon whether the plaintiff can show an arguable case that he will succeed at trial, whether the case is one where the plaintiff or defendant would not be adequately compensated by an award of damages at trial (e.g. because of the difficulty of proving loss), and upon the court's assessment of where the *balance of convenience* lies (see 10.21 CONTRACT OF EMPLOYMENT). It is often appropriate for a speedy trial to be ordered in such cases. The court should only resort to an attempt to assess the merits of the rival claims at the interlocutory stage if the restraint will have expired or largely expired before the action can be tried. (*Lawrence David Ltd v Ashton [1989] ICR 123; Dairy Crest Ltd v Pigott [1989] ICR 92*). This approach will tend to favour the employer, because (where the balance of convenience is otherwise even, as it often is) the court will tend to preserve the status quo by restraining the employee.

In *John Michael Design plc v Cooke [1987] ICR 445* the Court of Appeal indicated that, if the covenant appears *prima facie* good, it will normally be right to restrain the defendant, and that particular customers ought not to be excluded from the scope of the injunction merely because their loyalty to the employer is in any event in doubt.

Where there is good reason to believe that the defendant may have in his possession property belonging to the plaintiff or copies of information confidential to the plaintiff, it is common to seek further orders in addition to the basic injunction. One such order is for the delivery up of the items in question. Another is a form of relief known as the 'Anton Piller order', which instructs the defendant to allow the plaintiff's representatives access to particular premises in order to search for such property. The court will have to be persuaded that it is likely that the property is on the premises and that, without such an order, there is a real risk that it will be destroyed, hidden or tampered with. In a recent employment case, *Lock International plc v Beswick [1989] IRLR 481*, it was suggested that the court should be sparing in its exercise of the Anton Piller jurisdiction.

If the defendant has by some wrongful act (e.g. the copying of confidential information whilst still employed) obtained an advantage or 'springboard' in competition with the plaintiff, an injunction may be granted in such form as will neutralise that unfair advantage e.g. the ex-employee may be prevented from competing for a specified period of time until the confidential information loses its sensitive character. Such an order is known as a 'Bullivant order' after *Roger Bullivant Ltd v Ellis [1987] ICR 464*.

A plaintiff who obtains interlocutory orders will have to give a cross-undertaking in damages, that is, an undertaking to make good loss caused to the defendant if he eventually proves that the order should not have been made. On an *ex parte* application it is usual to adduce evidence of the plaintiff's financial standing, and any potential inability to make good the cross-undertaking must be drawn to the attention of the court. (*Swedac Ltd v Magnet & Southerns plc [1989] FSR 243*).

41.13 INTELLECTUAL PROPERTY RIGHTS

The law relating to intellectual property rights arising in the course of employment is complex and is beyond the scope of this book. What appears below is a bare outline of the rights which may subsist or arise.

The right of copyright subsists in categories of works listed in the *Copyright Designs and Patents Act 1988, s 1* and more fully defined in subsequent provisions. Of particular concern in employment relationships is the ownership of copyright in works created in the course of employment by an employee, such as reports, original compilations of information, computer programs, plans, diagrams and films. No act of registration is required. By *Sec 11(2)* of that Act the first owner of the copyright in a work made by an employee in the *course of his employment* is, subject to any contrary agreement, the employer. The question of who was first owner of copyright in an existing work is to be determined in accordance with the law in force at the time the work was made. [*1 Sch 11(1)*; see also *1 Sch 10*]. The *Copyright Act 1956* contained a similar provision to that contained in *Sec 11(2)* (see *Sec 4*).

The new Act has introduced for the first time a design right which broadly speaking is a right intended to replace copyright in designs for articles intended for industrial use having no intrinsic eye appeal and which are not themselves artisitic works. Where a design is created by an employee in the course of his employment, his employer is the first owner of any design right in the design. [*Sec 215(3)*]. The provisions relating to this new right are extremely complex. Note that these new design rights are distinct from the rights in designs registrable under the *Registered Designs Act 1949*.

A patent is a means of protecting an original invention capable of industrial application (see *Patents Act 1977, s 1*; the references below are to provisions of that Act). An invention made by an employee is taken, as between him and his employer, to belong to his employer for all purposes if but only if:

(*a*) it was made in the course of the employee's normal duties or of duties specially assigned to him, in circumstances such that an invention might reasonably be expected to result from the carrying out of those duties; or

(*b*) it was made in the course of the employee's duties and at the time the employee had (because of the nature of his duties and the particular responsibilities arising from them) a special obligation to further the interests of the employer's undertaking.

[*Sec 39(1)(2)*].

In certain circumstances, notably where the invention is of outstanding benefit to the employer, the employee may be awarded compensation such as to secure for him a fair share of that benefit. [*Secs 40, 41*].

Where the invention belongs to the employee, he may pursue an application for a patent and perform or work the invention without infringing any copyright or design right which the employer may have in related models or documents. [*Sec 39(3)* as inserted by *Copyright, Designs and Patents Act 1988, s 295, 5 Sch 11*].

Contractual terms which diminish the employee's rights in inventions are unenforceable to the extent that they do so, but this does not derogate from the employee's duty of confidentiality. [*Sec 42(2)(3)*].

42 Retirement

42.1 Unless a date for retirement is agreed with his employer, or there is a recognised customary date for retirement in a trade or industry, a person may continue in employment beyond pensionable age for so long as he is able to work. If an employer intends that an employee should retire at a certain age, he should specify that term in the letter of offer of employment. Retirement ages different from the state pensionable age are commonly specified for certain kinds of employment, e.g. for airline pilots, seamen and judges. Directors of a public company, or of a subsidiary of a public company, must retire at the next annual general meeting after attaining the age of 70, although this age limit does not apply if the director's appointment is approved by the company in general meeting by a resolution of which special notice, stating the director's age, has been given. [*Companies Act 1985, s 293(1)(2)(5)*]. Upon the employee's attainment of the specified age it is arguable, for the purposes of the unfair dismissal although not the sex discrimination legislation, that the contract of employment is terminated not by either of the parties, but by agreement.

The pensionable age for state retirement pension purposes is 65 for men and 60 for women. In certain circumstances employees may receive a state pension on reaching these ages whilst continuing to receive income from their employment.

42.2 EMPLOYMENT PROTECTION AND RETIRING AGE

An employee cannot bring a claim for unfair dismissal if on or before the effective date of termination he had attained the following age:

(*a*) if in the undertaking in which he was employed there was a normal retiring age for an employee holding the position which he held and the age was the same whether the employee holding that position was a man or a woman, that normal retiring age;
and

(*b*) in any other case, the age of 65.

[*EPCA s 64(1)(b)* as amended by *Sex Discrimination Act 1986 s 3*]. (See 54.14 UNFAIR DISMISSAL – I.)

This provision does not apply to 'union-related' dismissals. [*EPCA s 64(3); EA 1982, 3 Sch 19*].

An employee is not entitled to a redundancy payment if immediately before the date of his dismissal ('the relevant date') he had attained the following age:

(*a*) if in the business for the purposes of which he was employed there was a normal retiring age of less than 65 for an employee holding the position which he held, and the age was the same whether the employee holding that position was a man or a woman, that normal retiring age; and

(*b*) in any other case, the age of 65.

[*EPCA s 82(1)*as substituted by *EA 1989 s 16(1)*]. (See 38.10 REDUNDANCY – I.)

For 'normal retiring age', see 54.14 UNFAIR DISMISSAL – I.

43 Service Lettings

Cross-reference. See 3.3(*e*) BENEFITS IN KIND on provision of living accommodation.

43.1 Some employers provide residential accommodation for their employees. They may do so because the nature of the work is such that the job can be done more efficiently if the employee is close at hand. Another reason may be that the work is in a part of the country in which there is a shortage of accommodation, and the only way in which the employer can attract workers is to provide them with somewhere to live.

The provision of such accommodation poses a dilemma for both employee and employer when the employment relationship comes to an end. The interest in the employee retaining security of tenure in his home conflicts with the interest of the employer in regaining the accommodation so that he can use it for the employee's replacement. Another question is the extent to which rent controls apply.

It is not possible to give more than a broad outline of this area of law in a book on employment law, and those wishing to find more detailed discussion should consult such works as *Woodfall's Landlord and Tenant* or *Hill and Redman's Law of Landlord and Tenant*. That is particularly true of some of the complex transitional provisions associated with the change from the regime of the *Rent Act 1977 (RA 1977)* to that of the *Housing Act 1988 (HA 1988)*. Nor have we sought to deal here with matters such as the scope of the landlord's and the tenant's respective repairing obligations. A summary of the law as it affects employees is set out below. It has been assumed that situations such as that of a resident landlord are unlikely to arise in the employment context.

43.2 NATURE OF THE OCCUPANCY

It is of the greatest importance to distinguish between a *service tenancy* and a *service licence*. The grounds on which possession may be recovered from a tenant as opposed to a licensee are limited by statute (see below).

The test for distinguishing between a tenancy and a licence has been re-stated by Lord Templeman, giving the decision of the House of Lords in *Street v Mountford* [*1985*] *AC 809*. His Lordship also gave guidance about the position of service occupiers.

> 'To constitute a tenancy the occupier must be granted exclusive possession for a fixed or periodic term certain in consideration of a premium or periodical payments' (*p 818E*).
>
> 'A service occupier is a servant who occupies his master's premises in order to perform his duties as a servant. In those circumstances the possession and occupation of the servant is treated as the possession and occupation of the master and the relationship of landlord and tenant is not created; see *Mayhew v Suttle* (*1854*) *4 El & Bl 347*. The test is whether the servant requires the premises he occupies in order the better to perform his duties as a servant:
>
> "Where the occupation is necessary for the performance of services, and the occupier is required to reside in the house in order to perform those services, the occupation being strictly ancillary to the performance of the duties which the occupier has to perform, the occupation is that of a servant";

per Mellor J in *Smith v Seghill Overseers (1875) LR 10 QB 422, 428*' (*p 818G-H*).

A requirement that the employee live in certain accommodation for the better performance of his duties (so that he is a licensee and not a tenant) may be expressed in his contract of employment or may be implied. A chauffeur who is given a flat above the garage, or a housekeeper who is given accommodation in the premises she is charged with looking after, would, save in exceptional circumstances, be considered to be occupying that accommodation for the better performance of his or her duties. Employers may consider it wise to state expressly in any contract of employment or letter of offer of employment (where it is the case) that the employee will be required to occupy certain premises for the better performance of his duties and that his occupation is to cease upon the termination of the employment. But such a statement will not avail the employer if it does not accurately reflect the reality of the situation: cf. *Aslan v Murphy [1989] 3 AER 130*.

If the employee is not a service licensee in this sense, he may still be a lodger and not a tenant if the employer provides atttendance or services which require him or his servants to exercise unrestricted access to and use of the premises. Otherwise, however, the agreement to grant exclusive possession for a term at a rent points to the creation of a tenancy. Indeed, in *Ashburn Anstalt v Arnold [1989] Ch 1* the Court of Appeal held that even a rent was not an essential constituent of a lease. Two recent cases illustrate the application of these principles in employment cases.

In *Postcastle Properties Ltd v Perridge (1985) 276 EG 1063*, the plaintiffs brought a possession action for an estate cottage. The occupant, a man of 80 years, had been employed by the plaintiff's predecessor in title. He remained in occupation, and continued to work for and to pay £1.50 per week rent to the plaintiffs after they purchased the premises. He was held to have a tenancy. Strong evidence was needed to rebut the presumption of tenancy, which was not forthcoming in that case.

In *Royal Philanthropic Society v County (1985) 276 EG 1068*, the defendant was employed as a houseparent at the plaintiff's school. Initially he was provided with furnished accommodation in the school building. He was a licensee of the room. On marrying, he was provided with a house some miles from the school. Approximately one year later his employment came to an end, whereupon a notice to quit was served. Possession was successfully claimed in the county court. This was overturned on appeal, the Court of Appeal holding that the defendant was a tenant. Fox LJ said:

> 'The overall effect of *Street v Mountford* as we understand it is that an occupier of residential accommodation at a rent for a term is either a lodger or a tenant . . .' (*p 1071*).
>
> 'The employment, it seems to us, is material only if there is a true service occupancy, i.e. where the servant requires the premises for the better performance of his duties as a servant . . .' (*p 1072*).

Referring to a variety of factors put forward by counsel for the plaintiffs in his attempt to show that no tenancy was created, such as the informality of the paperwork, the relationship of the parties, and the fact that the previous occupancy was that of lodger, Fox LJ said:

> ' . . . it seems to us that they amount really to an attempt to go back to the approach, disapproved by the House of Lords in *Street v Mountford*, of

examining the circumstances with a view to ascertaining the intention of the parties. The only intention that is relevant under the law as it now stands "is the intention demonstrated by the agreement to grant exclusive possession for a term at a rent" (*Street v Mountford* at *p 891*).' (*p 1072*).

These decisions serve to demonstrate that, although the employment relationship continues as before, the nature of the employee's occupancy of premises may change.

43.3 RECOVERY OF POSSESSION

In order to recover possession from an occupying employee or ex-employee, the employer/landlord will first have to ensure that the employee's *contractual* right to occupy, whether under a licence or a tenancy, is brought to an end. If the employee does not leave voluntarily, it will then be necessary to obtain an order for possession, generally in the county court. In the case of a tenancy, the court's powers to make such an order are restricted by statute.

It is important that the employer does not seek to regain possession without recourse to court proceedings, whether by forcible eviction or by harassment. Such a course of action will contravene the *Protection from Eviction Act 1977* [*PFEA*].

Where premises are let as a dwelling, even under a tenancy which is not statutorily protected, it is not lawful for the owner to exercise a right of re-entry or forfeiture under the lease, or to enforce his right to recover possession, otherwise than by court proceedings. [*PFEA ss 2,3(1)*]. There is a deemed tenancy for these purposes whenever a person has exclusive possession of any premises under the terms of his employment. [*PFEA s 8(2)*].

It is a criminal offence unlawfully to deprive the employee of his occupation. [*PFEA s 1(2)*]. It is also an offence if a person, with the intention of causing the residential occupier to give up occupation or to refrain from exercising any rights or pursuing any remedy open to him, does acts which are likely to interfere with the peace and comfort of the occupier, or his family, or persistently withdraws or withholds services normally required for the occupation of the premises as a residence. [*PFEA s 1(3)*, as amended by *HA 1988, s 29*]. Where that intent cannot be shown, an offence is nonetheless committed if the employer or his agent, without reasonable grounds, does acts likely to interfere with the peace or comfort of the residential occupier or members of his household or persistently withdraws or withholds services reasonably required for the occupation of the premises as a residence, knowing or having reasonable cause to believe that that conduct is likely to cause the occupier to give up occupation or to refrain from exercising a right or remedy [*PFEA s 1(3A),(3B)*, as inserted by *HA 1988, s 29*].

Further, a right to damages for unlawful eviction (in addition to any existing rights to claim in tort or for breach of contract) is created by *HA 1988, s 27*.

Once the licence or tenancy has been brought to an end and the employer is seeking to recover possession, the employer ought not to accept further payments of rent (at least without making clear in writing the basis on which he does so), because the acceptance of such payments may lead to the creation of a fresh tenancy. If the employee continues to occupy the premises after he should have left, compensation will eventually be recoverable by order of the court (called 'mesne profits').

43.4 Service licence

A true *service licence* can be determined on termination of the relevant employment contract, with the notice period provided for in the contract. If the contract is silent on this point, then reasonable notice should be given. It is unlikely that a period of less than four weeks would be reasonable. If the licence is a *periodic licence* (i.e one which continues from week to week or month to month, rather than for a fixed term or until the end of the employment), a minimum of four weeks' notice to terminate it must be given in the prescribed form [*PFEA s 5(1A)* as inserted by *HA 1988, s 32*; *Notices to Quit etc. (Prescribed Information) Regulations 1988 (SI 1988 No 2201)*].

On the termination of a *service licence* the employer can take proceedings for possession. He will have to show

(*a*) that the premises were occupied by the employee for the duration of his employment (or for some agreed lesser period), and for the better performance of his duties;

(*b*) that the employment (or the lesser period) has ended, or that proper notice to determine the licence has been given;

(*c*) that either the agreed notice has been given or the former employee has been given an adequate period in which to vacate the premises;

(*d*) that no new arrangement has been created since the contract ended (therefore it is unwise to accept further payments of rent without specifying the basis on which this is done).

In *Whitbread West Pennines Ltd v Reedy* [*1988*] *ICR 807*, the former employee sought to argue that possession should not be ordered against him because there was pending an unfair dismissal claim in which he sought reinstatement (see 56.2 UNFAIR DISMISSAL – III). The argument failed. The Court of Appeal held that for the replacement employee to move into the accommodation would not make reinstatement any less practicable, and that in any event the employer could elect not to reinstate but to pay enhanced compensation instead. In a case where the licence to occupy terminates along with the employment, it does so notwithstanding that the dismissal is a wrongful dismissal. (*Ivory v Palmer* [*1975*] *ICR 340*).

43.5 Service tenancy

Tenancies in existence prior to 15 January 1989 continue to be governed by *RA 1977* or *Housing Act 1980* (*HA 1980*). New tenancies, however, are governed by *HA 1988*. Various kinds of tenancy therefore fall to be considered.

(i) *Protected tenancies* under *RA 1977*. These are automatically converted into *statutory tenancies* when the original, contractual tenancy expires through effluxion of time or a notice to quit is served.

(ii) *Protected shorthold tenancies* under *HA 1980*. These arose where, before the grant of the tenancy, the landlord served a prescribed notice indicating that this was the nature of the tenancy. The term must have been between one and five years, with the landlord having no right to end it sooner whilst the tenant complies with his obligations [*HA 1980, s 52*].

(iii) *Assured tenancies* under *HA 1988*. This will now be the normal basic type of tenancy. The tenant must be an individual who occupies the dwelling as his only or principal home, and the letting must not be one which is specifically excluded from protection [*HA 1988, s 1*].

(iv) *Assured shorthold tenancies* under *HA 1988*. These are similar in concept to the old protected shorthold tenancies, but their scope is less restricted. They must be for a fixed term of not less than six months, contain no landlord's right to terminate during the first six months if the tenant complies with his obligations, and the grant must be preceded by service of a notice in the prescribed form. [*HA 1988, s 20*].

In order to recover possession from a service tenant, the contractual tenancy must be terminated. This will occur if (in the case of a fixed-term tenancy) the term of the tenancy expires without being renewed, if the landlord claims to forfeit the lease where the lease makes provision for forfeiture for breach of certain terms in it, or (in the case of a periodic tenancy) if the landlord serves a notice to quit.

Expiry of term. If the tenancy is for a fixed term of, for example, two years, the contractual tenancy will automatically terminate on the expiry of the two-year period and it is not necessary for a notice to quit to be served.

Forfeiture for breach of a term of the lease. Except in the case of forfeiture for the non-payment of rent, the landlord must serve a notice under the *Law of Property Act 1925, s 146* on the tenant, specifying the breaches complained of and requesting him to remedy the same within a reasonable period of time and to pay reasonable compensation.

Notice to quit. A notice to quit should be in writing and some acknowledgement of receipt should be asked for. If sent by post, it should be sent by recorded delivery. To be valid the notice to quit must expire on the proper day. The notice to quit must expire at the end of the period of the tenancy. Because specifying a wrong date is fatal to a notice to quit, landlords should add the following saving clause in the notice to quit after the specified date: 'or at the expiration of the (week/month) of your tenancy which shall expire next after the expiration of four weeks from the service upon you of this notice'. The notice to quit must be served not less than four weeks before the date on which it is to take effect. [*Protection from Eviction Act 1977, s 5*]. Information prescribed by the *Notices to Quit etc. (Prescribed Information) Regulations 1988 (SI 1988 No 2201)* must be included in the notice to quit, otherwise it will be invalid.

No rent must be accepted after discovery of a breach of a term in the lease which gives the landlord the right to forfeit, such as unlawful sub-letting. Accepting rent may be construed as waiving the breaches complained of or creating a new tenancy.

43.6 Situations in which possession may be claimed from a tenant

Where a *protected shorthold tenancy* or an *assured shorthold tenancy* comes to an end, the court *must* grant the landlord possession if the proper procedure is followed. In the case of an assured shorthold tenancy, this involves giving the tenant not less than two months' notice that possession is required [*HA 1988, s 21*]. The procedural requirements in relation to the old protected shorthold tenancy were somewhat more complex: see *HA 1980, s 55; RA 1977, s 98(2), 15 Sch Case 19*. Possession of properties let on shorthold tenancies can also be recovered on the same grounds as are available in the case of ordinary tenancies.

In the case of a *protected tenancy* under *RA 1977*, the landlord must bring himself within one of a number of specified 'Cases' set out in *15 Sch*. Those Cases in *15 Sch*

Part I are 'discretionary' grounds, in that they require the court to be satisfied also that it is reasonable to grant possession; they include grounds such as arrears of rent or the causing of a nuisance. Those Cases in *15 Sch Part II* constitute mandatory grounds for possession. In addition, the court may make an order, if it is reasonable to do so, where suitable alternative accommodation is or will be available for the tenant. See generally *RA 1977, s 98*.

The ground particularly relevant to pre-1989 service lettings is *Case 8* (a discretionary ground): this arises if the landlord requires the premises for a whole-time employee, the existing tenant was granted a tenancy in consequence of his employment, and he has ceased to be in that employment.

A similar approach governs recovery of possession under *assured tenancies* under *HA 1988*. Again, there are both mandatory and discretionary grounds, and where one of the latter is established the court will have to be persuaded that it is reasonable to order possession [*HA 1988, s 7, 2 Sch*]. *Ground 16* is a discretionary ground which applies where the dwelling-house was let to the tenant in consequence of his employment by the landlord or a previous landlord, and the tenant has ceased to be in that employment. It will be seen that this is less stringent, from the landlord's point of view, than *Case 8* under *RA 1977* (see above), because it is not necessary to show that the accommodation is required for another employee. However, to do so would obviously assist the argument that it was reasonable to order possession. The availability of suitable alternative accommodation is another discretionary ground (*Ground 9*).

As in the case of *RA 1977* (see *Sec 100*), the court has a wide discretion under *HA 1988, s 9* to adjourn possession proceedings and to suspend the execution of orders.

43.7 Tenants of public authorities

Under *HA 1985*, security of tenure was conferred upon tenants of local authorities and of certain other public bodies. However, various categories are excluded from security of tenure. Those which are pertinent to employment include:

(*a*) Cases where the tenant is an employee of the landlord; or of

- (i) a local authority
- (ii) a new town corporation
- (iii) the governors of an aided school
- (iv) an urban development corporation
- (v) the Development Board for Rural Wales

and his contract of employment requires him to reside in the dwelling for the better performance of his duties.

(*b*) Where the tenant is a member of the police force, and the dwelling is provided rates and rent free by regulations made under the *Police Act 1964*.

(*c*) Where the tenant is employed by a fire authority; and

- (i) he is contractually bound to live close to a particular fire station; and
- (ii) the dwelling-house was let to him by the authority so that he could comply with the condition.

(*d*) Cases where temporary accommodation is granted in order to assist employees who are new to an area to find permanent accommodation there, provided that it is linked to an offer of employment to a person who was not resident in the district immediately before the grant, that it does not exceed one year and that the tenant is informed, in writing, of the circumstances in which the exception applies and that the landlord is of the opinion that it falls within that exception.

[*Housing Act 1985, 1 Sch, 2(1)(2)(3), 5(1)*].

43.8 RENT CONTROL

Occupation under a *licence* is not subject to rent control.

Where the employee went into occupation under a *RA 1977 protected tenancy* or a *protected shorthold tenancy*, he could apply under *Part IV* of that Act for a fair rent to be registered, and the landlord was not then entitled to charge a greater rent [*RA 1977, s 44*]. Now that new protected tenancies cannot be created, that provision will be of diminishing importance, although the possibility of such an application remains.

A tenant under an *assured tenancy* under *HA 1988* has no right to challenge the contractual rent which he has agreed to pay, whether the rent demanded of him is that originally agreed upon, or has subsequently been varied pursuant to a rent review clause. However, if the contractual tenancy comes to an end and the landlord wishes to increase the rent, he must serve notice of the proposed increase upon the tenant in a prescribed form [*HA 1988, s 13*]. The tenant may then go before a Rent Assessment Committee and seek a determination that the proposed new rent exceeds that which might reasonably be expected to be obtained in the open market, by a willing landlord, on the same terms of letting [*HA 1988, s 14*].

A tenant under an *assured shorthold tenancy* may refer the rent charged to the Rent Assessment Committee. However, the Committee may reduce the rent only if

(i) there is a sufficient number of similar dwelling-houses in the locality let on assured tenancies (whether shorthold or not) for a proper determination to be possible; and

(ii) the rent charged is *significantly* higher than the rent which the landlord might reasonably be expected to obtain having regard to the rents payable under other assured tenancies in the locality.

[*HA 1988, s 22*].

43.9 AGRICULTURAL TIED HOUSES

Where the employee is or was engaged in agriculture or forestry special rules may apply. A full discussion of these rules is beyond the scope of this book. They are to be found in the *Rent (Agriculture) Act 1976* as amended by *HA 1988*, and in *HA 1988, ss 24, 25*.

44 Sex Discrimination – I: Unlawful Discrimination

(See also EOC publications including 'Equality at Work', 'Equal Opportunities – a Guide for Employers' and the Code of Practice for the elimination of discrimination on the grounds of sex and marriage, and the promotion of equality of opportunity in employment (1985). The EOC has established an organisation called 'Equality Exchange', whose members receive information about and attend meetings relating to the furtherance of equal opportunities.)

Cross-reference. See EQUAL PAY (19) for the rules against sex discrimination in matters relating to contractual terms of employment.

44.1 Discrimination on grounds of sex or marital status is made unlawful by the *Sex Discrimination Act 1975 (SDA)*. Only the provisions of the Act relating to employment are considered below. Although they are worded in terms of sex discrimination against women, they should be read as applying equally to the treatment of men (with the exception of the special treatment afforded to women in connection with pregnancy or childbirth). [*SDA s 2*]. The provisions of *SDA* are similar to those relating to RACIAL DISCRIMINATION (37) in the *Race Relations Act 1976*, and readers should refer to decisions under that Act as well as *SDA*.

44.2 MEANING OF DISCRIMINATION

Discrimination may take place in three ways: direct discrimination, indirect discrimination and victimisation.

In deciding whether discrimination has taken place the position of the person allegedly discriminated against will be compared with that of a person of similar skill and qualification: like must be compared with like. [*SDA s 5(3)*].

The intention or motive of the alleged discriminator is irrelevant. (*R v Birmingham City Council, Ex parte Equal Opportunities Commission* [*1989*] *IRLR 173*).

44.3 Direct discrimination

This occurs where a woman is treated less favourably than a man, or a married person is treated less favourably than a single person. [*SDA ss 1(1)(a), 3(1)(a)*]. In order to establish that discrimination has taken place, it is not sufficient to show that certain treatment is different, it must be shown to be less favourable. Further, it is the treatment itself rather than its consequences which must be different and less favourable. (*Balgobin and another v Tower Hamlets London Borough Council* [*1987*] *ICR 829*). However, where a local education authority provided more places for boys than for girls in selective schools, the House of Lords held that it was not necessary for the complainant to show that selective education was 'better' than non-selective education. It was enough that, by denying the girls the same opportunity as the boys, the council was depriving them of a choice which was valued by them, or at least by their parents, and which is a choice obviously valued, on reasonable grounds, by many others. (*R v Birmingham City Council, Ex parte Equal Opportunities Commission* [*1989*] *IRLR 173*).

The dismissal of a woman because she is pregnant may amount to sex discrimination. In *Hayes v Malleable Working Men's Club and Institute* [*1985*] *ICR 703*, the Employment Appeal Tribunal held that the correct approach was to ask whether pregnancy was capable of being matched by analogous circumstances applying to a man and if so, whether they were closely enough matched to enable a fair comparison to be made between the treatment accorded to a woman in the one situation and a man in the other.

Although the woman need not show that her employer's intention or motive was to discriminate, there is no direct discrimination unless her sex was, subjectively, his *reason* for treating her less favourably. Thus it was not direct discrimination to make free entry to a swimming pool dependent upon state pensionable age. The Vice-Chancellor commented that a claim of indirect discrimination may have succeeded in these circumstances. (*James v Eastleigh Borough Council* [*1989*] *ICR 423*; this decision is likely to be appealed to the House of Lords).

44.4 Indirect discrimination

This occurs if an employer applies a requirement or condition to a woman or to a married person which he also applies to a man or an unmarried person but which is such that

(*a*) the proportion of women or married persons who are able to comply with it is considerably smaller than the proportion of men or unmarried persons; and

(*b*) he cannot show it to be justifiable irrespective of the sex or marital status of the person to whom it is applied; and

(*c*) which is to her, or that person's, detriment because she or he cannot comply with it.

[*SDA ss 1(1)(b), 3(1)(b)*].

If an employer imposes a requirement that all employees of his should be able to lift heavy weights, such a requirement would be discriminatory if applied to typists but not if applied to warehousemen. Similarly, a requirement that applicants should be six feet tall may be discriminatory depending on the circumstances. In each case the question will be: is that requirement justifiable in considering the duties to be performed?

In *Price v Civil Service Commission and the Society of Civil and Public Servants* [*1978*] *ICR 27*, the Employment Appeal Tribunal held that the maximum age limit of 28 for appointment as an Executive Officer in the Civil Service was discriminatory, as in practice it was harder for women to comply with than men since women in their twenties are commonly fully occupied with child bearing.

The case was remitted to an industrial tribunal on the question whether the condition could be justified irrespective of its discriminatory effect and in *Price v Civil Service Commission and Civil Service National Whitley Council (Staff Side) (No 2)* [*1978*] *IRLR 3* an industrial tribunal held that it was not justifiable. Note that a condition may be justified even though the employer has not produced detailed evidence to show that there was no other way of achieving his object. (*Cobb v Secretary of State for Employment* [*1989*] *ICR 508*).

An industrial tribunal in *Clarke and Powell v Eley (IMI Kynoch) Ltd* [*1982*] *IRLR 131* held, on the evidence before it, that the selection of part-time workers for redundancy before full-time workers irrespective of length of service constituted unlawful indirect discrimination. The requirement or condition that an employee had to work full-time before being considered for redundancy on the basis of 'last in, first out' was one with which a considerably smaller proportion of women than men could comply. It allowed one applicant's claim and dismissed the other claim. The EAT allowed the unsuccessful employee's appeal and dismissed the employer's appeal against the decision in relation to the other employee. ([*1983*] *ICR 165*). However, subsequently, different tribunals reached different conclusions upon whether a requirement that employees work full time is discriminatory. In *Home Office v Holmes* [*1984*] *ICR 678* at p 681E, it was held discriminatory; in *Kidd v DRG (UK) Ltd* [*1985*] *ICR 405*, in the absence of evidence, it was not. In *Kidd*, the EAT emphasised that each case turns on its own facts, and that it no longer has to be assumed without evidence that women are the providers of home care to young children. However, it is likely that after the decision of the European Court of Justice in *Bilka-Kaufhaus GmbH v Weber von Hartz* [*1987*] *ICR 110* (see 19.10 EQUAL PAY), industrial tribunals and courts will be more ready to hold that a requirement that an employee work full-time is discriminatory.

In determining the appropriate 'pool' for comparing the proportions of men and women who can comply with a requirement, the risk of a definition incorporating an element of discrimination must be avoided. There is a *prima facie* case of discrimination if in practice many more women than men are adversely affected by the requirement. (*R v Secretary of State for Education Ex parte Schaffter* [*1987*] *IRLR 53*). See also *Pearse v City of Bradford Metropolitan Council* [*1988*] *IRLR 379*.

A condition with which no woman can comply infringes *SDA s 1(1)(b)(i)*. (*Greencroft Social Club and Institute v Mullen* [*1985*] *ICR 796*).

The fact that a woman does not wish to comply with a condition does not mean she 'cannot' do so. Therefore in *Turner v The Labour Party and another* [*1987*] *IRLR 101* a condition that a member of a pension scheme only acquired certain rights if he or she died leaving a spouse was not discriminatory against a divorcee with no intention of remarrying.

An employer's policy not to employ men or women with small children was held not to be justifiable in the absence of evidence that employees with small children were unreliable. (*Hurley v Mustoe* [*1981*] *ICR 490*). In *Rainey v Greater Glasgow Health Board* [*1987*] *ICR 129* the House of Lords held that regard should be had to the efficiency of the business (see 19.10 EQUAL PAY). *Rainey* was an equal pay case, but it was said that the same principles were applicable to the question of justification under the *SDA*.

A number of the questions raised by a requirement to work full-time were considered in *Clymo v Wandsworth London Borough Council* [*1989*] *ICR 250*, where the employer refused to allow the employee to change to a job-sharing arrangement. The EAT held that the employer, having merely declined to provide an advantage not proffered to any employees in that grade, had not 'subjected' the employee to anything, and that there was no 'detriment'. It also suggested that to insist on full-time working does not amount to a 'requirement or condition' where a job by its very nature requires full-time attendance. It remains to be seen whether these *dicta* will be followed in the future.

44.5 Victimisation

If an employer treats any person less favourably than others because that person threatens to bring proceedings, to give evidence or information, to take any action or make any allegation concerning the employer with reference to *SDA* or the *Equal Pay Act 1970*, or has already done any of those things, then the employer is guilty of discrimination by victimisation. [*SDA s 4(1)*]. If, however, the allegation made against the employer is false and not made in good faith, any unfavourable treatment of that person by reason of the false allegation will not be considered discriminatory. [*SDA s 4(2)*].

44.6 DISCRIMINATION IN EMPLOYMENT

SDA forbids discrimination at every stage of employment: advertising vacancies, engagement of employees, promotion and other opportunities, dismissal. A person discriminated against by being dismissed does not have to have been employed for a qualifying period before being entitled to bring a claim, unlike other claims for unfair dismissal (cf 53.11 UNFAIR DISMISSAL – I).

Employment has a wider definition in the *Sex Discrimination Act 1975* than it does in some other employment protection legislation. It is defined in *Sec 82(1)* as

> 'employment under a contract of service or of apprenticeship, or a contract personally to execute any work or labour . . .'

In *Mirror Group Newspapers Ltd v Gunning [1986] ICR 145*, the Court of Appeal held that *Sec 82(1)* referred to a contract, the dominant purpose of which was the execution of personal work or services.

(Cf 37.8 RACIAL DISCRIMINATION.)

44.7 Advertising

An advertisement must not show any intention to discriminate unlawfully. [*SDA s 38*]. Both the publisher and the advertiser, who cause a discriminatory advertisement to be printed, are guilty of an unlawful act. [*SDA s 38(1)*].

'*Advertisement*' is defined by *Sec 82(1)* as including 'every form of advertisement, whether to the public or not, and whether in a newspaper or other publication, by television or radio, by display of notices, signs, labels, showcards or goods, by distribution of samples, circulars, catalogues, price lists or other material, by exhibition of pictures, models or films', or in any similar way. References to the publishing of advertisements will be interpreted accordingly.

The advertisement is not unlawful if the intended act which it indicates would not in fact be unlawful. [*SDA s 38(2)*]. Thus, for example, an advertisement inviting men only to apply for a sales post in Oman may not be unlawful because the work is to be carried out in a country whose laws or customs are such that the duties could not, or could not effectively, be performed by a woman. Being a man is a genuine occupational qualification for that job (see 44.13 below). [*SDA s 7(2)(g)*].

Use of a job description with a sexual connotation such as 'waiter', 'salesgirl', 'postman' or 'stewardess' will be taken to indicate an intention to discriminate unless the advertisement contains an indication to the contrary. [*SDA s 38(3)*]. Therefore, either a new word such as 'salesperson' will have to be used or the advertiser will have to insert a disclaimer such as 'applications are invited from men and women' or 'no intention to discriminate is meant by the use of the words in this advertisement'.

The publisher of a discriminatory advertisement may escape liability if he proves

(i) that the advertisement was published in reliance on a statement made to him by the person who caused it to be published to the effect that the advertisement was not in breach of the *Sex Discrimination Act 1975*; and

(ii) that it was reasonable for him to rely on the statement. [*SDA s 38(4)*].

An advertiser who knowingly or recklessly makes a statement regarding the legality of the advertisement which is in a material respect false or misleading, commits an offence and is liable on conviction in a magistrates' court to a fine not exceeding level 5 on the standard scale. [*SDA s 38(5)*; and see 1.10 INTRODUCTION]. Thus, for example, an advertiser who falsely assures a publisher that the people of Outer Monrovia would not accept women salespeople is guilty of a criminal offence, and the publisher of such an advertisement is guilty of an unlawful act unless he can establish that it was reasonable for him to rely upon that assurance.

44.8 Engagement

An employer may not discriminate directly or indirectly

(*a*) in the arrangements he makes for the purpose of determining who should be offered employment; or

(*b*) in the terms on which he offers employment; or

(*c*) by refusing or deliberately omitting to offer employment.

[*SDA s 6(1)*].

Thus, if an employer offers a woman three weeks' holiday, whereas a man doing the same job is entitled to five weeks, he is guilty of discrimination under the *Sex Discrimination Act 1975*. Also, the woman's contract will be modified by the *Equal Pay Act 1970* to give her the same holiday entitlement as that of the man (see EQUAL PAY (19)).

In *Saunders v Richmond-upon-Thames London Borough Council* [*1978*] *ICR 75*, it was assumed that questions asked at an interview constituted 'arrangements' within the meaning of (*a*) above. Whether or not the questions were unlawful was held to be a question of fact to be determined in each case. In *Brennan v JH Dewhurst Ltd* [*1984*] *ICR 52*, the arrangements made for interviewing applicants were operated so as to discriminate against women, and were therefore unlawful.

44.9 Opportunities

Once a woman is in a job, her employer may not discriminate against her in the way he affords her access to opportunities for promotion, transfer, training or to any other benefits, facilities or services, or by refusing or deliberately omitting to afford her access to them. [*SDA s 6(2)(a)*].

References in the Act to the granting of access to benefits, facilities or services are not limited to those provided by one person (who might be an employer), but include any means by which it is in that person's power to facilitate access to benefits, facilities or services provided by any other person ('the actual provider'). [*SDA s 50(1)*]. Thus, if there are two companies within a group, A and B, and employees are employed by B, but are afforded training facilities by A, both A and B may be liable for discriminatory training by A.

44.10 Dismissal

A dismissal on the grounds of an employee's sex or marital status is unlawful under *SDA s 6(2)(b)* as well as being unfair within the meaning of the *Employment Protection (Consolidation) Act 1978* (see UNFAIR DISMISSAL – I (54)).

Section 2(3) of the *Sex Discrimination Act 1986* provides for an extended definition of 'dismissal'. It provides that employees or partners whose employment or partnership comes to an end (and is not immediately renewed on the same terms) on the expiration of a certain period or the occurrence of a certain event are dismissed. So too are employees or partners who terminate their employment or partnership by acceptance of their employer's or fellow partners' repudiatory breach of contract.

The dismissal of a woman based on an assumption that men are more likely than women to be primary supporters of their spouses and children can amount to unlawful discrimination. (*Skyrail Oceanic Ltd v Coleman [1981] ICR 864*).

44.11 Subjection to any other detriment

Other detrimental measures taken by an employer on the grounds of sex such as demotion or withdrawal of privileges are unlawful under the *Sex Discrimination Act 1975*. Requiring only male supervisors to carry out dirty work was held to be an unlawful detriment in *Ministry of Defence v Jeremiah [1980] ICR 13*.

Sexual harassment does not, of itself, constitute a breach of *SDA*. However, the Scottish Court of Session has held, in effect, that sexual harassment which affects a woman's working conditions is contrary to *SDA*. (*Porcelli v Strathclyde Regional Council [1986] ICR 564*).

Discriminatory action taken by an employer to ensure the health and safety of his employees will not be considered unlawful if it is taken in compliance with his statutory obligations. (*Page v Freight Hire (Tank Haulage) Ltd [1981] ICR 299*).

44.12 Pensions

If an employer wishes to contract out of the state pension scheme he must give men and women equal access to pension benefits in his occupational pension scheme. [*Equal Pay Act 1970, s 6(1A)(a); Sex Discrimination Act 1975, 1 Sch 3; Social Security Act 1989, 5 Sch 13*; and see 44.20 below].

44.13 WHERE SEX IS A GENUINE OCCUPATIONAL QUALIFICATION

If an employer can establish that being a man is a genuine occupational qualification for a job he may discriminate lawfully in certain respects. He may discriminate in advertisements, interviewing procedures, and in offers for the post; also in refusing opportunities for promotion, training or transfer to that post. If, however, an employer takes on a woman to do a certain job, he cannot then offer her less favourable terms than those offered to a man, or dismiss her or discriminate against her in any other way, on the grounds that being a man is a genuine occupational qualification for the job. [*SDA s 7(1)*].

Being a man is a genuine occupational qualification for a job in the following circumstances.

(*a*) Where the essential nature of the job calls for a man for reasons of physiology (excluding physical strength or stamina) or, in dramatic performances or other entertainment, for reasons of authenticity, so that the essential nature of the job would be materially different if carried out by a woman.

Thus, a woman may not be discriminated against in jobs requiring physical strength and stamina provided that she is capable of performing those duties. However, employers may discriminate in seeking male models or actors.

(*b*) Where the job needs to be held by a man to preserve decency or privacy because

(i) it is likely to involve physical contact with men in circumstances where they might reasonably object to its being carried out by a woman; or

(ii) the holder of the job is likely to do his work in circumstances where men might reasonably object to the presence of a woman because they are in a state of undress or are using sanitary facilities.

If an employer required his employees to work stripped to the waist to establish that he was justified in refusing to offer employment to women, a court hearing a complaint against him would, it is thought, decide whether that requirement was necessary for the performance of the task, or mere whim on the part of the employer.

The *Sex Discrimination Act 1986 section 1(2)* provides for the addition of the following to the exception in the case of a job which needs to be held by a man to preserve decency or privacy:

> 'the job is likely to involve the holder of the job doing his work, or living, in a private home and needs to be held by a man because objection might reasonably be taken to allowing to a woman –
>
> (i) the degree of physical or social contact with a person living in the home; or
>
> (ii) the knowledge of intimate details of such a person's life
>
> which is likely, because of the nature or circumstances of the job or of the home, to be allowed to, or available to, the holder of the job.'

(*c*) Where the nature or location of the establishment makes it impracticable for the holder of the job to live elsewhere than in premises provided by the employer and

(i) the only such premises which are available for persons holding that kind of job are lived in, or normally lived in, by men and are not equipped with separate sleeping accommodation for women and sanitary facilities which could be used by women in privacy from men; and

(ii) it is not reasonable to expect the employer either to equip these premises with such accommodation and facilities or to provide other premises for women.

(See e.g. *Sisley v Britannia Security Systems Ltd [1983] ICR 628.*)

(*d*) Where the nature of the establishment, or the part of it within which the work is done, requires the job to be held by a man because

(i) it is, or is part of, a hospital, prison or other establishment for persons requiring special care, supervision or attention, and

(ii) those persons are all men (disregarding any woman whose presence is exceptional), and

(iii) it is reasonable, having regard to the essential character of the establishment or that part, that the job should not be held by a woman.

(*e*) Where the holder of the job provides individuals with personal services promoting their welfare or education or similar personal services, and those services can most effectively be provided by a man.

(*f*) Where the job needs to be held by a man because it is likely to involve the performance of duties outside the United Kingdom in a country whose laws or customs are such that the duties could not, or could not effectively, be performed by a woman.

(*g*) Where the job is one of two to be held by a married couple.

[*SDA s 7(2)* as amended by *Employment Act 1989, s 3(2)*].

These exceptions apply even where only some of the duties of the job fall within the above provisions. [*SDA s 7(3)*].

However, where an employer already has female employees who are capable of carrying out the duties of a vacant post, and whom it would be reasonable to employ on those duties and whose numbers are sufficient to meet his likely requirements in respect of those duties without undue inconvenience, then he may not discriminate by filling the vacancy with another woman, even if the vacancy falls within (*a*) to (*f*) above. [*SDA s 7(4)*]. (See e.g. *Etam PLC v Rowan [1989] IRLR 150*.)

44.14 EXCEPTIONS

Discrimination in training

Positive discrimination in favour of women or men, in affording access to training and encouragement to apply for particular work, is permitted to employers if at any time within the twelve months immediately preceding the doing of the act there were no persons of the sex in question among those doing that work or the number of persons of that sex doing the work was comparatively small. [*SDA s 48(1)(2)*].

Other persons or bodies may also discriminate in favour of women or men in similar circumstances. [*SDA s 47*, originally applicable to training bodies but extended by *Sex Discrimination Act 1986, s 4* so as to apply to 'any person'].

Positive discrimination is also permitted to encourage membership of and postholding in trade unions and employers' organisations where there are no or proportionally few postholders or members of that sex. [*SDA s 49*].

EA 1989, s 8 provides that the Secretary of State may by order make special provision for vocational training for lone parents. Where such an order is made, discrimination in favour of lone parents in accordance with the order will not be regarded as unlawful.

44.15 Communal accommodation

If an employer provides communal accommodation for his employees, he may discriminate in its provision if the accommodation is managed in a way which is as fair as possible to men and women. [*SDA s 46(3)*]. In deciding whether an employer has made fair provision, account is taken of (*a*) whether and how far it is reasonable to expect that the accommodation should be altered or extended, or that further alternative accommodation should be provided; and

(*b*) the frequency of the demand or need for use of the accommodation by men as compared with women.

[*SDA s 46(4)*].

If, for example, a company provided a holiday home for its employees but the sleeping arrangements were only suitable for men, then provided that it was only used occasionally and it was impractical to modify it for the use of the women or to build additional accommodation for them, such discrimination may be lawful.

Benefits dependent on communal accommodation. Discrimination on the grounds of sex is lawful in respect of the provision of any benefit, facility or service if

(i) the benefit, facility or service cannot be properly and effectively provided except for those using communal accommodation; and

(ii) in the relevant circumstances a woman could lawfully be refused the use of the accommodation under the rules above.

[*SDA s 46(5)*].

Therefore, if a firm ran a residential training course in Northern Scotland and accommodation could only be provided for men and it was fair so to do, failure to make the course available to women would not be discrimination.

Arrangements to compensate for detriment. It should be noted that sex discrimination is only permitted in the above circumstances where such arrangements as are reasonably practicable have been made to compensate for any detriment caused by the discrimination. [*SDA s 46(6)*]. For example, training courses run by the ABC Company for a few days in the North of Scotland are not available to women employees because of the unsuitability of the accommodation: the company will *not* have a defence against a claim alleging discrimination unless it can show either that an alternative course had been provided or that, having been considered carefully, it was thought with good reason not to be practicable to provide it.

44.16 Discrimination in compliance with the law

An employer is not guilty of an unlawful act if he discriminates in order to comply with a statute passed before the *Sex Discrimination Act 1975*, or a statutory instrument made or approved (whether before or after the passing of the *SDA*) by or under an Act passed before the *SDA*, if such provision is one concerning the protection of women. [*SDA s 51* as substituted by *EA 1989 s 3(3)*]. Thus, discrimination in order to comply with college statutes enacted under a statute prior to *SDA* was considered lawful in *Hugh-Jones v St John's College, Cambridge [1979] ICR 848*. Many such statutory requirements have been or will be removed as a result of *EA 1989*.

44.17 Discrimination to safeguard national security

Discrimination for the purpose of safeguarding national security is lawful. [*SDA s 52(1)*]. A certificate signed by, or on behalf of, a Minister of the Crown and certifying that an act specified in the certificate was done for the purpose of safeguarding national security is stated to be conclusive evidence that it was done for that purpose. [*SDA s 52(2)*].

However the European Court of Justice in *Johnston v The Chief Constable of the*

Royal Ulster Constabulary [*1987*] *ICR 83* held that a similar provision in a Northern Ireland Order was contrary to *Article 6* of the *Equal Treatment Directive No 76/207*. *SDA s 52(2)* has now been amended by the *Sex Discrimination (Amendment) Order 1988 (SI 1988 No 249)* so that it no longer applies to discrimination in employment and related areas.

44.18 Provision of benefits and services

An employer whose business consists of or includes the provision of benefits, facilities or services to the public may as a matter of *employment* law discriminate against a woman employee in the provision of those benefits or services to her unless

(*a*) the employer provides those benefits to his male employees, or

(*b*) their provision is regulated by the woman's contract of employment, or

(*c*) the benefits, facilities or services relate to training.

[*SDA s 6(7)*].

Thus, if an employer operates a public sports stadium, he may prevent a woman employee of his from using it unless, for example, he allows his male employees to use it. However, the employer will be liable to an action by that employee in the county court under the provisions of *SDA s 29* (discrimination in provision of goods, facilities or services).

44.19 Pay

Offering or paying a woman less remuneration than a man is not an act of unlawful discrimination [*SDA, s 6(5)(6)*], but if she is engaged on like work or on work rated as equivalent to that of a man or on work of equal value to that of a man, her contract is modified by the *Equal Pay Act 1970* so that she is able to claim pay equal to that of the man (see EQUAL PAY (19)).

44.20 Retirement and employment – related benefits

Since 7 November 1987, the date upon which the *Sex Discrimination Act 1986, s 2(1)* came into force, it has been contrary to *SDA 1975* to apply different compulsory retiring ages to men and women.

SDA s 6(4), as amended by *SDA 1986* and *Social Security Act 1989, 5 Sch 14* (a commencement order to bring into effect the relevant provisions is awaited), renders lawful discriminatory provision relating to death or retirement except insofar as, in their application to provision in relation to retirement, they render it unlawful for a person to discriminate against a woman –

(*a*) in such of the terms on which he offers her employment as make provision in relation to the way in which he will afford her access to opportunities for promotion, transfer or training or as provide for her dismissal or demotion; or

(*b*) in the way he affords her access to opportunities for promotion, transfer or training or by refusing or deliberately omitting to afford her access to any such opportunities; or

(*c*) by dismissing her or subjecting her to any detriment which results in her dismissal or consists in or involves her demotion; or

(*d*) in such of the terms on which he offers her employment as make provision in relation to the way in which he will afford her access to any benefits, facilities or services under an occupational pension scheme; or (*e*) in the way in which he affords her access to any such benefits, facilities or services; or

(*f*) by refusing or deliberately omitting to afford her access to any such benefits, facilities or services; or

(*g*) by subjecting her to any detriment in connection with any such scheme,

if the act of discrimination relates to a matter in respect of which an occupational pension scheme has to comply with the principle of equal treatment under *SSA 1989 5 Sch*. [*SDA s 6(4B)*]. That principle is set out in *SSA 1989 5 Sch 2*. It includes a bar upon indirect discrimination where the relevant requirement or condition cannot be justified irrespective of sex and (by *SDA s 6(4C)*) a bar on discrimination based on marital status. It applies only to employment-related benefit schemes as defined by *SSA 1989, 5 Sch 7*. This will include schemes for benefits payable in money or money's worth in respect of matters which include termination of service, retirement, death, sickness, industrial injury, unemployment or expenses connected with children or other dependants.

Also, claims relating to pay may be based directly on *Article 119* of the Treaty of Rome. 'Pay' includes purely contractual pension benefits which are not a substitute for a state pension. (*Bilka-Kaufhaus GmbH v Weber von Hartz [1987] ICR 110* but see *Burton v British Railways Board [1982] ICR 329*); *Newstead v Department of Transport [1988] ICR 332*. See also *Garland v British Rail Engineering Ltd [1982] ICR 420*, and the extremely important recent case of *Rinner-Kühn v FWW Spezial-Gebäudereinigung GmbH & Co KG [1989] IRLR 493*, which holds that a statutory restriction affecting a considerably greater number of women than men contravenes *Article 119* unless objectively justifiable on grounds unrelated to sex. See generally EUROPEAN COMMUNITY LAW (20), 19.9 EQUAL PAY and also *Hasley v Fair Employment Agency [1989] IRLR 106*.

If an employer wishes to contract out of the state pension scheme he must show that membership of his occupational pension scheme is available to women on the same terms as to men. [*Social Security Pensions Act 1975, s 53*].

44.21 EMPLOYEES TO WHOM THE ACT DOES NOT APPLY

(*a*) **Employees working outside Britain**

The *SDA* does not apply to employees who do their work wholly or mainly outside Great Britain. [*SDA ss 6(1), 10(1)*]. However the Act does apply to

(i) employment on board a ship registered at a port of registry in Great Britain; or

(ii) employment on aircraft or hovercraft registered in the United Kingdom and operated by a person who has his principal place of business, or is ordinarily resident, in Great Britain,

unless the employee does his work wholly outside Great Britain. [*SDA s 10(2)*]. By Order, Great Britain may be deemed to include the continental shelf, including foreign sectors of the continental shelf in relation to employment concerned with the exploration or exploitation of a cross-boundary petroleum field. [*SDA s 10(5)*]. The *Sex Discrimination and Equal Pay (Offshore Employment) Order 1987 (SI 1987 No 930)* has been made pursuant to this power.

(*b*) **Police officers**

Discrimination in height requirements and uniform or uniform allowances is lawful in the employment of police constables. [*SDA s 17(2)(3)*].

Application of a height requirement which women would find it harder to comply with than men would otherwise be unlawful unless shown to be justifiable. [*SDA s 1(1)(b)*].

(*c*) **Prison officers**

Discrimination is lawful between male and female prison officers as to requirements relating to height. [*SDA s 18(1)*]. Men may now be governors of women's prisons. [*SDA s 18(2)*].

(*d*) **Ministers of religion**

The Act does not apply to employment for purposes of an organised religion where the employment is limited to one sex so as to comply with the doctrines of the religion or to avoid offending the religious susceptibilities of a significant number of its followers. [*SDA s 19(1)*].

Since September 1983, employers have not been able to discriminate lawfully in the engagement, promotion, transfer or training of midwives. [*SDA s 20(1)(2); Sex Discrimination Act 1975 (Amendment of Section 20) Order 1983 (SI 1983 No 1202)*].

Section 1 of the *Sex Discrimination Act 1986* repeals *Sec 6(3), SDA 1975* whereby employment

(i) by a person employing five or fewer employees, or

(ii) in a private household

was excluded from the full protection of the legislation. *Section 1* was introduced to comply with *EC Directive 76/207 Article 2(2)* after the provisions of *section 6(3)* were held by the ECJ to conflict with the *Directive* (*Commission of the EC v UK* (*Case 165/82*) [*1984*] *ICR 192*). Some protection for employers in private households is retained by the extension (in *section 1(2)* of the *1975 Act*) of the defence of 'genuine occupational qualification' (see 44.13 above).

44.22 NON-EMPLOYERS COVERED BY THE EMPLOYMENT RULES

Users of contract workers

The person to whom an employer supplies labour (the principal) may not discriminate against a woman who is a contract worker

(*a*) in the terms on which he allows her to do that work; or

(*b*) by not allowing her to do it or continue to do it; or

(*c*) in the way he affords her access to any benefits, facilities or services or by refusing or deliberately omitting to afford her access to them (not being those which are supplied to the public at large unless, in relation to these, the woman is treated less favourably than other contract workers); or

(*d*) by subjecting her to any other detriment.

[*SDA s 9(2)*].

The exceptions available to employers relating to genuine occupational qualification apply equally to principals. [*SDA s 9(3)*].

44.23 Partnerships

It is unlawful for a partnership to discriminate against a woman in relation to a position as a partner in the firm

(*a*) in the arrangements they make for the purpose of determining who should be offered that position; or

(*b*) in the terms on which they offer her that position; or

(*c*) by refusing or deliberately omitting to offer her that position; or

(*d*) in a case where the woman already holds that position

(i) in the way they afford her access to any benefits, facilities or services, or by refusing or deliberately omitting to afford her access to them; or

(ii) by expelling her from that position, or subjecting her to any other detriment.

[*SDA s 11(1)* as amended by *Sex Discrimination Act 1986* which abolished an exception applying to partnerships of five or fewer partners].

These provisions also apply to persons proposing to form themselves into a partnership. [*SDA s 11(2)*]. However, the clauses relating to arrangements made for the purpose of determining who should be offered the position, and to refusing or deliberately omitting to offer a woman that position, do not apply where being a man is a genuine occupational qualification for the partnership. [*SDA s 11(3)*].

44.24 Trade unions and employers' organisations

Trade unions and employers' organisations may not discriminate against women in selecting their membership, in dispensing benefits or in subjecting members to any detriment, including expulsion. [*SDA s 12*].

44.25 Bodies conferring qualifications etc.

It is unlawful for an authority or body which can confer an authorisation or qualification which is needed for, or facilitates, engagement in a particular profession or trade to discriminate against a woman

(*a*) in the terms on which it is prepared to confer on her that authorisation or qualification; or

(*b*) by refusing or deliberately omitting to grant her application for it; or

(*c*) by withdrawing it from her or varying the terms on which she holds it.

[*SDA s 13(1)*].

In *British Judo Association v Petty [1981] ICR 660*, it was held that *SDA s 13* was to be widely construed so as to render unlawful a discriminatory restriction in a judo referee's certificate, since the certificate would in fact facilitate the holder's trade or profession.

Where the qualifying body must consider an applicant's character, if there is evidence to show that an applicant has practised unlawful discrimination in connection with the carrying on of any profession or trade, that must be taken into account in considering his character. [*SDA s 13(2)*].

44.26 Persons concerned with provision of vocational training

It is unlawful, in the case of a woman seeking or undergoing training which would help fit her for any employment, for any person who provides, or makes arrangements for the provision of, facilities for such training to discriminate against her

(*a*) in the terms on which that person affords her access to any training course or other facilities concerned with such training, or

(*b*) by refusing or deliberately omitting to afford her such access, or

(*c*) by terminating her training, or

(*d*) by subjecting her to any detriment during the course of her training.

[*SDA s 14; EA 1989, s 7(1)*].

These provisions apply to persons concerned with the provision of vocational training. They do not apply to the provision of training by employers to their employees to whom *SDA s 6(1) and (2)* apply to prohibit *inter alia* discrimination in access to training.

44.27 **Employment agencies**

It is unlawful for an employment agency to discriminate against a woman

(*a*) in the terms on which the agency offers to provide any of its services; or

(*b*) by refusing or deliberately omitting to provide any of its services; or

(*c*) in the way it provides any of its services.

[*SDA s 15*].

These provisions apply to guidance on careers and any other services related to employment. [*SDA s 15(3)*]. If, however, the employer could lawfully refuse to offer the job to a woman, discrimination in relation to that job by an employment agency is lawful. [*SDA s 15(4)*].

An employment agency may escape liability if it proves

(i) that it acted in reliance on a statement made to it by the employer to the effect that he could lawfully refuse to offer a woman employment; and

(ii) that it was reasonable for it to rely on the statement.

[*SDA s 15(5)*].

If, for example, an employment agency relied on the statement of an employer who had been guilty of discrimination in the past, to the knowledge of the employment agency, it may be difficult for that agency to establish that it had acted reasonably in acting upon that statement.

A person who knowingly or recklessly makes such a statement which in a material respect is false or misleading commits an offence and is liable on summary conviction to a fine not exceeding level 5 on the standard scale. [*SDA s 15(6)*; and see 1.10 INTRODUCTION].

It is also unlawful for the Secretary of State to discriminate in the provision of facilities or services under the *Employment and Training Act 1973 s 2*. [*SDA s 16*].

44.28 PERSONS RESPONSIBLE

Anything done by a person in the course of his employment shall be treated for the purposes of the Act as done by his employer as well as by him, whether or not it was done with the employer's knowledge or approval. [*SDA s 41(1)*]. However, it is a defence for an employer to prove that he took such steps as were reasonably practicable to prevent the employee from doing that act, or from doing in the course of his employment acts of that description. [*SDA s 41(3)*]. (See *Balgobin and another v Tower Hamlets London Borough Council* [*1987*] *ICR 829.*)

Anything done by a person as agent for another person with the authority of that person shall be treated as done by the principal as well as the agent. [*SDA s 41(2)*].

44.29 OTHER UNLAWFUL ACTS

Knowingly to aid another person in unlawful discrimination is itself an unlawful act. (See *Greater London Council v Farrer* [*1980*] *ICR 267.*) [*SDA s 42(2)*].

A person does not knowingly aid another to do an unlawful act if

(*a*) he acts in reliance on a statement made to him by that other person that, by reason of any provision of the Act, the act which he aids would not be unlawful; and

(*b*) it is reasonable for him to rely on the statement.

[*SDA s 42(3)*].

Knowingly to make a false statement is an offence punishable by a fine not exceeding level 5 on the standard scale. [*SDA s 42(4)*; and see 1.10 INTRODUCTION]. Thus, if an employer falsely assures his employee that a certain act is lawful, he is guilty of a criminal offence.

It is unlawful to give instructions to discriminate to a person over whom one has authority or to a person who normally acts in accordance with one's wishes. [*SDA s 39*]. Therefore, if a father, whose son normally acts in accordance with his wishes, orders him to discriminate in his business, the father acts unlawfully.

Direct or indirect pressure to induce or attempt to induce a person to discriminate is unlawful. [*SDA s 40*]. Such inducements may be either offering benefits or detriments.

44.30 EFFECT OF THE ACT ON CONTRACTS

A term of a contract is void where

(*a*) its inclusion renders the making of the contract unlawful by virtue of the Act;

(*b*) it is included in furtherance of an act rendered unlawful by the Act;

(*c*) it provides for the doing of an act which would be rendered unlawful by the Act.

[*SDA s 77(1)*].

Thus, a term in a contract for the provision of a discriminatory training programme would be rendered void by *Sec 77(1)*. A term in a contract for an advertisement which provided for the inclusion of a discriminatory expression would similarly be made void.

A term which constitutes (or is in furtherance of or provides for) unlawful discrimination against a party to a contract is not made void, but is unenforceable against that party. [*SDA s 77(2)*]. For example, a term in a contract with a woman which states that she cannot use a smoking room normally reserved for men is not enforceable in a court of law. A party to the contract may apply to a county court in England and Wales or a sheriff court in Scotland which may remove or modify the discriminatory term, provided that all persons affected have been notified of the application. [*SDA s 77(5)*].

(See also EQUAL PAY (19).)

Local authorities may not insert clauses into their contracts obliging the other party to comply with the discrimination legislation, because these are 'non-commercial matters'. [*Local Government Act 1988, s 17*]. (See *R v Islington London Borough Council, Ex parte Building Employers Confederation* [*1989*] *IRLR 382*.)

44.31 NO CONTRACTING OUT

A term in a contract which purports to exclude or limit any provision of the Act is unenforceable by any person in whose favour the term would operate. [*SDA s 77(3)*]. The inclusion of such a clause in a contract of employment would have no effect, leaving the employee free, despite its inclusion, to bring a complaint under the Act against the employer.

No agreement to compromise or settle a complaint brought under the Act is enforceable unless it has been made with the assistance of a conciliation officer. [*SDA s 77(4)*]. It is therefore essential that any settlement of such a complaint be approved by a conciliation officer. If this is not done, the employee may, despite the agreement, take her claim to an industrial tribunal. (For conciliation officers, see 2.3 ADVISORY, CONCILIATION AND ARBITRATION SERVICE.)

45 Sex Discrimination – II: Enforcement and Remedies

45.1 No legal action may be taken against an employer for a breach of any provision of the *Sex Discrimination Act 1975 (SDA)*, except where such an action is expressly provided for by the Act. The only means of direct enforcement open to an individual, for discrimination in relation to employment, is by application to an industrial tribunal (see 45.2 below). The Equal Opportunities Commission (EOC) has additional powers to hold formal investigations (see 45.8 below), issue non-discrimination notices (see 45.9 below) and may apply for an injunction in certain cases (see 45.10-45.11 below). Where *SDA* does not confer the rights granted by *EEC Directive 76/207*, individuals may rely upon the European Directive in claims against state authorities (see e.g. *Marshall v Southampton and South West Hampshire Area Health Authority (Teaching)* [*1986*] *ICR 335* and 44.20).

45.2 APPLICATIONS TO AN INDUSTRIAL TRIBUNAL

A person ('the complainant') may present a complaint to an industrial tribunal that another person has committed an act of discrimination against him or her which is unlawful by virtue of *SDA Part II* (the provisions relating to employment). By virtue of *SDA s 41* or *s 42*, the principal or employer of the discriminator will *also* be treated as having committed the discrimination (see 44.28 SEX DISCRIMINATION – I). [*SDA s 63(1)*]. Although the Act does not mention the 'burden of proof', in practice it is the complainant who must prove his or her case. (*Oxford v Department of Health and Social Security* [*1977*] *ICR 884*). However, industrial tribunals are entitled to draw an inference of sex discrimination from primary facts which indicate that there has been some discrimination, and if a complainant shows that he or she has been treated differently from other employees, it is for the respondent to establish that the discrimination was not on the ground of sex. (*Moberly v Commonwealth Hall (University of London)* [*1977*] *IRLR 176*). See also the draft EC directive set out at [*1988*] *3 CMLR 272*.

45.3 Time limit

A complaint must be presented to a tribunal before the end of the period of three months beginning when the act complained of was done. [*SDA s 76(1)*].

For the purposes of deciding when an act was done, in calculating the time limit

(*a*) where the inclusion of any term in any contract renders the making of the contract an unlawful act, that act shall be treated as extending throughout the duration of the contract; and

(*b*) any act extending over a period shall be treated as done at the end of that period (for an example, see *Calder v James Finlay Corporation Ltd* [*1989*] *ICR 157*); and

(*c*) a deliberate omission shall be treated as done when the person in question decided upon it.

[*SDA s 76(6)*].

If the cause for complaint is an omission rather than an act, the omission will be considered to have been decided upon when a person does something inconsistent with the omitted act or when the period within which he would reasonably have done the act has expired.

A tribunal may nevertheless consider any such complaint or application which is out of time if, in all the circumstances of the case, it considers that it is just and equitable to do so. [*SDA s 76(5)*]. One possible ground for doing so is that the complainant was unaware of his or her rights.

In *Stevens v Bexley Health Authority* [*1989*] *IRLR 240* the EAT appeared to consider that the statutory time limits were not applicable to claims brought directly under European law (see EUROPEAN COMMUNITY LAW (20) and 44.20 SEX DISCRIMINATION – I).

45.4 Conciliation

When a complaint has been presented to an industrial tribunal, the conciliation officer must endeavour to promote a settlement of the complaint if

(*a*) he is requested to do so both by the complainant and the respondent; or

(*b*) in the absence of requests by the complainant and the respondent, he considers that he could act with a reasonable prospect of success.

[*SDA s 64(1)*]. His services may also be sought by a prospective party before the presentation of a complaint. [*SDA s 64(2)*].

Information given to the conciliation officer in the performance of his duties is not admissible in evidence before the tribunal except with the consent of the giver of the information. [*SDA s 64(4)*]. Thus, frequently a conciliation officer will contact the employer to investigate the possibility of the removal of the cause of complaint. An employer is not obliged to give the conciliation officer information. See also ADVISORY, CONCILIATION AND ARBITRATION SERVICE (2).

45.5 Disclosure

An industrial tribunal may, on the application of a party to the proceedings, order the disclosure of a document which is relevant to the proceedings (see 27.7 INDUSTRIAL TRIBUNALS). However, the House of Lords in *Science Research Council v Nasse* [*1979*] *ICR 921* held that industrial tribunals should not order the disclosure of reports or references that have been given and received in confidence except where the Chairman of the tribunal decides that it is necessary in the interests of justice that the confidence should be overridden.In *Williams v Dyfed County Council* [*1986*] *ICR 449* the EAT offered guidance as to how essential information might be disclosed without breach of confidence.

45.6 Tribunal orders

Where an industrial tribunal finds that a complaint presented to it is well-founded, it may make such of the following orders as it considers just and equitable.

(*a*) An order declaring the rights of the complainant and the respondent in relation to the act to which the complaint relates. [*SDA s 65(1)(a)*]. Such a declaration may state, for example, that the complainant is entitled to certain training facilities or should be considered for a certain position.

(*b*) An order requiring the respondent to pay to the complainant compensation of an amount corresponding to any damages he could have been ordered by a county court to pay to the complainant. [*SDA s 65(1)(b)*]. Once a tribunal has decided to award compensation under *s 65(1)(b)*, the amount must be computed on the basis of what damages would be recoverable in a county court, and not on what the tribunal thinks is just and equitable. (*Hurley v Mustoe (No 2) [1983] ICR 422*). If the complainant was barred from applying for a particular benefit, the tribunal must in assessing compensation consider the percentage chance that her application would have succeeded (*Calder v James Finlay Corporation Ltd [1989] ICR 157*).

(*c*) A recommendation that the respondent take, within a specified period, action appearing to the tribunal to be practicable for the purpose of obviating or reducing the adverse effect on the complainant of any act of discrimination to which the complaint relates. [*SDA s 65(1)(c)*].

The amount of compensation awarded may not exceed the amount for the time being specified in *EPCA s 75(1) as amended* which is at present £8,925 where the act complained of occurred after 1 April 1989. [*Unfair Dismissal (Increase of Compensation Limit) Order 1989 (SI 1989 No 527)*]. It was previously £8,500. It has been held by an industrial tribunal that these limits do not apply where the successful claim is based upon EC law (*Marshall v Southampton and South West Hampshire Area Health Authority (No. 2) [1988] IRLR 325*). The tribunal also held that it was empowered to award interest on the compensation. The EAT overturned the award of interest *[1989] IRLR 459*; there was no appeal against the exceeding of the UK limit on compensation.

The amount awarded may include a sum for injury to feelings which results from the knowledge that it was an act of sex discrimination which brought about the employer's action. (*Skyrail Oceanic Ltd v Coleman [1981] ICR 864*). In that case the Court of Appeal considered a proper figure in the circumstances to be £100.(See also *Wileman v Minilec Engineering Ltd [1988] ICR 318*).

If without reasonable justification, the respondent to a complaint fails to comply with a recommendation made by an industrial tribunal that he take certain action under (*c*) above then, if it thinks it just and equitable to do so

(i) the tribunal may, subject to the limit in *Sec 65(2)*, increase the amount of compensation required to be paid to the complainant in respect of the complaint by an order made under *Sec 65(1)(b)*; or

(ii) if an order for compensation could have been made, but was not, the tribunal may make such an order.

[*SDA s 65(3)(a)(b)*].

45.7 THE EQUAL OPPORTUNITIES COMMISSION

The *Sex Discrimination Act 1975, s 53 and 3 Schedule* establishes the EOC which has the following duties

(*a*) to work towards the elimination of discrimination;

(*b*) to promote equality of opportunity between men and women generally; and

(*c*) to keep under review the working of the *Sex Discrimination Act* and the *Equal Pay Act 1970* and when it is required by the Secretary of State or otherwise thinks it necessary, to draw up and submit to the Secretary of State proposals for amending these Acts.

The EOC also has a duty to keep under review statutory provisions relating to health and safety at work which require men and women to be treated differently, to prepare reports on such matters and to prepare an annual report. [*SDA s 55; HSWA s 53*].

The EOC has the power to issue codes of practice, giving practical guidance. [*SDA s 56A*]. It has issued a code of practice 'for the elimination of sex and marriage discrimination and the promotion of equality of opportunity in employment' which came into force on 30 April 1985. A breach of the Code does not of itself render a person liable to proceedings, but any relevant provision of the Code may be taken into account by an industrial tribunal. [*SDA s 56A(10)*].

For inquiries, copies of the Code, leaflets etc. the address is Overseas House, Quay Street, Manchester M3 3HN.

45.8 Formal investigations

Apart from these general duties, the EOC may if it thinks fit, and shall if required by the Secretary of State for Employment, conduct a formal investigation for any purpose connected with the carrying out of its duties. [*SDA s 57(1)*]. The EOC or the Secretary of State for Employment must draw up terms of reference and give notice of the holding of the investigation either generally or to the particular persons named in the terms of reference.

Information. In order to conduct such an investigation, the EOC may issue a notice requiring the production of written information or documents or the attendance of witnesses for examination. A notice requesting information may only be issued where

(*a*) an investigation is being made into compliance with a non-discrimination notice [*SDA s 69*]; or

(*b*) service of the notice was authorised by or on behalf of the Secretary of State [*SDA s 59(2)(a)*]; or

(*c*) the terms of reference of the investigation show that the EOC believe that the person may have been or may be

  (i) carrying out unlawful discriminatory acts;

  (ii) applying discriminatory practices prohibited by *Sec 37*;

  (iii) issuing discriminatory advertisements, or issuing instructions to discriminate or pressurising others to discriminate (i.e. breach of *Secs 38, 39 or 40*);

  (iv) acting in breach of a term modified or included by virtue of an equality clause (see 19.4 EQUAL PAY).

[*SDA s 59(2)(b)*].

Such a notice cannot compel a person to disclose information or give evidence if he could not be compelled to do so in civil proceedings. Thus, communications with a solicitor relating to advice or discussions about the EOC's action would be privileged. The Act also states that necessary travelling expenses of persons required by notice to attend the EOC must be offered to them. If a person fails to comply with a lawful notice or the EOC has reasonable cause to suspect that he intends not to comply with it, the EOC may apply to a county court for an order requiring him to comply with it. Witnesses who fail to attend may be fined up to £400. [*SDA s 59(4); County Courts Act 1984, s 55(1)(2)*]. The EOC may have reasonable cause to believe that a person does not intend to comply with the order if he expresses his intention of non-compliance and also if he neglects to respond to requests which are proved to have been sent to him.

If a person is convicted in a magistrates' court of

(A) wilfully altering, suppressing, concealing or destroying a document required to be produced; or

(B) knowingly or recklessly making any statement which is false in a material particular,

he may be fined at level 5 on the standard scale. [*SDA s 59(6);* and see 1.10 INTRODUCTION].

EOC's report. The EOC may, as a result of its investigation, make recommendations to any person for changes in their procedures and to the Secretary of State for changes in the law or for other changes. [*SDA s 60(1)*]. *Sec 60* provides that the report of such an investigation and its recommendations may be published and inspected.

No information given to the EOC in connection with a formal investigation is to be disclosed by the EOC except

(*a*) on the order of any court; or

(*b*) with the informant's consent; or

(*c*) in the form of a summary or other general statement published by the EOC, which does not identify the informant or any other person to whom the information relates; or

(*d*) in a report of an investigation published by the EOC under *SDA s 60*; or

(*e*) to the Commissioner, additional Commissioners or employees of the EOC, or, so far as may be necessary for the proper performance of the functions of the EOC, to other persons; or

(*f*) for the purpose of any civil proceedings under the *Sex Discrimination Act 1975* to which the EOC is a party, or any criminal proceedings.

[*SDA s 61(1)*].

Contravention of these rules is made an offence punishable on summary conviction with a fine not exceeding level 5 on the standard scale. [*SDA s 61(2)*; and see 1.10 INTRODUCTION]. The EOC is under a general duty when preparing a report for publication or inspection to exclude, so far as is consistent with their duties and the object of the report, any matter which relates to the private affairs of any individual or the business interests of any person where the publication of that matter might in the opinion of the EOC prejudicially affect that individual or person. [*SDA s 61(3)*].

45.9 Non-discrimination notices

The EOC may issue a non-discrimination notice if during the course of a formal investigation, it is satisfied that a person has committed or is committing

(*a*) an unlawful discriminatory act;

(*b*) a discriminatory practice;

(*c*) a breach of the provisions relating to advertising, instructions to discriminate or pressure to discriminate; or (*d*) a breach of a term modified or included by virtue of an equality clause.

The non-discrimination notice may require the person

(A) not to commit any such acts; and

(B) where compliance involves changes in any of his practices or other arrangements

  (i) to inform the EOC that he has effected those changes and what those changes are; and

  (ii) to take such steps as may be reasonably required by the notice for the purpose of affording that information to other persons affected by those practices or arrangements.

[*SDA s 67(2)*].

The notice may require the person to supply information to show that the requirements of the EOC have been complied with. The time within which the notice must be complied with will be a date not later than five years from the date on which the notice became final. A non-discrimination notice or a finding by a court or tribunal becomes final when an appeal against the notice or finding is dismissed, withdrawn or abandoned or when the time for appealing expires without an appeal having been brought. An appeal against a non-discrimination notice will be taken to be dismissed if, notwithstanding that a requirement of the notice is quashed on appeal, a direction varying it is given under *Sec 68* (see below). [*SDA s 82(4)*].

The EOC may not issue a non-discrimination notice unless it has informed the relevant person of its intention and of the grounds of the notice and offered him an opportunity of making representations within a period of not less than 28 days specified in the notice and taken account of representations made by him. [*SDA s 67(5)*]. Thus, a company issuing an advertisement for male shop managers will be warned by the EOC of its intention of issuing a notice on the ground that it is contravening *Sec 38*. If the company then expresses its regret at having contravened the section and submits its proposed non-discriminatory advertisement, a notice may not be issued. If, however, it makes no such proposals, a notice will probably be issued which should then be complied with. If it is not, the EOC may apply to a county court for the issue of an injunction (see 45.10 below) against the employer.

It is therefore in the best interests of employers that

(i) they ensure that they are not in contravention of any of the provisions of the Act;

(ii) if they are in breach of any of the provisions and receive a notification of a proposal to issue a notice, they remedy the discrimination;

(iii) if a notice has been issued which they do not wish to challenge, they comply with it as soon as possible.

Appeal. If a person has any objection to a non-discrimination notice he may appeal against any requirement of the notice. Such an appeal must be lodged within six weeks of the service of the notice. The appeal must be made to an industrial tribunal or to a county court depending upon whether the acts to which the requirement relates are within the jurisdiction of the former or the latter. [*SDA s 68(1)*]. The appeal must be made to an industrial tribunal if the requirement relates to acts, such as dismissal, which are within its jurisdiction.

The *Industrial Tribunals (Non-discrimination Notices Appeals) Regulations 1977 (SI 1977 No 1094)* regulate the procedure to be adopted upon the hearing of such appeals.

Where the court or tribunal considers a requirement in a non-discrimination notice, in respect of which an appeal is brought, to be unreasonable because it is based on an incorrect finding of fact or for any other reason, the court or tribunal will quash the requirement. [*SDA s 68(2)*]. In addition to quashing the requirement, it may direct that a requirement be substituted in the terms specified in the direction. [*SDA s 68(3)*]. There is no appeal from such a direction. [*SDA s 68(4)*]. In appropriate circumstances application may be made to quash a non-discrimination notice under Order 53 of the Rules of the Supreme Court (judicial review).

Register of non-discrimination notices. A register is to be kept of non-discrimination notices which have become final. [*SDA s 70*]. The register is available for inspection and for copying. The EOC has to give general notice of the place or places where, and the times when, the register or a copy of it may be inspected. [*SDA s 70(4)*].

The EOC may, in certain circumstances, serve notices to investigate a person's compliance with a non-discrimination notice, without the consent of the Secretary of State. [*SDA s 69*].

45.10 INJUNCTIONS

Persistent discrimination

The EOC has certain powers to apply to the county court for an injunction where a person has been served with a non-discrimination notice or where a court or tribunal has found under *SDA s 63* (complaints relating to employment) or *Equal Pay Act 1970, s 2* that he has done an unlawful discriminatory act or an act in breach of a term modified or included by virtue of an equality clause (see 19.4 EQUAL PAY). If, within five years of the notice or of the court or tribunal finding becoming final, it appears to the EOC that unless restrained the person is likely to do an unlawful discriminatory act, breach an equality clause term or carry on a discriminatory practice made unlawful by *SDA s 37*, the EOC may apply for an injunction to restrain him from doing so. If satisfied that the application is well-founded, the court may grant the injunction in the terms applied for or on more limited terms. [*SDA s 71(1)*].

45.11 Advertisements and instructions or pressure to discriminate

Only the EOC may bring proceedings for breach of the provisions relating to advertisements and instructions or pressure to discriminate. It may make

(*a*) an application to an industrial tribunal or a county court for a decision whether the alleged contravention occurred; and/or

(*b*) an application to a county court for an injunction restraining continuance of such unlawful acts.

[*SDA s 72(1)(2)(4)*].

In all proceedings for an injunction, the EOC may not allege that a person has done an unlawful act which is within the jurisdiction of the industrial tribunal unless a finding of an industrial tribunal relating to that act has become final (see above). [*SDA s 72(5)*].

Additionally, in employment cases the EOC may, before applying for an injunction under *Sec 71(1)* or *72(4)*, present a complaint to an industrial tribunal that a person has done an act within the jurisdiction of the tribunal and the tribunal may

(i) make a finding of fact that the complaint is well-founded; and

(ii) make an order under *Sec 65(1)(a)* declaring the rights of the employer or person of whom the complaint is made, and the victim or the employee; and/or

(iii) make a recommendation under *Sec 65(1)(c)* that the employer (or person of whom complaint is made) take certain action within a specified period.

[*SDA s 73(1)*].

Applications by the EOC under *Sec 73(1)* to an industrial tribunal must be made before the end of the period of six months beginning when the act complained of was done. [*SDA s 76(4)*].

Similarly, application may be made to a county court or to an industrial tribunal within six months of the alleged act of discrimination within its jurisdiction, for a decision whether the alleged contravention occurred. [*SDA ss 72(2), 76(3)*].

Applications by the EOC under *SDA s 72(4)* to a county court for an injunction must be made before the end of the period of five years beginning with the original discriminatory act. [*SDA s 76(3)*]. A court or tribunal may nevertheless consider any such complaint, claim or application which is out of time if, in all the circumstances of the case, it considers it just and equitable to do so. [*SDA s 76(5)*].

45.12 ASSISTANCE FOR PERSONS DISCRIMINATED AGAINST

The Secretary of State is empowered to make orders to assist aggrieved persons who consider themselves to have been discriminated against. Forms are available to applicants by which they may question persons on matters relevant to the cause of their complaint. The *Sex Discrimination (Questions and Replies) Order 1975 (SI 1975 No 2048)* prescribes the form and procedure by which such questions may be asked. In proceedings before an industrial tribunal, a questionnaire is only admissible as evidence under *SDA s 74(2)(a)*

(*a*) where it was served before the presentation of a complaint, if it was served within the period of three months beginning when the act complained of was done;

(*b*) where it was served when a complaint had been presented, either if it was so served within the period of 21 days beginning with the day on which the complaint was presented, or if it was so served later with leave of the tribunal, within the period specified by the tribunal.

[*Reg 5*].

An employer may therefore be asked by which criteria he chose an employee for a particular post. But an employer is not obliged to answer an unreasonable question such as the name and address of a successful applicant for a post. (*Oxford v Department of Health and Social Security* [*1977*] *ICR 884*).

The EOC may also give assistance to claimants or prospective claimants (although not to respondents) if their case is of some complexity or raises a question of principle. That assistance may include obtaining or attempting to obtain a settlement, giving or arranging for the giving of advice or assistance, or representation by solicitor or counsel. The cost of this assistance constitutes a first charge for the benefit of the EOC on an award of costs made by the tribunal, or on any settlement whereby the respondent agrees to contribute to the complainant's costs. [*SDA s 75*].

45.13 SETTLEMENT OF CLAIM

An agreement settling a complaint relating to sex discrimination in employment or relating to *Equal Pay Act 1970, s 2* (see 19.11 EQUAL PAY) must be made with the assistance of a conciliation officer if it is to be enforceable by the respondent. [*SDA s 77(4)*]. Thus, if an employer agrees to compromise a complaint of discrimination brought against him, and in doing so pays a sum of money, unless the conciliation officer has assisted in reaching the agreement the applicant may pursue his/her claim despite the settlement.

46 Sickness and Sick Pay

Cross-references. See TERMINATION OF EMPLOYMENT (49) for sickness and frustration of contract of employment; for sickness and unfair dismissal, see 55.8 UNFAIR DISMISSAL – II.

46.1 In relation to pay for periods of sickness, the following may apply

(*a*) contractual provisions for sick pay (see 46.2 below);

(*b*) the statutory right to a specified level of sick pay ('statutory sick pay', see 46.3-46.8 below).

As in many areas of employment law, statutory payments are offset against contractual payments and vice versa. This 'offsetting' of payments during sickness is considered in 46.9-46.11 below.

Persistent illness may constitute such incapacity for work as to warrant dismissal (see 55.8 UNFAIR DISMISSAL – II).

In rare circumstances, sickness may render performance of the contract so radically different from that contemplated by the parties as to amount to a frustration of the contract (see 49.3 TERMINATION OF EMPLOYMENT).

46.2 CONTRACTUAL PROVISIONS FOR SICK PAY

An employer may agree to pay his employees while they are absent due to ill health. Such payments commonly run for a specified period of time and are subject to conditions.

The written particulars given to an employee setting out the terms and conditions of his employment must state whether or not the employer makes payments for periods of absence due to sickness and if so upon what terms (see 10.4 CONTRACT OF EMPLOYMENT). In *Mears v Safecar Security Ltd [1982] ICR 626*, the Court of Appeal held that where such a term is not specified or agreed, the tribunal must consider all the facts and circumstances to ascertain the term to be implied. There is no presumption of a contractual right to sick pay. An industrial tribunal must look to all the facts and circumstances and to the conduct of the parties since the contract began.

Where there is a contractual right to sick pay, but no provision as to its duration, the court will imply a reasonable term. (*Howman & Son v Blyth [1983] ICR 416*).

For the failure to comply with the statutory duty to specify in the written particulars of terms of employment what provisions for sick pay apply, see 10.9 CONTRACT OF EMPLOYMENT.

46.3 STATUTORY SICK PAY

(For further details see the DSS booklet 'Employers' Guide to Statutory Sick Pay', NI 227 and *Tolley's Guide to Statutory Sick Pay*, third edition (1988).)

From 6 April 1983, all employees, subject to certain specified exceptions (see 46.4 below), have been entitled to receive statutory sick pay ('SSP') from their employers, who may then recover it from national insurance contributions. The entitlement limit is, generally, twenty-eight weeks in a three-year period. The basic provisions are contained in the *Social Security and Housing Benefits Act*

1982 (SSHBA) as amended principally by the *Social Security Acts 1985* and *1986*. Regulations have been made under *SSHBA*, the main set of Regulations being the *Statutory Sick Pay (General) Regulations 1982 (SI 1982 No 894)* as amended, principally by the *Statutory Sick Pay (General) Amendment Regulations 1986 (SI 1986 No 477)* and the *Statutory Sick Pay (General) Amendment (No 2) Regulations 1987 (SI 1987 No 868)*.

The essential requirements for qualification are that an employee must

(*a*) have four or more consecutive days of sickness (including Sundays and holidays) during which he is too ill to be capable of doing his work (see further 46.5 below); and

(*b*) notify his absence to his employer, subject to certain statutory requirements and any agreement between them; and

(*c*) supply evidence of incapacity – this is also a matter for the employer: a common example of an employer's requirement would be

  (i) a 'self-certificate' for periods of four to seven days;

  (ii) a doctor's certificate or other evidence of sickness for periods after the first seven days.

[*SSHBA ss 2-6; Statutory Sick Pay (General) Regulations 1982, Reg 7*].

Employers may not contract out of the SSP provisions, and cannot require employees to contribute towards payments. [*SSHBA s 1(2)*].

46.4 Excluded employees

The following categories of employee are not entitled to receive SSP. These are an employee

(*a*) over state pension age on the first day of sickness;

(*b*) taken on for a specified period of not more than three months (unless the contract is extended beyond three months);

(*c*) having average weekly earnings less than the weekly lower earnings limit for National Insurance (NI) contribution liability;

(*d*) going sick within 57 days of having previously received one of a number of social security benefits;

(*e*) who has done no work for his employer under the contract of service;

(*f*) going sick during a stoppage of work at his place of employment due to a trade dispute, unless he has not taken part in the trade dispute, and has no direct interest in it;

(*g*) who is pregnant and goes off sick during the period starting eleven weeks before her expected week of confinement and ending six weeks after;

(*h*) who has already been due 28 weeks SSP from his employer in a period of entitlement of 3 years;

(*i*) who, subject to certain provisions, has already been due 28 weeks SSP from his former employer, and the gap between the first day of incapacity with the new employer and the last day on which SSP was paid by the former employer is eight weeks or less;

(*j*) who is in legal custody at any time on the first day of incapacity;

(*k*) who is abroad in a country which is outside the European Community at any time on the first day of the incapacity.

[*SSHBA 1 Sch; Social Security Act 1985, s 18(2)(d); Statutory Sick Pay (Mariners, Airmen and Persons Abroad) Regulations 1982 (SI 1982 No 1349); Statutory Sick Pay (General) Regulations 1982 (SI 1982 No 894); Statutory Sick Pay (General) Amendment Regulations 1986 (SI 1986 No 477)*].

Where the employer is notified that an excluded employee has been absent for four consecutive days or more, he is legally bound to send a form to the employee not later than seven days after being so notified. This form provides the explanation to the employee and the DSS of why SSP is not being paid, and allows the employee to claim State sickness benefit instead. [*Statutory Sick Pay (General) Regulations 1982 (SI 1982 No 894) Reg 15, as amended*].

46.5 The payment period

The period of four or more days of sickness (see 46.3(*a*) above) is called a 'period of incapacity for work' ('PIW'). Two or more PIWs which are separated by eight weeks or less are said to be 'linked' and are counted as one PIW. [*SSHBA s 2; Statutory Sick Pay (General) Amendment Regulations 1986 (SI 1986 No 477)*].

During a PIW, SSP is payable *only*

(*a*) while there is a 'period of entitlement', as defined (e.g. payment will cease, in the normal case, if the employment ends); *and*

(*b*) for days within the PIW which are 'qualifying days'.

The intention behind the idea of 'qualifying days' was that they would be the days on which the employee would normally be required to work, but it is open to employers in all cases to specify the pattern of qualifying days by agreement with the employees concerned. Each week must have at least one qualifying day, and qualifying days must not be defined by reference to the days of sickness. [*Statutory Sick Pay (General) Regulations 1982 (SI 1982 No 894); Statutory Sick Pay (General) Amendment Regulations 1985 (SI 1985 No 126)*].

SSP is not payable for the first three qualifying days in a PIW. It is paid for the fourth qualifying day onwards until either the employee becomes well again or the maximum payment period is reached.

The maximum entitlement to SSP is now 28 weeks in any period of entitlement of three years. A period of entitlement, as between an employee and his employer, is a period beginning with the commencement of a period of incapacity for work and ending with the earliest of

(i) the termination of that period of incapacity for work;

(ii) the day on which the employee reaches, as against the employer concerned, his maximum entitlement to statutory sick pay;

(iii) the day on which the employee's contract of service with the employer concerned expires or is brought to an end;

(iv) in the case of an employee who is, or has been, pregnant, the day immediately preceding the beginning of the disqualifying period (as defined by *SSHBA s 3(9)* as substituted). [*SSHBA s 3(2)*].

Therefore, an employer's liability to pay SSP will end if he has paid the employee SSP for twenty-eight weeks during a three-year period.

Days of entitlement to SSP from a previous employer, in a previous period of entitlement, will be taken into account in calculating whether maximum entitlement has been reached if

(A) the period of entitlement, as between the employee and his new employer, arose not more than 8 weeks after the last day in respect of which his previous employer had been liable to pay him SSP, and either

(B) the employee had provided the new employer with a leaver's statement (see 46.12 below) or

(C) the employer has himself issued such a statement to the employee.

[*Statutory Sick Pay (General) Amendment Regulations 1986 (SI 1986 No 477)*].

Employees who are still sick when their entitlement to SSP terminates may be entitled to State benefits. Employers of such employees must inform them in a prescribed form of the reason for the termination of SSP. [*SSHBA s 18; Statutory Sick Pay (General) Regulations 1982 (SI 1982 No 894), Reg 15, as amended by Statutory Sick Pay (General) Amendment Regulations 1986 (SI 1986 No 477)*].

46.6 The amounts payable and recoverable

Employees who earn less than the lower weekly earnings limit for National Insurance liability are excluded from SSP. In other cases the amount of SSP payable is related to the *average weekly earnings* of the employee, and SSP will be paid at either the standard or lower rate. The rates applicable from 6 April 1989 are

Earnings	SSP	28-week maximum
£84.00 and above	£52.10	£1,458.80
£43.00-£83.99	£36.25	£1,015.00

[*SSHBA s 7(1)* as substituted by *Social Security Benefits Up-rating Order 1989 (SI 1989 No 43), art 9*].

SSP is considered as earnings for PAYE income tax and NI contribution purposes. [*SSHBA s 23; Income and Corporation Taxes Act 1988, s 150*].

Recovery. The employer can deduct the gross amount of SSP from the total amount of employees' (primary) and employers' (secondary) Class I NI contributions due to the Collector of Taxes in respect of all employees for the tax month in which the SSP was paid, or from contributions due for subsequent months. From 6 April 1985, employers have also been able to deduct from contributions a sum equivalent to the employers' NI contributions due on SSP. In the tax year commencing 6 April 1989 that sum was 7½% of the SSP paid. [*Statutory Sick Pay (Additional Compensation of Employers and Consequential Amendments) Regulations 1985 (SI 1985 No 1411); Statutory Sick Pay (Additional Compensation of Employers) (Amendment) Regulations 1988 (SI 1988 No 431); Statutory Maternity Pay (Compensation of Employers) and Statutory Sick Pay (Additional Compensation of Employers) Amendment Regulations 1989 (SI 1989 No 286)*].

46.7 Records

Employers are obliged to keep records for SSP purposes. In particular, the following *minimum* information must be recorded by the employer and retained for at least three years.

- A note of the 'qualifying days' for SSP for each employee.
- Dates of each employee's PIWs.
- Days within each PIW on which SSP was not paid and the reasons why it was not paid.
- Copies of any leaver's statements (see 46.12 below) issued to an employee, as well as those statements provided by a previous employer and given to the employer by an employee.

[*Statutory Sick Pay (General) Regulations 1982 (SI 1982 No 894), Reg 13; Statutory Sick Pay (General) Amendment Regulations 1986 (SI 1986 No 477), Reg 5*].

The statutory records must be retained for at least three years, and must be stored in such a way that DSS inspectors can have access to them within a reasonable time, on request.

In addition, accounting records must be kept showing, *inter alios*, details of all SSP payments made, along with those of pay, NIC and PAYE income tax. Revenue records must be retained for seven years.

Employers may find it useful to keep fuller records, for example, self-certification forms, medical certificates, dates of all absences and the reasons for them. Such records can be used for the purposes of audit, and may also help to identify personnel problems.

Where personnel records are stored electronically, the provisions of the *Data Protection Act 1984* should be borne in mind.

46.8 Disputes

If an employer does not pay an employee SSP, the employee may ask him to give written reasons for the decision.

If the employee wishes to challenge the employer's decision, he may ask for a determination of the issue by an adjudication officer. There is a right of appeal from his decision to a Social Security Appeal Tribunal and thence to a Social Security Commissioner. There is a further right of appeal on a point of law, if leave is granted, to the Court of Appeal. [*Social Security Act 1980, s 14; Social Security (Adjudication) Regulations 1986 (SI 1986 No 2218)*].

It should be noted that the employer cannot ask the adjudication officer for a decision. He can be approached only by the employee or the DSS. However, if the employee has had four periods of self-certified sickness absence i.e. absences of between 4-7 days, in the past twelve months, and the employer doubts that the reasons given were genuine, he can seek help from the DSS on the fourth absence. He should inform the employee that the matter has been referred to the DSS.

As far as evidence of incapacity is concerned, the employer cannot require the employee to produce a medical certificate from a doctor for the first seven days of sickness. With that qualification, he can request the employee to provide reasonable evidence of incapacity, such as a self-certificate for absences of up to seven days. [*SSHBA s 17(2); Statutory Sick Pay (Medical Evidence) Regulations 1985 (SI 1985 No 1604)*].

46.9 OFFSETTING PAYMENTS MADE DURING SICKNESS AGAINST SSP

Any contractual remuneration paid to an employee for a day of sickness is to be offset against the SSP due for the *same day*. [*SSHBA s 10 and 2 Sch 2*]. However, SSP cannot be offset for days for which no remuneration is payable (e.g., probably, weekends). An employer can never pay the employee an amount in total which is *less* than the SSP due.

In personal injury actions, any special damages claimed will be subject to a deduction for SSP paid. (*Palfrey v GLC [1985] ICR 437*). The same principle was applied to payments under a non-contributory permanent health insurance scheme in *Hussain v New Taplow Paper Mills Ltd [1987] ICR 28*.

46.10 Contributory sickness schemes

An employee must not contribute to his own SSP. Thus, in the case of a jointly funded, i.e. 'contributory', sickness scheme, the amount of sick pay which will be offset against SSP must be in the proportion that the employer's contribution bears to the joint contributions to the scheme.

46.11 Contributory pension schemes

In the case of contributory pension schemes, offsetting will depend on how the pension scheme defines salary for calculation purposes: if salary is defined as 'earnings subject to PAYE income tax', then any SSP paid should be included in earnings for pension purposes. In that case the employee's pension contribution would be deducted from his full gross sick pay, i.e. including the SSP element. (See, in particular, the *Occupational Pensions Board Announcement No 2 (March 1983)*.)

46.12 ACTION WHEN EMPLOYEES LEAVE

If when an employee leaves there is a PIW which is separated from the date of termination by eight weeks or less, and SSP was payable for one week or more during the PIW, the employer must issue the employee with a 'leaver's statement'. This must be provided within seven days of the employment contract ending, and must state

(*a*) the date of the first day of the period of entitlement;

(*b*) the number of weeks of SSP payable (odd days of three will round down and four will round up to the nearest whole week) in that period of entitlement;

(*c*) the last day for which SSP was payable;

(*d*) the date the statement was made by the employer; and

(*e*) the full name, address and, if there is one, telephone number of the employer making the statement.

[*SSHBA s 3, as amended by Social Security Act 1985, s 18(5); Statutory Sick Pay (General) Amendment Regulations 1986 (SI 1986 No 477), Reg 7*].

46.13 PENALTIES

Non-compliance with the SSP provisions can amount to a criminal offence. [*Social Security Act 1986, s 54; Statutory Sick Pay (General) Regulations 1982 (SI 1982 No 894); Statutory Sick Pay (General) Amendment Regulations 1986 (SI 1986 No 477)*].

47 Strikes and Industrial Action

Cross-references. See PICKETING (34) for the specific rules on picketing; see TRADE UNIONS – I (51) for the liability of unions for industrial action.

47.1 LIABILITY FOR INDUSTRIAL ACTION – BACKGROUND

The right to take industrial action takes the form, in this country, of statutory *immunity* for action which would otherwise attract legal liability at common law. The statutory immunity first appeared in something like its present form in *Trade Disputes Act 1906, s 3*, and its scope has varied frequently since then. The current basic immunity is contained in the *Trade Union and Labour Relations Act 1974 (TULRA)*. The immunities in *TULRA* were amended by the *Trade Union and Labour Relations (Amendment) Act 1976 (TULR(A)A)* and have since been significantly limited by the *Employment Acts 1980* and *1982*, the *Trade Union Act 1984* and the *Employment Act 1988*.

The *Employment Act 1980* limited the immunity conferred on sympathy or 'secondary' action (see 47.6 below) and by *Sec 18* removed statutory immunity from certain acts to compel trade union membership. *Sec 18* was replaced by the *Employment Act 1982* which also introduced new restrictions by, in particular, limiting the scope of the term 'trade dispute' (see 47.4 below). In addition, trade unions may now be made liable in tort for industrial action for which there is no immunity (see 51.8 TRADE UNIONS – I). Previously it had been necessary to sue individual officials.

The *Trade Union Act 1984 (TUA)* further circumscribed the immunity given to trade unions from actions in tort, by limiting that immunity to industrial action supported by a ballot.

As a result of the *Employment Act 1988 (EA 1988)*, immunity has been removed from industrial action taken to enforce union membership, and there must be separate ballots for different workplaces involved in industrial action. *EA 1988* also provides a procedure for individual union members to insist upon ballots before industrial action.

At the time of writing, the Government has indicated that it will bring forward more legislation in the autumn of 1989. The Green Paper 'Removing Barriers to Employment' (Cm 655) proposes further restrictions on secondary action and the extension of balloting requirements to those who work under contracts for services (see EMPLOYEE OR SELF-EMPLOYED? (15)). Other possibilities which are apparently under consideration include making unions liable for unofficial action where they fail to discipline the strikers, provision for the attachment of earnings to pay fines for contempt of court and restrictions on industrial action in essential public services. (See now 'Unofficial Action and the Law' (Cm 821).)

In deciding whether legal proceedings can be taken against individuals (or unions) carrying on industrial action, it first must be ascertained whether a tort is being committed, for example, inducing a breach of contract (see 47.2 below). Then it must be ascertained whether that tort attracts the immunity conferred by *TULRA s 13* (as amended and limited by *TUA* and *EA 1988*).

The law relating to trade disputes is extremely complex. What appears below is an outline of the principles involved.

47.2 LIABILITY AT COMMON LAW

The law relating to the so-called 'economic torts' has developed gradually over the years; it is highly complex and in many respects still unclear. The most frequently encountered of the torts relate, broadly, to interference with contractual relations (note that *EA 1988, s 30(1)* deemed Crown servants to have contracts of employment for these purposes). They include:

(i) direct inducement of a breach of contract. A union which calls a strike will almost always induce the relevant employees to breach their contracts of employment, for example;

(ii) the indirect inducement or procurement of a breach of contract by unlawful means. For example, A may be able to sue the union if his contract to obtain goods from B is breached by B when the union induces B's employees to go on strike in breach of their contracts of employment;

(iii) interference with business by unlawful means. This may include the case where the performance of contracts is impeded but there is no actual breach;

(iv) intimidation. This is designed to deal with the situation where the harm results, directly or indirectly, not from the actual using of unlawful means, but from the threat of such use;

(v) conspiracy, i.e. an agreement either to do an unlawful act or to do a lawful act by unlawful means. The effect of the second limb is that an act done by two or more people may be unlawful even though it would have been lawful if done by one person acting alone.

Apart from the usual requirements of causation and foreseeability, it will usually be necessary to show that the defendant knows of the relevant contract and intends to procure its breach or the interference with its performance. Conspiracy is made out only where the defendant's predominant purpose is to injure the plaintiff, and not to further his own legitimate interests (see most recently *Metall und Rohstoff AG v Donaldson Lufkin & Jenrette Inc [1989] 3 WLR 563*).

Some of the most important of the many authorities on the economic torts are *D C Thomson & Co Ltd v Deakin [1952] Ch 646, J T Stratford & Son Ltd v Lindley [1965] AC 269, Torquay Hotel Co Ltd v Cousins [1969] 2 Ch 106, Merkur Island Shipping Corporation v Laughton [1983] ICR 490* and *News Group Newspapers Ltd v SOGAT '82 [1987] ICR 181*.

Although it is usually a breach of contract which is ultimately at the root of liability, that is by no means necessarily the case. See e.g. *Lonrho plc v Fayed [1989] 2 AER 65* (allegation of interference with business by unlawful means based upon fraudulent misrepresentation made to, but not causing loss to, third party). Doubt surrounds the extent to which breach of a statutory duty or a penal statute may be relied upon as unlawful means if the breach is not itself actionable. See *Lonrho Ltd v Shell Petroleum Co Ltd (No 2) [1982] AC 173; Barretts & Baird (Wholesale) Ltd v Institute of Professional Civil Servants [1987] IRLR 3; Associated British Ports v TGWU [1989] 1 WLR 939* (point not argued in the House of Lords).

Any successful picket will almost certainly involve the *prima facie* commission of a tort (see *Union Traffic Ltd v TGWU [1989] ICR 98*).

47.3 THE IMMUNITY FROM LIABILITY

TULRA s 13 provides as follows

'(1) An act done by a person in contemplation or furtherance of a trade dispute shall not be actionable in tort on the ground only –

(*a*) that it induces another person to break a contract or interferes or induces any other person to interfere with its performance; or

(*b*) that it consists in his threatening that a contract (whether one to which he is a party or not) will be broken or its performance interfered with, or that he will induce another person to break a contract or to interfere with its performance.

(4) An agreement or combination by two or more persons to do or procure the doing of any act in contemplation or furtherance of a trade dispute shall not be actionable in tort if the act is one which, if done without any such agreement or combination, would not be actionable in tort.'

[*TULRA s 13; TULR(A)A s 3(2); EA 1980, s 17(8) and 2 Sch; EA 1982, s 19(1) and 4 Sch*].

This formula provides immunity from actions based upon the most common of the economic torts. However, it is possible to formulate a cause of action which falls outside *Sec 13*. (See e.g. *Prudential Assurance Co Ltd v Lorenz (1971) 11 KIR 78* (inducing breach of fiduciary duty); *Associated British Ports v TGWU [1989] IRLR 291* and *[1989] 1 WLR 939* (inducing breach of statutory duty; the point was not argued in the House of Lords).) In such cases it is probably irrelevant that the act complained of may also constitute an inducement to breach of contract which does fall within the immunity.

47.4 'A TRADE DISPUTE'

'Trade dispute' is given a statutory definition in *TULRA s 29(1)* (as now restricted by *EA 1982, s 18*) as

'a dispute between workers and their employer which relates wholly or mainly to one or more of the following, that is to say

(*a*) terms and conditions of employment, or the physical conditions in which any workers are required to work;

(*b*) engagement or non-engagement, or termination or suspension of employment or the duties of employment, of one or more workers;

(*c*) allocation of work or the duties of employment as between workers or groups of workers;

(*d*) matters of discipline;

(*e*) the membership or non-membership of a trade union on the part of a worker;

(*f*) facilities for officials of trade unions; and

(*g*) machinery for negotiation or consultation, and other procedures, relating to any of the foregoing matters, including the recognition by employers or employers' associations of the right of a trade union to represent workers in any such negotiation or consultation or in the carrying out of such procedures.'

The test of whether there is a trade dispute is an *objective* test. (*NWL Ltd v Woods [1979] ICR 867*). A dispute for political reasons which is unconnected with terms and conditions of employment is not considered to be a trade dispute. One such case involved a refusal by broadcasting technicians to make a broadcast to South Africa. (*British Broadcasting Corporation v Hearn [1977] IRLR 273*). Similarly a proposed strike intended as a protest against Government policies was held not to be in contemplation or furtherance of a trade dispute. (*Express Newspapers Ltd v Keys [1980] IRLR 247*). In *Mercury Communications Ltd v Scott-Garner and another [1984] ICR 74*, an injunction was granted to restrain industrial action since the court held that the risk to jobs did not appear to be the major factor in the dispute. However, if the union genuinely wishes to achieve its demands, relating to terms and conditions of employment, it is not relevant to establish whether those demands are realistic (*Associated British Ports v TGWU [1989] IRLR 291*, a point not argued on appeal).

If workers take industrial action in this country in order to further a trade dispute abroad, then, provided that the outcome of the dispute relating to matters occurring outside the UK is likely to affect them in one or more of the aspects specified in *Sec 29(1)*, it will be considered to be a trade dispute for the purpose of the immunity conferred by *Sec 13*. [*TULRA s 29(3)*].

Although the dispute must be between workers (not merely the union) and their employer, it will be sufficient to show that it results from the breakdown of negotiations in which the union was acting on behalf of those workers; and in any event a 'yes' vote in the strike ballot will amount to an adoption of the dispute by the workers. (*Associated British Ports v TGWU [1989] IRLR 291*, a point not argued on appeal).

Thus, subject to the limits outlined above, a person or a trade union may take part in industrial action so long as it is in contemplation or furtherance of a trade dispute as defined. Further restrictions are imposed by *EA 1980*, *EA 1982* and *EA 1988*, considered in 47.6-47.7 below.

47.5 'In contemplation or furtherance . . .'

If there is a trade dispute, the question whether a particular act is in contemplation or furtherance of it is to be judged *subjectively*. In *Express Newspapers Ltd v McShane [1980] ICR 42*, the House of Lords held that 'If the party who does the act honestly thinks at the time he does it that it may help one of the parties to the trade dispute to achieve their objectives and does it for that reason, he is protected by the section'. (*Per* Lord Diplock at *p 57*). The House of Lords reversed the decision of the Court of Appeal which had applied a more objective test. The subjective test was also applied by the House of Lords in *Duport Steels Ltd v Sirs [1980] IRLR 116*. It is sufficient if one purpose of the strike is the furtherance of the dispute, even though there may be other purposes not within the immunity. (*Associated British Ports v TGWU [1989] IRLR 291*, a point not argued on appeal).

47.6 LIMITS IMPOSED ON SECONDARY ACTION

The *EA 1980, s 17* withdraws from individuals immunity from legal proceedings in tort in respect of certain kinds of industrial action. The immunity conferred by *TULRA s 13* is removed in the case of industrial action which consists of inducing a breach of a commercial contract (i.e. a contract which is not a contract of employment) by means of 'secondary action' (see below), unless that action can be brought within one of three exceptional categories. Liability for inducing a breach of a contract of employment which does *not* interfere with a commercial contract remains unaffected and enjoys complete immunity if done in contemplation or furtherance of a trade dispute. (For the scope of the term 'interference with a contract' see 47.2 above.)

'Secondary action' consists of any interference with a contract of employment under which the employer is not a party to the trade dispute concerned. Therefore, if there is interference with a commercial contract (whoever the parties to that contract are) there may be no immunity for the individuals who commit the interference if they do so by interfering with any contract of employment and the employer under that contract of employment is not a party to the trade dispute in question. The definition is thus aimed in particular at 'blacking' of goods or services, although other forms of industrial action are also covered.

In *Marina Shipping Ltd v Laughton* [*1982*] *ICR 215* and *Merkur Island Shipping Corporation v Laughton* [*1983*] *ICR 490*, it was held that blacking of ships caused by the International Transport Workers Federation was unlawful secondary action.

There will be immunity only if the secondary action is in one of the following categories.

(*a*) Lawful picketing at the premises of a *party to the trade dispute* [*EA 1980, s 17(5)*] (see PICKETING (34)).

(*b*) Interference with contracts of employment where the employer under that contract is an immediate supplier or customer of a party to the trade dispute and which is directly aimed at, and limited to, disrupting or preventing that employer's supply to or purchase from the party to the trade dispute and is likely to achieve that purpose. [*EA 1980, s 17(3)*].

(*c*) Interference with contracts of employment where: the employer under those contracts is *either* an *associated* employer of a party to the dispute *or* an immediate supplier or customer of such an employer, the principal purpose of the action is to prevent or disrupt the supply of goods or services between such persons, the action is likely to achieve that purpose, and the goods or services in question are in substitution for those which, but for the dispute, would have fallen to be supplied by or to the party to the dispute. [*EA 1980, s 17(4)*].

Categories (*b*) and (*c*) above apply to interference with contracts for the supply or purchase of services in the same way as to contracts for the supply or purchase of goods.

47.7 PRESSURE TO IMPOSE UNION MEMBERSHIP OR RECOGNITION

Under *EA 1982, s 14* and *EA 1988, s 10*, certain industrial action taken to impose union membership or recognition requirements does not have the protection of *TULRA s 13* and will therefore be unlawful. Specifically, there is no immunity from actions in tort for individuals who induce or attempt to induce another

(*a*) to incorporate in a contract to which that other person is a party, or proposed contract to which that other person intends to be a party, a term or conditions which would

(i) require that the whole, or some part, of the work done under the contract be done only by persons who are members or not members of trade unions or who are members or not members of a particular trade union; or

(ii) require that persons recognise one or more trade unions for the purpose of negotiating on behalf of workers employed by him, *or* negotiate or consult with an official of one or more trade unions;

(*b*) on grounds of union membership or union exclusion, to

(i) exclude a person from a list of approved suppliers or persons from whom tenders are invited;

(ii) terminate a contract for the supply of goods or services;

(iii) exclude a person from the group of persons from whom tenders for the supply of the goods or services are invited;

(iv) fail to permit a particular person to submit a tender;

(v) determine not to enter into a contract with a particular person for the supply of the goods or services.

[*EA 1982, ss 12(1)(2), 13(1)(2), 14(1)*].

Further, *EA 1988, s 10* provides that there is no immunity under *TULRA s 13* where the act concerned is done because, or partly because, a particular employer is employing, has employed or might employ a person who is not a member of any or any particular trade union, or because a particular employer refrains from discriminating against such a person, or because it is believed that any of these things has occurred. (See also 51.8 TRADE UNIONS - I.)

47.8 THE LIABILITY OF TRADE UNIONS

Trade unions are no longer immune from all proceedings in tort, arising from industrial action, as they were by virtue of *TULRA s 14*. They are now liable for tortious acts authorised or endorsed by a responsible person (see 51.8 TRADE UNIONS — I). They only enjoy the same statutory immunity as individuals if they fulfil the ballot requirements of *TUA*, as amended by *EA 1988*. The liability of trade unions in actions in tort is subject to statutory financial limits (see 51.9 TRADE UNIONS - I).

47.9 BALLOTS BEFORE INDUSTRIAL ACTION

In order to enjoy immunity from actions in tort for interfering with commercial contracts by inducing breaches of contracts of employment, trade unions must be supported by a ballot. [*TUA ss 10, 11* as amended by *EA 1988*]. The following are the prerequisites of a ballot before industrial action.

(*a*) All of those members who it is reasonable for the union to believe will be called upon in the industrial action, and no others must be balloted. If they have different places of work, *TUA s 11(1A)* (inserted by *EA 1988, s 17*) requires a separate ballot for each workplace, unless those balloted share a common feature of terms and conditions of employment or occupational description which is not shared by other members not balloted.

(*b*) So far as is reasonably practicable, every person entitled to vote must be supplied with a voting paper or have one made available to him at the workplace (or a place more convenient for him) during or immediately before or after his working hours. The words 'reasonably practicable' mean that inadvertent errors such as missing some members off the list will not necessarily invalidate the ballot. (*British Railways Board v National Union of Railwaymen* [*1989*] *IRLR 349*).

(*c*) The voting paper must contain at least one of the following questions –

(i) a question which requires the voter to say, by answering 'Yes' or 'No' whether he is prepared to take part, or to continue to take part, in a strike;

(ii) a question which requires the voter to say, by answering 'Yes' or 'No', whether he is prepared to take part, or as the case may be to continue to take part, in industrial action falling short of a strike;

Also, the following unqualified statement must appear without comment on every voting paper:

'If you take part in a strike or other industrial action, you may be in breach of your contract of employment.'

(*d*) So far as is reasonably practicable those voting must vote in secret.

(*e*) The votes must be fairly and accurately counted.

In order for the trade union to enjoy immunity from action

(*f*) the majority of those voting in the ballot must have answered 'Yes' to the appropriate question;

(*g*) the first authorisation or endorsement of industrial action must have taken place after the date of the ballot and before the expiry of the period of four weeks beginning with that date.

Where there are separate ballots for different workplaces, paragraphs (*b*) to (*f*) are to be tested in relation to the ballot for the workplace of the person whose breach or impaired performance of his contract of employment is relied upon to found the liability in tort. [*TUA s 10(3A)*, inserted by *EA 1988, s 17*].

If there is a suspension of industrial action for negotiations, a further ballot need not be held before industrial action is resumed, provided that the terms of the original ballot cover the reason for the resumed action. (*Monsanto plc v Transport & General Workers Union* [*1987*] *ICR 269*).

In *London Underground Ltd v National Union of Railwaymen* [*1989*] *IRLR 341* it was held that at the time of the ballot there must be a genuine, definite, substantial dispute (actual or reasonably foreseeable) between the parties, and that the ballot question must relate wholly to matters capable of constituting a trade dispute. However, in *Associated British Ports v TGWU* [*1989*] *IRLR 291* it was held that there was no need for the ballot information to describe or define every issue with which the dispute was concerned, provided that it was possible to identify the strike which was called with the strike which was voted for (the point was not argued on appeal).

Special provisions apply to overseas members. [*TUA s 11(9)(10)*]. A union which is a federation, and which does not have individual members whom it will call out on strike, cannot comply with *TUA ss 10 and 11* and therefore will enjoy no immunity from action when calling a strike. (*Shipping Company Uniform Inc v International Transport Workers Federation and others* [*1985*] *ICR 245*).

Funds are made available to trade unions for the conducting of ballots before industrial action. [*Funds for Trade Union Ballots Regulations 1984 (SI 1984 No 1654)*, as amended] (see 51.18 TRADE UNIONS – I). The Secretary of State is empowered by *EA 1980, s 3* as amended by *EA 1988, s 18* to issue a Code of Practice relating to the conduct by trade unions of ballots and elections (see CODES OF PRACTICE (7)). At the time of writing, a draft Code had been issued but had not yet been approved by Parliament.

47.10 EMPLOYER'S RIGHTS AND REMEDIES

The withdrawal of labour will usually amount to a breach of the contracts of employment of the individuals concerned. A strike notice may however, at least in theory, be construed as due notice to *terminate* the contracts of employment of the strikers. Whether this is so depends upon the words used and on the circumstances. (*Boxfoldia Ltd v National Graphical Association (1982) [1988] ICR 752*). Action taken in a go-slow or work-to-rule may also be considered a breach by each individual participant of his contract of employment. In *Secretary of State for Employment v Associated Society of Locomotive Engineers and Firemen [1972] ICR 7* at *p 56* Lord Denning MR said

> 'If [an employee] with . . . others, takes steps wilfully to disrupt the undertaking, to produce chaos so that it will not run as it should, then each one who is a party to those steps is guilty of a breach of his contract. It is no answer for any one of them to say "I am only obeying the rule book", or "I am not bound to do more than a 40-hour week". That would be all very well if done in good faith without any wilful disruption of services; but what makes it wrong is the object with which it is done.'

The lines of action open to an employer, and others affected by industrial action, include the following.

(*a*) An employer may try to conciliate, if necessary with the assistance of the ADVISORY, CONCILIATION AND ARBITRATION SERVICE (2).

(*b*) If employees are on strike or their work is disruptive within the meaning of Lord Denning's statement above, they do not have to be paid for the period during which industrial action persists. If employees are refusing to perform part of their contractual duties, employers may deduct an appropriate sum from their salaries. (*Sim v Rotherham Metropolitan Borough Council and others [1986] ICR 897; Miles v Wakefield Metropolitan District Council [1987] ICR 368; Wiluszynski v Tower Hamlets London Borough Council [1989] IRLR 259*; and see 31.8 PAY – I).

(*c*) If employees or unions are taking disruptive industrial action which is not in contemplation or furtherance of a trade dispute or is unprotected secondary action or action designed to create pressure in respect of trade union requirements as defined in *EA 1982, s 14* or *EA 1988, s 10*, or is action by trade unions taken without a ballot, an employer affected may apply to the High Court for an *injunction* to prevent them continuing such action. He may sue either the individuals involved or the union responsible, or both. Note that *TULRA s 17(1)* requires that any application for an injunction must be brought to the attention of the other party if it seems likely that he may claim that he is acting in contemplation or furtherance of a trade dispute. Unless the court is satisfied that all reasonable steps have been taken, an injunction will not be granted. However, it is important to apply to the court speedily.

In deciding whether or not to grant the injunction, a court must have regard to the likelihood of the defendant succeeding in establishing a defence under *TULRA s 13* or *s 15*. [*TULRA s 17(2)*]. Although the likelihood of establishing the defence is only one factor to be considered in deciding where the 'balance of convenience' lies (that being the test of whether to grant an interlocutory injunction if the plaintiff has an arguable case and an ultimate award of damages would not be an adequate remedy for either party), the injunction will normally be refused if it appears more likely than not that the statutory defence will be made out. (*NWL Ltd v Woods [1979] ICR 867*). The court will also have regard to whether it is likely that in practice the grant or refusal of the injunction will be decisive in determining the legal proceedings for an injunction (if so, it becomes more important to try to form a view of the ultimate chances of success), it will compare the disadvantage to the workers in being unable to strike while the iron is hot with the potential losses to the employer, in a proper case it may have regard to the public interest, and if all other considerations are evenly balanced it will usually attempt to preserve the status quo. (See e.g. *Dimbleby & Sons Ltd v NUJ [1984] ICR 386; Union Traffic Ltd v TGWU [1989] ICR 98; Associated British Ports v TGWU [1989] 1 WLR 939* (point not argued in the House of Lords).) The court will, however, under no circumstances grant an injunction if its effect would be to compel the employees to work.

If the union or the individuals against whom a court order is obtained act in breach of the order, proceedings may be taken for contempt of court. (See e.g. *Richard Read (Transport) Ltd and another v National Union of Mineworkers (South Wales Area) [1985] IRLR 67; Express & Star Ltd v NGA (1982) and others [1987] ICR 589; Kent Free Press v NGA and others [1987] IRLR 267*). The penalties which a court may impose if it finds a contempt proved are a fine, sequestration and imprisonment. A writ of sequestration will not affect the separate funds of a branch which is an unincorporated association (see *News Group Newspapers Ltd v Society of Graphical and Allied Trades (1982) [1986] ICR 716*). Note that the union will not be able to use its funds to indemnify individuals penalised for contempt of court, nor for certain criminal offences. [*EA 1988, s 8*; and see 51.10 TRADE UNIONS – I]. If industrial action is called without a ballot, union leaders can be required to rescind the instruction. (*Metropolitan Borough of Solihull v National Union of Teachers [1985] IRLR 211*).

(*d*) The employer may also claim *damages* against those taking part in or organising the industrial action, or against the union (see 51.8 TRADE UNIONS – I). A claim in tort for inducing breaches of contract (the most common cause of action) will only succeed if the statutory immunity does not apply. However, the immunity does not extend to straightforward actions for breach of contract, and individual strikers may be sued on that basis. However, this is rarely likely to be worthwhile for an employer. Damages are limited to the loss actually caused by the individual striker (*National Coal Board v Galley [1958] 1 WLR 16*), which may be difficult to prove, or confined to the extra cost of hiring a substitute; and to seek to enforce a substantial award of damages against ordinary employees, even if practicable, will not usually be conducive to good industrial relations.

(*e*) If necessary, an employer may dismiss all employees on strike (or taking other industrial action) and try to engage a new labour force. An industrial tribunal has no jurisdiction to hear a claim for unfair dismissal based on such a dismissal provided two conditions are met: *first*, all the employees in the employer's establishment who were taking part in the industrial action at the date when the complainant was dismissed must also be dismissed; *secondly*, none of those employees can be offered re-engagement by the employer until three months after the date of the dismissal, or else all of them must be offered re-engagement within that period. (See further 54.17 UNFAIR DISMISSAL – I.) [*EPCA s 62; EA 1982, s 9*].

47.11 THIRD PARTIES' RIGHTS AND REMEDIES

Parties whose contracts are interfered with by unlawful industrial action may apply to the High Court for an injunction and damages, provided that the loss caused is not too remote or unforeseeable. The holder of a train ticket was able to recover damages from the rail unions for wrongfully interfering with his contract with British Rail. (*Falconer v ASLEF and NUR [1986] IRLR 331*).

47.12 CONSEQUENCES FOR EMPLOYEES

For any industrial action, whether or not in contemplation or furtherance of a trade dispute,

(*a*) the employee loses his right to pay during the industrial action;

(*b*) he is not entitled to receive unemployment benefit, although his family may in some circumstances receive income support (see *Cartlidge v Chief Adjudication Officer [1986] ICR 256*);

(*c*) he is not entitled to any GUARANTEE PAYMENT (23) in respect of the days on which he is engaged in industrial action;

(*d*) if dismissed during a strike, a participant in that strike will not be able to claim compensation for UNFAIR DISMISSAL (54) if the two conditions in 47.10(*e*) above are met;

(*e*) so far as the computation of periods of continuous employment is concerned (for example, for redundancy and unfair dismissal claims), absence due to participation in a strike will not break continuity, but the period of absence is not counted in the computation. The start of the period of employment will be deemed to be postponed by the appropriate number of days (see 9.10 CONTINUOUS EMPLOYMENT).

47.13 EMPLOYEES WHO MAY NOT STRIKE

Some employees are forbidden by law to strike. These include members of the armed services and police officers. In a few cases employees, especially in industries which are or were within the public sector, may be under certain statutory duties. Attempts have been made to argue that, given that inducement of a breach of statutory duty does not fall within the *TULRA s 13* immunity (see 47.3 above), such provisions effectively prohibit organised strike action. But the recent decision of the House of Lords in *Associated British Ports v TGWU [1989] 1 WLR 939* at p *970* suggests that the courts will be reluctant to construe the relevant statutes so as to reach such a result.

It is a criminal offence for a person 'wilfully and maliciously [to break] a contract of service or of hiring, knowing or having reasonable cause to believe that the probable consequences of his so doing, either alone or in combination with others, will be to endanger human life, or cause serious bodily injury, or to expose valuable property whether real or personal to destruction or serious injury'. [*Conspiracy and Protection of Property Act 1875, s 5*]. The penalty is a fine not exceeding level 2 on the standard scale (see 1.10 INTRODUCTION) or imprisonment for not more than three months. However, there have been no recent prosecutions for this offence.

47.14 EMPLOYEE'S RIGHT TO A BALLOT

EA 1988, s 1, gives a remedy to a trade union member whose union seeks to involve him in industrial action without the support of a ballot. Such a person may apply to the High Court (the Court of Session in Scotland), which will make an order (see below) if he can demonstrate that:

(*a*) the union has, without the support of a ballot, authorised or endorsed any industrial action; and

(*b*) that members of the union, including the applicant, have been or are likely to be induced by the union to take part in or continue to take part in that action.

[*EA 1988, s 1(1), 1(2)*].

Again, any application should be made without undue delay.

For the purpose of deciding whether the members are induced by the union and whether action is authorised or endorsed by the union, reference is made to the test of liability of unions for official action contained in *EA 1982, s 15(2)*.[*EA 1988, s 1(3), (4)*; and see 51.8 TRADE UNIONS - I]. The fact that the inducement is ineffective is immaterial. [*EA 1988, s 1(6)*].

The action is authorised or endorsed without the support of a ballot unless, not more than four weeks before the commencement of the action, there has been a ballot complying with *TUA 1984, s 11* (see 47.9 above) in respect of the action, in which the applicant was entitled to vote. The majority of those voting must have answered 'yes' to a question asking them whether they are prepared to strike or take part in the industrial action concerned. [*EA 1988, s 1(5)*].

If the court upholds the complaint, it will make such order as it considers appropriate for requiring the union to take steps to ensure that there is no further inducement of members to take part in the action and that no member engages in any further conduct resulting from the prior inducement. The steps so required may include the withdrawal of any relevant authorisation or endorsement. [*EA 1988, s 1(2)*]. Disobedience to such an order will of course be a contempt of court.

48 Temporary and Seasonal Employees

Cross-references. See 15.3 EMPLOYEE OR SELF-EMPLOYED? for the distinction between a contract for services and a contract of service/employment. See 33.8 PAYE for vacation employment of students. See also ENGAGEMENT OF EMPLOYEES (18) and PROBATIONARY EMPLOYEES (35).

48.1 An employer may have to engage workers on a temporary basis. This might be to take over work while a permanent employee is away, or to cope with fluctuating work loads (e.g. due to seasonal work requirements). In this chapter the description 'temporary' is applied to a worker who is referred to an employer by an employment agency (the kind of worker commonly referred to as a 'temp') and to an employee who is employed for a limited period to do the work of an absent permanent employee. 'Seasonal worker' is applied to a person who enters into the direct employment of the employer for a limited period at a busy time of the year.

48.2 TEMPORARY WORKERS

Employment agencies

Employment agencies fulfil two main functions: they effect introductions of permanent staff to employers and they supply temporary staff for a short period of time. So far as the first category is concerned, after the introduction has been made, the employment agency drops out of the picture, and the employer enters into a direct relationship with the employee with all the attendant duties and responsibilities of a normal employment contract. If, however, the worker is supplied on a temporary basis, the agency charging the employer a weekly fee out of which it pays the worker, the employer is more accurately to be regarded in most circumstances as a user of that worker's services and not his employer. Thus, the employer may be vicariously liable for any wrong done by the worker while working for him (see 24.10 HEALTH AND SAFETY AT WORK – I) and liable to the worker for any claim by him for damages for personal injuries. (*Mersey Docks and Harbour Board v Coggins & Griffiths (Liverpool) Ltd [1947] AC 1; Denham v Midland Employers' Mutual Assurance Ltd [1955] 2 QB 437*). However, it is doubtful whether the employer would be liable to the worker for unfair dismissal or redundancy if the employment agency could be regarded as the primary employer who lends the worker's services to other employers. (*Cross v Redpath Dorman Long (Contractors) Ltd [1978] ICR 730*). In *Ironmonger v Movefield Ltd [1988] IRLR 461* it was held that the contract with the employment agency was one *sui generis*, somewhere between a contract of employment and a contract for services.

Statutory control of employment agencies. Persons who carry on employment agencies or employment businesses must be licensed by the Secretary of State. [*Employment Agencies Act 1973, s 1*]. There are certain specified grounds upon which a licence may be refused or revoked. [*s 2(3)(3A)*]. It is a criminal offence, punishable by a fine not exceeding level 5 on the standard scale (see 1.10 INTRODUCTION) to charge a person a fee for finding or seeking to find him employment, save in such cases as the Secretary of State prescribes. [*s 6*]. The classes which have been prescribed relate to occupations in the entertainment industry, to modelling and to au pairs. The conduct of employment agencies is further regulated by the *Conduct of Employment Agencies and Employment Businesses Regulations 1976 (SI 1976 No 715)*.

48.3 Employees

A temporary employee may accrue sufficient qualifying employment to present a complaint of unfair dismissal, although this has become unlikely in practice with the increase in the qualifying period to two years. If at the outset of his employment it was made clear to him that he was only engaged on a temporary basis, the employer's refusal to renew his temporary contract should be considered to be for a substantial reason falling within *EPCA s 57(1)(b)* and may well be considered fair. (See *Fay v North Yorkshire County Council [1986] ICR 133* approving *Terry v East Sussex County Council [1977] 1 AER 567*). The dismissal of replacement employees, taken on in place of permanent employees on medical suspension or absent because of pregnancy or confinement, will be considered to be for a reason falling within *Sec 57(1)(b)* provided that the employee was informed in writing at the time of the engagement that the employment was temporary and would be terminated when the permanent employee returned. [*EPCA s 61*]. The tribunal will then go on to decide whether the dismissal was fair within the meaning of *EPCA s 57(3)*.

48.4 SEASONAL WORKERS

Workers taken on for a limited period of time, such as seasonal sales staff or extra staff taken on to deal with the tourist season, are considered to be employees for all purposes. They enjoy all the normal employment protection rights provided that they have the necessary qualifying periods of employment.

Where such an employee is dismissed when the seasonal demand has ended, the fact that he was only taken on as a seasonal worker will not automatically make the dismissal fair. It is merely one of the circumstances which must be taken into account by an industrial tribunal in deciding whether the employer acted reasonably (see 55.4 UNFAIR DISMISSAL – II). Also a seasonal worker must be given at least the statutory minimum period of notice to terminate his contract of employment, unless the contract was for a fixed term (see 49.9 TERMINATION OF EMPLOYMENT).

If the period of unemployment between seasons is short and the employee is habitually re-engaged, his continuity of employment may be preserved during the period of his absence due to the temporary cessation of work. [*EPCA 13 Sch 9*]. (See 9.6 CONTINUOUS EMPLOYMENT and *Flack and others v Kodak Ltd [1986] ICR 775; Fitzgerald v Hall, Russell & Co Ltd [1970] AC 984*, but see also *Hellyer Brothers Ltd v McLeod [1987] ICR 526*.)

Employers should therefore take just as much care to comply with all the applicable employment rules regarding seasonal staff as they do in the case of their permanent staff.

49 Termination of Employment

49.1 A contract of employment may be terminated in several ways: by mutual agreement; by frustration; by expiry; by dismissal by the employer; by notice given by the employee; or by acceptance of a fundamental repudiatory breach of contract by the employer or the employee. The distinction between these different modes of termination may be of importance in determining whether the employee may bring a claim for UNFAIR DISMISSAL (54), WRONGFUL DISMISSAL (59) or REDUNDANCY (38).

The death of either party terminates the contract of employment, unless the contract expressly or impliedly provides otherwise. The bankruptcy of the employer does not operate as a dissolution of the contracts of employment between himself and his employees, but in general the winding-up of a company and the dissolution of a partnership do operate to terminate the contract, subject to the effect of the *Transfer of Undertakings (Protection of Employment) Regulations 1981 (SI 1981 No 1794)* (see TRANSFER OF UNDERTAKINGS (53)).

49.2 MUTUAL AGREEMENT

Termination by agreement between employer and employee may be effected either orally or in writing. The agreement to terminate may take effect on any day in the month or year, and does not have to coincide with a pay-day.

The courts will scrutinise an apparent agreement to terminate if the employee alleges that he was given no choice but to consent to the ending of his employment. The general principle which the courts will apply is that if the sole cause of the employee's willingness to agree to the termination of his employment is the threat of dismissal, he will be held to have been dismissed. If, however, other additional factors, such as financial inducements, affected his decision he will be taken to have resigned by mutual agreement. He will then not be entitled to bring any claim for unfair or wrongful dismissal.

In *Sheffield v Oxford Controls Ltd [1979] ICR 396* the employee was told that if he did not resign he would be dismissed. He signed an agreement to resign in return for certain financial benefits. The Employment Appeal Tribunal found that he had resigned and had not been dismissed because his resignation had been brought about not by the threat of dismissal but by other factors such as the offer of financial benefits. See also *Birch v University of Liverpool [1985] ICR 470* and *Scott and others v Coalite Fuels and Chemicals Ltd [1988] ICR 355*. But in *Caledonian Mining Co Ltd v Bassett and another [1987] ICR 425* an employer who dishonestly persuaded his employees to resign was treated as having dismissed them. The dishonesty in that case was held by the industrial tribunal to consist of a preconceived arrangement designed by the employers to avoid liability for redundancy payments.

An agreement for the automatic termination of a contract of employment on the occurrence of a certain event may be ineffective to exclude entitlement to statutory employment protection rights because of *EPCA s 140(1)* (see 54.18 UNFAIR DISMISSAL – I).

49.3 FRUSTRATION

Frustration occurs where the performance of the contract of employment becomes impossible or substantially different from that which the parties contemplated at the time of entering into the agreement. A contract will be terminated by frustration if performance becomes unlawful (for example by the passing of a statute after the contract is made). The question of termination by reason of frustration most frequently arises in cases of absence of the employee because of illness or imprisonment. Where the contract is frustrated, there is no dismissal (the essence of frustration is that in law termination is *automatic*), and hence no possible claim for wrongful or unfair dismissal or redundancy. The employee will be able to recover for services rendered prior to the frustrating event, relying if necessary upon *Law Reform (Frustrated Contracts) Act 1943, s 1(3)*.

49.4 Illness

In the past, it has been held that a contract of employment will be frustrated by illness where the illness interferes with the performance of an essential part of it or where the illness is likely to last for a long period.

In *Marshall v Harland & Wolff Ltd [1972] ICR 101*, the circumstances in which a contract of employment may be considered frustrated by absence due to illness were considered. Tribunals will have regard to

(i) the terms of the contract including the provisions as to sickness pay;

(ii) how long the employment was likely to last in the absence of sickness;

(iii) the nature of the employment;

(iv) the nature of the illness or injury and how long it has already continued and the prospects of recovery;

(v) the period of past employment.

In that case, the court held that an absence of 18 months was insufficient to frustrate the contract. However, in *Hart v A R Marshall & Sons (Bulwell) Ltd [1977] 1 WLR 1067*, it was decided that in the circumstances of that case an absence of four months frustrated the contract.

The Court of Appeal in *Notcutt v Universal Equipment Co (London) Ltd [1986] ICR 414* held that (despite earlier doubts) there was no reason in principle why, in appropriate circumstances, a contract terminable on notice could not be frustrated. In that case, the contract of an employee whose employment was terminable on the statutory minimum period of notice was held to be terminated by frustration due to ill health.

49.5 Imprisonment

In the most recent decision on the question, the Court of Appeal in *FC Shepherd & Co Ltd v Jerrom [1986] ICR 802* has held that a contract of employment was capable of being frustrated by the imposition of a custodial sentence. The rule that frustration could not be induced by a party's own default applied only to the party alleging that frustration had occurred.

49.6 EXPIRY

If a contract is for a fixed period, it will automatically terminate at the end of that period. No notice need be given. It should be noted that, for the purposes of a claim for redundancy pay or in respect of unfair dismissal, the expiry of a fixed term contract may nevertheless constitute a dismissal (see 38.6 REDUNDANCY – I and 54.4-54.6 UNFAIR DISMISSAL – I). If an employee remains in his employment after the expiry of the term, he will be considered to be working under the same terms and conditions as before, save only that his employment is subject to an implied term that it can be terminated by either party upon giving reasonable notice (see 49.8 below).

49.7 DISMISSAL BY THE EMPLOYER

'Dismissal' is here used in its popular sense, to mean termination of a contract of employment by the employer. For the purposes of the unfair dismissal and redundancy payments legislation, the concept of dismissal is given a special statutory meaning which includes both the expiry of a fixed term contract without its renewal and 'constructive dismissal' (see 38.6 REDUNDANCY – I and 54.4 UNFAIR DISMISSAL – I).

Sometimes there may be a dispute as to whether the words used by the employer (or the employee in the case of a resignation) in fact amount to a dismissal. Where those words are ambiguous, the court or tribunal should ask how they would have been understood by a reasonable listener in the circumstances. (*Sothern v Franks Charlesly & Co [1981] IRLR 278*). A party who has used unambiguous words cannot normally be heard to say that he did not mean what he appeared to mean. However, it seems that there may be exceptions to this rule. In *Barclay v City of Glasgow District Council [1983] IRLR 313* the EAT, dealing with a purported resignation by a mentally handicapped employee, held that there might be circumstances where words are spoken, for example under emotional stress, which the other party ought to know are not meant to be taken seriously. This approach was upheld in relation to words spoken in the heat of the moment by the Court of Appeal in *Sovereign House Security Services Ltd v Savage [1989] IRLR 115*.

Dismissal may be either *summary* or with *notice*. At common law, either party to the contract of employment is always free to terminate the relationship by giving the proper notice. Thus, if such notice is given, there can be no claim for WRONGFUL DISMISSAL (59). To be effective in law, the notice must expire on a certain specified day (*Morton Sundour Fabrics Ltd v Shaw (1966) 2 ITR 84*), or upon the occurrence of a specified event.

Summary dismissal is *prima facie* a breach of contract, but is justified in certain circumstances. Whether the dismissal is or is not fair is an entirely separate question. A dismissal may be fair even though proper notice is not given, and a dismissal on notice may nonetheless be unfair (see *Treganowan v Robert Knee and Co Ltd [1975] ICR 405; BSC Sports and Social Club v Morgan [1987] IRLR 391*; and UNFAIR DISMISSAL – II (55)).

49.8 Termination on notice – the contractual notice period

The contract of employment will usually specify the period of notice to be given to terminate the contract; indeed, the written particulars given to the employee must include the length of notice which the employee is obliged to give or entitled to receive (see 10.5 CONTRACT OF EMPLOYMENT).

49.9 Termination of Employment

If the contract is not for a fixed term and the notice period has not been expressly agreed, there is an implied term that it may be terminated upon reasonable notice. The court will determine what amounts to reasonable notice. Factors taken into account include the seniority and remuneration of the employee, his age, his length of service and what is usual in the particular trade. As a very rough guide, a period of two weeks or one month might be appropriate in the case of a manual worker, or three months in the case of senior skilled workers or middle management, and between three months and one year in the case of more senior managers. However, the period of notice must be determined on the particular facts of each case.

49.9 Termination on notice – statutory minimum notice

Whatever may be the contractual provisions – whether express or implied – for termination of the contract, the notice actually given must not be less than the statutory minimum period of notice. The contractual notice must be given if that is longer. The statutory rules are as follows:

(*a*) an employee who has been continuously employed for one month or more but less than two years is entitled to not less than one week's notice;

(*b*) an employee who has been continuously employed for two years or more but less than twelve years is entitled to one week's notice for each year of continuous employment;

(*c*) any employee who has been employed for twelve years or more is entitled to not less than twelve weeks' notice.

[*EPCA s 49(1); EA 1982, s 20, 2 Sch 3*].

This results in the following.

Table of statutory minimum notice

Period of continuous employment (years)	Minimum period (weeks)
Less than 2 (but one month or more)	1
At least 2 but less than 3	2
At least 3 but less than 4	3
At least 4 but less than 5	4
At least 5 but less than 6	5
At least 6 but less than 7	6
At least 7 but less than 8	7
At least 8 but less than 9	8
At least 9 but less than 10	9
At least 10 but less than 11	10
At least 11 but less than 12	11
12 or more	12

For example, if a clerk has been employed for twelve years under a contract which does not specify the period of notice to which he is entitled, a term of reasonable notice would be implied which in his case may well be one month. However, his length of service entitled him to twelve weeks' notice and that is the minimum notice he must be given.

An employee cannot contract out of his right to the statutory minimum period of notice. [*EPCA s 140*]. However, he may waive his right to notice on a particular occasion, or accept a payment in lieu of notice. [*EPCA s 49(3)*].

49.10 **Exceptions**

The following employees do not have the right to be given the statutory minimum period of notice

(*a*) employees engaged in work wholly or mainly outside Great Britain, unless the employee ordinarily works in Great Britain and the work outside Great Britain is for the same employer [*EPCA s 141(1)*];

(*b*) employees in employment under a contract made in contemplation of the performance of a specific task which is not expected to last for more than three months, unless they have been continuously employed for more than three months [*EPCA s 49(4A); EA 1982, s 20, 2 Sch 3*];

(*c*) certain seamen [*EPCA s 144*].

49.11 **Pay in lieu of notice**

An employer who intends to dismiss an employee may consider it desirable that the employee should cease work immediately and not work out his notice period. For example, some employers consider it unwise to let a sales representative, who knows that he is to be dismissed, have any further contact with the employer's customers, for fear of endangering their goodwill. If an employee is dismissed without notice or with short notice it is usual to give him pay in lieu of notice. It would be possible, although unusual, to give an employee notice to expire half way through the contractual or statutory notice period and to make a payment in lieu of notice in respect of the remainder of the period. Another possibility is to continue to pay the employee as usual, but to ask him to remain at home. This will not normally represent a breach of contract by the employer (but see 10.12 CONTRACT OF EMPLOYMENT). Even if he makes a payment in lieu of notice, an employer may nevertheless be liable to the employee for breach of contract if by the premature determination of his contract, the employee has been deprived of statutory rights. (See observations in *Robert Cort and Son Ltd v Charman* [*1981*] *ICR 816*.)

The practice of giving pay in lieu of notice is virtually universal, but it does not fit easily into the traditional legal framework. Two connected problem areas are

(*a*) whether pay in lieu of notice is taxable (see 49.12 below);

(*b*) if tax-free, whether it should be paid gross or net (see 49.13 below).

49.12 *Taxation of pay in lieu of notice*. The contract of employment may expressly empower the employer to dismiss the employee summarily on making a payment in lieu of notice. If the contract does set out such a right then the payment in lieu constitutes an 'emolument' of the employment, and tax should be deducted under PAYE in the usual way. It is probable that any appropriate National Insurance contributions should be paid as well.

Normally, there is no express contractual term relating to the making of payments in lieu of notice, but the employer may have an almost invariable custom of giving pay in lieu of notice. In a few such cases, inspectors of taxes have asserted that the payment in lieu was taxable under the general principles of Schedule E income tax as a payment which the employee has a 'reasonable expectation' that he will receive as a consequence of his having been employed. So far as is known, such an assessment has not been appealed, so there is no authoritative determination of this view.

It may be argued that the better view is that non-contractual pay in lieu of notice is a payment of *compensation* for the employer's breach of contract in not giving due notice, and escapes the general Schedule E tax charge accordingly. It would follow that neither the frequency with which such payments are made nor any expectation on the part of the employee would affect this. There is authority for the view that pay in lieu of notice is compensation. In *Dixon v Stenor Ltd [1973] ICR 157*, Donaldson J said (at p 158) 'if a man is dismissed without notice but with money in lieu, what he receives is, as a matter of law, damages for breach of contract'. Moreover, Inland Revenue booklet P 7 'The Employer's Guide to PAYE' (in paras 49, 51) appears to support the view above since it includes pay in lieu of notice in a list of types of termination payment which are stated not to be taxable under the general charge unless paid under a contract. (It should be remembered, however, that statements in IR booklets are not legally binding.)

Assuming that a non-contractual payment in lieu of notice falls to be regarded as compensation, it will be tax-free under the general rules. It may nevertheless be taxable under the special rules on compensation payments for loss of office (e.g. 'golden handshakes'), but only if the *total* amount paid to the employee, including any redundancy payment and any other termination payments, exceeds £30,000. [*Income and Corporation Taxes Act 1988, ss 148, 188(4); FA 1988, s 74*].

A non-contractual payment in lieu of notice is not subject to National Insurance contributions.

49.13 *Payment gross or net?* Many, if not most, employers who make a payment in lieu of notice which is tax-free, pay over to the employee his full gross wages or salary. Legally, however, if pay in lieu of notice is to be regarded as compensation for breach of contract (see above), it would follow that the employer is only liable to pay the net amount that the employee would have received after deduction of tax and National Insurance. This is because the measure of damages for breach of contract is calculated on the basis of *the amount lost* by the employee in not being allowed to work his notice.

However, there is nothing to prevent an employer from paying the gross amount and there may be sound reasons for doing so, e.g. to maintain good industrial relations or public relations. It is also conceivable, though unlikely, that an employer who had a consistent practice of making payments gross might be held liable to pay the gross amount to an employee on the ground that the consistent practice had given rise to an implied contractual term (see e.g. *Gothard v Mirror Group Newspapers Ltd [1988] ICR 729*). (To avoid the tax charge it would be necessary to establish that this term related only to the manner of calculating pay in lieu and not to the employer's liability to make the payment.)

A further complication is that in a number of recent industrial tribunal claims brought under the *Wages Act 1986* (see 31.5 PAY–I) it has been alleged that to pay wages in lieu of notice net rather than gross constitutes an unlawful deduction. This argument was upheld in *Jackson v Foster Wheeler [1989] IRLR 283*, a decision currently under appeal to the EAT.

49.14 **Summary dismissal**

If the employee acts in a way which is incompatible with the faithful discharge of his duty to his employer he may be dismissed instantly, without notice or wages in lieu of notice. Examples of misconduct which can in certain circumstances give rise to the right to dismiss summarily are wilful disobedience of a lawful order from the employer, theft of the employer's property, and drunkenness such as to impair the performance of his duties. The misconduct must be gross or grave, seen in the light of all the circumstances of the case. In general, employees should be given a clear indication of the type of conduct which the employer regards as warranting summary dismissal. (*ACAS Code No 1, para 8* – see Appendix).

Summary dismissal for misconduct which is not gross is a breach of contract rendering the employer liable in damages for WRONGFUL DISMISSAL (59).

For a recent discussion of the exact moment when a dismissal without notice takes effect, see *Octavius Atkinson & Sons Ltd v Morris* [*1989*] *ICR 431*.

49.15 Written statement of reasons for dismissal

An employee is entitled to be provided by his employer, on request, within 14 days of that request, with a written statement giving particulars of the reasons for his dismissal if

(*a*) he is given by his employer notice of termination of his contract of employment; or

(*b*) his contract of employment is terminated by his employer without notice; or

(*c*) where he is employed under a contract for a fixed term, that term expires without being renewed under the same contract.

[*EPCA s 53*]. The reasons given by an employer are admissable in evidence in any proceedings. The employer's reply to a request may refer to full reasons given in an earlier written communication, a copy of which should be sent with the reply. Where a legal adviser is appointed by the employee, as a duly authorised agent to receive the information, it is sufficient to communicate the information to the legal adviser. (*Gilham and others v Kent County Council (No 1)* [*1985*] *ICR 227*).

An employee is not entitled to written reasons unless he has been continuously employed for a period of six months ending with the effective date of termination. [*EPCA s 53(2); EA 1982, 2 Sch 4*]. This period is increased to two years by *EA 1989, s 15(1)*.

49.16 Remedy for failure to give reasons

A complaint may be made by the employee to an industrial tribunal on the grounds

(*a*) that his employer unreasonably refused to provide a written statement of the reason for dismissal; or

(*b*) that the particulars given are inadequate or untrue.

[*EPCA s 53(4)*].

In *Daynecourt Insurance Brokers Ltd v Iles* [*1978*] *IRLR 335*, the company failed to answer an employee's request for written reasons for his dismissal. Its justification for doing so was a general request by the police officer who investigated the alleged theft of company funds by the employee, that the company should not answer any correspondence or deal with any matter that related to the police investigations of the company's records. The EAT held that the industrial tribunal's finding, that the company should not have simply ignored the employee's statutory request but should have sought further advice of the police officer, was not wrong in law. In *Ladbroke Entertainments Ltd v Clark*

[*1987*] *ICR 585* the EAT held that there was no 'refusal' in the absence of evidence that the employers realised they had been asked to provide written reasons.

The time limit for presentation of the complaint is three months from the effective date of termination of employment. This period can be extended if the industrial tribunal is satisfied that it was not reasonably practicable to present it within the three-month period.

If the tribunal finds the complaint well-founded, it will make an award that the employer pay to the employee a sum equal to the amount of two weeks' pay. It may also make a decision as to what it finds that the employer's reasons were for dismissing the employee. A week's pay is calculated in accordance with the provisions of *EPCA 14 Sch* and the calculation date is

(*a*) where the dismissal was without notice, the date on which the employer's notice was given; or

(*b*) in any other case, the effective date of termination.

[*EPCA 14 Sch 7(f)(g)*].

(See further 'A WEEK'S PAY' (58).)

49.17 RESIGNATION BY THE EMPLOYEE

As in the case of dismissal by the employer, the employee may resign with or without notice. For the question of whether the words used will amount to a resignation, see 49.7 above. No particular terms of art are required for resignations. (*Walmsley v C&R Ferguson Ltd* [*1989*] *IRLR 113*). A failure to give due notice is *prima facie* a breach of contract, but may be justified in certain circumstances.

49.18 Termination by the employee giving notice

The statutory minimum period of notice to be given by an employee, who has been continuously employed for one month or more, is one week. [*EPCA s 49(2); EA 1982, s 20, 2 Sch 3*]. However, the contractual period of notice to be given will in most cases be longer. The contractual notice may be either expressly agreed upon or implied. If it is implied, the notice to be given is that which is a reasonable period in all the circumstances (see 49.8 above).

49.19 Summary termination by the employee

If an employer is in breach of a fundamental term of the contract of employment, the employee is entitled to leave the employment forthwith. Leaving the employment in these circumstances is known as 'constructive dismissal' for redundancy payments and unfair dismissal purposes, since although the employee takes the initiative in leaving his employment he will be considered to have been dismissed within the meaning of *EPCA s 83(2)* (see 38.6 REDUNDANCY – I) and *EPCA s 55(2)* (see 54.4 UNFAIR DISMISSAL – I). In such circumstances, the employee would also be able to claim damages for WRONGFUL DISMISSAL (59).

49.20 REPUDIATORY CONDUCT

It has already been seen (see 49.14 and 49.19 above) that a repudiatory breach of contract by either the employer or the employee entitles the other party to terminate the relationship without giving notice or by giving short notice. A dismissal in such circumstances is not necessarily fair, nor a constructive dismissal following the employer's breach necessarily unfair, although they often will be.

The courts have sometimes gone further, and suggested that a repudiatory breach *automatically* brings a contract of employment to an end (see e.g. *Marriott v Oxford & District Co-operative Society Ltd (No 2)* [*1970*] *1 QB 186*). Such a principle would be contrary to the normal rule in the law of contract, which is that the 'innocent' party always has the option whether to accept the breach (and thus bring the contract to an end) or to 'affirm' the contract.

Although the question is not finally resolved, and raises complex issues beyond the scope of this book, the better view appears to be that a contract of employment is no exception to the general rule. See *Thomas Marshall (Exports) Ltd v Guinle* [*1978*] *ICR 905; Gunton v Richmond-upon-Thames London Borough Council* [*1980*] *ICR 755; London Transport Executive v Clarke* [*1981*] *ICR 355; Rigby v Ferodo Ltd* [*1988*] *ICR 29*. This means that (leaving aside questions of frustration and expiry at a specified time or upon the occurrence of a specified event) there is no such thing as an automatic termination because of one party's conduct. There must always be an acceptance of the breach constituting a dismissal by the employer or a resignation by the employee.

However, it is of the nature of the employment relationship that, where one party is unwilling to perform the contract, it will be very difficult for the other party to say that the relationship remains alive. An acceptance of the breach by the innocent party will readily be inferred from his conduct.

49.21 RETRACTION OF RESIGNATION OR DISMISSAL

The general rule is that words of resignation or dismissal, once communicated to the other party and accepted by him, cannot unilaterally be withdrawn. (*Riordan v War Office* [*1959*] *3 AER 552*). However, the EAT has suggested that good industrial relations practice requires that an employer should be able to withdraw words of dismissal provided that he does so almost immediately. (*Martin v Yeoman Aggregates Ltd* [*1983*] *ICR 314*). If this view is correct, it should apply equally to a case of resignation by the employee.

49.22 REMEDIES FOR WRONGFUL TERMINATION

An employee who has been dismissed, or who has resigned in circumstances amounting to a constructive dismissal, may complain of UNFAIR DISMISSAL (54) to an industrial tribunal, whether or not proper notice was given to him. If proper notice was not given, or if he resigned summarily in response to the employer's repudiatory breach, he may bring a claim for WRONGFUL DISMISSAL (59) in the ordinary courts. Where the employee fails to give proper notice, the employer may also in principle sue for damages. Also, either party may in certain, limited circumstances be able to obtain an injunction restraining an unlawful termination. See further 10.21 CONTRACT OF EMPLOYMENT.

50 Time Off Work

(See also DE booklets No. 6 'Facing redundancy? – time off for job hunting or to arrange training' (PL 703) and No. 12 'Time off for public duties' (PL 702). ACAS Code of Practice No. 3 and the HSC Code on time off for training of safety representatives are set out in the Appendix.)

50.1 There are several distinct rights under which an employee may take time off work in specific circumstances.

— Trade union officials and members may take time off work for certain duties and activities (see 50.2-50.3 below).

— Employees have the right to take time off work to perform certain public duties (see 50.4 below).

— An employee under notice of redundancy may take time off to look for work etc. (see 50.6-50.7 below).

— Safety representatives must be given time off to perform their duties (see 50.8-50.9 below).

— A pregnant woman has a right to take time off for ante-natal care (see 50.10 below).

50.2 **TRADE UNION OFFICIALS**

An employer is obliged to permit an employee of his, who is an official of an independent trade union recognised by him, to take time off during his working hours to

(*a*) carry out –

(i) official duties which are concerned with negotiations with the employer that are related to or connected with any matters that fall within *TULRA s 29(1)* (see 47.4 STRIKES AND INDUSTRIAL ACTION) and in relation to which the trade union is recognised by the employer, or

(ii) any other such duties, which are concerned with the performance, on behalf of employees of the employer, of any functions that are related to or connected with any matters falling within *TULRA s 29(1)* that the employer has agreed may be so performed by the trade union, or

(*b*) undergo training in aspects of industrial relations which is

(i) relevant to the carrying out of any such duties as are mentioned in (*a*); and

(ii) approved by the Trades Union Congress or by the independent trade union of which he is an official.

[*EPCA s 27(1)*; *EA 1989, s 14*].

The Court of Appeal in *British Bakeries (Northern) Ltd v Aldington and others* [*1989*] *ICR 438* held that it was a question of fact, dependent on the particular circumstances of the case, whether a preparatory meeting was sufficiently proximate to carrying out duties concerned with (at that time) industrial relations to come within *Sec 27(1)(a)*. Although *Sec 27(1)(a)* has been amended since *Aldington*, it is thought that the decision is equally applicable to whether attendance at a meeting is sufficiently proximate to carrying out the duties now specified in *Sec 27(1)(a)*.

The amount of time a trade union official is permitted to take off in the exercise of his statutory right, the purposes for which, the occasions on which and any conditions subject to which, time off may be so taken are those that are reasonable in all the circumstances, having regard to any relevant provisions in the ACAS Code of Practice. [*EPCA s 27(2)*].

It is to be noted that the right accrues only to officials of independent trade unions recognised by the employer. (See 51.12 TRADE UNIONS – I.) The ACAS Code of Practice No. 3 on time off for trade union duties and activities lays down guidelines on the reasonable exercise of this right, in particular dealing with the position when the absence is requested in respect of duties connected with industrial action (the Code is reprinted in full in the Appendix). Note, however, that the Code predates the restriction of the right by *EA 1989*: previously it extended to all official duties concerned with industrial relations between the employer and his employees.

There is no right to time off if, for example, the purpose is to attend a demonstration in support of a dispute with another employer or to carry out internal union duties. Nor would the amended *s 27* extend to, say, taking part in a course on pension schemes if the employer does not consult or bargain with the union about pensions and has not agreed to it performing any pension-related functions on behalf of his employees.

In *Ashley v Ministry of Defence* [*1984*] *ICR 298*, the EAT held that unless it can be shown that the recognised union expressly or impliedly required the attendance of its official at a meeting, the attendance of the official at such a meeting cannot constitute the carrying out by the official of a duty within the meaning of *Sec 27*. The EAT further held that attendance at an advisory meeting could be a duty within the meaning of *Sec 27*; whether it is, is a question of fact. In deciding whether the right to time off is being exercised reasonably within the meaning of *EPCA s 27(2)*, the EAT in *Depledge v Pye Telecommunications Ltd* [*1981*] *ICR 82*, considered that where comprehensive arrangements existed for the discussion of industrial relations matters it would be reasonable for trade union officials to use them. In considering whether the request for time off is reasonable in all the circumstances, tribunals will take into account such matters as the nature, extent and purpose of time off already being taken by that employee. (*Wignall v British Gas Corporation* [*1984*] *ICR 716*).

The trade union official who is entitled to take time off work to perform his duties is entitled to be paid for the period of his absence. Where his pay does not vary with the amount of work done, he is paid as if he had worked during the period of absence. Where his pay does vary according to the amount of work done, the amount he is to be paid during his absence is calculated by reference to the average hourly earnings for that work. [*EPCA s 27(3)*].

If an employer is obliged under a contract of employment to pay an employee for time off taken to perform trade union duties then those payments will go to discharge any statutory liability he may have to make such payments, and vice versa. [*EPCA s 27(6)*]. For example, Bill Jones is entitled to receive £5 per hour under his contract of employment for time taken off on union business. His statutory entitlement (i.e. his normal pay) is £6 per hour. Since the *contractual payment* goes to discharge the employer's *statutory liability*, he will receive £6 per hour and not £6 plus £5.

An employee who is an official of an independent trade union recognised by his employer may present a complaint to an industrial tribunal that his employer has failed to permit him to take the time off or to pay him the whole or part of any amount to which he is statutorily entitled (and see 50.5 below). [*EPCA s 27(7)*].

50.3 TRADE UNION ACTIVITIES

An employer is obliged to permit an employee of his, who is a member of an independent trade union recognised by him, to take part in certain trade union activities during working hours. The activities are defined as

(*a*) any activities of the trade union of which the employee is a member; and

(*b*) any activities in relation to which the employee is acting as a representative of such union;

excluding activities which themselves consist of industrial action whether or not in contemplation or furtherance of a trade dispute. [*EPCA s 28(1)(2)*].

The amount of time that may be taken and the purposes for which and the occasions on which it may be taken are those that are reasonable in all the circumstances; the same test applies to the imposition of conditions by the employer. [*EPCA s 28(3)*]. The ACAS Code of Practice No. 3 lays down guidelines on the amount of time off which an employee is to be permitted. The Code is to be taken into account in determining what is reasonable.

The employee is not entitled to be paid for time he takes off to participate in trade union activities unless he is a trade union official and the time is taken in accordance with 50.2 above.

An employee who is a member of an independent trade union recognised by his employer may present a complaint to an industrial tribunal that his employer has failed to permit him to take time off to which he is entitled (and see 50.5 below). [*EPCA s 28(4)*].

50.4 PUBLIC DUTIES

An employer is obliged to permit an employee of his who is

(*a*) a justice of the peace;

(*b*) a member of a local authority;

(*c*) a member of any statutory tribunal;

(*d*) a member of, in England and Wales, a regional health authority or area health authority or, in Scotland, a health board;

(*e*) a member of, in England and Wales, the managing or governing body of an educational establishment maintained by a local education authority, or, in Scotland, a school or college council or the governing body of a central institution or a college of education; or

(*f*) a member of, in England and Wales, a water authority or, in Scotland, river purification board;

to take time off work to perform his duties. [*EPCA s 29(1)*].

In deciding when and how much time is to be taken off, regard will be paid to

(i) how much time off is required for the performance of the duties of the office, or as a member of the body in question, and how much time off is required for the performance of the particular duty;

(ii) how much time off has already been permitted for the performance of any relevant public duty, union duty or activity;

(iii) the circumstances of the employer's business and the effect of the employee's absence on the running of that business;

and these considerations will be applied in deciding what is reasonable in the circumstances. [*EPCA s 29(4)*].

Although there is no statutory provision entitling an employee to time off for jury service, prevention of a person from attending as a juror is both a crime and a contempt of court. Thus, it is probable that there is an implied term that an employee should be allowed time off to attend court for jury service. The same reasoning would imply a right to time off to attend court as a witness.

50.5 EMPLOYEE'S REMEDIES

An employee may present a complaint to an industrial tribunal that he has not been allowed time off to carry out (*a*) trade union duties or activities, or (*b*) public duties and (in the case only of a trade union official's duties) that he has not been paid for time he has been permitted to take off. [*EPCA ss 27(7), 28(4), 29(6)*].

If it finds such a complaint well-founded, the tribunal will make a declaration to that effect and may order the employer to pay the employee compensation for the default and for any loss caused thereby. [*EPCA s 30(2)*]. In the case of a union official who has not been paid for time taken off, the tribunal will order the employer to make the appropriate payment. [*EPCA s 30(3)*]. If the employee is a piece worker, the amount is calculated by reference to the average hourly earnings for that work. If there are no average earnings for that employee, those of a worker in comparable employment are taken. [*EPCA s 27(3)*].

An industrial tribunal does not have the power to impose conditions upon the parties as to the way in which the time off shall be taken or to specify the amount of time off which should be allowed. (*Corner v Buckinghamshire County Council [1978] IRLR 320*).

The time limit for presenting such complaints is three months from the date of the failure complained of. If the tribunal is satisfied that it was not reasonably practicable for the complaint to be presented within the period of three months (see 27.3 INDUSTRIAL TRIBUNALS), then this time limit may be extended. [*EPCA s 30(1)*].

50.6 TIME OFF TO LOOK FOR WORK OR MAKE ARRANGEMENTS FOR TRAINING

An employee who has been given notice of dismissal by reason of redundancy must be allowed, before the expiry of the notice, *reasonable* time off by his employer, during his working hours, to look for new employment or to make arrangements for training for future employment. [*EPCA s 31(1)*]. In order to qualify for this right, the employee must have been *continuously employed for a period of at least two years*, by the date on which (*a*) the notice is *due* to expire, or (*b*) the date on which it *would* expire had the statutory minimum period of notice been given, whichever is the longer. [*EPCA s 31(2)*]. (See CONTINUOUS EMPLOYMENT (9).)

An employee who is so allowed time off is entitled to be paid for the time taken off at the appropriate hourly rate, which is calculated by the amount of one week's pay divided by the number of normal working hours in a week, or where the number of those hours varies, by taking the average of the twelve weeks ending with the last complete week before the notice was given. [*EPCA s 31(3)(4)*]. The right to be paid is dependent upon the right to take time off. Thus, if an employee with less than two years' continuous service is given time off to seek other employment, there is no statutory obligation on the employer to pay him for time so taken.

An employee who is under notice of redundancy is entitled to time off to look for work irrespective of whether he has an appointment to attend a specific interview. (*Dutton v Hawker Siddeley Aviation Ltd [1978] IRLR 390*).

If an employer unreasonably refuses to allow an employee time off work when statutorily obliged to do so, the employee is entitled to be paid the remuneration to which he would have been entitled if he had been allowed time off *in addition* to his normal pay. [*EPCA s 31(5), (10)*].

50.7 **Remedy**

If an employer has unreasonably refused the employee time off or has failed to pay him, the employee may present a complaint to an industrial tribunal. [*EPCA s 31(6)*]. The time limit for the presentation of such a complaint is three months beginning with the day on which it is alleged that time off should have been allowed. If the tribunal is satisfied that it was not reasonably practicable for the complaint to be presented within the period of three months (see 27.3 INDUSTRIAL TRIBUNALS) then this time may be extended. [*EPCA s 31(7)*].

The employer may be made liable to pay (i) remuneration for the period of absence or (ii) remuneration for the period during which he should have allowed time off, or both. The maximum amount, where both these provisions are applicable together, cannot exceed two-fifths of a week's pay. [*EPCA s 31(9)*].

Any contractual remuneration paid to an employee for a period of time which he takes off to seek or train for new employment when he is under notice of dismissal for redundancy goes towards discharging the employer's statutory liability and vice versa. [*EPCA s 31(11)*].

50.8 **SAFETY REPRESENTATIVES**

The Safety Representatives and Safety Committees Regulations 1977 (SI 1977 No 500), Reg 4(2) impose a duty upon employers to allow safety representatives time off with pay for the performance of their duties as safety representatives, and to undergo training in health and safety matters. There are guidelines for the exercise of the latter right, and the Code of Practice approved by the Health and Safety Commission on time off for the training of safety representatives is reproduced in full in the Appendix.

50.9 **Remedy**

If an employer refuses a safety representative time off for these purposes or if he does not pay him for the time taken, the safety representative may present a complaint to an industrial tribunal. [*Safety Representatives and Safety Committees Regulations, Reg 11(1)*]. The time limit within which a complaint must be presented is three months from the date where the failure occurred, or within such further period as the tribunal considers reasonable in a case where it is satisfied that it was not reasonably practicable for the complaint to be presented within the period of three months. [*Reg 11(2)*]. Where an industrial tribunal finds the complaint well-founded, it may make an award of such an amount as the tribunal considers just and equitable in all the circumstances, having regard to the employer's default in failing to permit time off to be taken by the employee and to any loss sustained by the employee which is attributable to the employee's complaint. [*Reg 11(3)*]. Where the complaint is based upon the failure of the employer to pay remuneration due, the industrial tribunal will order that sum to be paid to the employee. [*Reg 11(4)*].

50.10 TIME OFF FOR ANTE-NATAL CARE

EPCA s 31A (as inserted by *EA 1980, s 13*) provides a statutory right for pregnant women not to be unreasonably refused time off with pay during working hours to keep an appointment for ante-natal care prescribed by a doctor, midwife or health visitor. There is no minimum qualifying period for this right nor does it depend on full-time employment. Complaint may be made to an industrial tribunal if such time off is unreasonably refused. (This right is considered in detail in 29.2-29.5 MATERNITY RIGHTS.)

51 Trade Unions – I: Nature and Liabilities

(See DE booklet No. 15 'Union secret ballots' (PL 701).)

Cross-references. See also CLOSED SHOP (6); TIME OFF WORK (50) for time off for trade union duties or activities; TRADE UNIONS – II (52) for individual rights and union membership; 55.3 UNFAIR DISMISSAL – II for dismissal for participation in union activities.

51.1 THE STATUS OF A TRADE UNION

The present law on the status and liability of trade unions is governed by the *Trade Union and Labour Relations Act 1974* (*TULRA*) as amended by the *Employment Acts 1980* and *1982*, the *Trade Union Act 1984* and the *Employment Act 1988*. 'Trade union' is statutorily defined in *TULRA s 28(1)* as

'. . . an organisation (whether permanent or temporary) which either –

(*a*) consists wholly or mainly of workers of one or more descriptions and is an organisation whose principal purposes include the regulation of relations between workers of that description or those descriptions and employers or employers' associations; or

(*b*) consists wholly or mainly of –

(i) constituent or affiliated organisations which fulfil the conditions specified in paragraph (*a*) above (or themselves consist wholly or mainly of constituent or affiliated organisations which fulfil those conditions), or

(ii) representatives of such constituent or affiliated organisations;

and in either case is an organisation whose principal purposes include the regulation of relations between workers and employers or between workers and employers' associations, or include the regulation of relations between its constituent or affiliated organisations.'

In *British Association of Advisers and Lecturers in Physical Education v National Union of Teachers and others* [*1986*] *IRLR 497*, the Court of Appeal construed this definition broadly so as to include an association 'concerned with the professional interests of its members'.

Several of the larger trade unions are made up of a number of constituent sections. The definition in *TULRA s 28(1)* ensures that both the conglomerate organisation and its constituent parts are considered to be trade unions. The National Union of Mineworkers is made up of a number of areas such as the National Union of Mineworkers (South Wales Area), all of which are, under *TULRA*, to be considered trade unions. Similarly, a branch of a trade union may be held to be a trade union (see *News Group Newspapers Ltd v SOGAT (1982)* [*1986*] *IRLR 337*).

51.2 Legal capacity

Unless a trade union is a special registered body which means, among other things, that it is a company registered under the *Companies Act 1985*, or is otherwise incorporated [*TULRA s 30*], it is not to be, or to be treated as if it were, a corporate entity. However, *TULRA s 2(1)* gives a trade union a statutory legal personality which it would otherwise lack so that it can (*a*) make contracts;

(*b*) own property which is to be vested in trustees;

(*c*) (subject to a trade union's limited immunity from legal actions concerning trade disputes – see 51.8 below) sue or be sued in its own name;

(*d*) be a defendant in criminal proceedings; and

(*e*) be subject to the enforcement of judgments, orders or awards made against it in just the same way as a company (thus trade union funds or property, with the exception of 'protected property' (see *EA 1982, s 17(2)*) may be seized to satisfy a judgment and a union may be ordered to pay a fine and is liable to have its assets sequestered in contempt proceedings).

51.3 CERTIFICATION OFFICER

The Secretary of State appoints a Certification Officer in consultation with ACAS under the *Employment Protection Act 1975 (EPA), s 7(1)*. He makes an annual report to the Secretary of State, who presents it to Parliament and publishes it [*EPA 1 Sch 13*]. His functions include:

(*a*) dealing with complaints relating to the keeping of the register of a union's members (see 51.5 below);

(*b*) dealing with complaints relating to trade union internal elections (see 51.6 below);

(*c*) dealing with complaints relating to political fund ballots (see 51.7 below);

(*d*) maintaining a list of trade unions (see 51.13 below).

(*e*) certifying whether trade unions are independent (see 51.14 below);

(*f*) certain supervisory functions in relation to trade union amalgamations (see 51.17 below); and

(*g*) administering the scheme for financial contributions towards trade union ballots (see 51.18 below).

51.4 OBLIGATIONS

Trade unions have statutory obligations to make annual returns, to appoint auditors and to make arrangements for the inspection of their members' superannuation schemes. [*TULRA ss 10, 11 and 2 Sch*]. The *Trade Union Act 1984 (TUA)* imposed additional statutory obligations to keep an up to date register of members, to hold periodic elections for membership of the principal executive committee and to hold ballots on the continued application of trade union funds for political purposes. *Paul v NALGO [1987] IRLR 43* is a decision of the Certification Officer which discusses several of these obligations. The *Employment Act 1988* makes certain of the existing obligations more stringent. By *Sec 6*, it also introduces a right for union members to inspect the union's accounting records within 28 days of making a request to do so. This includes the right to be accompanied by an accountant and to take copies of records. [*EA 1988, s 6(3)*].

51.5 Register of members

Every trade union is obliged by *TUA s 4* to compile and keep up to date a register of members.

A member of the union may apply to the Certification Officer, or to the High Court in England or the Court of Session in Scotland, for a declaration that this requirement has not been complied with. [*TUA s 5*]. The Court may also make an enforcement order requiring the union to compile or update the register. [*TUA s 5(5)(6)(7)*].

51.6 Elections

Trade unions are obliged to secure that, with certain exceptions, all members of the principal executive committee (including non-voting members, by virtue of *EA 1988, s 12(1)*), and other persons with the right to attend its meetings, stand for election at least every five years. The ballot must as far as is reasonably practicable be secret. *EA 1988, s 15* requires an independent scrutineer to be appointed to oversee the ballot. Candidates must so far as reasonably practicable be enabled to distribute election addresses without cost to themselves. The members entitled to vote must, so far as is reasonably practicable, be given a convenient opportunity to vote by post, the former provisions relating to a choice between workplace and postal ballots having been repealed by *EA 1988*. Government funding is available for the conduct of such elections (see 51.18 below).

[*TUA 1984, ss 1, 2* as amended by *EA 1988, ss 12, 14(2), 15*; *EA 1988, s 13*; *Trade Union Ballots and Elections (Independent Scrutineer Qualifications) Order 1988, as amended (SI 1988 No 2117 and SI 1989 No 131)*].

A person who claims that his union is in breach of the election provisions may apply to the Certification Officer, or to the High Court in England or to the Court of Session in Scotland. He must have been a member of the union at the date of the election, and at the date of the application. The application must be made within one year of the date the result of the election was announced. [*TUA s 5(1)(a),(2)*]. The Certification Officer or the court may make a declaration specifying the provisions with which the trade union has failed to comply. [*TUA s 5(3)*]. If it makes a declaration, the court must also, unless it considers that to do so would be inappropriate, make an enforcement order to secure the holding of an election specified in the order. [*TUA s 5(5)(7)(a)*].

The Secretary of State is empowered by *EA 1980, s 3* as amended by *EA 1988, s 18* to issue a Code of Practice relating to the conduct by trade unions of ballots and elections (see CODES OF PRACTICE (7)). At the time of writing, a draft Code had been issued but had not yet been approved by Parliament.

51.7 Political levy

The *TUA* obliges trade unions, which have passed a resolution (on the application of trade union funds for certain political purposes) pursuant to *Trade Union Act 1913, s 3* to hold ballots, at least every ten years, on the continued application of their funds for political purposes. [*TUA s 12*].

So far as is reasonably practicable, members of the union must be given the opportunity of voting by post in a secret ballot. [*TUA s 13(2); TUA 1913, s 4(1A)-(1F)* as amended by *EA 1988, s 14(1)*]. Funds are available for the conduct of such ballots (see 51.18 below). The ballot must be overseen by an independent scrutineer [*EA 1988, s 15*; and see the statutory instruments referred to in 51.6 above]. Complaints about the conduct of ballots may be made either to the Certification Officer or to the court by virtue of *EA 1988, s 16*.

51.8 LIABILITY IN TORT

EA 1982, s 15 has removed from trade unions the immunity they had previously enjoyed from certain actions in tort under *TULRA*. The immunity of trade unions in proceedings arising out of strikes or industrial action is now similar to that of individuals (cf. STRIKES AND INDUSTRIAL ACTION (47)). Such immunity only applies to action taken in contemplation or furtherance of a trade dispute. With certain narrowly defined exceptions, it does not protect secondary action or action taken to enforce trade union membership. Further, a trade union does not enjoy immunity from liability in tort for inducing breaches of contracts of employment unless its action has the support of a ballot complying with *TUA s 11*. [*TUA s 10*]. However, where proceedings in tort are brought against a trade union

(*a*) for a reason specified in *TULRA s 13(1)(a)* or *(b)* (see 47.2 STRIKES AND INDUSTRIAL ACTION); or

(*b*) in respect of an agreement or combination by two or more persons to induce or do an unlawful act;

then that act will only be taken to have been done by the union if it was authorised or endorsed by a responsible person. [*EA 1982, s 15(2)*]. An act will only be taken to have been authorised or endorsed if it was authorised or endorsed by one of the following:

(i) the principal executive committee; or

(ii) any other person who is empowered by the rules to authorise or endorse acts of the kind in question; or

(iii) the president or general secretary; or

(iv) any other official who is an employed official; or

(v) any committee of the union to whom an employed official regularly reports.

[*EA 1982, s 15(3)*].

An act will not be taken to have been endorsed by a person in category (iv) or (v) above if at the relevant time that person was prevented by the rules from authorising or endorsing acts of the kind in question, or the act had been repudiated as soon as was reasonably practicable by the principal executive committee or by the president or general secretary of the union. To be effective, the repudiation must be notified in writing. [*EA 1982, s 15(4)(5)*].

The union will not be able to rely upon such a repudiation if the principal executive committee, or president or general secretary has subsequently behaved in a way which is inconsistent with the purported repudiation. [*EA 1982, s 15(6)*]. (See also *Express and Star Ltd and others v NGA (1982) and another* [*1985*] *IRLR 455;* upheld on other grounds, [*1986*] *ICR 589*.) The liability of trade unions in such actions in tort is subject to financial limits, considered below.

51.9 Limits on damages awarded against a trade union

With the exception of amounts awarded in actions for personal injury or for breach of duty in connection with the ownership, occupation, possession, control or use of property, the amount of damages awarded (not including interest – see *Boxfoldia Ltd v National Graphical Association (1982)* [*1988*] *ICR 752*) in any proceedings in tort brought against a trade union must not exceed the following limits:

£10,000, if the union has less than 5,000 members;

£50,000, if it has 5,000 or more members but less than 25,000 members;

£125,000, if it has 25,000 or more members but less than 100,000 members;

£250,000, if it has 100,000 or more members.

[*EA 1982, s 16(3)*].

The Secretary of State may by order vary any of these sums. [*EA 1982, s 16(4)*].

51.10 LIABILITY OF INDIVIDUAL MEMBERS

The individual participants in industrial action have the same immunity as trade unions. Such immunity only applies to action taken in contemplation or furtherance of a trade dispute. There is, however, no limit on the damages which may be awarded if an individual is found liable. With certain narrowly defined exceptions, secondary industrial action is not protected. (See STRIKES AND INDUSTRIAL ACTION (47).)

EA 1988, s 8 renders unlawful the application of the property of a trade union towards the payment of any penalty imposed upon an individual for a relevant offence or for contempt of court, or towards any indemnity in respect of such liabilities. [*EA 1988, s 8(1)*]. All offences are relevant offences unless designated otherwise by order made by the Secretary of State. [*EA 1988, s 8(4)*]. However, the prohibition does not extend to civil liabilities, provided that the indemnity or contribution is otherwise lawful and intra vires the union. The union is given the right to recover property or its value applied in contravention of *Sec 8(1)*, and in the event of its unreasonable failure to take proceedings to this end, the court may order, upon application by a union member, that that member shall be authorised to do so in the union's name and at its expense. [*EA 1988, s 8(2), (3)*].

51.11 RECOGNITION, INDEPENDENCE AND RIGHTS

Sections 11-16 of the *Employment Protection Act 1975 (EPA)*, covering the statutory procedure by which independent trade unions could refer recognition issues to ACAS, were repealed with effect from 15 August 1980, save only for applications to the CAC alleging non-compliance with a recommendation for recognition. [*EA 1980, s 19(b); SI 1980 No 1170*].

Although the statutory recognition machinery has been repealed by *EA 1980*, the concepts of 'independence' and 'recognition' discussed below continue to be important for some purposes. One is the procedure for handling redundancies laid down in *EPA Part IV* (see REDUNDANCY – II (39)). Others are disclosure of information for collective bargaining purposes under *EPA s 17* (see 12.2 DISCLOSURE OF INFORMATION), the information and consultation requirements contained in the *Transfer of Undertakings Regulations 1981 (SI 1981 No 1794)* (see 39.7 REDUNDANCY – II and 53.18 TRANSFER OF UNDERTAKINGS) and the right to time off for trade union duties and activities. (See 50.2, 50.3 TIME OFF WORK.)

51.12 Voluntary recognition

An employer may voluntarily agree to recognise a trade union. Recognition can be express or implied. An employer need not have entered into a formal recognition agreement in order to be considered to have recognised a particular trade union. 'Recognition' is defined in *EPA s 126(1)* as 'the recognition of the union by an employer . . . to any extent, for the purpose of collective bargaining' and 'collective bargaining' includes: terms and conditions of employment; allocation of work; matters of discipline and facilities for officials of trade unions. [*EPA s 126*]. If management in fact consult a trade union about some or all of these matters they may be taken to have recognised that trade union. (*Joshua Wilson and Brothers Ltd v Union of Shop, Distributive and Allied Workers [1978] IRLR 120*). The evidence must be 'clear and unequivocal' for a court to reach the conclusion that an employer has recognised a trade union. In *National Union of Gold, Silver & Allied Trades v Albury Brothers Ltd [1979] ICR 84*, the Court of Appeal held that an act of recognition is such an important matter that it should not be held to be established unless the evidence is clear, either by actual agreement of recognition or clear and distinct conduct showing an implied agreement to recognise the trade union for the purposes of collective bargaining. In that case the Court of Appeal held that an attempt by the union to negotiate with the management increased wages for one man did not establish recognition by the employer. Recognition will not be inferred from the fact that a union has been given a right of representation in pay bargaining where that right is given by a third party over whom the employer has no control. (*Cleveland County Council v Springett and others [1985] IRLR 151*).

51.13 Listing

A list of trade unions is maintained by the Certification Officer. [*TULRA s 8(2)*]. Any trade union whose name is entered on the list may apply to the Certification Officer for a certificate that it is independent. [*EPA s 8(1)*]. A union which is not on the list maintained by the Certification Officer will automatically be refused a certificate of independence. [*EPA s 8(4)*].

51.14 Independence

If the union is listed, the Certification Officer will proceed to determine whether the applicant is an independent trade union. An independent trade union is defined in *TULRA s 30* as

'. . . a trade union which –

(*a*) is not under the domination or control of an employer or a group of employers or of one or more employers' associations; and

(*b*) is not liable to interference by an employer or any such group or association (arising out of the provision of financial or material support or by any other means whatsoever) tending towards such control.'

In *Squibb (UK) Staff Association v Certification Officer [1979] ICR 235*, the Certification Officer refused to grant a certificate of independence to a staff association which relied to a considerable extent upon facilities provided by the employers. He considered that the association could not be said to be free from liability to interference by the employers. The Court of Appeal upheld the refusal of the grant of the certificate.

51.15 Factors implying independence

In *Blue Circle Staff Association v Certification Officer [1977] 1 WLR 239*, some of the principles upon which the Certification Officer acts are set out (at pp 245-246).

'1 *Finance*: If there is any evidence that a union is getting a direct subsidy from an employer, it is immediately ruled out.

2 *Other assistance*: The Certification Officer's inspectors see what material support, such as free premises, time off work for officials, or office facilities a union is getting from an employer, and attempt to cost them out.

3 *Employer interference*: If a union is very small and weak and gets a good deal of help, then on the face of it its independence will be considered to be in danger and liable to employer interference.

4 *History*: The recent history of a union . . . is considered. It was not unusual for a staff association to start as a "creature of management and grow into something independent.".

5 *Rules*: The applicant union's rule book is scrutinised to see if the employer can interfere with or control it, and if there are any restrictions on membership. If a union is run by people near the top of a company it could be detrimental to rank and file members.

6 *Single company unions*: While they are not debarred from getting certificates, because such a rule could exclude unions like those of miners and railwaymen, they are considered to be more liable to employer interference. Broadly-based multi-company unions are considered more difficult to influence.

7 *Organisation*: The Certification Officer's inspectors then examine the applicant union in detail, its size and recruiting ability, whether it is run by competent and experienced officers, the state of its finance, and its branch and committee structure. Again, if the union was run by senior men in a company, employer interference was a greater risk.

8 *Attitude*: Once the other factors have been assessed, inspectors looked for a "robust attitude in negotiation" as a sign of genuine independence, backed up by a good negotiating record. . . .'

Before making a determination on the question of independence, the Certification Officer makes such inquiries as he sees fit and takes into account any relevant information submitted to him. [*EPA s 8(6)*]. In general he should not be cross-examined upon his reasons for his decision. (*Squibb* at 51.14 above.)

51.16 Withdrawal of certificate of independence

The Certification Officer may at any time withdraw a certificate, after giving notice to the trade union affected and determining the relevant questions, if he is of the opinion that the trade union in question is no longer independent. [*EPA s 8(7)*].

A trade union aggrieved by the refusal of the Certification Officer to issue it with a certificate, or by a decision of his to withdraw its certificate, may appeal to the Employment Appeal Tribunal. [*EPA s 8(9)*]. If the appeal is successful the Employment Appeal Tribunal will give directions to the Certification Officer to act according to its findings. A further appeal lies to the Court of Appeal on a point of law. [*EPA s 88(4)*].

51.17 AMALGAMATIONS AND TRANSFERS OF ENGAGEMENTS

One trade union may amalgamate with or transfer its engagements to another trade union. However, it may not do so unless a resolution which approves the amalgamation or transfer, in a form approved by the Certification Officer, has been passed by a vote of members. The *Trade Union (Amalgamations, etc.) Act 1964* and the *Trade Unions and Employers' Associations (Amalgamations, etc.) Regulations 1975 (SI 1975 No 536)*, as amended by *SI 1978 No 1344*, specify the information which must be given to union members and the manner in which the ballot must be taken. *Section 4* of the Act provides a remedy, by way of complaint to the Certification Officer, to a union member dissatisfied with the way in which the vote on the resolution was taken.

51.18 TRADE UNION BALLOTS

Payment of expenses of secret postal ballots

The Secretary of State was empowered under *EA 1980, s 1* to make a scheme, to be administered by the Certification Officer, providing for payment towards expenditure incurred by independent trade unions in conducting secret ballots. The Act, as amended by *TUA*, sets out a list of purposes to which a ballot question must relate for assistance to be available. Particulars of the scheme are laid down in the *Funds for Trade Union Ballots Regulations 1984 (SI 1984 No 1654)*, as amended by the *Funds for Trade Union Ballots (Amendment) Regulations 1988 (SI 1988 No 1123)*, which enable financial assistance to be given in relation to some or all of the following purposes:

(*a*) calling or ending a strike or other industrial action;

(*b*) holding elections to the principal executive committee required by *TUA s 2* or by the union rules, or to the positions of president, chairman, secretary or treasurer of the union, or to any position which the persons elected will hold as an employee of the union;

(*c*) amending union rules;

(*d*) obtaining a decision in accordance with the *Trade Union (Amalgamations, etc.) Act 1964* (see 51.17 above) on a resolution to approve an instrument of amalgamation or transfer;

(*e*) obtaining a decision on a resolution, for the purposes of *Trade Union Act 1913, s 3* (application of trade union funds for certain political purposes – see 51.7 above);

(*f*) obtaining a decision or ascertaining the views of members of a trade union as to the acceptance or rejection of a proposal made by an employer which relates in whole or in part to remuneration, hours of work, level of performance, holidays or pensions.

The Secretary of State may specify other purposes for which funds for the holding of ballots may be made available.

The Regulations lay down four essential conditions:

— The ballot must be conducted so as to secure, so far as reasonably practicable, that those voting may do so in secret.

— Those voting must be required to do so by marking a voting paper.

— Those voting must be required to return the voting papers individually by post to the trade union conducting the ballot or to another person responsible for counting the votes.

— In a ballot containing a question within (*f*) above, that only persons who are union members and are affected by the proposal are entitled to vote.

The Regulations lay down a number of other detailed conditions designed to ensure that payment is not made if the Certification Officer is not satisfied that the ballot was properly and fairly held in accordance with the requirements of *TUA* and *EA 1988*.

In general, a payment under the scheme will cover stationery and printing expenditure and, in certain circumstances, postal charges incurred by the trade union.

51.19 **The employer's obligations**

An employer is obliged, so far as is reasonably practicable, to comply with a request to use his premises for the purpose of giving a convenient opportunity of voting in a ballot to workers employed by him who are members of the union making the request. In order for this obligation to arise

(*a*) the employer, together with any associated employer, must employ more than 20 employees;

(*b*) the trade union must be recognised by the employer for collective bargaining purposes; and

(*c*) the ballot must satisfy the requirements of the Regulations introduced under *EA 1980, s 1*, as amended by *TUA* (i.e. the *Funds for Trade Union Ballots Regulations* referred to above).

[*EA 1980, s 2*].

The obligation is inapplicable in those cases where the *Employment Act 1988* makes a postal ballot mandatory. [*EA 1980, s 2(1)*, as amended by *EA 1988, 3 Sch 3(1)*].

If an employer fails to comply with a trade union's request under *EA 1980, s 2*, the union may present a complaint to an industrial tribunal that it has made a request in accordance with *EA 1980, s 2(1)* and that it was reasonably practicable for the employer to comply with it, but that he has failed to do so. [*EA 1980, s 2(4)*]. The complaint must be presented to the tribunal before the end of the period of three months beginning with the date of the failure, or within such further period as the tribunal considers reasonable in a case where it is satisfied that it was not reasonably practicable for the complaint to be presented before the end of the period of three months. [*EA 1980, s 2(5)*; and see 27.3 INDUSTRIAL TRIBUNALS].

Where a tribunal finds such a complaint well-founded, it will make a declaration to that effect. It may make an award of compensation to be paid by the employer to the union of such amount as it considers just and equitable in all the circumstances, taking into account the employer's default and any expense incurred by the union because of the failure. [*EA 1980, s 2(6)*]. An appeal lies to the Employment Appeal Tribunal on a question of law. [*EA 1980, s 2(7)*].

52 Trade Unions – II: Individual Rights and Union Membership

52.1 RIGHTS OF UNION MEMBERS IN RELATION TO EMPLOYER

An employee who is a member of a trade union has the following rights in relation to his employer.

(*a*) Dismissal for membership of, or for taking part in the activities of, an independent trade union is automatically unfair (see 55.3 UNFAIR DISMISSAL – II).

(*b*) Action short of dismissal by his employer for membership of, or for taking part in the activities of, an independent trade union gives the employee the right to complain to an industrial tribunal which may award him compensation (see 52.10 below).

(*c*) A trade union member has the right to time off work to take part in trade union activities (see 50.3 TIME OFF WORK).

(*d*) The right under *EA 1988, s 7* to require his employer to cease deducting from his wages moneys in respect of a union subscription.

In addition, a trade union *official* has the right to take time off with pay for his trade union duties (see 50.2 TIME OFF WORK).

52.2 RIGHTS OF UNION MEMBERS OR INTENDING MEMBERS IN RELATION TO UNION

A trade union member or would-be member has the following rights in relation to his union.

(*a*) Where there is a closed shop, the right not to be unreasonably excluded or expelled [*EA 1980, s 4*] (see 52.5 below).

(*b*) The right under *TULRA s 7* to terminate his membership with the union on giving reasonable notice and complying with any reasonable conditions.

(*c*) The right not to have disciplinary action taken against him by the union save in accordance with the rules of the union and further rights relating to disciplinary action conferred by *EA 1988* (see 52.7 and 52.8 below).

(*d*) The right under *EA 1988, s 1* to apply to the High Court (or, in Scotland, the Court of Session) if members of his union including himself have been called on to take industrial action which has not received prior ballot approval (see 47.14 STRIKES AND INDUSTRIAL ACTION).

(*e*) The right under *EA 1988, s 6* to inspect the union's accounting records.

(*f*) The right under *EA 1988, s 9* to apply for relief where the trustees of the union's property permit it to be applied unlawfully or comply with unlawful directions from the union.

An attempt to bring a common law claim against a union which had not achieved a result favouring a particular member was struck out as having no prospect of success in *Iwanuszezak v General Municipal Boilermakers and Allied Trades Union* [*1988*] *IRLR 219*. The union had to put the collective interests of its whole membership first.

52.3 EXCLUSION OR EXPULSION FROM A UNION — GENERAL

In the past, a person wishing to follow a certain occupation or take up employment for which it was necessary to belong to a particular trade union had little redress against such a union for its refusal of his application for membership. *EA 1980, s 4* confers upon persons seeking or in employment, in respect of which a closed shop agreement is in force, the right not to be unreasonably excluded or expelled from a trade union. The *Employment Act 1988* dramatically curtails the operation of the closed shop, but *EA 1980, s 4* has not been repealed, and will still be of importance in relation to the pre-entry closed shop, although that too may now be made unlawful (see 6.8 CLOSED SHOP).

The common law is still the only remedy for those who are not seeking *employment* but are seeking to work on a self-employed basis.

52.4 The common law

Since there is no contract in existence between an applicant for membership and a trade union, the only right he may have is not to have his application rejected arbitrarily or capriciously. The reason behind this right was stated in *Nagle v Feilden [1966] 2 QB 633* per Lord Denning MR, at *p 646*:

> 'The true ground of jurisdiction in all these cases is a man's right to work. I have said before, and I repeat it now, that a man's right to work at his trade or profession is just as important to him as, perhaps more important than, his rights of property.'

However, in *McInnes v Onslow-Fane [1978] 1 WLR 1520*, it was held that the British Boxing Board of Control in refusing a boxing manager's licence, while under a duty to reach an honest conclusion without bias and not in pursuance of any capricious policy, were under no obligation to give the plaintiff even the gist of their reasons for refusing, or proposing to refuse, his application, and were under no obligation to grant him an oral hearing.

Once a person has been accepted as a member of a union he may not be expelled except in accordance with the rules. (See, for example, *Edwards v Society of Graphical and Allied Trades [1971] 1 Ch 354*.) A union is not prevented from relying upon its rules in expelling a member in compliance with a decision of the TUC Disputes Committee enforcing the Bridlington Principles (which prohibit inter-union poaching). (*Cheall v APEX [1983] ICR 398*). The House of Lords in *Cheall* commented that different considerations might apply if the effect of the expulsion from the union was to have put Mr Cheall's job at risk. But in *Goring v British Actors Equity Association [1987] IRLR 122* the court took the view that the sole common law rights of a union member against the union were those conferred by its rules (including the implied obligation not to act capriciously or arbitrarily). The 'right to work' which might in certain circumstances be invoked by a non-member had no application. Further, in *Hamlet v General Municipal Boilermakers and Allied Trades Union [1987] ICR 150*, the court held that where a member of a union complained of the decision of a union, the court's function was not to review that decision but to ensure that the internal procedures of the union had been complied with.

52.5 The statutory right

New rights were created by *EA 1980, ss 4, 5* for employees who are or wish to be members of an independent trade union. The rights only exist, however, where there is a union membership agreement (closed shop) in force, the effect of which is to require all employees to belong to a trade union specified in the agreement. (For the definition of a 'union membership agreement', see below, and for the meaning of 'independence' see 51.14 TRADE UNIONS – I.) Since the coming into force of *s 11* of the *Employment Act 1988*, the importance of the closed shop has been much reduced, because closed shop dismissals are now automatically unfair. However, it may still be the case that job *applications* will be refused on the ground of non-membership of a trade union.

To come within the definition of a union membership agreement, the agreement must

(*a*) be made between an employer or employers and an independent union or unions; or

(*b*) identify the class of employees within the agreement; and

(*c*) have the effect in practice of requiring an employee in the class covered by the agreement to be or become a member of the union, or one of the unions which is or are party to the agreement, or of another specified independent trade union.

[*TULRA s 30; TULR(A)A s 3(3); EPCA s 153(1)*].

In order to enjoy a statutory right to complain of wrongful exclusion from a branch or section of a trade union, the branch or section must be specified in the union membership agreement. (*National Society of Operative Printers, Graphical and Media Personnel v Kirkham* [*1983*] *ICR 241*; and see *TGWU v Tucker, The Times, 2 March 1988*).

Where a closed shop agreement is in force, every person who is, or is seeking to be, in such employment will have the right

(i) not to have an application for membership of a specified trade union unreasonably refused;

(ii) not to be unreasonably expelled from a specified trade union.

For these purposes, if an application for membership of a trade union is neither granted nor rejected, it will be treated as having been refused on the expiry of the period within which it might reasonably have been expected to have been granted or refused. In addition, if under the rules of a trade union any person ceases to be a member of the trade union on the happening of an event specified in the rules, he will be treated as having been expelled from the union.

An employee, who had voluntarily surrendered his membership of a union, could not make a complaint under *EA 1980* that his resignation had been forced on him by the conduct of union officials, although there might be cases where the resignation was not truly voluntary. *(McGhee v Transport and General Workers Union* (*1985*) *82 L S Gaz 3696*).

These new rights are additional to present common law rights (see 52.4 above). [*EA 1980, s 4(3)*].

52.6 The remedy

The Act provides for a two-stage remedy for an employee who complains that he has been unreasonably expelled or excluded. He must begin by presenting a complaint to an industrial tribunal against the union in question, within the period of six months from the refusal or expulsion. Applications outside this time limit can only be heard if the tribunal is satisfied that it was not reasonably practicable to present the complaint in time and the complaint was presented within such further period as the tribunal considers reasonable. [*EA 1980, s 4(6)*].

At the first stage, the tribunal's function is limited to rejecting the application or finding that it is well-founded, and, if the latter, making a declaration that the refusal or expulsion was unreasonable. Under the *Employment Act 1988*, the refusal or expulsion will automatically be unreasonable if it takes place pursuant to unjustifiable disciplinary action within the meaning of *EA 1988, s 3*. [*EA 1988, s 4(6)(b)*]. There is a right of appeal from the tribunal's decision to the EAT. Such appeals are not limited to points of law, as are other such appeals to the EAT, but may extend to questions of fact. [*EA 1980, ss 4(8), 5(9)*].

Where the tribunal declares that the applicant has been wrongly refused or expelled from union membership, he will be entitled to compensation. However, he cannot apply for compensation until four weeks have elapsed after the declaration. This four-week period is designed to give the trade union an opportunity of admitting or readmitting the applicant to membership. The application must be made, however, within six months of the declaration. It will be made to an industrial tribunal if at the time of application the complainant has been admitted or readmitted to the union. Otherwise, the appropriate tribunal will be the EAT. [*EA 1980, s 5(2)(3)*].

Amount of compensation. The industrial tribunal and the EAT have different powers to award compensation. An industrial tribunal may award the applicant such amount 'as the tribunal considers appropriate for the purpose of compensating the applicant for the loss sustained by him in consequence of the refusal or expulsion which was the subject of the complaint'. The EAT on the other hand is given a much wider discretion and may award the applicant such amount 'as the Appeal Tribunal considers just and equitable in all the circumstances'. [*EA 1980, s 5(4)*].

There is also a difference in the maximum amount that can be awarded by the respective tribunals. The maximum awarded by an industrial tribunal cannot exceed an amount equal to thirty times the current maximum amount of a week's pay for the purposes of calculating the basic award in unfair dismissal cases (currently £172 per week, see 56.7 UNFAIR DISMISSAL – III) plus an amount equal to the current maximum compensatory award. The maximum the EAT can award is the above amount plus a sum equal to fifty-two times the maximum amount of a week's pay for the purposes of calculating additional awards of compensation in unfair dismissal cases (currently also £172 per week). [*EA 1980, s 5(7)(8)*].

The *maximum* that each tribunal can award is thus:

30 × £172	£5,160
Maximum compensatory award	£8,925
Maximum award of IT	**£14,085**
52 × £172	£8,944
Maximum award of EAT	**£23,029**

Whichever of the tribunals is to award compensation, it is the applicant's duty to take reasonable steps to mitigate his loss. The tribunal may reduce the award if it considers that the applicant failed to take such steps or if it considers that he caused or contributed to the action complained of (see e.g. *Howard v National Graphical Association* [1985] *ICR 101; Saunders v Bakers Food and Allied Workers' Union* [1986] *ICR 28*). There are the normal rights of appeal.

52.7 DISCIPLINING BY A TRADE UNION – COMMON LAW

A member of a trade union has a right to be dealt with in accordance with the rules of his union and in accordance with natural justice. If a union acts in breach of the rules or in breach of natural justice, the member affected may apply to the High Court for an injunction and a declaration of his rights. *EA 1988, s 2* directs the court to ignore provisions in the union's rules requiring disputes to be determined or settled in some other fashion in cases where the member applied to the union for such determination more than six months previously, unless the member has himself unreasonably delayed matters. Members of the National Union of Mineworkers, disciplined for breach of a union instruction given in breach of the rules, were held to be entitled to a declaration of the invalidity of the instruction and the unlawfulness of the disciplinary action. (*Taylor v National Union of Mineworkers (Derbyshire Area) and others* [*1984*] *IRLR 440*). Injunctions were granted to NUM members to restrain their union from instructing or seeking to persuade them or others not to work. The NUM had described the strike as official, where it had been called without a ballot as required by the rules, and had threatened disciplinary action. However, the courts will not review a decision of a trade union which is taken in accordance with the rules but which is attacked on the basis that it is one which no reasonable trade union could have reached in the circumstances. (*Hamlet v General Municipal Boilermakers and Allied Trades Union* [*1987*] *ICR 150*). For examples of the courts intervening where there has been a breach of natural justice (i.e. the right to a fair hearing before an unbiased decision-maker), see *Roebuck v National Union of Mineworkers (Yorkshire Area)* [*1977*] *ICR 573* and *Stevenson v United Road Transport Union* [*1977*] *ICR 893*.

52.8 DISCIPLINING BY A TRADE UNION – EMPLOYMENT ACT 1988

EA 1988, s 3 introduces an important new right 'not to be unjustifiably disciplined' by a union of which a person is or has at any time been a member. [*EA 1988, s 3(1)*]. This right is conferred in addition to any existing rights and the only remedies for any infringement are those conferred by *Secs 4 and 5*. [*EA 1988, s 3(7)*].

A person is unjustifiably disciplined if the supposed conduct falls within, or is believed by the union to fall within, any of the seven categories listed in *EA 1988, s 3(3)*. [*EA 1988, s 3(2)*]. In summary, the seven categories consist of:

(*a*) failing to participate in or support, or opposing, any industrial action;

(*b*) failing to break a contract of employment or other agreement with the employer for the purposes of industrial action;

(*c*) asserting, including by bringing proceedings, that the union or any of its officials or representatives is in breach of its obligations under the general law, its rules or any agreement; (However, false assertions made in bad faith are excluded by *s 3(4)*.)

(*d*) encouraging or assisting another person to fulfil obligations to the employer or to make assertions of the kind described in paragraph (*c*);

(*e*) consulting or requesting assistance from the Commissioner for the Rights of Trade Union Members (see 52.9 below) or the Certification Officer (see 51.3 above), or from any other person in relation to assertions of the kind described in paragraph (*c*);

(*f*) failing to comply with unjustifiable disciplinary action taken against himself or another;

(*g*) proposing to do any of these things, or doing acts which are preparatory or incidental to them, unless those acts could independently and justifiably lead to disciplinary action.

The disciplinary action against which members are protected includes expulsion, fines, deprivation of benefits or facilities, encouragement to another union not to accept him as a member, or subjection to any other detriment. [*EA 1988, s 3(5)*].

Complaints of unjustifiable disciplinary action are to be made to an industrial tribunal within three months of the determination complained of. [*EA 1988, s 4(1), (2)*]. However, time may be extended for such period as the tribunal considers reasonable, either where it was not reasonably practicable to present the complaint within three months (see 27.3 INDUSTRIAL TRIBUNALS), or where any delay is wholly or partly attributable to a reasonable attempt to pursue an appeal or otherwise to have the decision reconsidered. [*EA 1988, s 4(3)*]. If the complaint is well-founded, the tribunal will make a declaration to that effect. [*EA 1988, s 4(4)*]. If such a declaration is made, the complainant may make an application to seek compensation and/or the repayment of any sums paid by him as the result of the disciplinary action. [*EA 1988, s 5(1)*]. If the union has revoked the offending determination and taken all steps necessary to secure the reversal of steps taken to put it into effect, the application for compensation will be made to an industrial tribunal. Otherwise it will be made to the Employment Appeal Tribunal. Applications made in the wrong forum may be transferred. [*EA 1988, s 5(2), (4)*]. Applications for compensation are to be made not less than four weeks or more than six months after the disciplinary action is declared unjustifiable. [*EA 1988, s 5(3)*].

The compensation awarded will be that sum which is just and equitable in all the circumstances, taking account of the duty to mitigate loss and of any contributory fault. [*EA 1988, s 5(5)-(7)*]. Before dealing with mitigation or contribution, however, the tribunal or EAT is required to apply the statutory maxima and minima contained in *EA 1988, s 5(8)*. The maximum is the aggregate of (*a*) thirty times the maximum week's pay for calculating the basic award in unfair dismissal cases [*EPCA 14 Sch 8(1)(b)*], and (*b*) the maximum compensatory award in such cases [*EPCA s 75*]. These figures are at present £172 and £8,925 respectively, giving a maximum award under *EA 1988, s 5(8)* of £14,085. [*Unfair Dismissal (Increase of Compensation Limit) Order 1989 (SI 1989 No 527), Employment Protection (Variation of Limits) Order 1989 (SI 1989 No 526)*]. The minimum, which applies only in the case of applications to the EAT, is the amount for the time being specified in *EPCA s 73 (4A)*, which is at present £2,520. [*Unfair Dismissal (Increase of Limits of Basic and Special Awards) Order 1989 (SI 1989 No 528)*]. (See also 56.14 UNFAIR DISMISSAL – III, and 'A WEEK'S PAY' (58).)

52.9 THE COMMISSIONER FOR THE RIGHTS OF TRADE UNION MEMBERS

The office of Commissioner is created by *EA 1988, s 19*. The terms of appointment of the Commissioner and his staff are contained in *EA 1988, 1 Sch*. (At the time of writing, the Commissioner is a woman – see below.) Essentially, the Commissioner is empowered upon application to offer assistance with the costs of and associated with proceedings and prospective proceedings of the kind specified in *EA 1988, s 20(7)*. These include:

(*a*) applications to the court under *EA 1988, ss 1, 6, 9 and 16*, which relate respectively to the failure to hold a ballot prior to industrial action, the right to inspect the union's accounting records, the unlawful use by trustees of union property, and the failure to comply with rules relating to political fund ballots (note also that in respect of such applications *EA 1988, s 23* empowers the court to grant interlocutory relief);

(*b*) applications to the court under *EA 1988, s 8(3)*, which relate to the recovery of trade union property used to indemnify unlawful conduct;

(*c*) applications to the court under *TUA 1984, s 5*, which relate to the failure to hold proper ballots for trade union elections;

(*d*) proceedings under *Trade Union Act 1913, s 3(1)*, which relate to the unlawful application of union funds for political purposes.

By *EA 1988, s 20(7)(e)* the Secretary of State may by order add other categories of proceedings to this list.

In considering whether to assist an applicant, the Commissioner will have regard to, amongst other matters, whether the case raises a question of principle, whether the case is so complex that the applicant cannot reasonably be expected to deal with it unaided, and whether the case involves a matter of substantial public interest. [*EA 1988, s 20(4)*]. Assistance is mandatory where the proposed proceedings relate to the same matter as a declaration already made against the union by the Certification Officer about a union election or membership register or political fund ballot, provided that it appears to the Commissioner that there is a reasonable prospect of obtaining a court order under *TUA 1984, s 5* or *EA 1988, s 16*. [*EA 1988, s 20(5)*].

The present (and first) Commissioner is Mrs Gill Rowlands. Her office is at 1st Floor, Bank Chambers, 2A Rylands Street, Warrington, Cheshire, WA1 1EN, tel. 0925-415771.

The Green Paper 'Removing Barriers to Employment' (Cm 655), which is expected to lead to legislation being introduced in autumn 1989, proposes that the Commissioner should be able to appear in the title of assisted proceedings and (more importantly) that he should be able to assist in proceedings designed to enforce rights under unions' rules as well as statutory rights, provided that the application is a matter of 'substantial public interest'.

52.10 ACTION SHORT OF DISMISSAL FOR UNION MEMBERSHIP OR ACTIVITIES

EPCA s 23 (as now amended by *EA 1980*, *EA 1982* and *EA 1988*) concerns action short of dismissal taken by an employer against an employee

(*a*) to prevent him belonging to an independent trade union; or

(*b*) to prevent him taking part in the activities of an independent union; or

(*c*) to compel him to join any trade union.

An employee has a right to complain to an industrial tribunal for a declaration and compensation if he has suffered action short of dismissal for any of the above reasons.

An important discussion of these provisions is contained in the decision of the Court of Appeal in *National Coal Board v Ridgway and another* [*1987*] *ICR 641*, where it was held that they applied to a decision by the NCB to pay increased wages to members of the UDM at a particular colliery, but not to their workmates in the NUM. Amongst other points, the case is authority for the proposition that the expression 'an independent trade union' may refer to a particular union as well as to unions in general.

An employee also has the right not to have such action taken against him to require him to make payments in lieu of union subscriptions when he is not (or is no longer) a union member. [*EPCA s 23(1A); EA 1982, s 10(3)*].

52.11 **The remedy**

The employee may make a complaint to an industrial tribunal within three months of the action complained of, or within such further period as the tribunal considers reasonable in a case where it is satisfied that it was not reasonably practicable for the complaint to be presented within three months (see 27.3 INDUSTRIAL TRIBUNALS).

If the tribunal finds the complaint well-founded it will make a declaration to that effect and may order compensation to be paid. The compensation will be such amount as it considers just and equitable in all the circumstances, having regard to the right infringed and any loss sustained by the complainant. [*EPCA ss 24-26*].

Joinder of third parties. Where the employer was induced to take the action complained of by industrial action or threat of such action, although no account is to be taken by the tribunal of such pressure when deciding the complaint, the union (or unions) may be joined as a third party to the proceedings and may be ordered to pay all or part of the compensation as the tribunal considers just in the circumstances. [*EPCA s 26A; EA 1982, s 11*].

52.12 PROHIBITION ON UNION MEMBERSHIP AND UNION RECOGNITION REQUIREMENTS IN CONTRACTS FOR GOODS OR SERVICES

EA 1982, ss 12(1) and 13(1) provide that any term or condition of a contract for the supply of goods or services is void insofar as it purports

(*a*) to require that the whole, or some part, of the work done for the purposes of the contract is to be done only by persons who are or who are not members of trade unions or of a particular trade union [*EA 1982, s 12(1)(a)(b)*];

(*b*) to require any party to the contract to recognise one or more trade unions (whether or not named in the contract) for the purpose of negotiating on behalf of workers, or any class of worker, employed by him or to negotiate or consult with, or with any official of, one or more trade unions (whether or not so named). [*EA 1982, s 13(1)(a)(b)*].

Certain categories of people affected by action proscribed by *EA 1982, s 12(2)* and *13(2)* may bring an action based upon a person's failure to offer the opportunity to tender for a contract for the supply of goods or services, determination not to enter into such a contract, or termination of such a contract, if the person's decision was taken on the grounds of union membership or union recognition requirements.

The power of local authorities to have regard to non-commercial considerations in awarding contracts is limited by the *Local Government Act 1988, Part II*.

(For the prohibition of industrial action to impose union membership or recognition requirements, see 47.7 STRIKES AND INDUSTRIAL ACTION.)

53 Transfer of Undertakings

(See also DE booklet No 10 'Employment rights on the transfer of an undertaking' (PL 699).)

53.1 Far-reaching rules for the protection of employees' rights on the transfer of an undertaking were introduced by the *Transfer of Undertakings (Protection of Employment) Regulations 1981 (SI 1981 No 1794)* as amended by the *Transfer of Undertakings (Protection of Employment) (Amendment) Regulations 1987 (SI 1987 No 442)* (the Regulations). The purpose of the Regulations is to fulfil the United Kingdom's obligations under European Community law to give effect to the principles contained in *EC Council Directive 77/187*. In construing the Regulations, the British courts must have regard to the Directive (see *Robert Seligman Corporation v Baker [1983] ICR 770*; and the far-reaching approach taken by the House of Lords in *Litster v Forth Dry Dock and Engineering Co Ltd [1989] ICR 341*; see also 20.1 EUROPEAN COMMUNITY LAW). References below are to provisions of the Regulations unless stated.

53.2 Where an 'undertaking' (see 53.3 below) is 'transferred' (see 53.4 below) from the ownership of person *A* to person *B*

(*a*) individuals who are employed by *A* 'immediately before the transfer' (see 53.7, 53.11 below) automatically become the employees of *B* from the time of the transfer, on the terms and conditions they previously held with *A* (see 53.9 below);

(*b*) *B* inherits *A's* rights and liabilities in relation to those individuals (see 53.14 below);

(*c*) collective agreements, made by or on behalf of *A* with a trade union recognised by *A*, are inherited by *B* (see 53.16 below);

(*d*) where *A* recognises a union in respect of employees in the undertaking to be transferred and, following the transfer, the undertaking transferred maintains an identity distinct from any other undertaking owned by *B*, *B* must recognise the union in respect of those employees (see 53.17 below);

(*e*) *A* must inform recognised trade unions about the consequences of the transfer, and *B* must provide *A* with sufficient information in this regard (see 53.18 below);

(*f*) in certain circumstances, it may be necessary for *A* or *B* to consult with recognised trade unions concerning the transfer (see 53.18 below);

(*g*) dismissal of any employee (whether before or after the transfer) for any reason connected with the transfer is automatically unfair unless the reason is 'an economic, technical or organisational reason entailing changes in the workforce' in which case the dismissal is fair if reasonable in the circumstances (see 53.20 below).

53.3 **WHAT IS THE 'TRANSFER' OF AN 'UNDERTAKING'?**

Undertaking

'Undertaking' is defined as 'including' any 'trade or business' but not 'any undertaking which is not in the nature of a commercial venture'. With the same qualification, 'undertaking' is further defined as including a 'part' of an undertaking. [*Reg 2(1)*].

A 'part' of an 'undertaking' means a unit which is to some extent separate and self-contained from the remainder of the enterprise such as an operating division which is autonomous from the remainder of the business by virtue, for example, of having its own accounts, management structure, and product specialisation.

In addition to 'trade or business', 'undertaking' would appear to include a professional practice, such as that of an NHS doctor (see *Jeetle v Elster [1985] ICR 389*). Whether it also includes the operations of such organisations as statutory corporations or clubs and charities depends on whether the operations are in each case 'in the nature of a commercial venture'. This is very much a matter of first impression, although an interest in financial return may be an important indication. (*Woodcock v Committee of the Friends School Wigton and another [1987] IRLR 98*).

53.4 Transfer

An undertaking may be 'transferred' by sale or other 'disposition' or by operation of law. [*Reg 3(2)*]. That includes, for example, the case where the owner of a leased undertaking resumes the running of the business following a breach of covenant by the lessee. (*Landsorganisationen i Danmark v Ny Molle Kro [1989] IRLR 37*). A single transfer may be effected by a series of two or more transactions between the same parties. In determining whether or not such a series constitutes a single transfer regard is to be had to the extent to which the undertaking was controlled by the transferor and transferee respectively before the last transaction, to the lapse of time between each of the transactions, to the intention of the parties and to all the other circumstances. [*Reg 3(4)*].

In *Foreningen af Arbejdsledere i Danmark v Daddy's Dance Hall A/S [1988] IRLR 315* the European Court of Justice held that there was a relevant transfer where a lessee of restaurant premises gave notice to its employees upon the determination of the lease, and the lessor then granted a new lease to a third party which continued to run the business without any interruption. Where the identity of the economic unit was retained, it did not matter that the transfer took place in two phases. The same result was reached on similar facts in *Litster v Forth Dry Dock and Engineering Co Ltd [1989] ICR 341* and in *P Bork International A/S v Foreningen af Arbeidsledere i Danmark [1989] IRLR 41* (owner of leased undertaking repossessed it after forfeiture of the lease and then sold it on to a third party who resumed operation of the business). These decisions will be important where businesses are operated on a franchise.

It is thought that 'transfer' of the undertaking will only be held to have occurred if the undertaking itself is acquired 'as a going concern', so it is, effectively, the same concern in different hands.

The indicia of a transfer as a going concern have been well established by cases on the meaning of 'transfer of a business' and 'change of ownership of a business' under the redundancy payments provisions, now contained in the *Employment Protection (Consolidation) Act 1978* (see 38.5 REDUNDANCY - I). It is thought that these cases will be treated by the courts as authoritative guidance for the purpose of the Regulations. However, the exclusion of operations 'not in the nature of a commercial venture' from the definition of 'undertaking' means that 'transfer of an undertaking' has a slightly narrower meaning than 'transfer of a business' or 'change of ownership of a business' under *EPCA*.

The following have been treated as important indications that a transfer 'as a going concern' has taken place:

(i) assignment to the purchaser of the vendor's existing contracts with customers;

(ii) assignment to the purchaser of the vendor's existing contracts with suppliers;

(iii) an assignment to the purchaser of the trade debts of the vendor's business;

(iv) an assignment to the purchaser of the vendor's copyright patents, know-how, licences and other intellectual copyrights;

(v) a restrictive covenant prohibiting the vendor from competing with the purchaser;

(vi) an assignment of the vendor's trade name to the purchaser;

(vii) an assignment of goodwill from the vendor to the purchaser.

The most important single factor in determining whether a transfer as a going concern has taken place is that of 'goodwill', i.e. the custom of the vendor's business and the expectation that this custom will remain. An express assignment of goodwill is the strongest evidence of transfer as a going concern. This was important to the conclusion that there was no transfer in *Banking Insurance and Finance Union v Barclays Bank PLC [1987] ICR 495*. However, the absence of such an express assignment does not automatically lead to the conclusion that no transfer as a going concern has occurred, especially where goodwill is of little commercial significance because the business is at a low ebb or where the nature of the business is such that it can have no customers or goodwill in the ordinary sense (e.g. the doctor's practice in *Jeetle v Elster [1985] ICR 389*).

The recent decision of the European Court of Justice in *Landsorganisationen i Danmark v Ny Molle Kro [1989] IRLR 37* in effect recognises the significance of transfer as a going concern, but stresses that it need not matter that the business is temporarily closed at the time of the transfer: all the factual circumstances must be taken into account in determining whether the existing economic entity retains its identity.

53.5 Exclusion of share transfers

The Regulations apply only to the transfer of an undertaking from one legal person to another. They do not apply, for example, to the transfer of shares in a company which carries on the undertaking.

53.6 Exclusion of foreign undertakings

The Regulations do not apply to the transfer of an undertaking or part of an undertaking which is not situated in the United Kingdom 'immediately before the transfer'. [*Reg 3(1)*].

53.7 Time of the transfer

It may be important to identify the precise time of the transfer, because of the requirement (see 53.11 below) that the employee be employed by his old employer immediately beforehand (although, following the decision of the House of Lords in *Litster v Forth Dry Dock and Engineering Co Ltd* [1989] *ICR 341*, that requirement is effectively overridden if the employee is dismissed for a reason connected with the transfer, and some of the authorities would now be decided differently for that reason).

A number of cases have arisen where, for example, the employee has been dismissed between the exchange of contracts for the sale of the business and the completion date (*Wheeler v Patel* [1987] *ICR 631*), or joined the new employers after they were let into possession under a deed of assignment but before completion (*Brook Lane Finance Co Ltd v Bradley* [1988] *IRLR 283*). In these cases it was held that the contract of employment was not automatically continued by virtue of the Regulations. In both *Wheeler* and *Brook Lane* the EAT considered that it was bound by the decision of the Court of Appeal in *Secretary of State for Employment v Spence* [1986] *ICR 651* to hold that a transfer was only capable of taking place at a particular moment, and not over a period of time. However, in *Brook Lane* the EAT expressed concern that *Spence* had been decided without having regard to apparently conflicting dicta of the Court of Appeal in *Teeside Times Ltd v Drury* [1980] *ICR 338*. In *Litster* the House of Lords approved the reasoning in *Spence*, save as indicated above, but did not have to deal specifically with this point.

53.8 A special rule applies to 'hiving down' arrangements. Where a receiver or liquidator of a company (or an administrator, since the *Transfer of Undertakings (Protection of Employment) (Amendment) Regulations 1987 (SI 1987 No 442)*) transfers the business of a company to a wholly-owned subsidiary, the Regulations do not apply unless either

(*a*) the subsidiary ceases to be wholly owned; or

(*b*) the business is transferred from the subsidiary to a third party,

in which case there is deemed to be one transfer immediately before the first of these occurrences. The purpose of this rule is to prevent an automatic transfer of staff to the 'hived down' company, thereby defeating the object of the 'hive down' arrangement, namely to attract buyers for the viable part of the enterprise.

53.9 THE AUTOMATIC ASSIGNMENT OF CONTRACTS OF EMPLOYMENT AND ASSOCIATED RIGHTS AND LIABILITIES

The most drastic consequences of a transfer of an undertaking are specified in *Regulation 5(1)-(3)*. Those of the vendor's employees

(i) who were employed by the vendor immediately before the transfer, and

(ii) whose contracts would otherwise have been terminated by the transfer,

automatically become, from the moment of the transfer, employed by the purchaser on the terms and conditions which they enjoyed with the vendor. With certain specified exceptions, all the vendor's rights and liabilities connected with their contracts of employment are likewise assigned to the purchaser, and anything done by the purchaser prior to the transfer in relation to those employees or their contracts is deemed to have been done by the vendor.

Regulation 5(3) also deals with cases where there is more than one transaction by which the transfer is effected, and provides that *Regulation 5* catches any person employed immediately before any of the transactions in question.

53.10 'Employee'

Under the Regulations, an 'employee' covers an individual who works for another person under a contract of employment or apprenticeship, or otherwise, but does not include an independent contractor. [*Reg 2(1)*]

53.11 Immediately before the transfer

Formerly it was thought that *Regulation 5(1)* applied only to those contracts of employment subsisting *immediately* before the transfer. (*Secretary of State for Employment v Spence* [*1986*] *ICR 651*). Thus, if the transferor dismissed an employee even an hour or two before the transfer, the Regulations did not apply and that employee had no remedy against the transferee (which might be of great significance if, for example, the transferor was insolvent).

However, in *Litster v Forth Dry Dock and Engineering Co Ltd* [*1989*] *ICR 341* the House of Lords held that that approach was too simplistic. Although the rule in *Spence* held good where the dismissal was unconnected with the transfer, if the dismissal in fact took place solely or principally because of the prospective transfer, then the employee would be deemed to have been transferred immediately before the transfer. Their Lordships accepted the reasoning of the European Court of Justice in *P Bork International A/S v Foreningen af Arbejdslederen i Danmark* [*1989*] *IRLR 41*, namely, that the fact that *Directive 77/187* prohibited dismissal because of a transfer (see 53.20 below) meant that a dismissal in breach of that prohibition could not effectively exclude the operation of the Regulations.

53.12 'Would otherwise have been terminated'

Regulation 5 assigns the contracts of employment of those, and only those, whose contracts of employment would otherwise have come to an end by virtue of the transfer. The contracts of employment of individuals employed in a part of the undertaking which is not being transferred, or who agree with the vendor to continue working for the vendor under their existing contracts after the transfer, will not be assigned by the Regulations to the purchaser.

53.13 What the purchaser acquires

As noted above, the purchaser inherits those employees employed by the vendor immediately before the transfer on their existing terms and conditions. He has no power to impose, without the agreement of the individual employee, any different terms and conditions from those he has inherited from the vendor, however commercially convenient this may be. Equally, the transferred employee has no right to insist that he be given the benefit of any superior terms and conditions enjoyed by the purchaser's existing staff.

53.14 The purchaser inherits all accrued rights and liabilities connected with the contract of employment of the transferred employee. If, for example, the vendor was in arrears with wages at the time of the transfer, the employee can sue the purchaser as if the original liability had been the purchaser's. Equally, the purchaser can sue an employee for a breach of contract committed against the vendor prior to transfer. The purchaser will further inherit all the statutory rights and liabilities which are connected with the individual contract of employment. The transferred employee's period of continuous employment will date from the beginning of the period with the vendor and the statutory particulars of terms and conditions of employment, which every employer is obliged to issue under *Section 1* of *EPCA*, must take account of any continuity enjoyed by virtue of the Regulations.

Not every liability owed by the vendor to his employee will pass on the transfer. If the liability arises from breach of a duty owed to the union – for example, to consult over redundancy under *Sections 99 to 101, EPA 1975* – it is not sufficiently connected with the individual's contract and therefore does not pass to the purchaser (see *Angus Jowett v NUTGW [1985] ICR 646*).

53.15 Rights and liabilities which are not assigned under the Regulations

The Regulations do not have the effect of assigning

(i) criminal liabilities; or

(ii) rights and liabilities over or in relation to occupational pension schemes.

[*Regs 5(4), 7*].

53.16 TRANSFER OF AN UNDERTAKING AND THE TRADE UNION

Collective agreements

Under *Regulation 6(a)*, a collective agreement, which

(i) is made between the vendor and a union recognised by the vendor, and

(ii) applied to an employee whose contract has become automatically assigned to the purchaser by virtue of the transfer,

is automatically transferred to the purchaser in its application to that employee. Further, anything done by or under or in connection with that agreement by the vendor before the transfer is deemed to have been done by the purchaser.

The practical effect of this provision is minimal, since collective agreements are in English law presumed to be unenforceable (see *TULRA s 18*) unless, which is very rare, the contrary is stated in the agreement. It is only in this rare case where a binding agreement is entered into that *Regulation 6(a)* will pass any legal obligation to the purchaser. If the terms of a collective agreement are incorporated into the contract of employment of an individual whose service is automatically assigned on the transfer then its terms will bind the purchaser simply by virtue of the general rule that the purchaser inherits the rights and liabilities in the individual's contract.

Regulation 6(b) provides that any order made in respect of a collective agreement transferred under *Regulation 6(a)* takes effect as if the purchaser were a party to the agreement. In effect, this means that awards of the Central Arbitration Committee made against the vendor are binding against the purchaser to the extent that they previously bound the vendor.

53.17 Recognition

Where the vendor recognises a union in respect of employees in the undertaking to be transferred and, following the transfer, the undertaking transferred maintains an identity distinct from the rest of the purchaser's business or businesses, the purchaser must recognise the union in respect of those employees. [*Reg 9*].

Although machinery for enforcing trade union recognition (*Sections 11 to 16, EPA 1975*) has now been repealed and there is no penalty under the Regulations for refusal to recognise, the transfer of recognition may be significant when a transferred employee seeks to invoke against the purchaser a right which is dependent on the existence of a recognised union, e.g. the right to take time off for trade union activities under *Section 28, EPCA*.

53.18 Information and consultation

Under *Regulation 10*, the employer of employees affected by the transfer, whether he is the vendor or purchaser, must inform representatives of independent recognised trade unions, long enough before the transfer to enable consultations to take place between the employer and those representatives, of the following:

(i) the fact that a relevant transfer is to take place;

(ii) when it is to take place;

(iii) the reasons for it;

(iv) the legal, economic and social implications of the transfer for affected employees;

(v) the measures which he envisages taking in relation to those employees (and if no measures are envisaged, that fact);

(vi) if the employer is the vendor, the measures which the purchaser envisages that he will take in relation to those employees who are to be automatically assigned to him on the transfer (or if no measures are envisaged, that fact).

These provisions (as enacted in another context) were extensively discussed in *Institute of Professional Civil Servants and others v Secretary of State for Defence [1987] IRLR 373*, which is authority for several of the propositions referred to below, although not all of them were essential to the decision.

The purchaser must give the vendor the information necessary to enable him to comply in time with sub-paragraph (vi) above. But the purchaser is under no *obligation* to envisage any measures, and sometimes he may envisage them too late for there to be compliance with sub-paragraph (vi).

The information to be given to the representatives may be delivered to them personally or sent by post to the union's head office or other address notified by the representatives. [*Reg 10(4)*].

If either the vendor or the purchaser envisages that he will take measures in relation to employees represented by a recognised trade union, he must enter into consultation with the representatives of the union. (This is the only *obligation* to consult. Although, as stated above, there are other obligations to give information in time for consultation, consultation itself is voluntary.) The measures referred to must be definite plans or proposals, not mere hopes or possibilities, and must be such as would not have happened but for the transfer. The information to be disclosed does not include the calculations and assumptions underlying those plans. Consultation involves considering and replying to representations made by the union and, insofar as representations are rejected, stating the reasons for the rejection. Reasons need not be given in writing, though this may be advisable. [*Reg 10(5)*].

If an employer fails to inform or consult, then the union concerned may present a complaint to an industrial tribunal within three months of the date on which the relevant transfer is completed. If it is not reasonably practicable to bring the complaint within three months, it may be presented within a reasonable time thereafter. [*Reg 11(1)(8)*]. There is no need to wait for the transfer to take place before presenting the complaint, and it appears that the complaint may proceed even if in fact the transfer never takes place. (*Banking Insurance and Finance Union v Barclays Bank PLC* [*1987*] *ICR 495*).

Where a complaint succeeds, the tribunal must make a declaration to this effect and may order the employer to pay compensation to affected employees. [*Reg 11(4)*]. The maximum payable is two weeks' pay for each employee affected. [*Reg 11(11)*]. Moreover, there must be deducted from any liability

(i) any sum payable to the employee under a protective award [*Section 101, EPA 1975*]; and

(ii) any sum paid by way of damages for wrongful dismissal in respect of the protected period under *Section 99, EPA*.

[*Reg 11(7)(b)*].

It is a defence for the employer to show that there were special circumstances which rendered it not reasonably practicable to perform the duty in question, provided that he took whatever steps to perform that duty as were reasonably practicable in the circumstances. [*Reg 10(7)*]. By analogy with the case law on *Sections 99 to 101, EPA*, an employer is unlikely to show that a failure to inform or consult was due to 'special circumstances' unless the transfer has to be arranged or expedited because of a sudden and unforeseen emergency. However, the tribunal should look at the matter broadly, and ought not ordinarily to grant relief unless the employer has plainly been recalcitrant or neglectful of his obligations.

If a vendor wishes to allege that the reason for his default is the failure of the purchaser to supply him with information, he must give the purchaser notice of that fact and the purchaser must be made a party to the proceedings. [*Reg 11(3)*].

If an employer fails to pay compensation ordered to be paid by the tribunal, the employee concerned may present a complaint to an industrial tribunal. [*Reg 11(5)*].

53.19 DISMISSAL ON THE TRANSFER OF AN UNDERTAKING

If an individual employed in an undertaking is dismissed

(*a*) by the vendor in advance of the transfer of that undertaking, or

(*b*) by the purchaser after the transfer,

he may wish to bring a claim for unfair dismissal, a redundancy payment or wrongful dismissal.

53.20 Unfair dismissal and transfer of an undertaking

In order to complain of unfair dismissal the individual must first show that he has been dismissed within the statutory definition, that is to say

(i) that his contract of employment has been terminated by the employer (direct dismissal); or

(ii) that he was employed for a fixed term which has expired and not been renewed; or

(iii) that he resigned in circumstances where he was entitled to do so without notice on account of his employer's conduct (constructive dismissal).

[*EPCA s 55*].

(For a discussion of the statutory definition of dismissal see 54.4–54.10 UNFAIR DISMISSAL – I.)

The Regulations affect the operation of this definition in a number of ways.

First, the transfer itself cannot be treated as a dismissal. As can be seen from 53.12 above, the transfer operates to assign to the purchaser the contracts of employment of those who would otherwise have been dismissed upon the transfer.

Secondly, if the vendor refrains from dismissing employees before the transfer so that they are automatically assigned to the transferee, but the purchaser indicates – before the transfer – that he is unwilling to employ them, it appears that the employees will be treated as dismissed by the purchaser immediately after the transfer (see *Premier Motors (Medway) Ltd v Total Oil (Great Britain) Ltd [1984] ICR 58*).

Thirdly, if the purchaser substantially changes the terms and conditions of employment previously enjoyed by the transferred staff to their detriment, the staff may resign and treat themselves as constructively dismissed.

Fourthly, a transferred employee may be able to resign and assert constructive dismissal, even where the purchaser observes all the previous terms and conditions, if the change in identity of the purchaser is significant and is detrimental to the employee. This provision (*Regulation 5(5)*) may apply where, for example, the employee has been involved in personal conflict with the purchaser prior to the transfer.

If an employee has been dismissed by either the purchaser or the vendor and the reason for the dismissal is a reason connected with the transfer, the dismissal is automatically unfair unless it qualifies as an 'economic, technical or organisational reason entailing changes in the workforce' of either the vendor or the purchaser. [*Reg 8(1)(2)*]. If the reason falls within this category it will be held to be fair if the employer acted reasonably in all the circumstances in treating the reason as sufficiently justifying dismissal, within the meaning of *EPCA s 57(3)*, as amended.

The reason may be connected with the transfer, even though the employee dismissed was never employed in the undertaking or part transferred. If, for example, the purchaser dismisses his existing staff to accommodate the employees he is to inherit from the vendor, or if the job of an existing employee disappears following a reorganisation consequent upon the transfer, the dismissal will nonetheless be connected with the transfer.

It appears that a vendor may not invoke the defence of an 'organisational' or 'economic' reason where a purchaser is willing to acquire the undertaking only on terms that the vendor's staff are first dismissed, because the reason must relate to the conduct of the business for those words to apply. (*Wheeler v Patel [1987] ICR 631* and *Gateway Hotels Ltd v Stewart [1988] IRLR 287*, not following *Anderson v Dalkeith Engineering Ltd [1986] ICR 66*). The inconvenience to the purchaser of observing, in respect of transferred employees, terms and conditions different from those which are standard in the remainder of his enterprise does not give him an economic, technical or organisational reason for dismissing transferred staff who will not agree to changes (see *Berriman v Delabole Slate Ltd [1985] ICR 546*).

The words 'entailing changes in the workforce' impose important limitations on the defence of 'economic, technical or organisational reason'. It is only when the employer sets out to change the structure of his workforce, by reducing numbers or changing the functions which individuals perform, that the reason will entail a change in the workforce.

If an employer brings the case within the category of economic, technical or organisational reason entailing changes in the workforce, it will remain to be considered whether he acted reasonably in the circumstances. The considerations which will be relevant must vary with the circumstances of the individual case. It is fair to assume, however, that a failure to offer the employee an available job in some part of the business not affected by the economic technical or organisational problem in question, or a failure to consult the employee, will be grounds on which such dismissals may sometimes be considered unfair.

53.21 Redundancy payments

An employee dismissed by reason of redundancy is, subject to various qualifying conditions, entitled to a redundancy payment (see REDUNDANCY – I (38)). He is dismissed by reason of redundancy if the principal reason is that his employer has ceased or intends to cease carrying on business in the place where the employee was employed or if there is a diminution in the requirements of the employer's business for the work of the particular kind for which the employee is employed.

An employee whose contract is automatically assigned under the Regulations will not be dismissed by the vendor and cannot therefore become entitled to a redundancy payment unless and until he is dismissed by the purchaser by reason of redundancy.

If, however,

(i) an employee is dismissed by the vendor in advance of the transfer by reason of the fact that the vendor is to go out of business in the place where the employee was employed or no longer requires work of the particular kind done by the employee; or

(ii) following the transfer, the purchaser dismisses the employee for either of these reasons,

the employee is, on the face of it, entitled to a redundancy payment.

Despite Scottish EAT decisions to the contrary, the English Employment Appeal Tribunal has now confirmed that the employee will, in these circumstances, qualify for a redundancy payment even though the reason for his dismissal may qualify as an economic, technical or organisational reason entailing changes in the workforce. In *Gorictree Ltd v Jenkinson [1985] ICR 51*, it was held that the dismissal does not cease to be by reason of redundancy merely because it also qualifies as an economic, technical or organisational reason under the Regulations. It is likely that this decision, and not the earlier Scottish decisions, will be followed in future.

53.22 Wrongful dismissal

The impact of the Regulations on the law of wrongful dismissal is limited. An employee whose contract is automatically assigned to the purchaser on the transfer of an undertaking cannot, of course, treat the transfer as a dismissal or repudiation of his contract. Otherwise, the law as to wrongful dismissal is unaffected by the Regulations.

53.23 Commencement date

The Regulations covering the provision of information to, and consultation with, representatives of trade unions came into force on 1 February 1982. Those Regulations concerning the assignment of contracts of employment, unfair dismissal, and the transfer of collective agreements and union recognition came into force on 1 May 1982. [*Reg 1(1)*]. In deciding whether an employee working in a business which was transferred from one employer to another prior to that date maintained continuity of employment despite the transfer (see generally CONTINUOUS EMPLOYMENT (9)), it will be necessary to look to *EPCA 13 Sch 17* and *EPCA s 94*. For a recent discussion of those provisions, see *Dabell v Vale Industrial Services (Nottingham) Ltd* [*1988*] *IRLR 439*.

53.24 EXCLUSIONS

Employment abroad

The rules relating to unfair dismissal and the provision of information to, and consultation with, representatives of a trade union do not apply where under his contract of employment the employee ordinarily works outside the United Kingdom. [*Reg 13(1)*].

53.25 AVOIDING THE REGULATIONS AND THEIR CONSEQUENCES

An agreement to exclude or limit the application of the Regulations is invalid. [*Reg 12*]. The vendor and purchaser may, however, validly agree that one shall indemnify the other for sums payable in consequence of the operation of the Regulations. In practice, it is quite common for purchasers to take such indemnities from vendors.

54 Unfair Dismissal – I: The Right To Make A Claim

(See also DE booklets 'Fair and unfair dismissal – a guide for employers' (PL 714), No. 13 'Unfairly dismissed?' (PL 712) and 'The law on unfair dismissal – guidance for small firms' (PL 715).)

Cross-references. See TERMINATION OF EMPLOYMENT (49) for the various ways of terminating the contract at common law; 29.6 MATERNITY RIGHTS for the right not to be dismissed on grounds of pregnancy; UNFAIR DISMISSAL – II (55) for whether the dismissal was fair; UNFAIR DISMISSAL – III (56) for remedies for unfair dismissal.

54.1 The *Employment Protection (Consolidation) Act 1978 (EPCA)* re-enacted a right originally created by the *Industrial Relations Act 1971* – the right not to be unfairly dismissed. Since its introduction, an employer who dismisses an employee without good reason or without following a fair procedure lays himself open to a claim for unfair dismissal. When such a claim is brought, the employer has to establish the reason for the dismissal. The industrial tribunal will then consider whether the dismissal was fair in all the circumstances, neither party having the evidential burden in this enquiry. If the dismissal is held to be unfair, the employer can be ordered to re-engage, reinstate or to pay compensation to the ex-employee. The parties to a claim for unfair dismissal are known as the *applicant* (employee) and the *respondent* (employer).

54.2 PRE-CONDITIONS OF A CLAIM

A complaint of unfair dismissal must be presented to an industrial tribunal before the end of the period of three months beginning with the effective date of termination of the employment (or within such further period as the tribunal considers reasonable in a case where it is satisfied that it was not reasonably practicable for the complaint to be presented within the period of three months). [*EPCA s 67(2)*]. (See further 27.3 INDUSTRIAL TRIBUNALS.)

An applicant must also satisfy the conditions set out below if he wishes to bring a claim for unfair dismissal. If these conditions are not disputed by the respondent, no evidence need be brought by the applicant to establish them. If, however, there are grounds for suspecting that any of those necessary prerequisites is absent, the industrial tribunal will inquire into the matter, as it affects their jurisdiction to hear the case. The burden is on the applicant to show that he satisfies those conditions. The conditions are

(*a*) that the applicant was employed by the respondent under a contract of employment (see 54.3 below);

(*b*) that the applicant was dismissed, as defined (see 54.4 below); and

(*c*) that the applicant was employed for the necessary qualifying period (see 54.11 below). (The employer may sometimes argue that a claim cannot be brought because the employee did not work for the qualifying period under a *lawful* contract (see 54.16 below).)

In addition, certain employees are excluded from the right not to be unfairly dismissed

(i) employees over retirement age (see 54.14 below);

(ii) certain specified classes of employees (see 54.15 below);

(iii) those dismissed in connection with a lock-out or strike, provided certain conditions are satisfied (see 54.17 below).

54.3 EMPLOYMENT BY THE RESPONDENT

In order to bring a claim for unfair dismissal, an applicant must show that he was employed by the respondent under a contract of employment. Therefore, sub-contractors or consultants under contracts for services are not protected by the unfair dismissal provisions even though they may work regularly for one person or organisation. See 15.3 EMPLOYEE OR SELF-EMPLOYED?

54.4 DISMISSAL BY THE RESPONDENT

An employee is treated as having been dismissed if, but only if

(*a*) the contract under which he is employed by the employer is terminated by the employer, whether it is so terminated by notice or without notice; or

(*b*) where under that contract he is employed for a fixed term, that term expires without being renewed under the same contract; or

(*c*) the employee terminates that contract with or without notice in circumstances such that he is entitled to terminate it without notice by reason of the employer's conduct (usually called 'constructive dismissal').

[*EPCA s 55(2)*].

Where an employee who is entitled to return to work after a confinement is not permitted by her employer to do so, she will be considered to have been dismissed on her notified day of return. [*EPCA s 56*]. (See further 29.20 MATERNITY RIGHTS.)

54.5 Termination by notice

Notice of dismissal, once accepted, cannot be withdrawn. Thus, an employer who gives notice to an employee which is accepted cannot thereafter withdraw that notice without the consent of the employee.

Where an employer gives notice to an employee to terminate his contract of employment and, at a time within the period of that notice, the employee gives notice to the employer to terminate the contract of employment on a date earlier than the date on which the employer's notice is due to expire, the employee will nevertheless be taken to have been dismissed by his employer for the purposes of an unfair dismissal claim. [*EPCA s 55(3)*]. If an employee gives notice to terminate his employment and, during that period of notice, the employer summarily dismisses him, the employee will be considered to have been dismissed despite the fact that he first gave notice to terminate his contract. (*Harris and Russell Ltd v Slingsby [1973] 3 AER 31*). A contract of employment is only terminated by an employer if there is a specified or ascertainable date on which the contract is to cease. (*Haseltine Lake & Co v Dowler [1981] ICR 222*). Dismissal, to be effective, must be communicated to the employee. (*Hindle Gears Ltd v McGinty [1985] ICR 111*).

54.6 Expiry of a fixed term contract

It used to be thought that a fixed term contract was one which did not contain a provision for prior determination by notice. (*British Broadcasting Corporation v*

Ioannou [1975] *ICR 267*). However, in *Dixon v British Broadcasting Corporation* [*1979*] *ICR 281*, the Court of Appeal held that the words 'a fixed term' include a specified stated term even though the contract is determinable by notice within its term. A contract which is terminable on the occurrence of a specified event at some uncertain future time is not a contract for a fixed term within the meaning of the *EPCA*. (*Wiltshire County Council v National Association of Teachers in Further and Higher Education* [*1980*] *ICR 455*).

54.7 **Constructive dismissal**

In order to establish that he has been constructively dismissed, an employee must show that

(i) his employer has been in breach of an important term of the contract – this is known as a repudiatory breach (*Western Excavating (ECC) Ltd v Sharp* [*1978*] *ICR 221*) (it is not enough to show merely that the employer has behaved unreasonably – however, a serious breach of the implied term of trust and confidence may be sufficient);

(ii) he has left because of the breach (*Walker v Josiah Wedgwood & Sons Ltd* [*1978*] *ICR 744*);

(iii) he has not waived the breach. In other words, he must not delay his resignation too long, or do anything else which indicates acceptance of the changed basis of his employment. See the discussion in *W E Cox Toner (International) Ltd v Crook* [*1981*] *IRLR 443*.

Examples of breaches of contract upon which a complaint of constructive dismissal might be founded include: a reduction in pay (*Industrial Rubber Products v Gillon* [*1977*] *IRLR 389*); a complete change in the nature of the job (*Ford v Milthorn Toleman Ltd* [*1980*] *IRLR 30; Pedersen v Camden London Borough Council* [*1981*] *ICR 674*); or a failure to follow the prescribed disciplinary procedure (*Post Office v Strange* [*1981*] *IRLR 515*).

The employer may be held to be in repudiatory breach of contract not only if he breaks an express term but also if he infringes an implied term. Thus, an employer will be held guilty of a breach which entitles an employee to resign and claim that he has been constructively dismissed if the employer behaves in a way which destroys the relationship of trust and confidence with his employee. (*Bliss v South East Thames Regional Health Authority* [*1987*] *ICR 700*. See also *Wigan Borough Council v Davies* [*1979*] *ICR 411; Woods v WM Car Services (Peterborough) Ltd* [*1982*] *ICR 693*). Even if the 'last straw' was not by itself a fundamental breach of contract, the employee may be able to rely upon the employer's course of conduct considered as a whole.

Glidewell LJ conveniently summarised some of the relevant principles in *Lewis v Motorworld Garages Ltd* [*1986*] *ICR 157* at pp 169D – 170A.

> 'If the employer is in breach of an express term of a contract of employment, of such seriousness that the employee would be justified in leaving and claiming constructive dismissal, but the employee does not leave and accepts the altered terms of employment, and if subsequently a series of actions by the employer might constitute together a breach of the implied obligation of trust and confidence the employee is entitled to treat the original action by the employer which was a breach of the express terms of the contract as a part – the start – of the series of actions which, taken together with the employer's other actions, might cumulatively amount to a breach of the implied terms.'

Where there is a genuine dispute between parties about the terms of a contract of employment, it is not an *anticipatory breach* of the contract for one party to do no more than argue his point of view. (*Financial Techniques (Planning Services) Ltd v Hughes [1981] IRLR 32*; see also *Bridgen v Lancashire County Council [1987] IRLR 58*).

It has been suggested that the employee must make clear when he resigns that he regards himself as having been constructively dismissed (see *Walker*, above).

A constructive dismissal is not necessarily unfair. (*Savoia v Chiltern Herb Farms Ltd [1982] IRLR 166*).The tribunal will look at the conduct of the employer which amounted to the breach of contract and ask whether he acted reasonably, in the usual way. However, it is thought that it may be harder to demonstrate that a particular action is reasonable where it contravenes the contract of employment.

54.8 Forced resignation

If an employee resigns in circumstances where he is given no alternative but to resign or be dismissed, he will be considered to have been dismissed for the purposes of unfair dismissal. The question of whether the conduct of the employer caused the employee to leave is one of fact for the industrial tribunal. (*Martin v MBS Fastenings (Glynwed) Distribution Ltd [1983] ICR 511*). However, telling an employee that he would be dismissed at some unspecified date in the future does not give the employee the right to resign and claim that he has been constructively dismissed if the employer is guilty of no anticipatory breach of contract. (*Haseltine Lake & Co v Dowler [1981] ICR 222*; see also *Norwest Holst Group Administration Ltd v Harrison [1985] ICR 668*).

If an employee decides to leave because he has negotiated satisfactory terms for his departure, he will be considered to have resigned. In *Sheffield v Oxford Controls Ltd [1979] ICR 396*, Arnold J said, at p 402:

> 'It is plain, we think, that there must exist a principle . . . that where an employee resigns and that resignation is determined upon by him because he prefers to resign rather than to be dismissed (the alternative having been expressed to him by the employer in the terms of the threat that if he does not resign he will be dismissed), the mechanics of the resignation do not cause that to be other than a dismissal. The cases do not in terms go further than that. We find the principle to be one of causation.'

The Court of Appeal in *Birch v University of Liverpool [1985] ICR 470* held that an employee who took advantage of an early retirement scheme was not dismissed. Dismissal does not include termination by mutual consent.

54.9 Repudiatory conduct by the employee

Employers sometimes consider that an employee has 'dismissed himself' by breaching some fundamental term of his contract of employment such as failing to attend work. This is almost certainly not a correct approach. In *Thomas Marshall (Exports) Ltd v Guinle [1978] ICR 905*, Megarry VC held that an employee's repudiation of his contract of employment had to be accepted by the employer to bring the contract to an end. This 'acceptance' view was approved by a majority of the Court of Appeal in *Gunton v Richmond-upon-Thames London Borough Council [1980] ICR 755*, and by a majority of the Court of Appeal in *London Transport Executive v Clarke [1981] ICR 355*. However, the question of whether a repudiation of a contract of employment has to be accepted in order to bring the contract to an end has still not finally been decided. (*R v East Berkshire Health*

Authority, Ex parte Walsh [*1984*] *ICR 743* per May LJ at p 756F; and see *Rigby v Ferodo Ltd* [*1988*] *ICR 29*; TERMINATION OF EMPLOYMENT (49)).

54.10 **Situations of no dismissal**

There is *no dismissal* in the following cases.

(*a*) *Termination of the contract of employment by consent of both parties* (e.g. *Birch v University of Liverpool* [*1985*] *ICR 470*).

(*b*) *Termination by the employee whether with or without notice* in the absence of 'constructive dismissal' or forced resignation (see 54.7-54.8 above). A valid notice given by an employee cannot usually be withdrawn without the employer's consent. (*Riordan v War Office* [*1959*] *3 AER 522;* [*1960*] *3 AER 774*; *Sothern v Franks Charlesly & Co* [*1981*] *IRLR 278*). But it may be that words of resignation (or dismissal) spoken in the heat of the moment can be regarded as not being a true resignation, or else can be withdrawn if this is done quickly. (*Martin v Yeomen Aggregates Ltd* [*1983*] *ICR 314; Barclay v City of Glasgow District Council* [*1983*] *IRLR 313*).

(*c*) *Termination of employment by 'frustration'*. If the contract of employment cannot be performed or if its performance becomes radically different from that contemplated when the contract was entered into, it may be considered to have been terminated by frustration. (See further 49.3 TERMINATION OF EMPLOYMENT.)

(*d*) *Termination on the occurrence of an external event*. A contract for a voyage may be terminated 'automatically' when the voyage is completed. (*Ryan v Shipboard Maintenance Ltd* [*1980*] *ICR 88*). An appointment for 'as long as sufficient funds are provided either by the Manpower Services Commission or by other firms/sponsors to fund it' was held to come to an end automatically when the specified event took place. (*Brown v Knowsley Borough Council* [*1986*] *IRLR 102*).

54.11 EMPLOYMENT FOR QUALIFYING PERIOD

In order to bring a claim for unfair dismissal, the applicant must have been continuously employed for a period of two years ending with the 'effective date of termination' (see 54.13 below). [*EPCA s 64(1)(a); Unfair Dismissal (Variation of Qualifying Period) Order 1985 (SI 1985 No 782)*].

The period is calculated from the beginning of the employee's employment under the relevant contract of employment. This could be earlier than the date the employee starts performing duties under the contract. (*The General of the Salvation Army v Dewsbury* [*1984*] *ICR 498*).

If it is shown that the reason (or, if more than one, the principal reason) for the dismissal was a reason relating to trade union activities, see 55.3(*a*) below, the employee does *not* have to be continuously employed for any qualifying period in order to bring a claim. [*EPCA s 64(3); EA 1982, 2 Sch 5, 3 Sch 19*]. If an employee is dismissed on medical grounds in compliance with any law, regulation or code of practice providing for health and safety at work, the qualifying period for a claim is only one month. [*EPCA s 64(2); EA 1982, 2 Sch 5*].

54.12 **Calculation of period of continuous employment**

The detailed provisions relating to the calculation of a period of continuous employment are set out in *EPCA 13 Schedule* as amended by *EA 1982, 2 Sch.*

They are considered fully in CONTINUOUS EMPLOYMENT (9). They provide, for example, that there is continuity of employment when the business in which an employee works is transferred from one owner to another, when the employee is incapable of work because of sickness or injury, or absent from work wholly or partly because of pregnancy or confinement.

54.13 Effective date of termination

The qualifying period is calculated up to and including the effective date of termination. The effective date of termination is defined as

(*a*) in relation to an employee whose contract of employment is *terminated by notice*, whether given by his employer or by the employee, the date on which that notice expires;

(*b*) in relation to an employee whose contract of employment is terminated *without notice*, the date on which the termination takes effect; and

(*c*) in relation to an employee who is employed under a *contract for a fixed term*, where that term expires without being renewed under the same contract, the date on which that term expires.

[*EPCA s 55(4)*].

In most cases the effective date of termination is the date on which the employee ceases work. If an employer makes it clear to an employee that he is terminating his employment forthwith and pays him a sum of money in lieu of notice, the effective date of termination is the actual date of termination of the employment whether or not the employee was dismissed in breach of contract. (*Dedman v British Building Engineering Appliances Ltd [1974] ICR 53*; *Robert Cort and Son Ltd v Charman [1981] ICR 816;* see also *Leech v Preston Borough Council [1985] ICR 192*; *Batchelor v British Railways Board [1987] IRLR 136*). If, however, the contract continues although the employee stays away from work, the effective date of termination will be the date upon which the contract comes to an end in accordance with the notice. In *Crank v Her Majesty's Stationery Office [1985] ICR 1*, the EAT held that the employer and the employee can agree on a date of termination even though that may not be the date which would otherwise be held to be the effective date of termination within the meaning of *EPCA s 55(4)*. In *West v Kneels Ltd [1987] ICR 146* the EAT held that 'seven days' notice', used on dismissal, meant seven *clear* days.

Where an employee exercises a right of appeal against his dismissal but his appeal is not allowed, in the absence of any contrary contractual provision the effective date of termination will be the date of the original dismissal. (*J Sainsbury Ltd v Savage [1981] ICR 1*, approved in *West Midlands Co-operative Society Ltd v Tipton [1986] ICR 192*). However, for the purpose of deciding whether the employee had the necessary qualifying period of employment, if an employer dismisses an employee giving him no notice or less notice than that required by *EPCA s 49*, the effective date will be the date on which the statutory minimum period of notice would have expired had it been given. [*EPCA s 55(5); EA 1982, 3 Sch 1*]. (*Fox Maintenance Ltd v Jackson [1977] IRLR 306*). Thus, if an employer dismisses an employee after 103 weeks with wages in lieu of notice, the effective date of termination will be taken to be one week later, as the minimum period of notice after more than one month's employment is one week (see 49.9 TERMINATION OF EMPLOYMENT). The employee will thus be entitled to claim compensation for unfair dismissal. The extra time will not be added where an employee is summarily dismissed in circumstances where the employer is entitled to dismiss summarily, e.g. for gross misconduct (see 49.14 TERMINATION OF EMPLOYMENT), but an employer is not entitled simply to define a dismissal as being for gross misconduct without the tribunal investigating whether that description is justified. (*Lanton Leisure Ltd v White and Gibson* [*1987*] *IRLR 119*). The statutory extension applies even where the employee waives his right to notice. (*Secretary of State for Employment v Staffordshire County Council* [*1989*] *IRLR 117*), the Court of Appeal holding that the fact that an employee has waived his right to notice or accepted a payment in lieu of notice under *EPCA s 49(3)* is relevant only to his rights in contract.

For the purpose of calculating the qualifying period of employment where an employee terminates his contract of employment in circumstances in which he is entitled to do so by reason of his employer's conduct, the effective date of termination will be considered to be the date on which the statutory minimum notice required of the employer would have expired. [*EPCA s 55(6); EA 1982, 3 Sch 1*].

54.14 RETIRING AGE

No-one may complain of unfair dismissal if, on or before the effective date of termination, he has attained the age which, in the undertaking in which he was employed, is the normal retiring age for an employee holding the position which he held and the retiring age is the same for men and for women. [*EPCA s 64(1)(a)*, as substituted by *SDA 1986, s 3*]. 'Normal retiring age' is to be ascertained from the reasonable expectation of employees holding the position of the applicant at the date of dismissal. The contractual retiring age (if any) is *prima facie* the normal retiring age but it may be departed from in practice, with the result either that there is some other normal retiring age, or that there is no such normal age at all. Administrative policies communicated to the employees may give rise to such expectations, but when those policies are changed so too are those expectations. (*Waite v Government Communications Headquarters* [*1983*] *2 AC 714; Hughes Coy and Jarnell v Department of Health and Social Security and others* [*1985*] *AC 776*; *Whittle v Manpower Services Commission* [*1987*] *IRLR 441*).

Where there is no normal retiring age, employees aged 65 and over may not bring an application for unfair dismissal. [*EPCA s 64(1)(b)*, as substituted by *SDA 1986, s 3*].

An employee over normal retiring age or over the age of 65 *can* bring a claim for unfair dismissal if it is shown that the reason (or, if more than one, the principal reason) for the dismissal was 'union-related' (see 55.3(*a*) below). [*EPCA s 64(3); EA 1982, 3 Sch 19*].

54.15 EXCLUDED CLASSES OF EMPLOYEES

Certain classes of employment are excluded from the protection of the unfair dismissal provisions. If a respondent wishes to show that an applicant falls within an excluded class, the burden of proof is on him to do so. (*Kapur v Shields* [*1976*] *ICR 26*). The excluded cases are set out in *EPCA ss 141(2)(5), 142(1), 144(2), 145(2) as amended by EA 1982, 3 Sch 6* and *Dock Work Act 1989*.

(*a*) Any employment as a master or as a member of the crew of a *fishing vessel* where the employee is not remunerated otherwise than by a share in the profits or gross earnings of the vessel.

(*b*) Any employment where under his contract of employment *the employee ordinarily works outside Great Britain*. In deciding where an employee ordinarily works, one should look at the terms of the contract, express or implied, in order to ascertain where, looking at the whole period contemplated by the contract, the employee's base is to be. (*Wilson v Maynard Shipbuilding Consultants AB [1978] ICR 376* and *per* Lord Denning MR and Sir David Cairns in *Todd v British Midland Airways Ltd [1978] ICR 959*). Where the contract of employment is of little assistance, the tribunal should go by the conduct of the parties and the way they have operated the contract. (*Per* Lord Denning MR in *Todd* at p 964).

A person employed to work on board a ship registered in the United Kingdom (not being a ship registered at a port outside Great Britain) will be regarded as a person who under his contract ordinarily works in Great Britain unless

(i) the employment is wholly outside Great Britain, or

(ii) the employee is not ordinarily resident in Great Britain.

(See *Wood v Cunard Line Ltd [1989] ICR 398*.)

Employees engaged upon certain activities connected with offshore drilling were given employment protection rights by the *Employment Protection (Offshore Employment) Order 1976 (SI 1976 No 766)*.

(*c*) Dismissal from employment *under a contract for a fixed term of one year or more*, where the dismissal consists only of the expiry of that term without its being renewed if before the term so expires the employee has agreed in writing to exclude any claim in respect of rights to claim for unfair dismissal in relation to that contract. [*EPCA s 142; EA 1980, s 8(2)*].

(*d*) Dismissal from employment in respect of which the employee has validly contracted out of his right to claim compensation for unfair dismissal (see 54.18 below).

54.16 EMPLOYEE CANNOT ENFORCE RIGHTS IF CONTRACT ILLEGAL

The courts will not enforce an illegal contract. Thus, if it appears to an industrial tribunal that, for example, a contract of employment was entered into with an agreement that no tax be paid on some part or all of the remuneration, the tribunal will consider the agreement to be a fraud on the Inland Revenue and will dismiss the claim. (*Tomlinson v Dick Evans 'U' Drive Ltd [1978] ICR 639; Newland v Simons & Willer (Hairdressers) Ltd [1981] ICR 521; Napier v National Business Agency Ltd [1951] 2 AER 264*). It is only when the employee can establish that he was unaware that no deductions for tax were being made or where he made full declaration of his income to the Inland Revenue that he can pursue a claim for unfair dismissal.

54.17 DISMISSAL IN CONNECTION WITH A LOCK-OUT OR STRIKE

An industrial tribunal will not determine whether a dismissal (which includes for these purposes a failure to re-engage) is fair or unfair where at the date of the dismissal

(*a*) the employer was conducting or instituting a lock-out; or (*b*) the employee was taking part in a strike or other industrial action,

unless it is shown that either

(i) one or more relevant employees of the same employer have not been dismissed; or

(ii) that any such employee has, before the expiry of the period of three months beginning with that employee's date of dismissal, been offered re-engagement and that the employee concerned has not been offered re-engagement.

[*EPCA s 62; EA 1982, s 9*].

Any reference to an offer of re-engagement is a reference to an offer (made either by the original employer or by a successor of that employer or an associated employer) to re-engage an employee, either in the job which he held immediately before the date of dismissal or in a different job which would be reasonably suitable in his case. [*EPCA s 62(4)(c)*].

Thus, if all employees taking part in a strike or other industrial action are dismissed and none are subsequently reinstated or re-engaged, there can be no claims arising out of the dismissals. An employee may be taking part in industrial action even though he is not in breach of his contract of employment, for example by refusing to work overtime. (*Power Packing Casemakers Ltd v Faust and Others* [*1983*] *ICR 292*). If an employee is away sick or on holiday and has taken no part in the strike he should not be dismissed. If, however, an employee is away sick or on holiday but before his period of absence has taken part in the strike, and but for his absence would still be taking part, he will be considered one of the 'relevant' employees for the purposes of *EPCA s 62* so that if the strikers are to be dismissed, he should be dismissed as well. (*Williams v Western Mail & Echo Ltd* [*1980*] *ICR 366*; see also *Coates and Another v Modern Methods and Materials Ltd* [*1982*] *ICR 763*). In *Hindle Gears v McGinty* [*1985*] *ICR 111*, the EAT held that an employer's knowledge of an employee's participation in a strike will be taken into account but is not conclusive as to whether he is a 'relevant' employee or not. However, in *Bolton Roadways Ltd v Edwards* [*1987*] *IRLR 392* another division of the EAT held the employer's knowledge to be irrelevant. In the latter case it was also held that an offer of re-engagement could include a tacit, implied offer.

Provided that *all* employees who have taken part in a strike are dismissed before the conclusion of the hearing before an industrial tribunal (or the conclusion of the preliminary hearing if the jurisdiction point is dealt with separately), the tribunal will have no jurisdiction to entertain an application by any of the dismissed employees, even though not all the dismissals occurred while the strike was taking place. (*McCormick v Horsepower Ltd* [*1981*] *ICR 535; P & O European Ferries (Dover) Ltd v Byrne* [*1989*] *IRLR 254*; see also *Stock v Frank Jones (Tipton) Ltd* [*1978*] *1 WLR 231*). Similarly, offers of re-engagement to all dismissed employees made in two stages but within three months of their dismissals deprived all the employees of the right to claim unfair dismissal. (*Highland Fabricators Ltd v McLaughlin* [*1985*] *ICR 183*).

For the distinction between a lock-out and a strike, which affects the definition of 'relevant employees' see *Express & Star Ltd v Bunday and others* [*1987*] *ICR 379*.

In *Williams v National Theatre Board* [*1982*] *IRLR 377*, the Court of Appeal held that offers of re-engagement following a strike on condition that the employees would be treated as 'being on a second warning' under the employers' disciplinary procedure disentitled the applicants from bringing a claim for unfair dismissal;

despite that condition, the strikers were to be employed in the same capacity as before.

If, however, some employees are not dismissed or are reinstated or re-engaged, the tribunal will determine the reason for the dismissal or the failure to reinstate or re-engage the others, and decide whether it was fair to dismiss in all the circumstances of the case.

Action short of dismissal. Employers may not take action short of dismissal against employees for taking part in the activities of a trade union recognised by them (see 52.10 TRADE UNIONS – II). [*EPCA s 23*].

In *McLaren v National Coal Board [1988] ICR 370* the Court of Appeal discussed the general principles of fairness applicable, where a tribunal *does* have jurisdiction to hear a case, when the events occurred against a background of industrial action, and described the standards of procedural fairness as 'immutable'.

54.18 NO CONTRACTING OUT

With certain exceptions, any agreement to prevent any person from presenting or pursuing a complaint of unfair dismissal is void. [*EPCA s 140(1)*]. A clause in a contract of employment purporting to exclude this right will be ineffective, leaving the employee free to pursue a claim for unfair dismissal in the industrial tribunal. In *Igbo v Johnson Matthey Chemicals Ltd [1986] ICR 505* the Court of Appeal held that a variation of an employment contract which provided that if an employee failed to return from a period of leave on a certain date, her contract would be automatically terminated, converted a right not to be unfairly dismissed into a conditional right not to be dismissed, and accordingly it was void by reason of *EPCA s 140(1)*. But in *Scott and others v Coalite Fuels and Chemicals Ltd [1988] ICR 355*, an employee who had agreed to accept voluntary retirement as an alternative to redundancy was not successful in putting forward a similar argument. In *Logan Salton v Durham City Council [1989] IRLR 99*, a case where an employee under threat of dismissal agreed terms for termination, *Igbo* was distinguished on the grounds that this was a separate contract from the contract of employment, entered into without duress, after proper advice and for good consideration, and that termination was not contingent upon the happening of future events in circumstances which the parties might not have envisaged. The EAT granted leave to appeal.

Similarly, any agreement to pay an ex-employee money in consideration for his refraining from presenting or pursuing a complaint in an industrial tribunal is unenforceable unless a conciliation officer has taken action in reaching the agreement. [*EPCA s 140(2)(d),(e)*]. (See 2.3 ADVISORY, CONCILIATION AND ARBITRATION SERVICE.) Therefore, if a compromise of a claim or a potential claim is reached, an employer should request a conciliation officer to approve the settlement which should be drawn up on a form available from him. If this is not done, the ex-employee may pursue his claim before the industrial tribunal. If he succeeds, the tribunal will probably take into account any money paid under the agreement in making an order for compensation, but will not necessarily do so.

54.19 Exceptions

An agreement restricting the right to claim for unfair dismissal is enforceable if it is contained in the following agreements:

(*a*) a contract of employment for a fixed term of one year or more, where the dismissal consists only of the expiry of that term without its being renewed, if the provision has been recorded in writing before the expiry of that term;

(*b*) a dismissal procedure agreement reached between employers and one or more independent trade unions which has been approved by the Secretary of State;

(*c*) any agreement to refrain from presenting a complaint that he was unfairly dismissed where the conciliation officer has taken action in accordance with his statutory duties;

(*d*) any agreement to refrain from proceeding with a complaint where the conciliation officer has taken action in accordance with his statutory duties.

[*EPCA s 140(2)*].

55 Unfair Dismissal – II: The Fairness of the Dismissal

(See also DE booklets 'Fair and unfair dismissal – a guide for employers' (PL 714), No. 13 'Unfairly dismissed?' (PL 712) and 'The law on unfair dismissal – guidance for small firms' (PL 715).)

Cross-references. See UNFAIR DISMISSAL – I (54) for the right to make a claim; UNFAIR DISMISSAL – III (56) for remedies for unfair dismissal.

55.1 REASONS FOR DISMISSAL

Once the fact of dismissal has been established, it is for the employer to show

(*a*) what was the reason (or, if there was more than one, the principal reason) for the dismissal; and

(*b*) that it was one of the reasons set out in 55.2 below.

[*EPCA s 57(1)*].

An industrial tribunal will investigate the real reason for the dismissal of the employee. The fact that an employer told an employee that the reason for his dismissal was redundancy will not preclude the tribunal from deciding that, for example, the real reason for dismissal was lack of capability. (*Abernethy v Mott, Hay and Anderson* [*1974*] *ICR 323*). But the tribunal should not find for the employer on a ground not argued if the employee will be prejudiced in that he might have put his case differently if aware of that argument. (*Hannan v TNT-Ipec (UK) Ltd* [*1986*] *IRLR 165*). If the employee establishes that there is a dispute over the reason for the dismissal, the burden of proving which one of the competing reasons for the dismissal was the principal reason is on the employer. (*Maund v Penwith District Council* [*1984*] *ICR 143*). Also, the employer will only be allowed to rely upon facts known to him at the time of the dismissal to establish what the reason for the dismissal was. Thus, facts which come to light after the dismissal cannot be relied upon to justify the dismissal, though they may affect the level of compensation. (*W Devis & Sons Ltd v Atkins* [*1977*] *ICR 662*).

55.2 Acceptable reasons for dismissal

The following are acceptable reasons for dismissal:

(*a*) reasons related to the capability or qualifications of the employee for performing work of the kind which he was employed to do; or

(*b*) reasons related to the conduct of the employee; or

(*c*) that the employee was redundant; or

(*d*) that the employee could not continue to work in the position which he held without contravention (either on his part or on that of his employer) of a duty or restriction imposed by or under an enactment;

(*e*) some other substantial reason of a kind such as to justify the dismissal of an employee holding the position which that employee held.

[*EPCA s 57(1)(2)*].

If the employer fails to establish that the reason for the dismissal was an acceptable one, the tribunal *must* find the dismissal unfair. (*Earl v Slater and*

Wheeler (Airlyne) Ltd [*1973*] *1 AER 145*, observation of Sir John Donaldson *obiter* at p 149).

After a consideration of the *unacceptable* reasons for dismissal (see 55.3 below) and the criteria for assessment of the fairness of a dismissal where the reason is acceptable (see 55.4 below), the chapter looks at each of the acceptable reasons listed above in turn. Note that the term 'inadmissible reason' has been dropped from the legislation. [*EA 1982, 3 Sch*].

55.3 DISMISSALS WHICH ARE DEEMED UNFAIR

(*a*) **'Union-related' dismissals**

The dismissal of an employee will automatically be regarded as unfair if the principal reason for it was that the employee

(i) was, or proposed to become, a member of an independent trade union; or

(ii) had taken part, or proposed to take part, in the activities of an independent trade union at an appropriate time; or

(iii) was not a member of any trade union, or of a particular trade union, or of one of a number of particular trade unions, or had refused, or proposed to refuse, to become or remain a member.

[*EPCA s 58(1); EA 1982, s 3*]. (Note that there is no need for an employee to have been employed for any qualifying period to present a complaint on this ground.)

An 'independent trade union' is defined as any union which is not under the control or domination of an employer (see 51.14 TRADE UNIONS – I). [*TULRA s 30(1); EPCA s 153(1)*].

'An appropriate time', in relation to an employee taking part in the activities of a trade union, means a time which either

(*a*) is outside his working hours; or

(*b*) is a time within his working hours at which, in accordance with arrangements agreed with or consent given by his employers, it is permissible for him to take part in those activities.

[*EPCA s 58(2); EA 1982, s 3*]. 'Working hours', in relation to an employee, means any time when, in accordance with his contract of employment, he is required to be at work. In *Marley Tile Co Ltd v Shaw* [*1980*] *ICR 72*, the Court of Appeal held that such consent could be express or implied.

Closed shop. Under the relevant provisions of the *Employment Act 1988*, all dismissals to enforce a closed shop are now automatically unfair (see CLOSED SHOP (6)).

(*b*) **Dismissal on the ground of pregnancy**

An employee will be considered to have been unfairly dismissed or unfairly selected for redundancy if the reason or the principal reason for her dismissal or selection was that she was pregnant or is any other reason connected with her pregnancy, except one of the following reasons:

(i) that at the effective date of termination she is or will have become, because of her pregnancy, incapable of adequately doing the work which she is employed to do; or

(ii) that, because of her pregnancy, she cannot or will not be able to continue after that date to do that work without contravention (either by her or her employer) of a duty or restriction imposed by or under any enactment.

To be able to rely on one of these exceptions, the employer must have offered the pregnant employee suitable alternative employment or be able to show that there was no suitable alternative employment available.

[*EPCA s 60(1)-(4)*]. (See 29.6-29.9 MATERNITY RIGHTS.)

(*c*) **Unfair selection for redundancy**

The dismissal of an employee on the ground of redundancy will be considered unfair if the circumstances constituting the redundancy applied equally to one or more employees in the same undertaking who held positions similar to that held by the dismissed employee and who have not been dismissed by the employer, and either

(i) the reason (or if more than one the principal reason) for which he was selected for dismissal was union-related (see (*a*) above); or

(ii) he was selected for dismissal in contravention of a customary arrangement or agreed procedure relating to redundancy and there were no special reasons justifying a departure from that arrangement or procedure in his case.

[*EPCA s 59; EA 1982, 3 Sch 17*]. (See further 55.11 below.)

Selection of an employee for redundancy because she is pregnant is unfair (see 29.6 MATERNITY RIGHTS).

(*d*) **Dismissals on a transfer of an undertaking**

Where either before or after a relevant transfer, any employee of the transferor or transferee is dismissed, that employee shall *prima facie* be treated as unfairly dismissed if the transfer or a reason connected with it is the reason or principal reason for his dismissal. (*Transfer of Undertakings (Protection of Employment) Regulations 1981 (SI 1981 No 1794), Reg 8(1)*). However, the dismissal is not *automatically* unfair if the reason for it falls within *Reg 8(2)*, i.e. if it is for an economic, technical or organisational reason entailing changes in the workforce. See TRANSFER OF UNDERTAKINGS (53).

55.4 FAIRNESS IN THE CIRCUMSTANCES

If the employer establishes that the reason for the dismissal is an acceptable reason, the tribunal will proceed to determine whether the dismissal was fair or unfair, in all the circumstances, having regard to equity and the substantial merits of the case. [*EPCA s 57(3); EA 1980, s 6*]. Whereas the burden of establishing the reason for the dismissal is on the employer, the burden on this the second limb of the tribunal's inquiry has been placed neutrally. The tribunal will consider whether the employer acted reasonably or unreasonably in treating the reason for the dismissal as a sufficient reason for dismissing the employee. If *part* of the reason or principal reason was not reasonably relied upon, the dismissal will be unfair. (*Smith v Glasgow City District Council [1987] ICR 796*). Among the factors to be taken into account by the tribunal are the size and administrative resources of the employer's undertaking.

The EAT has held that the correct approach for an industrial tribunal, when applying *EPCA s 57(3)*, is to consider whether the employer's decision to dismiss fell within the band of reasonable responses to the employee's conduct which a reasonable employer could adopt. (*Iceland Frozen Foods v Jones [1983] ICR 17; British Leyland UK Ltd v Swift [1981] IRLR 91(CA); Gilham v Kent County Council (No 2) [1985] ICR 233*; and *Neale v Hereford and Worcester County Council [1986] ICR 471*). In other words, the tribunal must not ask itself whether it thinks the employer did the right thing, but must recognise that different employers may reasonably react in different ways to a particular situation.

The reason for and the fairness of the action taken is determined by examining the circumstances known to the employer at the time of the dismissal or when he maintains that decision at the conclusion of an internal appeal. (*West Midlands Co-operative Society Ltd v Tipton [1986] ICR 192*). The tribunal will take into account not only whether the employer had grounds for dismissing the employee, but also whether he adopted a fair procedure in dismissing him. In this context, the paragraphs in the *ACAS Code of Practice* relating to disciplinary practice and procedures (see Appendix) provide useful guidelines. The main points of these provisions are that *there should be a known disciplinary procedure which should be followed*. If there is a complaint against an employee, he should be informed in detail and preferably in writing of the complaint and given an opportunity to make representations, if necessary through, or in the presence of, an employee representative. (If the employee is a union member, his representative may be his shop steward.) He should also be given the opportunity, where practicable, to appeal to a level of management not previously involved. A dismissal may be held to be unfair when the employer has refused to entertain an appeal to which the employee was contractually entitled. In general, whether a dismissal has been carried out in breach of contract is a relevant factor in assessing its fairness, but is not conclusive either way. (*Hooper v British Railways Board [1988] IRLR 517*).

For several years it was thought that if an employer adopts an unfair procedure in dismissing an employee, but establishes on a balance of probabilities that if he had adopted a fair procedure the employee would still have been dismissed and his dismissal would have been fair, the dismissal may be held to be fair. But in *Polkey v A E Dayton Services Ltd [1988] ICR 142*, the House of Lords reaffirmed that the sole question for the tribunal is whether the employer acted reasonably at the time. There is no scope to consider what might have happened if the employer had acted differently, except at the stage of assessing compensation. But an employer may reasonably decide not to follow the normal procedure where it is clear that to do so would be utterly useless.

55.5 GROUNDS FOR DISMISSAL — LACK OF CAPABILITY OR QUALIFICATIONS

Capability means capability assessed by reference to skill, aptitude, health or any other physical or mental quality. *Qualifications* means any degree, diploma or other academic, technical or professional qualification, *relevant to the position which the employee held*. [*EPCA s 57(4)*].

55.6 Capability

In cases of lack of capability it is essential for the employer to show what was required of the employee, that the employee was informed of, or must have been aware of, those requirements, and that he fell short of them.

Dismissal procedure.

(i) If an employee falls short of the performance required of him, a meeting should be arranged with him and his representative at which he is informed of

(*a*) the respects (in detail) in which he falls short of the required standards;

(*b*) the time within which his performance must improve; and

(*c*) the fact that if he fails to improve he will receive a written warning and if he still fails to improve within a reasonable time he may be dismissed.

If possible, a witness should attend this meeting and take a contemporaneous note of what is said. If this cannot be done, a written record of what was said should be made as soon as possible after the meeting. The employee and his representative should be sent a summary of the meeting and of the conclusions reached.

(ii) If the employee's performance fails to improve, he should be sent a letter

(*a*) setting out the respects in which he has failed to improve; and

(*b*) inviting him and his representative to another meeting to explain this failure.

(iii) At the second meeting, at which again there should be a witness and a record kept,

(*a*) the complaints against the employee should be reiterated; and

(*b*) he should be given an opportunity to explain.

If he has no satisfactory explanation for his failure to improve, he should be informed that

(*c*) he has a further time in which to improve; and

(*d*) failure to improve within this time will result in dismissal.

The employee and his representative should again be sent a summary of the meeting.

(iv) If there is no improvement, repeat step (ii), warning him that his dismissal will be considered.

(v) At the third meeting, repeat steps (iii)(*a*) and (*b*) and if no satisfactory explanation is given, give notice of dismissal.

(vi) If the contract requires it, a manager or managers not involved in the original decision to dismiss should conduct an appeal hearing.

Other steps which may be taken are the offer of training to assist the employee's performance, and consultation with his union representative. Consideration should be given to whether the employer has other work available to which the employee would be better suited.

The importance of these steps will vary according to the circumstances. For example, it may be that a senior employee ought to be well aware of what is required of him and the consequences of failing adequately to perform his duties.

However, it is best to give warnings in cases of incapability, irrespective of the seniority of the employee.

55.7 **Qualifications**

Dismissal for lack of qualifications is not common since an employer will have difficulty in convincing a tribunal that an employee whom he engaged with full knowledge of his qualifications is not qualified for the job. If, however, the employee misled the employer into believing that he possessed certain qualifications which were essential for the performance of the task to which he was appointed, he may be dismissed for his lack of qualifications. Some of the cases on lack of qualifications have arisen where a man employed as a driver is disqualified from driving and therefore is no longer able to perform his duties. (*Appleyard v Smith (Hull) Ltd* [*1972*] *IRLR 19*). Consideration should be given to offering a disqualified employee suitable alternative employment.

55.8 **Lack of capability due to ill-health**

In cases of ill-health which make future performance of the contract of employment impossible, the contract may be considered to have been frustrated and the employee not to have been dismissed (see 49.3 TERMINATION OF EMPLOYMENT).

Before dismissing an employee for reasons of ill-health, an employer should find out the current medical position. This will involve obtaining, with the employee's consent, a report from the employee's general practitioner, and, if appropriate, his consultant (see 13.13 DISCLOSURE OF INFORMATION for the *Access to Medical Reports Act 1988*). In many cases it may be thought necessary to have the employee examined, with his consent, by a doctor appointed by the employer. Once the employer has properly informed himself of the employee's state of health and the prognosis, he should consider the requirements of his business, the employee's past sickness record and whether the employee could be offered an alternative position more suitable to his state of health. (*Spencer v Paragon Wallpapers Ltd* [*1977*] *ICR 301*). The employer should consult the employee and any representative before dismissing him. (*East Lindsay District Council v Daubney* [*1977*] *ICR 566; Merseyside & North Wales Electricity Board v Taylor* [*1975*] *ICR 185*).

Where the problem consists not of a long absence but of persistent short absences caused by unconnected minor ailments, a medical examination has little purpose. The employee should be told what level of attendance he is expected to attain, the period within which that is to be achieved and that dismissal may follow if there is no sufficient improvement. The situation should then be monitored to see whether absence is reduced below a reasonable level. A second warning would be appropriate in borderline cases. See *International Sports Co Ltd v Thomson* [*1980*] *IRLR 340; Rolls-Royce Ltd v Walpole* [*1980*] *IRLR 343; Lynock v Cereal Packaging Ltd* [*1988*] *ICR 670*.

55.9 **GROUNDS FOR DISMISSAL — MISCONDUCT**

In order to warrant dismissal, misconduct must be serious, or if not serious, repeated on more than one occasion. However fair the procedure adopted, a single incident of, for example, bad timekeeping, will not in most cases be considered sufficiently serious to justify a dismissal. Equally, the fact that an employee has recently been given a disciplinary warning (especially if it was for a similar offence) may make it more reasonable to dismiss. Where an appeal against a prior warning is pending, the employer ought to bear that in mind, although he is not precluded from dismissing before the appeal is heard. (*Tower Hamlets Health Authority v Anthony [1989] IRLR 394*). For the dismissal to be held fair, it must be a reasonable sanction for the offence and other possible penalties should be considered. The conduct for which an employee is dismissed usually relates to behaviour during working hours, but in certain cases an employee may be dismissed for other behaviour, if it is likely to affect the performance of his contract. If, for example, a play group leader is convicted of an indecent assault on a child outside his hours of work, his conviction for such an offence may make him unsuitable for carrying on his employment (e.g. *Nottinghamshire County Council v Bowly [1978] IRLR 252*, in which the EAT held to be fair the dismissal of a teacher after his conviction for an offence of gross indecency with a man).

The Court of Appeal in *W Weddel & Co Ltd v Tepper [1980] ICR 286* approved the approach to cases of misconduct formulated by Arnold J in *British Home Stores Ltd v Burchell [1980] ICR 303*. At p 304 he stated:

> 'What the tribunal have to decide every time is, broadly expressed, whether the employer who discharged the employee on the grounds of misconduct in question (usually, though not necessarily, dishonest conduct) entertained a reasonable suspicion amounting to a belief in the guilt of the employee of that misconduct at that time. That is really stating shortly and compendiously what is in fact more than one element. First of all, there must be established by the employer the fact of that belief; that the employer did believe it. Secondly, that the employer had in his mind reasonable grounds upon which to sustain that belief. And thirdly, we think, that the employer, at the stage at which he formed that belief on those grounds, at any rate at the final stage at which he formed that belief on those grounds, had carried out as much investigation into the matter as was reasonable in all the circumstances of the case.'

For a recent general discussion, see *ILEA v Gravett [1988] IRLR 497*, and also *Whitbread & Co plc v Mills [1988] ICR 776*.

But if the employer reasonably believes that one of a number of employees is guilty of dishonesty and, despite proper investigation, cannot identify the culprit, it may be reasonable to dismiss all those who could have been responsible. (*Monie v Coral Racing Ltd [1981] ICR 109; Whitbread & Co plc v Thomas and others [1988] ICR 135*).

Cases in which an employee is arrested by the police and charged with theft of his employer's property pose particular difficulties. Is it proper for the employer to conduct his own investigation and question the employee whilst the police investigations are proceeding? In *Harris and Shepherd v Courage (Eastern) Ltd [1982] ICR 530*, the Court of Appeal approved the decision of the EAT that there is no absolute rule that once an employee had been charged with an offence and advised to say nothing until his criminal trial, that an employer could not dismiss him for the alleged offence. Because of the long delay before a criminal prosecution is finally disposed of, it will often be necessary or desirable for the employer to act before its conclusion. Employers frequently carry out their own investigations and dismiss for dishonest conduct before a prosecution is concluded. If the employer awaits the outcome of a criminal trial and the employee is acquitted, he may find it harder to justify a subsequent dismissal, although the burden on the prosecution at the criminal trial is heavier than upon the employer in showing that he acted reasonably. The evidence which it is permissible for the employer to rely upon is less restricted than that which is admissible in the criminal trial, but how far it is reasonable for the employer to rely upon evidence which has been ruled inadmissible in a criminal trial depends on the facts in each case. (*Dhaliwal v British Airways Board [1985] ICR 513*).

Even if the employee may be charged with a criminal offence he must be given an opportunity by his employer to state his case. (*Read v Phoenix Preservation Ltd [1985] ICR 164*).

55.10 Dismissal procedure

The *ACAS Code of Practice No 1* stresses the importance of having a known disciplinary procedure. Paragraph 12 lays down guidelines for disciplinary action (see Appendix where the *Code* is reproduced in full). ACAS has also published a handbook, 'Discipline at Work'.

It should be noted in particular that an employer has no right to suspend an employee without pay unless this is expressly provided for in the contract of employment.

If an employee is suspected of misconduct, the employer should investigate the matter fully and give the employee an opportunity to explain himself. The extent of the investigation will depend on the circumstances. In *Royal Society for the Protection of Birds v Croucher [1984] ICR 604*, the EAT held that in a case in which an employee admitted offences of dishonesty there was very little scope for the kind of investigation referred to in *Burchell* (see 55.9 above). The employer does not have to prove beyond reasonable doubt that the employee was guilty of the misconduct, but merely that he had acted reasonably in treating the misconduct as sufficient for dismissing the employee in the circumstances known to him (or which he ought reasonably to have known) at the time. It does not matter if the employer's view is subsequently found to be mistaken. (*St Anne's Board Mill Co Ltd v Brien [1973] ICR 444; British Home Stores Ltd v Burchell [1980] ICR 303*). If the employer did not have reasonable grounds to dismiss at the time, the dismissal will be considered to be unfair even if subsequently evidence comes to light which proves him right. (*W Devis & Sons Ltd v Atkins [1977] ICR 662*).

The reasonableness of the employer's decision will be scrutinised at the time of the final decision to dismiss, namely at the conclusion of any appeal hearing. (*West Midland Co-operative Society v Tipton [1986] ICR 192*). Defects in the original procedure may be cured by a fair appeal, depending upon how bad the initial unfairness was and whether the appeal takes the form of a complete rehearing. (*Whitbread & Co plc v Mills [1988] ICR 776*).

It is important in considering the reasonableness of a dismissal that an employer's disciplinary procedures should follow the principles of natural justice, although a breach of the rules of natural justice does not automatically make a dismissal unfair. (*Slater v Leicestershire Health Authority [1989] IRLR 16*). The degree to which an industrial tribunal will scrutinise such procedures depends to a certain extent upon the size and resources of the employer's undertaking. In *Khanum v Mid-Glamorgan Area Health Authority [1979] ICR 40*, it was held that natural justice required that the employee should know the accusations made against her, that she should be given an opportunity to state her case and that the members of the management team and the appeals panel should act in good faith. Further, in *Bentley Engineering Co Ltd v Mistry [1979] ICR 47* the EAT held that natural justice required not merely that a man should have a chance to state his own case but that he must know sufficiently what was being said against him so that he could put forward his own case properly. For guidance in cases where an informant does not wish to be identified, see *Linfood Cash & Carry Ltd v Thomson [1989] ICR*

518. The EAT has held that unjustifiable delay in carrying out disciplinary proceedings can render unfair a dismissal which would otherwise have been held fair. (*Royal Society for the Prevention of Cruelty to Animals v Cruden* [*1986*] *ICR 205*). If possible, the employer should avoid a situation where the same members of management act as witnesses or complainants and as judges. (*Slater*, above – but the Court of Appeal recognised that this might sometimes prove impracticable).

Other points to bear in mind are: that the decision ought to be taken by those who conduct the hearing, and not by some more senior manager with only second-hand knowledge; that the employee should be given an opportunity to call witnesses if appropriate; and that the employee should be given reasonable advance warning of the hearing and that disciplinary action is under consideration.

In *Ulsterbus Ltd v Henderson* [*1989*] *IRLR 251* the Northern Ireland Court of Appeal applied the 'range of reasonable responses' test (see 55.4 above) to the procedure adopted, concluding that a reasonable employer could decide not to permit the confrontation and cross-examination of witnesses.

In *Bailey v B P Oil (Kent Refinery) Ltd* [*1980*] *ICR 642* the Court of Appeal held that the failure by employers to comply with a disciplinary procedure agreement was a factor to be taken into account, but that the weight to be given to it depended upon the circumstances.

55.11 GROUNDS FOR DISMISSAL — REDUNDANCY

Where the reason or the principal reason for the dismissal of an employee was that he was redundant (see REDUNDANCY – I (38)), the dismissal may be considered automatically unfair for one of two reasons.

(*a*) The dismissal will be considered unfair if the circumstances constituting the redundancy applied equally to one or more employees in the same undertaking who held positions similar to that held by the dismissed employee and who have not been dismissed by the employer, and either

   (i) the reason (or if more than one the principal reason) for which he was selected for dismissal was union-related; or

   (ii) he was selected for dismissal in contravention of a customary arrangement or agreed procedure relating to redundancy and there were no special reasons justifying a departure from that arrangement or procedure in his case.

   [*EPCA s 59; EA 1982, 3 Sch 17*]. (For union-related reasons, see 55.3 above.)

   An 'agreed procedure' is a procedure which has been agreed to by the employer and the workforce. The agreement may be made expressly or by implication. (*Henry v Ellerman Lines Plc* [*1985*] *ICR 57*). A 'customary arrangement' has been described as 'something which is so well known, so certain and so clear as to amount in effect to an implied "agreed procedure" which is the alternative contemplated by the paragraph'. (*Bessenden Properties Ltd v Corness* [*1973*] *IRLR 365; affirmed* [*1974*] *IRLR 338*; see also 39.10 REDUNDANCY – II). The most usual customary arrangement or agreed procedure is that of 'last in, first out', known as LIFO. Even in the absence of such an agreement or custom, it may be wise when considering selection for redundancy to dismiss the employee who joined the company most recently.

(*b*) Even if the dismissal is not considered unfair for the reasons set out in (*a*) above, it may be unfair 'in all the circumstances' within the meaning of *EPCA s 57(3)* as amended.

Among the circumstances which will be taken into account is the duty imposed by *EPA s 99* to consult trade union representatives where an independent trade union is recognised. A failure to comply with that requirement will almost certainly render the dismissal unfair. (*Kelly v Upholstery & Cabinet Works (Amesbury) Ltd* [*1977*] *IRLR 91; North East Midlands Co-operative Society Ltd v Allen* [*1977*] *IRLR 212*). In order to comply with the requirements of *Sec 99*, the employer must begin consultations before giving individual notices of dismissal. (*National Union of Teachers v Avon County Council* [*1978*] *ICR 626*). The EAT in *Williams v Compair Maxam Ltd* [*1982*] *ICR 156* listed the principles which, in the experience of the two lay members, reasonable employers adopt when dismissing for redundancy employees who are represented by an independent trade union recognised by them. The EAT stressed that the principles would not stay unaltered forever, and that they are not principles of law, but standards of behaviour. However, the principles outlined in *Williams* have been adopted by industrial tribunals and the EAT as standards by which to judge the fairness of dismissals for redundancy where a trade union is recognised by an employer. They are therefore of some importance and are set out below.

(1) The employer will seek to give as much warning as possible of impending redundancies so as to enable the union and the employees who may be affected to take early steps to inform themselves of the relevant facts, consider possible alternative solutions and, if necessary, find alternative employment in the undertaking or elsewhere.

(2) The employer will consult the union as to the best means by which the desired management result can be achieved fairly and with as little hardship to the employees as possible. In particular, the employer will seek to agree with the union the criteria to be applied in selecting the employees to be made redundant. When a selection has been made, the employer will consider with the union whether the selection has been made in accordance with those criteria.

(3) Whether or not an agreement as to the criteria to be adopted has been agreed with the union, the employer will seek to establish criteria for selection which so far as possible do not depend solely upon the opinion of the person making the selection but can be objectively checked against such things as attendance record, efficiency at the job, experience, or length of service.

(4) The employer will seek to ensure that the selection is made fairly in accordance with these criteria and will consider any representations the union may make as to such selection.

(5) The employer will seek to see whether instead of dismissing an employee he could offer him alternative employment.

(*Williams*, as above, *at p 162*). However, the extent to which any one or more of these principles apply depends on the circumstances of the particular case, and an employer's failure to adopt any one or more of these practices will not necessarily lead to a finding of unfair dismissal. (*Grundy (Teddington) Ltd v Plummer and Another [1983] ICR 367*). Moreover, the principles set out in *Williams* should not be treated as if they were a statute. (*Rolls-Royce Motors Ltd v Dewhurst [1985] ICR 869*). The position was summarised by Lord Bridge in *Polkey v A E Dayton Services Ltd [1988] ICR 142* at pages 162 to 163:

> '. . . in the case of redundancy, the employer will normally not act reasonably unless he warns and consults any employees affected or their representative, adopts a fair basis on which to select for redundancy and takes such steps as may be reasonable to avoid or minimise redundancy by redeployment within his own organisation . . . It is quite a different matter if the tribunal is able to conclude that the employer himself, at the time of dismissal, acted reasonably in taking the view that, in the exceptional circumstances of the particular case, the procedural steps normally appropriate would have been futile, could not have altered the decision to dismiss and therefore could be dispensed with.'

Even where no trade union is recognised for bargaining purposes, employers should consult with employee representatives before deciding which employees should be made redundant, in compliance with the *Industrial Relations Code of Practice para 46* (see Appendix). Employers should also consider the matters set out in *Code of Practice para 45* before deciding to implement redundancies. Where an employee has no representative, standards of good industrial relations practice require consultation with the employee before dismissing him as redundant, except in special circumstances. (*Freud v Bentalls Ltd [1983] ICR 77*). A tribunal may hold a redundancy dismissal to be unfair for lack of consultation with individual employees even where their union has been consulted. (*Walls Meat Co Ltd v Selby [1989] ICR 601*).

A dismissal of an employee may be considered unfair if no consideration is given to finding him another job within that company, or if the company is a member of a group, within that group. (*Vokes Ltd v Bear [1974] ICR 1*). The redundant employee should be offered an available vacancy even if it is at a lower salary or is of lower status than the post from which he is being made redundant. (*Avonmouth Construction Co Ltd v Shipway [1979] IRLR 14*).

The fairness of a dismissal for redundancy will be judged not at the date on which notice is given but at the date on which it takes effect. (*Stacey v Babcock Power Ltd [1986] ICR 221*).

If the employer can establish that had he taken reasonable steps to consult with the employee or find him other employment, he would still have been dismissed, an industrial tribunal may find the dismissal to be unfair but award no compensation, or compensate only for the wages and benefits which would have been received while consultation was taking place. (See also 55.4 above.)

55.12 **Dismissal procedure**

From decided cases (see 55.11 above and 39.9-39.13 REDUNDANCY – II) the following guidelines emerge:

(*a*) consult with employee representatives;

(*b*) consider possible alternatives to redundancies, e.g. short-time working, work sharing, other costs savings etc.;

(*c*) if redundancy becomes necessary, in consultation with employee representatives, agree objective criteria for selection for redundancy;

(*d*) apply the criteria objectively;

(*e*) inform the employees affected at the earliest opportunity;

(*f*) investigate the possibilities of offering them alternative employment within the company or group;

(*g*) give them time off to seek employment;

(*h*) pay all moneys due;

(*i*) conduct an appeal if the contract requires it.

55.13 GROUNDS FOR DISMISSAL — CONTRAVENTION OF ANY ENACTMENT

If an employer dismisses an employee because the employee could not continue to work in the position which he held without contravention (either on his part or on that of his employer) of a duty or restriction imposed by or under an enactment, the reason for the dismissal falls within *EPCA s 57(2)(d)*.

The fact that an employer genuinely but erroneously believes that he would be breaking the law by continuing to employ an employee, does not make the reason for the dismissal of that employee a reason falling within *EPCA s 57(2)(d)*, but it could be 'some other substantial reason' justifying the dismissal within *EPCA s 57(1)(b)* (see 55.14 below). (*Bouchaala v Trusthouse Forte Hotels Ltd* [*1980*] *ICR 721*).

Procedure. In these cases employers should

(*a*) arrange a meeting at which the employee should be informed of the situation and invited to express his views; and

(*b*) in appropriate cases, find out if the company or an associated company has a suitable vacancy which the employee can be offered instead.

55.14 GROUNDS FOR DISMISSAL — 'ANY OTHER SUBSTANTIAL REASON'

These reasons need not be of the same type as those that are specified in the Act. If the reason for dismissal is not one of those set out in *EPCA s 57(2)* (see 55.2 above), it may nevertheless be an acceptable reason if the employer can show that it was 'some other substantial reason of a kind such as to justify the dismissal of an employee holding the position which that employee held'. [*EPCA s 57(1)(b)*]. Examples of such reasons are the following.

(*a*) *Necessary re-organisation of the business*. (*Hollister v National Farmers' Union* [*1979*] *ICR 542; Richmond Precision Engineering Ltd v Pearce* [*1985*] *IRLR 179*). This may also apply in cases where changes in terms and conditions have led the employee to claim constructive dismissal. (*Genower v Ealing, Hammersmith & Hounslow Area Health Authority* [*1980*] *IRLR 297*). But note that the employee must be fairly considered for any new job created by the reorganisation. (*Oakley v The Labour Party* [*1988*] *ICR 403*).

(*b*) *Economic, technical or organisational reasons entailing changes in the workforce* of the transferor or the transferee before or after a relevant transfer within the meaning of the *Transfer of Undertakings (Protection of Employment) Regulations 1981 (SI 1981 No 1794), Reg 8(2)(b)*.

(*c*) Reasons of *necessary economies* such as in *Durrant and Cheshire v Clariston Clothing Co Ltd* [*1974*] *IRLR 360* in which a tribunal held that it was not unreasonable for a company to dismiss two employees who were earning £25.87 per week each but for whom they had to provide transport costing the company £24 per week each.

(*d*) *Protection of the interest of the business* such as in *R S Components Ltd v Irwin* [*1974*] *1 AER 41* in which the company were held to have fairly dismissed an employee for refusing to sign a reasonable restrictive covenant which was considered necessary.

(*e*) *Expiry of a fixed term contract* when it is shown that the contract was adopted for a genuine purpose and that fact was known to the employee, and it is also shown that the specific purpose for which the contract was adopted has ceased to be applicable. (*North Yorkshire County Council v Fay* [*1986*] *ICR 133*. See also *Terry v East Sussex County Council* [*1976*] *ICR 536*).

(*f*) The imposition of a *sentence of imprisonment*. (*Kingston v British Railways Board* [*1984*] *ICR 781*).

(*g*) *Dismissal of the replacement of an employee suspended on medical grounds.* [*EPCA s 61(2)*]. Where an employer suspends an employee on medical grounds in compliance with a statutory requirement and engages another in his place, he should inform the replacement employee in writing when engaging him that his employment will be terminated at the end of the suspension of the original employee. If he dismisses the replacement employee in order to allow the original employee to resume work, the dismissal will be regarded as having been for a reason falling within *EPCA s 57(1)(b)*.

(*h*) *Dismissal of the replacement of an employee absent due to pregnancy.* [*EPCA s 61(1)*]. Where an employer engages an employee to replace another employee who is absent due to pregnancy and on engaging the replacement employee he informs him in writing that his employment will be terminated on the return to work of the pregnant employee, a dismissal of the replacement employee to give work to the original employee will be considered as a dismissal for a reason falling within *EPCA s 57(1)(b)*.

As usual, dismissal for such a reason will be fair if it was within the 'range of reasonable responses' (see 55.4 above) and a fair procedure was followed.

55.15 DISMISSAL FOLLOWING AN INTERNAL APPEAL

If an employee uses an internal appeal procedure to challenge a decision to dismiss him, and his appeal is rejected, he will be regarded as having been dismissed from the date of his original dismissal, unless his contract provides otherwise (see e.g., *J Sainsbury Ltd v Savage* [*1981*] *ICR 1*, approved in *West Midlands Co-operative Society Ltd v Tipton* [*1986*] *ICR 192*).

The House of Lords in *West Midlands Co-operative Society* decided that the fairness of a dismissal is to be judged at the time of the final decision to dismiss, which, if there is an internal appeal, will be at the conclusion of such an appeal. Lord Bridge said at p 204D:

> 'A dismissal is unfair if the employer unreasonably treats his real reasons as a sufficient reason to dismiss the employee, either when he makes his original decision to dismiss, or when he maintains that decision at the conclusion of an internal appeal.'

In other words, facts and matters that come to light during the appeal hearing, whether in favour of the employee or against him, ought to be taken into account. However, if after an appeal the employer thinks that the employee ought to be dismissed not for the original reason but some completely different reason, the best course is to recommence the disciplinary procedure.

55.16 PRESSURE ON AN EMPLOYER TO DISMISS UNFAIRLY

In determining the reason for a dismissal, or whether it was fair in the circumstances, no account is taken of any pressure which by calling, organising, procuring or financing a strike or other industrial action, or threatening to do so, was exercised on the employer to dismiss the employee. Any question relating to dismissal will be determined as if no such pressure had been exercised. [*EPCA s 63*].

However, a trade union or an individual who induced the employer to dismiss an employee may in certain circumstances be joined in the proceedings and be ordered to pay all or part of any compensation awarded for unfair dismissal. [*EPCA s 76A; EA 1982, s 7*]. (See 56.20 UNFAIR DISMISSAL – III.)

56 Unfair Dismissal – III: Remedies

56.1 When an industrial tribunal finds that a complaint of unfair dismissal is well-founded it may make an order for the reinstatement or re-engagement of the complainant, or an order for compensation. This chapter deals with the remedies for unfair dismissal and the settlement of claims, as follows.

— Reinstatement (see 56.2 below) and re-engagement (see 56.3 below) and related rules (see 56.4-56.5 below).

— Awards of compensation (see 56.6-56.19 below), comprising
  - Basic award (see 56.7-56.8 below).
  - Compensatory award (see 56.10-56.13 below).
  - Maximum awards (see 56.14 below).
  - Additional award in case of non-compliance with order for reinstatement or re-engagement (except union-related cases) (see 56.15 below).
  - Union-related dismissals – special award (see 56 16-56.18 below) and reduction of total award (see 56.19 below).

— Joinder of parties (see 56.20 below).

— Interim relief (see 56.21 below).

— Settlement (see 56.22 below).

In practice, a successful complainant will in most cases receive an award of compensation which is made up of a basic award and a compensatory award. Orders for reinstatement and re-engagement are rare. Other payments are restricted to special circumstances as indicated in the relevant paragraphs.

The tribunal's first step on finding a dismissal to be unfair should be to explain to the employee the possibility of an order for reinstatement or re-engagement, and to ask him whether he wishes such an order to be made. [*EPCA s 68(1)*].

56.2 REINSTATEMENT

An order for reinstatement is defined as *an order that the employer shall treat the complainant in all respects as if he had not been dismissed*. In deciding whether to make such an order, the tribunal must consider

(*a*) whether the complainant wishes to be reinstated;

(*b*) whether it is practicable for an employer to comply with an order for reinstatement; and

(*c*) (in the case where the complainant wholly or partially caused or contributed to the dismissal) whether it would be just to order his reinstatement.

[*EPCA s 69(5)*].

In deciding whether to make an order for reinstatement, the tribunal will consider the effect that such an order would have on the respondent's business. If, as in *Coleman and Stephenson v Magnet Joinery Ltd* [*1974*] *ICR 25*, such an order would inevitably lead to industrial unrest, it should not be made.

If the tribunal orders reinstatement, it must specify

(i) any amount payable by the employer in respect of any benefit which the complainant might reasonably be expected to have received but for the dismissal, including arrears of pay, for the period between the date of termination of employment and the date of reinstatement;

(ii) any rights and privileges, including seniority and pension rights, which must be restored to the employee;

(iii) the date by which the order must be complied with.

[*EPCA s 69(2)*].

Moreover, if the complainant would have benefited from an improvement in his terms and conditions of employment had he not been dismissed, the order for reinstatement will require him to be treated as if he had benefited from that improvement from the date on which he would have done so had he not been dismissed. Thus, if an order for reinstatement is made, the applicant must be restored to his original job and receive back pay and benefits from the date of his dismissal.

56.3 RE-ENGAGEMENT

An order for re-engagement is defined as *an order that the complainant be engaged by the employer*, or by a successor of the employer or by an associated employer, *in employment comparable to that from which he was dismissed or other suitable employment* (i.e. not in the same job). [*EPCA s 69(4)*].

In deciding whether to order re-engagement the tribunal will take into consideration the same factors as for reinstatement above. The tribunal must specify the terms on which re-engagement will take place and, unless it considers that the complainant contributed to the dismissal, the terms of the re-engagement must be, as far as is reasonably practicable, as favourable as if reinstatement had been ordered. [*EPCA s 69(6)*].

In particular the tribunal will specify

(*a*) the identity of the employer;

(*b*) the nature of the employment;

(*c*) the remuneration for the employment;

(*d*) any amount payable by the employer in respect of any benefit which the complainant might reasonably be expected to have received but for the dismissal, including arrears of pay, for the period between the date of termination of employment and the date of re-engagement;

(*e*) any rights and privileges including seniority and pension rights which must be restored;

(*f*) the date by which the order must be complied with.

[*EPCA s 69(4)*].

56.4 GENERAL RULES ON REINSTATEMENT AND RE-ENGAGEMENT

For the purpose of deciding whether it is practicable to make an order for reinstatement or re-engagement, the tribunal will not take into account the fact that the employer has engaged a permanent replacement for the dismissed employee unless he can show *either* that it was not practicable for him to arrange for the dismissed employee's work to be done without engaging a permanent replacement, *or* that he engaged the replacement after the lapse of a reasonable period of time, without having heard from the dismissed employee that he wished to be reinstated or re-engaged, and that when the employer engaged the replacement it was no longer reasonable for him to arrange for the dismissed employee's work to be done except by a permanent replacement. [*EPCA s 70(1)*].

The continuity of employment of the employee is preserved, and any week falling between the effective date of termination and his re-employment counts towards his period of continuous employment. [*EPCA 13 Sch 20(1)(a); Labour Relations (Continuity of Employment) Regulations 1976 (SI 1976 No 660)*].

In calculating the amount payable on account of arrears of pay and benefits, the tribunal will take into account, so as to reduce the employer's liability, any sums received by the complainant in respect of the period between the date of termination of employment and the date of reinstatement or re-engagement by way of

(*a*) wages in lieu of notice or ex gratia payments paid by the employer;

(*b*) remuneration paid in respect of employment with another employer;

and such other benefits as the tribunal thinks appropriate in the circumstances. [*EPCA s 70(2)*].

If an order for reinstatement or re-engagement is made but the terms of the order are not fully complied with, the tribunal will make an award of compensation of such an amount as it thinks fit having regard to the loss sustained by the complainant as a result of the employer's failure to comply with the particular terms in question. [*EPCA s 71(1)*].

56.5 REFUSAL TO REINSTATE OR RE-ENGAGE

If an order for reinstatement or re-engagement is made but the employer refuses to comply with it, the tribunal will award the complainant additional compensation over and above the basic and compensatory awards (see 56.15 below), unless the employer can satisfy the tribunal that it was not practicable to comply with the order. [*EPCA s 71(2)*]. (See *Freemans plc v Flynn* [*1984*] *ICR 874*.) For the purpose of deciding whether it was practicable for the employer to comply with the order, the tribunal will not take into account the fact that he has engaged a permanent replacement unless the employer can show that it was not practicable for the dismissed employee's work to be done without engaging a permanent replacement. [*EPCA s 71(4)*]. Where the employee has indicated in his originating application that he will seek such an order, the employer must come ready with evidence as to the availability of the old job or comparable or suitable employment, or else bear the costs of any adjournment. [*Industrial Tribunals (Rules of Procedure) Regulations 1985 (SI 1985 No 16), 1 Sch 11(3)*].

The employee will usually want compensation to be awarded under *s 71* where compliance with the order is refused, but that may sometimes be less favourable to him than the initial financial award which accompanied the order (see 56.2, 56.3 above). The suggestion that he has the option simply to enforce that award (*Conoco (UK) Ltd v Neal* [*1989*] *ICR 114*) has since been rejected by the Court of Appeal in another, unreported case.

In practice, the employee rarely desires reinstatement or re-engagement and, even if he does, it is rarely ordered. If no such order is made, the amount of compensation will be calculated as set out below.

56.6 COMPENSATION

When a tribunal makes an award of compensation for unfair dismissal the award must consist of a *basic award* and a *compensatory award*. [*EPCA s 72*]. These awards are the most common and are often the only categories of award. They are considered first (see 56.7-56.13 below). There are statutory maxima for nearly all the awards and these are set out for reference in 56.14 below.

Some awards are made only in certain circumstances: these are the 'additional award' where there has been non-compliance with an order for reinstatement or re-engagement (see 56.15 below), and, in similar circumstances for union-related dismissals only, the 'special award' (see 56.16-56.18 below).

Recoupment provisions. Where the applicant has received statutory benefits, the respondent will be ordered to pay part of the compensation awarded not to the applicant but to the authority which paid the benefit, so that it recovers the money paid. This procedure, known as 'recoupment', is initiated by the service on the respondent of a 'recoupment notice' issued pursuant to the *Employment Protection (Recoupment of Unemployment Benefit) Regulations 1977 (SI 1977 No 674),* as amended by *SI 1980 No 1608*. It does not apply where a sum is paid by way of settlement of a dispute, before or after a finding of unfair dismissal is made.

56.7 BASIC AWARD

Amount

The calculation of the basic award is in principle similar to the calculation of a redundancy payment. It depends upon basic weekly pay, length of service and age. The maximum amount of a week's pay for the purpose of the calculation is £172 and the maximum number of years to be taken into account is 20. [*EPCA s 73(4) and 14 Sch 8(1)(b); Employment Protection (Variation of Limits) Order 1989 (SI 1989 No 526)*]. For dismissals before 1 April 1989 the maximum amount of a week's pay for these purposes was £164 (*SI 1988 No 276*). A week's pay is calculated in accordance with *EPCA 14 Sch* and is based on gross pay. (See 'A WEEK'S PAY' (58).) Subject to the exceptions set out below, the amount of the basic award is calculated by reference to the period, ending with the effective date of termination, during which the employee was continuously employed, by starting at the end of that period and reckoning backwards the number of complete years of employment falling within that period and allowing

(*a*) one and a half week's pay for each year of employment in which the employee was not below the age of 41;

(*b*) one week's pay for each year of employment not falling within (*a*) in which the employee was not below the age of 22;

(*c*) half a week's pay for each such year of employment not falling within either (*a*) or (*b*).

[*EPCA s 73(3); EA 1980, s 9; EA 1982, 2 Sch 5(2)*]. (See the table at the end of REDUNDANCY – I (38) (but note that in the case of redundancy payments employment prior to the 18th birthday is not counted).)

Where an employer is obliged but fails to give the statutory minimum period of notice, the effective date of termination for the purposes of calculating the basic award is taken as that upon which the notice would have expired had it been given. [*EPCA s 55(5)*]. Similarly, if the employee is constructively dismissed, and the employer has not given notice, the effective date of termination for the purposes of calculating the basic award is taken as that upon which the statutory minimum period of notice would have expired had it been given by the employer. [*EPCA s 55(6); EA 1982, 3 Sch 1*].

The basic award for employees nearing the age of 65 is reduced as follows: for every month by which the employee exceeds the age of 64, the total amount payable is reduced by 1/12. For example, an employee dismissed in the final month before his 65th birthday, would have the basic award reduced by 11/12. [*EPCA s 73(5)(6)* as amended by *SDA 1986, s 3(2)*].

Where an employee is dismissed both by the transferor and then (after being re-engaged) again by the transferee of a business, the transferee may be liable to pay two basic awards because of the provisions of the *Transfer of Undertakings (Protection of Employment Regulations) 1981. (Fenton v Stablegold (t/a Chiswick Court Hotel)* [*1986*] *ICR 236*). (See also TRANSFER OF UNDERTAKINGS (53).)

56.8 Exceptions

The amount of the basic award is *two weeks' pay* where the tribunal finds that the reason or the principal reason for the dismissal of the employee was that he was redundant and that

(*a*) he unreasonably refused or left suitable alternative employment; or

(*b*) his employment was renewed or he was re-engaged and he was therefore not considered dismissed under *EPCA s 84(1)*.

[*EPCA s 73(2)*].

The above provision has the curious effect that an employee is entitled to a basic award of compensation notwithstanding the fact that he is not considered as dismissed for the purposes of claiming a redundancy payment.

Where the dismissal is to be regarded as unfair by virtue of *EPCA s 58* or *s 59(a)* (i.e. for a 'union-related' reason) the amount of the basic award (before any reduction) will be not less than £2,520. [*EPCA s 73(4A); EA 1982, s 4(1); Unfair Dismissal (Increase of Limits of Basic and Special Awards) Order 1989 (SI 1989 No 528)*]. For dismissals between 1 April 1988 and 31 March 1989, the minimum award was £2,400.

56.9 Reduction of basic award

Where the tribunal considers that any conduct of the complainant before the dismissal (or, where the dismissal was with notice, before the notice was given) was such that it would be just and equitable to reduce or further reduce the amount of the basic award to any extent, the tribunal will so reduce the award. [*EPCA s 73(7B); EA 1980, s 9(4)*]. See also 56.13 below.

The amount of the basic award will not be reduced where the reason or principal reason for the dismissal was that the employee was redundant, unless the dismissal is to be regarded as unfair by virtue of *Sec 59(a)* (selection for redundancy for a 'union-related' reason) and in that event the reduction will apply only to so much of the basic award as is payable because of *Sec 73(4A)* (see 56.8 above). [*EPCA s 73(7C); EA 1982, s 4(2)*].

Where the tribunal finds that the complainant has unreasonably refused an offer by the employer which if accepted would have the effect of reinstating the complainant in his employment in all respects as if he had not been dismissed, the tribunal will reduce or further reduce the amount of the basic award to such extent as it considers just and equitable having regard to that finding. [*EPCA s 73(7A); EA 1980, s 9(4)*].

The amount of the basic award will be reduced, or, as the case may be, further reduced, by the amount of any redundancy payment awarded by the tribunal in respect of the same dismissal or of any payment made by the employer to the employee on the ground that the dismissal was by reason of redundancy, whether in pursuance of statutory provisions or otherwise. [*EPCA s 73(9)*].

Note that, where an employee had received an ex gratia payment from his former employers which included his statutory entitlement and which was sufficient to cover any basic or compensatory award, the EAT held that an industrial tribunal was not obliged to make a basic award. (*Chelsea Football & Athletic Co Ltd v Heath [1981] ICR 323*).

See also 56.19 below for reduction in union-related cases.

56.10 COMPENSATORY AWARD

The maximum amount of the compensatory award is now £8,925. [*Unfair Dismissal (Increase of Compensation Limit) Order 1989 (SI 1989 No 527)*]. (For dismissals before 1 April 1989, the limit was £8,500 (*SI 1986 No 2284*).) This limit is the last step in the calculation, applied after assessing the amount of loss and after taking into account any payments made by the respondent to the applicant and after any reduction required by any statute or rule of law. [*EPCA s 75(3)*]. Thus, an industrial tribunal must first deduct an ex gratia payment and then apply the statutory maximum. (*McCarthy v British Insulated Callenders Cables plc [1985] IRLR 94*).

For example, if an applicant's loss was assessed at £14,000 and the tribunal found that he was 50% to blame for the dismissal he would be awarded £14,000 *less* £7,000 (50% to blame), and not 50% of the statutory maximum.

However, it is not clear whether payments made by the employer should be deducted before or after deductions for contributory fault. See *Clement-Clarke International Ltd v Manley [1979] ICR 74* and *Parker and Farr Ltd v Shelvey [1979] ICR 896*.

56.11 Amount

The amount of compensation is such amount as the tribunal considers just and equitable in all the circumstances, having regard to the loss sustained by the complainant in consequence of the dismissal insofar as that loss is attributable to action taken by the employer. [*EPCA s 74(1)*].

The loss shall be taken to include

(*a*) any expenses reasonably incurred by the complainant in consequence of the dismissal; and

(*b*) loss of any benefit save for the contingent right to a redundancy payment which he might reasonably be expected to have had but for the dismissal.

[*EPCA s 74(2)(3)*].

56.12 **Assessment of compensatory award**

Since the decision in *Norton Tool Co Ltd v Tewson* [*1972*] *ICR 501*, the tribunal has a duty to show how compensation is made up. The most common heads of compensation are those set out below. Whereas the basic award is based upon *gross* pay, the compensatory award depends upon the *net* value of wages and other benefits.

Immediate loss of wages. This is the sum of the loss of wages from the date of termination until the date of the hearing. Account will be taken of wages paid in lieu of notice and earnings in other employments (see also 56.13 below).

Future loss of earnings. If the applicant is unemployed at the time of the hearing or is in less remunerative employment than that from which he was dismissed, he will be awarded a sum for future loss of earnings. The award will be based upon the applicant's net loss of earnings for such period as the tribunal considers reasonable, bearing in mind such matters as the length of time he may be unemployed. Compensation must be assessed on the basis of what has actually occurred by the time of the hearing rather than what might have been expected to occur at the time of the dismissal. (*Gilham v Kent County Council (No 3)* [*1986*] *ICR 52*). No allowance is made for statutory benefits receivable.

The award will take into account any increase in salary or any other benefit the applicant would have enjoyed had he not been dismissed. It will take account not only of regular wage or salary payments but also, for example, commission or bonus payments.

Loss of use of a company car. If the employee had the use of a company car not only for the purposes of his employment but also for private use, he will be compensated for the loss of that benefit. The tribunal will take into account whether or not the employer paid for the petrol for private motoring. The incidence of tax will be taken into account as it is in the assessment of loss of all benefits in kind. In assessing the value of a car, petrol and running costs, reference is sometimes made to annual estimates published by the AA. (*Shove v Downs Surgical plc* [*1984*] *ICR 532*).

Loss of benefits in kind. In assessing compensation, the tribunal will take into account other benefits in kind such as free accommodation, medical insurance and subsidised meals. It may do so even where there was no strict contractual entitlement to such benefits.

Pension rights. If the complainant was a member of a pension scheme which is transferable and has obtained employment in a company which operates a similar scheme, the pension should be transferred to avoid loss under this head of compensation. If the pension scheme is non-transferable, or if the applicant has failed to obtain new employment or has found a job where the employer contributes less to his pension than did the respondent, the task of assessing compensation for loss of pension rights is a hard one. One view was set out in detail by Sir John Donaldson in *Copson v Eversure Accessories Ltd* [*1974*] *ICR 636*. Another calculation was made by Lord Thompson in *Scottish Co-operative Wholesale Society Ltd v Lloyd* [*1973*] *ICR 137*. Since its publication, an approach in all but the simplest cases may be to follow the Government Actuary's guidelines for calculating loss of pension rights. ('A suggested method for assessing loss of pension rights under an occupational pension scheme following a finding of unfair dismissal by an industrial tribunal': Government Actuary's Department.) The guidelines must be applied with caution taking into account the possibility of obtaining pensionable employment. (*Manpower Ltd v Hearne*

[1983] ICR 567; Tradewinds Airways Ltd v Fletcher [1981] IRLR 272; see also *Willmont Bros Ltd v Oliver [1979] ICR 378*). Further guidance was given by the EAT in *Mono Pumps Ltd v Froggatt and Radford [1987] IRLR 368*. However, it is thought that an alternative approach may be for the tribunal to assess the period for which the employee should be compensated for loss of pension rights, and to make an award based upon the cost of purchasing a policy to make up the difference between the pension which he will receive and the amount he would have received had he remained in employment until the end of the period.

Loss of statutory rights. The tribunal will assess a nominal figure for loss of protection from unfair dismissal for the first two years (the period for acquiring unfair dismissal protection) of any new employment. The appropriate figure will normally be £100 (*S H Muffett Ltd v Head [1987] ICR 1*).

It will also award compensation for loss of the accrued right to the statutory minimum period of notice. The loss was assessed in *Daley v A E Dorsett (Almar Dolls) Ltd [1982] ICR 1* as half the wages due during that period, but it is thought that this may be too high in the ordinary case. See also *Arthur Guinness Son & Co (Great Britain) Ltd v Green [1989] ICR 241*.

56.13 Factors reducing the award

Contributory fault. Where the tribunal finds that the dismissal was to any extent caused or contributed to by any action of the complainant, it will reduce the amount of the compensatory award by such proportion as it considers just and equitable having regard to that finding. [*EPCA s 74(6)*]. The same percentage deduction will usually apply to both basic and compensatory award.

If, therefore, an employee was guilty of misconduct which was grave, but did not justify dismissal, or if the procedures used to dismiss him were unfair, but his own conduct to a certain extent contributed to his misfortune, the amount of compensation may be reduced. The reduction may be as much as 100% in an appropriate case. (*W Devis & Sons Ltd v Atkins [1977] ICR 662*). See also 56.19 below for reduction in union-related cases.

In order for a deduction for contributory fault to be made for the employee's misconduct, that conduct must be culpable or blameworthy in the sense that, whether or not it amounted to a breach of contract or tort, it was foolish or perverse or unreasonable in the circumstances. (*Nelson v British Broadcasting Corporation (No 2) [1980] ICR 110*). However, a deduction from an award may also be made for lack of capability. (*Finnie v Top Hat Frozen Foods Ltd [1985] ICR 433*). In *Courtaulds Spinning Ltd v Moosa [1984] ICR 218*, the EAT held that the taking of industrial action should not be characterised as contributory fault meriting a reduction in the amount of compensation.

Whether the unfairness made any difference. It was formerly thought that, if the employee would have been dismissed even if the employer had done all that he ought to have done, the dismissal ought not to be regarded as unfair. That approach was held to be wrong in *Polkey v A E Dayton Services Ltd [1988] ICR 142* (see 55.4 UNFAIR DISMISSAL – II), but to ask what would have happened if the employer had acted fairly is still relevant to compensation. For example, if the company shut down and all the employees were made redundant a few weeks after the applicant was unfairly dismissed, his compensatory award ought not to run beyond that date. Again, it may be that the tribunal considers that an employee dismissed for misconduct without a hearing could not in fact have said anything effective in his own defence, or that an employee dismissed without warning for lack of capability was not capable of improvement in any event.

The tribunal ought to assess the chances that a fair dismissal would have occurred and to apply a percentage deduction from the total loss accordingly (*Polkey*, above). It ought also to consider *when* that dismissal would have taken place, e.g. even if it is certain that a fair procedure would have led to the same result, it may be that its adoption would have prolonged the period of earning for a number of weeks (see *Mining Supplies (Longwall) Ltd v Baker [1988] ICR 676*). The tribunal may take account of the fact that an employee with a short period of service is more at risk of being selected for redundancy if job losses occur. (*Morris v Acco Co Ltd [1985] ICR 306*).

In a different context it has been suggested that it ought not to be assumed too readily that a failure to observe the principles of natural justice made no difference to the result. (*John v Rees [1970] Ch 345* at *p 402*).

The fact that the employer *could* have dismissed fairly on some other ground is irrelevant if he would not in fact have done so. (*Trico-Folberth Ltd v Devonshire [1989] IRLR 396*).

Mitigation of loss. The employee is under a duty to mitigate his loss. He must show that he has made active attempts to seek alternative employment. What employment he will be under a duty to accept is a matter to be determined by the tribunal. He must be realistic in his job expectations. He may not demand a salary or status higher than that which he previously enjoyed, and may have to accept some reduction. If the employee has not made reasonable efforts to find other work, his compensation will be reduced to reflect the tribunal's view of what would have happened if he *had* mitigated his loss.

Where an unfairly dismissed employee had unreasonably refused an employer's offer of reinstatement, he was rightly held only to be entitled to a basic award. (*Sweetlove v Redbridge and Waltham Forest Area Health Authority [1979] ICR 477*).

By failing to exercise a right of appeal, an employee may be held not to have mitigated his loss. (*Hoover Ltd v Forde [1980] ICR 239*). However this approach was not followed by the EAT in Scotland. (*William Muir (Bond 9) Ltd v Lamb [1985] IRLR 95*). There is no duty to mitigate until the dismissal has actually taken place. The employee's acts and omissions prior to dismissal will cause the award to be reduced either on the ground of contributory fault or not at all.

In *Daley v A E Dorsett (Almar Dolls) Ltd [1982] ICR 1*, the EAT did not interfere with an industrial tribunal's findings that an employee's decision not to accept full-time employment at a rate of earnings less than the amount of unemployment benefit was reasonable. It stressed, however, that industrial tribunals should be very slow indeed in finding reasonable a decision of a dismissed employee not to accept subsequent employment because he would be receiving less than unemployment benefit.

Expenses incurred in seeking to mitigate the loss suffered (e.g. the cost of travelling to job interviews) are recoverable as part of the compensatory award. That could include the cost of starting up a business of the employee's own, if that was a reasonable thing to do (see *Gardiner-Hill v Roland Berger Technics Ltd [1982] IRLR 498*). Legal expenses incurred in pursuing the unfair dismissal claim are not recoverable (for the award of costs see 27.22 INDUSTRIAL TRIBUNALS).

Payments made by the employer. Payments made by the applicant's former employer, whether under a contractual liability or *ex-gratia*, will generally be taken into account.

The applicant must give credit for pay in lieu of notice and other benefits received from the old employer during the notice period. (*Addison v Babcock FATA Ltd* [*1987*] *ICR 805*). He normally need not give credit for earnings from any new employment during the notice period, but this principle does not extend to cases where the notice period is very lengthy. (*Isleworth Studios Ltd v Rickard* [*1988*] *ICR 432*). Unemployment benefit received will not be taken into account (but see 56.6 above for the rules on recoupment).

56.14 MAXIMUM AWARDS

The maximum basic award is 20 × 1½ × £172 = £5,160 for dismissals on or after 1 April 1989. (For dismissals between 1 April 1988 and 31 March 1989, 20 × 1½ × £164 = £4,920.)

The maximum compensatory award is £8,925 for dismissals on or after 1 April 1989 (previously £8,500).

The maximum additional award which may be made in respect of non-compliance with an order is £4,472, or £8,944 in cases of race or sex discrimination (see 56.15 below).

The maximum special award in union-related cases is £25,040 (see 56.16-56.18 below).

[*Unfair Dismissal (Increase of Compensation Limit) Order 1989 (SI 1989 No 527); Employment Protection (Variation of Limits) Order 1989 (SI 1989 No 526); Unfair Dismissal (Increase of Limits of Basic and Special Awards) Order 1989 (SI 1989 No 528)*].

56.15 ADDITIONAL AWARD — NON-COMPLIANCE WITH AN ORDER

Additional compensation in cases where an order for reinstatement or re-engagement is made but not complied with (see 56.5 above) is calculated as follows (except union-related cases, see 56.16 below)

(*a*) if the dismissal is unfair by virtue of either the *Race Relations Act 1976* or the *Sex Discrimination Act 1975*, the amount of additional compensation will be not less than 26 or more than 52 weeks' pay;

(*b*) in any other case, the additional compensation will be not less than 13 or more than 26 weeks' pay.

[*EPCA s 71(2)(3); EA 1982, 4 Sch*].

The tribunal may not simply make the maximum award in order to force compliance with its order. It must consider factors such as the employer's conduct and the extent to which the compensatory award has met the actual loss suffered. (*Morganite Electrical Carbon Ltd v Donne* [*1988*] *ICR 18*).

The amount of a week's pay for the purpose of calculating an additional award will not exceed £172. [*EPCA 14 Sch 8(1)(a); Employment Protection (Variation of Limits) Order 1989 (SI 1989 No 526)*]. The maximum award in cases under (*a*) is therefore £8,944, and £4,472 under (*b*).

56.16 SPECIAL AWARD — 'UNION-RELATED' CASES

The *Employment Act 1982* introduced new provisions for a *special award* to be made to employees whose dismissals are to be regarded as unfair by reason of

EPCA s 58 or *s 59(a)*, namely where the reason for dismissal was that the employee

(*a*) was, or proposed to become, a member of an independent trade union; or

(*b*) had taken part, or proposed to take part, at any appropriate time in the activities of an independent trade union; or

(*c*) was not a member of any trade union, or of a particular trade union, or of one of a number of particular trade unions, or had refused or proposed to refuse to become or remain a member; or

(*d*) was selected for redundancy for a reason falling within (*a*) to (*c*) above.

[*EPCA s 72(c); EA 1982, s 5(2)*].

The special award is made only if the complainant requests the tribunal to make an order for reinstatement or re-engagement and such an order is either not made or not complied with. It is not made if the principal reason for the dismissal is redundancy and the complainant has unreasonably refused an offer of suitable alternative employment or if his contract has been renewed or he has been re-engaged.

56.17 Amount

The amount of the special award is

(*a*) one week's pay multiplied by 104; or

(*b*) £12,550

whichever is the greater, but it will not exceed £25,040. [*EPCA s 75A(1); EA 1982, s 5(3); Unfair Dismissal (Increase of Limits of Basic and Special Awards) Order 1989 (SI 1989 No 528)*].

If the tribunal makes an order for reinstatement or re-engagement which is not complied with, then unless the employer satisfies the tribunal that it was not practicable to comply with the order, the amount of the special award will be increased to

(*a*) one week's pay multiplied by 156; or

(*b*) £18,795

whichever is the greater. [*EPCA s 75A(2); EA 1982, s 5(3); SI 1989 No 528*].

The Secretary of State may by order increase the financial limits for the special award. [*EPCA s 75A(7); EA 1982, s 5(3)*].

The fact that an employer has engaged a permanent replacement for the complainant will not be taken into account in determining whether it was practicable to comply with an order for reinstatement or re-engagement, unless the employer shows that it was not practicable for him to arrange for the complainant's work to be done without engaging a permanent replacement.

Where the dismissal takes effect after the age of 64 the amount of the special award is reduced by 1/12 for every month by which the employee's age exceeds 64 (cf 56.7 above). [*EPCA s 75A(3); EA 1982, s 5(3); SDA 1986, s 3(2)(3)*].

56.18 Reduction of special award

Where the tribunal considers that any conduct of the complainant before the dismissal (or, where the dismissal was with notice, before the notice was given) was such that it would be just and equitable to reduce or further reduce the amount of the special award to any extent, the tribunal will reduce or further reduce that amount accordingly. [*EPCA s 75A(4); EA 1982, s 5(3)*].

Where the tribunal finds that the complainant has unreasonably

(*a*) prevented an order for reinstatement or re-engagement from being complied with; or

(*b*) refused an offer by the employer (not made in compliance with a tribunal order) which if accepted would have the effect of reinstating the complainant in his employment in all respects as if he had not been dismissed,

the tribunal will reduce or further reduce the amount of the special award to such extent as it considers just and equitable having regard to that finding. [*EPCA s 75A(5); EA 1982, s 5(3)*].

56.19 REDUCTION OF AWARD — 'UNION-RELATED' CASES

Where an award of compensation is made in respect of a dismissal which is to be regarded as unfair by virtue of *EPCA s 58* or *s 59(a)* a tribunal, in considering whether it would be just and equitable to reduce or further reduce the amount of *any part* of the award, will disregard any conduct or action which constitutes

(*a*) a breach or proposed breach of a requirement that the complainant should

(i) be or become a member; or

(ii) cease to be or refrain from becoming a member; or

(iii) not take part in the activities

of any trade union or a particular trade union or one of a number of particular trade unions;

(*b*) a refusal or proposed refusal to comply with a requirement to make a payment or payments in the event of his failure to become or his ceasing to remain a member of any trade union or of a particular trade union or of one of a number of particular trade unions; or

(*c*) an objection or proposed objection (however expressed) to the operation of a provision for the deduction of such a sum or sums from his remuneration.

[*EPCA s 72A; EA 1982, s 6*].

56.20 JOINDER OF THIRD PARTIES

If, in any proceedings before an industrial tribunal on a complaint of unfair dismissal, either the employer or the complainant claims

(*a*) that the employer was induced to dismiss the complainant by the actual or threatened calling, organising, procuring or financing of a strike or other industrial action and

(*b*) that such pressure was exercised because the complainant was not a member of any trade union or of a particular trade union or of one of a number of particular trade unions, the employer or the complainant may request the tribunal to direct that the person whom he claims exercised the pressure, be joined as a party to the proceedings. [*EPCA s 76A(1); EA 1982, s 7*].

A tribunal must grant such a request if it is made before the hearing of the complaint begins, but it may be refused if it is made after that time. The tribunal will refuse such a request if it is made after the tribunal has made an award of compensation.

If the tribunal makes an award of compensation and considers that the complaint of pressure is well-founded, it may make an order that the third party (joined according to the procedure outlined above) pay all or such part of the award as the tribunal may consider just and equitable in the circumstances. [*EPCA s 76A(3); EA 1982, s 7*].

56.21 INTERIM RELIEF IN RESPECT OF CERTAIN DISMISSALS

An employee who complains that he has been dismissed for

(*a*) being or proposing to become a member of an independent trade union; or

(*b*) taking part or proposing to take part in the activities of an independent trade union at an appropriate time; or

(*c*) not being a member of any trade union, or of a particular trade union, or of one of a number of particular trade unions, or refusing or proposing to refuse to become or remain a member,

may apply to an industrial tribunal for an order for interim relief. [*EPCA s 77(1); EA 1982, s 8*].

An order for interim relief may be made pending a substantive hearing where the tribunal considers that the complainant will succeed. The order is either for reinstatement or re-engagement, or for continuation of the terms of the contract.

An application for interim relief will only be entertained if it is presented to the tribunal within seven days following the effective date of termination and (where the complainant relies on (*a*) or (*b*) above) if there is also presented within that time a certificate from an authorised official of the union that the complainant was, or proposed to become, a member of the union and that there are good grounds for supposing that the reason or principal reason for the dismissal was one alleged in the complaint. [*EPCA s 77(2)*]. The tribunal should deal with the interim application as soon as possible. Both parties may be present at the hearing, the employer having had at least seven days' notice of the application. A party who has been joined to the proceedings in accordance with a request made under *EPCA s 76A* made at least three days before the hearing (see 56.20 above), must have as much notice as is reasonably practicable. [*EPCA s 77(3); EA 1982, s 8(2)*]. The hearing may only be postponed in special circumstances. [*EPCA s 77(3)(4); EA 1982, s 8(2)*].

If the tribunal considers that there are good grounds for considering that the complaint is well-founded, it will ask the employer, if he is present, whether he is willing to reinstate or re-engage the complainant pending the full hearing or settlement of the matter. If the employer states that he is willing to reinstate the employee, the tribunal will make an order to that effect.

If the employer states that he is willing to re-engage the employee in another job and specifies the terms and conditions on which he is willing to do so, the tribunal will ask the employee whether he is willing to accept the job on those terms and conditions, and

(*a*) if he is willing, make an order to that effect; and

(*b*) if he is unwilling to accept the job on those terms and conditions, then if the tribunal is of the opinion that the refusal is reasonable, it will make an order for the *continuation* of his contract of employment (a 'continuation order').

If the employer has failed to attend the hearing before the tribunal or states that he is unwilling either to reinstate the employee or re-engage him, the tribunal will make a continuation order. [*EPCA s 77(7)(8)(9)*].

A continuation order is an order that, until the complaint has been dealt with, the employee's contract will be treated as continuing for the purposes of his entitlement to benefits including pay and for the purposes of determining the length and continuity of his employment. If an employer fails to comply with a continuation order, compensation for such non-compliance may also be awarded if the complainant has thereby suffered loss, and the employer will be ordered to pay any amount of wages due under the continuation order. [*EPCA s 79(3)*].

At any time between the making of an order by an industrial tribunal under these interim provisions and the determination or settlement of the complaint to which it relates, the employer or the employee may apply to the tribunal for the revocation of the order on the ground of a relevant change of circumstances which has occurred since the making of the order. [*EPCA s 79(1)*].

56.22 SETTLEMENT

Employers may wish to settle a claim or a potential claim for unfair dismissal rather than proceed to a hearing (see INDUSTRIAL TRIBUNALS (27)). If this is done, a conciliation officer must take action for any agreement reached with the employee to be binding. [*EPCA s 140(2)(d), (e)*]. (See e.g. *Hennessy v Craigmyle and Co Ltd* [*1986*] *ICR 461*.) If this is not done an employee will be free to bring a claim notwithstanding that he has received a sum in settlement. Although this amount may be taken into account in assessing compensation (as in the example at 56.10 above), nevertheless it may not be sufficient to extinguish the employer's liability. If a compromise is reached after a tribunal has held a dismissal to be unfair but before making an award of compensation, a conciliation officer must be called upon to act in order for the agreement to be binding (see *Courage Take Home Trade Ltd v Keys* [*1986*] *ICR 874*). It was also held in *Courage* that where a settlement was fairly reached, but was not binding because of *EPCA s 140*, it might well not be 'just and equitable' to award any further compensation.

The settlement agreement should be recorded in writing, preferably on a form supplied by the conciliation officer. (*Duport Furniture Products Ltd v Moore and Advisory, Conciliation and Arbitration Service* [*1982*] *ICR 84*). (See 2.4 ADVISORY, CONCILIATION AND ARBITRATION SERVICE.)

56.23 ENFORCEMENT

Normally an employer who is ordered to pay compensation for unfair dismissal will do so promptly. If he does not, the employee must first apply to the county court for an order of execution. [*EPCA 9 Sch 7(1); County Court Rules 0.25 r 12*]. All the usual means of enforcement of a county court judgment will then become available, including execution against goods, winding-up and the garnisheeing of bank accounts. [*County Courts Act 1984, Parts V, VI*].

At present there is no power to award interest on industrial tribunal awards (see 27.21 INDUSTRIAL TRIBUNALS for proposed changes). But if the employer asks the county court to stay execution on an award pending an appeal, the employee should ask for that only to be done on terms that meanwhile the money is paid into an interest-bearing account.

57 Wages Councils

57.1 Wages Councils have regulated terms and conditions of employment for workers in certain industries by issuing orders. Substantial changes in their powers were effected by the *Wages Act 1986* (*WA*) which repealed the *Wages Councils Act 1979*. There are at present some two dozen wages councils whose orders affect around one tenth of the workforce, principally those engaged in retailing, catering and clothing manufacture. They consist of workers' and employers' representatives and independent members appointed by the Secretary of State. At the end of 1988 the Government published a consultation paper which suggested that wages councils should be abolished. Although no final decision had been announced at the time of writing, abolition was thought to be the most likely outcome.

57.2 WAGES COUNCILS

The *WA* provides for the abolition or variation of the scope of operation of wages councils by the Secretary of State. [*WA s 13*]. However, it does not give the Secretary of State power to set up new wages councils. Under the *WA*, wages councils make orders fixing

(*a*) basic rates of pay;

(*b*) overtime rates;

(*c*) amounts deductible for living accommodation.

[*WA ss 14, 15*].

Before making an order fixing minimum rates of remuneration, wages councils are now statutorily obliged to have regard to

(i) the effect that that rate will have on the level of employment among the workers to whom it will apply, and in particular in those areas where the remuneration received by such workers is generally less than the national average for such workers; and

(ii) such other matters as appear to it to be appropriate.

[*WA s 14(6)*].

Wages Councils now have no power to make orders affecting workers under the age of 21. [*WA s 12(3)*].

57.3 TRANSITIONAL PROVISIONS

Wages councils in existence on 25 July 1986 (the date of enactment of *WA*) continue to operate, although only in relation to workers aged 21 or more. However, orders previously made by them have all by now ceased to have effect, on the issue of a new order or otherwise [*WA s 24(2)*].

57.4 EFFECT OF WAGES ORDERS

If the contract of a worker, to whom a wages order applies, provides for the payment of less remuneration than the statutory minimum remuneration provided for him by the order, the contract has effect as if it instead provided for the payment of the statutory minimum remuneration. [*WA s 16(1)*]. Therefore, if a worker is being paid less than his entitlement under a wages order, he can pursue a claim in the county court or the High Court against his employer for breach of contract and for a declaration as to his entitlement. Further, if the employee is unfairly dismissed or is entitled to maternity pay, compensation will be calculated as if he or she had been paid the statutory minimum remuneration (*Cooner v PS Doal & Sons [1988] ICR 495*; see also 58.6 'A WEEK'S PAY').

In addition, an employer who fails to pay any worker of his, to whom a wages order made pursuant to *WA s 14* applies, a sum equal to or exceeding his entitlement under the order is guilty of an offence and liable on conviction in a magistrates' court to a fine. [*WA s 16(2)*].

57.5 COMPUTATION OF REMUNERATION

The *Wages Act 1986, s 11* replaced the restrictions on the payment of wages contained in the *Truck Acts* and the *Payment of Wages Act 1960*. Pursuant to *WA* the method of payment is to be determined by the contract. For the purpose of computing whether an employer is complying with a wages order in any week, there are added together

(*a*) the total amount of any money payments made by the employer to the worker on or before the relevant pay day, by way of remuneration in respect of time worked by him in that week, plus

(*b*) the total amount of deductions made by the employer from these money payments (such as deduction of tax) apart from

- (i) any deduction in respect of the worker's necessary expenditure in connection with his employment to the extent that the deduction is attributable to the week in question;
- (ii) any deduction in respect of the provision of living accommodation for the worker by the employer to the extent that the deduction exceeds any limit for the time being in force in relation to the worker by virtue of *Sec 14(1)(c)*, and
- (iii) with certain exceptions set out in *WA s 17(4)*, any other deduction made by the employer for his own use and benefit, less

(*c*) the worker's necessary expenditure in connection with his employment to the extent that such expenditure consists of payments to persons other than the employer, is attributable to that week and is not met, or designed to be met, by an allowance paid to him by the employer, and

(*d*) the total of any payments received from the worker by the employer falling within (*b*)(i) – (iii) above. [*WA s 17*].

57.6 ENFORCEMENT

Employers are obliged to keep records of payments and deductions for three years. [*WA s 19(1)*]. They are also obliged to post, in a way prescribed by the Secretary of State, notices informing workers of any wages order in force which affects them, and any proposal to make such an order. [*WA s 19(2)*; *Wages Councils (Notices) (No 2) Regulations 1987 (SI 1987 No 1852), Reg 6*].

An employer who fails to comply with these requirements is guilty of a criminal offence and is liable on conviction in a magistrates' court to a fine. [*WA s 19(4)*].

57.7 Wages Councils

The Secretary of State may appoint officers with wide powers, including power of inspection, to enforce the provisions relating to wages orders. Any person who knowingly makes a false record, or intentionally obstructs an officer or fails to comply with a requirement made by an officer in exercising his duties or who knowingly or recklessly makes a false statement, is guilty of an offence. [*WA s 20*].

57.7 **AGRICULTURAL WAGES BOARD**

The Agricultural Wages Board is constituted under the *Agricultural Wages Act 1948* (as amended by *ECA 1975, s 97*). It may make orders concerning remuneration, holidays and other terms and conditions of employment after having regard to representations made by the agricultural wages committees established for each county. Its powers are similar to, but now go beyond, those of wages councils. The Government regards itself as bound by international convention to leave this system in place until 1993. The address of the Board is Eagle House, 90-96 Cannon Street, London EC4N 6HT.

58 'A Week's Pay'

(See also DE booklet No. 11 'Rules governing continuous employment and a week's pay' (PL 711).)

58.1 The amount of money payable under several of the statutory employment protection rights depends upon a calculation based on the week's pay of the employee concerned. For example, a week's pay is the basis for the calculation of a redundancy payment and of the basic award in a claim for unfair dismissal.

The calculation of a week's pay differs according to whether the employee is in employment for which there are normal working hours or whether he is in employment for which there are no normal working hours.

58.2 EMPLOYMENTS FOR WHICH THERE ARE NORMAL WORKING HOURS

If the employee's normal working hours are the same every week and his remuneration for employment in normal working hours does not vary with the amount of work done in the period, the amount of a week's pay is the amount which is payable by the employer under the contract of employment in force on the calculation date if the employee works throughout his normal working hours in a week. [*EPCA 14 Sch 3(2)*].

Where the amount of the remuneration varies with the amount of work done but the number of normal working hours does not vary, the amount of a week's pay is the amount of remuneration for the number of normal working hours in a week calculated at the *average* hourly rate of remuneration payable by the employer to the employee in respect of the period of twelve weeks

(*a*) where the calculation date is the last day of a week, ending with that week;

(*b*) in any other case, ending with the last complete week before the calculation date.

[*EPCA 14 Sch 3(3)*]. This is the provision which must be applied even where the variation may be attributable to the amount of work done by other employees (*Keywest Club Ltd v Choudhury [1988] IRLR 51*; and see 58.6 below).

Where the employee is required under his contract to work during normal working hours on days of the week or at times of the day which differ from week to week or over a longer period so that the remuneration payable for or apportionable to any week varies, the amount of a week's pay is based upon the average remuneration paid and the average number of hours worked in the last twelve weeks before the calculation date. [*EPCA 14 Sch 4*; and see 58.3 below].

For the purposes of these calculations, weeks in which the employee was not paid because he was not working are excluded, and a previous working week is brought into account. [*EPCA 14 Sch 5*].

58.3 Overtime

Overtime hours and payment for them only fall within the calculation if the employer is obliged to provide, and the employee is obliged to work, the overtime. (*Tarmac Roadstone Holdings Ltd v Peacock and others [1973] ICR 273; Gascol Conversions Ltd v Mercer [1974] ICR 420*). In *British Coal Corporation v*

Cheesbrough [1988] ICR 769, the Court of Appeal held that overtime hours *must* be taken into account as if they were worked at the normal rate even if that had the effect of reducing the average hourly rate. This decision is being appealed to the House of Lords.

58.4 EMPLOYMENTS FOR WHICH THERE ARE NO NORMAL WORKING HOURS

The amount of a week's pay is the amount of the employee's average weekly remuneration in the period of twelve weeks

(*a*) where the calculation date is the last day of a week, ending with that week;

(*b*) in any other case, ending with the last complete week before the calculation date.

In arriving at the average weekly rate of remuneration no account shall be taken of a week in which no remuneration was payable by the employer to the employee, and remuneration in earlier weeks is brought in so as to bring the number of weeks of which account is taken up to twelve. [*EPCA 14 Sch 6*].

58.5 THE CALCULATION DATE

Where the calculation is for the purposes of assessing the amount of a basic award, the calculation date is the effective date of termination as defined by *EPCA s 55(4)* (see 54.13 UNFAIR DISMISSAL - I), or where the statutory minimum period of notice should have been given but was not, the date that notice would have expired. [*EPCA 14 Sch 7(1)(h)(i), (2)*].

Where the calculation is for the purposes of assessing the amount of a redundancy payment, the calculation date is the relevant date as defined by *EPCA s 90(1)* (see 38.4 REDUNDANCY - I). [*EPCA 14 Sch 7(1)(k)(l), (2)*].

For the calculation date for other employment protection rights, see *EPCA 14 Sch 7(1)*.

58.6 THE AMOUNT OF A WEEK'S PAY

For the purposes of calculating the amount of a week's pay, remuneration includes wages, salaries and expenses insofar as they represent profit in the employee's hands. (*S & U Stores Ltd v Wilkes [1974] 3 AER 401*). It also includes an incentive bonus, irrespective of whether the bonus is identifiably related to the particular employee's efforts (*British Coal Corporation v Cheesborough [1988] ICR 769*; the House of Lords has given leave to appeal). The amount of remuneration without deduction of tax is taken into account for the purposes of calculating a basic award and a redundancy payment. (*Secretary of State for Employment v John Woodrow & Sons (Builders) Ltd [1983] ICR 582*).

The amount of a week's pay for certain calculations is subject to statutory maxima. With effect from 1 April 1989, the limit on the amount of a week's pay for the purpose of calculating a basic award of compensation for unfair dismissal and for calculating a redundancy payment is £172. [*Employment Protection (Variation of Limits) Order 1989 (SI 1989 No 526)*]. It is to be noted that the amount of a week's pay for the purpose of calculating a special award under *EA 1982* is not subject to a statutory maximum. However, the total amount of a special award is subject to a statutory maximum. [*EPCA s 75A(1)(2); EA 1982, s 5(3)*].

Where a statutory minimum wage fixed by a Wages Council is in force, but the employee's actual wages have been less than that minimum, the statutory minimum wage should be used as the basis of that calculation (*Cooner v PS Doal & Sons [1988] ICR 495*).

59 Wrongful Dismissal

Cross-references. See TERMINATION OF EMPLOYMENT (49) for rules relating to dismissal on notice.

59.1 If an employer dismisses an employee and, in so doing, the employer acts in breach of his contractual obligations or of his statutory obligations to give him notice (see TERMINATION OF EMPLOYMENT (49)), he becomes liable to pay that employee damages for wrongful dismissal. This right derives from the common law relating to contract and is quite distinct from the employee's statutory employment protection rights (e.g. to claim compensation for unfair dismissal). Thus, unlike many of the remedies discussed in this book, the action for wrongful dismissal is brought in the county court or the High Court (see 59.10 below). In order to bring such a claim the ex-employee plaintiff must establish (i) that he was dismissed in breach of contract or with less than the statutory minimum period of notice, and (ii) that he has suffered loss as a result.

If an employer purports to dismiss an employee in breach of a contractual notice provision it is thought that the employee is in theory not bound to accept the breach and can maintain that the contract has not been determined (see e.g. *Shook v London Borough of Ealing* [*1986*] *ICR 314* and 49.20 TERMINATION OF EMPLOYMENT). However, acceptance of an employer's breach will be readily inferred. (See *Gunton v Richmond-upon-Thames London Borough Council* [*1980*] *ICR 755*).

59.2 DISMISSALS GIVING RISE TO THE ACTION

An employer who prematurely and without justification terminates a contract for a specific number of years (i.e. fixed term contract) will become liable to compensate his employee for loss of earnings up to the earliest date on which the contract of employment could lawfully have been terminated. Thus, if an engineer, engaged on a contract which is to run for three years without any provision for earlier determination by notice, is dismissed two years from the expiry of the term, he would be awarded damages based upon his loss over those two years. If, however, the contract provided that the employment could be terminated before the expiry of the three-year term by two months' notice on either side, the damages would only be calculated up to the point at which the contract could have lawfully been terminated (i.e. two months from the date of the dismissal).

59.3 Contracts terminable by notice

If a contract of employment is terminated by the employer giving no notice or shorter notice than is provided for in the agreement, in circumstances in which he is not entitled summarily to dismiss, the employee is entitled to damages to compensate him for the failure to give him the notice he should have received. Thus, if a manager entitled to three months' notice is only given one month's notice he is entitled to damages based upon two months' pay.

59.4 Contracts containing no provision for termination

Contracts which do not expressly provide for termination are subject to an implied term that they may be terminated by either party giving reasonable notice. What is reasonable notice will depend upon the particular circumstances (see 49.8 TERMINATION OF EMPLOYMENT). If no notice or less notice than is reasonable is given, the employee will be entitled to damages to compensate him for the loss.

59.5 Statutory minimum periods of notice

Apart from any contractual provision for notice, an employee whose contract is terminable by notice is entitled to the statutory minimum period of notice (see 49.9 TERMINATION OF EMPLOYMENT). If a book-keeper whose contract entitles her to four weeks' notice has been employed for twelve years, she will be entitled to twelve weeks' notice despite the contractual provision for four weeks.

59.6 DISMISSALS NOT GIVING RISE TO THE ACTION

Summary dismissals for misconduct

Despite the provisions of a fixed term contract or of a contract terminable on giving notice, an employer may dismiss an employee summarily, without having to pay him damages for wrongful dismissal, if the employee has been guilty of gross misconduct (see 49.14 TERMINATION OF EMPLOYMENT). Theft of the employer's property, disobedience of a lawful order or gross rudeness to the employer can justify summary dismissal if such acts are so serious as to destroy the employer/employee relationship. In *Laws v London Chronicle (Indicator Newspapers) Ltd [1959] 1 WLR 698* Lord Evershed said at p 701:

> '. . . one act of disobedience or misconduct can justify dismissal only if it is of a nature which goes to show (in effect) that the servant is repudiating the contract, or one of its essential conditions; and for that reason, therefore, I think that you find in the passages I have read that disobedience must at least have the quality that it is "wilful": it does (in other words) connote a deliberate flouting of the essential contractual conditions.'

The misconduct may occur outside the employment, but it must then be so serious that it strikes at the root of the confidence which must exist for the contract of employment to be effective. (*Jackson v Invicta Plastics Ltd [1987] BCLC 329*).

Unlike in respect of unfair dismissal, an employer may rely upon gross misconduct discovered *after* dismissal to justify a summary dismissal. (*Boston Deep Sea Fishing and Ice Co v Ansell (1888) LR 39 ChD 339*). Nor is the employer obliged to follow a fair procedure, although he will have to observe any procedural requirements stipulated by the contract.

59.7 Summary dismissals for incompetence

An employee may be summarily dismissed if he is grossly incompetent in the performance of his contractual duties. However, it is thought that the circumstances in which summary dismissal for incompetence would be held justified are relatively rare. This view is generally confirmed by the discussion in *Jackson* (above).

59.8 Dismissals with pay in lieu of notice

Frequently an employer who gives an employee notice does not require him to work out his notice period but gives him pay in lieu of notice.

Pay in lieu of notice is generally regarded as damages for wrongful dismissal, which implies that it should be paid net. In *Dixon v Stenor Ltd [1973] ICR 157*, Donaldson J said at p 158, 'if a man is dismissed without notice but with money in lieu, what he receives is, as a matter of law, damages for breach of contract'. However, if it is expressly or impliedly agreed that pay in lieu of notice is to be made gross, then a gross payment must be made (and see *Gothard v Mirror Group Newspapers [1988] ICR 729*). Even without such agreement, pay in lieu of notice is quite often based upon the employee's gross earnings. (See also 49.13 TERMINATION OF EMPLOYMENT.)

If there is a contractual right to terminate an employee's employment on making a payment in lieu of notice, the employer will not be in breach of contract by not giving notice but giving a payment in lieu. (*Rex Stewart Jeffries Parker Ginsberg Ltd v Parker [1988] IRLR 483*). If there is no contractual right to terminate by making a payment in lieu of notice, the making of such a payment may not extinguish his claim for damages unless, in all respects, the employee is put in the same situation as he would have been if notice had been given. It is also important to note that a dismissal in breach of contract will disentitle the employer to rely upon restrictive covenants in the contract, although this may not be the case if full payment in lieu of notice is made. See RESTRAINT OF TRADE, CONFIDENTIALITY AND EMPLOYEE INVENTIONS (41).

59.9 AMOUNT OF DAMAGES

The amount of damages for wrongful dismissal is based upon pay and other benefits, such as the use of a company car, which the employee would have received if the employer had complied with his contractual and statutory obligations. Notional national insurance deductions are made from this amount. Since the damages an ex-employee recovers are taxable to the extent that they exceed £30,000 (see *ICTA 1988, s 188(4)* as substituted by *FA 1988, s 74(1), (3)*), his liability to tax will be assessed and that sum taken into account in the calculation of damages. (*Shove v Downs Surgical plc [1984] ICR 532; Stewart v Glentaggart Ltd (1963) 42 ATC 318*).

At one time it was thought that damages for mental distress, caused by the breach of contract of employment, could be recovered. (*Cox v Philips Industries Ltd [1976] ICR 138*). However, in *Bliss v South East Thames Regional Health Authority [1987] ICR 700*, the Court of Appeal held that it is not permissible to award damages for frustration, mental distress, injured feelings or annoyance caused by a breach of contract. (See also *Addis v Gramophone Co Ltd [1909] AC 488*.)

The plaintiff must take all reasonable steps to mitigate his loss by seeking other employment. Sums he has received or should have received in other employment will be taken into account in calculating the loss.

For example, if a man is wrongfully dismissed from employment in which he was earning £500 per month net and obtains employment at £400 per month net one month after his dismissal, if he was entitled to three months' notice, his damages will be £700 (three months' entitlement at £500 less two months' salary at £400).

Statutory benefits received will be taken into account in assessing damages. For deduction of unemployment benefit see *Nabi v British Leyland (UK) Ltd [1980] 1 WLR 529*; and for deduction of supplementary benefit (now income support) see *Plummer v P W Wilkins & Son Ltd [1981] 1 WLR 831*.

59.10 THE COURT

Claims of up to £5,000 may be brought in the county court; claims over £5,000 must be brought in the Queen's Bench Division of the High Court. The recent

Civil Justice Review has made far-reaching proposals for extending the jurisdiction of the county court. In practice, claims of less than £50,000 which do not involve complex questions of fact or law are already transferred to the county court at an interlocutory stage. There is nothing to stop an employee simultaneously claiming unfair dismissal in the industrial tribunal and wrongful dismissal in the ordinary courts, but the employer may apply to have the tribunal proceedings stayed (see 27.23 INDUSTRIAL TRIBUNALS), and the employee cannot recover twice for the same loss.

59.11 TIME LIMIT

The time limit for bringing a claim for wrongful dismissal is the limitation period for all contractual claims – six years from the date of the breach of contract.

59.12 COMPROMISE OF CLAIMS

An employer and employee can agree that the employee will not bring or pursue any claim for wrongful dismissal provided that their agreement is supported by 'valuable consideration' (in other words, there must be some demonstrable material benefit to the employee who is party to the agreement). However, an employee may not contract out of his right to a statutory minimum period of notice [*EPCA s 140 (1)(a)*], although he may on a particular occasion waive his right to notice or accept a payment in lieu of notice (which payment may in any event extinguish his right to damages). [*EPCA s 49(3)*]. As the court may not 'rewrite' an agreement, but must strike out an offending clause altogether, any such agreement should be expressed only to apply to those rights where contracting-out is valid.

59.13 CONSULTANTS AND INDEPENDENT CONTRACTORS

Although all the discussion in this chapter has been directed at the termination of the contract of employment, if a consultancy agreement is terminated prematurely, the consultant may bring a claim for damages for breach of contract.

59.14 DIRECTORS

Certain payments made to directors on the termination of their appointment have to be disclosed in a company's accounts, and any such payments which are greater than the company's strict legal liability must have prior shareholder approval (see generally DIRECTORS (11)). [*Companies Act 1985 (as amended by Companies Act 1989), s 232, 6 Sch 8*].

60 Appendix: Codes of Practice

(See CODES OF PRACTICE (7) for information about the issuing of Codes and their legal effect.)

Contents

 The Codes are reproduced as issued and readers should note that some of the statutory references have been subsequently *amended* or *repealed*.

Industrial Relations Code of Practice

(This Code came into effect on 28 February 1972. It should be read together with the ACAS advisory handbook 'Discipline at Work', although the handbook does not have the legal status of a Code.)

INTRODUCTION

The purpose of the Code is to give practical guidance for promoting good industrial relations. It does so in accordance with the four general principles set out in the Industrial Relations Act. These stress the importance of freely conducted collective bargaining, orderly procedures for settling disputes, free association of workers and employers and freedom and security for workers.

The Code interprets industrial relations in the widest sense. It does not confine itself to procedural matters such as collective agreements and negotiating machinery. It is also concerned with human relations, and therefore with policies which directly affect the individual employee[1] in the performance of his job.

Two main themes underlie the Code

(i) the vital role of collective bargaining carried out in a reasonable and constructive manner between employers and strong representative trade unions[2];

(ii) the importance of good human relations between employers and employees in every establishment,[3] based on trust and confidence.

In any undertaking,[4] management needs to use its resources efficiently, while employees look for continuity of employment, security of earnings and satisfaction in their work. Both have a common interest in the undertaking's success because without it their aims cannot be achieved. But some conflicts of interest are bound to arise. With good industrial relations they can be resolved in a responsible and constructive way.

Good industrial relations are a joint responsibility. They need the continuing co-operation of all concerned – managements, trade unions, employers' associations and individual employees – and the discussion of day-to-day problems as they occur. The Code is designed to encourage and assist that co-operation.

Application and use

The Code applies wherever people are employed. Most of it will apply in most employment situations. But some of the detailed provisions may need to be adapted to suit particular circumstances, especially in small establishments, or particular types of employment. Any adaptations should be consistent with the Code's general intentions.

In this Code:

[1]employee includes any worker covered by the Industrial Relations Act (see Section 167 of the Act);

[2]trade union and employers' association include unregistered organisations, except where otherwise indicated;

[3]establishment means an individual factory, plant, office, shop, etc., in which employees work;

[4]undertaking means a business or organisation controlling one or more establishments.

In many cases, changes will be needed to meet the standards set by the Code. Where they cannot be made at once, those concerned should ensure that there is reasonable and continuing progress towards achieving the Code's standards.

The Code complements the provisions of the Industrial Relations Act. It provides guidelines for all concerned with the day-to-day problems of industrial relations, as well as for the Commission on Industrial Relations and for Courts of Inquiry and similar bodies.

The Code imposes no legal obligations. Failure to observe it does not by itself render anyone liable to proceedings. But Section 4 of the Industrial Relations Act requires any relevant provisions to be taken into account in proceedings under the Act before the National Industrial Relations Court or an industrial tribunal.

Revision

The Code sets standards which reflect existing good industrial relations practice. It is not meant to restrict innovation and experiment or to inhibit improvements on those standards.

Industrial relations can never be static. Just as individual undertakings should review and improve their own practices, so the Code will need to be revised periodically. Under the Industrial Relations Act this must be done after consultation with the Trades Union Congress and the Confederation of British Industry, and after taking account of advice from the Commission on Industrial Relations.

RESPONSIBILITIES

Management

1 The principal aim of management is to conduct the business of the undertaking successfully. Good industrial relations need to be developed within the framework of an efficient organisation and they will in turn help management to achieve this aim.

2 One of management's major objectives should therefore be to develop effective industrial relations policies which command the confidence of employees. Managers at the highest level should give, and show that they give, just as much attention to industrial relations as to such functions as finance, marketing, production or administration.

3 Good industrial relations are the joint responsibility of management and of employees and trade unions representing them. But the primary responsibility for their promotion rests with management. It should therefore take the initiative in creating and developing them.

4 Where trade unions are recognised for negotiating purposes management should

(i) maintain jointly with the trade unions effective arrangements for negotiation, consultation and communication, and for settling grievances and disputes;

(ii) take all reasonable steps to ensure that managers observe agreements and use agreed procedures;

(iii) make clear to employees that it welcomes their membership of an appropriate recognised union and their participation in the union's activities.

5 Where trade unions are not recognised for negotiating purposes management should

(i) maintain effective arrangements for consultation and communication and for settling grievances;

(ii) take all reasonable steps to ensure that managers use those arrangements;

(iii) make clear to employees that it respects their rights under the Industrial Relations Act to join a registered trade union and to take part in its activities, which include seeking recognition for negotiating purposes.

6 Effective organisation of work is an important factor in good industrial relations. Management should therefore ensure that

(i) responsibility for each group of employees is clearly defined in the organisational structure;

(ii) each manager understands his responsibilities and has the authority and training necessary to do his job;

(iii) individual employees or work groups know their objectives and priorities and are kept informed of progress towards achieving them.

7 All managers should receive training in the industrial relations implications of their jobs. This is as necessary for line managers, including supervisors, as for personnel managers.

8 The supervisor[5] is in a key position to influence industrial relations. Management should ensure that he

(i) is properly selected and trained;

(ii) has charge of a work group of a size that he can supervise effectively;

(iii) is fully briefed in advance about management's policies as they affect his work group;

(iv) is an effective link in the exchange of information and views between management and members of his work group.

9 Management should recognise that each employee has his individual needs and aspirations at work and should take this into account in its day-to-day conduct of business. In particular, management should recognise the employee's need to achieve a sense of satisfaction in his job and should provide for it so far as practicable.

Trade unions

10 The principal aim of trade unions is to promote their members' interests. They can do this only if the undertakings in which their members are employed prosper. They therefore have an interest in the success of those undertakings and an essential contribution to make to it by co-operating in measures to promote efficiency. They also share with management the responsibility for good industrial relations.

11 Trade unions should therefore

(i) where appropriate, maintain jointly with employers' associations and

---

[5] In this Code supervisor means a member of the first line of management, who is responsible for his work group to a higher level of management.

others concerned, effective arrangements at industry or other levels for settling disputes and for negotiating terms and conditions of employment;

(ii) maintain, jointly with individual managements, effective arrangements for negotiation, consultation and communication and for settling grievances and disputes;

(iii) take all reasonable steps to ensure that their officials, including shop stewards (see paragraph 100), and members observe agreements and use agreed procedures;

(iv) maintain effective procedures for resolving particular issues with other unions and, where appropriate, make full use of the procedures established by the Trades Union Congress for settling inter-union disputes.

12 Trade unions should ensure that officials, including shop stewards,

(i) understand the organisation, policies and rules of the union;

(ii) understand their powers and duties;

(iii) are adequately trained to look after their members' interests in an efficient and responsible way.

13 To ensure their organisation is effective, trade unions should also

(i) employ enough full-time officials to maintain adequate contact with management and with their members in every establishment where the union is recognised, and with any employers' associations concerned;

(ii) maintain effective communication, including the exchange of information and views, between different levels in the union;

(iii) encourage their members to attend union meetings and to take part fully in union activities by holding branch meetings at times and places convenient to the majority; and where there is a large enough membership, consider basing the branch organisation on the establishment;

(iv) maintain effective procedures for settling disputes within the union.

14 Members of a trade union should be prepared to provide their union with the authority and resources needed to carry out its functions.

Employers' associations

15 The principal aim of employers' associations is to promote those interests of their members which can best be served by co-operation at industry or other appropriate levels.

16 Employers' associations should therefore

(i) where appropriate, maintain jointly with the trade unions concerned effective arrangements at industry or other levels for settling disputes and for negotiating terms and conditions of employment;

(ii) encourage their members to develop effective arrangements for settling grievances and disputes at the level of the establishment or undertaking;

(iii) take all reasonable steps to ensure that their members observe agreements and use agreed procedures;

(iv) identify trends in industrial relations to help their members to anticipate and keep abreast of change;

(v) collect and analyse information about industrial relations and distribute it to their members;

(vi) provide an advisory service to their members on all aspects of industrial relations.

17 Members of an employers' association should be prepared to provide their association with the authority, resources and information needed to carry out its functions.

The individual employee

18 The individual employee has obligations to his employer, to his trade union if he belongs to one, and to his fellow employees. He shares responsibility for the state of industrial relations in the establishment where he works and his attitudes and conduct can have a decisive influence on them.

19 The legal relationship between employer and employee derives from the individual contract of employment. Often many of its terms are fixed by collective bargaining and stated in collective agreements. With certain exceptions, employees are entitled to a written statement about their main terms and conditions of employment (see paragraphs 60-61).

20 Each employee should

(i) satisfy himself that he understands the terms of his contract and abide by them;

(ii) make himself familiar with any arrangements for dealing with grievances and other questions which may arise on his contract, and make use of them when the need arises.

21 Some employees have special obligations arising from membership of a profession and are liable to incur penalties if they disregard them. These may include obligations, for example, in regard to health, safety and welfare, over and above those which are shared by the community as a whole.

22 A professional employee who belongs to a trade union should respect the obligations which he has voluntarily taken on by joining the union. But he should not, when acting in his professional capacity, be called upon by his trade union to take action which would conflict with the standards of work or conduct laid down for his profession if that action would endanger

(i) public health or safety;

(ii) the health of an individual needing medical or other treatment;

(iii) the well-being of an individual needing care through the personal social services.

23 Professional associations, employers and trade unions should co-operate in preventing and resolving any conflicts which may occur between obligations arising from membership of a profession and those which the professional employee owes to his employer and to his trade union if he belongs to one.

EMPLOYMENT POLICIES

24 Clear and comprehensive employment policies are essential to good relations between management and employees. They help management to make the most effective use of its manpower resources and give each employee opportunity to develop his potential.

25 Management should initiate and accept primary responsibility for these policies. But they should be developed in consultation or negotiation, as appropriate, with employee representatives.

26 The Race Relations Act 1968 makes it unlawful to discriminate on grounds of colour, race or ethnic or national origins about recruitment, terms and conditions of employment, training, promotion and dismissal. But management should not merely avoid such discrimination; it should develop positive policies to promote equal opportunity in employment.

27 Management should equally ensure that its employment policies are not influenced by conditions relating to age, sex or other personal factors except where they are relevant to the job.

Planning and use of manpower

28 Manpower planning in the undertaking consists of

(i) taking stock of existing manpower resources;

(ii) working out future manpower needs;

(iii) identifying what should be done to ensure that future manpower resources match those needs.

29 Manpower planning should be conducted in ways suited to the size and nature of the undertaking and should be

(i) backed by the authority of management at the highest level;

(ii) integrated with other aspects of planning in the undertaking;

(iii) based on adequate and up-to-date personnel records.

30 In operating its manpower policies management should

(i) avoid unnecessary fluctuations in manpower;

(ii) where changes are necessary, make them with as little disruption as is practicable to the employees concerned;

(iii) maintain arrangements for transferring employees from one job to another within the undertaking;

(iv) record information which will help it to identify the causes of, and to control, absenteeism and labour turnover.

Recruitment and selection

31 In recruiting and selecting employees management should

(i) decide the qualifications and experience needed by applicants;

(ii) consider filling vacancies by transfer or promotion from within the undertaking;

(iii) obtain as much information about applicants as is relevant to selection for the job, but avoid enquiries which are unnecessary for that purpose;

(iv) base selection on suitability for the job;

(v) explain the main terms and conditions of employment and give any relevant information about trade union arrangements before an applicant is engaged.

32 Management should also

(i) check recruitment and selection methods regularly to ensure that they are effective;

(ii) ensure that those who carry out recruitment and selection are competent to do so.

Training

33 Management should ensure that new employees are given

(i) induction training, including information about the matters referred to in paragraphs 60 and 62;

(ii) any training in the job needed to supplement previous education, training and experience.

34 Management should ensure that young people entering employment for the first time are also given broader initial instruction covering

(i) a general introduction to their working life, including the importance of health and safety precautions;

(ii) basic training in related skills, where appropriate, as well as specific training in their particular job.

35 Management should

(i) ensure that any necessary further education and training is provided when there is a significant change in the content or level of the job;

(ii) encourage employees to take advantage of relevant further education and training opportunities at all stages of their careers.

Payment systems

36 Payment systems vary according to the nature and organisation of the work, local conditions and other factors, but the following principles apply generally.

37 Payment systems should be

(i) kept as simple as possible, consistent with their purpose, so that employees can understand them;

(ii) based on some form of work measurement where payment is linked to performance;

(iii) jointly negotiated where trade unions are recognised.

38 Differences in remuneration should be related to the requirements of the job, which should wherever possible be assessed in a rational and systematic way in consultation with employee representatives.

39 Payment systems should be kept under review to make sure that they suit current circumstances and take account of any substantial changes in the organisation of work or the requirements of the job.

Status and security of employees

40 As far as is consistent with operational efficiency and the success of the undertaking management should

(i) provide stable employment, including reasonable job security for employees absent through sickness or other causes beyond their control;

(ii) avoid unnecessary fluctuations in the level of earnings of employees.

41 Where practicable, management should provide occupational pension and sick pay schemes.

42 Differences in the conditions of employment and status of different categories of employee and in the facilities available to them should be based on the requirements of the job. The aim should be progressively to reduce and ultimately to remove differences which are not so based. Management, employees and their representatives and trade unions should co-operate in working towards this objective.

43 In deciding how and when the changes mentioned in paragraphs 41 and 42 are to be introduced, their cost should be taken into account as part of total labour costs.

44 Responsibility for deciding the size of the work force rests with management. But before taking the final decision to make any substantial reduction, management should consult employees or their representatives, unless exceptional circumstances make this impossible.

45 A policy for dealing with reductions in the work force, if they become necessary, should be worked out in advance so far as practicable and should form part of the undertaking's employment policies. As far as is consistent with operational efficiency and the success of the undertaking, management should, in consultation with employee representatives, seek to avoid redundancies by such means as

(i) restrictions on recruitment;

(ii) retirement of employees who are beyond the normal retiring age;

(iii) reductions in overtime;

(iv) short-time working to cover temporary fluctuations in manpower needs;

(v) re-training or transfer to other work.

46 If redundancy becomes necessary, management in consultation, as appropriate, with employees or their representatives, should

(i) give as much warning as practicable to the employees concerned and to the Department of Employment;

(ii) consider introducing schemes for voluntary redundancy, retirement, transfer to other establishments within the undertaking, and a phased rundown of employment;

(iii) establish which employees are to be made redundant and the order of discharge;

(iv) offer help to employees in finding other work in co-operation, where appropriate, with the Department of Employment, and allow them reasonable time off for the purpose;

(v) decide how and when to make the facts public, ensuring that no announcement is made before the employees and their representatives and trade unions have been informed.

Working conditions

47 The Factories Act and other legislation lay down minimum standards about working conditions. Management should aim at improving on these standards in consultation and co-operation with employees and their representatives.

48 Management should therefore take all reasonable steps to

(i) improve standards of 'housekeeping', including the cleanliness, tidiness, lighting, heating, ventilation and general appearance of the workplace;

(ii) reduce noise, strain and monotony as far as practicable;

(iii) ensure that hazards are reduced to a minimum and the work done as safely as possible.

49 Management and employee representatives should

(i) take all reasonable steps to ensure that employees use protective equipment (for example, guards, safety helmets, goggles and ear defenders), observe the standards laid down by law and co-operate in agreed safety measures;

(ii) make the best use of arrangements for consultation about safety and health.

50 Every employee should

(i) ensure that he understands the health and safety precautions and observes them;

(ii) make use of protective equipment.

COMMUNICATION AND CONSULTATION

51 Communication and consultation are essential in all establishments. They are necessary to promote operational efficiency and mutual understanding, as well as the individual employee's sense of satisfaction and involvement in his job. Management, employee representatives and trade unions should co-operate in ensuring that effective communication and consultation take place.

52 Communication and consultation are particularly important in times of change. The achievement of change is a joint concern of management and employees and should be carried out in a way which pays regard both to the efficiency of the undertaking and to the interests of employees. Major changes in working arrangements should not be made by management without prior discussion with employees or their representatives.

53 When changes in management take place, for example, following a merger or take-over, the new managers should make prompt contact with employee representatives and take steps to explain changes in policy affecting employees.

Communication

54 In its day-to-day conduct of business, management needs both to give information to employees and to receive information from them. Effective arrangements should be made to facilitate this two-way flow.

55 The most important method of communication is by word of mouth, through personal contact between each manager and his immediate work group or individual employees, and between managers and employee representatives.

56 Personal contact should be supplemented as necessary by

(i) written information provided through, for example, notice boards, house journals or handbooks;

(ii) training, particularly induction courses for new employees;

(iii) meetings arranged for special purposes.

57 Subject to the limitations on disclosure of information, referred to in paragraph 98, management should regularly provide employees with information about

(i) the performance and plans both of the establishment and, so far as they affect it, of the undertaking;

(ii) organisational and management changes which affect employees.

58 Management should ensure that

(i) managers, including supervisors, regard it as one of their principal duties to explain management's policies and intentions to those responsible to them and have the information needed to do so;

(ii) work instructions are conveyed clearly.

59 Management, in co-operation with employee representatives, should

(i) provide opportunities for employees to discuss matters affecting their jobs with those to whom they are responsible;

(ii) ensure that managers are kept informed of the views of employees and of the problems which they may face in meeting management's objectives.

60 The Contracts of Employment Act, as amended in Schedule 2 of the Industrial Relations Act, entitles every employee, other than those in certain categories,[6] to be notified in writing within 13 weeks of starting a job, about

(i) his main terms and conditions of employment;

(ii) his rights under Section 5 of the Industrial Relations Act in respect of trade union membership;

(iii) how he can seek redress for a grievance.

61 The written statement should be as comprehensive and easy to understand as possible. Where it refers the employee to another document, the Act requires that he must have reasonable opportunities of reading that document in the course of his employment or that it must be made reasonably accessible to him in some other way. He should be told clearly, in the written statement, where he can see the document.

62 Apart from the statutory requirements, management should ensure that each employee is given information about

(i) the requirement of his job and to whom he is directly responsible;

(ii) disciplinary rules and procedures and the type of circumstances which can lead to suspension or dismissal;

(iii) trade union arrangements;

(iv) opportunities for promotion and any training necessary to achieve it;

(v) social or welfare facilities;

(vi) fire prevention and safety and health rules;

(vii) any suggestion schemes.

---

[6]Contracts of Employment Act 1963, Sections 4(8) and 6.

63 Employee representatives and trade unions should

(i) ensure that they have the means to communicate effectively with those whom they represent;

(ii) recognise that management has a responsibility for communicating directly with its employees.

64 Management, employee representatives and trade unions should co-operate in keeping employees informed of the conclusions reached through negotiation and consultation.

Consultation

65 Consultation means jointly examining and discussing problems of concern to both management and employees. It involves seeking mutually acceptable solutions through a genuine exchange of views and information.

66 Consultation between management and employees or their representatives about operational and other day-to-day matters is necessary in all establishments, whatever their size. Establishments with more than 250 employees should have systematic arrangements for management and employee representatives to meet regularly.

67 Management should take the initiative in setting up and maintaining consultative arrangements best suited to the circumstances of the establishment, in co-operation with employee representatives and trade unions concerned. The arrangements should not be used to by-pass or discourage trade unions.

68 In setting up the consultative arrangements, management should ensure that

(i) the arrangements provide opportunities for employees to express their views on proposed changes which affect them and encourage discussion, at whatever level is most appropriate, of matters closely associated with the work situation;

(ii) employee representatives have all the information they require to enable them to participate effectively in discussions;

(iii) senior managers take an active part in consultation;

(iv) the arrangements include effective means of reporting back to employees.

69 Where committees are set up, management and employee representatives should agree on

(i) the composition, objectives and functions of the committee and of any sectional or functional sub-committees;

(ii) the arrangements for the election or nomination of representatives;

(iii) the rules of procedure;

(iv) the range of subjects to be discussed.

70 Consultation and negotiation are closely related but distinct processes. Management and employee representatives should consider carefully how to link the two. It may often be advantageous for the same committee to cover both. Where they are separate bodies, systematic communication between those involved in the two processes is essential.

COLLECTIVE BARGAINING

71 Freely conducted collective bargaining is a joint activity which establishes a framework for relations between management and employees. It requires from both sides a reasonable and constructive approach in negotiation, with due regard to the general interests of the community, and a determination to abide by agreements which have been made.

72 Collective bargaining may take place at various levels, ranging from an industry or part of one to a group of employees within an establishment. Negotiations for the same group of employees may be conducted at different levels about different subjects.

73 Where negotiation takes place at more than one level, the matters to be bargained about at each level should be defined by agreement. The aim should be to assign to each level the matters which can be realistically settled at that level. Equally, whatever the level at which an agreement is reached, its terms should be capable of being applied effectively at the place of work.

Bargaining units

74 Collective bargaining in an establishment or undertaking is conducted in relation to defined groups of employees which can appropriately be covered by one negotiating process. In the Industrial Relations Act and in the Code these are called 'bargaining units'.

75 Although 'bargaining unit' is a new term, it describes what has long been established as part of the pattern of negotiation. Any negotiating arrangements need periodic review, but arrangements which are found to be working well should not be disturbed without good reason.

76 A bargaining unit should cover as wide a group of employees as practicable. Too many small units make it difficult to ensure that related groups of employees are treated consistently. The number of separate units can often be reduced by the formation of a joint negotiating panel representing a number of unions.

77 The interests of employees covered by a bargaining unit need not be identical, but there should be a substantial degree of common interest. In deciding the pattern of bargaining arrangements, the need to take into account the distinct interests of employees who form a minority group (including professional employees) should be balanced against the need to avoid unduly small bargaining units.

78 Factors which should be taken into account in defining a bargaining unit include

(i) the nature of the work;

(ii) the training, experience and professional or other qualifications of the employees concerned;

(iii) the extent to which they have interests in common;

(iv) the general wishes of the employees concerned;

(v) the organisation and location of the work;

(vi) hours, working arrangements and payment systems;

(vii) the matters to be bargained about;

(viii) the need to fit the bargaining unit into the pattern of union and management organisation;

(ix) the need to avoid disruption of any existing bargaining arrangements which are working well;

(x) whether separate bargaining arrangements are needed for particular categories of employees, such as supervisors or employees who represent management in negotiation.

79 When proposals are made for establishing or varying a bargaining unit, the first aim of management and unions should be to reach agreement on a voluntary basis. Where this proves impossible, either or both parties should consider

(i) referring the matter to the employers' association, where appropriate, and to a higher level within the trade union;

(ii) seeking advice and conciliation from the Department of Employment;

(iii) asking the Department of Employment to refer the matter to the Commission on Industrial Relations for examination and advice.

80 Failing a solution by any of these means, the employer, a registered trade union involved, or the Secretary of State may apply to the National Industrial Relations Court for a settlement under Sections 45-50 of the Industrial Relations Act.

81 In certain circumstances individual employees have a right under Sections 51-53 of the Industrial Relations Act to apply to the National Industrial Relations Court for their bargaining unit to be varied.

Recognition of trade unions

82 A trade union may claim recognition for negotiating purposes either where management already has agreed bargaining arrangements with other unions or where no arrangements exist. In either case management should take into account

(i) the extent of support for the claim among the employees concerned, whether members of the union or not;

(ii) the effect of granting recognition on any existing bargaining arrangements;

(iii) whether or not recognition should be granted to the same union (or section of a union) in respect of supervisors and of the members of their work groups.

83 Management is entitled to know the number, but not the identities, of the employees covered by the proposed bargaining unit who are members of the union making the claim. Where the extent of support cannot be agreed, it should be determined by arrangements agreed between the parties, for example, a secret ballot.

84 Where a trade union has members in a category of employees for which no union has secured negotiating rights, management should consider receiving representations from an official of the union on behalf of any of those members about grievances or other matters which can be dealt with on an individual basis.

85 Responsibility for avoiding disputes between trade unions about recognition lies principally with the unions themselves and, in the case of affiliated unions, with the Trades Union Congress. Unions concerned should make full use of the available procedures.

86 Claims for recognition should, as far as possible, be settled voluntarily between the parties. If they cannot reach agreement the procedures set out in paragraphs 79-81 may be used.

After recognition

87 Relations between management and trade unions which it recognises for negotiating purposes should be based on agreed procedures which provide a clear set of rules and a sound basis for resolving conflicts of interest.

88 Management should agree with recognised unions the provision of reasonable facilities to enable them to keep in touch with their members and to represent them effectively.

89 Management and recognised unions at the highest level should facilitate and encourage personal contact and discussion between managers and officials of the unions, including shop stewards. Contacts should not be left until trouble arises.

Collective agreements

90 Collective agreements deal with matters of procedure and matters of substance which are of joint concern to management and employees. A single agreement may contain provisions of both kinds or they may be dealt with in separate agreements. In either case, the agreement should be in writing and there should be agreed arrangements for checking that procedural provisions have not become out of date.

91 Procedural provisions should lay down the constitution of any joint negotiating body or specify the parties to the procedure. They should also cover

(i) the matters to be bargained about and the levels at which bargaining should take place;

(ii) arrangements for negotiating terms and conditions of employment and the circumstances in which either party can give notice of their wish to re-negotiate them;

(iii) facilities for trade union activities in the establishment and the appointment, status and functions of shop stewards;

(iv) procedures for settling collective disputes and individual grievances and for dealing with disciplinary matters;

(v) the constitution and scope of any consultative committees.

92 Substantive provisions settle terms and conditions of employment. They should indicate the period for which they are to apply, and cover

(i) wages and salaries and, where appropriate, overtime rates, bonuses, piecework and other systems relating earnings to performance;

(ii) hours of work, and, where appropriate, provisions for overtime, and shift working;

(iii) holiday entitlement and pay.

93 Agreements may also cover such matters as

(i) techniques for determining levels of performance and job grading, for example, work measurement and job evaluation;

(ii) procedures for handling redundancy and temporary lay-offs;

(iii) guaranteed pay, sick pay and pensions schemes;

(iv) the deduction by management of trade union contributions from the pay of members.

94 There is advantage in agreeing at industry level as much as is suitable for adoption over the industry as a whole, including

(i) terms and conditions of employment suitable for general application;

(ii) general guidelines for negotiating at a lower level matters which cannot be decided satisfactorily at industry level;

(iii) a procedure for settling disputes, either for the industry as a whole or as a model for individual undertakings to adopt by agreement.

95 To maintain fair and stable pay structures, an agreement reached at the level of the establishment or undertaking should define

(i) how and within what limits any negotiations at a lower level should be conducted;

(ii) how it relates to any relevant industry-wide agreement.

Disclosure of information

Paragraphs 96 to 98 have been superseded by ACAS Code No 2 infra, with effect from 22 August 1977.

EMPLOYEE REPRESENTATION AT THE PLACE OF WORK

99 Employees need representatives to put forward their collective views to management and to safeguard their interests in consultation and negotiation. It is also an advantage for management to deal with representatives who can speak for their fellow employees.

100 This function is widely carried out by employees who are accredited as union representatives to act on behalf of union members in the establishment where they themselves are employed. The title given to these representatives varies, but the most usual one is 'shop steward'. This is therefore used in the Code.

101 A shop steward has responsibilities both to trade union members in the establishment and to the union organisation outside it, in addition to his responsibilities as an employee. Most shop stewards spend only a part of their time in shop steward duties, but their role in the effective conduct of industrial relations at the place of work is always important.

102 Where there are shop stewards, trade unions should

(i) provide for their election or appointment;

(ii) define the manner in which they can be removed from office;

(iii) specify their powers and duties within the union.

Functions

103 A shop steward's functions at the place of work cover

(i) trade union matters such as recruitment, maintaining membership and collecting contributions;

(ii) industrial relations matters such as handling members' grievances, negotiation and consultation.

104 His role varies according to the industrial relations system in which he operates. Agreements at the level of the industry may lay down, or provide guidelines on, some of his functions. Others are best determined in the individual establishment. But all the functions of a shop steward should be clearly defined and those relating to industrial relations agreed between the parties.

105 A shop steward should observe all agreements to which his union is a party and should take all reasonable steps to ensure that those whom he represents also observe them.

Appointment and qualifications

106 Trade unions and management should seek agreement on

(i) the number of shop stewards needed in the establishment, including senior stewards and deputies;

(ii) the work groups for which each steward is responsible.

Both will depend on the size and organisation of the establishment and the number of union members employed.

107 Trade unions should decide on any conditions of eligibility for election and appointment such as a minimum age and length of service in the establishment. These matters may be the subject of consultation between management and unions.

108 To encourage union members to vote in elections of shop stewards, management should offer the trade unions facilities to conduct elections in the establishment and to publicise the dates and details.

109 Trade unions should notify management promptly in writing when shop stewards are appointed and when changes are made.

Status

110 Trade unions should

(i) give their shop stewards written credentials, setting out their powers and duties within the union, including any authority to call for industrial action;

(ii) seek agreement with management on the issue of joint written credentials setting out the relevant rights and obligations of the stewards and of management.

111 All credentials should state

(i) the period of office of the shop steward;

(ii) the work group he represents.

Co-ordination

112 In an establishment where there are a number of shop stewards of one trade union, they should consider electing a senior steward to co-ordinate their activities.

113 Where more than one union is recognised but each union has only a small number of members, the unions should seek to agree on the election of one steward to represent all their members in the establishment.

114 Where there are a number of senior shop stewards of different unions which negotiate jointly, the unions should seek to agree on the election of one of them to co-ordinate their activities in the establishment.

115 In each of these cases trade unions should seek agreement with management on the co-ordinating functions of the steward concerned.

Facilities

Paragraphs 116 to 118 have been superseded by ACAS Code No 3 infra, with effect from 1 April 1978.

Training

119 Each union should ensure that its own shop stewards are adequately informed about its policies and organisation and about the agreements to which it is a party. Management should ensure that the stewards are adequately informed about its objectives and employment policies.

GRIEVANCE AND DISPUTES PROCEDURES

120 All employees have a right to seek redress for grievances relating to their employment. Each employee must be told how he can do so (see paragraph 60).

121 Management should establish, with employee representatives or trade unions concerned, arrangements under which individual employees can raise grievances and have them settled fairly and promptly. There should be a formal procedure, except in very small establishments where there is a close personal contact between the employer and his employees.

122 Where trade unions are recognised, management should establish with them a procedure for settling collective disputes.

123 Individual grievances and collective disputes are often dealt with through the same procedure. Where there are separate procedures they should be linked so that an issue can, if necessary, pass from one to the other, since a grievance may develop into a dispute.

Individual grievance procedures

124 The aim of the procedure should be to settle the grievance fairly and as near as possible to the point of origin. It should be simple and rapid in operation.

125 The procedure should be in writing and provide that

(i) the grievance should normally be discussed first between the employee and his immediate superior;

(ii) the employee should be accompanied at the next stage of the discussion with management by his employee representative if he so wishes;

(iii) there should be a right of appeal.

Collective disputes procedures

126 Disputes are broadly of two kinds

(i) disputes of right, which relate to the application or interpretation of existing agreements or contracts of employment;

(ii) disputes of interest, which relate to claims by employees or proposals by management about terms and conditions of employment.

127 A procedure for settling collective disputes should be in writing and should

(i) state the level at which an issue should first be raised;

(ii) lay down time limits for each stage of the procedure, with provision for extension by agreement;

(iii) preclude a strike, lock-out, or other form of industrial action until all stages of the procedure have been completed and a failure to agree formally recorded.

128 The procedure should have the following stages

(i) employee representatives should raise the issue in dispute with management at the level directly concerned;

(ii) failing settlement, it should be referred to a higher level within the establishment;

(iii) if still unsettled, it should be referred to further agreed stages, for example, to a stage of an industry-wide procedure, or to a higher level within the undertaking.

129 Independent conciliation and arbitration can be used to settle all types of dispute if the parties concerned agree that they should. Arbitration by the Industrial Arbitration Board or other independent arbitrators is particularly suitable for settling disputes of right, and its wider use for that purpose is desirable. Where it is used the parties should undertake to be bound by the award.

DISCIPLINARY PROCEDURES

Paragraphs 130 to 133 have been superseded by ACAS Code No 1 infra, with effect from 20 June 1977.

ACAS Code No 1: Disciplinary practice and procedures in employment

(*This Code came into effect on 20 June 1977*. See also the ACAS handbook 'Discipline at Work' and 7.2 CODES OF PRACTICE.)

A failure on the part of any person to observe any provision of a Code of Practice shall not of itself render him liable to any proceedings; but in any proceedings before an industrial tribunal or the Central Arbitration Committee any Code of Practice issued under this section shall be admissible in evidence, and if any provision of such a Code appears to the tribunal or Committee to be relevant to any question arising in the proceedings it shall be taken into account in determining that question. (Employment Protection Act 1975 section 6(11).)

INTRODUCTION

1 This document gives practical guidance on how to draw up disciplinary rules and procedures and how to operate them effectively. Its aim is to help employers and trade unions as well as individual employees – both men and women – wherever they are employed regardless of the size of the organisation in which they work. In the smaller establishments it may not be practicable to adopt all the detailed provisions, but most of the features listed in paragraph 10 could be adopted and incorporated into a simple procedure.

Why have disciplinary rules and procedures?

2 Disciplinary rules and procedures are necessary for promoting fairness and order in the treatment of individuals and in the conduct of industrial relations. They also assist an organisation to operate effectively. Rules set standards of conduct at work; procedure helps to ensure that the standards are adhered to and also provides a fair method of dealing with alleged failures to observe them.

3 It is important that employees know what standards of conduct are expected of them and the Contracts of Employment Act 1972 (as amended by the Employment Protection Act 1975) requires employers to provide written information for their employees about certain aspects of their disciplinary rules and procedures.[1]

4 The importance of disciplinary rules and procedures has also been recognised by the law relating to dismissals, since the grounds for dismissal and the way in which the dismissal has been handled can be challenged before an industrial tribunal.[2] Where either of these is found by a tribunal to have been unfair the employer may be ordered to reinstate or re-engage the employees concerned and may be liable to pay compensation to them.

[1]Contracts of Employment Act 1972 S.4(2) as amended by Employment Protection Act Schedule 16 Part II requires employers to provide employees with a written statement of the main terms and conditions of their employment. Such statements must also specify any disciplinary rules applicable to them and indicate the person to whom they should apply if they are dissatisfied with any disciplinary decision. The statement should explain any further steps which exist in any procedure for dealing with disciplinary decisions or grievances. The employer may satisfy these requirements by referring the employees to a reasonably accessible document which provides the necessary information.

[2]The Trade Union and Labour Relations Act 1974 Schedule 1 para 21(4), as amended by the Employment Protection Act 1975 Schedule 16 Part III specifies that a complaint of unfair dismissal has to be presented to an Industrial Tribunal before the end of the 3-month period beginning with the effective date of termination.

Formulating policy

5 Management is responsible for maintaining discipline within the organisation and for ensuring that there are adequate disciplinary rules and procedures. The initiative for establishing these will normally lie with management. However, if they are to be fully effective the rules and procedures need to be accepted as reasonable both by those who are to be covered by them and by those who operate them. Management should therefore aim to secure the involvement of employees and all levels of management when formulating new or revising existing rules and procedures. In the light of particular circumstances in different companies and industries trade union officials[3] may or may not wish to participate in the formulation of the rules but they should participate fully with management in agreeing the procedural arrangements which will apply to their members and in seeing that these arrangements are used consistently and fairly.

Rules

6 It is unlikely that any set of disciplinary rules can cover all circumstances that may arise: moreover the rules required will vary according to particular circumstances such as the type of work, working conditions and size of establishment. When drawing up rules the aim should be to specify clearly and concisely those necessary for the efficient and safe performance of work and for the maintenance of satisfactory relations within the workforce and between employees and management. Rules should not be so general as to be meaningless.

7 Rules should be readily available and management should make every effort to ensure that employees know and understand them. This may be best achieved by giving every employee a copy of the rules and by explaining them orally. In the case of new employees this should form part of an induction programme.

8 Employees should be made aware of the likely consequences of breaking rules and in particular they should be given a clear indication of the type of conduct which may warrant summary dismissal.

Essential features of disciplinary procedures

9 Disciplinary procedures should not be viewed primarily as a means of imposing sanctions. They should also be designed to emphasise and encourage improvements in individual conduct.

10 Disciplinary procedures should

(*a*) Be in writing.

(*b*) Specify to whom they apply.

(*c*) Provide for matters to be dealt with quickly.

(*d*) Indicate the disciplinary actions which may be taken.

(*e*) Specify the levels of management which have the authority to take the various forms of disciplinary action, ensuring that immediate superiors do not normally have the power to dismiss without reference to senior management.

---

[3]Throughout this Code, trade union official has the meaning assigned to it by S.30(1) of the Trade Union and Labour Relations Act 1974 and means, broadly, officers of the union, its branches and sections, and anyone else, including fellow employees, appointed or elected under the union's rules to represent members.

(*f*) Provide for individuals to be informed of the complaints against them and to be given an opportunity to state their case before decisions are reached.

(*g*) Give individuals the right to be accompanied by a trade union representative or by a fellow employee of their choice.

(*h*) Ensure that, except for gross misconduct, no employees are dismissed for a first breach of discipline.

(*j*) Ensure that disciplinary action is not taken until the case has been carefully investigated.

(*k*) Ensure that individuals are given an explanation for any penalty imposed.

(*l*) Provide a right of appeal and specify the procedure to be followed.

The procedure in operation

11 When a disciplinary matter arises, the supervisor or manager should first establish the facts promptly before recollections fade, taking into account the statements of any available witnesses. In serious cases consideration should be given to a brief period of suspension while the case is investigated and this suspension should be with pay. Before a decision is made or penalty imposed the individual should be interviewed and given the opportunity to state his or her case and should be advised of any rights under the procedure, including the right to be accompanied.

12 Often supervisors will give informal oral warnings for the purpose of improving conduct when employees commit minor infringements of the established standards of conduct. However, where the facts of a case appear to call for disciplinary action, other than summary dismissal, the following procedure should normally be observed

(*a*) In the case of minor offences the individual should be given a formal oral warning or if the issue is more serious, there should be a written warning setting out the nature of the offence and the likely consequences of further offences. In either case the individual should be advised that the warning constitutes the first formal stage of the procedure.

(*b*) Further misconduct might warrant a final written warning which should contain a statement that any recurrence would lead to suspension or dismissal or some other penalty, as the case may be.

(*c*) The final step might be disciplinary transfer, or disciplinary suspension without pay (but only if these are allowed for by an express or implied condition of the contract of employment), or dismissal, according to the nature of the misconduct. Special consideration should be given before imposing disciplinary suspension without pay and it should not normally be for a prolonged period.

13 Except in the event of an oral warning, details of any disciplinary action should be given in writing to the employee and if desired, to his or her representative. At the same time the employee should be told of any right of appeal, how to make it and to whom.

14 When determining the disciplinary action to be taken the supervisor or manager should bear in mind the need to satisfy the test of reasonableness in all the circumstances. So far as possible, account should be taken of the employee's record and any other relevant factors.

15 Special consideration should be given to the way in which disciplinary procedures are to operate in exceptional cases. For example

(*a*) **Employees to whom the full procedure is not immediately available.** Special provisions may have to be made for the handling of disciplinary matters among nightshift workers, workers in isolated locations or depots or others who may pose particular problems for example because no one is present with the necessary authority to take disciplinary action or no trade union representative is immediately available.

(*b*) **Trade union officials.** Disciplinary action against a trade union official can lead to a serious dispute if it is seen as an attack on the union's functions. Although normal disciplinary standards should apply to their conduct as employees, no disciplinary action beyond an oral warning should be taken until the circumstances of the case have been discussed with a senior trade union representative or full-time official.

(*c*) **Criminal offences outside employment.** These should not be treated as automatic reasons for dismissal regardless of whether the offence has any relevance to the duties of the individual as an employee. The main considerations should be whether the offence is one that makes the individual unsuitable for his or her type of work or unacceptable to other employees. Employees should not be dismissed solely because a charge against them is pending or because they are absent through having been remanded in custody.

Appeals

16 Grievance procedures are sometimes used for dealing with disciplinary appeals though it is normally more appropriate to keep the two kinds of procedure separate since the disciplinary issues are in general best resolved within the organisation and need to be dealt with more speedily than others. The external stages of a grievance procedure may however, be the appropriate machinery for dealing with appeals against disciplinary action where a final decision within the organisation is contested or where the matter becomes a collective issue between management and a trade union.

17 Independent arbitration is sometimes an appropriate means of resolving disciplinary issues. Where the parties concerned agree, it may constitute the final stage of procedure.

Records

18 Records should be kept, detailing the nature of any breach of disciplinary rules, the action taken and the reasons for it, whether an appeal was lodged, its outcome and any subsequent developments. These records should be carefully safeguarded and kept confidential.

19 Except in agreed special circumstances breaches of disciplinary rules should be disregarded after a specified period of satisfactory conduct.

Further action

20 Rules and procedures should be reviewed periodically in the light of any developments in employment legislation or industrial relations practice and, if necessary, revised in order to ensure their continuing relevance and effectiveness. Any amendments and additional rules imposing new obligations should be introduced only after reasonable notice has been given to all employees and, where appropriate, their representatives have been informed.

ACAS Code No 2: Disclosure of information to trade unions for collective bargaining purposes

This Code supersedes paragraphs 96 to 98 (inclusive) of the Code of Practice in effect under Part 1 of Schedule 1 to the Trade Union and Labour Relations Act 1974. These paragraphs ceased to have effect when this Code came into force on 22 August 1977.

INTRODUCTION

1 Under the Employment Protection Act 1975 the Advisory, Conciliation and Arbitration Service (ACAS) may issue Codes of Practice containing such practical guidance as the Service thinks fit for the purpose of promoting the improvement of industrial relations. In particular, the Service has a duty to provide practical guidance on the application of sections 17 and 18 of the Act in relation to the disclosure of information by employers to trade unions for the purpose of collective bargaining.

2 The Act and the Code apply to employers operating in both the public and private sectors of industry. They do not apply to collective bargaining between employers' associations and trade unions, although the parties concerned may wish to follow the guidelines contained in the Code.

3 The information which employers may have a duty to disclose under section 17 is information which it would be in accordance with good industrial relations practice to disclose. In determining what would be in accordance with good industrial relations practice regard is to be had to any relevant provisions of the Code. However, the Code imposes no legal obligations on an employer to disclose any specific item of information. Failure to observe the Code does not by itself render anyone liable to proceedings, but the Act requires any relevant provisions to be taken into account in proceedings before the Central Arbitration Committee.[1]

Provisions of the Act

4 The Act places a general duty on an employer to disclose at all stages of collective bargaining information requested by representatives of independent trade unions. The unions must be either recognised by the employer for collective bargaining purposes, or fall within the scope of an ACAS recommendation for recognition. The representative of the union is an official or other person authorised by the union to carry on such collective bargaining.

5 The information requested has to be in the employer's possession, or in the possession of any associated employer, and must relate to the employer's undertaking. The information to be disclosed is that without which a trade union representative would be impeded to a material extent in bargaining and which it would be in accordance with good industrial relations practice to disclose for the purpose of collective bargaining. In determining what is in accordance with good industrial relations practice, any relevant provisions of this Code are to be taken into account.

6 No employer is required to disclose any information which would be against the interests of national security; would contravene a prohibition imposed by or under an enactment; was given to an employer in confidence, or was obtained by the employer in consequence of the confidence reposed in him by another person;

[1]Employment Protection Act 1975, sections 17(1)(b), 17(4) and 6(11).

relates to an individual unless he has consented to its disclosure; would cause substantial injury to the undertaking (or national interest in respect of Crown employment) for reasons other than its effect on collective bargaining; or was obtained for the purpose of any legal proceedings.

7 In providing information the employer is not required to produce original documents for inspection or copying. Nor is he required to compile or assemble information which would entail work or expenditure out of reasonable proportion to the value of the information in the conduct of collective bargaining. The union representative can request that the information be given in writing by the employer or be confirmed in writing. Similarly, an employer can ask the trade union representative to make the request for information in writing or confirm it in writing.

8 If the trade union considers that an employer has failed to disclose to its representatives information which he was required to disclose by section 17 of the Act, it may make a complaint to the Central Arbitration Committee.[2] The Committee may ask the Advisory, Conciliation and Arbitration Service to conciliate. If conciliation does not lead to a settlement of the complaint the Service shall inform the Committee accordingly who shall proceed to hear and determine the complaint. If the complaint is upheld by the Committee it is required to specify the information that should have been disclosed and a period of time within which the employer ought to disclose the information. If the employer does not disclose the information within the specified time the union may present a further complaint to the Committee and may also present a claim for improved terms and conditions. If the further complaint is upheld by the Committee an award, which would have effect as part of the contract of employment, may be made against the employer on the terms and conditions specified in the claim, or other terms and conditions which the Committee considers appropriate.

Providing information

9 The absence of relevant information about an employer's undertaking may to a material extent impede trade unions in collective bargaining; particularly if the information would influence the formulation, presentation or pursuance of a claim, or the conclusion of an agreement. The provision of relevant information in such circumstances would be in accordance with good industrial relations practice.

10 To determine what information will be relevant negotiators should take account of the subject-matter of the negotiations and the issues raised during them; the level at which negotiations take place (department, plant, division, or company level); the size of the company; and the type of business the company is engaged in.

11 Collective bargaining within an undertaking can range from negotiations on specific matters arising daily at the work place affecting particular sections of the workforce, to extensive periodic negotiations on terms and conditions of employment affecting the whole workforce in multiplant companies. The relevant information and the depth, detail and form in which it could be presented to negotiators will vary accordingly. Consequently, it is not possible to compile a list of items that should be disclosed in all circumstances. Some examples of information relating to the undertaking which could be relevant in certain

[2]Further information can be obtained from the Secretary of the Committee at 1 The Abbey Garden, London SW1P 3SE.

collective bargaining situations are given below.

(i) **Pay and benefits:** principles and structure of payment systems; job evaluation systems and grading criteria; earnings and hours analysed according to workgroup, grade, plant, sex, out-workers and homeworkers, department or division, giving, where appropriate, distributions and make-up of pay showing any additions to basic rate or salary; total pay bill; details of fringe benefits and non-wage labour costs.

(ii) **Conditions of service:** policies on recruitment, redeployment, redundancy, training, equal opportunity, and promotion; appraisal systems; health, welfare and safety matters.

(iii) **Manpower:** numbers employed analysed according to grade, department, location, age and sex; labour turnover; absenteeism; overtime and short-time; manning standards; planned changes in work methods, materials, equipment or organisation; available manpower plans; investment plans.

(iv) **Performance:** productivity and efficiency data; savings from increased productivity and output; return on capital invested; sales and state of order book.

(v) **Financial:** cost structures; gross and net profits; sources of earnings; assets; liabilities; allocation of profits; details of government financial assistance; transfer prices; loans to parent or subsidiary companies and interest charged.

12 These examples are not intended to represent a check list of information that should be provided for all negotiations. Nor are they meant to be an exhaustive list of types of information as other items may be relevant in particular negotiations.

Restrictions on the duty to disclose

13 Trade unions and employers should be aware of the restrictions on the general duty to disclose information for collective bargaining.[3]

14 Some examples of information which if disclosed in particular circumstances might cause substantial injury are: cost information on individual products; detailed analysis of proposed investment, marketing or pricing policies; and price quotas or the make-up of tender prices. Information which has to be made available publicly, for example under the Companies Acts, would not fall into this category.

15 Substantial injury may occur if, for example, certain customers would be lost to competitors, or suppliers would refuse to supply necessary materials, or the ability to raise funds to finance the company would be seriously impaired as a result of disclosing certain information. The burden of establishing a claim that disclosure of certain information would cause substantial injury lies with the employer.

Trade union responsibilities

16 Trade unions should identify and request the information they require for collective bargaining in advance of negotiations whenever practicable. Misunderstandings can be avoided, costs reduced, and time saved, if requests state as

[3]Employment Protection Act 1975, section 18. See paragraphs 6 and 7 of this Code.

precisely as possible all the information required, and the reasons why the information is considered relevant. Requests should conform to an agreed procedure. A reasonable period of time should be allowed for employers to consider a request and to reply.

17 Trade unions should keep employers informed of the names of the representatives authorised to carry on collective bargaining on their behalf.

18 Where two or more trade unions are recognised by an employer for collective bargaining purposes they should co-ordinate their requests for information whenever possible.

19 Trade unions should review existing training programmes or establish new ones to ensure negotiators are equipped to understand and use information effectively.

Employers' responsibilities[4]

20 Employers should aim to be as open and helpful as possible in meeting trade union requests for information. Where a request is refused, the reasons for the refusal should be explained as far as possible to the trade union representatives concerned and be capable of being substantiated should the matter be taken to the Central Arbitration Committee.

21 Information agreed as relevant to collective bargaining should be made available as soon as possible once a request for the information has been made by an authorised trade union representative. Employers should present information in a form and style which recipients can reasonably be expected to understand.

Joint arrangements for disclosure of information

22 Employers and trade unions should endeavour to arrive at a joint understanding on how the provisions on the disclosure of information can be implemented most effectively. They should consider what information is likely to be required, what is available, and what could reasonably be made available. Consideration should also be given to the form in which the information will be presented, when it should be presented and to whom. In particular, the parties should endeavour to reach an understanding on what information could most appropriately be provided on a regular basis.

23 Procedures for resolving possible disputes concerning any issues associated with the disclosure of information should be agreed. Where possible such procedures should normally be related to any existing arrangements within the undertaking or industry and the complaint, conciliation and arbitration procedure described in the Act.[5]

---

[4]The Stock Exchange has drawn attention to the need for employers to consider any obligations which they may have under their Listing Agreement.

[5]Employment Protection Act 1975, sections 19 to 21. See paragraph 8 of this Code.

ACAS Code No 3: Time off for trade union duties and activities

(*This Code came into effect on 1 April 1978.*)

This Code supersedes paragraphs 116 to 118 (inclusive) of the Code of Practice in effect under Part 1 of Schedule 1 to the Trade Union and Labour Relations Act 1974, which paragraphs shall cease to have effect on the date on which this Code comes into effect.

INTRODUCTION

1 Under section 6 of the Employment Protection Act 1975 (referred to hereafter as the Act) the Advisory, Conciliation and Arbitration Service (ACAS) has a duty to provide practical guidance on the time off to be permitted by an employer

(*a*) to a trade union official in accordance with section 57 of the Act; and

(*b*) to a trade union member in accordance with section 58 of the Act. This Code is intended to provide such guidance.

2 Section 57 of the Act requires an employer to permit an employee of his or hers, who is an official of an independent trade union which is recognised by the employer,[1] to take reasonable paid time off during the employee's working hours for the purpose of enabling the employee

(*a*) to carry out those duties which are concerned with industrial relations between his or her employer and any associated employer[2] and their employees; or

(*b*) to undergo training in aspects of industrial relations which is

(i) relevant to the carrying out of those duties; and

(ii) approved by the Trades Union Congress or by the independent trade union of which he or she is an official.

3 An employer who permits an employee time off under this section is required to pay him or her for the time off taken. Where the employee's pay does not vary with the amount of work done, the employer is required by the Act to pay the employee as if he or she had worked during the period when the time off was taken. Where the employee's pay does vary according to the amount of work done then payment for the time off permitted is to be calculated by reference to the average hourly earnings for the work the employee is employed to do.

4 For the purposes of section 57 of the Act the word 'official' means an employee who has been elected or appointed in accordance with the rules of the union to be a representative of all or some of the union's members in a particular company or workplace.

---

[1]Section 62 of the Act provides that a trade union shall be treated as recognised not only if it is recognised for the purpose of collective bargaining but also if ACAS has made a recommendation for recognition which is operative within the meaning of section 15 of the Act.

[2]Any two employers are to be treated as associated if one is a company of which the other (directly or indirectly) has control, or if both are companies of which a third person (directly or indirectly) has control: Trade Union and Labour Relations Act 1974, section 30(5). This definition is appropriate to the private sector of employment.

5 Section 58 of the Act requires an employer to permit an employee of his or hers who is a member of an appropriate trade union[3] to take reasonable time off during the employee's working hours for the purpose of taking part in any trade union activity to which the section applies. Trade union activities to which the section applies are any activities of an appropriate trade union of which the employee is a member; and any activities in relation to which the employee is acting as a representative of such a union; but excluding activities which themselves consist of industrial action whether or not in contemplation or furtherance of a trade dispute. There is no requirement under section 58 that union members or representatives be paid for time off taken on union activities.

6 The amount of time off under sections 57 and 58 of the Act, the purposes for which, the occasions on which and any conditions subject to which time off may so be taken are those that are reasonable in all the circumstances having regard to any relevant provisions of this Code of Practice.

7 Sections 57 and 58 of the Act provide that a trade union official or member may present a complaint to an industrial tribunal that his or her employer has failed to permit the taking of time off as required by these sections or, in the case of an official, to pay him or her the whole or part of any amount required by the Act to be paid. Such complaints may be resolved by conciliation by ACAS, and if such a resolution is achieved no tribunal hearing will be necessary. This Code will be taken into account in determining any question arising during tribunal proceedings on sections 57 and 58, although failure to observe any provision of the Code will not of itself render a person liable to any proceedings.

General considerations for time off arrangements

8 The general purpose of the statutory provisions on time off for trade union duties and activities is to aid and improve the conduct of industrial relations. These provisions apply to all employers without exception as to size or type of business or service. But trade unions should be aware of the wide variety of circumstances and the different operational requirements which will have to be taken into account in any arrangements for dealing with time off. For example, some employers face particular exigencies of production, services and safety in process industries. Others operate in the special circumstances of the small firm. In enterprises large and small the workforce may be fragmented. Proper regard will therefore have to be paid to particular operational requirements and obligations of different industries and services.

9 Union officials and members may face particular problems of effective representation and communication, and employers in their turn should be aware of these. They may arise, for example, from the differing hours or shifts worked by members in a single negotiating area; from employment part-time; from the scattered or isolated locations of workplaces and, particularly in the case of some married women, from domestic commitments which limit the possibilities of active participation in their union outside the workplace and outside the hours of normal day working.

10 To take account of this wide variety of circumstances and problems, employers and unions should reach agreement on arrangements for handling time off in ways appropriate to their own situations. Subsequent advice in the Code should be read

[3]Appropriate trade union for the purposes of the section means, in relation to an employee of any description, an independent trade union which, in respect of that description of employee, either is recognised by his or her employer or is the subject of an operative ACAS recommendation for recognition.

in the light of this primary point of guidance which ACAS considers fundamental to the proper operation of time off facilities. The absence of a formal agreement dealing specifically with time off for trade union duties and activities should not of itself preclude the granting of release.

11 Employers and unions, at the appropriate level, will need to review jointly their current time off provisions bearing in mind the statutory requirements, this Code of Practice and the particular workplace circumstances. Where existing arrangements meet these requirements and are working to the satisfaction of both parties they need not be changed. In some situations time off arrangements will have to be revised and it may be helpful to set out any such revised arrangements in formal agreements.

12 Arrangements for the handling of time off for union duties, industrial relations training and union activities should accord with agreed procedures for negotiation, consultation, grievance handling and dispute settlement. Agreements on time off and on other facilities for union representation should be consistent with wider agreements which should deal with such matters of workplace representation as constituencies, number of representatives and the form of any joint credentials.

Trade union officials' duties concerned with industrial relations

13 In addition to his or her work as an employee a trade union official may have important duties concerned with industrial relations. An official's duties are those duties pertaining to his or her role in the jointly agreed procedures or customary arrangements for consultation, collective bargaining and grievance handling, where such matters concern the employer and any associated employer and their employees. To perform these duties properly an official should be permitted to take reasonable paid time off during working hours for such purposes as

(*a*) collective bargaining with the appropriate level of management;

(*b*) informing constituents about negotiations or consultations with management;

(*c*) meetings with other lay officials or with full-time union officers on matters which are concerned with industrial relations between his or her employer and any associated employer and their employees;

(*d*) interviews with and on behalf of constituents on grievance and discipline matters concerning them and their employer;

(*e*) appearing on behalf of constituents before an outside official body, such as an industrial tribunal, which is dealing with an industrial relations matter concerning the employer; and

(*f*) explanations to new employees whom he or she will represent of the role of the union in the workplace industrial relations structure.

Training of officials in aspects of industrial relations

14 To carry out their duties effectively officials need to possess skills and knowledge. In addition to the practical experience obtained from holding office officials should undertake training in relevant subjects when necessary.

15 Training should be relevant to the industrial relations duties of an official. It should be approved by the TUC or the official's union. An official's industrial relations duties will vary according to the collective bargaining arrangements at

the place of work, the structure of the union and the role of the official. Accordingly there is no universally applicable syllabus for training.

16 An official who has duties concerned with industrial relations should be permitted to take reasonable paid time off work for initial basic training and such training should be arranged as soon as possible after the official is elected or appointed.

17 An official should be permitted to take reasonable paid time off work for further training relevant to the carrying out of his or her duties concerned with industrial relations where he or she has special responsibilities or where such training is necessary to meet circumstances such as changes in the structure or topics of negotiation at the place of employment or legislative changes affecting industrial relations.

18 When the trade union has identified a need for basic or further training and wishes an official to receive training it should inform management what training it has approved for the purpose and, if the employer asks for it, supply a copy of the syllabus or prospectus indicating the contents of the training course or programme.

19 The number of officials receiving training from any one place of employment at any one time should be that which is reasonable in the circumstances, bearing in mind such factors as the operational requirements of the employer and the availability of relevant courses. Trade unions should normally give at least a few weeks' notice of their nominations for training.

20 Unions and management should endeavour to reach agreement on the appropriate numbers and arrangements and should refer any problem which may arise to the relevant procedure.

Trade union activities

21 To operate effectively and democratically trade unions need the active participation of members in certain union activities. A member should therefore be permitted to take reasonable time off during working hours for union activities such as taking part, as a representative, in meetings of official policy-making bodies of the union such as the executive committee or annual conference, or representing the union on external bodies such as the committees of industrial training boards.

22 Members should be permitted to take reasonable time off during working hours for such purposes as voting at the workplace in union elections. Also there may be occasions when it is reasonable for unions to hold meetings of members during working hours because of the urgency of the matter to be discussed or where to do so would not adversely affect production or services. Employers may also have an interest in ensuring that meetings are representative.

Conditions relating to time off

23 For time off arrangements to work satisfactorily the trade union should ensure that its officials are fully aware of their role, responsibilities and functions. The union should inform management, in writing, as soon as possible after officials are appointed or have resigned and should ensure that officials receive any appropriate written credentials promptly. Management at all levels should be familiar with agreements and arrangements relating to time off.

24 Management should make available to officials the facilities necessary for them to perform their duties efficiently and to communicate effectively with members,

fellow lay officials and full-time officers. Such facilities may include accommodation for meetings, access to a telephone, notice boards and, where the volume of the official's work justifies it, the use of office facilities.

25 Management is responsible for maintaining production and service to customers, and for making the operational arrangements for time off. Union officials should bear in mind management's problems in discharging these responsibilities. The union official who seeks time off should ensure that the appropriate management representative is informed as far in advance as is reasonable in the circumstances. The official should indicate the nature of the business for which time off is required, the intended location and the expected period of absence. Management and the union should seek to agree arrangements, where necessary, for other employees to cover the work of officials or members taking time off.

26 Where it is necessary for the union to hold meetings of members during working hours it should seek to agree the arrangements with management as far in advance as is practicable. Where such meetings necessarily involve a large proportion of employees at the workplace at any one time, management and unions should agree on a convenient time which minimises the effects on production or service – for example, towards the end of the shift or the working week or just before or after a meal break.

27 When a number of members need time off at any one time there should be agreement to leave at work such members as are essential for safety or operational reasons – for example, to keep premises open to the public or to provide necessary manning in a continuous process firm.

28 Management may want time off work for union duties or activities to be deferred because, for example, problems of safety or of maintenance of production or service would ensue if time off were taken at a particular time. The grounds for postponement should be made clear and parties should endeavour to agree on an alternative time for the union duty or activity. In considering postponement parties should weigh the urgency of the matter for which time off is required against the seriousness of any problems arising.

29 The union official and union member should not unduly or unnecessarily prolong the time they are absent from work on union duties or activities.

30 A dispute or grievance in relation to time off work for union duties or activities should be referred to the relevant procedure.

Industrial action

31 Management and unions have a responsibility to use agreed procedures to resolve problems constructively and avoid industrial action. Time off should be provided for this purpose. Satisfactory time off arrangements are particularly needed where communication and co-operation between management and unions are in danger of breaking down. Where industrial action has not occurred employers and unions should avoid hastily altering these arrangements since to do so may damage relationships.

32 A distinction should be made between situations where an official is engaged in industrial action along with his or her constituents and those where the official is not – for example, where only some of the constituents are taking unofficial action. Where an official is not taking part in industrial action but represents members involved, normal arrangements for time off with pay for the official should apply.

33 There is no obligation on employers to permit time off for union activities which themselves consist of industrial action but where a group of members not taking part in such action is directly affected by other people's industrial action these members and their officials may need to seek the agreement of management to time off for an emergency meeting.

DE Code of Practice: Picketing

(This Code came into effect on 17 December 1980.)

Section A

INTRODUCTION

1 The Code is intended to provide practical guidance on picketing in trade disputes for those who may be contemplating, organising or taking part in a picket and for those who as employers or workers or members of the general public may be affected by it.

2 There is no legal 'right to picket' as such but peaceful picketing has long been recognised as being lawful. However, the law imposes certain limits on how and where lawful picketing can be undertaken so as to ensure that there is proper protection for those who may be affected by picketing, including those who want to go to work normally.

3 It is a *civil* wrong, actionable in the civil courts, to persuade someone to break his contract of employment or to secure the breaking of a commercial contract. But the law exempts from this liability those acting in contemplation or furtherance of a trade dispute, including pickets, provided that they are picketing only at their own place of work.* The *criminal* law, however, applies to pickets just as it applies to everyone else: they have no exemption from the provisions of the criminal law (e.g. as to obstruction and public order).

4 The Code outlines the law on picketing (although it is of course for the courts and industrial tribunals to interpret and apply the law in particular cases). Sections B and C outline the provisions of the civil and criminal law respectively and Section D describes the role of the police in enforcing the law. The Code – in Sections E, F and G – also gives guidance on good practice in the conduct of picketing.

5 The Code itself imposes no legal obligations and failure to observe it does not by itself render anyone liable to proceedings. But Section 3(8) of the Employment Act 1980 provides that any provisions of the Code are to be admissible in evidence and taken into account in proceedings before any court or industrial tribunal or the Central Arbitration Committee where they consider them relevant.

Section B

PICKETING AND THE CIVIL LAW

6 Section 15 of the Trade Union and Labour Relations Act 1974 (as amended by the Employment Act 1980) provides the basic rules for lawful industrial picketing:

(i) it may only be undertaken in contemplation or furtherance of a trade dispute;

* Subject additionally in cases of secondary action to the limitations described in paragraph 9 below.

(ii) it may only be carried out by a person *attending at or near his own place of work*; a trade union official in addition to attending at or near his own place of work may also attend at or near the place of work of a member of his trade union whom he is accompanying on the picket line and whom he represents;

(iii) its only purpose must be peacefully obtaining or communicating information or peacefully persuading a person to work or not to work.

7 Picketing commonly involves persuading employees to break their contracts of employment by not going into work and, by disrupting the business of the employer who is being picketed, interfering with his commercial contracts with other employers. If pickets follow the rules outlined in paragraph 6 they are protected by Section 13 of the Trade Union and Labour Relations Act 1974 (as amended)* from being sued in the civil courts for these civil wrongs. These rules are explained more fully in paragraphs 10 to 19 below.

8 These rules apply in the normal cases where employees picket at their own place of work in support of a dispute with their own employer. Cases may arise, however, where employees picket at their own place of work in support of a dispute between another employer and his employees, for example, where employees at one place are involved in a strike in support of a dispute elsewhere and have mounted a picket line at their own place of work in the course of that strike.

9 In such cases the picketing, in order to be protected, must further satisfy the requirements of lawful secondary action contained in Section 17 of the Employment Act 1980. (These are described in detail in the Annex.) In practice this means that these pickets will have to target their picketing precisely on the supply of goods or services between their employer and the employer in dispute. If they impose or threaten an indiscriminate blockade on their employer's premises, they will be liable to be sued in the civil courts.

In contemplation or furtherance of a trade dispute

10 Picketing is lawful only if it is carried out in contemplation or furtherance of a trade dispute. A trade dispute is defined in Section 29 of the Trade Union and Labour Relations Act 1974 (as amended). It covers all the matters which normally occasion disputes between employers and workers such as terms and conditions of employment, the allocation of work, matters of discipline, trade union recognition and membership or non-membership of a trade union.

Attendance at or near his own place of work

11 It is lawful for a person to induce a breach of contract in the course of picketing only if he pickets at or near his own place of work.

12 'At or near his own place of work' is not defined in statute. In general, however, except for those covered by paragraphs 13 and 14 below, lawful picketing normally involves attendance at an entrance to or exit from the factory, site or office at which the picket works. It does not enable a picket to attend lawfully at an entrance to or exit from any place of work which is not his own, even if those who work there are employed by the same employer or covered by the same collective bargaining arrangements. The law does not protect anyone who pickets without permission on or inside any part of premises which are private property.

* Unless otherwise stated by the Trade Union and Labour Relations (Amendment) Act 1976.

Pickets who trespass may be sued in the civil courts.

13 Section 15 of the 1974 Act (as amended by the Employment Act 1980) distinguishes two specific groups of employees:

— those (e.g. mobile workers) who work at more than one place; and

— those for whom it is impracticable to picket at their own place of work because of its location.

It declares that it is lawful for such workers to picket those premises of their employer from which they work or from which their work is administered. In the case of lorry drivers, for example, this will usually mean in practice those premises of their employer from which their vehicles operate.

14 Special provisions also govern people who are not in employment and who have lost their jobs for reasons connected with the dispute which has occasioned the picketing. This might arise, for example, where the dismissal of a group of employees has led directly to a strike, or where in the course of a dispute an employer has terminated his employees' contracts of employment because those employees refuse to work normally. In such cases Section 15 declares that it is lawful for a worker to picket *at his former place of work*. This does not apply, however, to any workers who have subsequently found a job at another place of work. Such workers may only picket lawfully at their new place of work in the course of a dispute with their new employer or in the course of lawful secondary action.

Trade union officials

15 For the reasons described in Section F it is often helpful to the orderly organisation and conduct of picketing for a trade union official to be present on a picket line where his members are picketing. Section 15 of the 1974 Act (as amended by the Employment Act 1980) therefore makes it lawful for a trade union official to picket at any place of work provided that:

(i) he is accompanying members of his trade union who are picketing lawfully at or near their own place of work; and

(ii) he personally represents those members within their trade union.

If these conditions are satisfied then a trade union official has the same legal protection as other pickets who picket lawfully at or near their own place of work.

16 Under Section 15 of the 1974 Act (as amended by the Employment Act 1980) an official* – whether a lay official or an employee of the union – is regarded for this purpose as representing only those members of his union whom he has been specifically appointed or elected to represent. An official cannot, therefore, claim that he represents a group of members simply because they belong to his trade union. He must represent and be responsible for them in the normal course of his trade union duties. For example, it is lawful for an official (such as a shop steward) who represents members at a particular place of work to be present on a picket line where those members are picketing lawfully; for a branch official to be present only where members of his branch are lawfully picketing; for a regional official to be present only where members of his region are lawfully picketing; for a national official who represents a particular trade group or section within the

---

* as defined in Section 30 of the Trade Union and Labour Relations Act 1974 (as amended by the Employment Protection Act 1975).

union, to be present wherever members of that trade group or section are lawfully picketing; and for a national official such as a General Secretary or President who represents the whole union to be present wherever any members of his union are picketing lawfully.

17 Trade union officials may, of course, picket lawfully at their own place of work, whether or not their members are also picketing. However, to be entitled to picket at a place of work other than their own, they must satisfy the conditions laid down in Section 15 of the Trade Union and Labour Relations Act 1974 (as amended by the Employment Act 1980) and described in paragraphs 15 and 16 above.

Lawful purposes of picketing

18 The only purposes of picketing declared lawful by section 15 are:

— peacefully obtaining and communicating information; and

— peacefully persuading a person to work or not to work.

Pickets may, therefore, seek to explain their case to those entering or leaving the picketed premises and to ask them not to enter or leave the premises where the dispute is taking place. This may be done verbally or it may involve the distribution of leaflets or the carrying of banners or placards putting the pickets' case. Pickets have, however, no powers to require other people to stop or to compel them to listen or to do what they have asked them to do. A person who decides to cross a picket line must be allowed to do so.

19 Picketing which is accompanied by, for example, violent, threatening or obstructive behaviour goes beyond peaceful persuasion and is therefore unlawful. As explained in Section C, a picket who threatens or intimidates someone, or obstructs an entrance to a workplace, or causes a breach of the peace commits a criminal offence. But in addition pickets who commit such criminal offences, may forfeit their immunity under the civil law and may be liable to be sued for inducing or threatening to induce a breach of contract.

Seeking redress

20 An employer or an employee whose contracts are interfered with by picketing which does not comply with the rules described in paragraphs 10-19 above has a civil law remedy. He may start an action for damages against those responsible and also ask the court to make an order* stopping the unlawful picketing.

21 An order will normally be sought against the person on whose instructions or advice the picketing is taking place, but it will usually apply not only to him but to any others acting on his behalf or on his instructions. Thus an organiser of picketing cannot avoid liability by, for example, changing the members of the picket line each day. Moreover, if a person knows that such an order has been made against someone and yet aids and abets him in breaking it, he may be in contempt of court himself and liable to be punished by the court.

* An injunction in England and Wales and an interdict in Scotland.

Section C

PICKETING AND THE CRIMINAL LAW

22 If a picket commits a criminal offence he is just as liable to be prosecuted as any other member of the public who breaks the law. The immunity provided under the civil law does not protect him in any way.

23 The criminal law protects the right of every person to go about his lawful daily business free from interference by others. No one is under any obligation to stop when a picket asks him to do so or, if he does stop, to comply with the picket's request, for example, not to go into work. Everyone has the right, if he wishes to do so, to cross a picket line in order to go into his place of work or to deliver or collect goods. A picket may exercise peaceful persuasion, but if he goes beyond that and tries by means other than peaceful persuasion to deter another person from exercising those rights he may commit a criminal offence.

24 Among other matters it is a criminal offence for pickets (as for others)

— to use threatening or abusive language or behaviour directed against any person, whether a worker seeking to cross a picket line, an employer, an ordinary member of the public or the police;

— to use or threaten violence to a person or to his family;

— to intimidate a person by threatening words or behaviour which cause him to fear harm or damage if he fails to comply with the pickets' demands;

— to obstruct the highway or the entrance to premises or to seek physically to bar the passage of vehicles or persons by lying down in the road, linking arms across or circling in the road, or jostling or physically restraining those entering or leaving the premises;

— to be in possession of an offensive weapon;

— intentionally or recklessly to damage property;

— to engage in violent, disorderly or unruly behaviour or to take any action which is likely to lead to a breach of the peace;

— to obstruct a police officer in the execution of his duty.

25 A picket has no right under the law to require a vehicle to stop or to be stopped. The law allows him only to ask a driver to stop by words or signals. A picket may not physically obstruct a vehicle if the driver decides to drive on or, indeed, in any other circumstances. A driver must – as on all other occasions – exercise due care and attention when approaching or driving past a picket line, and may not drive in such a manner as to give rise to a reasonably foreseeable risk of injury.

Section D

ROLE OF THE POLICE

26 It is not the function of the police to take a view of the merits of a particular trade dispute. They have a general duty to uphold the law and keep the peace, whether on the picket line or elsewhere. The law gives the police discretion to take whatever measures may reasonably be considered necessary to ensure that picketing remains peaceful and orderly.

27 The police have *no* responsibility for enforcing the *civil* law. An employer cannot require the police to help in identifying the pickets against whom he wishes to seek an order from the civil court. Nor is it the job of the police to enforce the terms of an order. Enforcement of an order on the application of a plaintiff is a matter for the court and its officers. The police may, however, decide to assist the officers of the court if they think there may be a breach of the peace.

28 As regards the *criminal* law the police have considerable discretionary powers to limit the number of pickets at any one place where they have reasonable cause to fear disorder.* The law does not impose a specific limit on the number of people who may picket at any one place; nor does this Code affect in any way the discretion of the police to limit the number of people on a particular picket line. It is for the police to decide, taking into account all the circumstances, whether the number of pickets at any particular place is likely to lead to a breach of the peace. If a picket does not leave the picket line when asked to do so by the police, he is liable to be arrested for obstruction either of the highway or of a police officer in the execution of his duty if the obstruction is such as to cause, or be likely to cause, a breach of the peace.

Section E

LIMITING NUMBERS OF PICKETS

29 The main cause of violence and disorder on the picket line is excessive numbers. Wherever large numbers of people with strong feelings are involved there is a danger that the situation will get out of control and that those concerned will run the risk of arrest and prosecution.

30 This is particularly so whenever people seek by sheer weight of numbers to stop others going into work or delivering or collecting goods. In such cases, what is intended is not peaceful persuasion, but obstruction, if not intimidation. Such a situation is often described as 'mass picketing'. In fact, it is not picketing in its lawful sense of an attempt at peaceful persuasion and may well result in a breach of the peace or other criminal offences. Moreover, anyone seeking to demonstrate support for those in dispute should keep well away from any picket line so as not to create the risk of a breach of the peace or other criminal offence being committed on that picket line.

31 Large numbers on a picket line are also likely to give rise to fear and resentment amongst those seeking to cross that picket line even where no criminal offence is committed. They exacerbate disputes and sour relations not only between management and employees but between the pickets and their fellow employees. Accordingly pickets and their organisers should ensure that in general the number of pickets does not exceed six at any entrance to a workplace; frequently a smaller number will be appropriate.

---

* In Piddington v Bates (1960) the High Court upheld the decision of a police constable in the circumstances of that case to limit the number of pickets to two.

Section F

ORGANISATION OF PICKETING

Functions of the picket organiser

32 An experienced person, preferably a trade union official who represents those picketing, should always be in charge of the picket line. He should have a letter of authority from his union which he can show to police officers or to people who want to cross the picket line. Even when he is not on the picket line himself he should be available to give the pickets advice if a problem arises.

33 An organiser of pickets should maintain close contact with the police. Advance consultation with the police is always in the best interests of all concerned. In particular the organiser and the pickets should seek directions from the police on the number of people who should be present on the picket line at any one time and on where they should stand in order to avoid obstructing the highway.

34 The other main functions of the picket organiser should be:

— to ensure that pickets understand the law and the provisions of this Code and that the picketing is conducted peacefully and lawfully;

— to be responsible for distributing badges or armbands, which authorised pickets should wear so that they are clearly identified;

— to ensure that employees from other places of work do not join the picket line and that any offers of support on the picket line from outsiders are refused;

— to remain in close contact with his own union office, and with the offices of other unions if they are involved in the picketing;

— to ensure that such special arrangements as may be necessary for essential supplies or maintenance (see paragraph 38) are understood and observed by the pickets.

Consultation with other trade unions

35 Where several unions are involved in a dispute, they should consult each other about the organisation of any picketing. It is important that they should agree how the picketing is to be carried out, how many pickets there should be from each union and who should have overall responsibility for organising them.

Right to cross picket lines

36 Everyone has the right to decide for himself whether he will cross a picket line. Disciplinary action should not be taken or threatened by a union against a member on the ground that he has crossed a picket line which it had not authorised or which was not at the member's place of work. Under Section 4 of the Employment Act 1980 exclusion or expulsion from a union in a closed shop on such grounds may be held to be unreasonable.

Section G

ESSENTIAL SUPPLIES AND SERVICES

37 Pickets should take very great care to ensure that their activities do not cause distress, hardship or inconvenience to members of the public who are not involved in the dispute. Pickets should take particular care to ensure that the movement of essential goods and supplies, the carrying out of essential maintenance of plant and equipment and the provision of services essential to the life of the community are not impeded, still less prevented. Arrangements to ensure this should be agreed in advance between the unions and employers concerned.

38 The following list of essential supplies and services is provided as an illustration but it is not intended to be comprehensive:

— supplies for the production, packaging, marketing and/or distribution of medical and pharmaceutical products;

— supplies essential to health and welfare institutions, eg hospitals, old peoples' homes;

— heating fuel for schools, residential institutions and private residential accommodation;

— other supplies for which there is a crucial need during a crisis in the interests of public health and safety (e.g. chlorine, lime and other agents for water purification; industrial and medical gases; sand and salt for road gritting purposes);

— supplies of goods and services necessary to the maintenance of plant and machinery;

— livestock;

— supplies for the production, packaging, marketing and/or distribution of food and animal feeding stuffs;

— the operation of essential services, such as police, fire, ambulance, medical and nursing services, air safety, coastguard and air sea rescue services and services provided by voluntary bodies (e.g. Red Cross and St. John's ambulances, meals on wheels, hospital car service) and mortuaries, burial and cremation services.

Annex

SECONDARY ACTION AND PICKETING

1 This Annex amplifies the description of lawful secondary action in paragraph 9 of Section B (Picketing and the Civil Law).

2 It is lawful for employees who are in dispute with their own employer to picket peacefully at their own place of work. As the Code explains such pickets have immunity from civil actions if in the course of picketing they interfere with contracts.

3 Anyone who contemplates picketing at his own place of work in furtherance of a dispute between another employer and his workers is subject to separate and more restrictive provisions. In such cases picketing must satisfy the requirements of Section 17 of the Employment Act 1980 (as set out in paragraphs 4 and 5 below).

4 If such pickets interfere only with contracts of employment then they are protected by the statutory immunity. If, however, they also interfere with commercial contracts (by means, for example, of inducing breaches of contracts of employment), their activities will be immune from civil proceedings only if:

(*a*) their employer is a supplier to, or customer of, the employer in dispute under a contract to provide goods or services; and

(*b*) the principal purpose of the picketing is directly to prevent or disrupt the supply of goods or services during the dispute between their employer and the employer in dispute; and

(*c*) the picketing is likely to achieve that purpose.

5 Employees of an associated employer* of the employer in dispute and of suppliers and customers of that associated employer may also picket lawfully at their own place of work if:

(*a*) their principal purpose is to disrupt the supply of goods and services between the associated employer and his supplier or customer; and

(*b*) those goods or services are in substitution for goods or services which but for the dispute would have been supplied to or by the employer in dispute; and

(*c*) the secondary action is likely to achieve the purpose in (*a*) above.

6 In practice this means that any picketing by employees who are not in dispute with their own employer must be very specifically targeted

— in the case of customers and suppliers of the employer in dispute, on the business being carried out during the dispute between the customer or supplier and the employer in dispute; or

— in the case of the associated employer, on work which has been transferred from the employer in dispute because of the dispute.

There is no immunity for interfering with commercial contracts by indiscriminate picketing at customers and suppliers or at associated employers of the employer in dispute.

---

* Two employers are associated if one is a company of which the other has control or both are companies of which a third has control (Section 30(5) of the Trade Union and Labour Relations Act 1974).

HSC Code of Practice: Safety Representatives and Safety Committees

(*This Code came into force on 1 October 1978.*)

1 The Safety Representatives and Safety Committees Regulations 1978 concern safety representatives appointed in accordance with Section 2(4) of the Act and cover:

(*a*) prescribed cases in which recognised trade unions may appoint safety representatives from amongst the employees;

(*b*) prescribed functions of safety representatives.

Section 2(6) of the Act requires employers to consult with safety representatives with a view to the making and maintenance of arrangements which will enable him and his employees to cooperate effectively in promoting and developing measures to ensure the health and safety at work of the employees, and in checking the effectiveness of such measures. Under section 2(4) safety representatives are required to represent the employees in those consultations.

2 This Code of Practice has been approved by the Health and Safety Commission with the consent of the Secretary of State for Employment. It relates to the requirements placed on safety representatives by section 2(4) of the Act and on employers by the Regulations and takes effect on the date the Regulations come into operation.

3 The employer, the recognised trade unions concerned and safety representatives should make full and proper use of the existing agreed industrial relations machinery to reach the degree of agreement necessary to achieve the purpose of the Regulations and in order to resolve any differences.

INTERPRETATION

4 (*a*) In this Code, 'the 1974 Act' means the Health and Safety at Work etc. Act 1974 and 'the Regulations' means the Safety Representatives and Safety Committees Regulations 1978;

(*b*) words and expressions which are defined in the Act or in the Regulations have the same meaning in this Code unless the context requires otherwise.

FUNCTIONS OF SAFETY REPRESENTATIVES

5 In order to fulfil their functions under section 2(4) of the Act safety representatives should:

(*a*) take all reasonably practicable steps to keep themselves informed of:

(i) the legal requirements relating to the health and safety of persons at work, particularly the group or groups of persons they directly represent,

(ii) the particular hazards of the workplace and the measures deemed necessary to eliminate or minimise the risk deriving from these hazards, and

(iii) the health and safety policy of their employer and the organisation and arrangements for fulfilling that policy;

(*b*) encourage co-operation between their employer and his employees in promoting and developing essential measures to ensure the health and safety of employees and in checking the effectiveness of these measures;

(*c*) bring to the employer's notice normally in writing any unsafe or unhealthy conditions or working practices or unsatisfactory arrangements for welfare at work which come to their attention whether on an inspection or day to day observation. The report does not imply that all other conditions and working practices are safe and healthy or that the welfare arrangements are satisfactory in all other respects.

Making a written report does not preclude the bringing of such matters to the attention of the employer or his representative by a direct oral approach in the first instance, particularly in situations where speedy remedial action is necessary. It will also be appropriate for minor matters to be the subject of direct oral discussion without the need for a formal written approach.

INFORMATION TO BE PROVIDED BY EMPLOYERS

6 The Regulations require employers to make information within their knowledge available to safety representatives necessary to enable them to fulfil their functions. Such information should include:

(*a*) information about the plans and performance of their undertaking and any changes proposed insofar as they affect the health and safety at work of their employees;

(*b*) information of a technical nature about hazards to health and safety and precautions deemed necessary to eliminate or minimise them, in respect of machinery, plant, equipment, processes, systems of work and substances in use at work, including any relevant information provided by consultants or designers or by the manufacturer, importer or supplier of any article or substance used, or proposed to be used, at work by their employees;

(*c*) information which the employer keeps relating to the occurrence of any accident, dangerous occurrence or notifiable industrial disease and any statistical records relating to such accidents, dangerous occurrences or cases of notifiable industrial disease;

(*d*) any other information specifically related to matters affecting the health and safety at work of his employees, including the results or any measurements taken by the employer or persons acting on his behalf in the course of checking the effectiveness of his health and safety arrangements;

(*e*) information on articles or substances which an employer issues to homeworkers.

HSC Code of Practice: Time off for the Training of Safety Representatives

(*This Code came into force on 1 October 1978.*)

PREFACE

This document sets out a Code of Practice, which has been approved by the Health and Safety Commission, relating to the time off with pay which a Safety representative is to be permitted to take during his working hours for the purpose of undergoing training approved by the TUC or by independent unions. It should be read in conjunction with the Safety Representatives and Safety Committees Regulations 1977, with particular reference to Regulation 4, which sets out the functions of a safety representative and the time off for training necessary to perform these functions.

The Advisory, Conciliation and Arbitration Service has also prepared a Code of Time Off for trade union duties and activities generally under Section 57 of the Employment Protection Act. However, this Code, approved by the Health and Safety Commission, is concerned with time off for training of safety representatives appointed under the Regulations.

Issues which may arise are covered by paragraph 3 of the Code of Practice on Safety Representatives approved by the Health and Safety Commission. The schedule to the Regulations deals with the computation of pay for the time off allowed. Regulation 11 contains provisions as to reference of complaints to industrial tribunals about time off and the payment to be made.

To complement training approved by the TUC or by independent unions for safety representatives, an employer should make such arrangements as are necessary to provide training in the technical hazards of the workplace and relevant precautions on safe methods of work, and on his organisation and arrangements for health and safety.

CODE OF PRACTICE

1 The function of safety representatives appointed by recognised trade unions, as set out in Section 2(4) of the Health and Safety at Work etc. Act 1974, is to represent employees in consultations with employers about health and safety matters. Regulation 4(1) of the Safety Representatives and Safety Committee Regulations (SI 1977 No 500) prescribes other functions of safety representatives appointed under those Regulations.

2 Under Regulation 4(2)(*b*) of those Regulations the employer has a duty to permit those safety representatives such time off with pay during the employee's working hours as shall be necessary for the purpose of 'undergoing such training in aspects of those functions as may be reasonable in all the circumstances'.

3 As soon as possible after their appointment safety representatives should be permitted time off with pay to attend basic training facilities approved by the TUC or by the independent union or unions which appointed the safety representatives. Further training, similarly approved, should be undertaken where the safety representative has special responsibilities or where such training is necessary to meet changes in circumstances or relevant legislation.

4 With regard to the length of training required, this cannot be rigidly prescribed, but basic training should take into account the functions of safety representatives placed on them by the Regulations. In particular, basic training should provide an understanding of the role of safety representatives, of safety committees, and of trade union policies and practices in relation to:

(*a*) the legal requirements relating to the health and safety of persons at work, particularly the group or class of persons they directly represent;

(*b*) the nature and extent of workplace hazards, and the measures necessary to eliminate or minimise them;

(*c*) the health and safety policy of employers, and organisation and arrangements for fulfilling those policies.

Additionally, safety representatives will need to acquire new skills in order to carry out their functions, including safety inspections, and in using basic sources of legal and official information and information provided by or through the employer on health and safety matters.

5 Trade unions are responsible for appointing safety representatives and when the trade union wishes a safety representative to receive training relevant to his functions it should inform the management of the course it has approved and supply a copy of the syllabus, indicating its contents, if the employer asks for it. It should normally give at least a few weeks' notice of the safety representatives it has nominated for attendance. The number of safety representatives attending training courses at any one time should be that which is reasonable in the circumstances, bearing in mind such factors as the availability of relevant courses and the operational requirements of the employer. Unions and management should endeavour to reach agreement on the appropriate numbers and arrangements and refer any problems which may arise to the relevant agreed procedures.

CRE Code of Practice: Race Relations

(*This Code came into effect on 1 April 1984.*)

PART 1: THE RESPONSIBILITIES OF EMPLOYERS

1.1 Responsibility for providing equal opportunity for all job applicants and employees rests primarily with employers. To this end it is recommended that they should adopt, implement and monitor an equal opportunity policy to ensure that there is no unlawful discrimination and that equal opportunity is genuinely available.

1.2 This policy should be clearly communicated to all employees — e.g. through notice boards, circulars, contracts of employment or written notifications to individual employees.

1.3 An equal opportunity policy aims to ensure:

(*a*) *that no job applicant or employee receives less favourable treatment than another on racial grounds;*

(*b*) *that no applicant or employee is placed at a disadvantage by requirements or conditions which have a disproportionately adverse effect on his or her racial group and which cannot be shown to be justifiable on other than racial grounds;*

(*c*) *that, where appropriate and where permissible under the Race Relations Act, employees of under-represented racial groups are given training and encouragement to achieve equal opportunity within the organisation.*

1.4 In order to ensure that an equal opportunity policy is fully effective, the following action by employers is recommended:

(*a*) allocating overall responsibility for the policy to a member of senior management;

(*b*) discussing and, where appropriate, agreeing with trade union or employee representatives the policy's contents and implementation;

(*c*) ensuring that the policy is known to all employees and if possible, to all job applicants;

(*d*) providing training and guidance for supervisory staff and other relevant decision makers, (such as personnel and line managers, foremen, gatekeepers and receptionists) to ensure that they understand their position in law and under company policy;

(*e*) examining and regularly reviewing existing procedures and criteria and changing them where they find that they are actually or potentially unlawfully discriminatory;

(*f*) making an initial analysis of the workforce and regularly monitoring the application of the policy with the aid of analyses of the ethnic origins of the workforce and of job applicants in accordance with the guidance in paragraphs 1.34-1.35.

SOURCES OF RECRUITMENT

Advertisements

1.5 *When advertising job vacancies it is unlawful for employers: to publish an advertisement which indicates, or could reasonably be understood as indicating, an intention to discriminate against applicants from a particular racial group. (For exceptions see the Race Relations Act).*

1.6 It is therefore recommended that:

(*a*) employers should not confine advertisements unjustifiably to those areas or publications which would exclude or disproportionately reduce the numbers of applicants of a particular racial group;

(*b*) employers should avoid prescribing requirements such as length of residence or experience in the UK and where a particular qualification is required it should be made clear that a fully comparable qualification obtained overseas is as acceptable as a UK qualification.

1.7 In order to demonstrate their commitment to equality of opportunity it is recommended that where employers send literature to applicants, this should include a statement that they are equal opportunity employers.

Employment Agencies

1.8 *When recruiting through employment agencies, job centres, careers offices and schools, it is unlawful for employers:*

(*a*) *to give instructions to discriminate, for example by indicating that certain groups will or will not be preferred. (For exceptions see the Race Relations Act);*

(*b*) *to bring pressure on them to discriminate against members of a particular racial group. (For exceptions, as above).*

1.9 In order to avoid indirect discrimination it is recommended that employers should not confine recruitment unjustifiably to those agencies, job centres, careers offices and schools which, because of their particular source of applicants, provide only or mainly applicants of a particular racial group.

Other Sources

1.10 *It is unlawful to use recruitment methods which exclude or disproportionately reduce the numbers of applicants of a particular racial group and which cannot be shown to be justifiable.* It is therefore recommended that employers should not recruit through the following methods:

(*a*) recruitment, solely or in the first instance, through the recommendations of existing employees where the workforce concerned is wholly or predominantly white or black and the labour market is multi-racial;

(*b*) procedures by which applicants are mainly or wholly supplied through trade unions where this means that only members of a particular racial group, or a disproportionately high number of them, come forward.

SOURCES FOR PROMOTION AND TRAINING

1.11 *It is unlawful for employers to restrict access to opportunities for promotion or training in a way which is discriminatory.* It is therefore recommended that:

— job and training vacancies and the application procedure should be made known to all eligible employees, and not in such a way as to exclude or disproportionately reduce the numbers of applicants from a particular racial group.

1.12 *It is unlawful to discriminate, not only in recruitment, promotion, transfer and training, but also in the arrangements made for recruitment and in the ways of affording access to opportunities for promotion, transfer or training.*

Selection Criteria and Tests

1.13 In order to avoid direct or indirect discrimination it is recommended that selection criteria and tests are examined to ensure that they are related to job requirements and are not unlawfully discriminatory. For example:

(*a*) a standard of English higher than that needed for the safe and effective performance of the job or clearly demonstrable career pattern should not be required, or a higher level of educational qualification than is needed;

(*b*) in particular, employers should not disqualify applicants because they are unable to complete an application form unassisted unless personal completion of the form is a valid test of the standard of English required for safe and effective performance of the job;

(*c*) overseas degrees, diplomas and other qualifications which are comparable with UK qualifications should be accepted as equivalents, and not simply be assumed to be of an inferior quality;

(*d*) selection tests which contain irrelevant questions or exercises on matters which may be unfamiliar to racial minority applicants should not be used (for example, general knowledge questions on matters more likely to be familiar to indigenous applicants);

(*e*) selection tests should be checked to ensure that they are related to the job's requirements, i.e. an individual's test markings should measure ability to do or train for the job in question.

Treatment of Applicants, Shortlisting, Interviewing and Selection

1.14 In order to avoid direct or indirect discrimination it is recommended that:

(*a*) gate, reception and personnel staff should be instructed not to treat casual or formal applicants from particular racial groups less favourably than others. These instructions should be confirmed in writing;

(*b*) in addition, staff responsible for shortlisting, interviewing and selecting candidates should be:

— clearly informed of selection criteria and of the need for their consistent application;

— given guidance or training on the effects which generalised assumptions and prejudices about race can have on selection decisions;

— made aware of the possible misunderstandings that can occur in interviews between persons of different cultural background;

(*c*) wherever possible, shortlisting and interviewing should not be done by one person alone but should at least be checked at a more senior level.

Genuine Occupational Qualification

1.15 *Selection on racial grounds is allowed in certain jobs where being of a particular racial group is a genuine occupational qualification for that job.* An example is where the holder of a particular job provides persons of a racial group with personal services promoting their welfare, and those services can most effectively be provided by a person of that group.

Transfers and Training

1.16 In order to avoid direct or indirect discrimination it is recommended that:

(*a*) staff responsible for selecting employees for transfer to other jobs should be instructed to apply selection criteria without unlawful discrimination;

(*b*) industry or company agreements and arrangements of custom and practice on job transfers should be examined and amended if they are found to contain requirements or conditions which appear to be indirectly discriminatory. For example, if employees of a particular racial group are concentrated in particular sections, the transfer arrangements should be examined to see if they are unjustifiably and unlawfully restrictive and amended if necessary;

(*c*) staff responsible for selecting employees for training, whether induction, promotion or skill training should be instructed not to discriminate on racial grounds;

(*d*) selection criteria for training opportunities should be examined to ensure that they are not indirectly discriminatory.

Dismissal (including redundancy) and Other Detriment

1.17 *It is unlawful to discriminate on racial grounds in dismissal, or other detriment to an employee.*

It is therefore recommended that:

(*a*) staff responsible for selecting employees for dismissal, including redundancy, should be instructed not to discriminate on racial grounds;

(*b*) selection criteria for redundancies should be examined to ensure that they are not indirectly discriminatory.

Performance Appraisals

1.18 *It is unlawful to discriminate on racial grounds in appraisals of employee performance.*

1.19 It is recommended that:

(*a*) staff responsible for performance appraisals should be instructed not to discriminate on racial grounds;

(*b*) assessment criteria should be examined to ensure that they are not unlawfully discriminatory.

1.20 *It is unlawful to discriminate on racial grounds in affording terms of employment and providing benefits, facilities and services for employees.* It is therefore recommended that:

(*a*) all staff concerned with these aspects of employment should be instructed accordingly;

(*b*) the criteria governing eligibility should be examined to ensure that they are not unlawfully discriminatory.

1.21 In addition, employees may request extended leave from time to time in order to visit relations in their countries of origin or who have emigrated to other countries. Many employers have policies which allow annual leave entitlement to be accumulated, or extra unpaid leave to be taken to meet these circumstances. Employers should take care to apply such policies consistently and without unlawful discrimination.

1.22 *It is unlawful to discriminate in the operation of grievance, disputes and disciplinary procedures,* for example by victimising an individual through disciplinary measures because he or she has complained about racial discrimination, or given evidence about such a complaint. Employers should not ignore or treat lightly grievances from members of particular racial groups on the assumption that they are over-sensitive about discrimination.

1.23 It is recommended that:
in applying disciplinary procedures consideration should be given to the possible effect on an employee's behaviour of the following:

— racial abuse or other racial provocation;

— communication and comprehension difficulties;

— differences in cultural background or behaviour.

1.24 Where employees have particular cultural and religious needs which conflict with existing work requirements, it is recommended that employers should consider whether it is reasonably practicable to vary or adapt these requirements to enable such needs to be met. For example, it is recommended that they should not refuse employment to a turbaned Sikh because he could not comply with unjustifiable uniform requirements.

Other examples of such needs are:

(*a*) observance of prayer times and religious holidays;

(*b*) wearing of dress such as sarees and the trousers worn by Asian women.

1.25 *Although the Act does not specifically cover religious discrimination, work requirements would generally be unlawful if they have a disproportionately adverse effect on particular racial groups and cannot be shown to be justifiable.*

1.26 Although there is no legal requirement to provide language training, difficulties in communication can endanger equal opportunity in the workforce. In addition, good communications can improve efficiency, promotion prospects and safety and health and create a better understanding between employers, employees and unions. Where the workforce includes current employees whose English is limited it is recommended that steps are taken to ensure that communications are as effective as possible.

1.27 These should include, where reasonably practicable:

(*a*) provision of interpretation and translation facilities, for example, in the communication of grievance and other procedures, and of terms of employment;

(*b*) training in English language and in communication skills;

(*c*) training for managers and supervisors in the background and culture of racial minority groups;

(*d*) the use of alternative or additional methods of communication, where employees find it difficult to understand health and safety requirements, for example:

— safety signs; translation of safety notices;

— instructions through interpreters;

— instruction combined with industrial language training.

1.28 *It is unlawful to instruct or put pressure on others to discriminate on racial grounds.*

(*a*) An example of an unlawful instruction is:

— an instruction from a personnel or line manager to junior staff to restrict the numbers of employees from a particular racial group in any particular work.

(*b*) An example of pressure to discriminate is:

— an attempt by a shop steward or group of workers to induce an employer not to recruit members of particular racial groups, for example by threatening industrial action.

1.29 *It is also unlawful to discriminate in response to such instructions or pressure.*

1.30 The following recommendations are made to avoid unlawful instructions and pressure to discriminate:

(*a*) guidance should be given to all employees, and particularly those in positions of authority or influence on the relevant provisions of the law;

(*b*) decision-makers should be instructed not to give way to pressure to discriminate;

(*c*) giving instructions or bringing pressure to discriminate should be treated as a disciplinary offence.

1.31 *It is unlawful to victimise individuals who have made allegations or complaints of racial discrimination or provided information about such discrimination, for example, by disciplining them or dismissing them.*

1.32 It is recommended that:
— guidance on this aspect of the law should be given to all employees and particularly to those in positions of influence or authority.

1.33 It is recommended that employers should regularly monitor the effects of selection decisions and personnel practices and procedures in order to assess whether equal opportunity is being achieved.

1.34 The information needed for effective monitoring may be obtained in a number of ways. It will best be provided by records showing the ethnic origins of existing employees and job applicants. It is recognised that the need for detailed information and the methods of collecting it will vary according to the circumstances of individual establishments. For example, in small firms or in firms in areas with little or no racial minority settlement it will often be adequate to assess the distribution of employees from personal knowledge and visual identification.

1.35 It is open to employers to adopt the method of monitoring which is best suited to their needs and circumstances, but whichever method is adopted, they should be able to show that it is effective. In order to achieve the full commitment for all concerned the chosen method should be discussed and agreed, where appropriate, with trade union or employee representatives.

1.36 Employers should ensure that information on individuals' ethnic origins is collected for the purpose of monitoring equal opportunity alone and is protected from misuse.

1.37 The following is the comprehensive method recommended by the CRE.

Analyses should be carried out of:

(*a*) the ethnic composition of the workforce of each plant, department, section, shift and job category, and changes in distribution over periods of time;

(*b*) selection decisions for recruitment, promotion, transfer and training, according to the racial group of candidates, and reasons for these decisions.

1.38 Except in cases where there are large numbers of applicants and the burden on resources would be excessive, reasons for selection and rejection should be recorded at each stage of the selection process, e.g. initial shortlisting and final decisions. Simple categories of reasons for rejection should be adequate for the early sifting stages.

1.39 Selection criteria and personnel procedures should be reviewed to ensure that they do not include requirements or conditions which constitute or may lead to unlawful indirect discrimination.

1.40 This information should be carefully and regularly analysed and, in order to identify areas which may need particular attention, a number of key questions should be asked.

1.41 Is there evidence that individuals from any particular racial group:

(*a*) do not apply for employment or promotion, or that fewer apply than might be expected?

(*b*) are not recruited or promoted at all, or are appointed in a significantly lower proportion than their rate of application?

(*c*) are under-represented in training or in jobs carrying higher pay, status or authority?

(*d*) are concentrated in certain shifts, sections or departments?

1.42 If the answer to any of these questions is yes, the reasons for this should be investigated. If direct or indirect discrimination is found action must be taken to end it immediately.

1.43 It is recommended that deliberate acts of unlawful discrimination by employees are treated as disciplinary offences.

1.44 *Although they are not legally required, positive measures are allowed by the law to encourage employees and potential employees and provide training for employees who are members of particular racial groups which have been under-represented in particular work*. Discrimination at the point of selection for work, however, is not permissible in these circumstances.

1.45 Such measures are important for the development of equal opportunity. It is therefore recommended that, where there is under-representation of particular racial groups in particular work, the following measures should be taken wherever appropriate and reasonably practicable:

(*a*) job advertisements designed to reach members of these groups and to encourage their applications: for example, through the use of the ethnic minority press, as well as other newspapers;

(*b*) use of the employment agencies and careers offices in areas where these groups are concentrated;

(*c*) recruitment and training schemes for school leavers designed to reach members of these groups;

(*d*) encouragement to employees from these groups to apply for promotion or transfer opportunities;

(*e*) training for promotion or skill training for employees of these groups who lack particular expertise but show potential: supervisory training may include language training.

PART 2: THE RESPONSIBILITIES OF INDIVIDUAL EMPLOYEES

2.1 While the primary responsibility for providing equal opportunity rests with the employer, individual employees at all levels and of all racial groups have responsibilities too. Good race relations depend on them as much as on management, and so their attitudes and activities are very important.

2.2 *The following actions by individual employees would be unlawful*:

(*a*) *discrimination in the course of their employment against fellow employees or job applicants on racial grounds*, for example, in selection decisions for recruitment, promotion, transfer and training;

(*b*) *inducing, or attempting to induce other employees, unions or management to practise unlawful discrimination*. For example, they should not refuse to accept other employees from particular racial groups or refuse to work with a supervisor of a particular racial group;

(*c*) *victimising individuals who have made allegations or complaints of racial discrimination or provided information about such discrimination*.

2.3 To assist in preventing racial discrimination and promoting equal opportunity it is recommended that individual employees should:

(*a*) co-operate in measures introduced by management designed to ensure equal opportunity and non-discrimination;

(*b*) where such measures have not been introduced, press for their introduction (through their trade union where appropriate);

(*c*) draw the attention of management and, where appropriate, their trade unions to suspected discriminatory acts or practices;

(*d*) refrain from harassment or intimidation of other employees on racial grounds, for example, by attempting to discourage them from continuing employment. Such action may be unlawful if it is taken by employees against those subject to their authority.

2.4 In addition to the responsibilities set out above individual employees from the racial minorities should recognise that in many occupations advancement is dependent on an appropriate standard of English. Similarly an understanding of the industrial relations procedures which apply is often essential for good working relationships.

2.5 They should therefore:

(*a*) where appropriate, seek means to improve their standards of English;

(*b*) co-operate in industrial language training schemes introduced by employers and/or unions;

(*c*) co-operate in training or other schemes designed to inform them of industrial relations procedures, company agreements, work rules, etc;

(*d*) where appropriate, participate in discussions with employers and unions, to find solutions to conflicts between cultural or religious needs and production needs.

PART 3: THE RESPONSIBILITIES OF TRADE UNIONS

3.1 Trade unions, in common with a number of other organisations, have a dual role as employers and providers of services specifically covered by the Race Relations Act.

3.2 In their role as employer, unions have the responsibilities set out in Part 1 of the Code. They also have a responsibility to ensure that their representatives and members do not discriminate against any particular racial group in the admission or treatment of members, or as colleagues, supervisors, or subordinates.

3.3 In addition, trade union officials at national and local level and shopfloor representatives at plant level have an important part to play on behalf of their members in preventing unlawful discrimination and in promoting equal opportunity and good race relations. Trade unions should encourage and press for equal opportunity policies so that measures to prevent discrimination at the workplace can be introduced with the clear commitment of both management and unions.

3.4 *It is unlawful for trade unions to discriminate on racial grounds:*

(*a*) *by refusing membership;*

(*b*) *by offering less favourable terms of membership.*

3.5 *It is unlawful for trade unions to discriminate on racial grounds against existing members:*

(*a*) *by varying their terms of membership, depriving them of membership or subjecting them to any other detriment;*

(*b*) *by treating them less favourably in the benefits, facilities or services provided.* These may include:

training facilities;

welfare and insurance schemes;

entertainment and social events;

processing of grievances;

negotiations;

assistance in disciplinary or dismissal procedures.

3.6 In addition, it is recommended that unions ensure that in cases where members of particular racial groups believe that they are suffering racial discrimination, whether by the employer or the union itself, serious attention is paid to the reasons for this belief and that any discrimination which may be occurring is stopped.

3.7 It is recommended that deliberate acts of unlawful discrimination by union members are treated as disciplinary offences.

3.8 *Although they are not legally required, positive measures are allowed by the law to encourage and provide training for members of particular racial groups which have been under-represented in trade union membership or in trade union posts.* (Discrimination at the point of selection, however, is not permissible in these circumstances.)

3.9 It is recommended that, wherever appropriate and reasonably practicable, trade unions should:

(*a*) encourage individuals from these groups to join the union. Where appropriate, recruitment material should be translated into other languages;

(*b*) encourage individuals from these groups to apply for union posts and provide training to help fit them for such posts.

3.10 Training and information play a major part in the avoidance of discrimination and the promotion of equal opportunity. It is recommended that trade unions should:

(*a*) provide training and information for officers, shop stewards and representatives on their responsibilities for equal opportunity. This training and information should cover:

the Race Relations Act and the nature and causes of discrimination;

the backgrounds of racial minority groups and communication needs;

the effects of prejudice;

equal opportunity policies;

avoiding discrimination when representing members.

(*b*) ensure that members and representatives, whatever their racial group, are informed of their role in the union, and of industrial relations and union procedures and structures. This may be done, for example:

through translation of material;

through encouragement to participate in industrial relations courses and industrial language training.

3.11 *It is unlawful for trade union members or representatives to induce or to attempt to induce those responsible for employment decisions to discriminate:*

(*a*) *in the recruitment, promotion, transfer, training or dismissal of employees;*

(*b*) *in terms of employment, benefits, facilities or services.*

3.12 For example, they should not:

(*a*) restrict the numbers of a particular racial group in a section, grade or department;

(*b*) resist changes designed to remove indirect discrimination, such as those in craft apprentice schemes, or in agreements concerning seniority rights of mobility between departments.

3.13 *It is unlawful to victimise individuals who have made allegations or complaints of racial discrimination or provided information about such discrimination.*

3.14 *Where unions are involved in selection decisions for recruitment, promotion, training or transfer, for example through recommendations or veto, it is unlawful for them to discriminate on racial grounds.*

3.15 It is recommended that they should instruct their members accordingly and examine their procedures and joint agreements to ensure that they do not contain indirectly discriminatory requirements or conditions, such as:

unjustifiable restrictions on transfers between departments or irrelevant and unjustifiable selection criteria which have a disproportionately adverse effect on particular racial groups.

3.16 It is recommended that:

(*a*) unions should co-operate in the introduction and implementation of full equal opportunity policies, as defined in paras 1.3 & 1.4;

(*b*) unions should negotiate the adoption of such policies where they have not been introduced or the extension of existing policies where these are too narrow;

(*c*) unions should co-operate with measures to monitor the progress of equal opportunity policies, or encourage management to introduce them where they do not already exist. Where appropriate (see paras 1.33-1.35) this may be done through analysis of the distribution of employees and job applicants according to ethnic origin;

(*d*) where monitoring shows that discrimination has occurred or is occurring, unions should co-operate in measures to eliminate it;

(*e*) although positive action is not legally required, unions should encourage management to take such action where there is under-representation of particular racial groups in particular jobs, and where management itself introduces positive action representatives should support it;

(*f*) similarly, where there are communication difficulties, management should be asked to take whatever action is appropriate to overcome them.

PART 4: THE RESPONSIBILITIES OF EMPLOYMENT AGENCIES

4.1 Employment agencies, in their role as employers, have the responsibilities outlined in Part 1 of the Code. In addition, they have responsibilities as suppliers of job applicants to other employers.

4.2 *It is unlawful for employment agencies: (For exceptions see Race Relations Act)*

(*a*) *to discriminate on racial grounds in providing services to clients;*

(*b*) *to publish job advertisements indicating, or which might be understood to indicate, that applications from any particular group will not be considered or will be treated more favourably or less favourably than others;*

(*c*) *to act on directly discriminatory instructions from employers to the effect that applicants from a particular racial group will be rejected or preferred or that their numbers should be restricted;*

(*d*) *to act on indirectly discriminatory instructions from employers i.e. that requirements or conditions should be applied that would have a disproportionately adverse effect on applicants of a particular racial group and which cannot be shown to be justifiable.*

4.3 It is recommended that agencies should also avoid indicating such conditions or requirements in job advertisements unless they can be shown to be justifiable. Examples in each case may be those relating to educational qualifications or residence.

4.4 It is recommended that staff should be given guidance on their duty not to discriminate and on the effect which generalised assumptions and prejudices can have on their treatment of members of particular racial groups.

4.5 In particular staff should be instructed:

(*a*) not to ask employers for racial preferences;

(*b*) not to draw attention to racial origin when recommending applicants unless the employer is trying to attract applicants of a particular racial group under the exceptions in the Race Relations Act;

(*c*) to report a client's refusal to interview an applicant for reasons that are directly or indirectly discriminatory to a supervisor, who should inform the client that discrimination is unlawful. If the client maintains this refusal the agency should inform the applicant of his or her right to complain to an industrial tribunal and to apply to the CRE for assistance. An internal procedure for recording such cases should be operated;

(*d*) to inform their supervisor if they believe that an applicant, though interviewed, has been rejected on racial grounds. If the supervisor is satisfied that there are grounds for this belief, he or she should arrange for the applicant to be informed of the right to complain to an industrial tribunal and to apply to the CRE for assistance. An internal procedure for recording such cases should be operated;

(*e*) to treat job applicants without discrimination. For example, they should not send applicants from particular racial groups to only those employers who are believed to be willing to accept them, or restrict the range of job opportunities for such applicants because of assumptions about their abilities based on race or colour.

4.6 It is recommended that employment agencies should discontinue their services to employers who give unlawful discriminatory instructions and who refuse to withdraw them.

4.7 It is recommended that employment agencies should monitor the effectiveness of the measures they take for ensuring that no unlawful discrimination occurs. For example, where reasonably practicable they should make periodic checks to ensure that applicants from particular racial groups are being referred for suitable jobs for which they are qualified at a similar rate to that for other comparable applicants.

Index

Index

Index